The SAGE Guide to Key Issues in

MASS MEDIA
ETHICS AND LAW

EDITORIAL BOARD

The SAGE Guide to Key Issues in
MASS MEDIA
ETHICS AND LAW

Editors

William A. Babcock and William H. Freivogel
Southern Illinois University Carbondale

2

$SAGE reference

Los Angeles | London | New Delhi
Singapore | Washington DC | Boston

Los Angeles | London | New Delhi
Singapore | Washington DC | Boston

FOR INFORMATION:

SAGE Publications, Inc.
2455 Teller Road
Thousand Oaks, California 91320
E-mail: order@sagepub.com

SAGE Publications Ltd.
1 Oliver's Yard
55 City Road
London, EC1Y 1SP
United Kingdom

SAGE Publications India Pvt. Ltd.
B 1/I 1 Mohan Cooperative Industrial Area
Mathura Road, New Delhi 110 044
India

SAGE Publications Asia-Pacific Pte. Ltd.
3 Church Street
#10-04 Samsung Hub
Singapore 049483

Acquisitions Editor: Jim Brace-Thompson
Editorial Assistant: Jordan Enobakhare
Project Development, Editing, &
   Management: Laurie Collier Hillstrom
Production Editor: Tracy Buyan
Reference Systems Coordinator:
   Anna Villaseñor
Typesetter: Hurix Systems Pvt. Ltd.
Proofreaders: Lawrence W. Baker,
   Tricia Currie-Knight
Indexer: David Luljak
Cover Designer: Candice Harman
Marketing Manager: Carmel Schrire

Printed in the United States of America.

Library of Congress Cataloging-in-Publication Data

The SAGE guide to key issues in mass media ethics and law
/ Editors William A. Babcock & William H. Freivogel.

pages cm
Includes bibliographical references and index.

ISBN 978-1-4522-7435-5 (hardcover : alk. paper)

1. Mass media—Law and legislation—United States.
2. Mass media—Moral and ethical aspects—United States.
I. Babcock, William A. (Professor of journalism), editor.
II. Freivogel, William H. editor. III. Title: Guide to key issues
in mass media ethics and law.

KF2750.S34 2015
174'.93840973—dc23   2014047305

15 16 17 18 19 10 9 8 7 6 5 4 3 2 1

CONTENTS

VOLUME 2

SECTION 4

REPORTING AND REPUTATION

Now, a half-century after the granddaddy of all American media cases, *New York Times v. Sullivan*, legal scholars are increasingly asking whether this case that freed the press to be tough might not today be seen as a case encouraging unethical, unfair, and inaccurate journalism. Have we have come to a time when the *Onion*, and also possibly many grocery-store tabloid publications, will be required to carry a "fiction" label/disclaimer on each page?

What today constitutes opinion, libel, and false light may not be as clear as it was in the latter part of the twentieth century, given the makeup of the U.S. Supreme Court and the prevalence of new media. Is it possible that the First Amendment allows reporters and publishers to be punished for disparaging crops, farm practices, or agricultural producers? Or does it permit the government to ban newsgathering drones over industrial farms and puppy mills?

Sports news and reporting have been impacted by new media. Social media have provided evidence against high school and college athletes in high-profile sexual assault cases. Too, courts have ruled video game makers cannot steal a college football player's identity without compensation.

And when, if ever, is it justified for a government to censor communications in the online era? Does such censorship result in greater social harmony and unity, or does it lead to social repression?

Legislators have answered the latter question by providing Internet sites with almost unlimited immunity from the defamatory, pornographic, nasty, false posts of third parties. That protection, provided by Section 230 of the Communications Decency Act, gives Internet news organizations even more protection than *New York Times v. Sullivan* has provided traditional news organizations.

James Goodale, the *New York Times* lawyer who fought in favor of the libel decision, acknowledges that its legal protections along with those of Section 230 mean that "you have two million people libeling each other all day long."

Section 4 of *The SAGE Guide to Key Issues in Mass Media Ethics and Law* highlights these and other topics dealing with information gathering.

29

JOURNALISM

Communications Decency and Indecency

Section 230 of the Communications Decency Act is the statutory little brother of the First Amendment. Like the First Amendment, it protects crude and distasteful expression. The revolutionary development of the Internet as a robust source of news, information, entertainment, gossip, misinformation, and vitriol has occurred under the mantle of Section 230 of the Communications Decency Act of 1996 (CDA). A string of federal court decisions has recognized a safe harbor of immunity for interactive computer services, protecting them from suits for third-party postings.

Concerns about the breadth of the Section 230 immunity grow out of instances of anonymous Internet abuse that have grabbed headlines and largely escaped legal consequences. These abuses include cyberbullying of teens, the humiliation of female college students, racially discriminatory housing postings, ubiquitous pornography, websites that solicit unchecked gossip about public figures,

YouTube postings that allegedly promote terrorism, and boyfriends humiliating ex-girlfriends online. The widely publicized abuses have led to state and local laws criminalizing cyberbullying and to calls for national legislation and court action to curb immoral and unethical conduct.

The debate about Section 230 involves a clash among important American values of free expression on the one hand and tolerance, civility, privacy, and equality on the other. Because most of the offensive third-party postings are anonymous, the debate also challenges the special place that anonymous speech has enjoyed since the days of the Federalist Papers and *Common Sense*. The defamatory Web poster of today is a poor cousin of the patriot-pamphleteer, yet seeks the same protection. The debate also highlights different value systems in different societies, pitting the primacy of free expression in the United States against the protected place that privacy has in Europe, where the "right to be forgotten"—to have dated personal information scrubbed from the Web—recently was recognized in courts.

Section 230 fits comfortably into the American constitutional architecture of free expression. In interpreting the First Amendment, the Supreme Court of the United States has recognized that free expression requires the protection of profane speech, hate speech, anonymous gossip, flag-burning, cross-burning, and advocacy of violent revolution. It has rejected laws requiring newspapers to publish rights-of-reply. It has ruled that even carelessly erroneous content about public officials deserves constitutional protection. As Justice William J. Brennan Jr. wrote famously in *New York Times v. Sullivan*, "Erroneous statement is inevitable in free debate" and must be protected if free expression is to have the "breathing space" that it requires to survive.

Section 230 is the breathing space for the Internet's extraordinarily freewheeling expression. Like the First Amendment, it protects speech that is indecent, nasty, careless, hateful, misleading, and false. The First Amendment does not require Section 230. But the broad safe harbor of Section 230 protects the same kinds of expression as the First Amendment protects. Nevertheless, as the name of the law suggests, Congress was not trying to protect indecency when it passed the Communications Decency Act.

Development of Section 230

Courts have searched for the right legal analogy to apply to third-party postings on interactive computer services. Is an Internet site a publisher who should be held liable for defamation and other causes of action growing out of third-party postings, the same way that newspapers are responsible for letters to the editor? Or is an Internet site like a distributor, liable after it is informed of problematic content—like bookstores or libraries? Or, is the analogy of a common carrier most apt? That would leave the Internet site no more responsible for the content of a posting than the telephone company is for an obscene telephone call.

The first answer came in 1991 in *Cubby, Inc. v. CompuServe, Inc.*, in which the Court likened an Internet site to a library, which, as a distributor, could only be liable if it took no action after being notified of offending speech. But four years later, a New York court subjected an online computer service to broad publisher liability in *Stratton Oakmont, Inc. v. Prodigy Services Corporation.* Stratton Oakmont, an investment firm, complained that Prodigy had defamed it on the "Money Talk" bulletin board by failing to remove an anonymous posting claiming that Oakmont acted fraudulently during an initial public offering. Prodigy had claimed publicly that it would correct false material on its site. For that reason, the court ruled, Prodigy could be held legally responsible. Because of its high-minded promise to monitor comments and delete those violating its guidelines, it was acting as a publisher and was subject to defamation claims.

The *Stratton* decision led to Section 230. Congress thought the decision discouraged Internet sites from removing obscene content because the only way to avoid publisher liability was to avoid acting like a publisher. Under *Stratton,* Internet sites had to refuse to take down any content if they were to avoid publisher liability. *Stratton* both promoted indecency and interfered with the quickly developing Internet by subjecting it to liability for third-party postings.

Two differently motivated legislative efforts came together in the CDA. One, led by Senator James Exon (R-OK), targeted online obscenity. The second originated in the House, where Representatives Christopher Cox (R-CA) and Ron Wyden (D-OR) introduced an amendment to the Telecommunications Act to encourage filtering software so parents could keep their children from accessing porn sites. Cox-Wyden overruled *Stratton* because that decision had discouraged use of filtering software; the filtering software, like Prodigy's promise to edit its site, could trigger publisher liability under *Stratton*.

A conference committee report specified, "One of the specific purposes of this section is to overrule *Stratton-Oakmont v. Prodigy* and any other similar decisions which have treated such providers and users as publishers. . . . The conferees believe that such decisions create serious obstacles to the important federal policy of empowering parents to determine the content of communications their children receive through interactive computer services."

Congress also stated in its statutory findings on Section 230 the importance of the rapid development of the Internet, and its policy of promoting the Internet's continued development and vibrancy.

After stating these dual goals—deterring indecency and promoting the Internet—Congress laid out the safe harbor provision titled "Protection for 'Good Samaritan'

Blocking and Screening of Offensive Material." The two parts of this provision appear to be aimed at accomplishing Congress's two purposes. The first states, "No provider or user of an interactive computer service shall be treated as the publisher or speaker of any information provided by another information content provider." In other words, service providers are not publishers of third-party postings and are not liable the way publishers are. The second part of the provision states, "No provider or user of an interactive computer service shall be held liable on account of . . . any action voluntarily taken in good faith to restrict access to or availability of material that the provider or user considers to be obscene, lewd, lascivious, filthy, excessively violent, harassing, or otherwise objectionable." This provision was intended to open the door to service providers taking down objectionable work without subjecting themselves to publisher's liability.

Court Interpretation

The Cox-Wyden amendment had greater impact than Senator Exon's effort because the Supreme Court decided in 1997 that the Exon provisions violated the First Amendment.

But Section 230 received a broad interpretation in *Zeran vs. America Online, Inc.,* in 1997. The decision by Chief Judge J. Harvie Wilkinson III of the Fourth Circuit ensured that courts would not treat online computer services like publishers or distributors. The case had a highly unfavorable set of facts for AOL. Kenneth M. Zeran ran a business out of his Seattle home. He received a flood of calls after an anonymous posting on AOL listed his phone number in an advertisement for "Naughty Oklahoma T-Shirts." The T-shirts featured offensive slogans related to the bombing of the Alfred P. Murrah Federal Building in Oklahoma City in 1995. The posting occurred six days after the Murrah bombing. AOL said it would remove the posting, but the next day there was another anonymous post. An Oklahoma radio station passed on the false message, triggering more calls. Zeran claimed AOL was unreasonably slow in removing the defamatory messages. Nevertheless, Judge Wilkinson said that the plain language of Section 230 "creates a federal immunity to any cause of action that would make service providers liable for information originating with a third-party user of the service." He pointed out that the law bars suits against online computer services when they are performing any of the traditional roles of a publisher—"such as deciding whether to publish, withdraw, postpone or alter content." Judge Wilkinson wrote, "The specter of tort liability in an area of such prolific speech would have an obvious chilling effect," adding, "It would be impossible for service providers to screen each of their millions of postings for possible problems."

Zeran argued that AOL should nevertheless be held liable as a distributor, and should have been subject to suit once it had notice of the posting and failed to remove it. But Judge Wilkinson said that "distributor liability" was a "subset" of "publisher liability" because it also involves whether a statement should be published. He also pointed out that if an online computer service were subject to distributor liability every time it was put on notice about a potentially defamatory statement, the online service "would have a natural incentive simply to remove messages upon notification, whether they were defamatory or not." That, Judge Wilkinson said, would be "directly contrary" to Congress's purpose in Section 230.

Other federal courts followed *Zeran,* which held sway for much of the next decade, guaranteeing the growing number of online computer services broad immunity from suits involving third-party content. In addition, Congress explicitly approved of the *Zeran* interpretation of Section 230(c) in the Committee Report to the Dot Kids Implementation and Efficiency Act.

Abuses of Section 230's Safe Harbor

In recent years, three important federal appeals court judges—Judges Frank Easterbrook, Alex Kozinski, and Diarmuid O'Scannlain—have questioned *Zeran*'s breadth, arguing that it is at odds with the anti-obscenity name and purpose of the statute. This creates a legal debate among four of the most renowned federal appeals court judges appointed by former president Ronald Reagan—Wilkinson, Easterbrook, Kozinski, and O'Scannlain.

The foment on the federal bench regarding the correctness of *Zeran* occurs against the backdrop of high-profile stories about Internet abuses that have roiled public opinion. The public is regularly shocked by the destructive and sometimes fatal consequences of cyberbullying and cyber-harassment. One high school student was so humiliated by a Web page mocking him that he stayed home from school for his senior year. The suicides of two teens in MySpace-related incidents frustrated the public because of the absence of legal consequences for the abusers. Megan Meier, a fourteen-year-old from St. Charles, Missouri, hung herself after reading a fake post from a person she thought was a boy her age telling her, "The world would be a better place without you." The posting had actually been written by a mother in the neighborhood. The mother was prosecuted under federal hacking laws and eventually acquitted. Kristin Helms, fifteen, of Orange County, California, committed suicide after she had sex with a twenty-seven-year-old man she had communicated with through MySpace. Helms's parents sued MySpace for negligence in failing to adequately police its site, but MySpace has consistently succeeded in persuading courts to dismiss negligence suits under Section 230.

In Texas, Jane Doe, as the next friend of minor plaintiff "Julie Doe," sued MySpace for negligently failing to protect Julie. Julie Doe was thirteen when she signed up for the social networking site claiming to be eighteen. She met a nineteen-year-old through the site and maintained he sexually assaulted her; the man was charged with felony sexual assault. The district court, citing Section 230, dismissed a suit against MySpace, and appeals courts upheld the decision.

MySpace has provided two state attorneys general with the names of 90,000 registered sex offenders it had banned from its site—a number 40,000 greater than MySpace had acknowledged

previously. Jack Bennett, an FBI special agent in charge of the Cyber Crime Unit, told a conference in 2009 that one in three children would be cyberbullied and one in seven solicited for sex online.

Beyond cyber-harassment, former senator Joseph I. Lieberman, the Connecticut Independent, joined with officials of the Department of Homeland Security in a successful public call for YouTube to take down third-party postings advocating terrorism against the United States— postings for which YouTube claimed Section 230 protection. YouTube complied.

The proliferation of Internet gossip sites and rumor mills has led to noteworthy episodes of abuse. Two notorious ones ironically involved former journalists as the victims. In *Blumenthal v. Drudge,* the "Drudge Report" on America Online published a defamatory statement that Sidney Blumenthal, formerly of the Clinton White House, was a spouse abuser. The court ruled that AOL enjoyed Section 230 immunity from suit. Defamatory statements also appeared on Wikipedia making false allegations against John Seigenthaler Sr., a journalist who had worked in the Kennedy Justice Department and later, ironically, founded the First Amendment Center. The Wikipedia entries claimed Seigenthaler was involved in both Kennedy assassinations. The author, who kept adding new defamatory claims as Wikipedia deleted old ones, eventually apologized, and Wikipedia removed the false information from public access.

In recent years, gossipy websites invited people to post complaints or rumors about bad neighbors (GossipReport.com), bad boyfriends (TheDirty.com), bad colleagues (GossipReport.com), and "bad girls" on campus (JuicyCampus.com). By 2008, fifty-seven campuses had Juicy Campus.com pages on which students debated the promiscuity of various female students by name. The New Jersey attorney general filed a consumer fraud complaint against JuicyCampus for not removing objectionable material when told about it. Early in 2009, JuicyCampus shut down, a victim, it said, of the economic downturn.

A vicious online gossip episode involved the anonymous rumormongering directed at two young women in Yale Law School, Brittan Heller and Heide Iravani. Beginning in 2005, anonymous posters left false, crude messages on AutoAdmit, which calls itself "the most prestigious law-school discussion board in the world." The men who ran the site ignored requests to take down the postings, claiming that there was insight to be found in "the ugliest depths of human opinion." When Heller was shut out after applying for sixteen summer jobs, she discovered that the firms had searched for her name using Google and come up with AutoAdmit postings such as "Stupid Bitch to Attend Yale Law." Section 230 barred a successful suit against AutoAdmit.com, but the women had a strong enough case to persuade a court to strip away the anonymity of the defamers, including one who styled himself AK47. They eventually identified eight of the men and obtained settlements.

Even when Section 230 protects a website in the United States, it does not protect the site overseas. In 2010, three Google executives were sentenced by an Italian magistrate to six months in prison for not moving quickly enough to block a video of an autistic boy being bullied by students. Privacy trumps free expression in Europe.

Judicial Narrowing of Section 230

Judge Easterbrook raised questions about *Zeran* in dicta in the 2003 decision *Doe v. GTE Corporation.* The dicta had no force of law, but were a sign of emerging discontent with *Zeran.* Hidden video cameras in the locker rooms, bathrooms, and showers of Illinois college sports teams had captured male players in various stages of undress without their consent. The only viable defendant was GTE, which hosted the website young-studs.com, where the videos were for sale. Judge Easterbrook questioned the broad interpretation of *Zeran,* which other circuits had adopted by then. If *Zeran* were correct, Judge Easterbrook reasoned, then online computer services would be "indifferent to the content of information they host or transmit" because they get immunity from suit regardless of whether they "take precautions" to avoid obscene material. Judge Easterbrook's law and economics background emerged as he argued that "As precautions are costly, not only in direct outlay but also in lost revenue from the filtered customers, ISPs [Internet Service Providers] may be expected to take the do-nothing option and enjoy immunity under Section 230(c)(1)." Yet that interpretation, Judge Easterbrook pointed out, conflicts with the title of the law—the Communications Decency Act—and the title of the provision—"Protection for 'Good Samaritan' Blocking and Screening of Offensive Material." This is "hardly an apt description" of the law "if its principal effect is to induce ISPs to do nothing about the distribution of indecent and offensive materials via their services."

Judge Easterbrook acknowledged the caption of a statute had to yield to the text where the text is clear, but he said it was not clear. By reading Section 230(c)(1) as definitional rather than as a grant of immunity, the text and the caption are harmonized, Judge Easterbrook argued. An online computer service would remain a "provider or user" and eligible for the immunity grant in Section 230(c)(2) as long as the information on its site came from a third party; it would become a publisher or speaker if it generated the content and would lose the immunity grant of Section 230(c)(2). Judge Easterbrook's opinion laid the groundwork for later decisions cutting back on Section 230.

The *Doe* dicta were picked up by U.S. District Judge Amy J. St. Eve in a fair housing suit by the Chicago Lawyers' Committee against Craigslist. Third parties posted discriminatory ads on Craigslist rental and sales listings. Some examples were: "NO MINORITIES," "Women of Color NEED NOT APPLY," and "looking for gay latino (sic)." Judge St. Eve held that Section 230 immunity applies not to "any cause of action," but only to causes of action where publishing is a necessary element of the case. Winning a fair housing case requires proof of publication of the discriminatory ad, she concluded, so Section 230 is broad enough to protect Craigslist

from the Chicago Lawyers' Committee suit.

On appeal, the case came back to Judge Easterbrook, giving him an opportunity to reiterate his dicta from *Doe* in an opinion affirming the district court. He wrote that the *Zeran* interpretation did not find "much support in the statutory text" because the text does not contain the word "immunity or any synonym." Judge Easterbrook pointed to the recent decision in *Metro-Goldwyn-Mayer Studios Inc. v. Grokster Ltd.*, in which a movie studio sued a company that developed peer-to-peer file-sharing software, as supporting his view. *Grokster* held that an Internet content provider is liable for contributory copyright infringement for a system designed to encourage infringement. Easterbrook said *Grokster* was incompatible with treating Section 230(c)(1) as an absolute grant of immunity for content provided by third parties. Online computer services designed to encourage illegal postings should be subject to court action just as Grokster was subject to suit because its design encouraged illegal activity. Judge Easterbrook concluded that Section 230(c)(1) provides that an online computer service must not be treated as a speaker or publisher when the content comes from someone else.

Because the Fair Housing Act penalizes acts of publishing, Section 230's safe harbor protects Craigslist from a fair-housing suit. Judge Easterbrook also acknowledged the reality of the Internet, agreeing it would be impractical for an online service, such as Craigslist, to hire a staff to check ads. Users post thirty million housing ads every month involving 450 cities, making it impossible for the staff of thirty to even try to verify them.

Roommates

A potent challenge to the Section 230 safe harbor is Judge Kozinski's 2008 decision in *Fair Housing Council of San Fernando Valley v. Roommates.com, LLC*. Judge Kozinski made it easier for a court to find that an online computer service had forfeited its immunity by turning, chameleon-like, from a service provider to a content provider. Roommates.com is an online classified ad service that helps people find suitable roommates; it has approximately 150,000 active listings and gets a million page views a day. Users fill out online questionnaires choosing answers from drop-down menus; the words in the drop-down menus are words of Roommates' choosing. The questionnaire asks the user's age, sex, and various characteristics. In choosing a roommate preference, the user picks among "Straight or Gay" males, "Straight" males, only "Gay" males, or "No males." In addition, the Roommates questionnaire has a space for users to provide "additional comments." The Fair Housing Councils of San Fernando Valley and San Diego filed suit claiming that these questionnaires violated the Fair Housing Act (FHA) and state laws. Roommates maintained the Section 230 safe harbor protected it from the housing discrimination claim, and the district court agreed. The fair-housing groups appealed, and the three-judge panel of the Ninth Circuit reversed.

The Ninth Circuit panel ruled that Roommates took on the role of an "information content provider" by using a questionnaire and channeling users' answers, thus shedding the immunity enjoyed by an "interactive computer service provider." Judge Kozinski pointed to the definition of an information content provider as anyone "responsible, in whole or in part, for the creation or development of information provided through the Internet."

By composing the questionnaire, Roommates is partly responsible for developing the content, the court ruled. Judge Kozinski wrote that Roommates was responsible for the questionnaires and for sending out the resulting member profiles by e-mail. Roommates is not responsible, however, for the "additional comments" provided by users. This is an ironic result in that most of the racially motivated comments—such as "NOT looking for black Muslims"—were in answer to this portion of the questionnaire. But Judge Kozinski concluded that Roommates' additional comments question was open-ended, suggesting "no particular information that is to be provided by members." For that reason, Roommates retained its identity as an online computer service in respect to these comments because it had not helped develop the content.

The Ninth Circuit agreed to rehear the Roommates case, and, once again, Judge Kozinski wrote the majority opinion, this time for the en banc court. He confessed during public remarks in the spring of 2009 that his en banc opinion was not as sweeping as his earlier panel decision. "I had to write a somewhat more moderate opinion," he said. "We had to add in every line 'don't worry Google is safe.' We said it every way we could."

In the en banc decision, Judge Kozinski did not provide much analysis to determine that Roommates was a content provider when it came to the wording of the questionnaire. "Roommates is undoubtedly the 'information content provider' as to the questions and can claim no immunity for posting them on its site, or for forcing subscribers to answer them as a condition of using its services," he wrote. By requiring users to choose from "pre-populated answers," Judge Kozinski wrote, Roommates "becomes the developer, at least in part, of that information." Roommates asks discriminatory questions, which, Judge Kozinski argued, "is no different from a real estate broker in real life saying, 'Tell me whether you're Jewish or you can find yourself another broker.'"

The Kozinski court also concluded that Roommates' search system did not warrant immunity because it distributes housing information based on the same discriminatory criteria it extracts from its questions. "If Roommates has no immunity for asking the discriminatory questions, as we concluded above . . . it can certainly have no immunity for using the answers to the unlawful questions to limit who has access to housing," the court held.

Judge Kozinski sought to ease the fears of Google, Yahoo!, Bing, and other online computer services that their search processes might also be seen as either discriminatory or part of content development. Roommates "differs materially" from those sites, he wrote, in that Roommates' search was designed to use allegedly unlawful criteria. By contrast, ordinary search engines "do not use unlawful criteria to limit the scope of searches conducted on them. . . . Therefore, such search engines play no part in the 'development' of any unlawful searches."

Kozinski said that close cases should be resolved in favor of immunity. "There will always be close cases where a clever lawyer could argue that something the website operator did encouraged the illegality," he wrote. "Such close cases, we believe, must be resolved in favor of immunity, lest we cut the heart out of section 230 by forcing websites to face death by ten thousand duck-bites, fighting off claims that they promoted or encouraged—or at least tacitly assented to—the illegality of third parties."

For Section 230 not to apply, a plaintiff has to show that it is "very clear that the website director participates in developing the illegality." Otherwise, the "message to website operators is clear: If you don't encourage illegal content, or design your website to require users to input illegal content, you will be immune."

Finally, he responded to the dissent's worry about chilling the growth of commerce on the Internet: "The Internet has outgrown its swaddling clothes and no longer needs to be so gently coddled." Judge Kozinski elaborated on this sentiment in public remarks shortly after the decision. He ridiculed the sky-is-falling reaction of computer services to every challenge to Section 230. He said the computer services always argue that if plaintiffs win, then "Google will die. We couldn't get it to go under if we tried. It's like a big battleship and if we blew a hole in the side it wouldn't sink," he said.

In the Section 230 cases decided since *Roommates,* the en banc decision has become an important point of reference with many courts accepting it as the prevailing law. Nevertheless, the large majority of courts, while following *Roommates,* have distinguished it from the facts of the cases they were deciding and refused to pierce the veil of Section 230 immunity.

In a later Craigslist case, Cook County Sheriff Thomas Dart tried to use *Roommates* as support for the proposition that the online classified service did not have immunity with respect to its erotic listings because it helped generate the content. But a court rejected the sheriff's claim. It ruled that Craigslist does not induce posters to provide anything in particular, making it like the open commentary portion of the Roommates questionnaire, which was upheld.

What could not be won in court was won politically, however. In September 2010, Craigslist bowed to pressure from the attorneys general of seventeen states and took down its erotic website, temporarily replacing it with the word "Censored." Section 230 apparently does not protect a computer service from a concerted campaign of public officials only too happy to attack lurid content.

Perils of Promises

Judge O'Scannlain's decision in *Barnes v. Yahoo!* narrows the Section 230 safe harbor in a different way, by holding that Section 230 does not protect a computer service if it makes a promise to take down illegal material and then fails to do it.

Cecilia Barnes's former boyfriend created a fake profile in her name and posted nude photos and a solicitation to sex. The boyfriend entered Yahoo! chat rooms to direct men toward the profile, resulting in calls seeking sex from Barnes. Barnes sent letter after letter to Yahoo!, in accordance with company policy, requesting the fake profile be removed. After a local news program prepared a story, Barnes received a telephone call from the director of communications promising to "personally walk the statements over to the division responsible for stopping unauthorized profiles and they would take care of it." Two months passed with no action until Barnes finally sued. Then the profiles disappeared.

Judge O'Scannlain read Barnes's complaint to include a claim of promissory estoppel, alleging that Yahoo! had failed to follow through on a promise. Promissory estoppel is a contract claim, not a tort, he wrote, and does not itself involve the act of publishing; Section 230 is therefore irrelevant because it applies to torts involving publishing.

One difficulty in Judge O'Scannlain's argument is that it raises the same problems as *Stratton,* which was the original stimulus for Section 230. In *Stratton,* Prodigy lost its legal protection because it was a high-minded site that promised to remove objectionable content and then failed to follow through. In *Barnes,* Yahoo! ran into the same problem. It promised to remove false profiles, but ended up facing liability because it did not keep the promise. Moreover, Yahoo! could have avoided liability just the way Prodigy could have—by refusing to remove any content from the Web.

If Congress passed Section 230 because it was unhappy that *Stratton* encouraged sites to take no responsibility for content, then *Barnes* might be criticized because it encourages the same irresponsibility.

Shortly after the *Barnes* decision, attorney Jim Dempsey of the Center for Democracy and Technology told a conference on Internet and the law that he did not expect a major impact from the ruling, noting that there are "relatively few winning promissory estoppel cases." Still, he said, "I think it is a terrible decision. The whole structure of 230 was supposed to both protect the post and allow the site to take Good Samaritan measures. . . . One response of companies would be to tell people nothing on the phone. People will say, 'Say you will look into it, but don't say you will do anything.' That will stop the estoppel."

Proposals for Reform

Judge Kozinski, who is funny and outspoken, left little doubt at a conference in the spring of 2009 that he thinks courts should and will further rein in Section 230. He likened trashy Internet posting to "peeing in the swimming pool," predicting that some set of facts will provoke a strong judicial response. "It will have to be the right kind of case where the information is obtained in some illicit way," he said, like "a camera in a bathroom or bedroom without consent." He noted that some computer services were making certain they did not obtain identifying information about anonymous third-party posters so that they would have nothing to surrender during a legal proceeding seeking the poster's identity. That practice could provoke a judicial response, he said. "One solution" to this situation, according to Judge Kozinski, is that a computer service loses its Section 230 immunity "if you willingly want to set up not knowing who are the original content providers."

Judge Kozinski is not alone in thinking that online news sites could lose Section 230 by protecting the anonymity of third-party posters. George Freeman, former lawyer for the *New York Times,* told a First Amendment conference in late 2009 that news organizations are misguided in using "shield laws" to protect the identity of anonymous posters to websites. Freeman does not believe that anonymous Internet posters are analogous to anonymous news sources. "We really risk losing the war, that is the immunity Congress has given us. . . . That kind of 230 immunity is in jeopardy if we play this out to the hilt." Freeman, who has spent his career protecting his newspaper's confidential sources, pointed out that anonymous posters have not asked journalists to promise to protect their identities before providing information, nor has a journalist vetted the poster's comments. "You are dealing with a poster you have no contact with," he said. "You don't know them at all, you have no contact with them and it is really a stretch to call this newsgathering. Many are nutty. What they said may well be defamatory. Should I be protecting their right to be nutty?"

Legal commentators have advocated a variety of reforms to Section 230 that go beyond Judge Kozinski's cosmetic surgery in *Roommates.* Robert G. Magee and Tae Hee Lee questioned the medium-based approach of Section 230, arguing that "information content providers should be subject to the same rules regarding liability for defamation, regardless of the nature of the medium, whether it be a book, a magazine, a chat room or a Web site." Eric Weslander suggested a "modified notice-and-takedown scheme, similar but not identical to what exists under copyright law, which would allow people who were directly affected by objectionable content to petition to have the content removed from the site and which would provide a mechanism for deterring frivolous requests." Cara J. Ottenweller, who focuses on cyberbullying, suggested proposals to void *Zeran*'s inclusion of distributor immunity as a subset of publisher immunity. Frank Pasquale argued that a "right of reply" would allow those who thought they were damaged to asterisk the post and alert readers to a reply, offering victims meaningful recourse on the Internet. Paul Ehrlich suggested stripping the poster of anonymity—a solution that would provide the victim with recourse against the perpetrator, serve as a deterrent to irresponsible posts, and avoid chilling innocent speech.

But Cecilia Ziniti argued that these proposals would not work well on the Web. Ziniti maintained that distributor liability does not make sense in light of the increased interactivity of Web. 2.0 and would result in "service provider over-precaution and its accompanying chilling effect on free speech." "Search engines might abandon indexing any unknown content" if knowledge leads to liability, Ziniti argued. "The marginal effect—that some providers will avoid creating new Web 2.0 services to avoid liability—eliminates much of the social value of the Web 2.0." A notice-and-takedown procedure modeled after the Digital Millennium Copyright Act would avoid the problem that scanning equals knowledge. It also would give victims a way to request removal of illegal content. But online computer services would overreact because each post represents potential liability, Ziniti reasoned. This notice-and-takedown approach would create a "heckler's veto," she wrote, like the one that the Supreme Court frowned upon when it struck down much of the rest of the Communications Decency Act in *Reno v. ACLU.* Ziniti also knocked down the suggestion that a *Grokster*-style standard could be employed, under which a website would lose immunity only if it had taken affirmative steps to invite illegal activity. Ziniti believed this approach would have some of the same problems as the notice-and-takedown procedure. The "right-of-reply" solution would give alleged victims a more satisfactory way to respond to defamatory posts, directing readers to the victim's reply, Ziniti wrote. But she questioned whether readers would follow the asterisk to look at the reply.

Danielle Keats Citron wrote passionately about the need for a cyber civil rights agenda to counter the online mob, which she likened to the Ku Klux Klan or a gang of rapists. She offered a way to protect free-speech interests without ignoring civil rights concerns. Citron proposed that immunity should be determined by a "standard of care," like that used in the area of torts. The most important element of the standard of care would be "traceable anonymity," under which ISPs would retain the identifying information of posters, which would be turned over only under court order. "This would allow posters to comment anonymously to the outside world but permit their identity to be traced in the event they engage in unlawful behavior," she wrote.

Even some of the most moderate of the reforms suggested by commentators—a mandated right of reply and restricting anonymity—could themselves raise First Amendment problems. A right-of-reply requirement might run afoul of *Miami Herald Publishing Company v. Tornillo,* where the Court found that government-imposed right-of-reply requirements for newspapers violated the First Amendment, even though broadcasters had long been required to offer a right of reply. The Supreme Court held in *Reno v. ACLU* that Internet sites receive the highest level of First Amendment protection—like newspapers and unlike the traditionally regulated broadcast industry. For that reason, the Constitution may not permit Congress to impose a right of reply upon websites. In *Reno*—where the Court struck down the portion of the Communications Decency Act written by Senator Exon—Justice John Paul Stevens wrote about the Internet in glowing terms, writing that "any person with a phone line can become a town crier with a voice that resonates farther than it could from any soapbox."

Measures to restrict anonymity might have fewer constitutional problems. *McIntyre v. Ohio Elections Commission* upheld the right of citizens to publish campaign materials anonymously. But the Supreme Court ruled in *Branzburg v. Hayes* that the First Amendment did not protect a reporter-anonymous source privilege. There is less reason to protect the names of anonymous Internet posters than anonymous sources of reporters because the Internet posters did not obtain an agreement of confidentiality before offering the information.

Newsrooms versus Google

Even the judicial and academic critics of the broad interpretation of Section 230 acknowledge that many traditional legal solutions are not up to the reality of the Internet with its millions of postings every day. A notice-and-takedown procedure likely would result in sites taking down every piece of content about which a complaint is filed—whether that content was objectionable or not. It simply would be too hard to review the validity of all of the complaints.

The situation is different for the small, but important, subset of sites covered by Section 230: traditional news sites. They do not face the millions of posts of a Craigslist. For them, the best approach might be to retool newsroom policies already in existence. The *New York Times* has adopted a policy of monitoring all anonymous comments before they are posted; the *Wall Street Journal*'s policy favors subscribers' comments over anonymous comments from nonsubscribers; and the *Washington Post* is considering a plan to give greater prominence to comments with names over those without names. During the past decade, after Jayson Blair's journalistic fraud at the *Times,* newsrooms have cracked down on the handling of anonymous sources. Professional journalism organizations have put into place newsroom policies designed to minimize the use of confidential sources and to require greater oversight by editors. Newsrooms do not need to wait for a Jayson Blair–type problem to address anonymous poster abuses.

News organizations can ban racist, sexist, defamatory, and otherwise objectionable comments, either before they are posted or afterwards. Tight control of poster comments is contrary to the ethic of the Internet culture. Those who want to democratize the news process might oppose these restrictions on posters as a violation of the democracy of the net. But the credibility and accountability that these moves would achieve are consistent with a journalistic culture. When a posting harms someone, the newsroom can look at its truthfulness: Does the poster have firsthand knowledge? Is there confirmation?

Bartnicki v. Vopper protected news organizations that broadcast or publish illegally wiretapped conversations, if they were not involved in the illegal activity.

The First Amendment does not require Section 230. Still, the protections that Section 230 offers to expression on the Web are analogous to the protections that the First Amendment offers free expression in many contexts. Like the First Amendment, Section 230 protects indecent expression, hate speech, and the disclosure of national security secrets. Just as Justice Brennan wrote in *New York Times v. Sullivan* about the importance of providing speech with the breathing room for mistakes, the immunity of Section 230 is the breathing room for speech on the Internet.

Pro

The nation does not need the First Amendment to protect popular speech, but rather to protect the speech people hate. *New York Times v. Sullivan* protected careless, incorrect statements about public officials. *Hustler Magazine v. Falwell* protected the ugliest of speech as parody. *R.A.V. v. St. Paul* freed skinheads who had burned a cross on the lawn of a young, black family. *Cohen v. California* protected a man's right to wear a jacket in a courthouse with the words "F— the draft"; "one man's vulgarity is another's lyric," wrote Justice John Marshall Harlan. *Texas v. Johnson* protected the right to burn the American flag. *Stanley v. Georgia* protected a person's right to possess obscene material in his own home.

Con

Section 230 has transformed the Communications Decency Act into the Communications Indecency Act. The goal of encouraging service providers to police their sites and take down objectionable content was laudable. But it has not worked. Service providers have no incentive to review content of third-party postings. There is no liability for those who do not review the postings. So it does not make sense for a service provider to spend money on employees to review millions of posts. After all, reviewing the posts can just lead to trouble if employees make promises to take down material and then fail to keep the promises.

Section 230 encourages a reckless, no-holds-barred brawl on the Web that damages reputations, threatens the well-being of young people, and harms society's need for truth, civility, or community. The Web is a strong young adult now, not a toddler. Google, Facebook, and Twitter are far more powerful media enterprises than the *New York Times* or *Time* magazine. Yet Section 230 gives the Internet companies legal immunity for third-party posts when print newspapers still are liable for the letter to the editor. Just as the First Amendment has its limits, so too should Section 230. In addition to the limits of *Roommates* and *Barnes,* Congress should consider requiring a right-of-reply, notice-and-takedown procedures like those used in digital copyright cases, and record-keeping to keep track of poster information.

Looking to the Future

The Wild West of the Web, protected by Section 230, has become an accepted part of our lives in the twenty-first century. The Web's robust and burgeoning contributions to free expression and to social dialogue are generally viewed as outweighing the dark side of the Web. It is possible, as Judge Kozinski predicts, that a dramatic or tragic incident will focus national attention on Section 230 in such a way that limitations will be imposed on service providers. But there already have been dramatic events that have not resulted in pressures to limit the Section 230 safe harbor. The Googles, Facebooks, and Twitters are so strong today that they could defeat any attempt to limit their legal immunity.

Even if Congress or the courts were to narrow Section 230, they probably would

not protect the Julie Does of the world. The racial epithets on Craigslist are unfit for a twenty-first-century mode of communication, but, as Judge Easterbrook admits, there is no way a staff of thirty can cull them from a universe of thirty million messages a month. Nor is anyone, including Judge Easterbrook, ready to sacrifice the convenient and economical online housing ads in order to root out all sexual and racial innuendo. Nor are decisions such as *Roommates* and *Yahoo!* going to solve the most egregious cases of abuse because the rulings are narrow, limited to solicitation of illegal content in *Roommates* and to the rare cases of promissory estoppel in *Yahoo!*

Instead of amending Section 230, communities and states probably will continue to pass cyber-harassment laws of dubious constitutionality and federal judges will put some limitations on service providers who induce posters to submit illegal content.

Conclusion

Every day, vast, almost unquantifiable numbers of messages, solicitations, attacks, enticements, lies, and bits of truth flash around the Web. The thirty million Craigslist postings a month are a tiny tip of a Web where there are tens of millions of bloggers. The sheer size of the marketplace of ideas in cyberspace makes it impossible to apply customary rules that worked for a quantifiable and visible set of publications, broadcasts, and advertisements. Nor does the chaos of the Web leave much room for polite debate.

When Oliver Wendell Holmes spoke of his marketplace of ideas or when John Milton spoke about Truth and Falsehood grappling on the field of battle, they could not have imagined the sheer size of the marketplace or the contours of the enormous battle. Holmes and Milton would be horrified by the nasty, mean, and obscene turns that the human mind takes when it is truly set free. But there is no turning back with the tens of millions of postings that are published each day. The notion that a free market of ideas is the best way for society to find the truth is being tested for its own truthfulness on the battlefield of cyberspace.

William H. Freivogel
Southern Illinois University Carbondale

See also Cyberbullying and Student Expression; Reader Comments; Twitter and Traditional Media

Further Reading

Citron, Danielle Keats. "Cyber Civil Right." *Boston University Law Review* 89 (2009): 61.

Kozinski, The Honorable Alex. Remarks at the 22nd Annual Media and Law Conference, Kansas City, MO, April 17, 2009.

Liptak, Adam. "When American and European Ideas of Privacy Collide." *New York Times,* February 26, 2010.

Magee, Robert G., and Tae Hee Lee. "Information Conduits or Content Developers? Determining Whether News Portals Should Enjoy Blanket Immunity from Defamation Suits." *Communication Law and Policy* 12 (2007): 369–404. doi: 10.1080/10811680701558048.

Margolick, David. "Slimed Online." *Portfolio .com*, March 11, 2009.

Ottenweller, Cara J. "Cyberbullying: The Interactive Playground Cries for a Clarification of the Communications Decency Act." *Valparaiso University Law Review* 21 (2007): 1285.

Pasquale, Frank. "Ranking, Reductionism, and Responsibility." *Cleveland State Law Review* 54 (2006): 115, 135–136.

Poulsen, Kevin. "MySpace Sued over 2006 Teen Suicide." *Wired,* February 25, 2008. http://www.wired.com/threatlevel/2008/02/myspace-sued-ov.

Weslander, Eric. "Murky 'Development': How the Ninth Circuit Exposed Ambiguity within the Communications Decency Act, and Why Internet Publishers Should Worry." *Washburn Law Journal* 48 (2008): 267.

Ziniti, Cecilia. "The Optimal Liability System for Online Service Providers: How *Zeran v. America Online* Got It Right and Web 2.0 Proves It." *Berkeley Technology Law Journal* 23 (2008): 583, 600.

30

DRONES

Call it the dawning of journalism's Drone Age.

Unmanned aerial vehicles—aka drones—have left the realm of science fiction and are making their way into use by businesses, the Department of Homeland Security, law-enforcement officials, and news organizations in the United States. Their potential as a newsgathering tool is only just now being explored—but can these machines maneuver around the ethical and legislative obstacles that threaten to block their use?

To answer that question, we first have to try to define what the word *drone* encompasses. In the spring 2013 issue of *News Media and the Law,* Lilly Chapa provided this description: "Technically, any aircraft that is controlled remotely is an unmanned aerial vehicle (UAV), or drone. Most modern drones are controlled by Global Positioning System-based commands programmed through a computer. Drones can cost anywhere from $300 to $5 million and can be as small as a dinner plate or as large as a Cessna. They can be equipped with a variety of tools, including cameras, GPS trackers, infrared sensors and weapons."

As journalists, we know the power of words. The phrase "the pen is mightier than the sword" was coined for a reason—and when our words are backed up by facts and evidence gathered with all the tools at our disposal, our words can have a significant impact. How then, ethically, will we use this new technology to wield the power of the pen to tell our stories?

Pros

In the book *Media Ethics: Issues and Cases,* co-authors Philip Patterson and Lee Wilkins make the case that "moral systems are not synonymous with ethics. *Ethics begins when elements within a moral system conflict* [italics in original text]. Ethics is less about the conflict between right and wrong than it is about the conflict between equally compelling (or equally unattractive) alternatives and the choices that must be made between them."

A group of journalists with a focus on the future has made it its mission to keep the attention on ethics. The Professional Society of Drone Journalists, which formed in 2011, bills itself on its website as "the first international organization dedicated to establishing the ethical, educational and technological framework for the emerging field of drone journalism." The organization's founder is Matthew Schroyer, a drone expert who works on a National Science Foundation grant at the University of Illinois. In a July 2013 interview, Schroyer said he has developed a preliminary code of conduct for drone journalism. His hope is that the code will be interactive at some point, so members of the society can alter the code to keep up with developments in the drone journalism field.

The code lays out the additional responsibilities that drone journalists take on when controlling these unmanned vehicles, and it also emphasizes the potential risks of operating unmanned aerial vehicles (UAVs) in populated urban areas as the speed, range, and size of these machines undergo further development. Being able to take aerial photographs when reporting on a story makes a drone a valuable resource, but in this regard the code also warns that the chance for abuse—especially when it comes to matters of privacy and safety—is also increased.

New Technology for an Old Idea

Aerial newsgathering is nothing new, noted New York media lawyer Nabiha Syed in a May 3, 2013, *Slate* article. Syed, a visiting fellow at the Yale Law School Information Society Project, detailed how, in 1906, a commercial photographer named George R. Lawrence hoisted a 46-pound camera into the air above San Francisco with the help of seventeen kites and steel wire to take panoramic shots of the earthquake and fire devastation in that city. Fast-forward five decades, to 1958, and television news reporter John Silva altered the media landscape even further through his use of the KTLA "Telecopter" in Los Angeles— ushering in the modern reality of live traffic updates (and car chases, too) to the city's residents.

But whenever the subject of drones comes up in American society, ethical conflicts and controversies invariably seem to follow. Consider the uproar regarding Americans' privacy when Amazon's Jeff Bezos announced to CBS's "60 Minutes" correspondent Charlie Rose in 2013 that his company aims to someday use "octocopters" to deliver packages to customers.

The drones do not have pilots sitting in front of a screen to fly them to their destination, Bezos said. Unlike a remotely piloted aircraft, these devices use GPS coordinates to zero in on their landing sites. His announcement prompted members of Congress to introduce legislation to deal with this potential invasion of privacy. U.S. Representative Ted Poe, R-Texas, had this to say not long after Bezos's interview: "Think how many drones could soon be flying around the sky. Here a drone, there a drone, everywhere a drone in the United States. . . . The issue of concern, Mr. Speaker, is surveillance, not the delivery of packages. That includes surveillance of someone's backyard, snooping around with a drone, checking out a person's patio to see if that individual needs new patio furniture from the company."

What the drone movement has going for it, however, is historical record: Many of the technological advances in cars and planes that Americans enjoyed after World War II can be directly traced to advances made in the war effort against Germany and Japan. In this same way, the conflicts in Iraq and Afghanistan have helped fuel the advances in the unmanned aircraft industry. Armed drones still are being used to eliminate terrorists overseas, but the unarmed civilian versions of these machines are now available to any hobbyist (or journalist) with the money to spend on them.

At Present, There's a Future

Whether Americans are ready for them or not, drones are already being deployed within the borders of the United States. They have been in use by the Customs and Border Protection agency along the U.S.-Mexico border and by law-enforcement personnel as well, bringing us closer to what the American Civil Liberties Union has termed a "surveillance society" government. Meanwhile, the Federal Aviation Administration, under the aegis of the 2012 FAA Modernization and Reform Act passed by Congress, has been tasked with integrating commercial drones into U.S. airspace by 2015. The FAA estimates that 7,500 commercial drones could be flying in national airspace in just a few years, and that number could rise to 30,000 by the year 2030, agency officials reported. The FAA is not constrained by the act to address privacy concerns related to the use of commercial drones, and FAA officials said the agency does not have the authority to make or enforce any rules related to privacy concerns.

All the attempts by municipalities and states to regulate how drones are operated by media organizations could eventually involve issues of prior restraint. The First Amendment Handbook of the Reporters Committee for Freedom of the Press says that prior restraint occurs when a government agency restricts what a media outlet can publish. The FAA could be in violation of First Amendment protections of the press if it denies a news organization's request to fly a drone because of the subject matter being covered. Existing laws provide First Amendment protection to drones equipped with cameras that are engaged in communicative photography, despite the obstacles posed by considerations of property law, public safety, and trespass, to name a few. The right of free expression using drones for filming events currently is only constrained by reasonable time, manner, and place restrictions, and a core justification for the right to use drones in this manner also includes government oversight.

Commercially, when the United States finally relents on the FAA drone restrictions currently in place ("if" this will happen seems a foregone conclusion), the country will have come catching up to do in the creativity department for drone uses. In the town of Northam, South Africa, at its annual Oppikoppi music festival August 8–10, 2013, UAVs were scheduled to deliver cold beers to concert attendees via a parachute. At the present time, civilians and businesses in the United States are barred by FAA regulations from using drones for compensation or for hire by others, although the owner of a dry-cleaning business in Philadelphia did hit upon the novel idea of delivering freshly laundered shirts to his customers via drone as a marketing gimmick. The owner of the business, 24-year-old Harout Vartanian, told Philadelphia NBC affiliate WCAU-TV's Vince Lattanzio that he was looking for a way to grab some attention for his business, and the drone delivery idea has done just that. The drones are too small to carry more than a pound or two (which roughly equals a couple of shirts), so the service is not really practical. But it shows what the future might hold for like-minded business owners.

Follow the Money

With Bezos's Amazon, as well as with Vartanian's dry-cleaning business, part of the drive behind the expanded use of UAVs in the United States stems from nothing more than capitalistic ambition. A Bloomberg.com story written by David Mildenberg and posted online December 16, 2013, examines the competition among two dozen U.S. states to win the right to open testing facilities that will determine whether drones can operate in the same airspace as passenger jets. In his story, Mildenberg reveals just how much is at stake, financially, for companies such as Amazon that enter into the drone arena. Almost a quarter-million UAVs are forecast to be in use by the year 2035, according to a study by the U.S. Transportation Department, and less-stringent regulations could lead to the creation of 70,000 jobs over the next

few years. Mildenberg also revealed details from a report drawn up by the Teal Group Corporation—a Fairfax, Virginia-based aerospace research company—that predicts expenditures on civilian and military drones worldwide will total $89 billion during the next decade.

Even with all that money being spent, drones still have the potential to save news organizations even more precious cash in the long run. Matthew Waite, director of the drone journalism program at the University of Nebraska–Lincoln, told Chapa that the helicopters used by morning television programs to report on the rush-hour traffic jams are a huge waste of money. The money spent on the maintenance of the aircraft, plus fuel and insurance, in addition to the pilot's salary, can make the yearly cost hover in the millions. But, for a whole lot less money, these same news programs could buy and fly a drone with a camera that could do the exact same job.

As these UAVs have begun to show their potential as useful tools that can be wielded by journalists and non-journalists alike, there has been an attempt to ease Americans' fear of drones. One such effort involved the Association for Unmanned Vehicle Systems International's three-day trade fair at the Washington Convention Center August 12–15, 2013. The event, which took place less than a mile away from the White House, featured more than 500 exhibits whose main intent was to show how these pilotless machines and other robotic inventions can participate in law-enforcement maneuvers, search-and-rescue operations, traffic control, the sale of houses and real estate, checking remote and inaccessible areas for pipeline problems and forest fires, and much more.

A D(r)one Deal

The use of drones by journalists already is a *fait accompli*—something that has already been done and cannot be undone—and reporters overseas have offered up tantalizing glimpses of the future of drone-enhanced journalism. For example, a video on CNN's website, shot from a drone and narrated by reporter Karl Penhaul 10 days after Typhoon Haiyan ravaged the Philippines in early November 2013, showed what the people of the community of Tacloban, Philippines, had to deal with in the storm's aftermath. The video in which Penhaul appears could be considered a glimpse of the future of journalism—and that same video footage would be completely illegal to shoot in the United States at the present time.

What makes drones so appealing to journalists is that they give reporters access to the sky. That is something that was not nearly so accessible before these machines made their presence known. To get aerial shots used to require a helicopter, a hot-air balloon, or an airplane, all of which are dependent on others to operate and cost money to use. The downside of using drones, especially in populated areas, is that they can come crashing down on the very citizens they were sent up to look down on. In two such recent instances, a drone crashed into skyscrapers in midtown Manhattan and fell to a sidewalk, while another drone spun out of control and crash-landed into a crowd at a bull-running event in Virginia.

Here in the United States, journalism students are experimenting with how to use UAVs to gather information for stories. At the University of Missouri's School of Journalism, students are taking courses that are designed to teach them how to operate drones for news reports. In a story by ABC News' Colleen Curry, journalism professor William Allen said the university has a class in which journalism students are cutting their teeth on the use of "J-bots," which is the term he used to describe these "journalism robots," or drones. The students are using the J-bots to take drone-based photography and video, all in an attempt to see if the machines will be useful to their chosen profession. Because of FAA restrictions, these journalism students can only use their drones in rural areas, limiting their subject matter to agricultural and conservation stories, Allen said.

Schroyer, in a story posted November 19, 2013, on the PSDJ website, used a drone to capture aerial footage of the devastation in Gifford, Illinois, after an outbreak of severe weather swept across the nation's midsection. His article noted that the video was shot with a remote-controlled helicopter that has four motors and can be bought online. A camera capable of shooting 720p video was attached to the drone, and the video footage was transmitted to an Apple iPad on the ground. (He noted, too, that the iPad also was used to control the drone.) Schroyer said he believes that his story represents what drone journalists are capable of doing through the use of these low-cost systems.

Lest anyone think that Schroyer was running afoul of FAA restrictions on drone use by shooting his video, he added a disclaimer at the end of his story that said the drone's flight followed the protocols laid out in FAA advisory circular (AC) 91–57. The FAA document, dating from June 9, 1981, addresses the subject of "model aircraft operating standards." The advisory circular encourages voluntary compliance with safety standards outlined for operators of model aircraft. Some of the operating standards set for model-aircraft operators in the document include the selection of an operating site for the aircraft that keeps a "sufficient" distance from populated areas, and a caution not to fly the machine any higher than 400 feet off the ground.

Waite, who worked for the *St. Petersburg Times* (which changed its name to the *Tampa Bay Times* on January 1, 2012) and PolitiFact, told Chapa that he envisions a time in the not-too-distant future when news organizations have several of these UAVs at the ready to use during breaking news, such as a traffic accident or a house fire. The device could be sent out and flown over the news scene, where it could take a photograph or video and let the workers in the newsroom evaluate whether the story warrants further involvement.

Cons

Chapa's fairly succinct descriptor for these flying machines may not be that easy to apply to all of this burgeoning technology. A Future Tense event that took place May 7, 2013, at the New America Foundation in Washington, D.C., invited speakers to discuss "The Drone Next Door." (Future Tense is a project of *Slate,* the New America Foundation, and Arizona State University that looks at the implications of new technologies, and Torie Bosch is its editor.) In a story about the event, Bosch identified half a dozen hot topics that were debated by the speakers in attendance. What characteristics qualified one of these devices to be called a drone drew comments from Michael Toscano, president and chief executive officer of the Arlington, Virginia–based Association for Unmanned Vehicle Systems International. It is his belief that the use of the word is inaccurate to describe a flying machine in which a human is in control of the system, Bosch reported.

Another speaker at the event, Daniel Rothenberg, said drones have become a catchall for many different forms of surveillance technology, from people wielding video-capturing cell phones to security cameras in buildings—and everything else in between. The word *drone* is an inaccurate term for these machines, said Rothenberg, a professor of practice at ASU's School of Politics and Global Studies. He maintained in his conversation with Bosch that the machines are neither good nor bad in and of themselves; it is the way they are used that leads us to describe them in those terms. He also noted that drones are the face of the future—and that face can instill fear and foreboding in some who do not know what the future holds.

Yet another Future Tense participant, ASU's Brad Allenby, wondered in an article posted online April 30, 2013, why Americans are so worked up about the possible privacy risks posed by drones when our society has been exposed to far more serious and wide-ranging breaches by other technologies. Allenby—the Lincoln professor of engineering and ethics at ASU, and a professor of civil, environmental, and sustainable engineering—penned an article for *Slate* in which he argued that the mountains of data being amassed by Internet behemoths Facebook and Google (as well as tech giants Apple and Microsoft) pose a far greater danger to Americans' privacy than do drones. It also should be noted that Allenby wrote his article in April 2013, months before the Target data-breach fiasco that could have affected up to 110 million shoppers at its stores, but he was prescient enough to mention that financial institutions that possess consumers' credit-card data could have a "far more caustic" effect on privacy than drones. And that is not to mention the growing ability technology has given all of us to record almost everything going on around us today.

What Should We Call These Machines?

Jay Stanley, a senior policy analyst at the American Civil Liberties Union, pointed to the use of the word *drone* as the source of the trouble. He said proponents of the technology would prefer that these machines be referred to by the term *UAV* (for "unmanned aerial vehicle") or *UAS* ("unmanned aerial system") to accurately describe the whole system, from the vehicle itself to the person on the ground controlling it—and the communications connection that links the two. Using these acronyms, Stanley said, is

one way to distance the unmanned (and unarmed) devices deployed in civilian settings from the deadly attacks carried out by the Central Intelligence Agency and U.S. military via Predator and Reaper drones.

At the website of the Drone Journalism Lab, established by the College of Journalism and Mass Communication at the University of Nebraska–Lincoln in 2011, there is a post dated November 14, 2013, that shows the width and breadth of the debate over what definition fits when someone says "drone." The headline for the entry reads, "Why We Argue the Word Drone Is Meaningless," and it links to a story written by David R. Arnott of NBC News that tells how Syrian rebels were showing off a government drone they claimed to have brought down. The Web post encourages readers to click on the link to the report about the captured drone. It reveals that what the rebels brought down was an unmanned aerial vehicle with a camera attached to it. The machines are readily available online and sell for around $500, he said, so trying to equate that device to the unmanned aircraft used by the U.S. military to launch missiles in the course of its antiterrorist operations shows the problems inherent in such a definition.

In the United States, the conflict over drone use involves First Amendment and Fourth Amendment freedoms, possible issues of prior restraint by the federal government, privacy issues with regard to new technology, and state and municipal legislation to rein in what can be done with these machines. Clearly this is a complicated issue, with no immediately obvious answer as to what is "right."

The *Christian Science Monitor*'s website features an article dated April 1, 2013, that was written by Jack L. Amoureux and sports the headline "Are U.S. Drones Ethical?" Amoureux, a visiting assistant professor of politics and international affairs at Wake Forest University, wondered in his article if it is ethical to use drones anywhere. The possibility that an armed drone could someday hover over the heads of Americans in their own backyards might finally spur a debate about U.S. drone policy, he said—especially if it makes those same Americans think about how citizens of other nations feel about these lethal machines buzzing through their airspace.

In a separate opinion column on the *U.S. News & World Report* website, Amoureux noted the legal maelstrom surrounding drone use by saying that opposition to them now revolves around the constitutional rights enjoyed by U.S. citizens. This opposition has led to calls for more regulation of domestic drones, he wrote, especially in light of the fact that the administrations of both George W. Bush and Barack Obama have shown how easy it is to legally justify controversial policies. These legal debates can ultimately serve as a distraction from pressing ethical questions.

Privacy Concerns

The use of drones as a surveillance tool by journalists and law-enforcement officials has stirred up privacy concerns at the state level, drawing efforts by legislators to limit their use in forty-three of the fifty states as of January 2, 2014, according to information posted on the American Civil Liberty Union's website by advocacy and policy strategist Allie Bohm. Of those forty-three states, nine have enacted drone legislation, and bills were still active in five more. But because these drones are being operated in public, there is not much in the way of U.S. privacy laws that prevent their use. The Fourth Amendment provides the "right of the people to be secure in their persons, houses, papers, and effects, against unreasonable searches and seizures." But is that enough in the face of this technological advancement?

For some, including the *Guardian*'s Glenn Greenwald, it is not. In an online article posted March 29, 2013, he wrote that the spreading use of domestic drones for surveillance purposes has not engendered concern among civilians because their use can be equated to the same type of work that police helicopters and satellites perform. That attitude is a sorely misinformed one, Greenwald said, adding that the ACLU's 2011 report on domestic drone use makes that abundantly clear.

Greenwald also noted how American writer Howie Klein has been following the flow of money from the drone industry to members of Congress in an attempt to influence the political response to the use of UAVs in the United States. Those political contributions, Greenwald wrote, have helped squelch congressional action on domestic drone legislation.

Legal Considerations

The prospect of a federal law governing the use of UAVs in the United States is a bridge too far for some. Margot E. Kaminski, in an article published in the May 2013 issue of the *California Law Review Circuit,* wrote that the use of drones by nonpublic entities constitutes the most difficult piece of the privacy puzzle. Kaminski, executive director of the Information Society Project, a research scholar, and a lecturer in law at Yale Law School, said that laws governing the use of civilian drones could restrict the ability of private citizens to conduct legal information gathering. Laws that restrict how drones can be used will offer up privacy concerns as the stated purpose behind them, but she contended that the laws still will constitute restrictions on free speech.

Kaminski added that courts have not determined yet whether privacy rights or free-speech rights will ultimately win out in this debate, and it also remains to be seen how privacy and speech interests interact. She advocates a "drone federalism" approach to legislation, where states take the lead in enacting privacy regulations for UAVs. This will allow for what she terms "necessary experimentation" on how to balance privacy concerns with First Amendment rights.

The issue of invasion of privacy is at least a century old in our American society. Case in point: M. Ryan Calo, director for privacy and robotics at the Center for Internet and Society, wrote an article for the *Stanford Law Review* that considered the role of drones in the privacy debate surrounding these machines. In his article, posted online December 12, 2011, Calo noted that Samuel Warren and Louis Brandeis had a good idea of what a violation of privacy looked like when they wrote their 1890 article "The Right to Privacy." The "yellow journalism" that employed the use of "instantaneous

photographs splashing pictures of a respectable wedding on the pages of every newspaper" was their way to represent a world where technology ran rampant. It was the reason they gave to advance the cause of privacy law in the United States.

In his article, Calo said drones could provide the impetus to refine privacy law to fit modern-day realities, since it is not too far-fetched to imagine a time when everyone from hobbyists to policemen could be using UAVs. It will be up to privacy advocates to ensure that privacy rights are not further eroded.

Entrenched Resistance

Public radio reporter Scott Pham, in an article posted online July 28, 2013, at the website Mashable.com, wrote down what he thinks is the most obvious use for drones in journalism: covering events that pose the most difficulty for photojournalists on land, including public protests and natural disasters. Pham, who noted that he played a role in getting the Missouri Drone Journalism Program (a collaboration that involves the University of Missouri's Information Technology Program, the Missouri School of Journalism, and National Public Radio member station KBIA in Columbia, Missouri) off the ground in 2012, harbored a hunch that Americans' resistance to drone use within their country's borders could be worn down by showing how UAVs could be used for good instead of evil. But Pham reported that he misread the situation regarding drones. In particular, he said he deeply underestimated the drone skeptics, including members of the Missouri General Assembly, who introduced legislation to ban the use of UAVs in the Show-Me State. Pham acknowledges that the use of drones in America is a very controversial topic, but he said he had hoped that people would not be threatened by the use of a drone by a public radio station, which he regards as one the least-threatening entities that could deploy one of these unmanned machines in civilian airspace.

The Missouri bill says that no person, group, or organization, including journalists and news organizations, will be permitted to use an unmanned aircraft to conduct surveillance of any individual or property without consent. In a separate article, Pham called the bill "anti-free speech, anti-journalism and altogether backward."

Akin to pouring salt into an already open wound, the FAA sent a letter to the drone journalism programs of both the University of Nebraska–Lincoln and the University of Missouri, spelling out different standards that the schools would have to follow to fly their unmanned aircraft. This standard, designed for public entities, requires a "Certificate of Authorization" for any outdoor flight of a drone—a process that can take a minimum of two months to complete, reported Yahoo News' Rob Walker in a story posted online August 28, 2013. Walker's story noted that the new FAA hurdle makes turning out even a timely feature story much more difficult than it should be, especially in the context of an academic semester. Walker, who described the process as a "blunt regulatory instrument," said the FAA missed out on a

chance to advance the use of drones in a responsible fashion. To bolster his argument, he pointed out the abundance of unauthorized drone experimentation that is taking place with increasing frequency, which is completely the opposite of what these news programs are attempting to do.

An Abundance of Caution

Part of the resistance to the widespread deployment of UAVs appears to stem from the surreptitious nature in which they can be deployed. After all, people sunbathing in their own backyards can be filmed by a cameraman flying aloft in a helicopter just as easily as by a drone—and with the exception that the aircraft cannot be less than 500 feet off the ground, where private property protection ends, there is nothing illegal about that cameraman being up in the sky. (The U.S. Supreme Court, in the 1946 case *United States v. Causby,* ruled 5–2 that the ancient common-law doctrine that land ownership extended to the space above the earth "has no place in the modern world." Justice William O. Douglas's opinion noted that, if the doctrine were valid, "every transcontinental flight would subject the operator to countless trespass suits. Common sense revolts at the idea.") U.S. citizens have not voiced the same level of concern—or outrage—about security cameras in department stores, banks, or even public streets, so is the real impetus for all this new drone legislation a fear of potential abuse by journalists and the government?

Schroyer, in his International Human Press interview, said that people have every right to be cautious about drone use, but the rules and regulations being formulated in the state legislatures—and even down at the municipal level—sometimes do not grasp the reality of the situation. He did add, though, that states are passing good laws that allow for the use of drones by law-enforcement personnel only when those agencies obtain a warrant.

The recent controversy about drones—and the ultimate impact they will have on journalists and American society as a whole—has been spurred by the use of weaponized UAVs against suspected terrorists in countries such as Afghanistan, Pakistan, Somalia, and Yemen. These Predator and Reaper drones, which are manufactured by General Atomics and operated by the CIA and the U.S. military, have grabbed headlines internationally in America's ongoing war on terror. The use of these drones for air strikes on suspected terrorists has resulted in civilian casualties, even as U.S. officials insist that the attacks have eliminated terrorist threats.

Could these UAVs be weaponized for certain uses in the United States? Information obtained by the Electronic Frontier Foundation in response to a Freedom of Information Act lawsuit against the federal Customs and Border Protection agency shows that idea is not as far-fetched as it sounds. In a 2010 "Concept of Operations" report, the CBP noted that it has considered equipping its drones with nonlethal weapons designed to neutralize "targets of interest." EFF senior staff attorney Jennifer Lynch noted in a blog post that this is the first

that anyone has heard of a federal agency proposing to use weapons in a domestic setting.

Ominous Overseas Reports

Overseas, where U.S. combat missions target religious extremist groups such as al-Qaida and the Taliban, the debate regarding drone technology takes on a lethal tone. In these foreign countries, drones are viewed as harbingers of death and destruction. For example, information found December 22, 2013, on the website of the Bureau of Investigative Journalism estimates that, in Pakistan, between 2,534 and 3,642 people have been killed in 380 drone strikes since 2004. Of those killed, the bureau estimates that between 416 and 951 of them were civilians. Similarly, information on the website estimates that, in Yemen, anywhere from 283 to 412 people have been killed in 57 to 67 air strikes, of which the civilian casualties number between 27 and 71.

These overseas casualty reports that stem from UAVs with ominous-sounding names bring to mind reports of CIA detention programs with "black sites," where suspected terrorists could be subjected to "enhanced interrogation" far away from the prying eyes of the press, as well as the policy of "extraordinary rendition," which U.S. officials began using after the 9/11 terrorist attacks to apprehend suspected terrorists and move them from one country to another. *Fast Company*'s Neal Ungerleider wrote in an article posted online February 6, 2013, that drones still occupy a place in the American psyche that is bounded by assassinations, terrorist attacks, and unintended deaths and injuries to civilians overseas.

In a May 6, 2013, article for *Slate,* Rothenberg wrote that the debate over drone use encompasses much more than the surgical strikes to eliminate terrorists and the potential privacy threats that some experts foresee in the United States. It also includes how the UAVs have become symbols of the disorder, uncertainty, and threats that surround us in a rapidly changing world. To Rothenberg, the greatest challenge we face in our society is how to conduct the debate over this emerging technology in a way that acknowledges the very real fears some people have about these machines. From this learning experience, he said, will come a better, more educated way to regulate drones.

Ethical Considerations

So, assuming Waite is correct in his prediction, what are some of the ethical models that can encompass the complexities of using drones in journalism?

One ethical approach that merits consideration is Aristotle's Golden Mean, in which the virtue of something can be found between the extremes on either end. In the case of drones, one could make the argument that the extremes range from no restrictions at all on domestic drone use—a kind of "anything goes" scenario—all the way to an Orwellian "Big Brother"–style clampdown on any drone use whatsoever. With the number of state legislatures that are considering (or have enacted) some sort of drone legislation,

any solution to be found is likely to fall somewhere in the middle between the two extremes—but that solution will take on a patchwork appearance without some form of overarching regulation from the federal government. That being said, this ethical approach has real potential to help shape the debate regarding drone use, as private citizens, law-enforcement personnel, and legislators hammer out agreements on what can be considered justifiable uses of UAVs. The problem with Aristotle's Golden Mean is that it relies on individuals to act virtuously and not simply follow a set of rules (or a political donor's contributions). Unfortunately, what qualifies as a virtue in one individual may not be a virtue in someone else, so what some may see as an altruistic use of UAVs in the United States may be seen as a massive intrusion into personal privacy by others. There may be no way to find common ground.

German philosopher Immanuel Kant's categorical imperative also could be considered as a potential alternative to address the ethical debate surrounding drones. His ethical model could be described as "acting as though your choices could be considered a universal law." This approach differs from Aristotle's Golden Mean in that it places the emphasis on the actions each individual takes, rather than on the individual. In other words, it takes the focus of acting in an ethical manner out of the realm of the individual and places it instead on what the individual does. Kant's categorical imperative placed at its center the concept of duty. If a person feels that his or her action is dictated by duty, then that action is both moral and ethically correct.

Kant's approach seems to be best suited for members of the military, who are expected to follow orders from their superiors without question. It could be adapted for use by journalists who are considering how to tackle the drone issue, but with such a rapidly changing set of criteria that defines what a drone is in today's world, such a rigid view of what is "right" may not be possible to achieve—at least not in humans. But in machines such as UAVs, what once was considered science fiction may actually be looming on the technological horizon. A Georgia Institute of Technology professor named Ronald C. Arkin has developed a hypothesis for lethal weapons systems on the battlefield that could be ethically superior to human soldiers, wrote Don Troop in the *Chronicle of Higher Education.* Troop's article details how Arkin, a professor of robotics and ethics, has developed algorithms for an "ethical governor" that could someday dictate to a drone or other robotic device whether to shoot (or hold its fire) in a battle environment. The actions of these machines would follow the rules of war that would be agreed upon by international law. Arkin's mention of lethal robots (including drones) sounds eerily similar to the world envisioned in the science-fiction "Terminator" movies, where cybernetic organisms are sent back in time in an attempt to wipe out the human race.

Troop's article also highlights the thoughts of Noel Sharkey, a professor of artificial intelligence and robotics at the England's University of Sheffield. Sharkey pointed out that the Geneva Conventions require that newly developed weapons systems undergo testing during the development process to guard against inadvertent harm to civilians, but no such requirement exists for systems designed strictly for surveillance. Until the 9/11 terrorist attacks in New York and Washington, D.C., surveillance was the name of the game for Predator drones, Sharkey told Troop—but, once those attacks took place, the CIA and the Air Force moved quickly to equip these unmanned aerial vehicles with Hellfire missiles. This creeping militarization of surveillance technology may be the very thing that is creeping out Americans when they think of drones zipping through the skies they sleep under.

A third way to approach the drone debate would be to advocate John Stuart Mill's utility principle. Mill, an English philosopher, was a proponent of 18th-century philosopher Jeremy Bentham's ethical theory of utilitarianism, which can be described as "the greatest good for the greatest number of people." In other words, he emphasized the outcome of an ethical situation over an individual's ethics or the actions of an individual. In their book *Media Ethics: Issues and Cases,* Patterson and Wilkins described how utilitarianism can make some people happy, while at the same time it can make others miserable. For Mill, both outcomes could be valued at the same time; this delicate balancing act, by its very nature, forces discussions regarding the effects on those involved in a particular situation.

Utilitarianism has much to offer in this drone debate; after all, its ultimate goal is the "greatest good," and that is what a great deal of journalists strive for in their profession. But it is also worth noting that Bentham, who inspired Mill, was also the same philosopher who came up with a unique idea for a prison: the "panopticon." Bentham's prison was a place where inmates could be monitored at all times, but they would never be able to see the prison officials who were capable of keeping them under constant surveillance. This could be a representation of how utilitarianism, taken to its extreme, could trample on the rights of a societal minority.

A fourth ethical model for considering the use of drones in U.S. civilian airspace is communitarianism. This approach, according to book authors Patterson and Wilkins, puts the outcome of individual ethical decisions in the spotlight, where they are evaluated based on how the decisions will affect society as a whole. The communitarian approach means that journalism must be part and parcel of both the economic and political systems with which it coexists. Thinking as a communitarian makes it possible for journalists to analyze whether what they consider "news" is a proper mechanism for the community in which they work to grow and transform itself.

In communitarian thinking, values such as altruism and benevolence have just as big a part of any ethical discussion as the elements of loyalty and truth telling, and cooperation among individuals yields desirable results that were once thought to be possible only through competition. It is through this idea of cooperation and benevolence that a middle ground on the issues of privacy and press freedom can be worked out, according to Harvard University professor and American political philosopher Michael J. Sandel, since the word *community* describes for communitarians what they have as citizens. It quite literally is a core part of their societal destiny.

Conclusion

All of these ethical models offer different ethical approaches that journalists can analyze for the best way to deploy drones (and the technology that goes with them) in a responsible manner within newsgathering organizations. Drones represent the latest, but certainly not the only, technological advance in our profession that has raised issues of privacy, morality, and ethics in American society, and it is up to us, as journalists, to find an ethical system that allows media to use these machines in a manner that benefits mankind.

On that point, Waite, in an opinion column posted December 11, 2013, on Al Jazeera's website, wrote that the Society of Professional Journalists' Code of Ethics directs journalists to "seek truth and report it, minimize harm and be accountable." This code, and others like it, can be adapted fairly easily to address the use of drones in journalism, he said. Professional journalists conduct their business ethically, and although that does not mean they will not make mistakes (they will), the fact that they are voluntarily willing to operate under a code of ethics at all proves that the alternative for our society could be much worse.

John Jarvis
Southern Illinois University

See also Invasion of Privacy; New Technology: Free Speech Messiah or First Amendment Traitor; Richard Jewell and the 2013 Boston Marathon

Further Reading

Allenby, Brad. "The Golden Age of Privacy Is Over." *Slate,* April 30, 2013. http://www.slate.com/articles/technology/future_tense/2013/04/domestic_drone_surveillance_the_golden_age_of_privacy_is_over.html.

Amoureux, Jack L. "America Is Asking All the Wrong Questions about Drones." *U.S. News & World Report*, March 19, 2013. http://www.usnews.com/opinion/articles/2013/03/19/were-asking-the-wrong-questions-about-drones.

Amoureux, Jack L. "Are U.S. Drones Ethical?" *Christian Science Monitor*, April 1, 2013. http://www.csmonitor.com/Commentary/Opinion/2013/0401/Are-US-drones-ethical.

Bohm, Allie. "Status of Domestic Drone Legislation in the States." American Civil Liberties Union, February 15, 2013. https://www.aclu.org/blog/technology-and-liberty/status-domestic-drone-legislation-states.

Bosch, Torie. "How to Have a Constructive Discussion about Drones: A Future Tense Event Recap." *Slate,* May 7, 2013. http://www.slate.com/blogs/future_tense/2013/05/07/future_tense_event_recap_how_to_have_a_constructive_discussion_about_domestic.html.

Calo, M. Ryan. "The Drone as Privacy Catalyst." *Stanford Law Review* 29 (2011). http://www.stanfordlawreview.org/online/drone-privacy-catalyst.

Chapa, Lilly. "Drone Journalism Begins Slow Takeoff." *News Media and the Law* 37 (2013): 9–12.

Curry, Colleen. "Drones Eyed by Paparazzi, J-School Teaching Reporters How to Fly Them." *ABC News*, March 22, 2013. http://abcnews.go.com/US/drones-eyed-paparazzi-school-teaching-reporters-operate/story?id=18782432.

Federal Aviation Administration. Advisory Circular 91–57, June 9, 1981. http://www.faa.gov/documentlibrary/media/advisory_circular/91–57.pdf.

Greenwald, Glenn. "Domestic Drones and Their Unique Dangers." *Guardian*, March 29, 2013. http://www.theguardian.com/commentisfree/2013/mar/29/domestic-drones-unique-dangers.

Horsey, David. "Jeff Bezos' Amazon Drone Fleet Raises Premature Privacy Fears." *Los Angeles Times,* December 5, 2013. http://www.latimes.com/opinion/topoftheticket/la-na-tt-amazon-drone-fleet-fears-20131204,0,1849862.story#axzz2n2EKU2s6.

"Interview with Drone Expert and Advocate Matthew Schroyer." International Human Press, July 20, 2013. http://www.ithp.org/articles/droneexpert.html.

Kaminski, Margot E. "Drone Federalism: Civilian Drones and the Things They Carry." *California Law Review Circuit* 57 (2013): 57–74.

Kaufman, Leslie, and Ravi Somaiya. "Drones Offer Journalists a Wider View." *New York Times,* November 24, 2013. http://www.nytimes.com/2013/11/25/business/media/drones-offer-journalists-a-wider-view.html?pagewanted=1&_r=0.

Lynch, Jennifer. "Customs and Border Protection Logged Eight-Fold Increase in Drone Surveillance for Other Agencies." *Electronic Frontier Foundation*, July 3, 2013. https://www.eff.org/deeplinks/2013/07/customs-border-protection-significantly-increases-drone-surveillance-other.

Mildenberg, David. "Freight-Drone Dream Has U.S. States Vying for Test Sites." *Bloomberg.com,* December 16, 2013. http://www.bloomberg.com/news/2013–12–16/dream-of-drone-commerce-has-24-u-s-states-vying-for-test-sites.html.

Patterson, Philip, and Lee Wilkins. *Media Ethics: Issues and Cases.* New York: McGraw-Hill, 2011.

Pham, Scott. "When Journalism Becomes a Game of Drones." *Mashable.com*, July 28, 2013. http://mashable.com/2013/07/28/game-of-drones-journalism.

Rose, Charlie. "Amazon's Jeff Bezos Looks to the Future." *CBS News*, December 1, 2013. http://www.cbsnews.com/news/amazons-jeff-bezos-looks-to-the-future.

Rothenberg, Daniel. "What the Drone Debate Is Really About." *Slate*, May 6, 2013. http://www.slate.com/articles/technology/

future_tense/2013/05/drones_in_the_united_states_what_the_debate_is_really_about.html.

Schroyer, Matthew. "Drone Over Storm-Ravaged Illinois Village Documents Aftermath of Historic Tornado Outbreak." *Dronejournalism.org,* November 19, 2013. http://www.dronejournalism.org/news/2013/11/drone-over-storm-ravaged-illinois-village-documents-aftermath-of-historic-tornado-outbreak.

Stanley, Jay. "'Drones' vs 'UAVs'—What's Behind a Name?" *Free Future,* May 20, 2013. https://www.aclu.org/blog/technology-and-liberty-national-security/should-we-call-them-drones-or-uavs.

Syed, Nabiha. "Privacy Concerns Shouldn't Ground Journalism Drones." *Slate,* May 3, 2013. http://www.slate.com/blogs/future_tense/2013/05/03/drone_regulations_need_to_protect_the_first_amendment_as_well_as_citizens.html.

Troop, D. "'Moral' Robots: The Future of War or Dystopian Fiction?" *Chronicle of Higher Education* 59, no. 3 (2012): 23.

Ungerleider, Neal. "Test Flying a Drone That Makes Anyone an Aerial Photographer." *Fast Company*, February 6, 2013. http://www.fastcompany.com/3005534/test-flying-drone-makes-anyone-aerial-photographer.

Waite, Matthew. "Journalists: Good Early Drone Adopters." *Al Jazeera*, December 11, 2013. http://www.aljazeera.com/indepth/opinion/2013/11/journalists-good-early-drone-adopters-20131123125221676178.html.

Walker, Rob. "The U.S. Government Is Making It Very Difficult for Journalists to Use Drones. That's a Problem." *Yahoo! News*, August 28, 2013. http://news.yahoo.com/drone-journalism-faa-restrictions-164543522.html.

"Why We Argue the Word Drone Is Meaningless." *Drone Journalism Lab,* November 14, 2013. http://www.dronejournalismlab.org/post/66983379659/why-we-argue-the-word-drone-is-meaningless.

31

New York Times v. Sullivan

New York Times v. Sullivan was one of the greatest victories in history for free speech and a free press. But what is lost in the mists of time is that the Supreme Court viewed the case more as a civil rights case than one about the First Amendment.

The case was argued on January 6, 1964, with the Reverend Dr. Martin Luther King Jr. in the courtroom. Five months earlier, Dr. King had led the huge March on Washington for Jobs and Freedom. The largest crowd in U.S. history marched on the National Mall for civil rights. Five months later, Congress passed the Civil Rights Act of 1964. On the day of the oral argument, Justice Arthur Goldberg sent down to King a copy of King's book of the Montgomery bus boycott—*Stride Toward Freedom*—asking for an autograph.

Half a century after the Court's decision, *Sullivan* is more about press freedom than civil rights. The decision constitutionalized defamation and just about insulated the press from suits over stories about public officials or public figures—whether or not the stories were true. To win, a public official or public figure must prove not just falsity but also "actual malice," by which the Court meant "reckless disregard of the truth" or knowledge of the falsity of the allegation.

The decision was a monumental blow on behalf of what Justice William J. Brennan Jr. called the necessity of providing "breathing space" for democracy by allowing the media to make mistakes in their pursuit of a story.

"We consider this case," wrote Brennan, "against the background of a profound national commitment to the principle that debate on public issues should be uninhibited, robust and wide-open, and that it may well include vehement, caustic, and sometimes unpleasantly sharp attacks on government and public officials. . . . Erroneous statement is inevitable in free debate, and [it] must be protected if the freedoms of expression are to have the 'breathing space' they 'need to survive.'"

Debate about Decision

To most First Amendment advocates, *New York Times v. Sullivan* is a touchstone of press freedom. Without it, timid editors would pull their punches and self-censor to avoid costly libel suits. Public officials would use libel as a way to bludgeon media with the temerity to portray them in an unfavorable light—the way that public officials and public figures use defamation in Great Britain.

But not all First Amendment advocates are entirely pleased with the results half a century later. "I wonder if there is libel anymore," said former *New York Times* lawyer Jim Goodale at a public American Bar Association (ABA) event commemorating the fiftieth anniversary of *Sullivan*. *Sullivan*—together with Section 230 of the Communications Decency Act governing online defamation—has resulted in "egregious examples of outrageous libel," he said. "You have two million people libeling each other all day long."

Geoffrey Stone, the noted First Amendment expert and professor at the University of Chicago Law School, said at the same event that Brennan's blow for giving the democracy "breathing space" may have instead damaged political discourse. When Brennan wrote *Sullivan* he was "thinking about mainstream, professional reporters," said Stone, who was a clerk for Brennan. Now, with the Internet,

> people engaged in professional discourse . . . are not professional at all. . . . Instead of dealing with professional reporters it now includes every Tom, Dick and Harry on the Internet. . . . One can make the argument that the long-term consequence of *Sullivan* is to destroy credibility and that has a damaging impact on democracy. . . . *Sullivan* was situation driven—it was about the civil rights movement, not the First Amendment. . . . But as a First Amendment decision it left a lot of the justices uncomfortable. . . . Its

consequences for public discourse became much more problematic. . . . False statements don't advance public discourse . . . they poison discourse.

As a result of *New York Times v. Sullivan*, the law is more protective of free expression than are the ethical codes of major news organizations. The decision protects those who carelessly make false allegations about public figures and public officials. For that reason, it can protect poor, careless, unethical reporting that violates journalistic norms. Yet Justice Brennan's call for protecting the "breathing space" of a democracy is a kind of utilitarian "greater good" argument that democracy will work better if it protects the freedom to be wrong than if the media are afraid to disclose the wrongdoing of the powerful.

"Heed Their Rising Voices"

Sullivan was about civil rights from the start. The controversy began with a mistake-riddled full-page advertisement in the March 29, 1960, edition of the *New York Times* with the stirring title "Heed Their Rising Voices." That admonition was aimed straight at Congress, quoting a *New York Times* editorial that had urged, "Let Congress heed their rising voices for they will be heard." The ad had been placed by southern ministers leading the civil rights movement and by noted entertainers such as Harry Belafonte, Sidney Poitier, and Marlon Brando and celebrities such as Jackie Robinson and Eleanor Roosevelt.

The ad contained several mistakes. Most were minor, but at least one could have justified a libel judgment even under the actual malice standard. The minor mistakes were that Dr. King had been arrested four, not seven times. Students were not singing "My Country 'Tis of Thee" on the steps of the State Capitol in Montgomery, Alabama; they were singing the National Anthem. Students were expelled by the State Board of Education not for leading the demonstration at the Capitol, but rather for demanding service at a lunch counter in the Montgomery County Courthouse on a different day. Most of the student body, not the entire student body, protested the expulsion. They did it by boycotting class, not refusing to re-register. The biggest mistake was the claim that armed police had ringed student protesters at Alabama State and padlocked their dorm to "starve them into submission." The dorm had not been surrounded, nor were the officials trying to starve the students.

The *New York Times* advertising department made no effort to check the facts, instead relying on the good name of civil rights leader A. Philip Randolph, who vouched for the signatures on the ad. Had the *Times* checked its own morgue, it could have discovered the errors. As the text of the ad demonstrates, the mistakes were a small part of the message. The mistakes are in boldface.

"The growing movement of peaceful mass demonstrations by Negroes is something new in the South, something understandable. . . . Let Congress heed their rising voices, for they will be heard."

—*New York Times* editorial
Saturday, March 19, 1960

Heed Their Rising Voices

As the whole world knows by now, thousands of Southern Negro students are engaged in widespread non-violent demonstrations in positive affirmation of the right to live in human dignity as guaranteed by the U.S. Constitution and the Bill of Rights. In their efforts to uphold these guarantees, they are being met by an unprecedented wave of terror by those who would deny and negate that document which the whole world looks upon as setting the pattern for modern freedom. . . .

In Orangeburg, South Carolina, when 400 students peacefully sought to buy doughnuts and coffee at lunch counters in the business district, they were forcibly ejected, tear-gassed, soaked to the skin in freezing weather with fire hoses, arrested en masse and herded into an open barbed-wire stockade to stand for hours in the bitter cold.

In Montgomery, Alabama, after **students sang "My Country, 'Tis of Thee"** on the State Capitol steps, **their leaders were expelled from school, and truckloads of police** armed with shotguns and tear-gas **ringed the Alabama State College Campus**. When the **entire student body** protested to state authorities by **refusing to re-register**, **their dining hall was padlocked in an attempt to starve them into submission.**

In Tallahassee, Atlanta, Nashville, Savannah, Greensboro, Memphis, Richmond, Charlotte, and a host of other cities in the South, young American teenagers, in face of the entire weight of official state apparatus and police power, have boldly stepped forth as protagonists of democracy. Their courage and amazing restraint have inspired millions and given a new dignity to the cause of freedom.

Small wonder that the Southern violators of the Constitution fear this new, non-violent brand of freedom fighter . . . even as they fear the upswelling right-to-vote movement. Small wonder that they are determined to destroy the one man who, more than any other, symbolizes the new spirit now sweeping the South—the Rev. Dr. Martin Luther King, Jr., world-famous leader of the Montgomery Bus Protest. For it is his doctrine of non-violence which has inspired and guided the students in their widening wave of sit-ins; and it this same Dr. King who founded and is president of the Southern Christian Leadership Conference—the organization which is spearheading the surging right-to-vote movement. Under Dr. King's direction the Leadership Conference conducts Student Workshops and Seminars in the philosophy and technique of non-violent resistance.

Again and again the Southern violators have answered Dr. King's peaceful protests with intimidation and violence. They have bombed his home almost killing his wife and child. They have assaulted his person. **They have arrested him seven times**—for "speeding," "loitering" and similar "offenses." And now they have charged him with "perjury" under which they could imprison him for *ten years*. Obviously, their real purpose is to remove him physically as the leader to whom the students and millions of others—look for guidance and support, and thereby to intimidate *all* leaders who may rise in the South. Their strategy is to behead this affirmative movement, and thus to demoralize Negro Americans and weaken their will to struggle. The defense of Martin Luther King, spiritual leader of the student sit-in movement, clearly, therefore, is an integral part of the total struggle for freedom in the South.

Decent-minded Americans cannot help but applaud the creative daring of the students and the quiet heroism of Dr. King. But this is one of those moments in the stormy history of Freedom when men and women of good will must do more than applaud the rising-to-glory of others. The America whose good name hangs in the balance before a watchful world, the America whose heritage of Liberty these Southern Upholders of the Constitution are defending, is *our* America as well as theirs. . . .

We must heed their rising voices—yes—but we must add our own.

We must extend ourselves above and beyond moral support and render the material help so urgently needed by those who are taking the risks, facing jail, and even death in a glorious re-affirmation of our Constitution and its Bill of Rights.

We urge you to join hands with our fellow Americans in the South by supporting, with your dollars, this Combined Appeal for all three needs—the defense of Martin Luther King— the support of the embattled students—and the struggle for the right-to-vote.

Your Help Is Urgently Needed . . . NOW!!

The Trial

Almost no one read the ad in Alabama. Only about 394 copies of the editorial circulated in the state, about thirty-five of which were distributed in Montgomery County, where L. B. Sullivan was the police commissioner. Sullivan was not named in the ad, a fact that became important in the decision.

The person who noticed the ad and got the controversy started was himself a journalist, Grover C. Hall Jr., editorial editor of the *Birmingham Advertiser*. Hall wrote an editorial condemning the ad, titled "Lies, Lies, Lies." Hall himself opposed segregation and was the son of a *Birmingham Advertiser* editor who won the Pulitzer Prize for opposing the Ku Klux Klan in the 1920s. But Hall Jr.

thought that northern pressure caused pushback from the South. He also was irritated that the northerners turned a blind eye to racism in their own backyards.

The judicial handling of Sullivan's lawsuit against the *Times* was infected by segregationist bias. First, the *Times* had trouble finding a lawyer who would represent it in Alabama. Then the trial judge, Walter Burgwyn Jones, denied the *Times*'s efforts to remove the case to federal court, even though that ruling was contrary to a legal treatise on the subject of jurisdiction that Jones himself had written. The one hundredth anniversary of the Confederacy fell during the trial, and Jones allowed the jurors to wear Confederate uniforms and pistols to court to commemorate the occasion. Sullivan could not prove damages, but several witnesses testified that they knew the ad referred to him because he was in charge of the Montgomery police. The jury returned a verdict of $500,000, a large sum at the time.

Nor was the verdict the only one that the *Times* faced in the South. Harrison Salisbury, the legendary *Times* reporter and editor, estimated that the *Times* faced about $3 million in libel and criminal libel verdicts in the South, all flowing from civil rights coverage. Justice Hugo Black noted in his concurrence that the *Times* had eleven libel suits against it in Alabama alone, seeking a total of $5.6 million. CBS faced another $1.7 million, he noted. This situation came at a time when the nation's leading newspaper was financially vulnerable, having just started to recover from a financially damaging strike. George Freeman, a former *New York Times* lawyer, said that the advertising side of the

Times argued in favor of the paper pulling out of the South editorially because of the financial threat of the libel suits.

Brennan addressed the issue of self-censorship in his opinion. "Whether or not a newspaper can survive a succession of such judgments, the pall of fear and timidity imposed upon those who would give voice to public criticism is an atmosphere in which the First Amendment freedoms cannot [survive]. . . . A rule compelling a critic of official conduct to guarantee the truth of all his factual assertions—and to do so on pain of libel judgments virtually unlimited in amount—leads to . . . self-censorship."

More than once, Brennan alluded to the civil rights backdrop of the case. He wrote that the ad communicated "information, expressed opinion, recited grievances, protested claimed abuses, and sought financial support on behalf of a movement whose existence and objectives are matters of the highest public interest and concern." And later: "The present advertisement as an expression of grievance and protest on one of the major public issues of our time, would seem clearly to qualify for the constitutional protection."

Brennan gave several reasons for providing more protection for speech critical of public officials than of private individuals. One was that American history demonstrates that the First Amendment does not permit seditious libel. Seditious libel punishes criticism of the government. Brennan referred to the famous crisis of 1798 regarding the Sedition Act. That law made it a crime punishable by prison and steep fines to criticize public officials, including the president, then

John Adams. The law was used to jail newspaper editors who supported Adams's political opponent, Thomas Jefferson. Brennan noted that the Sedition Act never had been tested in the Supreme Court. The controversy preceded the establishment of judicial review in the 1803 *Marbury v. Madison* decision. But Brennan said that the "attack upon the Sedition Act's validity has carried the day in the court of history" and that "its invalidity has been assumed" by the justices of the Supreme Court.

Brennan went on to note that a judgment of the size involved in the *Sullivan* case could be a greater punishment than was meted out by seditious libel laws. Because the history of the Sedition Act of 1798 showed that seditious libel violates the First Amendment, then the use of state libel laws to punish criticism of public officials even more harshly must also violate the amendment.

Another reason for removing some libel protection from public officials was that the Court had recognized that statements made by public officials acting within their public duties could not be actionable unless made with actual malice. Citizen critics should be on a level playing field with public officials, he wrote.

Finally, the Court ruled that Sullivan could not collect because he was not named in the ad. The ad was not "of and concerning" Sullivan.

The Supreme Court could have thrown the case out on a jurisdictional question. Judge Jones's refusal to remove the case against the *Times* from state court was most likely wrong. The doctrine of judicial restraint would counsel that the Court should decide the case on the most narrow grounds possible, rather than reaching out to the constitutional question. But had the Supreme Court ruled for the *Times* on the jurisdictional issue, then Sullivan would most likely have prevailed against the four ministers he had also sued and over whom the state court in Alabama had jurisdiction. Plus, the press would have been denied a signal victory.

Chief Justice Earl Warren had chosen Brennan to write the opinion because he was the most likely justice to win over the entire Court for a unanimous opinion. Brennan was known as a schmoozer on the Court who was extremely successful in creating majorities and sometimes unanimous opinions. Brennan succeeded in the *Sullivan* case when Justice John Harlan withdrew his dissent at the last moment.

As a matter of First Amendment theory, the *Sullivan* decision was viewed as a victory for the argument advanced by Alexander Meiklejohn basing First Amendment theory on self-government. As Meiklejohn put it, "The principle of free speech springs from the necessities of the program of self-government. It is not the Law of Nature or of Reason in the abstract. It is a deduction from the basic American agreement that public issues shall be decided by universal suffrage." Meiklejohn went on to stress that his source of protection for free speech protected speech about public matters rather than private ones. Because the source of the freedom flows "from the necessities of self-government by universal suffrage," it assures protection only to "speech which bears directly, or indirectly, upon issues with which the voters have to deal . . . considerations of matters of public interest." It does not protect private speech about private matters in the same way, he argued.

Public Figure, Public Concern

In 1967, soon after *Sullivan,* the Court extended the actual malice standard to public figures. The Court took the action in two cases involving famous figures, one of whom is more remembered for his notoriety than fame. He was retired major general Edwin Walker, who was accused in an Associated Press story of having urged students at the University of Mississippi to riot to bar the admission of the first black student, James Meredith. The other public figure case involved Georgia football coach Wally Butts, who was accused in an article in the *Saturday Evening Post* of fixing a 1962 football game with legendary Alabama football coach Bear Bryant. The Court decided that both Butts and Walker were public figures. Butts won and Walker lost. The Court differentiated the two stories because the AP story on Walker was on deadline and did not show any violation of journalistic standards. The Butts story, on the other hand, was an investigative report that the magazine had plenty of time to research. The non-sports reporter who wrote the story based it on a source who claimed to have overheard a telephone conversation between Butts and Bryant. The source was unreliable, having written bad checks. In addition, the reporter did not check out the story thoroughly. For example, he did not interview another person who was said to have overheard the conversation.

Chief Justice Warren explained the extension of *Sullivan* to public figures by noting that the political process does not provide a check on the activities of public figures as it does on public officials. For that reason, he concluded, "public opinion may be the only instrument by which society can attempt to influence their conduct." In a society where the distinctions between the public and private sphere are blurred, public figures "often play an influential role in ordering society," and they have access to the media to "influence policy and to counter criticism of their views and activities."

A high-water mark for Brennan's expansion of *Sullivan* was the 1967 *Time v. Hill* decision, when the Court extended the *Sullivan* standard from public affairs to coverage of entertainment. The case was not a defamation case but rather a false light privacy decision. In 1952 the Hill family was held hostage in its home for nineteen hours by three escaped convicts, who treated the family courteously. A play inspired by the incident injected violence into the plot. *Life* magazine ran a picture story showing scenes from the play in the Hills' former house. Hill sued under New York's Right to Privacy law, which recognized a cause of action where there was a "material and substantial falsification" of a newsworthy event. The case gained extra attention because former vice president Richard M. Nixon argued the case for the family. Initially, when discussing the case in its secret conference, the Court voted 7–2 in favor of Hill, according to published accounts. Justice Abe Fortas, a liberal who was under attack in the media for questionable investments, wrote a bitter draft opinion attacking the press. But then Brennan began to pick off members of the majority until he controlled the opinion. Brennan wrote, "We have no doubt that the subject of the *Life* article, the opening of a new play linked to an actual incident, is a matter of public interest. The line between the informing and the entertaining is too elusive for the protection of [freedom of the press.] Erroneous statement is no less inevitable in such case than in the case of comment upon public affairs, and in both, if innocent or merely negligent, [it] must be protected if the freedoms of expression are to have the 'breathing space' that they 'need to survive.'"

For a time, it seemed the Court was ready to extend the *Sullivan* standard to protect false statements about private individuals if the publication involved matters of public concern. In *Rosenbloom v. Metromedia* in 1971, Brennan wrote a plurality opinion making that extension. A defamatory broadcast had reported that George Rosenbloom, the distributor of nudist magazines in Philadelphia, was guilty of a crime when he had only been arrested. Rosenbloom was a private citizen, but the issue was one of public concern, the Court said. But soon the court pulled back from that extension of *Sullivan.*

Public Figure versus Private Figure

By *Gertz v. Robert Welch* three years later, the composition of the Court had changed, and so too had its view on matters of public concern. Justice Lewis F. Powell Jr.

returned to *Sullivan*'s emphasis on public officials rather than matters of public concern. In *Gertz,* a John Birch Society publication called *American Opinion* had claimed that a prominent Chicago lawyer, Elmer Gertz, was the "architect" of a "communist frameup" of a policeman convicted of killing a young man. Gertz represented the family in a civil case related to the murder. Powell explained that the *Sullivan* actual malice standard was better applied to public officials rather than private individuals involved in matters of public concern. He noted that public officials have connections to the press and can defend themselves by getting out their point of view. In addition, he noted that public officials had voluntarily stepped into the public spotlight and "must accept certain necessary consequences of that involvement in public affairs."

Powell began to try to explain who would be a public figure and who would be a private one. "In some instances," he wrote, "an individual may achieve such pervasive fame or notoriety that he becomes a public figure for all purposes and in all contexts. More commonly, an individual voluntarily injects himself into a particular public controversy and thereby becomes a public figure for a limited range of issues." Gertz did not meet this standard, Powell said. He had served as an officer in civil and professional groups and published books and articles that made him well-known in certain circles. But he had achieved "no general fame or notoriety in the community." None of the jurors knew of him. Powell said that the Court would not lightly classify an involved citizen as a public figure. "Absent clear evidence of fame or notoriety in the community, and pervasive involvement in the affairs of society, an individual should not be deemed a public personality for all aspects of life."

Powell provided some protection for the press in libel cases filed by private individuals. A private individual did not have to meet the *Sullivan* actual malice standard to collect actual damages, but did have to meet the standard and prove falsity in order to collect punitive damages.

Having decided to go the public figure rather than public concern route, the Court soon found that drawing the line between the public officials and figures and private individuals was difficult. For example, a police officer is a public official but a firefighter generally is not. The police officer's authority to use deadly force is the rationale for this seemingly arbitrary line drawing. A person who is a public official for part of his or her career can return to private life. For example, a Justice Department official running an organized crime task force is a public official for his actions in that role. But after returning to the private practice of law he is not a public official or public figure for his run-of-the-mill legal work, even though he would remain a public official for subsequent stories about his work in the Justice Department.

In a 1976 decision, Justice William H. Rehnquist wrote the Court's opinion determining that the heiress to the Firestone tire fortune—from one of the wealthiest families in America—was not a public figure when it came to stories about a messy divorce involving extramarital sex. Rehnquist wrote that people who have not taken on special prominence in the affairs of society are not

public figures unless they "thrust themselves to the forefront of particular public controversies in order to influence the resolution of the issues involved." Filing divorce papers in court and holding press conferences to answer reporters' questions was not determined to transform a private figure into a public one.

Brennan's Fight to Save *Sullivan*

Although *Sullivan* appears to be firmly rooted in the law today, it faced severe challenges in the 1970s and 1980s on the Court and in society. Lee Levine, a noted First Amendment lawyer, told the ABA forum on the fiftieth anniversary of *Sullivan* that the threat was real. "Yes, there definitely was a time and place when Brennan was afraid *Sullivan* was at risk," he said.

During the 1980s two big national libel suits by two generals left media lawyers wondering how much protection *Sullivan* provided. General William Westmoreland sued CBS for its stories criticizing the general's conduct of the Vietnam War. Israeli General Ariel Sharon sued *Time* magazine for its stories about his involvement in the Israeli killing of Palestinian refugees in camps in Lebanon during the Israeli invasion of Lebanon. Both lawsuits were wars of attrition that involved huge defense costs and that damaged the credibility of the media involved.

But the challenge within the Court was more serious. *The Progeny,* a book published on the fiftieth anniversary of the decision, describes Brennan's successful effort to nurture and save *Sullivan.* The book is written by Levine and Steve

Wermiel, the former *Wall Street Journal* Supreme Court correspondent who conducted extensive interviews with Brennan before the justice's death. The book injects an ironic footnote to history: There was a marked difference between the public Brennan, who believed passionately in the press, and the private Brennan, who had an uncomfortable relationship with the press.

Brennan had a close relationship with Anthony Lewis, the *New York Times* reporter who popularized the *Sullivan* decision with his book *Congress Shall Make No Law*. But Brennan confided that he did not think the press did a good job of reporting on legal issues because reports on the Supreme Court lacked depth. He thought the press did not respect people's privacy and he refused to hold press conferences because of the risk of being misquoted or misconstrued. The press coverage of Abe Fortas that led to his resignation from the Court hurt Brennan. Brennan himself invested in a real estate trust recommended to him by another federal judge. When that became the subject of press reports, Brennan sold his interest, canceled all speaking engagements, and quit the American Bar Association and the New Jersey bar as well.

But on the Court, Brennan continued his all-out effort to defend *Sullivan* against former allies and new conservative opponents.

Justice Byron R. White, who had joined *Sullivan* in 1964, soon served notice within the Court that he did not entirely buy into the decision. He had been on board in *Sullivan* partly because of the civil rights backdrop. White had been president John F. Kennedy's assistant attorney general for civil rights before joining the Court in 1962. But the same year *Sullivan* was decided, he had grave reservations about the application of *Sullivan* in *Garrison v. Louisiana*. That case involved Jim Garrison, the controversial district attorney from New Orleans who later went on to claim he had found proof of a New Orleans conspiracy that led to the assassination of President Kennedy. The libel case did not involve the Kennedy assassination, however. Garrison had been in a fight with the judges in his parish and held a press conference in which he attributed the big backlog of criminal cases to inefficiency, laziness, and excessive vacations of the judges. He also accused the judges of refusing to cover the expenses of undercover investigations of vice in New Orleans. He said: "The judges have now made it eloquently clear where their sympathies lie in regard to aggressive vice investigations by refusing to authorize use of the DA's funds to pay for the cost of closing down the Canal Street clip joints. . . . This raises interesting questions about the racketeer influences on our eight vacation-minded judges." Garrison was convicted under Louisiana's criminal libel law.

White drafted a strongly worded dissent saying that he would not protect the malicious liar's calculated falsehood. Brennan adopted much of the language from White's dissent and incorporated it into his majority opinion. The dissent did not see the light of day. In this part of the opinion, Brennan stated, "Calculated falsehood falls into that class of utterances '[of] such slight social value as a step to truth that any benefit that may be derived from them is clearly outweighed by the social interest in order and morality.'" The internal quotes are from the *Chaplinsky v. New Hampshire* case, where the Court declared that "fighting words" were not protected by the First Amendment.

But the overall ruling of the Court was that Louisiana's criminal libel law violated *Sullivan* and was unconstitutional. The Court ruled that the law violated *Sullivan* for two reasons. First, it permitted a person to be jailed for criminal libel for even truthful statements, if the statements were made with ill will. "Truth may not be the subject of either civil or criminal sanctions where discussion of public affairs is concerned," wrote Brennan. The other reason that the Louisiana law violated *Sullivan* was that it did not require the actual malice standard where the criticism of a public official was directed at the official's private conduct and amounted to a personal attack, like Garrison's. Brennan rejected the distinction. He wrote,

The *New York Times* rule is not rendered inapplicable merely because an official's private reputation, as well as his public reputation, is harmed. The public-official rule protects the paramount public interest in a free flow of information to the people concerning public officials, their servants. To this end, anything which might touch on an official's fitness for office is relevant. Few personal attributes are more germane to fitness for office than dishonesty, malfeasance, or improper motivation, even though these characteristics may also affect the official's private character.

Chief Justice Warren E. Burger, who came on the Court after *Sullivan,* had

joined Brennan in the *Rosenbloom* case involving the pornographer. But later Burger took steps to deny Brennan the chance to write opinions in defamation cases. When the majority of the Court was ready to rule for the press, Burger would join the majority so he could assign the opinion to someone other than Brennan. By most accounts, the justices resented the obvious gamesmanship and appreciated the more straightforward way that Burger's successor, Chief Justice Rehnquist, assigned opinions.

Brennan still managed to outmaneuver Burger. In *Philadelphia Newspapers, Inc. v. Hepps,* the Court had initially voted to require that a media defendant disprove the falsity of a story. But it was a thin and fragile majority that emerged from the Court's conference and soon Justice Sandra Day O'Connor began having her doubts. Brennan was able to pick up O'Connor and take away the majority from Burger. He assigned the case to O'Connor to make sure that he kept that majority. The Court ruled that a private figure plaintiff has the burden of proving falsity when the topic is a matter of "public concern" where a media defendant is involved.

The differences between White and Brennan were particularly sharp in *Dun & Bradstreet, Inc. v. Greenmoss Builders, Inc.* in 1985. In that case, the credit-reporting service reported to five clients that Greenmoss was about to file for bankruptcy and that it had fewer assets than it actually controlled. Greenmoss won actual and punitive damages from the Vermont Supreme Court. The Supreme Court upheld that award, saying that *Gertz*'s rule on punitive damages did not apply because the issue was not a matter of public concern and the story was not widely distributed. White initially wrote a strong draft dissent in which he said that *Sullivan* had been wrongly decided. A worried Brennan wrote an elaborate defense of his landmark opinion. But that defense never saw the light of day because Justice John Paul Stevens came to Brennan to say he did not feel comfortable with it and suggest that it was unwise to publicize the split on the court over *Sullivan.* Brennan pulled back.

Is There False Opinion?

The Court had said in some of its libel decisions that there was no such thing as a false opinion. That had led many libel lawyers to assume that statements of opinion were immune from libel suits. That assumption turned out to be off base.

In *Milkovich v. Lorain Journal Company*, 1990, Chief Justice Rehnquist said the Court had not actually meant that there is no such thing as a false opinion. In some instances, opinions appear to be based on the assertion of particular facts; if a news organization has shown reckless disregard of the truth in basing its opinion on a false set of facts, then a statement of opinion can be susceptible to a libel suit.

Mike Milkovich was a legendary wrestling coach at Maple High School in Ohio. His squads often won the state title. During one big wrestling meet, a fight broke out between communities. Milkovich denied instigating the fight when he testified under oath to a hearing of state education officials. A sports columnist, Ted Diadiun, wrote, "Anyone who attended the meet . . . knows in his heart that Milkovich . . . lied at the hearing after . . . having given his solemn oath to tell the truth." Milkovich sued. He lost in the lower courts, which took the Supreme Court at its word when it said there was no such thing as a false opinion. But Rehnquist concluded that a published statement of opinion that implies the truth of a set of facts can be the basis of a libel suit if the underlying facts are wrong and the paper was malicious in its use of the false information. In this instance, the claim that Milkovich had lied under oath implied that he had perjured himself by misstating facts under oath. That could be the basis of a lawsuit.

Media lawyers were surprised and mildly panicked. But the *Milkovich* decision never turned out to have as much impact as it first seemed it might. Milkovich himself settled for an uncertain amount and the decision did not lead to a spate of libel suits aimed at opinion.

Parody

Even though Rehnquist had appeared to be a threat to *Sullivan* in both *Milkovich* and *Firestone,* he ended up expanding *Sullivan* in an important decision involving parody: *Hustler Magazine v. Falwell,* 1988.

The Reverend Jerry Falwell was a nationally prominent and politically influential preacher who frequently provided important support to conservative candidates and causes.

Larry Flynt, the publisher of pornographic *Hustler Magazine,* printed an ad parody patterned after the Campari liquor advertising campaign in which celebrities talked about their "first times." Although the ad suggested through double entendre that the celebrities were talking about the first time they had sex, the ads actually talked about the first time they had drunk Campari. The *Hustler* parody said that Falwell's first time having sex was with his mother in an outhouse when they were both drunk. It also said Falwell only preached when he was drunk. A label in small type at the bottom of the ad read: "Ad parody—not to be taken seriously."

Falwell sued for emotional distress and had home-court advantage in his home state of Virginia, where he won a big judgment against *Hustler* for infliction of emotional stress—$100,000 in compensatory damages along with additional punitive damages. What few people knew about Rehnquist was that he had once been an avid amateur cartoonist in his days at Stanford University. One of the influential amicus briefs in the case was filed by the nation's editorial cartoonists. They pointed out that exaggeration, parody, sarcasm, and hyperbole were their bread and butter. One cartoon that the lawyer preparing the brief left out was drawn when Rehnquist was in the midst of a difficult confirmation fight. That one showed Rehnquist in Ku Klux Klan robes trying to deny blacks the right to vote in his native Arizona. The cartoon played off of Rehnquist's controversial role as a young Republican election judge challenging the voting credentials of African Americans in Arizona.

The brief—minus the Rehnquist cartoon—was obviously influential, as Rehnquist cited it in his opinion providing

First Amendment protection to the *Hustler* cartoon. The chief justice wrote about the long history of hyperbolic political cartoons dating back to the cartoons that ridiculed Boss Tweed during the Tammany Hall corruption of the nineteenth century. He wrote,

> The political cartoon is a weapon of attack, of scorn and ridicule and satire; it is least effective when it tries to pat some politician on the back. It is usually as welcome as a bee sting, and is always controversial in some quarters. . . . Several famous examples of this type of intentionally injurious speech were drawn by Thomas Nast, probably the greatest American cartoonist to date, who was associated for many years during the post–Civil War era with *Harper's Weekly*. In the pages of that publication Nast conducted a graphic vendetta against William M. "Boss" Tweed and his corrupt associates in New York City's "Tweed Ring." It has been described by one historian of the subject as "a sustained attack which in its passion and effectiveness stands alone in the history of American graphic art." Another writer explains that the success of the Nast cartoon was achieved "because of the emotional impact of its presentation. It continuously goes beyond the bounds of good taste and conventional manners."

Despite their sometimes caustic nature, from the early cartoon portraying George Washington as an ass down to the present day, graphic depictions and satirical cartoons have played a prominent role in public and political debate. Nast's castigation of the Tweed Ring, Walt McDougall's characterization of presidential candidate James G. Blaine's banquet with the millionaires at Delmonico's as "The Royal Feast of Belshazzar," and numerous other efforts have undoubtedly had an effect on the course and outcome of contemporaneous debate. Lincoln's tall, gangling posture, Teddy Roosevelt's glasses and teeth, and Franklin D. Roosevelt's jutting jaw and cigarette holder have been memorialized by political cartoons with an effect that could not have been obtained by the photographer or the portrait artist. From the viewpoint of history, it is clear that our political discourse would have been considerably poorer without them.

Rehnquist conceded that "there is no doubt that the caricature of respondent and his mother published in *Hustler* is at best a distant cousin of the political cartoons described above, and a rather poor relation at that. If it were possible by laying down a principled standard to separate the one from the other, public discourse would probably suffer little or no harm. But we doubt that there is any such standard, and we are quite sure that the pejorative description 'outrageous' does not supply one."

Rehnquist extended the *Sullivan* actual malice standard to parody and other hyperbolic speech. It is a somewhat-unusual application of a standard that requires proof of actual malice, reckless disregard of the truth, and knowledge of falsity. The *Hustler* ad was published with the knowledge that the claim of Falwell having sex with his mother in an outhouse was actually false.

Wermiel, the *Progeny* author, said at the ABA conference on *Sullivan* that Brennan was ecstatic with Rehnquist's opinion. "Rehnquist . . . wrote an opinion that Brennan could have written. Brennan said the press should just kiss Rehnquist for his opinion in *Hustler v. Falwell*. He could leave the Court in peace. If Rehnquist could write that opinion, *New York Times v. Sullivan* was safe."

Alternatives to *Sullivan*

Some critics of *Sullivan* have advocated allowing a judicial determination of falsity, without damages. But Stone, the former Brennan clerk and *Sullivan* critic, said that neither plaintiffs nor press defendants like that solution. For plaintiffs there is no money, and the press risks its reputation.

Ethicists have advocated the creation of national or regional news councils. The council is composed of retired judges, journalists, lawyers, and other notables. Under this approach, the panel of notables hears evidence from both an aggrieved official and the editors and reporters. The aggrieved party agrees in advance not to seek money damages.

Some news councils were created in the last part of the twentieth century, and there were a few examples of what supporters consider to be successes. One much-publicized example was Northwest Airlines' complaint against WCCO and Don Shelby. The airline complained about an investigative report that asserted Northwest had a large number of safety violations. Some of the video that accompanied the report had been doctored to appear to show airplanes coming in for landings at such a steep angle that they would have crashed. The news council found that the TV station had exaggerated its report, a conclusion with which the broadcasters strongly disagreed.

But news councils never have caught on. The Minnesota News Council recently disbanded, as have others around the country.

Pro

New York Times v. Sullivan provides the breathing space for robust public debate essential to a democracy. Without the actual malice standard, public officials could use the threat of big libel judgments to intimidate the press into submission and self-censorship. The *New York Times* came face-to-face with that pressure with its coverage of the civil rights movement in the South and its publication of an ad in support of the Reverend Martin Luther King Jr. *Times* ad executives proposed pulling out of the South because of the pressure. In the balance, it is better to protect a robust press that accidentally makes some mistakes when writing about public officials than to open up the press to pressures that can lead to self-censorship of truthful, important, but controversial news concerning public officials and public figures. In the final analysis, the *Sullivan* actual malice standard protects the greater good of a democratic society.

Con

New York Times v. Sullivan has protected poor journalism by allowing journalists to escape court censure even when they carelessly report false information. Rather than advancing public discourse, *Sullivan* contributes to poisoning that discourse by protecting false information. *Sullivan*—in combination with Section 230's absolute protection of Internet companies from libel suits for false third-party postings to websites—floods the public arena with false information, hard to sort from truthful information. Some have suggested a judicial determination of falsity, without money damages. Others have suggested news councils to evaluate reporting without damages. But neither alternative has taken hold.

Looking to the Future

New York Times v. Sullivan appears to be safe from judicial revisionism. It will continue to provide journalists—whether they be professional or citizen journalists—with protection against libel suits designed to silence or intimidate. The robust public discussion that Justice Brennan sought to encourage has become increasingly robust—and sometimes ugly. Self-styled journalists who lack the professional ethics that news organizations instill publish rumor and innuendo that would never make the news standards of traditional news organizations. Information posted to the Web is especially problematic in that it often lacks the internal editing and application of journalistic standards that traditional journalism imposes. If there are to be limits imposed on the robust public debate that currently exists, those limits would more likely be imposed on Internet postings by making websites more responsible for third-party postings. There is no current move in that direction, however, as the spirit of the Web favors greater rather than less freedom.

Conclusion

New York Times v. Sullivan was the product of the most controversial years of the civil rights movement. At the time, the Warren Court was ten years into its effort to tear out segregation "root and branch." The libel judgments that had been won in the South against the *New York Times* and other northern media pressured those companies to cut back on their support of a reporting and editorial commentary critical of the South's segregation. The $3 million of libel judgments facing the *Times* threatened the robust debate of that scourge on American society.

While rooted in the civil rights movement, *New York Times v. Sullivan* became one of the great First Amendment and free press landmarks, providing broad protection for the press, even when it makes mistakes. The decision was followed by a golden age of investigative reporting about the wrongdoing of public officials, an era symbolized by Bob Woodward and Carl Bernstein's Watergate reporting that contributed to the resignation of President Nixon.

The expansion of *Sullivan* from public officials to public figures, from public affairs to the entire range of news coverage, from factual accounts to cartoons and parodies, has been one of the most important developments of the past half century in the debate of public issues.

William H. Freivogel
Southern Illinois University Carbondale

See also False Light; First Amendment Theory; Free Press versus Public Safety; Opinion and Libel; Parody, Satire, and the First Amendment

Further Reading

American Bar Association, Forum on Communications Law. "*New York Times v. Sullivan:* A 50th Anniversary Celebration." February 7, 2014.

Babcock, William A. "News Councils." *Gateway Journalism Review,* Winter 2014.

Brauer, David. "Not Everyone Sad to See the Minnesota News Council Go." *MinnPost,* February 3, 2011. http://www.minnpost .com/braublog/2011/02/not-everyone-sad-see-minnesota-news-council-go.

Fein, Bruce. "*Hustler Magazine v. Falwell:* A Mislitigated and Misreasoned Case." *William and Mary Law Review* 30 (1989): 905.

Levine, Lee, and Stephen Wermiel. *The Progeny: Justice William J. Brennan's Fight to Preserve the Legacy of* New York Times v. Sullivan. Chicago: American Bar Association, 2014.

Media Law Staff Reporter. *Libel on Trial: The Westmoreland and Sharon Cases.* BNA Special Report, 1985.

32

PARODY, SATIRE, AND THE FIRST AMENDMENT

Shortly before Egyptian satirist Bassem Youssef canceled his popular political TV comedy program, *Al-Bernameg,* in 2014, his American counterpart, Jon Stewart, appeared on his show in Cairo, after Youssef had been a guest on Stewart's show in New York City. With an audience of thirty million viewers, Youssef had been previously arrested and interrogated for insulting the country's president and Islam.

"Let me ask you this," Youssef said to Stewart in a mock interrogation. "Does satire put you, does it get you in trouble? How about the love you feel from the people?"

"I'll tell you this," Stewart replied, laughing. "It doesn't get me into the kind of trouble that it gets you into. I get in trouble, but nowhere near what happens to you."

A segment on CBS News's *60 Minutes* titled "The Jon Stewart of Egypt" featured both men discussing their shows, their relationship, and differences in constitutional protection for their satirical commentary. While Stewart can freely criticize American public officials without fear of government reprisal, pressure from the Egyptian government and fear for his family's safety motivated Youssef to curtail his satirical expression.

American political satire is protected by the First Amendment, but does that same degree of protection also apply to satires that create fake news stories, or comedic parodies involving well-known trademarked commercial products or someone else's copyrighted original expression?

What about fair or unfair use of copyrighted works and protected trademarks exploited for fun, such as singer-songwriter "Weird Al" Yankovic's musical parodies inspired by Top 40 songs? What about liability for a popular New York City morning radio host who recently quipped, after playing a promotion jingle mocking several commercials, "I hope I don't get sued"? Or trademark plaintiffs recovering for jokes about their products or slogans, such as "Michelob Oily," "Hard Rain Café,"

"Mutant of Omaha," "Lardashe Jeans," or "Muppet Spa'am"?

Satires and Parodies: Distinctions and Protections

The distinctions between satire and parody are both literary and legal. Satire mocks a culture, society, or individual in general without using copyrighted work or protected trademarks. Constitutionally, satire merits strong First Amendment protection.

According to Gilbert Highet in his 1962 book *The Anatomy of Satire,* satire "deals with actual cases, mentions real people by name or describes them unmistakably (and often unflatteringly), talks of this moment and this city, and this special, very recent, very fresh deposit of corruption whose stench is still in the satirist's curling nostrils."

Among the classic satires is Jonathan Swift's 1729 essay "A Modest Proposal," intended to ridicule English economists and landlords. Among Swift's satirical suggestions was a moneymaking proposal to slaughter poor Irish children and sell their remains for human consumption. But like his contemporary colleagues, not everyone enjoyed the joke, such as when the satirical newspaper the *Onion* posted a fake 2011 story that armed U.S. House members took a group of schoolchildren hostage in the Capitol.

In discussing the need for constitutional protection for satire, Robert D. Sack in his seminal work *Sack on Defamation* stated, "Humor is an important medium of legitimate expression and central to the well-being of individuals, society, and their government. Despite its

typical literal 'falsity,' any effort to control it runs severe risks to free expression as dangerous as those addressed to more 'serious forms of communication.'"

Parody is more particular in its humorous targets since the expression relies on a copyrighted work or a protected trademark. Considered under intellectual property law, parody's protection falls under fair use of copyrighted material or trademarks. As defined by *Black's Law Dictionary,* parody is "a transformative use of a well-known work for purposes of satirizing, ridiculing, critiquing, or commenting on the original work, as opposed to merely alluding to the original to draw attention to the later work."

In the 1994 landmark parody copyright case *Campbell v. Acuff-Rose Music, Inc.,* the Supreme Court cited definitions of parody from "modern dictionaries" as a "literary or artistic work that imitates the characteristic style of an author or work for comic effect or ridicule" and a "composition in prose or verse in which the characteristic turns of thought and phrase in an author or class of authors are imitated in such a way as to make them look ridiculous."

That distinction between parody and satire can cause legal confusion, especially in predicting how courts will decide. As the American Civil Liberties Union notes in an online essay, "Satire and Parody and the First Amendment," that uncertainty over the "parody-satire distinction has a chilling effect on speech." For example, the Ninth Circuit (*Dr. Seuss v. Penguin Books*) found that the "poetic account" about the O.J. Simpson Trial, *The Cat NOT in the Hat: A Parody by Dr. Juice,* was not a parody, but a copyright infringement of the Dr. Seuss classic *The Cat in the Hat.* However, the Eleventh Circuit (*Suntrust Bank v. Houghton Mifflin*) considered Alice Randall's 2001 *Wind Done Gone* a fair use parody of Margaret Mitchell's 1936 classic *Gone with the Wind,* and vacated a federal district court injunction against its publication. But why did Mitchell's estate not sue over other parodies, such as Carol Burnett's TV skit about life on the "Terra Plantation somewhere in Georgia?"

First Amendment protection for parody and satire involves two distinct areas of media law: intentional infliction of emotional distress and intellectual property.

While the 1988 landmark parody case *Hustler Magazine v. Falwell* is sometimes considered as a libel case, the opinion also deals with the tort of intentional infliction of emotional distress. That tort includes three elements: conduct by the defendant considered intentional or reckless, conduct offending accepted standards of decency, and conduct causing the plaintiff severe emotional distress. Whether the plaintiff sues for libel or emotional distress, the outcome relies on whether the reasonable reader would understand the material as a parody or a satire.

That "reasonable reader" standard applies in suits regarding parody and satire in intellectual property law: copyright and trademark. Even though the primary purpose of a parody or satire is humor, the holder of a mimicked trademark or copyright might not find the use to be humorous, especially if there is a commercial use, public confusion, or damage to the protected mark. In the past three decades, the number of such suits by intellectual property owners has substantially increased, even though the courts have given humorous commentary considerable latitude.

An example of such frivolous suits involved comedian Al Franken's 2003 book examining America's conservative news media called *Lies and the Lying Liars Who Tell Them: A Fair and Balanced Look at the Right.* Fox News Channel attempted to stop Franken, who has since become a U.S. Senator representing Minnesota, from using the registered trademark slogan "fair and balanced" used to identify the cable news service. Even though Fox News commentator Bill O'Reilly appeared on the book's cover, Franken argued the satirical work examined other conservative media besides Fox, and the use of the slogan was protected parody. In *Fox News Network LLC v. Penguin Group (USA), Inc.*, the U.S. District Court of the Southern District of New York denied Fox's motion for a temporary restraining order to prevent publication of Franken's book with that title. In denying the motion, Judge Denny Chin called the case "wholly without merit, both factually and legally." It would be "highly unlikely" that the public would mistake Franken's book for a Fox product. "Here, whether you agree with him or not in using the mark, Mr. Franken is clearly mocking Fox," Chin wrote. Fox dropped the suit, and the book soared to the top of the best-seller charts.

In defending copyright- and trademark-infringement suits, a humorist could argue the fair use defense, particularly when the parody or satire involves a well-known word, slogan, or symbol that represents a "public figure." But how far should that fair use go? Should it cover any funny work borrowed from the original, or must the humor result from expression concerning the original work? Is the parodist creating something new and fresh, or just exploiting the original work for attention? How crucial is the humorist's intent—to comment or copy—in determining fair use?

In clarifying any confusion about the nature of the parody, the creator must send two messages, both "simultaneous and contradictory," even though some might not understand the humor. As the Second Circuit stated in a trademark infringement case, *Cliffs Notes, Inc. v. Bantam Doubleday Dell Publishing Group, Inc. (1989),* the messages must "convey . . . that [the parody] is the original, but also that it is not the original and is instead a parody."

Fair Use in Parodies: Copyright and Trademark

As stated in Section 107, Title 17 (limitations of exclusive rights) of the U.S. Code, the current fair use doctrine considers four factors to determine the fair use of copyrighted material: "(1) the purpose and character of the use, including whether such use is of a commercial nature or is for nonprofit educational purposes; (2) the nature of the copyrighted work; (3) the amount and substantiality of the portion used in relation to the copyrighted work as a whole; and (4) the effect of the use upon the potential market for or value of the copyrighted work."

The Supreme Court applied the copyright fair use test for parody in its 1994 opinion in *Campbell v. Acuff-Rose Music,*

Inc. Prior to that decision, parody copyright decisions were limited to federal circuit cases, such as those in the Ninth and Second Circuits, particularly regarding musical parodies, as discussed by Charles L. Sanders and Steven R. Gordon in their 1990 article "Strangers in Paradise: Weird Al and the Law of Musical Satire."

The *Campbell* decision concerned the unauthorized use of Roy Orbison's 1964 hit rock ballad "Oh, Pretty Woman" by the rap group 2 Live Crew. One of the world's largest music publishers, Acuff-Rose Music Inc., which owned the copyright to the song written by Orbison and William Dees, claimed the rap group's 1989 commercial parody, written by Luther R. Campbell, was a copyright infringement on the original work. The publisher had refused 2 Live Crew's previous request to pay a fee to use the song, but the group released their parody version anyway.

Orbison's hit describes a lonely man, who pleads with a beautiful woman to spend time with him by saying, "Pretty woman, don't walk on by. Pretty woman, don't make me cry. . . ." Instead of ignoring him, the woman does walk his way. The parody copied the original song's first line and guitar riff, before degenerating into a social commentary on the life and culture depicted by the song, with the "pretty woman" becoming quite the opposite. As the federal district court wrote, the parody turned "predictable lyrics into shocking ones" and showed "how bland and banal the Orbison song seemed to them."

The original song stated, "Pretty woman, walking down the street. Pretty woman, the kind I like to meet." The 2 Live Crew parody rephrased the original song,

"Ball-headed woman, girl your hair won't grow. Ball-headed woman, you got a teeny-weeny afro."

The case pitted the nation's parodists and satirists against the nation's copyright holders and songwriters. Was 2 Live Crew's parody a fair use of the copyrighted song, or did the mocking version's "commercial character and excessive borrowing" negate a fair-use defense under the Copyright Act of 1976?

The Sixth Circuit overturned the district court's granting of summary judgment for 2 Live Crew and its music company, Luke Skywalker Records. In unanimously overruling the Circuit Court in favor of 2 Live Crew, the Supreme Court weighed the "nature" of the parody in using the original song against its for-profit nature or "commercial character." Using the Copyright Act's four-pronged test to determine the parody's fair use of the original song, the Court, in an opinion written by Justice David Souter, held that the parody's commercial nature was "only one element" to consider, and that "insufficient consideration was given to the nature of the parody in weighing the degree of copying" of the original song.

Determining fair use for a parody must also consider whether the new work is "transformative" or whether it "merely supercedes the objects" of the original creation. How much and to what extent does the parody "alter" the original work "with new expression, meaning, or message?" The Court stated, "The more transformative the new work, the less will be the significance of other factors, like commercialism, that may weigh against a finding of fair use." Acuff-Rose did not deny that the parody has "transformative

value," but the Court found that 2 Live Crew's version provides "social benefit, by shedding light on an earlier work, and, in the process, creating a new one."

Fair use allows a certain amount of copying (not excessive) in order for the public to recognize the original (e.g., Orbison's opening line). The parody must quote "the original's most distinctive or memorable features" since "it is the heart at which the parody takes aim." In order to do that, "the parody must be able to 'conjure up' at least enough of the original to make the object of its critical wit recognizable," the Court stated.

A parody does not have to be labeled as such, and does not lose protection because some readers, viewers, or listeners do not understand the humor. The Court quoted a 1992 trademark case from the Southern District of New York, *Yankee Publishing Inc. v. News America Publishing, Inc.,* "First Amendment protections do not apply only to those who speak clearly, whose jokes are funny, and whose parodies succeed."

With parody, "context is everything," the Court continued, since not "anyone who calls himself a parodist can skim the cream and get away scot free." What else did the parodist do "besides go to the heart of the original?" In the parody, 2 Live Crew used the first line and opening riff, but then "departed markedly" from Orbison's lyrics, while copying and repeating the bass riff. "Like any other comment or criticism," parody "may claim fair use" under federal law. As for the 2 Live Crew parody's impact on the market value of the original song, the Court stated, "The cognizable harm is market substitution, not any harm from criticism. As to parody pure and simple, it is unlikely that the work will act as a substitute for the original, since the two works usually serve different market functions."

In determining fair use for parodies in copyright infringement cases, the courts do not always accept a fair use defense for all parodies. Parodies must have more than a humorous element, and must make a critical commentary on a copyrighted work to be "fair," not just bring the original work into the public mind to draw attention to the new work. For a parody to succeed, it must use a sufficient amount of material to "evoke" the original work.

As discussed by copyright attorney Alan R. Friedman at the Practising Law Institute's "Fundamentals of Copyright Law in the Data Era 2014," decisions in copyright infringement cases regarding fair use defenses for parodies "are not always consistent." That was demonstrated by two 1998 fair use cases, *Leibovitz v. Paramount Pictures Corporation* and *Columbia Pictures Industries v. Miramax*.

In the first case, Paramount Pictures created a marketing poster for the feature film *Naked Gun 33 1/3* with actor Leslie Neilsen's smiling face imposed on a pregnant woman's naked body. The poster was intended to replicate a *Vanity Fair* magazine cover with a photograph by Annie Leibovitz of actress Demi Moore posing serious, naked, and pregnant. Leibovitz claimed copyright infringement, while Paramount argued a fair use defense. In applying *Campbell*'s fair use analysis, the Second Circuit agreed with Paramount that the use was fair since the parody poster was a critical comment by

making fun of the "seriousness, even the pretentiousness" of the original cover photograph.

In the second case, the fair use parody defense was rejected. Columbia Pictures created a promotional poster for the feature film *Men in Black* with the movie's intimidating heroes, played by actors Will Smith and Tommy Lee Jones, holding large weapons. To promote the documentary film *The Big One,* Miramax created a promotional poster with a smiling filmmaker Michael Moore dressed in a black suit, white shirt, black tie, and sunglasses, while holding a large microphone. The U. S. District Court for Central California held that the Miramax poster was a copyright infringement, since it did not critically comment on the *Men in Black* poster, but only conjured up the original for an advertising campaign.

Parody can also be a defense in trademark infringement claims unless the parody is intended to be an actual trademark used in commerce, which might not qualify as protected First Amendment speech. As discussed by trademark attorney Vijay Toke at the Practising Law Institute's "Fundamentals of Trademark Law in the Global Marketplace 2014," the parody must be "obvious" to the public as an amusing joke, and not cause confusion with a protected trademark. "If you make the judge laugh, you win," Toke stated in describing a successful defense.

Successful examples of the parody trademark defense would be "Lardashe" jeans for "large size women" instead of Jordache jeans, or dog toys shaped like Louis Vuitton handbags. A more "subtle" parody could cause confusion and not qualify for a parody defense, such as "Dom Popingnon" popcorn marketed in bottles resembling Dom Pérignon.

A nominative fair use defense can also be used to defeat a trademark infringement claim, since courts may recognize parodies as protected First Amendment speech, as discussed in the *Intellectual Property Book 2014*. To qualify for that protection, the parody's humor must target the protected trademark for an expressive, not a commercial purpose. For example, in *Mattel Inc. v. MCA Records Inc.*, the Ninth Circuit ruled in favor of MCA Records for the song "Barbie Girl" as a fair use of the Barbie doll trademark owned by Mattel. The court ruled that such lyrics as "I'm a blond bimbo girl in a fantasy world" mocked the iconic doll without mentioning its name, the use of the Ken and Barbie doll trademark was necessary to fulfill the parody's purpose, and such steps by the record company as a disclaimer on the album avoided confusion of any affiliation with the doll's manufacturer.

A trademark holder can also sue by claiming that the parody causes dilution or public confusion with a major trademark, as Siegrun D. Kane discussed in *Kane on Trademark Law*. While the purpose of a parody is to poke fun at a famous trademark, the owner can argue that the parody could cause dilution to tarnish the mark. Is the parody trademark intending to sell competing products and benefit from the famous trademark, or is it intended to be a social commentary or pure entertainment? Will the consumer public interpret the parody trademark as a joke and not be confused with the famous trademark? In recent years, Kane stated, courts tend to be more liberal toward a parody use of protected trademarks.

But not all parodies of famous trademarks merit First Amendment protection. Some examples likely to cause confusion would be "Michelob Oily" mocking Michelob Ultra beer and "Mutant of Omaha" instead of the insurance company Mutual of Omaha. Lardashe jeans (Jordache jeans) and Muppet Spa'am (Spam meat) parodies did not cause public confusion.

The parody slogan "Condom, don't leave home without it" was found to cause dilution of the trademarked slogan, "The American Express card, don't leave home without it." The "Petley Flea" parody did not cause dilution of the Tetley tea trademark.

First Amendment Protection: Libel and Emotional Distress

In an ironic parallel with another famous plaintiff in *New York Times v. Sullivan*, the Reverend Jerry Falwell first heard about *Hustler* magazine's ad parody through a newspaper journalist. Alabama public service commissioner Lester Bruce "L. B." Sullivan first saw the 1960 editorial advertisement "Heed Their Rising Voices" after a *Montgomery Advertiser* journalist discovered it few days after its publication in the *New York Times*, and paid little heed—at first. Falwell was asked about *Hustler*'s ad parody by a reporter when leaving a news conference in Washington, D.C., and replied, "That is probably nothing new."

Falwell and *Hustler* publisher Larry Flynt had been trading attacks for several years prior to the Campari ad parody. The TV evangelist regularly attacked the "Big Three" of pornography, namely *Playboy, Penthouse,* and *Hustler,* particularly the latter. In return, *Hustler* and Flynt regularly lampooned Falwell with several cartoons.

Once back at his Lynchburg, Virginia, headquarters, Falwell sent a staffer to buy *Hustler*'s November 1983 issue. According to Rodney Smolla's 1988 book *Jerry Falwell v. Larry Flynt: The First Amendment on Trial* and Falwell's trial testimony, the parody nearly brought the evangelist to tears. In response, he filed a $45 million lawsuit for libel, invasion of privacy, and intentional infliction of emotional distress.

As Falwell described his initial reaction during his trial testimony, "I think I have never been as angry as I was at that moment. . . . My anger became a more rational and deep hurt. I somehow felt that in all of my life I had never believed that human beings could do something like this. I really felt like weeping. I am not a deeply emotional person; I don't show it. I think I felt like weeping."

Meanwhile, Flynt had his own legal problems, being in prison at time of complaint over his refusal to disclose his source in automobile executive John DeLorean's cocaine-smuggling trial. "I didn't know [about the lawsuit] until my attorney came and told me," Flynt recalled in Joseph Russomanno's 2002 book *Speaking Our Minds: Conversations with the People behind Landmark First Amendment Cases.*

Between 1981 and 1983, Campari liqueur, an Italian aperitif, ran advertisements in several national magazines, including *Cosmopolitan, People,* and *Playboy,* featuring such celebrities as Geraldine Chaplin, Elizabeth Ashley, and Johnny Carson describing their "first time" with the liqueur. As *Hustler*'s publisher stated, Falwell "seemed like an appropriate candidate" for a parody of the Campari advertisement describing another fictional "first time" experience of having sex with his mother in an outhouse. The full-page ad parody with Falwell's smiling photograph featured a mock interview describing the fictional sexual encounters, and getting intoxicated on the liqueur before preaching. Below Falwell's photograph, the "interview," and a Campari bottle, a small-type caption read, "Ad parody—not to be taken seriously."

"We just thought it would be great to use Falwell in the ad parody because he would be an unlikely person that you would see doing a liquor ad," Flynt told Russomanno. "So we all thought it was funny. Apparently Falwell didn't."

Nor did others. For example, the Fourth Circuit's opinion stated, "In this interview Falwell allegedly details an incestuous rendezvous with his mother in an outhouse in Lynchburg, Virginia. Falwell's mother is portrayed as a drunken and immoral woman and Falwell appears as a hypocrite and habitual drunkard."

Thus began a four-year battle between one of America's most famous televangelists and one of its most infamous pornographers featuring a lawsuit, trial, appeal, and landmark First Amendment Supreme Court decision, all covered in detail by the national media. As Smolla described, "The case was at once high moral drama and farcical passion play, a tragicomic mélange of bombastic law-yers, contemptuous witnesses, and scath-ing cross-examinations."

With the defense denied a change of venue motion, the six-day "wild circus" trial in December 1984 was held in the U.S. District Court for the Western District of Virginia in Roanoke, not far from Falwell's home base, which included his Thomas Road Baptist Church mega-congregation, his Moral Majority conser-vative political organization, and his Liberty University. Flynt also lost an infringement of copyright suit and appeal in Los Angeles, after Falwell distributed a copy of the ad parody in a direct mail campaign to his followers to fund the law-suit. Falwell successfully claimed fair use to republish the ad parody.

Flynt and *Hustler* were represented by Los Angeles–based attorney Alan Isaacman, assisted by David Carson. For decades, Isaacman had represented his client in several cases around the coun-try. Across the aisle for the plaintiff was New York City attorney Norman Roy Grutman, who had represented Bob Guccione and *Penthouse*. That represen-tation included victories in *Falwell v. Penthouse* over a published interview given to two freelance reporters, in *Pring v. Penthouse* against celebrity attorney Gerry Spence, and in a case against *Hustler* and Flynt.

Judge James Clinton Turk did not allow the jury to consider Falwell's appro-priation claim for invasion of privacy, but did allow deliberation on the claims of libel and intentional infliction of emo-tional distress. Using the latter claim against a media defendant was "a rela-tively new idea," Smolla stated. Although

"highly experimental," the strategy was "ingenious"—and it worked, at least with the Roanoke jury.

Although no one could understand the Campari ad parody to be factual and it did offend the generally accepted standards of decency, the jury did not find it libel-ous. But Flynt and *Hustler* published it with the intent to cause Falwell emotional distress. The plaintiff was awarded $100,000 in compensatory damages, $50,000 in punitive damages against Flynt, and $50,000 in punitive damages against *Hustler*.

"I was happy at the trial level when they found no libel," Flynt told Russomanno. "I would have gladly paid the $200,000. But I felt these jurors wanted me to pay Jerry Falwell $200,000 for hurting his feelings. That's just not right. That's why I told my attorney that I wanted to appeal it."

Falwell doubled his damage claim after *Hustler* ran the ad a second time in its March 1984 issue.

From a First Amendment perspective, the jury verdict was the first time that a public figure, who was actively involved in national politics, electronic media, and evangelism, could use tort law to punish the media for publishing offensive and potentially harmful content, even though not considered factual.

Flynt appealed the intentional inflic-tion of emotional distress claim to the Fourth Circuit in Richmond. Falwell appealed the appropriation claim, but not the libel claim. On August 5, 1986, the three-judge panel announced its deci-sion to uphold the jury verdict and dam-ages. The jury's denial of Falwell's appropriation claim was upheld. Citing the plaintiff's failure to establish the actual malice standard, the court denied the libel claim. But that did not prevent Falwell from recovering for the emotional distress. In his deposition, Flynt admitted that he intended to harm Falwell, and the republication of the ad parody after trial indicated "outrageousness." Again, the judges applied actual malice, this time in Falwell's favor. The opinion stated, "We, therefore, hold that when the First Amendment requires application of the actual malice standard, the standard is met when the jury finds that the defendant's intentional or reckless misconduct has proximately caused the injury complained of. The jury made such a finding here, and thus the constitutional standard is satisfied."

Hustler's opinion argument also failed. The Fourth Circuit ruled that liability resulted from the intent to cause emotional distress, not the intent to spread false information or defame. Was this a First Amendment inconsistency—that liability could be based on intent to cause emotional harm, even if there was no libelous speech or invasion of privacy? While a victory for Falwell, the Fourth Circuit decision was a major defeat for Flynt, *Hustler,* and the American media.

As Isaacman later told Russomanno about his reaction, "All it is, is poking fun at a person. We didn't defame him; we just poked fun at him. We might have ridiculed him, and might have hurt his feelings in the process, but if you can't do that to a celebrity—to a public figure—then that applies not just to Larry Flynt and *Hustler* magazine, but to everybody else—Jay Leno, David Letterman, the newspapers, cartoonists, and sportswriters."

Flynt and *Hustler* were denied an *en banc* hearing before the entire Fourth Circuit panel. Judge J. Harvie Wilkinson III dissented from the denial and defended satire's First Amendment protection as "particularly relevant to political debate." Satire was intended to be "outrageous," that protection was "not diminished" by humor, "unfair or offensive speech," Wilkinson stated, while using political cartoons mocking American presidents (Washington, Jefferson, Grant, Garfield, Cleveland) as examples.

The next and final stop was the U.S. Supreme Court, with oral arguments slated for December 2, 1987. Despite the dangerous implications of the Fourth Circuit's opinion for protection of parody, satire, or opinion, major media outlets "weren't very anxious" to aid the plaintiffs, Isaacman told Russomanno. The consensus from some attorneys in Supreme Court practice leaned against Flynt and *Hustler* before the conservative-prone justices. Yet amicus curiae briefs were filed by such major media outlets as the *New York Times*, Times Mirror Company, and Home Box Office, as well as professional organizations and advocacy groups, including the American Newspaper Publishers Association, the Reporters Committee for Freedom of the Press, and the American Civil Liberties Union Foundation.

Larry Flynt's life, particularly the *Falwell* case, was dramatized in the 1996 feature film *The People vs. Larry Flynt.* The film features a condensed, but accurate version of Isaacman's thirty-minute argument (performed by Edward Norton), but none of Grutman's argument (played by New York University law professor

Burt Neuborne, with only one line of dialogue). The film sets the Supreme Court
arguments on a sunny spring day, while in
real life, it was a cold winter morning.

While relaxed about his debut before
the nation's highest court, Isaacman wondered about how his client would behave,
since Flynt was arrested for yelling
obscenities at the justices during oral
arguments for *Keeton v. Hustler* in 1983.
During his rehearsals with numerous
prominent members of the Supreme
Court Bar, Isaacman was cautioned not to
inject humor into his arguments, despite
the nature of the complaint.

Isaacman opened his argument with
the First Amendment's protection for satire, and the jury's verdict that the ad could
not be understood as factual. In referring
to the Court's landmark decision in *New
York Times v. Sullivan*, he cited the need
for "uninhibited, robust, and wide-open"
debate about public figures.

"The First Amendment protects all
speech except for certain narrowly drawn
categories," Isaacman argued. "False
statement of facts made with requisite
fault, fighting words, obscenity. . . . In
this situation the new area that is sought
to be protected is satiric or critical commentary of a public figure which does not
contain any assertions of fact."

Answering pointed questions from
Justices Sandra Day O'Connor, William
Rehnquist, and Thurgood Marshall,
Isaacman, perhaps unintentionally, pro-
voked rare laughter in the solemn cham-
bers of the High Court.

"And *Hustler* has every right to say
that somebody who's out there campaign-
ing against it . . . has every right to say
that man is full of 'B.S.'," Isaacman

argued. "*Hustler* is saying, let's deflate
this stuffed shirt, let's bring him down to
our level, or at least to the level where you
will listen to what we have to say. . . .
Well, maybe not quite there."

With that remark, Chief Justice
Rehnquist doubled over, bending at the
waist in laughter, joined by the rest of the
Court, including his fellow justices.
A few moments later, Justice Antonin
Scalia got into the comedy act. When the
conservative justice countered that free
speech was "an important value, but not
the only important value," Isaacman
offered the example of a political cartoon
mocking George Washington (as
Wilkinson's Fourth Circuit dissent did).
Provoking more laughter in the court,
Scalia replied, "But that's a far cry from
committing incest with your mother in an
outhouse. . . . Is there no line between the
two?" Isaacman insisted that *Hustler* did
not state that Falwell committed such an
act, and no one believed he did.

The humorous response encouraged
Isaacman; as he later recalled to
Russomanno, "There was good humor
around, and I said, 'Boy, this is finally an
encouraging sign in this case.'"

In conclusion, Isaacman argued that
allowing a public figure to sue for emotional distress was a "meaningless standard" and would allow punishment of
unpopular speech.

Grutman's argument to the Court
focused on the "back side" of the First
Amendment by pointing out that not all
speech is protected, such as "deliberate,
malicious character assassination" motivated by the satirist's state of mind to
inflict harm. The government has the
power to curtail such "repulsive and

loathsome" speech to protect "other vital social interests." The tort of emotional stress was not a "new tort," as the justices suggested, but rested on historical foundation dating back to the 1900s.

"This case is no threat to the media," Grutman concluded. "It will be a rare case indeed where this kind of behavior will ever be replicated, but where it occurs, it deserves condemnation, which the jury gave it, which the Fourth Circuit [affirmed]."

Written by Chief Justice Rehnquist, the Supreme Court's unanimous decision reversing the Fourth Circuit ruling was announced on February 24, 1988. Only eight justices participated in the decision, since Anthony Kennedy was confirmed on February 3. All agreed with the opinion's reasoning except Justice Byron White, who wrote a two-sentence concurrence.

The majority opinion held that a public figure or official may not recover for intentional infliction of emotional distress unless the publication contains a false statement of fact made with "actual malice." The government's interest in protecting public figures from emotional distress, the outrageousness of the material, or the intent to inflict emotional distress did not overcome First Amendment protection. Falwell was clearly a "public figure," and the Court accepted the trial jury's finding that the ad parody "was not reasonably believable."

"At the heart of the First Amendment is the recognition of the fundamental importance of the free flow of ideas and opinions on matters of public concern," the opinion stated. Citing the Supreme Court's 1984 decision in *Bose Corporation v.*

Consumers Union of United States, Rehnquist continued, "The freedom to speak one's mind is not only an aspect of individual liberty—and thus a good unto itself—but also is essential to the common quest for truth and the vitality of society as a whole."

In rejecting the respondent's argument for a "different standard" for "severe emotional distress" for "the subject of an offensive publication" through "outrageous" conduct, the Court stated, "But in the world of debate about public affairs, many things done with motives that are less than admirable are protected by the First Amendment."

Reviewing the vital legacy of American political cartoonists, especially those creating caricatures of politicians and presidents, the Court stated, "Were we to rule otherwise, there can be little doubt that political cartoonists and satirists would be subjected to damage awards without showing that their work falsely defamed its subject." While the *Hustler* "caricature" differs from the political cartoons mentioned, the Court declined to establish an "outrageousness" standard "to separate one from the other."

Hustler republished the Falwell ad parody for a third time after the Supreme Court's ruling. Reacting to the Court's decision, Flynt called the ruling "a victory not just for *Hustler*, but for all satirists and members of the press."

Falwell and Grutman were less gracious in defeat.

"No sleaze merchant like Larry Flynt should be able to use the First Amendment as an excuse for attacking public figures," Falwell said. "The Supreme Court has given the green light to Larry Flynt and his ilk."

"If we left the field vanquished, we did not leave with dishonor," Grutman said. "We left with glory."

The Flynt-Falwell feud did not last forever, however. In 1997, the two were interviewed together by Larry King, shortly after the motion picture premiered and Flynt's autobiography, *An Unseemly Man*, was published. Shortly after the interview, Falwell showed up unexpectedly at Flynt's Beverly Hills office. That began a friendship that lasted until the televangelist's death in 2007, as described in the publisher's remembrance, "My Friend, Jerry Falwell," featured in the *Los Angeles Times*.

Some scholars consider the *Hustler* ruling as a landmark First Amendment decision, while others reject it as "misreasoned" bad law and being among the High Court's "worst" decisions.

Smolla called the opinion "a triumphant decision of freedom of speech," written by a conservative First Amendment chief justice with a "strongly anti-press record."

"Far from signaling the disintegration of America's moral gyroscope, the opinion reaffirms the most powerful magnetic force in our constitutional compass: that essential optimism of the American spirit, an optimism of wild-eyed, pluralistic, free-wheeling debate," Smolla wrote. "When all is said and done, Americans have the good common sense to distinguish between the hustler and the real thing, and we have established as a first principle the censorship of neither."

Even though Rehnquist included the actual malice standard, the ruling "absolutely barred" public figures from recovering damages for nonfactual communication that hurt one's feelings, Smolla added. The opinion invites lower courts to "embark on a more complex analysis for private figure cases."

In marking the twenty-fifth anniversary of the decision in 2013, Roy S. Gutterman stated that the case ranks among "the most important" First Amendment cases by presenting a "history lesson" about the role of political satire in "the marketplace of ideas."

"*Hustler v. Falwell*'s scope continues to grow and the precedent helps not only to clarify important First Amendment principles, but to protect them as well," Gutterman wrote in a Huffington Post op-ed piece. "It has been influential in helping courts clarify protections on a range of speech issues. . . . The *Hustler* case is what gives an entire spectrum of citizens, particularly comedians and satirists, the protection to do what they do—make fun of people, politicians and public policy."

Others, such as Bruce Fein and John Kang, disagreed with this assessment of the case's legacy and have criticized the Supreme Court's decision and reasoning.

In a 1989 review of Smolla's book published the previous year, Fein called *Hustler v. Falwell* "a mislitigated and misreasoned case," even though he praised the book. The "vulgar" advertisement "undercut reasoned discourse and debate" in order to "evoke an unthinking dislike" of Falwell and to satisfy Flynt's "perverse sense of joy" in mocking moral values. "The advertisement was no more worthy of legal protection than a spite fence constructed to inflict harm for its own sake," Fein argued.

Rather than to contribute to public debate about the televangelist, Flynt's intent was to hurt Falwell's reputation and provoke emotional distress, while bringing *Hustler* magazine publicity and profit. While protecting political cartoonists using "contemplative faculties," Rehnquist should have "drawn a principled line" to deny the ad parody First Amendment protection, and Falwell should have recovered damages under the "fighting words" exception, Fein concluded.

In his 2012 *Nevada Law Review* article, Kang ranks the decision as one of the worst ever handed down by the Supreme Court. First, the Court acted with "moral indifference" and violated "basic expectations for moral decency" by making public figures "appallingly vulnerable to emotional injury." Second, the "atrocious" opinion still stands as "good law" since most have not considered it "a sham" in the same category as *Bush v. Gore*. Third, Kang's students have praised the decision as "eminently sensible and a logical victory for the Enlightenment."

Federal Circuit Court Judge Robert Sack, in his seminal treatise *Sack on Defamation: Libel, Slander and Related Torts*, called *Hustler v. Falwell* a "resounding endorsement" of the *New York Times v. Sullivan* actual malice standard, and the Court's "first extension" of the doctrine "to a new area of the law [intentional infliction of emotional distress] since its application in [*Time, Inc. v.*] *Hill* to the law of privacy." In the *Hustler* decision, Sack stated, "The Court was, in effect, declaring that it would not permit states to avoid constitutional safeguards by inventing new torts or by calling old ones (libel, slander, or invasion of privacy), by

new names, such as "intentional infliction of emotional harm" or "outrage."

While the *Hustler* decision prevents plaintiffs from making an "end run" around a defamation suit by recovering for intentional infliction of emotional stress, the case also affirmed First Amendment protection for satire and parody. Courts have applied the "reasonable person" standard requiring consideration of how an objectively reasonable reader or viewer would view the material—that is, would the reasonable person understand the parody or satire as factual? Such speech should not be interpreted literally, but viewed in the context of humorous commentary on matters of public interest.

One example of this application was the 2004 Texas Supreme Court decision in *New Times Inc. v. Isaacks*, which gave First Amendment protection to a fictional satirical news story. In 1999, a thirteen-year-old student, Christopher Beamon, in Ponder, Texas, was arrested and detained for five days after writing a violent Halloween story, for which he received a perfect 100 grade as well as extra credit, and read for the class. After some parents complained, school authorities considered details in his story about the fatal shootings of a teacher and two classmates as "terroristic threats." Denton County Juvenile Court Judge Darlene Whitten ordered Beamon jailed for ten days, but allowed his release after five. Denton County District Attorney Bruce Isaacks did not prosecute the juvenile.

Beamon's arrest and detention attracted international news attention and criticism. The *Dallas Observer*, an alternative weekly newspaper, published a satirical nonfactual report based on the incident. Titled "Stop the Madness," it detailed a fictional arrest and ten-day jail sentence of a six-year-old girl over her book report about Maurice Sendak's 1963 children's classic *Where the Wild Things Are*. The story included fabricated quotes from Isaacks and Whitten. It also falsely quoted then–Texas governor George W. Bush, who was running for president, condemning the book.

Isaacks and Whitten sued for libel, and a trial court ruled against the newspaper's owners (New Times, Inc.) and its editors, who appealed to the Court of Appeals of Texas. That court held that "satire or parody that conveys a substantially false and defamatory impression is not protected under the First Amendment as mere opinion or rhetorical hyperbole, but instead is subject to scrutiny as to whether it makes a statement of fact under defamation case law." It also found the newspaper and its editors liable under the actual malice standard.

In overruling the appeals court, the Texas Supreme Court cited the standard of the Tenth Circuit's 1982 decision in *Pring v. Penthouse International, Ltd.*: "The test is not whether the story is or is not characterized as 'fiction,' 'humor,' or anything else in the publication, but whether the charged portions in context could be reasonably understood as describing actual facts about the plaintiff or actual events in which she participated. If it could not be so understood, the charged portions could not be taken literally."

Even though a reasonable reader might not understand the satire, which did not contain a disclaimer, the reader would not consider it factual, and the newspaper did not act with actual malice. Calling for an "objective, not subjective" inquiry, the court stated, "In a case of parody or satire, courts must analyze the words at issue with detachment and dispassion, considering them in context and as a whole, as the reasonable reader would consider them."

Conclusion

While American humorists engaging in satire or parody might not fear governmental prior restraint or the threat of imprisonment for mocking public officials, satire and parody do not have absolute First Amendment protection. Courts tend to protect such humorous speech by creating a high bar for plaintiffs seeking to recover damages for intentional infliction of emotional distress. Trademarks and copyrighted materials can also be used in satire and parody, especially under a fair use defense, as long as the joke remains a joke and not a clear commercial use meant to profit from protected speech.

Jack Breslin
Iona College

See also False Light; *New York Times v. Sullivan*; Opinion and Libel

Further Reading

Carvath, Swaine, and Moore, LLP. *Intellectual Property Answer Book 2014*. New York: Practising Law Institute, 2013.

Dorsen, Harriette K. "Satiric Appropriation and the Law of Libel, Trademark, and Copyright: Remedies without Wrong." *Boston University Law Review* 65 (1985): 923.

Fein, Bruce. "Book Review: *Hustler Magazine v. Falwell*: A Mislitigated and Misreasoned Case, *Jerry Falwell v. Larry Flynt: The First Amendment on Trial* by Rodney A. Smolla." *William and Mary Law Review* 30 (Summer 1989): 905.

Flynt, Larry. "Larry Flynt: My Friend, Jerry Falwell." *Los Angeles Times*, May 20, 2007. http://touch.latimes.com/#section/-1/article/p2p-29891784/.

Friedman, Alan R. "Enforcing Copyrights: Copyright Litigation and Available Defenses." In *Fundamentals of Copyright Law in the Data Era 2014*. New York: Practising Law Institute, 2014.

Gutterman, Roy S. "*Hustler v. Falwell:* 25 Years of Protected Satire." *Huffington Post*, February 28, 2012. http://www.huffingtonpost.com/roy-s-gutterman/hustler-v-falwell-25-year_b_2783713.html.

Highet, Gilbert. *The Anatomy of Satire.* Princeton, NJ: Princeton University Press, 1962.

Kane, Siegrun D. *Kane on Trademark Law,* 6th ed. New York: Practising Law Institute, 2013.

Kang, John M. "*Hustler v. Falwell:* Worst Case in the History of the World, Maybe the Universe." *Nevada Law Journal* 12 (Summer 2012): 582–590.

Pollack, Malla. "Satire and Parody and the First Amendment." American Civil Liberties, February 9, 2012. http://uscivilliberties.org/themes/4440-satire-and-parody-and-the-first-amendment.html.

Russomanno, Joseph. *Speaking Our Minds: Conversations with the People behind Landmark First Amendment Cases.* Mahwah, NJ: Lawrence Erlbaum Associates, 2002.

Sack, Robert D. *Sack on Defamation: Libel, Slander, and Related Problems,* 4th ed. New York: Practising Law Institute, 2014.

Sanders, Charles L., and Steven R. Gordon. "Stranger in Parodies: Weird Al and the Law of Musical Satire." *Fordham Entertainment Media and Intellectual Property Law Forum* 1 (1990): 11–22.

Smolla, Rodney A. "Emotional Distress and the First Amendment: An Analysis of *Hustler v. Falwell*." *Arizona State Law Journal* 20 (1988): 423.

Smolla, Rodney A. *Jerry Falwell v. Larry Flynt: The First Amendment on Trial.* New York: St. Martin's Press, 1988.

Toke, Vijay K. "Trademark and Unfair Competition Litigation: A Primer." In *Fundamentals of Trademark Law in the Global Marketplace 2014,* 333–374. New York: Practising Law Institute, 2014.

33

OPINION AND LIBEL

Fact and opinion seem to be two mutually exclusive categories. Accusations of fact, which are verifiable in their truth or falsity, can be actionable as defamation. Expressions of opinion, inherently unverifiable as true or false, are protected speech. It is that simple. Or is it?

For decades, defamation law (the law of libel and slander, though I will sometimes use "libel" as shorthand) has struggled with the distinction between fact and opinion. It has never been as simple as it would seem at first blush, though the simple fact-opinion distinction has many adherents and refuses to die, even, it seems, when the Supreme Court decrees that it must.

This article will examine the fact-opinion distinction in libel law over the years, and most especially since the Supreme Court's dictum in *Gertz v. Robert Welch, Inc.*, 418 U.S. 323 (1974), that "there is no such thing as a false idea" seemed to provide an Olympian endorsement of everyone's gut feeling that there really is a simple, black-and-white, fact-and-opinion distinction.

Fair Comment and Criticism at Common Law

English common law distinguished between fact and opinion in libel law, and recognized an opinion defense under the name "fair comment and criticism." The defense was designed to shield mere statements of good-faith belief and opinion from libel liability. The defense is explained as follows in Peter Carter-Ruck's treatise *On Libel and Slander*:

Comment is statement of opinion: it is the inference which the writer or speaker draws from facts. Assertions of facts are not protected by this defence. Comment must appear as comment; it must not be so mixed up with statements of fact that the reader or listener is unable to distinguish between report of facts and comment. "Any matter, therefore, which does not indicate with reasonable clearness that it purports to be comment, and not statement of fact, cannot be protected by the plea of fair comment." The reason is apparent: to state accurately and clearly what a man has done and then to express an opinion is comment which cannot do any harm or work injustice. The reader is then put in a position to judge for himself whether the opinion expressed is well-founded or not. If there is any doubt whether the words are statements of fact or comment the question is one to be decided by the jury subject to the judge ruling that the words are reasonably capable of being comment.

For the defence of fair comment to succeed it must be proved that the subject matter of the comment is a matter of legitimate public interest; that the facts upon which the comment is based are true; and that the comment is fair in the sense that it is relevant to the facts and in the sense that it is the expression of the honest opinion of the writer or speaker.

This passage is revealing, for while it suggests a broad defense for "comment," it also shows that English law imposed a number of qualifications and hurdles for the comment defense to be met.

Initially, under the English test, the subject of the comment must have been a matter of "legitimate public interest," which typically meant matters of government and public administration, and criticism in the fields of art, literature, and entertainment. But the issue of the "legitimacy" of any comment injected an unwelcome subjectivity into the defense. When is an aspect of the private life of someone, even one involved in government, a "legitimate" subject of commentary? Such matters were left to the jury, which was free to conclude that, for example, a speaker went too far when he not only criticized another's actions but also expressed a good-faith skepticism of that person's motives. See *Campbell*

v. Spottiswoode, 3 B & S 769, 122 E.R. 288 (1863; opinion of Crompton, J.): "It is always to be left to a jury to say whether the publication has gone beyond the limits of a fair comment on the subject-matter discussed. A writer is not entitled to overstep those limits and impute base and sordid motives which are not warranted by the facts, and I cannot for a moment think that, because he has a bona fide belief that he is publishing what is true, that is any answer to an action for libel." This notion that an opinion can and should be expressed without attacking one's opponent's motives, of course, must seem quaint and foreign to many modern Americans.

Next, fair comment in English law required the defendant to prove that his comment was based upon true facts or privileged reports. Finally, it required the defendant to prove, in Carter-Ruck's words, "that the comment in question is in the first place comment which an honest minded man could make upon the facts, and secondly that the comment is the defendant's honest opinion." The "first place" test, a purportedly objective measure of the protectability of the opinion, created a huge amount of uncertainty for any speaker. It meant, essentially, that a jury would second-guess whether the speaker's opinion is allowable. A leading judicial test, though meant to be permissive of many opinions, illustrates that ultimately the jury was allowed to rule based on its after-the-fact determination of fairness: "The question which the jury must consider is this: would any *fair* man, however prejudiced he may be, however exaggerated or obstinate his views, have said that which this criticism has said"

(*Broadway Approvals Limited v. Oldhams Press Limited*, 2 All E.R. 904 [1964; emphasis added]).

The Fair Comment and Criticism Defense in America

The states of the United States inherited the British fair comment and criticism defense, and made it a mainstay of their laws of libel and slander for many years. In the late nineteenth and early twentieth centuries it was one of the privileges most often raised in defense of libel claims, and indeed it was described in one memorable case as the "brightest jewel in the crown of the law" for its role in protecting freedom of discussion.

The Missouri case of *Diener v. Star-Chronicle Publishing Co.*, 230 Mo. 613, 132 S.W. 1143 (1910; *Diener I*), which applied and explained fair comment, illustrates its importance in American libel law at a time before the First Amendment was found to affect that body of law. In *Diener I*, the plaintiff, a chauffeur for the city health commissioner, had sued a newspaper over an editorial that implicitly criticized him and his boss for an incident in which the plaintiff (while driving his boss) negligently killed a small child. The editorial suggested that the chauffeur's boss was responsible for having "run down and killed a small child in the street," and that the coroner who exculpated the health commissioner had acquiesced in "the mangling of . . . little tots."

Automobiles were new at the time, and the ordinary reader of the day, who certainly understood the dangerousness of autos and how easily they could go out of control, would not have understood the phrase "killed a small child," or even the harsher "mangling of little tots," to refer to the crime of murder. Rather, when a car runs someone down, "it is by means of a collision, through negligence, or accident," as the court noted. So the court held that the newspaper's editorial did not impute commission of a crime to Diener, and was not libelous *per se*. But the court went on to address the fair comment privilege, as well. It summarized the defense as follows:

> So long as a publication is not directed to a public officer by charging corruption or other criminal malfeasance or nonfeasance, so long as it is not directed to the defamation of a individual in his private character or business, but is directed to a matter of live public concern and is for an honest and not a defamatory purpose, it is qualifiedly privileged.

Within those lines, the court stated, everyone is entitled to "comment fairly, freely, with vigor and severity." After reviewing the policy behind the fair comment privilege, applauding it as "the brightest jewel in the crown of the law," the court explained the reasons why the privilege applied in this case. First, the office of coroner and its business—particularly its inquiry into the death of a child—were matters of public interest and concern. Second, the editorial was fair and had an honest purpose and was "in no wise earmarked with abuse and vituperative indications of malice." Hence, the editorial was privileged as a matter of law under the fair comment doctrine.

If the secondary holding status of fair comment in *Diener I* left any doubt as to the importance of the doctrine, that doubt was resolved by a related case a few months later. At issue in *Diener v. Star-Chronicle Publishing Co.,* 232 Mo. 416, 135 S.W. 6 (1911; *Diener II*), was a second, somewhat-embellished petition filed by the plaintiff after his original petition had been dismissed by the trial court. Among other things, the *Diener II* petition pled that the editorial had effectively branded Diener a "killer." The court held that even the harshest invective would be protected if the fair comment doctrine otherwise fit:

> Libel cannot hang on so slender a thread as a mere matter of taste in the penman's selection of one word instead of another one, interchangeable as a synonym, or (by condensation) in using laconically one word instead of expanding and diluting his idea into a phrase, thereby toning and softening it down. The use of a given word often makes the stroke that of a feather. The use of another may make the stroke that of a hammer. When the purpose is honest, as gathered from the whole publication, when the discussion is on a matter of live and present public concern (as here) and there are no earmarks of malice through invective, vituperation, or calumny, and where the publication does not pertain to the private business and the private character of an individual, or charge corruption or other misdemeanor to one clothed with authority, in a defamatory way, we say, when such condition of things appears, then a writer may use a hammer, instead of a feather, in fulminating argumentatively.

No wonder the court in *Diener I* had identified fair comment as "the brightest jewel in the crown of the law" as it sought to "seek and maintain the golden mean between defamation on the one hand, and a healthy and robust right of free public discussion, on the other." Before *New York Times v. Sullivan*, the fair comment defense was the crucial doctrine that permitted writers to "use a hammer, instead of a feather, in fulminating argumentatively."

In the area of literary and artistic criticism, American courts generally readily accepted the right of writers to criticize authors and artists who offer their works to the public. The Iowa Supreme Court's ruling in *Cherry v. Des Moines Leader*, 114 Iowa 298, 86 N.W. 323 (1901), is a landmark decision protecting criticism. The *Leader*'s critic could hardly have been more harsh in his review of the Cherry Sisters, a vaudeville singing and dancing team. The review included this classic passage:

> Effie is an old jade of fifty summers, Jessie a frisky filly of forty, and Addie, the flower of the family, a capering monstrosity of thirty-five. Their long, skinny arms, equipped with talons at the extremities, swung mechanically, and anon waved frantically at the suffering audience. The mouths of their rancid features opened like caverns, and sounds like the wailings of damned souls issued therefrom. They pranced around the stage with a motion that suggested a cross between the danse du ventre and fox trot—strange creatures with painted faces and hideous mien. Effie is spavined, Addie is string-halt, and Jessie, the only one who showed her stockings, has legs with calves as classic in their outlines as the curves of a broomhandle.

Yet the court, basing its opinion both on the entertainer's solicitation of the public and the "manifest distinction between matters of fact and comment on or criticism of undisputed facts or conduct," held the review fully protected as fair comment:

> One who goes upon the stage to exhibit himself to the public, or who gives any kind of a performance to which the public is invited, may be freely criticised. He may be held up to ridicule, and entire freedom of expression is guaranteed dramatic critics, provided they are not actuated by malice or evil purpose in what they write. Fitting strictures, sarcasm, or ridicule, even may be used, if based on facts, without liability, in the absence of malice or wicked purpose.

The court ruled within the strictures of the fair comment defense, but, like the court in *Diener I* and *II*, interpreted that defense as supportive of free expression. A dramatic critic, it wrote, "should be allowed considerable license" in a situation like this, because of the value of informing the public of the character of the entertainment.

The fair comment and criticism defense was a mainstay of libel law throughout the nineteenth century and most of the twentieth century. It was the means by which statements of opinion, particularly in literary and artistic reviews, and in political discourse, were protected.

Legal reformers, at times, attempted to broaden the fair comment defense. Thomas Cooley, one of the nineteenth century's most widely read and cited legal commentators, and a member of the Michigan Supreme Court for twenty-one years, urged a broad view of fair comment in which criticism of public

officials would be limited only "by good faith and just intention." In a prescient passage in his 1868 treatise, he argued, for example, against the English law limitation of the fair comment privilege to comments about the *public* acts of officials and candidates. This rule, he noted, assumes "that the private character of a public officer is something aside from, and not entering into or influencing, his public conduct, and that a thoroughly dishonest man may be a just minister, and that a judge who is corrupt and debauched in private life may be pure and upright in his judgments; in other words, that an evil tree is as likely as any other to bring forth good fruits." That assumption, he asserted, "is false to human nature," and thus Cooley concluded that the English fair comment doctrine, which limited criticism about private matters, was not sufficiently comprehensive.

Despite the efforts of Cooley and others, however, most American courts accepted all the limitations on the fair comment defense found in English law, and those limitations at times prevented the defense from applying to political and other commentary that today most Americans would view as well within the realm of free speech. Professor George Chase of Columbia Law School, for example, in reviewing one fair comment decision, pooh-poohed the assertion that the fair comment defense established "a full and free right of criticism." Professor Chase called the Maryland Supreme Court's decision in *Nagley v. Farrow*, upholding a judgment against a newspaper for criticizing a public official, "a mockery."

Rhetorical Hyperbole

What would eventually become one of the most important aspects of the opinion defense in American libel law entered Supreme Court jurisprudence through a back door in 1970. In the years following the constitutionalization of libel law brought about by *New York Times Co. v. Sullivan*, 376 U.S. 254 (1964), the Supreme Court took a number of libel cases to clarify, apply, and, in some cases, expand the *Sullivan* rule. *Greenbelt Cooperative Publishing Association v. Bresler*, 398 U.S. 6 (1970), was one such case. In that public official libel case, the trial court had instructed the jury that it could find *Sullivan* "actual malice" simply by examining the alleged defamatory language coupled with evidence of the defendant's hostility to the plaintiff.

The Supreme Court found the trial court's instruction to be "error of constitutional magnitude" because of its misinterpretation of the *Sullivan* "actual malice" standard. In so doing, the Court addressed the plaintiff's contention that because the newspaper repeatedly used the word *blackmail*, and it was obvious that the plaintiff had committed no such crime, an inference of knowledge of falsehood was permissible. The Court noted that in the circumstances at issue, the word *blackmail* could not reasonably be interpreted as referring to the crime of blackmail. Bresler, the plaintiff, was a real estate developer who was negotiating with the Greenbelt City Council to obtain zoning variances. During certain city council and community meetings, various persons characterized Bresler's negotiating position as *blackmail*, and the newspaper reported those accusations. The Supreme Court readily concluded that the word *blackmail* in the context of the news reports of the real estate negotiations and its public debate carried a quite different meaning than the accusation of the crime of blackmail:

> It is simply impossible to believe that a reader who reached the word "blackmail" in either article would not have understood exactly what was meant: It was Bresler's public and wholly legal negotiating proposals that were being criticized. No reader could have thought that either the speakers at the meetings or the newspaper articles reporting their words were charging Bresler with the commission of a criminal offense. On the contrary, even the most careless reader must have perceived that the word was no more than rhetorical hyperbole, a vigorous epithet used by those who considered Bresler's negotiating position extremely unreasonable.

Thus the Court interpreted the use of the word *blackmail* in the context of the newspaper's reports of the public debate as "rhetorical hyperbole," in contradistinction to an accusation of the crime of blackmail. This passage would become one of the crucial precedents of the libel opinion doctrine as it developed.

The *Gertz* Dicta

The law of comment and opinion took a dramatic turn in 1974 when the Supreme Court issued its decision in *Gertz v. Robert Welch, Inc.* The issue there was the application and extent of the constitutional protection first recognized in *New York Times Co. v. Sullivan*—specifically, did it cover statements made about persons who were neither public officials nor public figures, and, if so, what fault standard applied? It was not a case about a statement of opinion; the core alleged libelous statements, accusing Elmer Gertz, an esteemed civil rights attorney, of various misdeeds and unsavory associations, were clearly factual assertions that Gertz had proven at trial to be false.

Nonetheless, in the course of the Court's decision, perhaps hoping to better frame the constitutional status of false factual assertions, Justice Lewis Powell waxed eloquent about the opposite of factual statements—namely, statements of opinion. He began Section III of the *Gertz* decision with this paean to the place of opinion in discourse, and the sharp distinction between protected opinion and actionable fact:

> We begin with the common ground. Under the First Amendment there is no such thing as a false idea. However pernicious an opinion may seem, we depend for its correction not on the conscience of judges and juries but on the competition of other ideas. But there is no constitutional value in false statements of fact. Neither the intentional lie nor the careless error materially advances society's interest in "uninhibited, robust, and wide-open" debate on public issues (*New York Times Co. v. Sullivan*, 376 U.S., at 270). They belong to that category of utterances which "are no essential part of any exposition of ideas, and are of such slight social value as a step to truth that any benefit that may be derived from them is clearly outweighed by the social interest in order and morality" (*Chaplinsky v. New Hampshire*, 315 U.S. 568, 572 [1942]).

These statements about "no such thing as a false idea" and about opinions depending "on the competition of other ideas," not "the conscience of judges and juries," were all dicta—observations not essential to the case at hand, and hence not binding on other courts. But they came from the Supreme Court. They seemed to express legal truisms. They confirmed what many judges, attorneys, and ordinary Americans believe: that the First Amendment gives free reign to expressions of opinion. And, most appealingly, they offered an easy out for courts in deciding many of the borderline libel and slander cases that came before them.

Letter Carriers: More Rhetorical Hyperbole

On the same day that *Gertz* was decided, the Supreme Court also decided a labor-dispute case involving alleged libelous statements made during the course of a union-organizing campaign, *Old Dominion Branch No. 496, National Association of Letter Carriers, AFL-CIO v. Austin*, 418 U.S. 264 (1974). Replacement workers sued a union for publishing a "List of Scabs" in its newsletter. Right above the list, the newsletter, among other things, published a lengthy, highly disparaging essay, attributed to Jack London, describing a scab as a rattlesnake, toad, and traitor. Plaintiffs, pointing to that essay, asserted that identifying them as "scabs" was tantamount to accusing them of being traitors.

The union initially sought a ruling that federal labor law preempted state libel law in cases arising from labor disputes, but the court found that this dispute was not preempted. The Supreme Court, however, went on to apply the *Sullivan/Gertz* "actual malice" standard to non-preempted labor libel cases. The Court also went on, much as it did in *Greenbelt*, to determine that the language in question was rhetoric and comment, not factual assertion. The Court found that the mere use of the word *scab*, even together with the Jack London definition, "cannot be construed as representations of fact." Citing an earlier labor case, *Linn v. United Plant Guard Workers of America, Local 114*, 383 U.S. 53 (1966), the Court held that in the course of union picketing, use of "loose language or undefined slogans that are part of the conventional give-and-take in our economic and political controversies" is allowable. Citing *Greenbelt* as well, the Court held that the word *scab* was obviously used "in a loose figurative sense to demonstrate the union's strong disagreement with the views of those workers who opposed unionization." Expressions of such opinions "even in those pejorative terms" are protected. The Court even cited its own "no such thing as a false idea" dictum the same day in *Gertz*. *Letter Carriers* thus lined up with *Greenbelt*, and *Linn*, in immunizing "exaggerated rhetoric" from libel law.

The Post-*Gertz* Definitional Opinion Defense

Soon after the *Gertz* ruling, lower courts began citing Justice Powell's "no such thing as a false idea" dictum as if it had laid down or discovered a new libel defense or a new First Amendment doctrine. Two

months later, a district court in *Holodnak v. Avco Corp., Avco-Lycoming Division, Stratford, Connecticut*, 381 F.Supp. 191 (D. Conn. 1974), resolved a labor dispute by finding an employee's expression of opinion protected, relying in large part on the *Gertz* dictum. Within a few years, the dictum was becoming more frequently cited, often as key authority, in libel cases. See, for example, *Pierce v. Capital Cities Communications, Inc.*, 427 F.Supp. 180 (E.D. Pa. 1977), in which a statement the plaintiff described as "immoral" was held to be constitutionally protected opinion; *Steaks Unlimited, Inc. v. Deaner*, 468 F.Supp. 779 (W.D. Pa. 1979), which suggested that if the statements at issue in the case had been ones of opinion, they then could not have been defamatory; *Church of Scientology of California v. Siegelman*, 475 F.Supp. 950 (S.D.N.Y. 1979), which dismissed libel claims based on various statements as non-actionable opinion, or as "a mix of opinion and unflattering, but non-defamatory, factual statements."

Ollman v. Evans, 479 F.Supp. 292 (D.D.C. 1979), was a key step in the development of a new opinion defense based on the *Gertz* dictum. It involved a professor of political science, as plaintiff, who sued the well-known newspaper columnists Rowland Evans and Robert Novak. Evans and Novak wrote a scathing column about the plaintiff, an admitted Marxist, who had been nominated to serve as chairman of the Department of Government and Economics of the University of Maryland. After their column appeared, the plaintiff was denied the nomination. He claimed that the column damaged his reputation as a scholar. In particular, the plaintiff claimed the article was defamatory because it portrayed him as a political activist rather than a scholar, and because it contended that he desired to use the classroom as a tool for preparing for "the revolution."

The district court began its analysis of the defendant's motion for summary judgment with a flat-out statement that "the First Amendment precludes liability based on the utterance of defamatory opinions." It cited the famous *Gertz* dictum for that proposition. It then noted, however, that common law drew a distinction between pure opinion and an opinion that includes an implied statement of facts. For this the court relied on Section 566 of the *Restatement (Second) of Torts,* which noted that an opinion can be actionable "only if it implies the allegation of undisclosed defamatory facts as a basis of the opinion." Accordingly, the court held that if an author bases his opinion on disclosed facts, the opinion itself does not give rise to a cause of action. But if the author supplies no such facts, but utters a defamatory opinion, a claim arises, not because of the opinion but because of the libelous underlying facts that are implied. The court found this distinction between pure opinion, and opinions implying defamatory facts, to strike an appropriate balance "between competing legitimate needs." Specifically, "it encourages unfettered inquiry, contemplation, and communication, yet does not preclude redress to individuals for damage to their reputation." The court went on to distinguish between statements of opinion and assertions of fact, admitting that the difference "may be hazy at times" but concluding that at least in the case of loosely defined or variously interpretable

statements that are made in the context of social, political, or philosophical debate, those statements are opinion. By contrast, "statements imputing objective reality, uncolored by possible interpretation or bias, are statements of fact."

Applying that analysis, the court concluded that the newspaper column in question, while based on a selective reporting of the plaintiff's positions, reported merely the defendant's opinions. Accordingly, the court found that under "*Gertz* and its progeny," the opinions of the defendants were fully constitutionally protected unless they implied defamatory facts. Finding no such implied defamation facts, and finding that the defendants sufficiently disclosed the basis for their opinions, the court granted the summary judgment.

Ollman v. Evans was not the only libel case in which the *Gertz* opinion defense was being asserted or used as a basis for decision. By the early 1980s, the *Gertz* dictum was being asserted in scores of cases across the country, and was generally received approvingly by courts, many of which were eager to dismiss borderline libel claims rather than permit them to move ahead through extensive pretrial proceedings, including intrusive discovery. Nonetheless, *Ollman*, which occurred and was decided in the nation's capital, a news center, became the focus of much of the attention concerning the opinion defense. The long and rocky course of the case on appeal, and the differing opinions reached by many distinguished appellate judges, only added to the case's interest and focus.

The District of Columbia Circuit first ruled on the case in 1983 with a *per curiam* judgment of reversal and three separate opinions (*Ollman v. Evans*, 713 F.2d 838 [D.C. Cir. 1983]). Judge Spottswood W. Robinson III, who wrote the longest separate opinion, began with recognition of the "special solicitude for unfettered expression of opinion" that he understood *Gertz* compelled. But while he accepted the *Gertz* dictum as a binding pronouncement of a new absolute opinion defense, he noted that neither *Gertz* nor any other Supreme Court decision "has provided much guidance for recognizing statements that are 'opinion' for First Amendment purposes." He acknowledged that both *Greenbelt* and *Letter Carriers* suggested that rhetorical hyperbole qualified as opinion.

Judge Robinson concluded that statements of opinion could not be neatly divided from statements of fact: "Fact is the germ of opinion, and the transition from assertion of fact to expression of opinion is progression on a continuum." Nonetheless, he attempted to classify statements of opinion and fact in a range, including (1) pure opinion, relating to matters of "personal taste, aesthetics, literary criticism, religious beliefs, moral convictions, political views, and social theories," (2) loosely definable various interpretable remarks that are often "flung about in colloquial argument and debate," (3) metaphorical language that clearly could not be proven true or false, and (4) "hybrid opinions"—statements that are neither pure fact nor pure opinion but often evaluations and conclusions "laden with factual contents." He viewed the statements at issue in *Ollman* as hybrid facts and thus analyzed each of the assertions to determine whether the background facts were fully and accurately set forth. With respect to one of the statements, "that Ollman lacks a reputation in his field as a scholar," he concluded that the statement had factual elements and that its ultimate analysis depended upon the background facts and whether they were true or not. The two other judges on the panel took different approaches, but agreed to send the case back for more analysis.

Eventually the D.C. Circuit *en banc* ruled on *Ollman v. Evans*, 750 F.2d 970 (D.C. Cir. 1984). The majority decision was written by Judge Kenneth Starr (who later became well-known as the special prosecutor whose report led to the Clinton impeachment). At the outset, Judge Starr noted that the court faced the "delicate and sensitive task" of reconciling First Amendment rights with the plaintiff's interest in his reputation. He noted the common law fair comment defense, but viewed the *Gertz* dicta (which he acknowledged as such) as "fundamentally" changing the law—"elevating" the fact-opinion distinction to constitutional dimension. Like Judge Robinson, he identified the problem as distinguishing between fact and opinion. In this regard, he first found guidance from *Greenbelt* and *Letter Carriers*: they squarely put rhetorical hyperbole in the opinion camp. And he looked to how other lower courts had navigated the "largely uncharted seas" left by *Gertz*. Some treated the fact-opinion distinction as a judgment call; some focused almost exclusively on the verifiability of the assertions; others applied multi-factor analyses.

Creating any test for distinguishing fact from opinion was difficult, Judge Starr noted,

In formulating a test to distinguish between fact and opinion, courts are admittedly faced with a dilemma. Because of the richness and diversity of language, as evidenced by the capacity of the same words to convey different meanings in different contexts, it is quite impossible to lay down a bright-line or mechanical distinction. Judicial decisions, however, that represent mere *ad hoc* judgments or which, in contrast, lay down rules of excessive complexity may deter publication of the very opinions which the *Gertz*-mandated distinction is designed to protect, inasmuch as potential speakers or writers would, under such regimes, be at a loss to predict what courts will ultimately deem to be opinion. While this dilemma admits of no easy resolution, we think it obliges us to state plainly the factors that guide us in distinguishing fact from opinion and to demonstrate how these factors lead to a proper accommodation between the competing interests in free expression of opinion and in an individual's reputation.

Ultimately, Judge Starr concluded that a "totality of the circumstances" approach was best, considering (1) the common usage or meaning of the language of the challenged statement, (2) the statement's verifiability, (3) the full context of the statement, and (4) the broader context or setting in which the statement appears. He rejected applying the analysis of Section 566 of the *Restatement (Second) of Torts* (the search for implied factual assertions within a statement in the form of an opinion) on top of the multi-factor test, on the grounds that the multi-factor analysis sufficiently tests whether the statement implies the existence of undisclosed facts. In the *Ollman* case, for example, he concluded that even if all

underlying facts had not been disclosed, readers would understand the Evans and Novak column, an opinion column appearing on the opinion page, to be offering only opinions, and not making implied assertions of fact.

Applying the totality of the circumstances approach, Judge Starr found the Evans and Novak column to be one of opinion and not fact, and hence totally nonactionable as libel. Even with respect to the most troublesome statement, the suggestion that Ollman did not have a reputation in his field as a scholar, Judge Starr concluded that the opinion-column context signaled to the reader that this assertion was meant as opinion, not fact. Judge Robert Bork concurred in the result (in partnership with, among others, Judge Ruth Bader Ginsburg), with a somewhat different analysis, relying on both contextual and intuitive signals and policy principles (including deference to free speech when language falls in a gray area, particularly in the public arena). Three dissents were filed, including one by Judge Antonin Scalia, which sharply criticized Judge Bork's policy-informed approach.

Despite the many differing approaches displayed in the *Ollman en banc* opinions, Judge Starr's "totality of the circumstances" approach, with its four clear factors to be analyzed, was subsequently adopted or applied by many other courts. But even as *Ollman* went on to become a leading precedent for the post-*Gertz* opinion defense, a disquieting concern about it lingered, because of an unusual written opinion by Justice William Rehnquist in 1985 when the Supreme Court denied certiorari (*Ollman v. Evans,* 471 U.S.

1127 [1985; Rehnquist, J., dissenting from denial of certiorari]). The *Ollman* case was untested under *New York Times Co. v Sullivan*, Justice Rehnquist noted, suggesting that First Amendment protection depended solely upon the *Sullivan* doctrine. He characterized the appeals court's ruling based on the opinion defense as "nothing less than extraordinary." As law students are taught, dissents are worth reading. At times, the dissenter's views can become the majority rule.

Hustler v. Falwell: The Missing Opinion Defense

In 1988, the Supreme Court issued a landmark ruling with respect to expressions of opinion, *Hustler Magazine, Inc. v. Falwell*, 485 U.S. 46 (1988). It is an odd-fitting, almost inexplicable decision, however.

Hustler v. Falwell came to the U.S. Supreme Court with its libel claims already resolved. A jury verdict rejected libel claims of the Reverend Jerry Falwell, because the parody ad that he complained of, published by *Hustler* magazine, clearly did not make any factual assertion about Falwell. It was a mean, nasty publication (it portrayed Falwell boasting of having raped his mother in an outhouse) that no one could reasonably interpret as an assertion of fact. But the jury did enter a judgment on Falwell's intentional infliction of emotional distress claim, based on the outrageous nature of the publication and the evidence that *Hustler*'s publisher, Larry Flynt, intended to hurt Falwell and damage his reputation and feelings. The question presented to the Supreme Court,

thus, was whether this intentional infliction of emotional distress tort could be applied to publication that was clearly meant to express a political opinion, albeit a mean and hurtful one.

Before the U.S. Supreme Court, a group of editorial cartoonists and political parodists, in an amicus brief, strongly asserted that the tort of intentional infliction of emotional distress should not be allowed to chill and punish many legitimate political commentaries. They gave as illustrations many important historical political cartoons and other political commentaries, which often employed ridicule, caricature, and other techniques similar to those used by *Hustler* magazine. They requested, essentially, recognition of constitutional immunity for political opinion.

The Supreme Court could have found a First Amendment exemption from tort liability when the liability is deposited on such statements of opinion expressed in artistic and other forms. In *Falwell*, rather, the Court, in a unanimous decision written by Chief Justice William Rehnquist, held that expressive content must be judged by the standard of *New York Times v. Sullivan*. Thus, the *Hustler* parody ad in issue was evaluated by the Court under the *Sullivan* standard: had it been published with knowledge of falsity or reckless disregard of truth or falsity? The Court concluded there was no such knowledge of falsity or reckless disregard of truth, and hence the plaintiff could not succeed. It was a victory for opinion and the right to express political commentary, but an odd one analytically. The *Sullivan* standard, meant solely to be applied where the truth or falsity of a statement was at issue, was applied to an admittedly non-factual commentary that clearly could not be judged true or false.

The problems with this analysis may arise from Chief Justice Rehnquist's First Amendment position. Whereas *Sullivan*'s author, Justice William J. Brennan Jr., worked hard to expand *Sullivan*'s reach in various ways, Rehnquist regularly resisted any such extensions of the *Sullivan* rule. Some lower courts took the constitutional deference to free expression articulated by *Sullivan* as a reason to narrowly construe foreign jurisdiction over publishers and broadcasters. Rehnquist, by contrast, opposed any special deference on summary judgment or *de novo* appellate review in libel cases, or any special jurisdictional rules protecting speakers from libel lawsuits in foreign states. See *Lawrence v. Bauer Pub. & Printing Ltd.*, 459 U.S. 999 (1982; Rehnquist, J., dissenting from denial of certiorari); *Keeton v. Hustler Magazine, Inc.*, 465 U.S. 770, 781 n.12 (1984); *Calder v. Jones*, 465 U.S. 783 (1984). Logically and analytically, one could easily make a case for the policy behind *Sullivan* requiring new limits on libel claims based on opinion, or tort claims based on expression. Rehnquist responded, however, that the "actual malice" defense of *Sullivan* was sufficient protection for the press, and all activities of the media should be subject to laws of general application. (This position also seemed to explain his dissent from the denial of certiorari in *Ollman*.) This feeling that *Sullivan* sufficiently protects the media, and that common law should otherwise apply, may underlie his reluctance in *Milkovich* to recognize any new

constitutional protection for opinion, and his use of the *Sullivan* standard as the sole protection of free speech.

The ultimate ruling in *Falwell* affirmed the right to critically comment through artistic and other means, and upheld that right not only against libel claims, but also against tort claims, in this case intentional infliction of emotional distress. Though odd in its analysis and particular holding, the *Falwell* decision nonetheless stands as another affirmation of the constitutional right to express opinions.

Milkovich and Its Foundations

For more than a decade after *Gertz*, most federal and state courts treated the *Gertz* dicta, as *Ollman v. Evans* did, as a clear doctrine of constitutional law—namely, a definitive direction that opinion was automatically exempt from libel law. The only question—the one that bedeviled the many judges of *Ollman v. Evans*—was how to distinguish protected opinion from unprotected fact. The comfortable certainty of the absolute opinion defense came to an end, however, when the U.S. Supreme Court ruled directly on opinion as a defense in libel law, in *Milkovich v. Lorain Journal Co.*, 497 U.S. 1 (1990).

The plaintiff, Michael Milkovich, had been a high school wrestling coach whose team had been declared ineligible for a state tournament because of a fight at a wrestling match. A sports columnist, Theodore Diadiun, covered the hearing at which Milkovich and his school superintendent testified. The writer did not believe the two officials' testimony and said so, writing in his column that anyone who attended the meet at which the fight occurred "knows in his heart that Milkovich and Scott lied at the hearing after each having given his solemn oath to tell the truth." Scott (the school superintendent) and Milkovich, the wrestling coach, sued for libel. The Ohio Supreme Court, applying what it understood as *Gertz* absolute protection for opinion and assessing the column under a totality of the circumstances approach, concluded the statements in issue were assertions of opinion, not fact, and not actionable.

When the case reached the U.S. Supreme Court, the Court (again in a decision by Chief Justice Rehnquist) examined the *Gertz* dicta, and labeled it as just that—statements not binding on itself or other courts. The Court rejected a pure textual analysis of whether a statement appeared to be opinion or fact, noting that such a simplistic distinction could lead to abuses. If someone labels a statement as one opinion but it nonetheless asserts facts or implies defamatory facts, it should not be protected as opinion. Essentially, the Supreme Court returned to the distinction made by the *Restatement (Second) of Torts* that one must look at not only the statement itself but also whether it implies or could be seen to imply defamatory facts:

> If a speaker says, "In my opinion John Jones is a liar," he implies a knowledge of facts which lead to the conclusion that Jones told an untruth. Even if the speaker states the facts upon which he bases his opinion, if those facts are either incorrect or incomplete, or if his assessment of them is erroneous, the statement may still imply a false assertion of fact. Simply couching such statements in terms of

opinion does not dispel these implications; and the statement, "In my opinion Jones is a liar," can cause as much damage to a reputation as the statement, "Jones is a liar." . . . It is worthy of note that, at common law, even the privilege of fair comment did not extend to "a false statement of fact, whether it was expressly stated or implied from an expression of opinion" *Restatement (Second) of Torts,* supra § 566 comment a (1977).

Thus, there being no automatic exemption for opinion, the dispositive question in the *Milkovich* case became whether or not a reasonable fact finder could conclude that the statements in the newspaper column "imply an assertion that petitioner Milkovich perjured himself in a judicial proceeding." The Court determined that a reasonable fact finder could so conclude. Indeed, the Court distinguished the columnist's statement from the kind of language used in *Greenbelt*: "This is not the sort of loose, figurative, or hyperbolic language which would negate the impression that the writer was seriously maintaining that the petitioner committed the crime of perjury."

In his dissent in *Milkovich*, Justice William J. Brennan Jr. described the Court's theoretical analysis as "almost entirely correct." He acknowledged the appropriateness of an analysis looking to whether implied factual assertions are made within the scope of a reported opinion. He parted company with the majority, however, as to the application of that rule. In the context of the *Milkovich* newspaper column, Justice Brennan stated, "no reasonable reader could understand Diadiun to be impliedly asserting—as fact—that Milkovich had perjured himself."

Stressing that contextual analysis used in *Greenbelt*, *Letter Carriers,* and *Falwell*, Justice Brennan stated that the context of the newspaper sports column in issue, and the columnist's own language of surmise, sufficiently conveyed to readers that the columnist was asserting only opinions and not facts. Such a complete contextual analysis was essential, Justice Brennan emphasized: "Distinguishing which statements do imply an assertion of a false and defamatory fact requires the same solicitous and thorough evaluation that this Court has engaged in when determining whether particular exaggerated or satirical statements could reasonably be understood to have asserted such facts." He quoted as well Justice Oliver Wendell Holmes's famous statement in *Towne v. Eisner*, 245 U.S. 418, 425 (1918), about the importance of context in language interpretation: "A word is not a crystal, transparent and unchanged, it is a skin of a living thought and may vary greatly in color and content according to the circumstances and time in which it is used."

The end result of *Milkovich* was an odd one. *Milkovich* had directly referred to the *Greenbelt* "rhetorical hyperbole" doctrine, thus formally placing *Greenbelt*'s conclusion that "rhetorical hyperbole" was not actionable within the clarified opinion defense. Yet *Milkovich* had held that a newspaper columnist's admittedly opinion-based column about public officials was not protected by the opinion defense. It thus left the opinion defense in a somewhat-counterintuitive position: the more outrageous your opinions, in style and content, the more likely they are to be protected. After *Milkovich*, commentary that uses concrete words and facts and understated expression—the kind that really makes you think—could for the most part subject the speaker to full libel liability. But overstated and grossly exaggerated rhetoric—even when it used highly charged words like *blackmail* and *treason*—would be fully protected.

One can question the advisability of this distinction as a matter of policy. Participants in today's information-based society need the ability to communicate freely and effectively to influence a resolution of important issues, and decision makers need low-key, thoughtful, and fact-based opinions and analyses to rely upon. Commentators in the media need to be able to express opinions in such understated language in order to give readers what Walter Lippmann described as "a picture of reality on which men can act." On the other side, we hardly need to encourage sensationalized, hyped, and exaggerated commentary. Such commentary is commonplace and the source of major criticisms of "the media" today, and the extreme political division that it supports is viewed as one of the biggest problems in the political arena. Yet *Milkovich* immunizes rhetorical hyperbole, while leaving less extreme statements of opinion to potential trials.

The Opinion Defense after *Milkovich*

The opinion defense did not die after *Milkovich*, which, technically analyzed, merely tweaked it by requiring careful analysis of whether any purported opinion implied defamatory facts. But if the

Supreme Court in *Milkovich* also sought to slow down, or discourage, recognition of an opinion defense, it has failed in that respect. The response from most courts after *Milkovich* has not been a retreat from recognition of the opinion defense, but rather an intellectual effort to keep that defense alive.

After *Milkovich*, several state courts explicitly recognized state constitutional privileges for opinion. For example, the Oklahoma Supreme Court recognized in *Magnusson v. New York Times Co.*, 98 P.3d 1070 (Ok. 2004), that the common law fair comment privilege, and the pre-*Milkovich* cases on opinion, together afford "individuals the opportunity for honest expressions of opinion on matters of legitimate public interest based on true or privileged statements of facts, to defend against a defamation cause filed by a private person." Other states that have adopted opinion privileges as a matter of state constitutional law include New York, Ohio, and Utah. See *Immuno AG v. Moor-Jankowski*, 77 N.Y.2d 235, 567 N.E.2d 1270 (1991); *Vail v. The Plain Dealer Publishing Co.*, 649 N.E.2d 182 (Ohio 1995); *West v. Thomson Newspapers*, 872 P.2d 999 (Utah 1994). See also *Lyons v. Globe Newspaper Co.*, 415 Mass. 258, 612 N.E.2d 1158 (1993), which suggested state constitutional privilege would be recognized in appropriate cases.

A number of federal courts, though bound by *Milkovich*, have continued to apply *Ollman*-like totality-of-the-circumstances approaches in analyzing whether the statements in issue express opinions or facts. This was, of course, the means by which Justice Brennan in his *Milkovich* dissent reached the conclusion

that the sports column there did not really imply any defamatory facts.

Yet another possible approach for those who seek a broader opinion privilege would be to encourage courts to recraft the fair comment and privilege defense for modern times. Only a few tweaks to that privilege could adapt it into a broader opinion privilege. Its "matter of public interest" element, for example, could be adapted to the twenty-first century with the recognition that today's public sphere is occupied not only by government officials and politicians but also by businesses, nonprofit and nongovernmental entities, and even entertainment and sports celebrities. The limitation of the privilege to comment can be addressed through the popular totality of the circumstances test. And the concern with the speaker's motive embodied in the third element of the common law doctrine could be handled through application of the *Milkovich* "implied facts" analysis, which prevents a speaker from using a comment as a disguise for a malicious attack. Such updates to the fair comment common law defense could revive that defense and make it more meaningful today.

The Progress of the Opinion Defense

Beyond the analytical ups and downs charted above, one can detect significant progress in judicial treatment of opinion. The fair comment defense in English and early American law was limited—to matters of legitimate public interest (whatever that was), and to some kind of subjective good-faith fairness in the origin of the opinion. Perhaps in an era when written and memorable expressions were largely the products of elites who played by the same rules and had relatively equal access to the judicial system, these rules worked. But in modern times, as speech was democratized and extended to all areas of life, as we came to recognize the value of robust debate on all issues, and as broader recognition of First Amendment rights spawned a social ethos of free expression, those common law limitations became too restrictive. Reformers like Thomas Cooley fought for broader rules of the right to express comment, and landmarks like *Diener* and the *Cherry Sisters* case recognized broad rights of commentary, even within the general outlines of the fair comment defense.

By the post-*Sullivan* era, the time was ripe for shedding the fair comment limitations. If indeed public debate was designed to be "uninhibited, robust, and wide-open," as *Sullivan* held, and if even factual misstatements and some harm to reputation were inevitable and acceptable consequences of the right of free expression, then some broader protection for comment and opinion seemed appropriate. When the Supreme Court gave an opening in *Gertz*, lower courts readily overlooked its status as dicta and applied it as if it were the most carefully thought-out rendition of new law. The opinion defense, unburdened by the limitations of the common law fair comment doctrine, offered a wonderful new technique for sending disputes out of the courtroom and back into the arena of public debate.

Considering this enthusiasm (and perhaps over-enthusiasm) for a new absolute defense, perhaps Chief Justice Rehnquist and the *Milkovich* Court were correct to remind lower courts that absolute doctrines often lead courts astray, and that well-established cautions about defamatory factual assertions hidden in the form of opinion must not be forgotten. *Milkovich* was not a reversal of the recognition of opinion, but a caution and a reminder that in law, simplistic litmus tests often lead us astray. Even as states like New York constitutionalize an opinion protection, and even as other states rediscover fair comment and reapply that doctrine to modern circumstances, the *Milkovich* reminder that opinions cannot be used to hide assertions of defamatory facts is a necessary element of opinion law.

Fact and opinion are indeed mutually exclusive, as libel law, in its choppy course, has recognized. But the law has also recognized that separating out facts from opinion cannot be done simplistically, and requires at times a complex analysis, including a gimlet eye for factual assertions hidden or implicit in statements framed as opinions. Statements of opinion are now more protected in American law than they ever have been before. There is indeed no such thing as a false idea. But there also is not—and never was—any such thing as a simple, magical divide between assertions of opinion and of fact.

Mark Sableman
Thompson Coburn

See also False Light; *New York Times v. Sullivan*; Right of Publicity

Further Reading

Carter-Ruck, Peter F. *On Libel and Slander.* London: Butterworths, 1973.

Chase, George. "Criticism of Public Officers and Candidates for Office." *American Law Review* 23 (1889): 346, 353.

Cooley, Thomas. *A Treatise on the Constitutional Limitations Which Rest Upon the Legislative Powers of the States of the American Union.* 1868.

Levine, Lee, and Stephen Wermiel. *The Progeny: Justice William J. Brennan's Fight to Preserve the Legacy of* New York Times v. Sullivan. Chicago: ABA Publishing, 2014.

Lippmann, Walter. *Public Opinion.* New York: Harcourt, Brace & Co., 1922.

Rosenberg, Norman L. *Protecting the Best Men: An Interpretative History of the Law of Libel.* Chapel Hill: University of North Carolina Press, 1986.

Sableman, Mark. "Fair Comment, the Brightest Jewel in the Crown of the Law: As Protection for Free Speech and against Abusive SLAPP Suits." *Journal of the Missouri Bar* 61 (2005): 132.

34

FALSE LIGHT

The Tortured and Troubled Tort That Survives

As the global scope and probing ability of new technology quickly outdistances existing media law protections, the right to privacy has been threatened by growing public concerns about data collection, mass surveillance, and Internet exposure. As a result, what was once considered a safeguarded right with adequate remedies of recovering damages has turned into a fading concept unable to cope with government snooping, unwarranted access, and anonymous online publishing.

These issues make privacy protections a "hot button" issue in media law, with calls for stronger state and federal legislation to address new concerns caused by new media. Meanwhile, lobbyists for the data-collection industry have managed to stall proposed federal legislation, such as president Barack Obama's proposed consumer privacy bill of rights from 2012. While some states have passed statutes addressing such concerns as law enforcement warrants for e-mail searching, drone surveillance, and schools collecting student data, can stronger federal legislation catch up with privacy problems caused by ever-expanding technology?

With this increased collection of personal information about individuals over the past decade, polls indicate that most Americans believe the right to privacy has been compromised and consider it "already lost" or "under serious threat." Their privacy is being threatened by banks and credit-card agencies, the federal government, and law enforcement, with little legal protection. Yet the public wants the government to investigate terrorism, even if these activities invade their personal privacy.

In addition to the public's outrage over government surveillance, Hollywood celebrities continue to lobby for stronger California statutes to protect them and their families from paparazzi photographers. These star-stalkers sometimes recklessly disregard trespass and traffic laws as they pursue six-figure bounties offered by entertainment and gossip media for exclusive shots.

Perhaps the current debate over privacy protection was best summed up by the whistleblower-fugitive Edward J. Snowden, the former federal security contractor who leaked government information about electronic surveillance by the National Security Agency. From his temporary asylum in Russia, Snowden stated in his 2013 Christmas message broadcast on British television: "A child born today will grow up with no conception of privacy at all. They'll never know what it means to have a private moment to themselves—an unrecorded, unanalyzed thought. . . . Privacy matters; privacy is what allows us to determine who we are and who we want to be."

In addition to these concerns over invasion of privacy by data collection, newsgathering, and publication on global media platforms, is the constitutional right of privacy and the recovery of damages adequately protected by existing tort remedies and criminal sanctions, while balanced with First Amendment freedoms of speech and press?

False Light: The Most Controversial of Privacy Torts

Although recognition varies among the fifty states, four tort remedies are available: intrusion, publication of embarrassing facts, false light, and appropriation/right of publicity. These tort remedies protect our right of privacy, including one's physical space, embarrassing (but true) personal information, and unauthorized commercial use of one's image.

Intrusion is a newsgathering tort that occurs prior to publication or broadcast, such as photography, surveillance, or recording. The intrusion tort protects against offensive entries into private places without consent, such as peering through windows, tape-recording conversations or copying private documents without permission, or the use of high-tech surveillance technology to photograph or record inside someone's home without consent. In some circumstances, the courts have extended a public person's expectation of privacy into public places, such as harassing and dangerous stalking of celebrities by paparazzi photographers.

The private-facts tort involves publication or broadcast of private or embarrassing, but truthful, information that interferes with the right to be left alone. With libel law, the plaintiff sues because the published information is false and damaging. The troubling element of privacy law is that the information is true, but of a highly personal nature. The plaintiff is trying to prevent the facts from being published because they are true. Even if the information is true, however, it is nobody's business. As a result, the plaintiff considers the facts to be embarrassing and private, and the publication/broadcast of those facts to be "objectionable." A "cause of action" can result even if the published information is "true and nondefamatory."

Similar to private facts, false light is a publication or broadcast tort since the information has already been obtained. The common law concern is preventing individuals from being publicized in an erroneous and offensive manner. While resembling or even duplicating libel, false light protects one's self-esteem or emotional well-being rather than public reputation. Similar to the other torts, false light protects the right to be left alone and the right to an inviolate personality.

Sometimes occurring in journalism, but most often in public relations and advertising, appropriation is a commercial tort regarding use of a private person's likeness, voice, name, or image. Many states also recognize the right of publicity concerns about the unauthorized commercial use of a celebrity or famous person's image, which has value.

Of the four privacy torts, false light is the most controversial and unpredictable, as demonstrated by the varying interpretations among states in recognizing or rejecting it. While roughly two-thirds of the states recognize this tort, about one-third reject or have not decided about false light. Of the four torts, false light has caused the most controversy primarily due to its "elusive and amorphous nature," similarity to defamation, and chilling effect on the media's First Amendment rights.

Those who oppose the tort label false light as "an unnecessary and redundant legal claim," "too amorphous a tort," "a misunderstood tort," "a hybrid between two insufficient causes of action," "largely duplicative of existing torts," "sloppy and overgrown," and "a social construction," and claim that it "has nothing to do with privacy."

Besides this confusion over the tort's rationale, the overlap between false light and defamation is another major source of objection from courts, scholars, and attorneys. Critics have described false light as a "lite" version of defamation, "simply a defamation claim in sheep's clothing," "a

sickly stepchild of defamation," "seemingly transformed defamation," "more to do with a property claim in one's reputation," having "no separate intellectual foundation [from defamation]," "a claim for defamation that cannot succeed because falsity [is] insufficiently derogatory," and "an adjunct of sorts . . . a modestly convenient add-on [to defamation]."

As a threat to press freedom, false-light critics term the tort "an end run around the First Amendment," "an unacceptable chill on those in the media seeking to avoid liability," and "without the attendant protections of the First Amendment," and argue that it "unnecessarily threatens free press."

While plaintiffs have difficulty in pursuing successful false light claims, some do succeed, and so, as Bruce W. Sanford stated in *Libel and Privacy* (2008), "the spectre of them should not be ignored."

Origins of the Right to Privacy and False Light Tort

The "right of privacy" is defined in *Black's Law Dictionary* (2009) as "the right to personal autonomy" and "the right of a person and the person's property to be free from unwarranted public scrutiny or exposure." This right is a relatively new area of law, having been principally developed in the second half of the twentieth century. As noted above, the Constitution does not "explicitly provide" for the right, but the Supreme Court (first case in 1965) has recognized "zones of privacy" created by specific guarantees in the Bill of Rights. Others disagree, such as Judge Robert H. Bork, who told the

Senate Judiciary Committee in 1987 during his unsuccessful Supreme Court nomination hearings, "I have not heard anybody yet root it [the right to privacy] in the Constitution."

The public's perception of the right of privacy ranks high among our constitutional freedoms, as indicated by the First Amendment Center's "State of the First Amendment" reports. In surveys taken in 1997, 2002, and 2007, 99 percent of those polled considered the right to privacy to be either "essential" or "important."

The roots of today's right to privacy can be traced to Great Britain and Colonial America, where citizens enjoyed no such protection. If you were accused of treason or blasphemy, the king's men could search your home, seize your possessions, and arrest you without a warrant for an indefinite period. The Founding Fathers created the Fourth Amendment to prevent warrantless searches and seizures, but they did not enumerate a specific right to privacy. Before 1890, according to the *Restatement (Second) of Torts,* no English or American court "had ever expressly recognized" the right, but some decisions "appeared to protect it in one manner or another."

The origins of legal protection and remedies for American privacy can be traced to seminal arguments for the right of privacy and legal claims for its invasion made by two Boston attorneys, Samuel Warren and Louis Brandeis, in 1890. Their *Harvard Law Review* article "The Right of Privacy" proposed a separate legal claim for invasion of privacy, which would hold newspapers liable for publishing truthful information, and even suggested criminal sanctions.

Warren and Brandeis were concerned with protecting "intimate" information from being published in a growing newspaper industry prone to sensationalism and "unseemly gossip." Coming from a wealthy, Boston society background, Warren was reacting to newspaper coverage of his family, particularly about his wife, the daughter of a U.S. senator and secretary of state under president Grover Cleveland.

Arguing that people had "the right to be left alone," Warren and Brandeis stated that accepted common law and tort law doctrine confirmed the right of privacy, the violation of which would be actionable. Neither "the truth of the matter published" nor "the absence of 'malice' in the publisher" would "afford a defence." Brandeis and Warren discussed what could today be considered disclosure and appropriation, but not false light.

Justice Brandeis elaborated on his privacy arguments when dissenting from the U.S. Supreme Court ruling in the 1928 wiretapping case of *Olmstead v. United States*. In citing "the makers of our Constitution," he stated, "They conferred, as against the Government, the right to be let alone—the most comprehensive of rights and the right most valued by civilized men."

In addition to federal protection, every state recognizes the right to privacy in various degrees by their constitutions, statutes, common law, or court decisions. That was not always the case, however. For example, in 1999, Minnesota was one of three states, along with South Dakota and Wyoming, without privacy rights by legislation or common law. In *Lake v. Wal-Mart Stores, Inc.*, the state established the right to privacy when the Supreme Court of Minnesota ruled that the tort of invasion of privacy could be used as a common law cause of action. The ruling allowed two women to sue a Wal-Mart store in Dilworth, Minnesota, when photographs taken of them naked while showering on a Mexican vacation were wrongfully developed and distributed. As tort remedies, the Minnesota court recognized intrusion, private facts, and appropriation, but not false light.

Ten states recognize a right to privacy in their constitutions (Alaska, Arizona, California, Florida, Hawaii, Illinois, Louisiana, Montana, South Carolina, and Washington), while court decisions in others confirm the right as constitutional. The top ten states for protecting their citizens against invasions of privacy are California, Connecticut, Florida, Hawaii, Illinois, Massachusetts, Minnesota, New York, Washington, and Wisconsin, according to the *Privacy Journal* (2012). The newsletter ranks twelve states at the bottom for privacy protection: Arkansas, Delaware, Idaho, Iowa, Kansas, Kentucky, Mississippi, Missouri, North Carolina, South Dakota, Texas, and Wyoming.

In 1903, New York became the first state legislature to recognize a statutory right of privacy by creating a commercial appropriation tort remedy to recover damages for using a person's likeness for commercial or trade purposes without their knowledge or consent. The law followed *Roberson v. Rochester Folding Box Company,* a state case involving commercial use of a young girl's image on flour boxes and promotional materials without her knowledge or consent, in which the New York Court of Appeals ruled there

was no precedent for the so-called right of privacy or cause of action for invasion of privacy. Two years later, Georgia was the first state to recognize a common law right of privacy in *Pavesich v. New England Life Insurance Company*, when the Georgia Supreme Court ruled that an insurance company's commercial use of the plaintiff's picture without permission was a violation of that right.

On the federal level, the Supreme Court in 1965 used five amendments of the Bill of Rights to guarantee a "penumbra" zone of privacy. In *Griswold v. Connecticut*, Estelle Griswold, executive director of the Planned Parenthood League of Connecticut, and Dr. C. Lee Buxton, a Yale Medical School professor and the league's medical director, challenged a Connecticut criminal law banning the use of contraceptives or counseling others in their use. Arguing that the state law violated the "right of marital privacy," Justice William O. Douglas stated that "specific guarantees in the Bill of Rights have penumbras, formed by emanations from those guarantees that help give them life and substance. Various guarantees create zones of privacy." Douglas specified those guarantees as coming from the First (right of free association), Third (prohibition against quartering of troops), Fourth (security against unreasonable search and seizure), Fifth (privilege against self-incrimination), and Ninth Amendments (rights not enumerated are retained by the people).

In his landmark 1960 article "Privacy" in the *California Law Review*, William L. Prosser discussed four privacy torts:

1. Intrusion upon the plaintiff's seclusion or solitude, or into his private affairs.

2. Public disclosure of embarrassing facts about the plaintiff.

3. Publicity that places the plaintiff in a false light in the public eye.

4. Appropriation, for the defendant's advantage, of the plaintiff's name or likeness.

Like Warren and Brandeis, Prosser recognized disclosure and appropriation, but he also distinguished false light, which he noted that the two Boston attorneys "do not appear to have had in mind." False light, he stated, first appeared in 1816 during Lord Byron's dispute with an English publisher who attempted to circulate an inferior poem falsely attributed to him. That case and others illustrated the elements of "publicity falsely attributing to the plaintiff some opinion or utterance" or "an obvious innuendo . . . which places him in a false light before the public" or generates "false publicity." Both private facts and false light "concern the interest in reputation, and move into the field occupied by defamation." Noting an overlap between defamation and false light, Prosser stated that privacy cases afford a "needed remedy" for uncovered claims. He questioned whether false light "is not capable of swallowing and engulfing the whole law of public defamation."

Although the U.S. Supreme Court did not explicitly reference by name or define the false light tort in *Time v. Hill* (1967), the decision affirmed its existence using such terms as *calculated falsehood, falsely reported*, and *erroneous statements about matters of public interest.* The court applied the actual malice standard for such privacy claims, borrowed from defamation law regarding public figures, as the level of fault for plaintiffs involved in newsworthy events (as will be discussed below). This affirmation, along with definitions in the *Restatement of Torts* (1977, 1990), encouraged judicial support of the false light tort, and launched a trend of recognition by more states accepting the tort. But these milestones did not secure the future of false light by eliminating the tort's confusing flaws, as other states still rejected it.

Similarities and Distinctions between Defamation and False Light

While resembling or even duplicating defamation, false light is aimed at protecting one's self-esteem rather than one's public reputation. Recognizing the "differences" between the two claims, some states require plaintiffs to choose between libel and false light, while others allow suits for both.

Due to that possible overlap between false light and defamation, some states refuse to recognize this privacy tort outright, while others have accepted then rejected it, or have not considered its status. Why is false light necessary, critics charge, since it overlaps with defamation law?

Defamation hinges on falsity, but a false light claim can proceed if nothing incorrect has been stated. As for dissemination, false light requires wider communication, namely "publicity," while defamation requires "publication," which is simply communication to a third party. Defamation focuses on injury to one's reputation, and false light involves harm to an individual's dignity or emotional well-being. As for limitations on claims, some states restrict defamation claims yet apply no limit to false light claims.

These distinctions set a lower bar for false light claims. In defamation suits, plaintiffs must demonstrate that the statement was false. In some states, false light plaintiffs need only demonstrate that the statement placed the plaintiff in a false light. So the false light claimant can file suit even if the defendant's statement was arguably true, and did not damage the plaintiff's reputation. Since false light does not require reputational harm, the plaintiff can recover for false light even if the statement improves one's reputation.

Defamation protects the objective interest of reputation; false light protects the subjective interest of emotional injury (e.g., hurt personal feelings, embarrassment, helplessness). Not being required to show reputational damage, the false light plaintiff must prove the vaguer standard "highly offensive to the reasonable person" (HORP), which can chill otherwise-protected speech. Yet there are similar defenses between false light and libel, such as opinion, fair comment, truth, and consent. Those can make false light claims more difficult to win than libel actions.

In a 1989 article for the *New York University Law Review,* Diane L. Zimmerman stated that false light "encompasses a broader class of speech than can be reached by defamation," which applies to a narrow class of falsehoods regarding reputation. But "false light can be brought for virtually any untruth on the ground that it caused hurt feelings." By being "unencumbered by common law restrictions," she noted, the false light tort creates a "serious challenge to First Amendment values."

Even though defamation and false light are distinct by definition and theory, the differences are not practical, as courts rely on differing interpretations of state statutes. As Deckle McLean stated, "By definition, all defamations are false light privacy invasions. Not all false light privacy invasions are defamation." According to their definitions, all public defamation puts plaintiffs in a false light, but the converse is not true, since being put in a false light does not necessarily mean being placed in a defamatory light in the public eye. As David A. Elder wrote in *Privacy Torts,* "Defamation and false light are neither identical nor mutually exclusive." In practice, there is a danger of the "spectre" of false light "swallowing up" the law of defamation.

A 1984 Fifth Circuit decision in *Braun v. Flynt* held that a plaintiff cannot recover damages for both false light and defamation. Jeannie Braun worked at an amusement park performing an act called "Ralph the Diving Pig," during which a pig dove into a pool and Braun fed it with a milk bottle. *Chic,* an adult magazine owned by Larry Flynt, ran a photograph of the act in a section called "Chic Thrills," implying something kinky. Braun, mortified and depressed, could not return to work. She sued Flynt for defamation and false light. A jury awarded her damages for both causes of action, but the Fifth Circuit applied *Gertz v. Welch* (1974), ruling that Braun was not a public figure and allowing her to recover damages, but not for both claims.

Plaintiff's Cause of Action

A woman is strolling down a busy sidewalk with other pedestrians in downtown

Washington, D.C., on a lovely spring afternoon. Little does she know, but a camera crew from the local ABC station, WJLA-TV, is videotaping her for an "on-the-street" news report. That night the station's 6:00 p.m. newscast shows a "clearly recognizable" close-up of her face, followed by a reporter saying, "For the 20 million Americans who have herpes, it's not a cure." In the 11:00 p.m. news show, the anchor reads the same words with the same video of her face.

The woman, Linda Duncan, filed defamation and invasion-of-privacy claims against the station for showing her close-up image in a story about "the development of a new medical treatment for genital herpes." As a pedestrian on the corner behind the reporter, she was in plain view, unknowingly turned toward the camera, and paused on a public street, but the story did not state that she had the disease. From the image and report, however, Duncan asserted that the audience would infer she did. In 1984, the District of Columbia court dismissed her defamation and privacy claims related to the 6:00 p.m. newscast, but allowed her suit regarding the 11:00 p.m. newscast to proceed.

Citing the *Restatement (Second) of Torts*, the court stated that the false light tort requires that "the publicity forming the basis for the false light claim be reasonably capable of being understood as singling out, or pointing to, the plaintiff." In considering Duncan's defamation claim the court held that her "acquaintances and friends" could identify the plaintiff from "the juxtaposition of closely cropped film and commentary of the report" about the herpes epidemic, which "may support the inference that the plaintiff has genital herpes." The analysis was "directly applicable" to the false light claim. The court ruled that a jury should determine her defamation and false light claims for the eleven o'clock report.

Instead of being defamatory, as required in libel, the portrayal must be highly offensive to the reasonable personable (HORP). The harm is more subjective, based on personal or emotional injury, such as embarrassment, rather than objective, such as damage to one's reputation. The level of fault resembles actual malice. With regard to giving publicity "that places the other before the public in a false light," the *Restatement (Second) of Torts* stated liability for invasion of privacy if:

a. the false light in which the other was placed would be highly offensive to the reasonable person, and
b. the actor had knowledge of or acted in reckless disregard as to the falsity of the publicized matter and the false light in which the other would be placed.

With the HORP standard applied to false light claims, a media outlet can be held liable for truthful publications or broadcasts that create a false impression or implication that may be considered highly offensive to the reasonable person. For example, the *Pensacola News Journal* accurately reported that a local businessman, Joe Anderson Jr., had shot and killed his wife in a hunting accident. While Anderson admitted those facts were true, he claimed that the newspaper had failed to immediately mention that authorities ruled the shooting accidental.

That reporting created the false impression that he escaped prosecution for her murder due to his community standing.

In *Anderson v. Gannett Company, Inc.*, the plaintiff sued for libel in 2001 over a series of articles that appeared between December 13, 1998, and July 12, 2000. When the libel claim was dismissed due to the two-year state statute of limitations, he amended his claim to false light. The trial jury awarded Anderson an $18.28 million damage award, but the state's First District Court of Appeals ruled that both claims involved the same facts and reversed the award under the limitations statute. In 2009, the Florida Supreme Court ruled in a companion case, *Jews for Jesus v. Rapp*, that the state did not recognize the false light tort, and affirmed the *Anderson* verdict dismissal.

Fault

The Supreme Court's decision in *Time, Inc. v. Hill* (1967) established the actual malice standard as the level of fault in false light claims, even if plaintiffs are private individuals and voluntary public figures, such as public officials. The case was decided prior to the Court's ruling in *Gertz v. Robert Welch, Inc.,* which more clearly differentiates the status of private and public individuals. But *Gertz* did not overrule *Hill*, and even cited the decision with approval. The High Court has never explicitly applied *Gertz* to false light claims. The lower courts are split in cases involving private figures as to whether *Gertz* applies to false light or whether all false light claims must satisfy the more difficult *New York Times v. Sullivan* standard.

In 1952, James Hill and his family were held hostage in their home outside Philadelphia by three escaped convicts and eventually released unharmed. Even though the Hills had moved and discouraged publicity, a novel, *The Desperate Hours*, was written about the incident, which included fictionalized accounts of violence and oral sexual insults. The novel was subsequently made into a Broadway play and two feature films. *Life* magazine published an account of the play, which described it as a reenactment of the Hill incident and used photographs of scenes staged in the former Hill home. Claiming that *Life* had given a knowingly false impression that the play depicted the actual incident, Hill sued for damages under a New York statute. *Life* maintained that the article concerned a topic of public interest and was published in good faith.

In setting aside the lower-court rulings and a trial-court judgment for Hill, the Supreme Court applied the actual malice rule of *New York Times v. Sullivan* in favor of *Life*. The Court stated that the New York statute "affords 'little protection' to the 'privacy' of a newsworthy person, 'whether he be such by choice or involuntarily.'" Instead, the Court applied a different standard by holding that the First Amendment's protections for speech and press "precluded the application of the New York statute to redress false reports of matters of public interest" without evidence of knowing and reckless disregard of the truth.

In examining the statute only with regard to a libel action by a private individual, the decision declines to address whether the actual malice test should be applied "both to persons voluntarily and involuntarily thrust into the public limelight." Considering the overlap of libel and false light in *Hill*, the court accepted the argument that they were "in effect twin torts." Proof of actual malice was required without regard to whether the plaintiff is a private or public figure. Public interest in an event or person brought the newsworthy defense into false light. The falsity of dramatic account depicted in the novel, play, and article was not addressed. Citing this ruling seven years later in *Cantrell v. Forest City Publishing Company*, the Court found "no occasion" to "apply a more relaxed standard of liability" for "false statements injurious to a private individual" in false light invasions.

The novel's closing paragraphs contain an ironic coincidence, considering the resulting lawsuit. Coming out of the hospital after the ordeal, the young son was "surrounded" by three newspaper reporters. The youth ended his interview by telling the three reporters, "Only if you tell him I said so, I'll sue you for libel."

If this happened to the Hill family, who were embarrassed about their portrayals, how about other plaintiffs whose newsworthy life experiences are dramatized on television or in feature films? If writers and producers use actual events as research, they can argue "public record" or "based on a true story" defenses, such as reliance on police reports, trial transcripts, or accurate news stories.

False Light and Docudramas

Even before Prosser's discovery of the false light torts, docudramas—first in motion pictures, then on broadcast network and cable TV—have resulted in defamation and invasion-of-privacy claims. While based on true events, docudramas often contain a mix of fact and fiction and are presented with knowledge of falsity, which is an element of a false light claim.

In contesting docudrama portrayals, plaintiffs tend to file more defamation suits, in which courts tend to be more lenient with docudramas involving matters of public importance and interest. If a docudrama subject files a defamation suit, courts allow docudrama producers the actual malice standard, which makes successful damage recovery claims difficult.

The increase of false light claims from docudramas, in feature films and on television, resulted in scholarly attention to the issue, such as articles by Tim A. Pilgrim (1990), Matthew Stohl (2002), and Susan Hallander (2005).

Stohl called docudramas "True Lies" since this genre often misses the essence of historical event and rewrites a complete fiction with little regard for truth or individual dignity. They also cause ambiguity over consent and the subject's rights. Without obtaining rights, a reasonably accurate portrayal becomes more difficult. Therefore, rights are obtained from primary subjects, secondary identifiable characters, or other sources, such as journalists or investigators. But when these subjects refuse to sign away rights, fictionalization of facts occurs, resulting in false light claims.

In order to avoid false light suits over fictionalized and HORP portrayals, media law scholars recommended such remedies as avoiding the real name of the subject, using disclaimers, presenting evidence to defend accuracy, and limiting the use of living persons refusing consent. With the increase of docudramas in network TV in the 1970s and 1980s, according to Pilgrim, the three broadcast networks (ABC, NBC, and CBS) developed standards/guidelines for producing docudramas, such as substantiating material, omitting factual material that would distort perception of a historical event, changing the sequence of events, using disclaimers, and getting releases.

Arguing that defamation and right of publicity adequately protect docudrama plaintiffs, Hallander stated that these false light plaintiffs rarely prevail, and many jurisdictions do not recognize the tort as pertaining to docudramas: "The false light invasion of privacy action, when applied against docudrama moviemakers, unnecessarily wastes judicial resources, restricts movie producers' rights to free expression, and indirectly damages the very people it is designed to protect."

Typical False Light Instances

With regard to false but nondefamatory statements, the falsehood is usually implied rather than explicit, with the plaintiff portrayed in an inaccurate or embarrassing situation. Typical instances resulting in false light claims include: distortion, coincidental or accidental use of names in a play or novel, fictionalization, embellishment, or misuse of names or misplacement of photographs in otherwise legitimate news stories.

Unauthorized fictionalization of actual events or identifiable persons can also lead to successful false light claims. Minor falsehoods that offend only hypersensitive individuals are not sufficiently offensive to support these claims. Yet is any news story absolutely accurate? As the *Restatement (Second) of Torts* stated, "Complete and perfect accuracy in published reports about any individual is seldom attainable by any reasonable efforts." It continues, "Plaintiff's privacy is not invaded when the unimportant false facts are made, even when they are made deliberately." A "serious offense" may be taken by "a reasonable man" when there has been "a major misrepresentation for his character, history, activities, or beliefs."

A freelance writer, Milton Shapiro, wrote a flattering but unauthorized biography of Hall of Fame baseball pitcher Warren Spahn based on secondary sources. Without interviewing his subject, the author exaggerated details about Spahn's family life, marriage, military experience, and thoughts while pitching, and he fictionalized conversations between Spahn and associates. In *Spahn v. Jullian Messner, Inc.*, a New York trial court ruled that the fictionalized biography was "unauthorized exploitation of his personality," stopped further publication, and awarded financial damages, which the New York Court of Appeals upheld in 1967.

Before becoming a successful author and Hollywood screenwriter (*Basic Instinct*), Joe Eszterhas learned a costly lesson about fictionalizing news stories. In December 1967, Melvin Cantrell and forty-three others died when the Silver Bridge across the Ohio River collapsed at Point Pleasant, West Virginia. Eszterhas covered the disaster for the *Cleveland Plain Dealer*, particularly in a news feature on the impact of Cantrell's death on the Cantrell family. Five months later, the reporter and a photographer visited the family home in Pomeroy, Ohio. They interviewed and photographed Cantrell's children, but their mother was not home. Eszterhas's Sunday magazine feature story included fabricated statements from the mother and descriptions of the poverty-stricken family living in "dirty and dilapidated conditions." The Cantrell family sued, claiming that the story had "unreasonably placed their family in a false light before the public through its many inaccuracies and untruths." The trial jury ruled for the Cantrell family with compensatory damages.

Although the Court of Appeals for the Sixth Circuit reversed the jury verdict, the Supreme Court in 1974 upheld the trial ruling. The Court cited the application of *Time v. Hill*'s actual malice standard to false light by the district judge, but did not reexamine the previous decision. In fabricating his interview with Mrs. Cantrell, the reporter's "calculated falsehoods" deliberately misled readers. The Court stated that the reporter and newspaper "had portrayed the Cantrells in a false light through knowing or reckless untruth." The decision left actual malice as an issues (newsworthy) test for false light, but did not apply the *Gertz* approach as persons test. The falsification did not defame Mrs. Cantrell, but subjected her to public sympathy that she did not desire.

Omission of facts can create a false light claim as much as additions or embellishments. For example, in the 1968 Second Circuit case *Varnish v. Best Medium Publishing Company*, the *National Enquirer*'s article "'Happiest Mother' Kills Her Three Children and Herself" omitted half of a wife's suicide note, which created the false image of an insensitive, uncaring husband. While the court agreed with the appellant that "minor inaccuracies and fictionalized dialogue will not alone defeat the privilege granted to truthful publications of public interest," it also found that the article "was sufficiently untruthful and offensive to support a judgment for invasion of privacy." But the omission of facts does not necessarily establish actual malice in false light claims for a public figure.

Proper context should also be considered with publishing photographs. Without "their knowledge or consent," a photographer took a picture of John Gill and his wife "seated in an affectionate pose" outside their ice cream concession at the Farmers Market in Los Angeles. The couple sued twice over its publication. In first instance, the photograph was included in an article in the May 1949 issue of the *Ladies' Home Journal* about different kinds of love, both desirable and not. The caption with the Gills' photograph read, "Publicized as glamorous, desirable, 'love at first sight' is a bad risk." The "happily married" couple with a "high moral reputation" claimed the publication exposed them to public "scorn, ridicule, hatred, contempt and obloquy" and damaged their social and business contacts. Ruling that the publication served "no legitimate interest," the Supreme Court of California in 1952 ruled for the plaintiffs in *Gill v. Curtis Publishing Company*, stating that "their feelings were hurt and they suffered mental anguish." The court stated,

It is not unreasonable to believe such would be seriously humiliating and disturbing to plaintiffs' sensibilities, and it is so alleged, especially when we consider it deals with the intimate and private relationship between the opposite sexes and marriage.

In the second claim, the photograph appeared in the October 1947 issue of *Harper's Bazaar,* in an article titled "And So the World Goes Round" with a short commentary about love. In ruling for the publisher in *Gill v. Hearst Publishing Company,* the California Supreme Court in 1953 stated that the photograph of the plaintiffs, even considered "complimentary and pleasing," was "portraying nothing to shock the ordinary sense of decency or propriety."

Context and juxtaposition can also be relevant in false light claims involving promotion of stories and photographs in print publications and other media outlets. *Playgirl* magazine featured a cover photograph of TV actor Jose Solano Jr. (*Baywatch*) in its January 1999 issue. In the photograph, Solano was shirtless and wore red swim trunks like his TV character. On top of the cover, running through Solano's forehead, was the promotional headline "TV Guys. Prime-Time's Sexy Young Stars Exposed," with the caption "*Baywatch*'s Best Body, Jose Solano" below his image. Inside the magazine, Solano's head shot (dressed in T-shirt and sweater) appeared next to a quarter-page, bullet-point profile, but no nude or explicit photographs of him were included.

Solano did not pose for photographs or give an interview to the magazine. Claiming that the magazine damaged his business and social contacts, Solano filed a false light suit alleging that *Playgirl* "deliberately created the false impression that he did so, making it appear he was willing to degrade himself and endorse such a magazine." Although the district court granted summary judgment for *Playgirl,* the Ninth Circuit in 2002 reversed in Solano's favor by stating that "a jury reasonably could conclude that the *Playgirl* cover conveyed the message that Solano was not the wholesome person he claimed to be, that he was willing to—or was 'washed up' and had to—sell himself naked to a women's sex magazine."

States Rejecting False Light

As of 2014, eleven states have rejected the false light tort by statute or common law. They include Colorado (2002), Florida (2009), Massachusetts (2004), Minnesota (1998), Missouri (2013), New York (1982), North Carolina (1984), Texas (1994), Virginia (1981), Washington (1989), and Wisconsin (1997). State courts give common reasons, such as its similarity to defamation, potential chilling of media, or the vagueness of the concept as only the substance or "gist" of the statement was false.

Citing the tort's potential to muffle the media, the Colorado Supreme Court rejected the false light claim. In *Denver Publishing Company v. Bueno* (2002), the court found Eddie Bueno's false light and defamation claims to be "nearly identical." The *Rocky Mountain News* published a 1994 story about the criminal activities of the family of Pete and Della Bueno, which included eighteen children.

Fifteen of the children had criminal records, and one died in 1977. One of the two children who lived crime-free lives, Eddie, sued the newspaper and the reporter. A family-tree mug-shot caption did not distinguish Eddie as never being arrested. Only the end of the article mentioned two siblings, Eddie (oldest) and Freddie (youngest), as having "stayed out of trouble." Bueno sued for defamation and false light. In rejecting Bueno's false light claim, the court said he could have a defamation claim by proving that a statement about him was false.

The court ruled that false light was superfluous because it was "highly duplicative of defamation both in the interests protected and conduct averted." The tort "applies only to a narrow band of cases such that any potential gain in individual protection is offset by the chilling effect the new, undefined tort would have on speech." Recognition of different interests of false light and defamation "rests primarily on parsing too subtle distinction between an individual's personal sensibilities and his or her reputation in the community," the court noted, and consequently "false light is too amorphous a tort for Colorado."

In rejecting false light, the North Carolina Supreme Court's ruling in *Renwick v. News and Observer* (2002) was grounded in the overlap of false light and defamation as indistinguishable. Stating that false light lacks the "procedural limitations" that accompany defamation actions, the Texas Supreme Court ruled in *Cain v. Hearst* (1994) that false light duplicated defamation without protecting free-speech interests, and overlapped with misappropriation.

Recognizing three of the four privacy torts in *Lake v. Wal-Mart Stores, Inc.* (1998), Minnesota rejected false light. The Minnesota Supreme Court stated, "We decline to recognize the tort of false light privacy at this time. We are concerned that claims under false light are similar to claims of defamation, and to the extent that false light is more expansive than defamation, tension between this tort and the First Amendment is increased." Citing other states in its denial of the tort, the court noted, "False light is the most widely criticized of the four privacy torts and has been rejected by several jurisdictions."

As mentioned above, Florida no longer recognizes the false light tort since the state's supreme court ruled in *Anderson v. Gannett Co., Inc.* (2003). The court stated that the tort was "largely duplicative of existing torts, but without the attendant protections of the First Amendment." False light "allows the plaintiff to circumvent the strict requirements that have been adopted by statute and developed by case law to ensure the right to freedom of expression," the justices warned.

States Recognizing or Not Ruling on False Light

Nine states—Alaska, Hawaii, Michigan, North Dakota, Oregon, South Carolina, South Dakota, Vermont, and Wyoming—have not had the opportunity to rule on whether they recognize false light or not. In the remaining thirty states and the District of Columbia, false light claims are viable.

One example of a state justifying recognition would be Ohio, which approved the false light tort along with an actual malice standard in *Welling v. Weinfeld* (2007), a case involving invasion of privacy between private individuals, not by a media respondent. In one suit between the feuding neighbors, a couple claimed that their neighbor had distributed handbills at their children's school and near the husband's workplace for tips about who threw rocks through a window of her banquet facility.

In recognizing the false light tort, the Ohio Supreme Court stated, "Today, thanks to the accessibility of the Internet, the barriers to generating publicity are slight, and the ethical standards regarding the acceptability of certain discourse have been lowered. As the ability to do harm has grown, so must the law's ability to protect the innocent."

Prospects for False Light: Survive or Expire?

Will the false light tort continue as a remedy for invasion of privacy? Will more states join the minority that reject the tort? Will states and federal courts recognizing the tort create difficult standards or dismiss suits? If so, even where the tort is recognized, the chances of a false light plaintiff recovering damages will be slim.

Has there been a noticeable trend among states in recognizing or rejecting false light that would indicate the tort's future? The states expressly recognizing the tort did so in 1960s and 1970s, before courts realized how false light could be expanded and misused against the media. In rejecting the tort, the Colorado

Supreme Court noted "a slow but important trend among states that have decided that this controversial form of privacy has no place in their courts." The attorney for the original private plaintiff in the Colorado case argued there was an "ongoing trend" of states rejecting false light beginning in the 1980s and 1990s. That included North Carolina, Texas, and Minnesota, but then Tennessee recognized the tort in 2001. Most recently, Missouri reaffirmed its rejection. Neither side can claim a noticeable trend today either way.

Defenders of false light have insisted that the tort protects concerns not covered by existing remedies, and they have dismissed any overlap with defamation claims. In defending false light, Bryan R. Lasswell stated in a 1993 article for *South Texas Law Review* that false light and defamation serve "unique interests" and cannot replace each other. Although admitting that the "biggest disadvantage" of false light is the defamation similarity, Lasswell wrote, "The greatest advantage presented by a false light action is that an action or publication need not be defamatory before it is actionable." In explaining the "special needs" regarding mental anguish provided by false light, Lasswell quoted the 1985 Seventh Circuit decision in *Douglass v. Hustler Magazine, Inc.*, "False light tort, to the extent distinct from tort of defamation . . . rests on an awareness that people who are made to seem pathetic or ridiculous may be shunned, and not just people who are thought to be dishonest or incompetent or immoral."

In a 1991 article for the *Case Western Reserve Law Review,* Gary T. Schwartz argued that false light might have "suffered from excessive constitutionalization." To remedy this confusion, he proposed that "a well-defined false light tort can be effective in discouraging the commission of false light violations." As for the defamation, false light does not allow plaintiffs to "bypass defamation restrictions." Schwartz favored "a limited false light doctrine," while proposing "a certain division of responsibility between defamation and false light torts." In defending the tort, he stated, "After balancing several factors, I conclude that a limited doctrine of false light is desirable."

As Nathan E. Ray argued in a 2002 article in the *Minnesota Law Review,* false light can protect an individual's "distinct interest—self-determination" to "curb media abuses." This would allow citizens to determine for themselves how "they are presented to the public."

As for those who argue against the tort, they claim that the confusion over its purpose and application has chilled First Amendment media protections, and they insist that defamation provides adequate protection for plaintiffs.

As Sanford argued against false light, "Ostensibly, the tort purports to allow recovery for misrepresentations and inaccuracies that do not rise to the level of libel or slander. In practice, a misrepresentation that does not amount to a defamatory remark may be difficult for a publisher to detect or avoid."

Insisting that "injuries from untruths" belong in defamation actions, Zimmerman stated that the "empty" and "unworkable" false light tort has resulted in confusion in First Amendment theory and "a severe chilling effect on the communication of accurate information."

Zimmerman concluded that false light was "unsalvageable as currently conceived and should be stricken from common law as a cognizable cause of action." While "a much-reduced, but acceptable scope for false light could be retained," Zimmerman stated that noticeable problems would still occur. "Current conception of false light invasions should be approached with skepticism and caution. . . . Its splendid pedigree notwithstanding, false light has proved in practice to illuminate nothing. From the viewpoint of coherent First Amendment theory, it has served instead to deepen the darkness."

In a 2013 article titled "Ray of Hope to Eliminate False Light" on the Privacy Association website, Kosseff noted two federal decisions (Sixth Circuit and Seventh Circuit) and two state decisions (Missouri and Iowa) that "indicate that courts are generally holding false light plaintiffs to a high standard." As "an outdated and unnecessary privacy tort," false light must be eliminated by courts and legislatures, Kosseff concluded.

In a 2012 review of developments in invasion of privacy at the Practicing Law Institute's annual "Communications Law in the Digital Age" seminar, Kelli L. Sager's course materials listed fifteen state and federal false light cases that indicate no significant changes in the tort. In considering a variety of issues regarding the tort, seven focused on cases involving both false light and defamation claims. Of the fifteen false light decisions discussed, twelve favored the defendants, and two involved media defendants.

The false light tort continues to divide scholars, courts, and legislatures while creating debate and confusion over its necessity, validity, and existence. Despite its disputed purpose and legacy, this controversial tort will remain—barring individual state rejections—in at least two-thirds of the country.

Jack Breslin
Iona College

See also Invasion of Privacy; Opinion and Libel

Further Reading

Elder, David A. *Privacy Torts.* St. Paul, MN: West Group, 2002. Cumulative Supplement. New York: Thomson Reuters, 2013.

Hallander, Susan. "Call for the End of the False Light Privacy Action as It Relates to Docudramas." *Seton Hall Journal of Sports & Entertainment Law* 15 (2005): 275.

Kosseff, Jeff. "A Ray of Hope to Eliminate False Light." Privacy Association, September 11, 2013. https://www.privacyassociation.org/privacy_perspectives/post/a_ray_of_hope_to_eliminate_false_light.

Lasswell, Bryan R. "In Defense of False Light: Why False Light Must Remain a Viable Cause of Action." *South Texas Law Review* 34 (1993): 149–180.

McLean, Deckle. "False Light Privacy." *Communications & the Law* 19, no. 1 (March 1997): 63–81.

Pilgrim, Tim A. "Docudramas and False-Light Invasion of Privacy." In *Privacy and Publicity,* edited by Theodore Kupferman, 223–257. Westport, CT: Meckler, 1990.

Prosser, William L. "Privacy." *California Law Review* 48, no. 3 (August 1960): 383–423.

"Ranking of States in Protections." *Privacy Journal* (2012). http://www.privacyjournal.net/events.htm.

Ray, Nathan E. "Let There Be False Light: Resisting the Trend against an Important Test." *Minnesota Law Review* 84 (February 2000): 713.

Russo, Brent T. "Survey of Ohio Law: Ohio Supreme Court III. Cases Concerning Tort Law." *Ohio Northern University Law Review* 34 (2000): 980.

Sager, Kelli L. "Recent Developments in Defamation, Invasion of Privacy and Other Content-Based Claims." *Communications Law in the Digital Age* 3 (2012): 252–257.

Sanford, Bruce W. *Libel and Privacy,* 2nd ed. Upper Saddle River, NJ: Prentice Hall, 1991.

Schwartz, Gary T. "Explaining and Justifying a Limited Tort of False Light Invasion of Privacy." *Case Western Reserve Law Review* 41 (1991): 885

Segal, William D. "Torts: Right of Privacy: Is 'False Light' Recognized in California?" *California Law Review* 50, no. 2 (May 1962): 357–364.

Solove, Daniel J., Marc Rotenberg, and Paul M. Schwartz. *Information Privacy Law,* 2nd ed. New York: Aspen Publishers, 2006.

Stohl, Matthew. "False Light Invasion of Privacy in Docudramas: The Oxymoron Which Must Be Solved." *Akron Law Review* 35 (2002): 251.

Tannenbaum, Wendy. "A Recent Decision Calls False Light Outdated." *News Media & the Law* 22 (Fall 2002).

Warren, Samuel D., and Louis D. Brandeis. "The Right to Privacy." *Harvard Law Review* 4, no. 5 (December 1890): 193–220.

Zimmerman, Diane Leenheer. "False Light Invasion of Privacy: The Light That Failed." *New York University Law Review* 64 (May 1989): 364.

35

ETHICAL CENSORSHIP

The first e-mail sent from China was transmitted on September 20, 1987, and said, "Across the Great Wall we can reach every corner in the world." Much has occurred since that time. China now is infamous for its Golden Shield Project, dubbed the Great Firewall of China, a massive and ubiquitous surveillance project operated by the Ministry of Public Security to scrutinize the gateways through which content on foreign websites enters China. Except for those adequately tech-savvy to bypass this censorship—referred to as "climbing over the wall"—most Chinese Internet users are still confined to the world within the Wall. Precisely what constitutes the censorship process—algorithms, individual censors, a censoring bank of people, some combination, etc.—is not known, and is a well-guarded governmental secret.

By the end of December 2013, there were 618 million Chinese Internet users, 45.8 percent of the nation's population, according to the China Internet Network Information Center (CNNIC). The diffusion of the Internet, especially mobile Internet via devices such as smartphones and tablets, has caused the Chinese government to be fearful of how easy it is for its citizens to communicate with one another, especially in the aftermath of the Arab Spring uprisings in 2010.

On June 6, 2013, Edward Snowden, a former U.S. National Security Agency (NSA) contractor, disclosed America's mass surveillance program to the *Guardian* and the *Washington Post*. This revelation has stirred a debate on national security and citizens' privacy in the United States.

So when is it justified for a government to censor communications in the online era, and if censorship is to occur, when and under what circumstances might it be responsible for such censorship to take place? This article focuses on the evolution of online censorship in China, the rationale for such censorship, and the latest censorship rules, actions, and trends. In addition, this article examines how China and the United States handle online surveillance.

The Evolution of Online Censorship in China and Its Justifications

How Online Censorship Works in China

The Internet was opened to the Chinese public in January 1995. Ever since then, the Chinese government has been aware of the Internet's potential threat to its existence. Following Singapore's model, China adopted an ever-more-rigorous program of online censorship. Such censorship comprises a legal and administrative framework, overseeing organizations, and technical methods.

The Chinese government has issued laws and regulations to monitor the operation of Internet companies. Among them, the 2005 Provisions on the Administration of Internet News Information Service set the tone for future development. According to the provisions, government-licensed and approved news agencies must get state approval for covering specific events. Internet news services shall not conduct any journalistic interviews, but only reprint news from those approved news outlets. Thus, the censorship criteria are unclear. This interference actually is a kind of censorship since Internet news services may not run their own news stories, but only parrot what has been already audited by the government.

On May 4, 2011, the State Internet Information Office was set up under the State Council to be in charge of directing, coordinating, and supervising online content management as well as implementing the Internet information dissemination policy. This office also oversees the approval of online news-reporting businesses. In general, online publication industries are under the supervision of this office.

Different censoring measures have been used to supervise the Internet in addition to setting up a specific organization. Technically, the censorship system blocks websites by using "blacklists," and monitors some important websites in particular. It has several tiers, ranging from local to international. The monitoring at city telecoms is looser and at international gateways much more intense.

Some foreign websites, such as some human rights organizations and news organizations, were first blocked in 1996. YouTube was blocked in March 2008, after riots in Tibet, and Facebook and Twitter in July 2009, after riots in Xinjiang, another autonomous region where ethnic minorities live. Bloomberg and the *New York Times* have been blocked since June and October 2012, respectively, after publishing stories about the finances of former Chinese leaders' relatives. The most recent clampdown happened in November 2013, to the Chinese-language websites of the *Wall Street Journal* and Reuters. Other high-profile websites on the list include Dropbox, Vimeo, Reporters Without Borders, Blogspot, and Wordpress. According to Greatfire.org, 3,004 of 24,296 domains, 2,176 of 11,389 Google searches, and 262 of 976 Wikipedia pages are blocked in China as of May 14, 2014, when this article was written.

Search-results removal is also imposed on Internet corporations; otherwise they cannot get licenses to run their business.

This often is considered to be self-censorship of Internet content and service providers, even though these content and service providers have little choice but to comply with governmental "suggestions." Technical improvements have made it possible to sift specific search terms rather than blocking the whole site. For example, after a search term is blocked at Google.com.hk, a message will pop up saying, "Search results may not comply with the relevant laws, regulations, and policy, and cannot be displayed." Users who search banned terms at Google may be blocked for ninety seconds before search functions resume. Because in mainland China, even if users type in Google.com, their Internet explorers are automatically redirected to Google.com.hk, it means they cannot have access to some search results unless they take further measures.

In addition to the computerized system, China employs Internet police, dubbed "public opinion analysts," to erase anti-government comments and post pro-government opinions. What is discussed in this article only applies to censorship- and propaganda-related police and excludes police dealing with Internet crimes. Public opinion analysts steer online discussion on bulletin board systems and in chat rooms under false names or anonymously. Because *Global Times* reported that for each such post commentators were paid fifty fen, or Chinese cents, by the government, they are dubbed as "The Fifty Cent Party," a Chinese Internet users' satire. The salaries vary from place to place. Some commentators are out-of-work college graduates. The use of Internet commentators shows the

party is using different methods to shape online opinions. Unlike deleting opposing and negative opinions, "guiding public opinions" is considered less offensive and more effective.

Monitoring and guiding opinions is a gigantic project, considering the mammoth amount of user-generated online content every day. Sina.com, a portal website headquartered in Beijing that provides the most popular weibo (Chinese Twitter) service, monitors some 100 million messages every day sent by its 500 million users. Even so, weibo contains sensitive words that are removed quickly, most within twenty-four hours.

Why Censor and Self-Censor?

Justifications for restrictions on Internet access include concerns over the influence of Western ideology and culture, public activism for democracy, and the spread of pornography. Some researchers say maintaining national and cultural stability—not deterrence—is the real goal of China's online censorship.

Article 19 of the 2005 provisions stipulates that Internet news services shall not provide any cultural product that may defy the basic principles of the Constitution; endanger national security, divulge state secrets, subvert national sovereignty or territorial integrity; do harm to state interest; undermine ethnic unity or religious policies; spread rumors and destroy public stability; spread obscenities, pornography, gambling, and violence; humiliate or libel others; or disturb the public order by instigating illegal gatherings, associations, demonstrations, or assemblies.

The guiding principle of supervising the Internet saw a transition from "controlling" the Internet to making full use of it when then-president Hu Jintao gave a speech in January 2007 in which he stressed "asserting supremacy over online public opinion" and "studying the art of online guidance."

The Information Office of the State Council of China published a white paper on the Internet in China on June 8, 2010. It said China "endeavored to create a healthy and harmonious Internet environment" and emphasized that "China advocates the rational use of technology to curb dissemination of illegal information online" and "to prevent and curb the harmful effects of illegal information on state security, public interests, and minors." What is prohibited includes "information that contains content subverting state power, undermining national unity, infringing upon national honor and interests, inciting ethnic hatred and secession, advocating heresy, pornography, violence, terror, and other information that infringes upon the legitimate rights and interests of others." This mirrors the 2005 provisions. Such a broad definition of prohibitions gives the government the ability to censor virtually any content at will. As it says in the white paper, "Basic telecommunication business operators and Internet information service providers shall establish Internet security management systems and utilize technical measures to prevent the transmission of all types of illegal information."

Chinese president Xi Jinping delivered a speech on ideology on August 19, 2013, at the National Propaganda Work Conference. Xi called for seizing the ground of new media and for building a strong army within the party's propaganda organization. Qian Gang, a former journalist and director of the China Media Project at the University of Hong Kong, scrutinized the Chinese media's response and offered a lens through which this issue may be viewed. Though Xi himself did not use the phrase *yulun douzheng*, or "public opinion struggle," follow-up comments and editorials from the party's media outlets, such as the *People's Daily*, and propaganda officials stressed the importance of this struggle. Later, Li Congjun, chief of Xinhua News Agency, pointed out that "new media were a priority field of this struggle." The *Beijing Daily* ran a story titled "In the Struggle in the Ideological Sphere, We Must Have the Courage to Show Our Swords," followed by the *People's Liberation Army Daily*'s "Capturing the Initiative in the Online Public Opinion Struggle." Xu Qiliang, a politburo member and vice-chair of the Central Military Commission, warned that the Internet should be brought under control in case hostile forces may use it for "ideological infiltration."

Internet users, Internet Service Providers (ISPs), and Internet Content Providers (ICPs) are all accountable for illegal content online in China. This applies to ISPs and ICPs whose servers or operations are located in China. ISPs and ICPs should stop the transmission of impressible content when it is detected and report it to the authorities. The definition of *impressible content* is broad. It includes opposing China's constitution, divulging state secrets, subverting state power, damaging national unity, disseminating rumors, obscenity, or pornography, and insulting or slandering a third party. ISPs and ICPs will be unable to get their licenses renewed if they do not fulfill their monitoring responsibilities. Therefore, they self-censor online content. Because the list of sensitive words is changeable and vague, Internet companies tend to remove even more than necessary to make their business safe and sustainable. Being cooperative to the government is rewarded. In 2009, Baidu, China's largest search-engine company, was awarded the China Internet Self-Discipline Award for its contribution to harmonious and healthy Internet development.

If they post anything that may be considered impressible content, Internet users are worried about potential persecution that may jeopardize themselves and their family. Therefore, they do not comment or air opinions on sensitive issues. Such deterrence results in the self-censorship of both Internet companies and Internet users. Content most likely to be censored includes posts calling for collective action rather than those criticizing the state and its leaders, according to a Harvard research group led by Gary King. Another goal of censorship is to prevent political activity from happening when the Internet is used as a tool for organizing such gatherings.

China's government is not alone in collecting data on its citizens. Edward Snowden's disclosure of how the NSA had conducted massive data mining of online communications started the debate about whether he was a traitor or a patriot. Many in the United States chastised the NSA's invasion of the privacy rights of Americans. The spokesman of China's Ministry of Defense grasped the opportunity and asserted the importance of protecting Internet security and national security.

According to Snowden, the NSA's PRISM program accesses users' private communications via Internet and tele-communications companies, such as Google and Verizon. Immunized under Section 702 of the Foreign Intelligence Surveillance Act (FISA) of 2008, intelligence agencies can monitor the phone, e-mail, and other communications of U.S. citizens for up to a week without obtaining a warrant.

The U.S. government justifies NSA's collection of communications of non-Americans outside of the United States and American citizens in the United States by saying that the surveillance helps prevent acts of terrorism and thus protects the American people. As George Washington University professors Henry Farrell and Martha Finnemore argued, in terms of international relations, Snowden "has revealed nothing that was really unexpected."

Justifications and Repercussions of Online Censorship

The chronology of online censorship in China reveals that China's position focuses on preventing the invasion of Western ideology and the spread of rumors, as well as protecting Chinese citizens—minors, in particular—from pornography. Underneath, the long-term pursuit is political stability.

Anti-Pornography

In general, it is easy to get public support for anti-pornography Internet censorship, as pornography is considered a big threat to social order in Asian countries such as China, South Korea, and Singapore. Since the New China was founded in 1949, pornography, together with prostitution, drug use, and gambling, have been considered bad legacies from Old China, and thus subject to elimination. China's anti-pornography laws appear draconian, targeting anything violating public morality and harming the physical and psychological well-being of youth. The Law of Obscenity stipulates that selling, producing, and spreading obscene materials are banned. Sociologists such as Li Yinhe consider such laws outdated, as they oppose freedom of speech and human desires.

Online pornography and gambling are singled out for heavy punishment because they are viewed as great challenges to the Socialist social order. In 2010, a professor from Nanjing was sentenced to three and a half years in jail for "group licentiousness." He was charged with using online chat rooms to arrange gatherings for group sex. Those such as the professor and his cohorts, most of whom were convicted, may not be punished in other countries since it is considered a private matter among consenting parties.

Juveniles are often emphasized as the potential victims of online pornographic and obscene materials. However, most of the cases prosecuted by Chinese police targeted adults. Third-person effects research shows people perceive a bigger impact of media on others than on themselves, and Chinese may have collective anxiety over Internet pornography's negative effects on the society as a whole. Such perceptions encourage policymakers to censor online content.

The 2010 white paper specifies that the "state guarantees online safety for minors." The Law of the People's Republic of China on the Protection of Minors stipulates that "the state shall take measures to prevent minors from overindulging in the Internet; prohibit any organization or individual from producing, selling, renting, or providing by other means electronic publications and Internet information containing pornography, violence, murder, terror, gambling, or other content harmful to minors."

On May 19, 2009, the Ministry of Industry and Information Technology (MIIT) issued a notice requiring that all personal computers sold in mainland China after July 1, 2009, install the Green Dam Youth Escort software, which filters pornography or violence. MIIT explained the aim was "to build a green, healthy, and harmonious online environment, and to avoid the effects on and the poisoning of our youth's minds by harmful information on the Internet." Although discontinued later due to cybersecurity and economic concerns, this project raised censorship concerns since the software could keep a record of all Web pages users had viewed. It also likely could filter out politically sensitive words. Thus, the measures and actions taken are more sweeping and proactive, going far beyond simple protection of minors.

China launched its Anti-Pornography Campaign in 1989. In the 1990s, copyright was added, which made it transform into the Anti-Pornography and Anti-Piracy Campaign in 1999. The campaign is under the leadership of the National Anti-Pornography and Anti-Piracy Office, which is affiliated with the General

Administration of Press and Publication. It coordinates with twenty-eight government divisions. The focus of the campaign varies each year, especially before significant events, such as the run-up to the 2008 Olympics. In the first half of that year, 46.1 million illegal publications were seized, 1.6 million of which were pornographic. The Spring Festival, International Children's Day, and National Day are some of the peak seasons for the campaign during regular years.

Since 2009, online censorship has gained strong momentum with the increased penetration of the Internet. Chinese police launched a campaign against Internet pornography in 2009 to protect the "emotional health of the children." It ended with 5,394 arrests and 4,186 criminal investigations, which represented an increase of 40 percent compared with the previous year. More than 9,000 porn websites and programs were closed in 2009. About 97,000 blogs and microblogs involved in disseminating pornographic content were shut down, 287 Internet companies investigated, and 2,446 pornography cases cracked down upon in the first half of 2012. The Ministry of Public Security vowed to intensify its monitoring of information. In the summer of 2013, Xinhua News Agency announced another anti-porn campaign to create a benign Internet environment for Chinese youth during summer break and prevent "spiritual pollution," or sex and pornography. The campaign focused on porn websites, online games, blogs, and microblogs carrying crude and vulgar content.

If, indeed, such campaigns reduce the dissemination of graphic and obscene photos and videos online, they are beneficial to minors, social harmony, and the greater good. However, most cases target adult pornography. Western countries, on the other hand, tend to protect the use of sexually explicit materials by adults. Although the official Chinese media often report on such anti-pornography campaigns, China's post-1980s and post-1990s generations, or Chinese who were born in these two decades, are dismissive of such cleanups and the underlying surveillance. Thus, while Chinese society is becoming more liberal toward sexuality, old anti-sex laws still exist. Katrien Jacobs, associate professor of visual cultural studies at Chinese University of Hong Kong, and her research group found it was easy to access hard-core pornography websites and images in cafeterias in Shenzhen via the Chinese search engine Baidu. At best, the supervision department only selectively monitors online pornography. It is only targeted when intimidation of Internet users is needed. While some websites were shut down for posting pictures of young women in bikinis, similar photos were easily found at the website of the party's official news outlets.

Pornography is also mixed with crimes and dissidents as "unhealthy" information, and politically sensitive terms are actually blocked by software. In this way, anti-pornography campaigns are employed as an excuse to legitimize online censorship.

Anti-Rumors

New media, such as social networking sites, have provided a new conduit for Internet users to set up networks where they can share ideas. To some extent, these networks could function as a marketplace of ideas, especially in countries such as China, where the ruling party tightly controls traditional media. Such online networks are important to Chinese because the structure of Chinese society, to use sociologist Fei Xiaotong's words, is "like the circles that appear on the surface of a lake when a rock is thrown into it. Everyone stands at the center of the circles produced by his or her own social influence." Chinese society is highly relational. The online network is only the virtual reality of the actual world.

With the exponential increase of microbloggers, "public opinion struggle" is a convenient governmental excuse to censor domestic online opinion leaders and even ordinary Internet users. The most recent campaign was waged to crack down upon "rumormongering."

"Big Vs," or those verified active commentators with millions of followers on weibo, have been under intense surveillance and even detention since August 2013, charged with fabricating and spreading false claims. Charles Xue, a sixty-year-old naturalized American venture capitalist and Big V known as Xue Manzi to his 12 million Sina Weibo followers, was charged with having group sex and confessed in front of a video camera on CCTV, China's state-run national television channel. Xue gained his stardom on weibo for promoting a campaign that helped rescue abducted children. He also shared his musings on corruption and political reform with his followers. Xue told CCTV that he had spread irresponsible posts online and that freedom of speech could not override the law. His three-minute confession aired on evening prime time. Xue's scenario is telling and chilling enough to make other active and articulate online opinion leaders know how social elites may be easily humiliated. Wang Qinglei, a former CCTV producer, was fired in December with the given reason of violating relevant rules about how journalists use their weibo accounts. Wang had criticized his former employer for abusing its power in the coverage of Xue before he could get a fair trial.

While the ripple effects caused by Xue's detention and confession were still being felt, on September 9, 2013, the Supreme People's Court and the Supreme People's Procuratorate announced that if defamatory content is forwarded 500 times and viewed 5,000 times, the person who posts it will face up to three years in jail.

About a week after the new rule became effective, a sixteen-year-old boy in western Gansu Province was placed under administrative detention for posting inaccurate information online. The teenager claimed in his post that a suspect died as a result of police brutality. He was the first publicly acknowledged victim of the 500 rule. Several other activists with many followers were arrested or detained afterward.

The chilling effect of such rigorous laws may make the Chinese society fragmented, as Murong Xuecun worried. Murong is the pen name of Hao Qun, an award-winning writer who has criticized China's censorship. He has about 8.5 million weibo followers across accounts on four portal websites. On May 11, 2013, his posts were deleted simultaneously by these weibo services. There was no claimed reason for the closure, which happened within five minutes. But his Sina Weibo account resumed on May 17.

Some microbloggers, in a joking way, pleaded with other weibo users to not forward their posts more than 500 times. But some users forwarded posts from government weibo accounts more than 500 times, since at least 50,000 Chinese government departments at all levels have official weibo accounts.

The anti-rumor campaign is censorship that stifles criticism of the government. The 500 bar is set quite low when compared to the 500 million registered weibo users. The result of such a censorship policy would be harmful to countless Internet users. There are rumors online and not enough protection for those who are defamed. But most posts just constitute people's comments and opinions. The 500 and 5,000 rule suppresses people's freedom of speech. Withholding information from the public means people remain uninformed and thus are unable to knowledgeably participate in the decision-making process. This prohibits citizens from being civically engaged, as they are not fully able to partake of any semblance of a marketplace of ideas.

National Security

If neither anti-pornography nor anti-rumor discourse appears to justify censorship, what about national security?

President Obama defended the NSA surveillance program, PRISM, by saying it was "a circumscribed, narrow system directed at us being able to protect our people." To Keith B. Alexander, director of the NSA, the aim of the surveillance was to protect Americans from "imminent threats, from terrorism to devastating cyberattacks." On the other hand, John McLaughlin says in his article in *Foreign Policy,* "The effectiveness of our democracy depends on an informed citizenry; effective intelligence depends on withholding and protecting information deemed sensitive."

China has maintained that online surveillance is justified, as the nation needs to defend itself from the encroachment of Western ideology and domestic ethnic riots.

Chinese education emphasizes the century of humiliation that began when China was first invaded by Western powers following the Opium War in 1840 and culminated in the founding of the People's Republic of China in 1949. Currently, nationalism is enhanced and consolidated by the media. "Road to Rejuvenation," for instance, is a series of TV programs, a book, and a long-term exhibition in 2011 that all have the same name, showing China is prepared to realize its dream of establishing its former greatness. Nationalist ideology resonates with young Chinese urbanites who are the beneficiaries of China's economic reform. Therefore, it is not surprising to find China's government eager to stamp out any Western ideology in its online discourse.

In 1983, there was a campaign called "anti-spiritual pollution." Its apparent aim was to wipe out pornography, but it actually was a crusade against the encroachment of Western ideology. Lieutenant General Liu Yazhou, political commissar of the People's Liberation Army's University of National Defense, published an article on October 15, 2013, titled

"Western Hostile Forces Attempt to Defeat China with the Internet." In the article, General Liu warned that China should take proactive measures in the Internet era to control the discourse. He underlined the importance of microblogs as the venue for different voices. Chinese are indoctrinated with a nationalistic historical view and political discourse, which affect how Chinese perceive their identity and the potential threat from outside. It can be found in China's recent stance on territorial claims with its neighbors. As a world power, the United States, in particular, is considered by some Chinese as a potential threat. And this threat is on the rise.

Confucius emphasized relationship-defined ethics. The relationship is inclusive—monarchs and subjects, fathers and sons, husbands and wives, to name a few. To maintain good relationships, one needs to follow customs, called *li*. *Li* can be defined as imperatives of conduct. *Liji*, or the *Book of Rites*, is a whole collection of rites and rules pertinent to daily life. *Kejifuli*, or to constrain oneself to follow rituals and norms, is one of the key principles of Confucius's philosophy. It can be found in many conversations between the Master and his disciples in the *Analects*. Chinese are educated to constrain themselves to follow social norms and rituals for the interest of the state and the community. The emphasis by national propaganda on not spreading rumors, the policies aimed at eliminating pornographic and obscene content, as well as draconian laws all accentuate the greater good and promote cultural harmony.

Chinese officials appear beleaguered by hostile Western forces taking advantage of the Internet to hinder, as they see it, their nation's economic development and the stability of its social order. Online censorship can counter any action that may bring social turmoil, even when it is still burgeoning.

On the one hand, such propaganda has been effective. Some Chinese Internet users are self-disciplined and self-censoring of their Internet footprints. Especially when considering whether or not online surveillance may help the government detect potential threats, some Internet users may favor censorship. However, such censorship eliminates different opinions and severs individuals from a larger and more heterogeneous community.

On the other hand, Sina Weibo did not strictly follow the real-name registration rule—which required Internet users to register their real names and national identification numbers with online service providers before posting comments on providers' websites—so tweeters still enjoyed their anonymity online after the deadline. And Fang Bingxin, former president of Beijing University of Posts and Telecommunications and father of the Great Firewall, was hit by a shoe thrown by a student when he lectured at Wuhan University. It shows how resentful the younger generation is about censorship and surveillance, though some people are sympathetic to Fang, saying he simply has been fulfilling his responsibilities as an intellectual.

In 2009 a meme called the Baidu Ten Mythical Creatures went viral. Topping the list was the Grass Mud Horse, a translation of the homophone of *cao ni ma* (fuck your mother) in Mandarin. Chinese Internet users created such words to bypass the filtering software that claimed to protect them from vulgar and profane content.

The Grass Mud Horse's biggest enemy is the River Crab, or *he xie* (harmony), since foul words are often eliminated for the sake of creating a harmonious society.

John Stuart Mill argued for the free-dom to express and debate competing ideas:

> The peculiar evil of silencing the expression of an opinion is, that it is robbing the human race; posterity as well as the existing generation; those who dissent from the opinion, still more than those who hold it. If the opinion is right, they are deprived of the opportunity of exchanging error for truth: if wrong, they lose, what is almost as great a benefit, the clearer perception and livelier impression of truth, produced by its collision with error.

In China, harmony has for countless centuries been a goal. Thus, silencing of dissent or whatever might erode harmony is nothing new to the world's most populous nation. The advent of new/computer/Internet technology has brought with it new challenges to a Communist government determined to keep out dangerous, foreign messages and information. Just as Mongols and Manchus were able to scale China's Great Wall, members of today's tech-savvy young generation have found that the nation's Great Firewall can be breached. They know how to circumvent the Firewall by using proxy servers and virtual private networks (VPNs). Those with more computer knowledge can even get rid of the fetters without VPNs by copying and pasting new addresses in a host file that is a list of Internet Protocol addresses. Then entering the most up-to-date addresses of blocked websites after "http://" or "https://" will make these sites accessible. Software and tips for bypassing the Wall are easily searchable.

Only when the public is well informed can the society make progress. In the video, the Grass Mud Horse finally defeats the River Crab. But in a nation espousing the greater good of social communitarianism, harmony has for many governments and dynasties trumped personal freedoms and privacy. Tens of thousands of educated young Chinese may well see governmentally forced harmonization to be an ineffective sham. But in a land where the River Crab has for centuries successfully navigated numerous dangerous shoals, reversing this tide will likely prove to be as difficult as is swimming upstream against a swift current.

Tao Fu
University of International Business
and Economics
William A. Babcock
Southern Illinois University Carbondale

See also China Worried?; Global First Amendment: The China Question and an Onion-Peeling Approach

Further Reading

"The Astonishing Speed of Chinese Censorship." BBC, March 26, 2013. http://www.bbc.co .uk/news/world-asia-china-21743499.

Buckley, C. "Chinese Defense Ministry Accuses U.S. of Hypocrisy on Spying."

New York Times, June 27, 2013. http://rendezvous.blogs.nytimes .com/2013/06/28/u-s-prism-meet-chinas-golden-shield/?_r=0.

Buckley, C. "Crackdown on Bloggers Is Mounted by China." *New York Times,* September 10, 2013. http://www.nytimes.com/2013/09/11/

world/asia/china-cracks-down-on-online-opinion-makers.html?_r=0&adxnnl=1&ref=internetcensorship&adxnnlx=1384172902-H8FD9781nJvyEiNrqubr/Q.

"Cat and Mouse: How China Makes Sure Its Internet Abides by the Rules." *Economist,* April 6, 2013. http://www.economist.com/news/special-report/21574629-how-china-makes-sure-its-internet-abides-rules-cat-and-mouse.

China Internet Network Information Center. "The 33rd Statistical Report on Internet Development (*2014 zhongguo hulian wangluo fazhan zhuangkuang tongji baogao*)," January 2014. http://www.cnnic.net.cn/hlwfzyj/hlwxzbg/hlwtjbg/201401/P020140116395418429515.pdf.

"China's Newest Online Campaign against Pornography and Vulgar Content Is Hypocritical." *International Business Times,* July 17, 2013.

"China Says 5,349 Arrested in Internet Porn Crackdown." Reuters, December 31, 2009. Retrieved from http://www.reuters.com/article/2010/01/01/us-china-internet-idUSTRE60004220100101.

"China Shuts Down 97,000 Blog, Microblog Accounts in Anti-Porn Campaign." *People's Daily,* September 29, 2012. http://english.peopledaily.com.cn/90882/7965475.html.

Chu, K., and W. Launder. "U.S. Media Firms Stymied in China." *Wall Street Journal,* December 6, 2013. http://online.wsj.com/news/articles/SB10001424052702303722104579242431330313584.

Congressional-Executive Commission on China. *Annual Report.* Washington, DC: U.S. Government Printing Office, 2013. http://www.gpo.gov/fdsys/pkg/CHRG-113hhrg85010/html/CHRG-113hhrg85010.htm.

Congressional-Executive Commission on China. "Provisions on the Administration of Internet News Information Services," 2006. http://www.cecc.gov/resources/legal-provisions/provisions-on-the-administration-of-internet-news-information-services.

Davison, W. P. "The Third-Person Effect in Communication." *Public Opinion Quarterly* 47 (1983): 1–15.

Deal, J. "China's Nationalist Heritage." *National Interest* 123 (2013): 44–53.

Dimitrov, M. *Piracy and the State: The Politics of Intellectual Property Rights in China.* Cambridge, UK: Cambridge University Press, 2009.

Farrell, H., and M. Finnemore. "The End of Hypocrisy." *Foreign Affairs* 92, no. 6 (2013): 22–26.

"Father of Great Firewall Pelted at Wuhan University." *WantChinaTimes*, May 19, 2011. http://www.wantchinatimes.com/news-subclass-cnt.aspx?id=20110519000158&cid=1103.

Fei, X. *From the Soil: The Foundations of Chinese Society.* Translated by G. G. Hamilton and Z. Wang. Berkeley, CA: University of California Press, 1992.

Feng, G. C., and S. Z. Guo. "Tracing the Route of China's Internet Censorship: An Empirical Study." *Telematics and Informatics* 30 (2013): 335–345.

FlorCruz, J. A. "Online Popularity Can Be Perilous as China Obsesses about Internet Rumors." *CNN*, September 13, 2013. http://www.cnn.com/2013/09/13/world/asia/china-online-rumors-crackdown-florcruz/.

Foster, P. "China Suffering from 'Confucian Confusion' over Sex." *Telegraph,* September 22, 2011. http://www.telegraph.co.uk/news/worldnews/asia/china/8780976/China-suffering-from-Confucian-confusion-over-sex.html.

"A Giant Cage." *Economist,* April 6, 2013. http://www.economist.com/news/special-report/21574628-internet-was-expected-help-democratise-china-instead-it-has-enabled.

Gordon, A. D., J. M. Kittross, J. C. Merrill, W. A. Babcock, and M. Dorsher. *Controversies in Media Ethics,* 3rd ed. New York: Routledge, 2011.

"The Great Firewall: The Art of Concealment." *Economist,* April 6, 2013. http://www.economist.com/news/special-report/

21574631-chinese-screening-online-material-abroad-becoming-ever-more-sophisticated.

Gries, P. H., Q. Zhang, H. M. Crowson, and H. Cai. (2011). "Patriotism, Nationalism and China's U.S. Policy: Structures and Consequences of Chinese National Identity." *China Quarterly* 205 (2011): 1–17.

Haley, U. "China's Fifty Cent Party for Internet Propaganda." *Huffington Post,* October 4, 2010. http://www.huffingtonpost.com/usha-haley/chinas-fifty-cent-party-f_1_b_749989.html.

"How Does China Censor the Internet?" *Economist,* April 21, 2013. http://www.economist.com/blogs/economist-explains/2013/04/economist-explains-how-china-censors-internet.

Huang, C., and K. Zhai. "Xi Jinping Rallies Party for Propaganda War on Internet." *South China Morning Post,* September 4, 2013. http://www.scmp.com/news/china/article/1302857/president-xi-jinping-rallies-party-propaganda-war-internet?page=all.

Hunt, K., and C. Y. Xu. "China Employs 2 Million to Police Internet." *CNN,* October 7, 2013. http://www.cnn.com/2013/10/07/world/asia/china-internet-monitors.

"The Internet in China." GOV.cn, June 8, 2010. http://english.gov.cn/2010-06/08/content_1622956_6.htm.

Jacobs, K. *People's Pornography: Sex and Surveillance on the Chinese Internet.* Chicago: University of Chicago Press, 2012.

"Journalist Wang Qinglei Allegedly Fired after Criticizing Chinese State TV." *Huffington Post,* December 2, 2013. http://www.huffingtonpost.com/2013/12/02/wang-qinglei-cctv-letter-confession_n_4370956.html.

King, G., J. Pan, and M. E. Robert. "How Censorship in China Allows Government Criticism but Silences Collective Expression." *American Political Science Review* 107, no. 2 (2013): 326–343.

Kshetri, N. "Cyber-Victimization and Cybersecurity in China." *Communications of the ACM* 56, no. 4 (2013): 35–37. doi:10.1145/2436256.2436267.

Lee, B., and R. Tamborini. "Third-Person Effect and Internet Pornography: The Influence of Collectivism and Internet Self-Efficacy." *Journal of Communication* 55 (2005): 292–310.

Lee, J. "First Amendment Essay: Regulating Blogging and Microblogging in China." *Oregon Law Review* 91 (2012).

Leo, L. "Teen Arrest Puts 300m Tweeters on Edge." *Times*, September 21, 2013.

Liang, B., and H. Lu. "Fighting the Obscene, Pornographic, and Unhealthy: An Analysis of the Nature, Extent, and Regulation of China's Online Pornography within a Global Context." *Crime, Law, and Social Change* 58, no. 2 (2012): 111–130.

Liu. Y. "*Xifang didui shili wangtu yi hulianwang bandao zhongguo* (Western Hostile Forces Attempt to Defeat China by the Internet)." *Xinhua News,* October 25, 2013. http://news.xinhuanet.com/world/2013-10/15/c_125537518.htm.

Lo, K. "Sinicizing Žižek? The Ideology of Inherent Self-Negation in Contemporary China." *Positions* 19, no. 3 (2011): 739–761. doi:10.1215/10679847-1369289.

Madison, L. "Obama Defends 'Narrow' Surveillance Programs." *CBS News*, June 19, 2013. http://www.cbsnews.com/8301–250_162-57590025/obama-defends-narrow-surveillance-programs.

McLaughlin, J. "The Real Reason You Are Mad at the NSA." *Foreign Policy,* June 17, 2013. http://www.foreignpolicy.com/articles/2013/06/16/the_real_reason_youre_mad_at_the_nsa?page=0,0.

Mill, J. S. *On Liberty*. New York: Gateway Editions, 1955.

Mozur, P. "No VPN? No Problem. A New Way around China's Great Firewall." *Wall Street Journal,* November 29, 2012. http://blogs.wsj.com/chinarealtime/2012/11/29/no-vpn-no-problem-a-new-way-around-chinas-great-firewall.

Murong, X. "Chinese Internet: A New Censorship Campaign Has Commenced." *Guardian,* May 15, 2013. http://www.the

guardian.com/world/2013/may/15/chinese-internet-censorship-campaign.

Nakashima, E., and J. Warrick. "For NSA Chief, Terrorist Threat Drives Passion to 'Collect It All,' Observers Say." *Washington Post,* July 14, 2013. http://www.washingtonpost.com/world/national-security/for-nsa-chief-terrorist-threat-drives-passion-to-collect-it-all/2013/07/14/3d26ef80-ea49–11e2-a301-ea5a8116d211_story.html.

"Online Censorship in China." GreatFire.org, 2013.

OpenNet Initiative. "Country Profile: China." *Access Contested,* 2012. http://access.opennet.net/wp-content/uploads/2011/12/accesscontested-china.pdf.

Qian, G. "Parsing the 'Public Opinion Struggle.'" *China Media Project,* September 24, 2013. http://cmp.hku.hk/2013/09/24/34085.

Rajagopalan, M., and A. Rose. "China Crackdown on Online Rumors Seen as Ploy to Nail Critics." *Reuters*, September 18, 2013. http://www.reuters.com/article/2013/09/18/net-us-china-internet-idUSBRE98H07X20130918.

Ramzy, A. "A Swinger's Case: China's Attitude toward Sex." *Time,* May 22, 2010. http://content.time.com/time/world/article/0,8599,1991029,00.html.

Sebag-Montefoire, C. "Beijing's Play for Porn." *New York Times,* July 26, 2013. http://latitude.blogs.nytimes.com/2013/07/26/beijings-play-for-porn/?ref=internetcensorship.

Shen, L. "*Tanmi saohuangdafei ban* (The Mystery of the National Anti-Pornography and Anti-Piracy Office)." Infzm.com, January 21, 2010. http://www.infzm.com/content/40655.

Subramanian, R. "The Growth of Global Internet Censorship and Circumvention: A Survey." *Communications of the IIMA* 11, no. 2 (2011): 69–90.

Tatlow, D. K. "U.S. Prism, Meet China's Golden Shield." *New York Times,* June 28, 2013. http://rendezvous.blogs.nytimes.com/2013/06/28/u-s-prism-meet-chinas-golden-shield/?_r=0.

Wine, M. "A Dirty Pun Tweaks China's Online Censors." *New York Times,* March 11, 2009. http://www.nytimes.com/2009/03/12/world/asia/12beast.html?_r=0.

Wu, G. "In the Name of Good Governance: E-Government, Internet Pornography and Political Censorship in China." In *China's Information and Communications Technology Revolution: Social Changes and State Responses,* edited by X. Zhang and Y. Zheng, 68–83. New York: Routledge, 2009.

36

FARM PROTECTION AND AGRICULTURE DISPARAGEMENT LAWS

Since the 1990s, the agriculture industry has used various pieces of state-level legislation, such as "Farm Protection" and "Agriculture Disparagement" laws, to limit media coverage and restrict public discourse. Media and public organizations have continually challenged this strategy and question the constitutionality of these laws. Agribusiness has been successful in lobbying state lawmakers to pass laws that make creating and withholding video or audio recordings of animal abuse and neglect a criminal offense. Criticizing and questioning various food- and crop-production techniques can result in civil and criminal charges.

Farm protection or "ag-gag" laws are crafted to limit access to agriculture facilities, and specifically restrict the use of audio and video recording of working agriculture operations. Members of the media and political action groups such as the Humane Society of the United States and People for the Ethical Treatment of Animals, as well as the average citizen, are affected by farm protection laws. Nine states currently have farm protection laws,

and more than a dozen states have attempted to pass similar legislation. Farm protection law advocates cite reasons such as trespassing, damage to property, and preventing animal cruelty when pushing for such statutes. Opponents claim farm protection laws protect unethical agriculture producers and punish whistleblowers.

Agriculture disparagement or "veggie libel" laws are designed to limit what media and individuals can say about agriculture products and production practices. To date thirteen states have agriculture disparagement laws. These laws expand traditional defamation law to specifically protect the agriculture industry. Agriculture is a significant economic contributor to most states. Protecting this important industry and providing financial stability to the state economies are cited as reasons for having such laws. The 1996 lawsuit by a cattlemen's association called the Texas Beef Group against television talk-show host Oprah Winfrey is a highly publicized case involving an agriculture disparagement law. Despite the media attention surrounding the Winfrey case, and the skepticism of First Amendment scholars, no court has ruled on the validity of any agriculture disparagement laws. This puts media and citizens in a precarious position when questioning agriculture products and production methods.

Farm Protection Laws

Eleven states introduced farm protection legislation in 2013. The legislation was defeated in most of these states, but more bills were introduced at the state level again in 2014. Despite national public and media attention, conservative lawmakers in states with substantial and influential agriculture organizations are seeing some success.

The Farm Animal and Field Crop and Research Facilities Protection Act (K.S.A. 47–1825) was passed into law in Kansas in 1990, making it the first farm protection legislation in the United States. Through this legislation the agriculture industry was able to make it a felony, if found guilty, to gain unauthorized access to a crop, livestock, or agricultural research facility.

The impetus for this legislation is linked to the increase in the number of hog-production mega-farms. During the 1980s, the pork industry started constructing large hog farms in Kansas, Colorado, Nebraska, and Oklahoma. These farms were capable of producing 300,000 hogs per year, as reported by the U.S. Department of Agriculture. The benefits to the hog industry made these mega-farms an attractive prospect. In a time of waning pork prices, these operations offered to lower input costs while increasing product output.

However, issues related to wastewater runoff, air quality, and land value made mega-hog farms undesirable to many of the communities in these states. In addition, animal rights groups were very concerned with the treatment of animals in these large facilities. Construction of mega-facilities was often met with protests and vandalism, and destruction of property was not uncommon. Some operations even had hogs taken from the site by protesters and people who entered the facility after hours. In response to the theft of product and damage to property, the hog industry began to lobby state legislatures to pass laws that would limit access to the mega-farms. The industry cited the financial loss incurred by loss of product or vandalism, as well as the potential risk to the animals (and humans) when unauthorized access occurs.

Organizations and members of the media challenged the industry's claims. These groups believed the proposed laws were designed to protect the pork industry and maintain its veil on unethical production practices. Despite these protests, the Kansas legislature moved forward with passing the legislation. The next year, the North Dakota and Montana state legislatures followed suit and adopted versions of farm protection laws. It would be twenty years before the next farm protection bill would pass into law.

Farm Security in a Post–September 11 World

The Iowa legislature passed H.F. 589 in early 2012 and launched a new era of farm protection legislation. Utah state lawmakers passed a similar bill after Iowa. The

Iowa and Utah laws make violations a misdemeanor crime, not a felony like previous laws. Also unlike the versions from the 1990s, the new set of bills hinged on the buzzword *biosecurity* and specifically addressed the issues of undercover access to information and facilities and investigative reporting.

Biosecurity is a post–9/11 buzzword used to address many issues in the food production system. Originally designed to protect the food supply from the threat of a foreign terrorist attack, the term now encompasses domestic issues as well. Agribusiness argues security measures are needed at animal and food production operations for many reasons. One is to prevent a person from intentionally, or unintentionally, contaminating plants or animals with a foreign substance. Many threats to food safety, such as *Salmonella* strains, can be carried into a facility on clothing, hair, and shoes. Another reason to restrict access to facilities is to prevent human injury. Producers state that agriculture operations are dangerous places for people who are not properly trained to be there. Farm protection law supporters also cite the issue of trespassing on private property as a reason to enact the legislation.

"The U.S. constitution says that you cannot enter a person's private property without formal knowledge," said Joe Seng, a veterinarian and Iowa state senator who cosponsored that state's legislation, during a 2012 National Public Radio interview. "Even a policeman has to obtain a search warrant to get on a piece of property. These are private properties owned by either farmers or corporations that have strict bio-security facilities that

do not want either birds, mice, vermin, anything like that, even cockroaches entering into these facilities—people included."

In addition to addressing biosecurity concerns, new farm protection laws restrict and criminalize unauthorized audio and video recording at agriculture production sites. The laws also criminalize gaining access to a facility under false pretenses, such as applying for a job with the intent to write an undercover news article. The practice of taking jobs at operations to gain information has been used by both professional journalists and activist groups. The industry states that this approach is unethical, and that editing of audio and video files can make any situation look worse than it might really be. Mark Bittman of the *New York Times*, who first used the term *ag-gag* in a 2011 article, disagreed: "Videotaping at factory farms wouldn't be necessary if the industry were properly regulated. But it isn't. And the public knows this."

Harper's Goes Undercover

Harper's Magazine reporter Ted Conover used this tactic as a way to gain access to the meat industry for a 2013 special report. Conover spent several months undercover at a Cargill Meat Solutions plant in Nebraska. He was hired as a full-time U.S. Department of Agriculture meat inspector. Conover had planned for the assignment for nearly two years. He even completed required college-level courses that would make him qualified for the job. Conover stated that he believed this was the best way to get inside the meat industry and to see, and then report, firsthand what happens inside a major meat production facility. Conover also stated this article, and the public's right to know about the workings of slaughterhouses, was a good example of why farm protection laws should be blocked and questioned.

Critics of this tactic questioned Conover's ability to inspect meat and do investigative work at the same time, thus questioning the safety of the meat Conover was supposed to be certifying. Critics also cited the cost incurred by USDA and Cargill to unknowingly train, certify, and employ an undercover reporter. Despite the visually striking images Conover gained from the assignment, some critics thought the article revealed very little new information about meat processing. This called into question the overall necessity of such a report.

Protecting Animals or Sensationalizing Cruelty?

Activists and journalists see farm protection laws as a direct infringement on First Amendment rights, as well as an attempt by the agriculture industry to limit public knowledge of unscrupulous business practices. Animal rights activists are particularly concerned as to what the lack of transparency means for meat, poultry, dairy, and animal production operations. The Humane Society of the United States (HSUS) and People for the Ethical Treatment of Animals (PETA) both have worked to block this state-level legislation. In spring 2013 HSUS and PETA spent considerable man-hours and money protesting farm protection bills.

In Tennessee HSUS initiated a media campaign after a bill had been passed by the state legislature and was awaiting governor Bill Haslam's signature. Haslam did not sign the bill into law. He said that he believed the law would go against what was in the best interest of the animals. It is hard to say what the outcome would have been had HSUS not conducted the costly public advocacy campaign to urge the governor not to sign the legislation. HSUS did not wait as long in North Carolina before it joined other advocacy groups in a media campaign to defeat similar legislation. It is estimated that more than $100,000 was spent to sway the public, and then in turn convince the state legislators to not pass the bill. The North Carolina legislature adjourned in 2013 without approving the measure.

Animal abuse in Tennessee was the center of considerable media attention prior to the HSUS campaign. In May 2012 HSUS released videos that organization members had taken while undercover at a Tennessee walking-horse farm, Whitter Stables. The video was obtained over several months in 2011. It documented trainers pouring caustic chemicals on the front legs of horses. This would force horses to walk with an exaggerated gait for competitions. The Federal Horse Protection Act makes the practice, known as soring, illegal.

The HSUS website indicated: "The footage also shows horses being brutally whipped, kicked, shocked in the face, and violently cracked across the heads and legs with heavy wooden sticks. The investigator documented the cruel practice of 'stewarding'—training a horse not to react to pain during official show inspections of their legs for soreness, by striking them in the head when they flinch during mock inspections in the training barn. The investigation also uncovered the illegal use of numbing agents for the purpose of temporarily masking a horse's reaction to pain so it can pass official horse show inspections."

HSUS turned over all evidence to local law enforcement officials and the U.S. Department of Agriculture in May 2012. The lead trainer at the farm, Jackie McConnell, eventually pleaded guilty to felony abuse charges. McConnell was fined $75,000 and given three years' probation. Almost a year later the USDA was again called to Tennessee to investigate another walking-horse abuse case documented by the Humane Society. In this case nineteen horses were taken into protective custody and the owner faced felony charges.

Animal rights activists saw these cases as reasons for citizens and journalists to be able to make undercover recordings and take photographs. HSUS and many members of the media cited the viral videos as the key factors in bringing the abusive trainers to justice, and in saving the horse from further torture. The U.S. Department of Agriculture relied heavily on the videos as part of the prosecution of the trainers.

Critics of HSUS, however, asked: why, if the primary concern was the well-being of the animals, was the video withheld from law enforcement for months? Supporters of the farm protection bill in Tennessee, and several other states, push the aspect of the bills that makes withholding documentation from law enforcement a punishable crime. Missouri, Arkansas, and South Carolina are states that have adopted into law farm protection statutes that focus on the issue of animal cruelty.

Mandatory Reporting

Many of the farm protection bills set up seventy-two-hour windows in which employees, activists, or journalists that have video or audio proof of animal abuse must turn it over law enforcement. Posting the audio or video files on activists' websites or turning them over to media would violate the law. Furthermore, some of the farm protection bills would bar citizens who gathered the documentation from talking with media. Failure to turn over documentation could land the person in jail. This is what happened in the case of Taylor Radig of Colorado, who in November 2013 was charged with animal cruelty in Colorado. The case received national attention as it was one of the first of its kind.

Radig was an animal rights activist with the nonprofit group Compassion Over Killing. She took a job with the Quanah Cattle Company in Kersey, Colorado, where over time she covertly recorded cattle being abused. Radig's video showed calves being kicked and being violently thrown into trucks. Many of the calves were newborns. Radig did not turn over the video or contact law enforcement about the abuse at the time it happened. Instead she waited nearly two months before turning over the footage, which had been used in the meantime by Compassion Over Killing.

In a media statement the Weld County Sheriff said that Radig had failed to report the alleged abuse in a timely manner.

This, in the sheriff's opinion, meant she was negligent and subject to criminal charges. Radig was arrested and charged with animal cruelty, along with three other Quanah Cattle Company workers. Farm owners said they were unaware of the abuse. Compassion Over Killing called the arrest an outrage and an attempt by big agriculture to silence whistleblowers.

This case, like so many others, went viral. Over the months following the arrest the activists' website Change.org collected more than 200,000 signatures on a petition objecting to Radig's arrest. In January 2014 the Weld County District Attorney dropped all charges against Radig. Colorado is not a state with a farm protection law. However, the Radig arrest for failing to comply with the mandatory reporting element is in line with farm protection legislation.

Same Bill, New Name

Even though 2013 was not a successful year for farm protection supporters, they continued to push for more laws in 2014. Indiana's state legislature kicked off the year by introducing a bill that was clearly a farm protection bill. However, due to the high-profile media attention and the use of the term *ag-gag*, crafty legislatures developed a new name for such a bill. This bill would have created a crime called "agriculture mischief." It was designed to stop undercover recordings and photography on farms. The bill did not pass. Indiana had previously attempted to pass a farm protection bill in 2013, but it failed as well.

Supporters of the new "agriculture mischief" bill stated that it does not name specific actions that would be criminalized, as the 2013 version had. Indiana Farm Bureau was involved in the debate. That organization supported the legislation, stating that Indiana farmers should have the right to determine who is on their property and what they do while they are there.

New Hampshire lawmakers also were trying to succeed where they failed in 2013. A new bill was introduced that would have criminalized witnessing animal cruelty and not reporting it. This bill would have given anyone who witnessed cruelty to livestock forty-eight hours to report the incident to law enforcement or face a $250 fine. The proposed legislation was quickly defeated.

Idaho Becomes the First State to Have Both Farm Protection and Agriculture Disparagement Laws

On February 28, 2014, the Interference with Agriculture Production law was signed into effect in Idaho, making that state the first to have both a modern-day farm protection and an agriculture disparagement law. The bill criminalized unauthorized access, while also criminalizing audio and video recording of agriculture records, operations, or production processes.

The Idaho law came on the heels of public outrage surrounding animal abuse at one of the state's dairy farms. The non-profit group Mercy for Animals released a video that documented extreme abuse of dairy cows at Bettencourt Dairies. After the Idaho law was introduced, the organization released additional footage that showed a cow being sexually assaulted.

Producers from the state's multibillion dollar dairy industry said that footage represented an isolated incident. The Idaho Dairymen's Association and other agriculture groups lobbied aggressively to get the law passed quickly. One prominent member of the Idaho dairy industry who spoke out against the statute was Hamdi Ulukaya, founder and chief executive officer of Chobani yogurt. In a letter to the governor, Ulukaya said he believed the law would limit transparency and that it went against his company's values and views.

Idaho and Utah Face Lawsuits

Within weeks of the law's passage a group of nearly twenty nonprofit organizations, advocacy groups, and freelance journalists filed a lawsuit claiming the law violated the First Amendment, the Supremacy Clause, and the Fourteenth Amendment of the U.S. Constitution. The Animal Legal Defense Fund, PETA, the American Civil Liberties Union of Idaho, and the Center for Food Safety are among the plaintiffs. The group asked the court to immediately repeal the law.

One of the plaintiff attorneys is Justin Marceau, a law professor at the University of Denver. Marceau was also counsel for a group that filed a similar lawsuit against Utah's farm protection law in July 2013. That state's law passed in 2012. In April 2013 prosecutors in Draper City, Utah, charged a woman who recorded footage of a slaughterhouse from a public street where she could see through a fence. All charges were dropped due to heightened media coverage of the incident.

The sticking point is the battle between what opponents of the statute see as free-press and free-speech issues, and what supporters feel are property rights and farm owners' rights to control undercover recordings on their property. The defendants in the lawsuits have asked that the cases be dismissed. They believe the laws address specific actions and not free speech. There also is a question of the plaintiffs meeting the "of and concerning" requirement for the lawsuits, which requires plaintiffs to prove a defamatory statement refers to them. The plaintiffs believe the laws punish whistleblowers.

No farm protection laws have been repealed, and no one has been convicted of a crime as a result of these laws. The outcome of the Idaho and Utah lawsuits, both of which are pending as of the summer of 2014, will have an impact on the long-term feasibility and enforceability of these laws.

Agriculture Disparagement Laws

Agriculture and aquaculture disparagement laws are laws enacted at the state level that allow producers of agriculture and aquaculture products to sue individuals and/or companies that purportedly make statements about the product that directly result in a loss of profit for the producer. The purpose of these laws is to provide economic stability for states whose economies are primarily dependent on agriculture and aquaculture production and distribution monies. Each state law defines the producer and the pool of possible plaintiffs differently. Currently, one state has such a broad definition that any group along the distribution chain from growers to shippers can file a suit. However, most limit the possible plaintiffs to those who directly produce the product. Given the corporatization of agriculture, however, this can still lead to a debate about who the actual producers are and who can recoup damages.

Many citizens first learned of agriculture disparagement laws when watching the documentary *Food, Inc.* (2008). In this documentary a woman from Colorado, whose young son had died from *Escherichia coli* O157:H7 (commonly called *E. coli*), spoke about food-safety issues and the process used to issue recalls on tainted food products. At one point during the interview, she said she was reluctant to say too much because of the so-called veggie libel laws and the possibility of litigation against her under these laws.

As of mid-2014 thirteen states have agriculture and aquaculture disparagement laws in effect: Alabama, Arizona, Colorado, Florida, Georgia, Idaho, Louisiana, Mississippi, North Dakota, Ohio, Oklahoma, South Dakota, and Texas. Additionally, more than thirty states have considered enacting such legislation. With the exception of the *Texas Beef Group v. Oprah Winfrey* and *Beef Products, Inc. v. ABC News* cases, both of which will be discussed in depth later in this chapter, there has been very little public discussion about the constitutional implications of such laws.

"A Is for Apple"

The case that launched the agriculture disparagement law initiative was *Auvil v. CBS "60 Minutes"* (1989). The CBS newsmagazine program *60 Minutes*, in February 1989, aired a segment based on a report from the National Resources Defense Council (NRDC) that discussed possible hazards related to the use of Alar. Alar was a pesticide commonly used on apples. The NRDC report indicated that Alar remained on the apples and in the skin of the apple, even after washing. This led to consumption of the pesticide by consumers. The report went further to suggest that since children consume significant portions of commercial apples, the use of Alar was a direct threat to the health and safety of children.

After the "A Is for Apple" story aired there was a substantial downturn in the purchasing of apples. Reportedly more than $3 million was lost due to the perishable nature of the product. Subsequently, several small apple producers were forced into bankruptcy, and the entire industry and tertiary industries dependent on apples sales were hit with financial losses. A group of apple growers from the state of Washington filed a lawsuit against CBS, its local affiliates, the NRDC, and the public-relations firm hired by NRDC to promote the Alar report findings. The suit sought to recoup the financial loss suffered through common law product disparagement laws.

The defendants sought a summary judgment to have the case dismissed. The local CBS affiliates and the NRDC public-relations firm were granted the judgment and absolved of culpability. The court stated the plaintiff's claim did not meet the "of and concerning" precedent set forth by *New York Times v. Sullivan* (1964), the benchmark case by which most defamation and First Amendment cases are judged. In this case, L. B. Sullivan, an Alabama sheriff, filed a defamation lawsuit against the *New York Times* for an advertisement that ran in the newspaper. Sullivan stated that the advertisement was detrimental to his good standing and thus caused harm to his reputation. The *New York Times'* defense was that under the First Amendment, the press has the freedom to discuss public issues and public figures as part of a democratic society. Further, under the protection of the First Amendment citizens have the right to state their opinions and engage in public debate.

The *New York Times* did eventually win this case, and many important precedents were set. First, the criteria for a "public figure" were discussed and expanded. The Court determined that given the public nature of Sullivan's job, he was indeed a public figure. As a public figure the possibility of criticism and discussion regarding performance and actions is not only more likely to occur than with private individuals but also necessary. If speech is limited due to the threat of legal action, debate will be chilled and democracy will not be possible. Citizens must be allowed to discuss the performance of public figures and exchange multiple, and oftentimes conflicting, ideas. Furthermore, the court determined that people could become public figures both willingly and unwillingly. Second, a set of criteria was established to judge future First Amendment cases. There were three key components to the criteria: a defamatory statement must be *of and concerning* the plaintiff, a libelous statement must be made with *actual malice,* and the plaintiff bears the *burden of proof* regarding the defendant's

knowledge and intentions. Sullivan did not meet the "of or concerning" requirement because he was not named in the ad. These are the standards by which press freedom and defamation cases have been judged since the early 1960s.

The *Auvil v. CBS "60 Minutes"* case progressed though the judicial system up to the U.S. Court of Appeals for the Ninth Circuit. The Ninth Circuit Court granted a summary judgment to CBS and NRDC; thus the case was defunct. The Ninth Circuit was concerned that due to the nature of the program, an array of opinions had been sought and differing views could be formed from the coverage. Clearly there were free-speech issues related to the case. The court stated that failing to grant a summary judgment could result in a chilling effect on journalistic speech.

The Ninth Circuit cited precedent set by *Bose Corporation v. Consumer Union of the United States, Inc.* (1984), a product disparagement case. In this case the Bose Corporation, which produces stereo equipment, sought damages due to a report published in *Consumer Reports* magazine that questioned the product's reliability. This is a benchmark case for disparagement claims. There are three significant implications from the ruling in this case. The first is that all courts must conduct their own investigation into the truthfulness of the claim published and the facts surrounding the case. This part of the ruling resulted from a state-level appeals court using previous court findings as the basis of its decision, and not conducting an independent review of the case. This is particularly relevant to state-level agriculture disparagement laws. Requiring higher courts to conduct an independent review into the matter can protect consumers and journalists from high-powered and well-financed big agriculture companies that are politically connected.

The second important implication of *Bose* is that the court determined a business should be considered a public figure and thus is open to public discourse about its product. Just as public officials are subject to public debate about their competence, consumers must be able to discuss the benefits and limitations of products and corporations. Lastly, this ruling upheld and strengthened the criteria of actual malice. It was judged that *Consumer Reports* had gone to reasonable lengths to insure the validity of the information it printed and thus no actual malice occurred. Under this precedent the plaintiff is required to prove actual malice by the defendant; that is, that the defendant knowingly and willingly published false information about a product. Since the "A Is for Apple" story and the NRDC report on pesticide use on apples were scientifically valid, this could not be proven. The case was dismissed.

Pushing for Agriculture-Specific Laws

As a result of the *Auvil v. CBS "60 Minutes"* case, many agriculture and aquaculture associations began to discuss what they saw to be holes in common law tort. A significant sector of agriculture producers thought that these standards did not adequately reflect and protect their products. They sought remedies that would allow recovery of monies lost due to a decrease in sales as a result of publicly made disparaging comments about their products. Advocates for a new law wanted a means through which companies could seek restitution from consumers, media, and advocacy groups. The new law would differ from common law of trade disparagement that typically granted relief when one business disparaged another.

Proponents of the agriculture disparagement laws lobbied that there should be a special set of laws to protect this industry from junk science or malicious statements, since unlike other industries most agriculture products cannot be warehoused or held to "ride the market." The perishable nature, or shelf life, of various agriculture products is the reasoning offered by the agriculture industry to enact this legislation. Large producers and a variety of agriculture-related associations began to lobby their respective state legislatures to enact laws that would provide both protection from disparaging comments, as well as the ability to recover financial losses resulting from negative public comments.

In 1991 Colorado was the first state to consider an agriculture disparagement law. As stated previously, the grounds for the introduction of the bill to the Colorado legislature were to protect the state economy, which is largely based on agriculture goods and labor. This first attempt was not successful; it would be a few years before Colorado would enact its agriculture disparagement law, which would prove to be one of the most stringent of the statutes. Louisiana was the first state to enact an agriculture disparagement law. The legislature in that state was under pressure from cantaloupe producers, who had just suffered market losses from media coverage of an *E. coli* outbreak that had been traced back to the fruit. Twelve more states would follow and enact "veggie libel" laws between 1991 and 1997.

Not All Agriculture Disparagement Laws Are the Same

Each state's version of the law is different. Under most laws awards for both pecuniary and punitive damages can be sought. Idaho is the only state that limits plaintiffs to seek recovery of only pecuniary damages. South Dakota and Ohio statutes permit all plaintiffs to receive three times the damages as compensation. Court costs and legal fees can be awarded in Ohio and Arizona. Uniquely, in Colorado, defendants are subject to criminal charges as well as civil. All state laws have a statute of limitations of one to two years. What party may file a lawsuit is different in each state. Agriculture producers are allowed to bring suit in all of the states with agriculture disparagement laws. Colorado, Idaho, Louisiana, Mississippi, Oklahoma, South Dakota, and Texas are limited to only producers. Some states go further by broadening the scope of the statute to include other parties in the agriculture industry, such as:

Alabama	Marketer and seller
Arizona	Marketer, seller, shipper, or association thereof
Florida	Association thereof
Georgia	Marketer, processor, seller, or consumer
North Dakota	Distributor, manufacturer, producer, seller, or association thereof
Ohio	Distributor, producer, seller, or association thereof

Additionally, the types of products protected under these agriculture disparagement laws vary from state to state. An example of this can be seen in a comparison between the neighboring states of North Dakota and South Dakota. The South Dakota statute protects any *consumable food item* produced in the state. However, North Dakota's statute is much broader in that it extends protection to any *agriculture product* from the state. A difference such as this is significant to the public discourse on both food safety and agriculture production methods. According to an article from the *North Dakota Law Review,* the agriculture disparagement law in that state was introduced and supported by a group of equine ranchers. The ranchers had been the targets of an animal rights campaign exposing the ill-treatment of horses used to generate and harvest estrogen-rich equine urine for the production of Premarin. Premarin is a conjugated estrogen cream that is produced by Pfizer pharmaceutical company. It is a multi-billion-dollar product.

Disseminating statements to the public that are disparaging or include false information is actionable under all of the laws. A higher standard of accountability regarding public disparaging remarks is found in five states: Louisiana, Mississippi, Ohio, South Dakota, and Texas. In these states the defendant must have had or should have had knowledge that the comments made about the safety of a perishable food product were false. It is this expansion to include issues of food safety that becomes of great importance in the 2012 South Dakota case discussed below, *Beef Products, Inc. v. ABC News.* But no knowledge or awareness of falsity is required under Oklahoma's or Alabama's laws. False information just has to be disseminated in these two states to make the claim actionable.

Even more noteworthy features of these laws are they shift the burden of proof from the plaintiff to the defendant, and they narrow the acceptable standards for evaluating the truthfulness of public comments. Disregarding the precedent set by *New York Times v. Sullivan*, these laws place the burden of proving the truthfulness of the claim squarely on the shoulders of the defendant. Rather than entering the courtroom under a presumption of innocence, these defendants and their claims are presumed to be at fault. Furthermore, these agriculture disparagement laws established that there must be sound, widely accepted, scientific proof to support the claims and statements made by the defendants. The financial burden of conducting such scientific research as required by some states makes this unfeasible for small groups or individuals. *False information* is defined differently by the various states. South Dakota does not define *false information*.

Red Flags for First Amendment Scholars

These alterations have raised red flags for First Amendment scholars. Law professors David Bederman and Eileen Jones first wrote of the potential negative effects agriculture disparagement laws could have on free speech. Across the board, scholars agree these laws violate the First Amendment protection of freedom of speech and freedom of the press.

Agriculture disparagement laws make actionable speech that is protected.

Shifting the burden of proof to the defendant makes people become reluctant to discuss issues in an open manner, or to challenge current practices and ideas. The threat of possible litigation, in which the defendant is assumed culpable, has a chilling effect on public discourse. Additionally, when discussion of public concerns takes place, there are inevitably errors made without malicious intent. In order for free debate to occur and for democracy to be achieved, people cannot be afraid of participating in critical, public discourse.

Critics of agriculture disparagement laws agree that states have the right to enact libel, disparagement, and defamation statutes; however, they argue that states cannot give the agriculture industry special privileges. The public has a right to know about issues of food safety and to be able to have free, open debate on food safety and public health issues.

While many scholars believe agriculture disparagement laws are unconstitutional, to date there has been no court ruling on the constitutionality of the laws. Since 1991, six cases have been brought to court under agriculture disparagement laws. A Texas emu producer sued a Honda automobile dealer over a negative portrayal of emus in an advertisement. In another Texas case a lawn turf grower sued a county extension agent for stating the type of turf grown by the producer was not viable for Texas lawns. Egg producers in Ohio sued a consumer group that exposed the tactic of placing old eggs in new containers with new eggs. These three cases did not result in written decisions. The first two cases were dismissed for not meeting the "of and concerning" standard. The third case was dismissed because the defendant had proof that the claim was true and thus no actual malice could be determined. Only two cases have resulted in written decisions by the courts. One is pending. None has made it past the lower courts.

One of the two cases that have resulted in a written decision was brought against the State of Georgia by law professor and attorney David Bederman on behalf of two consumer groups. This suit asked the state court to rule on the constitutionality of the Georgia agriculture disparagement law. However, rather than doing so, the Georgia court dismissed that case, ruling that neither Bederman nor the consumer groups met the "of and concerning" criteria; thus the issue could not be decided.

Texas Beef Group v. Oprah

The second case with a written decision is by far the more prominent case, widely covered by U.S. media. It is *Texas Beef Group v. Oprah Winfrey* (1996). In addition to the talk-show host, her production company and her guest in the episode in question also were sued. The group of Texas cattlemen stated they had suffered losses into the millions of dollars as a result of an *Oprah* episode in which she spoke with food-safety experts about the growing concern of bovine spongiform encephalopathy (BSE), commonly known as mad-cow disease. In this episode the BSE expert stated that "mad-cow disease is the AIDS of the future." Winfrey commented that fact had "stopped [her] from ever eating a burger again."

The cattlemen said that, due to Winfrey's public prominence, she had incredible impact on consumers and their purchasing patterns. They also claimed that a source from the cattle industry, who was interviewed, was not allowed equal airtime. Furthermore, they claimed that comments from the cattle-industry representative were edited out so as to make the episode more powerful, and subsequently biased against the beef industry.

Winfrey's legal team fought these allegations under First Amendment protection. The Winfrey team said they had done all that was reasonably expected to prove the validity of the claims made by the BSE expert, and the program had the right to debate issues of public concern freely.

After months of litigation, the Texas court ruled that the cattlemen's group could not sue because their product was not perishable. The court stated that while the value may decrease over time, the cattle could be held from the market until the market recovered. The case was dismissed against Winfrey and associates. Winfrey's defense cost more than $500,000 and consisted of multiple attorneys from across the nation. Again, the court ruling did not address the constitutionality of the law, but rather who may bring a suit under the law.

Beef Products, Inc. v. ABC News

There were no new cases under agriculture disparagement laws for the next ten years. Some interpreted this as a sign of support for the position of law scholars who said these laws are clear First Amendment violations. Furthermore, some thought agriculture producers and associations may have seen the unlikelihood of winning a case under an agriculture disparagement law, and thus chose to save the money and time by not filing suit. To date, none of these laws has been repealed. They are all still "on the books," looming off in the distance waiting to be used.

In September 2012 Beef Products Inc., a South Dakota–based ground beef distributor, filed a $1.2 billion defamation suit against ABC News under that state's agriculture disparagement law. The claim centers on ABC News coverage in March 2012 of Beef Products' lean finely textured beef product (LFTB). ABC News and other media outlets had taken to calling LFTB "pink slime." The 257-page suit named the ABC network, host Diane Sawyer, and ABC correspondents Jim Avila and David Karley as defendants. It also named Gerald Zirnstein, a U.S. Department of Agriculture microbiologist who named the product "pink slime," Carl Custer, a former federal food scientist, and Kit Foshee, a former Beef Products quality-assurance manager who was interviewed by ABC News. ABC News was not the first media organization to do an exposé on LFTB.

In 2009 the *New York Times* published a detailed report on LFTB. The report explained that beef processing plants set aside cartilage and meat scraps that cannot be sold as stand-alone products. These byproducts are then ground and mixed together. The media coverage highlighted Beef Products' practice of using low levels of ammonium hydroxide gas to prevent the growth of *E. coli* and other pathogens in ground beef. The LFTB is pink in appearance, which helps it blend in with raw ground beef. The reports questioned the safety of this practice, as well as the overall nutritional value of the product.

In 2011 celebrity chef Jamie Oliver doused beef trim with liquid ammonia during an episode of *Jamie Oliver's Food Revolution* on the Food Network. He contended that using ammonia to treat the beef trim made it unfit for consumption, much less suitable for school lunches. Industry supporters argued that his treatment of the beef product in that manner was outrageous and inaccurate. Following that episode Beef Products turned to leading researchers in beef production and the U.S. Department of Agriculture experts, all of whom held fast on the position that LFTB is completely safe to eat.

Public outcry followed the combined media attention and hit a high following the 2012 ABC reports. There was considerable concern about the new $5 million contract that had just been inked between the U.S. Department of Agriculture and Beef Products to use ground beef containing LFTB in the nation's school lunch programs. Several large supermarket chains cancelled contracts with Beef Products as a result of the public uproar. In the following months Beef Products closed three of its four plants, and more than 750 Beef Products employees lost their jobs due to these closures. Cargill Meat Solutions, another major producer of LFTB, also noted a financial loss due to decline in demand for the product. Cargill uses a different method to treat the LFTB for pathogens—not the ammonium hydroxide. A third LFTB supplier, Pennsylvania-based AFA Foods, declared Chapter 11 bankruptcy in April 2012. The company already had been struggling to pay its bills; the negative media attention and decrease in LFTB sales was more than it could handle.

The Internet again played a key role in the expanse of media and public attention given to the original reports and the defa-mation lawsuit. Following the March 2012 broadcasts, Texas mom Bettina Siegel started a Change.org petition to get the U.S. Department of Agriculture to stop using ground beef containing LFTB in the school lunch program. It took just nine days for her petition to get more than 200,000 signatures. As a result of this effort and the media attention, the USDA started giving schools the option to pur-chase ground beef that did not contain LFTB. Many schools, fully aware of the public attention on the matter, started pur-chasing the more expensive ground beef that did not contain the filler product. However, it should be noted that in 2013 many school districts went back to pur-chasing ground beef containing LFTB because dwindling school lunch budgets could not sustain the more expensive product. Ground been containing LFTB has always been certified as safe by the U.S. Department of Agriculture.

Beef Products, along with BPI Technology Inc. and Freezing Machines Inc., two other entities owned by Eldon and Regina Roth, claims that ABC News disseminated false and misleading infor-mation about its product and the safety of the product, which resulted in substantial financial loss. This qualifies as grounds for a lawsuit under the South Dakota law. ABC News holds the position that its reporting was fair and that there are no grounds for a defamation suit.

Attorneys for ABC News asked that the case be dismissed and stated a num-ber of reasons to support their request. For instance, the media giant's lawyers argued Beef Products cannot state a claim under South Dakota's Agricultural Food Products Disparagement Act because ABC did not question the safety of Beef Products' meat product. ABC also asked the court to dismiss claims of disparagement of an agricultural food product, libel, and tortious interference with business relationships.

The case was not dismissed, but rather returned to South Dakota State Circuit Court by U.S. District Court Judge Karen E. Schreier. Defendants asked that all claims by BPI Technology and Freezing Machines be dismissed. The argument was that these two entities, which are incorporated and based in Delaware, not South Dakota, are not real parties of interest. Schreier did not agree with ABC News. Judge Schreier cited several legal standards, including the burden the defen-dants have in establishing federal juris-diction by a preponderance of the evidence. If the defendant fails to meet that burden, the judge wrote, the court must remand the case. The judge deter-mined BPI Tech and FMI had the right to action under South Dakota law. ABC News and the other defendants had claimed that false statements about Beef Products were only "of and concerning" it and not the other two entities.

Two additional lawsuits related to the case were subsequently filed in December 2013. A former Beef Products employee who lost his job because of the plant clo-sures sued ABC, ABC News, chef Jamie Oliver, and food activist Bettina Siegel for damages. The family of a sixty-two-year-old Minnesota man filed a lawsuit against Beef Products and other meat producers JBS Swift and Tyson Fresh Meat. The man died from complications related to eating *E. coli*–contaminated ground beef. Beef Products claimed the meat consumed by the man was not from one of its facilities and the lawsuit was a ploy to garner public support against Beef Products.

Due to the nature of the South Dakota agriculture disparagement statute, and the media frenzy around this case, the Beef Products lawsuit is viewed as a precedent-setting opportunity. South Dakota Circuit Judge Cheryle Gering heard oral arguments in December 2013 and in March 2014 ruled that the case would move forward. ABC News filed a motion with the South Dakota Supreme Court asking that the case be dismissed. In May 2014 the South Dakota Supreme Court denied the appeal by ABC News and the other defendants. The case is pending as of mid-2014.

Pro

Supporters of farm protection and agriculture disparagement laws consist primarily of large agriculture companies, agriculture special-interest associations, and conservative lawmakers. They cite trespassing, biosecurity, and economic stability as core reasons farmers need protection.

Supporters assert that farm operators should have the right to determine who has access to facilities and what happens on a farm. These laws help prevent unauthorized access, which can protect animals on the farms. Furthermore, such legislation protects farm operators from investing time and money in training people posing as employees, when they are not in fact there to work. If preventing animal cruelty is the primary goal, then it would make sense that all documentation of such acts should be turned over to law enforcement as soon as possible. Holding on to such evidence may help news ratings, but it does not help the animals being mistreated.

In the case of Beef Products and ABC News more than 700 people lost their jobs. Agriculture disparagement laws have been put in place to protect companies in this type of situation. Food production is a highly technical industry. If information is taken out of context or edited in a certain manner, the public can be misled on the actual impact of a practice. Advocates for these statutes say that agriculture companies need to be protected from tidal waves of bad publicity. In the era of digital media, false or misleading news spreads quickly. Agriculture companies that produce products that do not have a substantial shelf life need an outlet to protect investments and reputations.

Con

Opponents of farm protection and agriculture disparagement laws worry about the chilling effect on free speech. Journalists have the responsibility to bring issues to the public's attention, and they can use whatever means necessary to do so. This can include undercover, secret recordings of animal abuse or unsafe food-handling tactics. When the public is allowed to see what happens in a production facility, the farm operator is more likely to conduct business in a humane, ethical manner.

Opponents argue that farm protection bills protect farm owners but not the public or livestock. In recent years many animal abuse cases have been made public due to the efforts of HSUS and PETA. Without this type of undercover work, many atrocities would continue on farms. If farm operators are practicing ethical and safe methods, they should not worry about public awareness.

Media need the freedom to question businesses and the government. Agriculture disparagement laws directly jeopardize this freedom. With the threat of multi-billion-dollar defamation suits, media might begin to self-censor content or decide not to cover an important issue. In either case the public interest will not be served, but rather the interest of big agriculture.

Looking to the Future

Journalists, animal rights activists, farm workers, and citizens have joined together to leverage online content to fight the passage of new farm protection laws. In this digital age of bloggers, online activists and hackers, and freelance journalists, the issue of who (if anyone) can enjoy journalistic protections from these laws is an important issue to consider.

Passing these restrictive laws at the state level is much more cost-effective than trying to do so at a national level. At the state level special interest groups such as the Farm Bureau Federation carry considerable political clout. Oftentimes passage of state legislation receives very little media or public attention. Agriculture disparagement laws passed in the 1990s were rarely heard of before the *Food, Inc.* documentary. Farm protection legislation of the 1990s also went underreported. It was not until these bills were given the moniker of "ag-gag" laws that the public started paying attention and began questioning the statutes. It will be important to continue to monitor state legislation, especially as lawmakers introduce bills under new names.

A court ruling on the validity of agriculture disparagement laws will set the tone for the future. If the case can make its way to the Supreme Court there could finally be a ruling on the constitutionality of these laws. If Beef Products is successful in its lawsuit against ABC News, the media industry could see a wave of future lawsuits. If it is not, states most likely will not enact new agriculture disparagement laws, and the agriculture industry will find a new way to protect its interests.

Conclusion

From a media perspective, farm protection and agriculture disparagement laws are state-level statutes that directly conflict with First Amendment freedoms. These laws put the needs of an industry and corporations before the rights of consumers and the public. Large agribusiness and special-interest groups have the financial and political resources to continue to introduce this type of legislation, and to challenge free-speech advocates in court.

Preventing animal abuse is the latest mantra of farm protection and agriculture mischief backers, but many see this as a thin shroud hiding the real motives behind the laws. Currently, nine states have such laws, but each year more states are trying to pass farm protection bills. Whistleblowers and undercover reporters could face criminal charges under these laws. Online media has played an important role in blocking the expansion of farm protection statutes, but the agriculture industry continues to try. The outcome of the lawsuits in Idaho and Utah will have a significant impact on the long-term implementation of farm protection laws.

Agriculture disparagement laws are in place in thirteen states. The Oprah Winfrey case brought the issue of agriculture disparagement into the headlines, but very little media attention has been given to the topic as a whole. The 2012 lawsuit by Beef Products against ABC News could be the case that finally settles the issue of constitutionality of agriculture disparagement laws. If ABC News successfully defends its coverage, then media most likely will not again face the threat of such a lawsuit. However, if Beef Products wins, media and consumers could face even more lawsuits for questioning the agriculture industry. This would be a serious blow to the First Amendment and a substantial victory for the big agriculture business.

Sam Robinson
California State University at Monterey Bay

See also Deceptive Newsgathering; Invasion of Privacy; Investigative Reporting; *New York Times v. Sullivan*

Further Reading

Bederman, David J. "Food Libel: Litigating Scientific Uncertainty in a Constitutional Twilight Zone." *DePaul Business Law Journal* 10 (1997–1998): 192–231.

Bederman, David J., Scott M. Christensen, and Scott Dean Quesenberry. "Of Banana Bills and Veggie Hate Crimes: The Constitutionality of Agriculture Disparagement Statutes." *Harvard Journal on Legislation* 34 (1997): 135–168.

Bittman, Mark. "Who Protects the Animals?" *New York Times*, April 26, 2011. http://opinionator.blogs.nytimes .com/2011/04/26/who-protects-the-animals/?_php=true_type=blogs_r=0.

Conover, Ted. "The Way of All Flesh." *Harper's Magazine*, May 2013. http:// harpers.org/archive/2013/05/the-way-of-all-flesh.

Dane, Keith. "A Sore Subject: The Tennessee Walking Horse Industry." *Humane Society of the United States*, April 12, 2013. http:// www.humanesociety.org/issues/tenn_ walking_horses/facts/sore_subject_ tennessee_walking_horse_091407.html# .UtwVLxDTnIU.

Isern, Kevin A. "When Is Speech No Longer Protected by the First Amendment: A Plaintiff's Perspective of Agriculture Disparagement Laws." *DePaul Business Law Journal* 10 (1997–1998): 233–257.

Jones, Eileen Gay. "Forbidden Fruit: Talking about Pesticides and Food Safety in the Era of Agriculture Product Disparagement Laws." *Brooklyn Law Review* 66 (2000): 1–26.

Mattson, Jennifer J. "North Dakota Jumps on the Agriculture Disparagement Law Bandwagon by Enacting Legislation to Meet a Concern Already Actionable under State Defamation Law and Failing to Heed

Constitutionality Concerns." *North Dakota Law Review* 74 (1998): 1–26.

Robinson, Sam. "Agriculture Disparagement Laws Take Root." *Gateway Journalism Review*, October 12, 2012. http://gatewayjr.org/2012/10/12/ag-disparagement-laws-take-root.

Robinson, Sam. "More States Considering 'Ag-Gag', Farm Protection Bills." *Midwest Center for Investigative Reporting*, March 14, 2013. http://investigatemidwest.org/2013/03/14/more-states-considering-ag-gag-laws-farm-protection-bills.

37

COVERING CRIME VICTIMS

Plaintiff Rights and Media Liability

Violent crimes make media headlines every day in American journalism. In the middle of these stories are the victims of these crimes or the survivors they leave behind. Suddenly these people are involuntarily thrust into the media spotlight with their personal tragedies and lives laid open for public consumption.

In covering crime victims and survivors, the media has often been accused of sensationalism, insensitivity, and exploitation. Yet these people's stories are often newsworthy and should be covered in the public interest. In some cases, the victims need publicity, such as the parents of missing children who need media coverage to help locate them. As a result of the crimes that changed their lives, some victims have become advocates and celebrities, actively seeking media attention. But others have objected to media coverage and filed suits for invasion of privacy, negligence, and infliction of emotional distress. In some cases, the media has been found liable for violations of criminal and tort law in newsgathering activities.

This chapter studies the relevant legal case history and potential media liabilities in newsgathering and publication concerning crime victims, including newsgathering torts, invasion of privacy, and negligence, balanced against First Amendment protections and defenses, such as newsworthiness, public figure status, and matters of public record. From privacy case law, it considers relevant cases and precedents from physical intrusion, false light, and publication of embarrassing facts. Standards involving potential negligence claims, such as wrongful death and risk of physical harm, are studied for potential media liability in publishing and newsgathering.

The Legal Status of Crime Victims

Public Figure Status of Crime Victims in Media Coverage

While the courts and legislatures have granted crime victims limited standing in the criminal justice system, they have received no such advantage over the media in civil suits or criminal actions regarding newsgathering or publication. The courts have consistently with rare exceptions supported the media's First Amendment rights over the claims of crime victims.

In some circumstances selected media's sympathy with the tragic plight of crime victims jeopardizes the Sixth Amendment rights of criminal defendants. Media reports more often feature interviews with victims, some of whom actively seek publicity, than criminal defendants, who are often advised by attorneys to shun media attention. On other occasions, selected media outlets have been accused of intrusion on seclusion in times of bereavement, the publication of embarrassing facts unrelated to a crime, or negligence in newsgathering resulting in wrongful death. Following a crime the victim and survivors are usually seeking privacy, while the media wants to cover them as part of a newsworthy public interest story. Sometimes after the initial tragedy, the victims seek media publicity to convict the offender, find a missing person, or advocate a particular cause.

The conflict between media and crime victims first arises in the newsgathering stage, when the victims are suddenly and involuntarily thrust into the limelight. With the exception of the public figure or celebrity who becomes the victim of crime, most victims are not prepared to deal with the unexpected and intense media scrutiny surrounding a sensational crime.

The courts have not specifically defined crime victims in any particular category (e.g., all-purpose, limited, involuntary) of public figures. No specific case focuses on the public figure status of crime victims. A landmark false light privacy case, *Time, Inc. v. Hill* (385 U.S. 374, 1967), however, distinguishes crime victims as "private individuals" as opposed voluntary public figures, such as public officials. The case was decided prior to the Supreme Court's ruling in *Gertz v. Robert Welch, Inc.* (418 U.S. 323, 1974), which more clearly defines the differing status of private and public individuals.

James Hill and his family in 1952 were held hostage in their home outside Philadelphia by three escaped convicts, and eventually released unharmed. Even though the Hills had moved and discouraged publicity, a novel, *Desperate Hours*, was written about the incident that included fictionalized violence and verbal sexual insults. The novel was subsequently made into a Broadway play and two feature films. *Life* magazine published an account with photographs of scenes staged in the former Hill home. Claiming that *Life* had given a knowingly false impression that the play depicted the actual incident, Hill sued for damages under a New York appropriation statute. *Life* maintained that the article concerned a topic of public interest and was published in good faith.

The initial court ruling stated that the New York statute "affords 'little protection' to the 'privacy' of a newsworthy person, 'whether he be such by choice or involuntarily.'" Instead the court applied a different standard by holding that the First Amendment's protections for speech and press "precluded the application of the New York statute to redress false reports of matters of public interest" without evidence of knowing and reckless disregard of the truth. The court's consideration of the statute was limited to the context of an action by a "private individual." The decision declined to address whether the actual malice test should be applied "both to persons voluntarily and involuntarily thrust into the public limelight."

In setting aside the lower-court rulings and a trial-court judgment for Hill, the Supreme Court applied the *New York Times v. Sullivan* (376 U.S. 254, 1964) actual malice rule in favor of *Life*. Considering the overlap of libel and false light in *Hill*, the Court applied the actual malice test and accepted the argument that they were "twin torts." Public interest in an event or person brought the newsworthy defense into false light. Proof of actual malice was required without regard to whether the plaintiff is a private or public figure. The falsity of the dramatic account depicted in the novel, play, and article were not addressed. The Court did not consider crime victims in a special category of public figures, nor did it create any special circumstances regarding coverage of crime victims.

Seven years later in *Gertz*, the Court dealt with the status of private persons in libel law. Part of the Court's rationale for distinguishing private individuals is the understanding that public officials and public figures maintain more access to media attention as part of their status. Hence they have "a more realistic opportunity to counteract false statements" than private persons do. Public figures have "thrust themselves to the forefront of particular public controversies," as opposed to private figures who do not

seek publicity. The state has a greater interest in protecting private persons from injury by such statements.

It is hard to imagine any sane person wanting to be a victim of a crime in order to gain publicity. Based on this assumption, no person would voluntarily seek the public limelight of media attention by means of being a crime victim. Except for celebrities and public officials who become victims of crime, most crime victims would be considered private persons prior to being a victim. Once a crime has occurred, particularly one that attracts media attention, the criminal justice process regarding that crime becomes a "particular public controversy." The crime victim's role in the process becomes a matter of public importance and legitimate news value.

The *Restatement (Second) of Torts* defines involuntary public figures as "individuals who have not sought publicity or consented to it, but through their own conduct or otherwise have become a legitimate subject of public interest. They have, in other words, become 'news.'" The definition mentions "the victims of crime or those who are so unfortunate as to be present when it is committed." It also allows some publication of private facts about victims by stating: "As in the case of the voluntary public figure, the authorized publicity is not limited to the event that itself arouses public interest, and to some reasonable extent includes publicity given to the facts about the individual that would otherwise be private."

As they are unexpectedly thrust into the limelight, most crime victims would be considered involuntary public figures, although there are those who actively seek media attention after the initial crime to help convict the defendant, advocate for legislative change, or educate the public about victims' rights and public safety. The public figure status of crime victims who later seek media attention would change from involuntary to limited voluntary, not all-purpose, since, as stated in *Gertz*, they have voluntarily injected themselves "into a particular public controversy and thereby [become] a public figure for a limited range of issues." Notable examples would be New York state congresswoman Carolyn McCarthy, Texas state senator Suzanna Gratia Hupp, and John Walsh, host of the Fox TV show *America's Most Wanted.*

This change in public figure status—from involuntary or limited to all-purpose—would cause a victim to surrender a greater degree of privacy or libel protection than a private individual. Once a "celebrity victim" or victim lobbyist thrusts herself/himself into the limelight, the rules regarding libel, for example, change from a negligence standard to actual malice, a much more difficult burden to prove.

Should a particular crime victim's motivation for becoming a limited public figure be a factor in determining public figure status? Is there a "grey area" of liability between publishing details concerning the crime and irrelevant details after the victim has withdrawn from the public limelight following a trial or funeral?

Elected legislators who were private individuals before becoming crime victims, such as McCarthy and Hupp, clearly became public officials as defined in *Sullivan.* By running for political office, they voluntarily thrust themselves into the limelight and the public debate over controversial issues. An entertainment celebrity, such as Walsh, would be considered an all-purpose public figure by voluntarily thrusting himself into particular controversies with his lobbying for legislation and advocacy for victims' rights.

Privacy

Common Law Right of Privacy and Intrusion

In a 2003 Oklahoma case (*Anderson v. Blake* and *Anderson v. Suiters aka Lohman,* 35 Med. L. Rptr. 823, 790–1), Aundra Anderson, who claimed that she had been raped by her estranged husband while unconscious, entrusted a videotape depicting the attack to a Norman police officer, Don Blake, "only for law enforcement purposes" to prosecute the crime. Blake asked the alleged victim to speak with a reporter for KOCO-TV, Kimberly Lohman Suiters, about the ordeal, but she declined. The officer put the reporter on the telephone anyway, and Anderson refused to answer most of the reporter's questions.

Without the alleged victim's knowledge or consent, Blake allowed Suiters to view the tape, copy portions, and play the sexually explicit contents on the local news on July 2, 2003. Since Anderson refused to cooperate with the district attorney's office, the charges against her husband were dropped.

In Anderson's suit against Blake, the original court agreed with the plaintiff's assertion of her privacy interest in the "personal" video, which "depicted the most private of matters," but the federal district court later dismissed her intrusion upon seclusion claim. In Anderson's suit against the media defendants, the court ruled that the plaintiff failed to show that they acted as state actors with the police or acted jointly to violate her right to privacy. A summary judgment dismissed her publication of private facts claim since the published portions were substantially related to a matter of legitimate public concern. The Tenth Circuit upheld the district court rulings (499 F.3d 1228, 2007).

Identification of Sexual Assault Victims

The ethical debate over the treatment and identification of sexual assault victims continues among news organizations. Some claim that publishing victims' names gives realism to a crime story, while others counter that identification retraumatizes the victim. Privacy suits by victims over identification have usually failed unless some injury can be proven to be a direct result of the publication. A plaintiff proving that identification in a news story directly caused an injury or death to a victim would be a difficult standard to reach.

For example, an assailant could obtain a victim's identity and address through available public and private sources (e.g., witnesses, driver's license records, city directories) other than a published newspaper article. Punishing a media outlet for broadcast/publication or prior restraint of using such information would not prevent a suspect/defendant from obtaining that information elsewhere. Courts have usually

found that victims' names add credibility to stories, and such information obtained from police reports and other public documents is considered accessible public information.

In two rulings the U.S. Supreme Court considered the legal aspect of the privacy issue in the identification of sexual assault victims by knocking down two state statutes proscribing such publications, although the ethical debate resurfaces whenever a high-profile case emerges. In order to justify a statute restraining such publications of identifications of sexual assault victims from public record, the state must show a compelling interest to outweigh the First Amendment defense of publishing truthful information lawfully obtained. Once a media outlet lawfully obtains information about a matter of public interest, publication cannot be restrained. That erects a formidable obstacle for victims to win privacy suits over media identification.

In *Cox Broadcasting Corporation v. Cohn* (420 U.S. 469, 1975), an Atlanta TV reporter heard the name of a rape victim, Cynthia Cohn, in court as five defendants entered guilty pleas. He also found her name and details of the crime in the indictments. Despite a Georgia statute making publication of rape victims' names a misdemeanor, the reporter broadcast her name, much to her family's distress. The victim's father, Martin Cohn, sued television station WSB-TV for invasion of privacy under the statute.

When the trial court ruled for Cohn, Cox Broadcasting appealed to the Georgia Supreme Court, which ruled that the statute only applied to criminal, not civil, prosecutions, and sent the case back to the trial court. The plaintiff could sue under common law invasion of privacy, even though his daughter, not Cohn, was named in the broadcast. The media defendant argued that her name was a matter of public interest, which could be published without penalty, but the Georgia Supreme Court did not agree and upheld the statute as constitutional (231 Ga. 60, 200 SE2d 127).

Cox appealed to the U.S. Supreme Court, which ruled that the government could not punish the publication of information, such as a rape victim's name, obtained from public records. Information and accurate details about crimes and subsequent trials is in the public interest. By putting the victim's name in court documents, they placed it in the public domain and made it a matter of public interest. State governments can ensure victims' privacy by leaving their names out of public documents and proceedings or by using aliases or initials (as done in the case that follows), instead of the victims' real names.

The high court's second case regarding publication of a rape victim's name, *Florida Star v. B.J.F.* (491 U.S. 524, 1989), involved a Florida statute forbidding such publication or broadcast. A reporter-trainee for the *Florida Star* in the Jacksonville Sheriff Department's pressroom copied an incident report containing the name of a rape-robbery victim. The sheriff's department was not required to disclose such reports. Despite a policy of not naming rape victims, the newspaper printed the victim's name in a "Police Reports" item. The victim, B.J.F., sued the sheriff's department and the newspaper claiming a privacy right under the state statute. The sheriff's department settled the claim, but the *Star* lost in trial court

and appealed to the state court of appeals. That court upheld the decision allowing a *per se* invasion of privacy under the statute, and the Florida Supreme Court refused to hear the case (499 So. 2d 883).

The U.S. Supreme Court reversed the Florida courts, saying that imposing damages on the news media for publishing the victim's name violated the First Amendment, if such truthful information about a matter of public importance was lawfully gathered. Not relying on the precedent in *Cox*, which the newspaper argued, the Court instead focused on the press's role in covering trials and relied on *Smith v. Daily Mail Publishing* (443 U.S. 97, 1979) regarding the publication of names of juvenile offenders.

The Court did state that "the interests in protecting the privacy and safety of sexual assault victims and in encouraging them to report offense without fear of exposure are highly significant." It did not hold that "truthful publication was automatically protected," that there was "no zone of personal privacy" for the individual that the state could protect from "intrusion by the press," or that the state could never punish such publication. To impose liability on the *Florida Star*, however, was "too precipitous a means of advancing those interests" and did not serve a "state interest of the highest order." Punishing the press for publishing truthful information could result in self-censorship of the press as the government's watchdog.

Despite both decisions, the legal and ethical debate continues over publication/broadcast of the identities of sexual assault victims, whether obtained legally or illegally, or from public records or private sources. Following the Court's decision in

Florida Star, several states proposed or passed "victim name bills" that would prohibit disclosure, and in some circumstances would punish the publication of names of sexual assault victims. In a case involving a tabloid's publication of the name of the alleged rape victim in the William Kennedy Smith trial, the Florida Supreme Court upheld a lower-court ruling that a state statute criminalizing publishing the victim's name "in an instrument of mass communication," no matter how it had been obtained, was an unconstitutional selective ban on the media, being overbroad and underinclusive (*Florida v. Globe Communications Corporation*, 23 Med. L. Rptr. 1116, 1994).

The court did mention the possibility of narrowly tailored statutes imposing sanctions for publication of a rape victim's name "in a proper case." As a result, neither *Cox* nor *Florida Star* grants absolute protection for such disclosure in all circumstances. The latter decision did not hold that a state "may never punish publication of the name of a victim of a sexual offense," as demonstrated in the state statutes mentioned above. *Florida Star* does give the media some protection, especially for truthful publication that has been lawfully obtained.

Even with the above precedents safeguarding selected publication of the identities of sexual assault and rape victims, the decision to publish remains a sensitive ethical issue for the media. A majority of the public believes that such information should not be published, even though the media has certain legal protections. While it might be legal to publish such information in a high-profile case, such publication might not always be the wisest public-relations decision. Many media outlets have internal guidelines that prohibit the identification of sexual assault and rape victims. As demonstrated in the ethical debate following the identification of alleged victims in high-profile cases, such as those involving Kobe Bryant, William Kennedy Smith, or Dominique Strauss-Kahn, some media outlets might abandon those policies under the pressure of competition.

Private Facts

Although some lower-court decisions considered in this chapter offer little precedential value at the national level, the kinds of judicial reasoning outlined often reflect guidance given by higher courts to balance the privacy interests of crime victims with the First Amendment guarantees of a free press reporting on matters of public interest.

For example, under the protection of the First Amendment, a claim of the private facts tort depends on an analysis measuring "newsworthiness of facts" about limited involuntary public figures, according to the Supreme Court of California's 1998 decision in *Shulman v. Group W Productions, Inc.* (18 Cal. 4th 200), involving a private facts and intrusion claim by an accident victim against the producers of a television documentary, *On Scene: Emergency Response*. The newsworthiness analysis gives "considerable deference" to news media reporters and editors. This avoids the "likelihood of unconstitutional interference with freedom of the press to report truthfully on matters of legitimate public interest." Thus private facts and false light claims against news organizations by crime victims usually fail under the newsworthiness and public interest defenses.

When Georgia resident Nancy Tomlinson Tatum shot and killed an intruder with a knife in his hand and his pants unzipped, the police ruled the case to be a justifiable homicide. Having obtained her name and address from police, and despite the prohibition of publication of the name of a sexual assault victim under the Georgia Rape Shield Statute, the *Macon Telegraph* ran two stories about the incident using Tatum's name and address. Tatum sued the newspaper for invasion of privacy in *Macon Telegraph Publishing Company v. Tatum* (21 Med. L. Rptr 1117, 1993).

After considerable debate in the trial court over whether Tatum was a sexual assault victim and the newspaper having been given her name by police, the jury awarded her $100,000 in general and punitive damages. On appeal, the *Macon Telegraph* argued that the U.S. Supreme Court's decision in *Florida Star* should prevent media liability in a civil suit. The Georgia Court of Appeals disagreed, stating that the jury had correctly determined that the published facts were not a matter of public record prior to publication, and the *Telegraph*'s action was "in willful disregard" of Tatum's privacy rights. But the Georgia Supreme Court (436 S.E. 2d 655, GA., 1993) reversed the appeals court, using *Florida Star* to rule that a newspaper could not be punished for publishing truthful information that was lawfully obtained without a state interest of the highest order. The right of a free press to publish and the public's need to know outweighed the victim's right to privacy.

Once she committed the homicide, though justified, Tatum lost "the right to keep her name private" by becoming the object of legitimate public interest, the Georgia court ruled.

The Georgia high court acknowledged that Tatum committed the homicide in self-defense, and so by protecting her life she became a public figure, surrendering her right of privacy. Would the court apply a different standard if she had not resisted and survived the act, then sued the paper for damages? Probably not, since the Georgia court would once again rely upon *Florida Star*'s rule regarding publication of legally obtained truthful information.

Despite the *Florida Star* ruling, the number of cases filed under state statutes demonstrates that the right of the news media to publish or broadcast information from public records or public sources regarded as public information is not absolute.

For example, in *Times Mirror Company v. Superior Court of San Diego; Jane Doe* (198 Cal. App. 3d 1420, 1988), a California Court of Appeal rejected First Amendment arguments concerning public information. In July 1981, a San Diego woman, using the alias "Jane Doe" in the case, discovered her roommate's dead body in their apartment and confronted a man there. Fleeing the apartment, she reported the discovery to the police. Doe's name was withheld by police for her protection and to further the investigation. A summer intern at the San Diego office of the *Los Angeles Times* called the coroner's office and obtained Doe's name from "an unknown person." The resulting *Times* story about the murder included Doe's name as the discoverer of the body.

Doe sued the *Times* for invasion of privacy and intentional and negligent infliction of emotional distress.

The California court rejected the *Times*'s argument that the First Amendment privilege in printing Doe's name outweighed her right to privacy. Where a crime victim's safety is involved, the news media could be subject to liability. Especially when a suspect is at large, "the First Amendment provides no absolute protection from liability for printing the witness's name." The witness's safety and the state interest in furthering the criminal investigation take precedence over the public's right to know the individual's name. Even though names appear in public records, the press cannot "print names in connection with sensitive information with impunity." Although the subject of the roommate's murder was newsworthy, the publication of Doe's name was not. The *Times* did not obtain her name in open court or from public records open for inspection.

In two federal district court decisions, the survivors of two different homicide victims were not successful in invasion of privacy actions against the media involving public disclosure of private facts. In *Andren v. Knight Ridder Newspapers* (10 Med. L. Rptr. 2109, 1984), the family of murder victim Judith Bucknell sued Knight Ridder, owner of the *Miami Herald*, which published an account of the homicide with quotations from the victim's diary obtained from a Miami police detective. The story was reprinted in the *Detroit Free Press*, also a Knight Ridder newspaper.

The U.S. District Court, Eastern District of Michigan, dismissed the claims for disclosure of private facts and intentional or negligent infliction of emotional distress. Though the victim's mother, Dorothy Andren, claimed her privacy had been violated by the publication, the court determined that she had no standing to assert the postmortem invasion of her deceased daughter's privacy. The "savage" murder was a newsworthy event in Michigan, even though it occurred in South Florida.

In *Justice v. Belo Broadcasting* (4 Med. L. Rptr. 2067, 1979), the parents of Texas murder victim Ivan M. Justice sued Belo Broadcasting, owner of TV station WFAA-TV, for broadcasting allegedly false information about a homosexual relationship between Justice and his employer, Richard Lamport, who was abducted and murdered at the same time. The U.S. District Court, Northern District of Texas, determined that the deceased victim's relatives could not maintain an invasion of privacy action, based on their own interests or as a representative for the deceased, "where the alleged invasion was directed primarily at the deceased." The court recognized cases, such as *Cox Broadcasting,* that allowed survivors to recover for their own privacy interests invaded by broadcast or publication, even though they were not mentioned in the story about the victim. Using an analogy from Texas defamation law denying recovery for slander or libel of the deceased, the court denied the Justices' privacy action since the broadcast made no mention of them. Nor could they claim a violation of their son's right of privacy, "since the right is personal."

In *Barger v. Courier Journal and Louisville Times* (20 Med. L. Rptr. 118, 1991), a Kentucky case involving a newspaper's publication of a photograph of a dead or dying victim of a shooting rampage at a manufacturing plant, the Kentucky Court of Appeals ruled that the deceased victim's family lacked standing to bring a tort action for invasion of privacy and outrageous conduct in newsgathering. In its publication of the photograph, the newspaper did not disclose the identities of his family members, and so their privacy was not invaded. Although the *Courier* photograph omitted the victim's name, the court stated, "Few in our society would argue that the publication and distribution of the photograph was not in poor taste, insensitive and indelicate." While the court stated that the publication of the photograph was "highly offensive to most reasonable persons," the shooting rampage, which killed seven people and wounded thirteen others, was newsworthy as "a matter of legitimate public interest" occurring in a public place where media are normally granted access.

Elizabeth Ann Holloway, the mother of Natalee Holloway, who disappeared during a 2005 senior trip to Aruba, lost a 2012 suit against the *National Enquirer* charging intentional infliction of emotional distress and invasion of privacy over three articles about her daughter's case.

In these cases, the courts did not recognize the survivors as crime victims, even though the crimes greatly impacted their lives, nor did they grant them any favored legal status as such.

Intrusion and Trespass

Crime victims have also unsuccessfully attempted privacy suits against the media based on intrusion claims or separate claims

of the trespass tort. In some cases, it does not matter who gives the consent to enter the victim's property, even if the property's owner, such as an absent or deceased victim, did not. But plaintiffs' claims of intrusion and trespass could gain more sympathy from courts in light of the Supreme Court's decision on media ride-alongs with police entering private residences in *Wilson v. Layne* (526 U.S. 603, 1999). Although the Court's decision in *Wilson* focuses on the violation of the private citizens' Fourth Amendment rights, the ruling emphasizes their right of privacy weighed against the media's presence as unnecessary in the execution of a search warrant. While the court acknowledged a need for accurate reporting on law enforcement activities to protect suspects and minimize police abuse, that need did not justify the media's intrusion by accompanying law enforcement officials into the Wilsons' private home.

In *Florida Publishing Company v. Fletcher* (2 Med. L. Rptr. 1088, Fla. Sup. Ct. 1976), the plaintiff was away visiting friends when a 1972 fire damaged her home, and also killed her seventeen-year-old daughter. Based on standard procedure, Jacksonville fire marshals and police allowed a photographer from the *Florida Times-Union* to enter the burned-out home and photograph the "silhouette" left on the floor after the girl's body was removed. The plaintiff claimed that she first learned about the exact details of her daughter's death when she saw the photograph and accompanying story.

The Florida Supreme Court ruled that the news media's entry into the home was made at the express invitation of the police and fire officials, according to accepted policy of allowing media to enter private property. The photographer accompanying the fire marshal was not liable for intrusion under the theory of implied consent based upon "the common usage, custom and practice for news media." The plaintiff's claim was not an actionable invasion of privacy, nor did the media involved commit unlawful trespass. In this case the invitation by law enforcement was not connected to the execution of a fugitive warrant, as in *Wilson*, but was connected to the investigation of a fatal fire in a private home.

The New York State Supreme Court denied both a privacy claim and a trespass claim based on legitimate public interest and accurate portrayal of the events reported. In *Costlow v. Cusimano* (34 A.D. 2d 196, 1970), the parents of two children who died by suffocation by being trapped in a refrigerator sued radio reporter Robert Cusimano, who took photographs of the deceased children at the family's residence and wrote an article about the tragedy. Although the photographs and article were not published in a print or broadcast outlet, Costlow argued that Cusimano had "published" them by exhibiting to find a potential publisher, and thus intentionally subjected the family to "public shame."

In denying the privacy claim, the New York court ruled that the tragedy, "while necessarily unpleasant to the children's parents, is a matter of public concern" and public record, so must be defined as newsworthy. Cusimano's account was not false, nor did he exhibit actual malice in his attempts to secure a publisher by maliciously intending to injure the plaintiffs. In denying the trespass claim, the court stated that although Cusimano may be liable for "physical harm done while on the land, irrespective of whether his conduct would be subject to liability were he not a trespasser," any damages for injury to reputation or for emotional distress alleged by the parents were not a "natural consequence" of the trespass, and were "more properly allocated under other categories of liability."

In a 1997 Ohio case, *Barrett v. Outlet Broadcasting* (22 F. Supp. 2d 726, 1997), the family of a suicide victim cited not privacy claims, but violations of their Fourth and Fourteenth Amendment rights, as well as tort claims of trespass and intentional infliction of emotional distress, in a civil suit against the City of Columbus police and a local TV station. A reporter and cameraman for WCMH-TV, Channel 4 News, a station owned by Outlet Broadcasting, accompanied the Columbus Homicide Squad under the department's ride-along policy for a local news story to promote the 1993 premiere of NBC's drama series *Homicide: Life on the Street*. The plaintiff's mother committed suicide in her home after shooting her common law husband in a minor dispute. The police and emergency squad responded to a 911 call from the family, and later the homicide investigators and accompanying media entered the home.

Whether the police or the residents gave actual consent remained unclear. The cameraman stated that the detectives set no limitations on what he could do, yet granted him "no special privileges at crime scenes." The media did accompany the investigators to the victim's bedroom and photographed the bullet wound in her naked upper torso. The broadcast segment contained graphic photographs of the victim's body, but not her naked upper torso in light of the station's policy regarding sensitive material.

The U.S. District Court for the Southern District of Ohio dismissed the claims against the city and media defendants, but did chastise the media's conduct. Even though the media's presence was "not inherently unconstitutional," the court held that a reasonable jury "could find this conduct an unreasonable intrusion" violating the Fourth Amendment. The consent given to enter the house did not include going to the second floor and photographing the victim's body to broadcast on television. The media defendants were not privileged by the First Amendment to enter the home without the residents' permission, or to film and broadcast the victim's corpse or the interior of her home.

Consent has covered the media in other intrusion and emotional distress cases, even if it was not expressly given or even if the media do not properly identify themselves.

In *Baugh v. CBS* (21 Med. L. Rptr. 2065, N.D. Cal, 1993) a federal district court ruled that a CBS crew acted within the scope of an alleged victim plaintiff's consent, even though she did not expressly consent to her image being broadcast. A crew from the CBS-TV show *Street Stories* accompanied an Alameda County District Attorney's Office mobile crisis intervention team into the Oakland home of Yolanda Baugh and her daughter, Donyella, regarding Yolanda's assault complaint against her husband. Even though the plaintiff allowed the team and crew to enter, she later claimed that she believed the camera crew was with the district attorney's office, not media. The camera crew members not only did not identify themselves as media representatives, but also never stated that the tape would be broadcast nationally.

The federal court ruled in favor of the media defendants in denying the plaintiff's trespass complaint, since under California law even when consent to enter is fraudulently induced, consent is nonetheless given. The court refused to dismiss the plaintiff's intentional infliction of emotional distress and disclosure of private facts claims since even though the assault complaint was part of a public police report, the broadcast included Baugh's emotional reaction to the incident, which was not included in the public report.

Perhaps these intrusion-trespass cases would have had different dispositions in light of the U.S. Supreme Court's ruling in *Wilson v. Layne* (526 U.S. 603, 1999). The Court ruled that media ride-alongs in a home violate the Fourth Amendment's "right of residential privacy" and right against unreasonable searches when the media presence does not aid in the execution of a warrant. As discussed above, the need for accurate reporting on police issues or good public relations for police does not justify the intrusion of media ride-alongs into private homes, the Court stated. Hence, in future cases of this nature, plaintiffs could be more successful in seeking damages for unconstitutional trespass or intrusions by relying on the *Wilson* precedent regarding the Fourth Amendment.

Negligence

While crime victims have been frustrated in privacy suits against the media, suits involving negligence claims could have more successful results under certain conditions under the precedents of particular state cases.

In *Hyde v. City of Columbia, Missouri, et al.* (637 S.W.2d 251, 1982), the Court of Appeals of Missouri ruled in favor of a victim plaintiff, stating that the release of information by the police and media defendants created a foreseeable risk of injury to the victim by an at-large assailant. The U.S. Supreme Court (cert. denied, 459 U.S. 1226, 1983), allowed the case to stand, which meant that newspapers could be held liable for a story that exposed a specific victim to an unreasonable, foreseeable risk of harm, even if the information was obtained from public record.

The plaintiff, Sandra Hyde, alleged that on August 20, 1980, she was abducted at gunpoint by an unknown male, but escaped from his car. She made an incident report to the Columbia, Missouri, police department. Without her knowledge, the department released her name and address to reporters from the *Missouri Daily Tribune* and the *Columbia Missourian*, which both published the information with the knowledge that her unknown assailant was still at large. Using that information, the plaintiff alleged that the assailant continued to terrorize her on several occasions. Hyde sued the police department and the *Daily Tribune* for defamation, negligence, outrageous conduct, and invasion of privacy. The trial court dismissed the petition, and Hyde appealed.

The plaintiff claimed that the police owed her a duty not to disclose her identity and address to the media. The newspaper had a duty not to publish the information in order to protect her from the "foreseeable risk of intentional harm" by the assailant, who was still at large. The police department's policy also prohibited releasing the identity of a "sex crime victim" or "a victim who can positively identify the assailant." The publication of such information was also forbidden by the newspaper's internal policy. The defendants argued against such duties and claimed that the policy on release and publication of "public record" information varied in each case. The information here was both newsworthy and public record.

According to the state appeals court, not disclosing records of a criminal investigation is justified by legislation, such as Missouri's Sunshine Law exemptions, based on law enforcement needs, rights of the accused to a fair trial, and the protection of innocent persons involved. Opening all criminal investigation information to anyone violates the constitutional rights of the accused and the privacy of a victim or witness. The name and address of a crime victim who can identify an at-large assailant is not public record under the Sunshine Law. The disclosure served "no essential criminal investigation role" and was "a threat to the very personal safety of the victim." The police had a duty to foresee the risk of injury by the disclosure, which did not serve "a substantial interest of the public." In balancing the public's right to know and the individual's right to personal security, the newspaper owes a duty to exercise reasonable care not to allow the at-large assailant to injure the plaintiff by the publication.

The state court stated that the plaintiff is a private person who has become the unwilling victim of a crime, and is allowed to sue the newspaper for negligence under Missouri law, which does not extend a privilege for reporting that does not deal with matters of legitimate public concern. To delete the name and address of the abduction victim from the report would not impair a significant news function.

Missouri law imposes negligence for an intentional injury where the actor creates a "foreseeable risk" of injury by the assailant to the victim. The release and publication of such information encourages an injury and additional crime. The media and police defendants had the duty to prevent that "foreseeable risk," as supported by the pleadings and the facts of discovery of the petition.

In reversing the trial court's dismissal, the Missouri Court of Appeals remanded it for trial, but the case was settled out of court. Hyde agreed to a $6,000 settlement from the city, but received nothing from the *Daily Tribune*.

Such a precedent could be cited by other jurisdictions in making rulings favoring victim plaintiffs in cases of an unreasonable and foreseeble risk created by a media defendant. For example, in *Times Mirror,* as discussed above, the California Court of Appeal cited *Hyde* in ruling in favor of a victim plaintiff in a privacy invasion action, stating "Where a crime victim's safety is involved, at least one case has found that the news media may be subjected to liability for printing the victim's name and address."

In a previous case involving the victim of a robbery who was also the sole witness to a murder, the Court of Appeals of Missouri upheld a trial court's summary judgment in favor of a media defendant who published the victim plaintiff's name and address. In *Hood v. Naeter Brothers Publishing* (562 S.W.2d 770, 1978), Roger Hood was working in a liquor store when two masked men robbed the store and fatally shot a fellow employee. The Cape Girardeau police department released a report to the press, which included Hood's name and address. Having recently moved there, Hood was not listed in the local telephone directory. The *Southeast Missourian*, owned by Naeter Brothers Publishing, published a front-page account of the robbery-murder, which identified Hood and printed his address. At the time of publication, the two suspects were still at large. In a suit charging that the newspaper's outrageous conduct of publication caused him severe emotional distress, Hood claimed that he had changed his residence several times and that he constantly feared bodily harm from the at-large suspects.

In upholding the trial court's summary judgment against Hood, the Missouri Court of Appeals stated that the newspaper's conduct was not "extreme and outrageous." The published material was "a matter of public record and readily available to all interested persons." The publication of such information about a sole witness when the suspects are at large "may be unwise but it does not go beyond the bounds of human decency."

Could a TV station be held negligent for a reporter's call to a distressed man that allegedly caused him to commit suicide? In May 1993, a mentally ill Rhode Island man, Bruce Clift, telephoned his wife and threatened suicide. When she arrived home, he had turned on the gas jets and was firing guns from his perch in an upstairs window. While she was trying to dissuade his attempts, a police car arrived. The police soon surrounded the house, and a trained negotiator began talking to Clift. As the press attention surrounding the incident grew, an enterprising reporter for a local TV station, Channel 12, owned by Narragansett Television, called Clift for an exclusive telephone interview to be broadcast later. The interview was played on the 6 p.m. news, during which Clift carried out his suicide threat. When police entered the home, they noted that the television sets were tuned to Channel 12, which had just broadcast the interview.

Claiming that the TV station's negligent action caused her husband's death, Clift's wife, Judith, launched a civil suit against Narragansett Television on nine claims of action, including negligence, willful misconduct, trespass, and the right of privacy. Narragansett moved to dismiss, and the trial judge granted the motion.

The Rhode Island Supreme Court reinstated the suit. In *Clift v. Narragansett Television* (688 A.2d 805, 1996), the court decided that a medical doctor's affidavit supplied facts that "suggest the decedent's suicide resulted from an uncontrollable impulse that was brought about by a delirium or insanity caused by Narragansett's negligence." The trial judge should have let the jury decide the affidavit's truth rather than dismiss the case. The jury would have to decide whether the reporter's actions "exacerbated" Clift's preexisting impulses of self-destruction and violence, and if there was a likelihood that he would have killed himself whether the reporter called or not.

The media defendant could be held liable, "notwithstanding the absence of any uncontrollable impulse, if the suicide was a foreseeable risk from the defendant's negligent acts." The press is not immune from liability for its negligence, and the First Amendment is not "an impenetrable shield from a negligence claim," the court stated.

The question of media negligence relating to crime victims was also addressed in a U.S. District Court decision involving a suit filed by fifty plaintiffs—including survivors of the slain Bureau of Alcohol, Tobacco, and Firearms (ATF) agents, and a surviving agent, John Risenhoover— following the raid of the Branch Davidian compound outside Waco, Texas. The plaintiffs claimed that the media's presence alerted the Davidians prior to the impending ATF raid, resulting in the death of the agents. In *Risenhoover v. England* (936 F. Supp. 392, 1996), the court granted summary judgment in favor of the *Waco Tribune-Herald* and television station KWTX-TV to all claims except negligence. The court chastised the media for not avoiding detection in covering a secret law enforcement operation: "Instead, the media arrogantly descended on the compound as if the First Amendment cloaked them with immunity from acting as reasonable individuals under the circumstances. Their actions are particularly egregious when considered in light of the fact that they knew how dangerous [Branch Davidian leader David] Koresh and his followers were."

Incitement

The federal case of *Paladin Enterprises, Inc. v. Rice et al.* (128 F.3d 233, 1997) involved the family and guardians of three homicide victims, who filed an incitement wrongful death action against the publishers of *Hit Man: A Technical Manual for Independent Contractors,* intended to be an instruction book for hired killers. Following details in the manual, James Perry murdered Mildred Horn, her eight-year-old quadriplegic son Trevor, and his nurse Janice Saunders on the night of March 3, 1993, in the Horns' suburban home in Montgomery County, Maryland. Perry had been hired as a contract killer by Horn's ex-husband, Lawrence, so he would receive Trevor's $2 million medical settlement.

The district court (940 F.Supp. 836, 1997) granted Paladin's motion for summary judgment, citing *Brandenburg v. Ohio* (395 U.S. 444, 1969) to support its finding that the First Amendment protected Paladin from the plaintiff's claim that the publisher had aided and abetted Perry. While the comprehensive manual advocated murder and the company's marketing campaign was intended to assist criminals in committing crimes, Paladin did not incite the triple homicides.

The Fourth Circuit reversed the summary judgment motion and remanded the case for trial, saying that the First Amendment did not bar finding Paladin civilly liable for aiding and abetting the murders. The district court misunderstood *Brandenburg*, which did not protect teaching "the technical methods of murder." Rather, "the prose of *Hit Man* is at the other end of the continuum from the ideation at the core of advocacy protected by the First Amendment."

As demonstrated by numerous amicus briefs filed for both sides, the case did provoke considerable concern among publishers and news media that recognizing the potential for civil action against Paladin would having a chilling effect on First Amendment speech and press freedoms. In response the court assumes that news reporting "could never serve as a basis for aiding and abetting liability consistent with the First Amendment," since a reporter does not intend "to facilitate the repetition of the crime," but merely to report the event and inform the public.

The Supreme Court denied the petition for writ of certiorari (523 U.S. 1074, 1998). Shortly before the trial was scheduled to begin, a settlement was reached in which Paladin's insurance company agreed to "multimillion dollar compensation payments to the families" and annual charitable contributions to two organizations designated by the plaintiff. Paladin also agreed to take *Hit Man* out of publication.

In his book about the case, *Deliberate Intent,* attorney/law professor Rod Smolla, a member of the plaintiff's legal team, concluded: "We had achieved total victory. . . . But if their lives cannot be retrieved, in their deaths there is now perhaps at least a measure of redemption and meaning. The law will never be the same. We have struck a blow against the culture of violence. Freedom to speak is not freedom to kill."

The Fourth Circuit's unanimous opinion was written by Judge Michael Luttig, whose father was murdered in 1994. Even though he was a sitting federal court of appeals judge, Luttig was allowed by federal law to make a victim impact statement at the killer's sentencing on behalf of his father and family. In discussing the potential impact of the judge's experience on their case, Smolla mentions the suggestion by another plaintiff attorney that Luttig should have recused himself from the case. Smolla disagreed, however, because Luttig had previously addressed the issue by saying his experience as a crime victim did not prevent him from being fair and impartial in murder cases. However, the author does note "an intensity" that echoed throughout Luttig's opinion, which Paladin "tried to capitalize on" in its petition to the Supreme Court.

Would a judge who was not directly affected by violent crime have read *Hit Man* with a different perspective and written a less "intense" opinion than Luttig? Would the court's unanimous decision have remained intact? Luttig's colleagues were mindful of his crime-victim experience and allowed him to author the decision regardless. But could the experience of being a victim of a violent crime or a family member of a crime victim unfairly influence a judge or jury against a media defendant in other areas of litigation?

Fraud and Misrepresentation

In isolated incidents following tragedies, such as after the 1995 bombing of the Murrah federal office building in Oklahoma City and the 1991 mass shooting in Killeen, Texas, certain media representatives were discovered to be impersonating hospital workers, clergymen, rescue personnel, or law enforcement officials to gain access to victims or survivors for interviews.

While none of these individuals were arrested or prosecuted for such alleged actions, they could potentially have been found criminally liable under state statutes, as demonstrated in *New Jersey v. Cantor* (221 N.J. Super. 219, 1987). The mother of a homicide victim alleged that the defendant, Carla Cantor, a newspaper reporter, did not identify herself as a member of the media when asking personal questions about the deceased victim. Instead, Cantor allegedly identified herself as a county official, namely a lady "from the morgue." Cantor insisted that she properly identified herself as a newspaper reporter before interviewing the woman, but was found guilty by a municipal court judge. Upon subsequent appeals and retrials, she was continually (three trials) found guilty of impersonating a public official according to the state penal code.

In affirming Cantor's conviction, the Superior Court of New Jersey, Appellate Division, rejected the defendant's First Amendment arguments under state and federal constitutional protections, stating "a pressperson has no special immunity from the application of general laws and no special privilege to invade the rights and liberties of others." In regards to the circumstances of the victim, the court stated that the "alleged deceit was practiced on an individual who was particularly vulnerable by virtue of her daughter's death and the surrounding circumstances."

In a federal case involving a cause of action for intentional misrepresentation, a minor victim's mother, Diane Morgan Chambon, alleged that a newspaper reporter, Mark Celender, promised to keep certain private information confidential, then breached that promise by publishing those facts as part of his article in the *Valley News Dispatch*. The child's father, a former police chief, was being prosecuted for sexually abusing her, and some of the published information (e.g., name and age of the victim) had been legally obtained from public records.

In *Morgan v. Celender* (19 Media L. Rep. 1862 , 1992), a federal district court ruled that the publication did not constitute disclosure of embarrassing facts, even if Celender had obtained some of the information deceptively from Morgan. Her allegation that Celender breached his promise did not allow a tort action for intentional misrepresentation. The court stated that "failure to keep a promise to do something in the future does not constitute fraud," and Morgan had failed to prove any monetary loss to support her fraud claim as required under Pennsylvania law.

While the plaintiff relied on the Supreme Court's standard for breach of a promise of confidentiality as established in *Cohen v. Cowles Media* (501 U.S. 663, 1991), the district court stated that in *Cohen*, the Minnesota Court of Appeals "held that the breach of the agreement by the newspaper did not establish a cause of action for fraudulent misrepresentation."

Both cases demonstrate that the media will be subject to appropriate laws of general applicability as stated in *Cohen*. In some cases, such as *Cantor*, the media can be found guilty of violating penal codes in illegal newsgathering activities, such as that particular case involving criminal impersonation while interviewing a crime victim. In other cases, such as *Morgan*, the media will not be found liable for alleged tortious actions. While these newsgathering practices might be considered unethical by some, when appropriate they will be considered legal under the relevant statutes and precedents. Courts might state some regard for the victim's circumstances, as in *Cantor*, but will grant no special standing or privilege.

Discussion

The courts have consistently acknowledged the vital role of crime victims in all phases of the criminal justice system. Through legislation and precedent, victims have been given limited status to participate in criminal proceedings, particularly through victim impact statements.

In making these decisions and statutes, both courts and legislatures have acknowledged the violence and emotional trauma experienced by crime victims and their survivors. This concern has been balanced by guaranteeing certain procedural rights within the criminal justice system. But this favor does not extend to balancing the media's right to publish and the crime victim's right to privacy.

The media show sympathy to crime victims in particular circumstances, but as the discussed cases demonstrate, there are consistent alleged invasions of privacy in publication of private facts, intrusion, trespass, infliction of emotional distress, and negligence. The courts have generally ruled in favor of media defendants in criminal actions and civil suits filed by crime victims. While judges are also sympathetic to victims' trauma and right to privacy, their rulings have recognized the collective public right to know about crime and its victims as a matter of legitimate concern.

In selected cases, victims have been able to recover damages after invasions of privacy that have endangered their safety. For example, in *Hyde, Times Mirror*, and *Risenhoover*, the courts left the door open for successful actions when the media's publication of public information creates an unreasonable and foreseeable risk of danger to a crime victim. In particular, these cases provide potential precedent for media negligence liability, but privacy actions remain a formidable obstacle for crime victims and survivors as involuntary, but newsworthy, public figures. To be successful they must prove a compelling state interest in protecting victims' privacy over the media's First Amendment publishing rights and the public's right to know. It is unlikely that crime victims will be able to overcome such media defenses as newsworthiness, legitimate public interest, or publication of public information.

One of the more controversial areas of this topic is the identification of sexual assault victims. Guided by *Florida Star*, media outlets can print such information, if truthful and legally obtained through public record. Many outlets have chosen to not disclose victims' names due to ethical considerations, however. While the ethical debate is far from settled, the willingness of states to adopt statutes forbidding publication, even after *Florida Star*, demonstrates that the legal question has not been absolutely determined either. Media outlets could be left open for criminal or civil liability for publication/broadcast of truthful, legally obtained public information when prosecuted under these state statutes, if certain conditions for proving resulting harm are met. In these selected states, if an identified crime victim could prove resulting injury, such as in *Hyde* or *Times Mirror*, could the media outlet that

published/broadcast or the law enforcement agency that released the information, be held liable for such injury? What if the information could be obtained by a suspect from sources other than law enforcement or media publication?

If the safety of a crime victim, particularly a potential witness in a criminal trial, would be considered a compelling state interest under appropriate victims' rights statutes, then should not the state provide protection, such as a police bodyguard or safe location? The media should not be punished for publication when other remedies are available, and suspects can obtain such information elsewhere. Why should the media bear the burden, when law enforcement can assume the obligation, and liability if violated, to refrain from inadvertent release of potentially harmful or sensitive information about a victim?

The potential for media liability in harm to victims directly resulting from such publication/broadcast poses troubling distinctions. In determining the resulting harm, should it matter whether the victim's safety is actually compromised, the victim is merely fearful, or actual harm comes to the victim? What if the harm is inflicted not by the suspect, but by a confederate, who could also use alternative sources to obtain such information? To what extent would the media's liability depend upon the foreseeability of harm from the release of particular information? Is negligence enough, or should liability be imposed only if the media outlet recklessly or intentionally endangers a victim/witness?

Then should the decision to publish be left up to the individual sexual assault or rape victim? Should a media outlet allow a victim to determine whether or not her/his name should be published, even if it has been included in a police report, which would be considered public record that the outlet could legally obtain? For example, the Indiana University–Bloomington student newspaper, the *Indiana Daily Student*, briefly adopted that policy following a 2000 incident during which an unknown suspect exposed himself to two female students. The students were identified in the newspaper's report and complained to the staff that such identification endangered their safety since the suspect was still at large. For a brief period afterwards, the staff decided to let the victims of a crime or an alleged criminal act decide whether they should be identified. The policy later reverted to one that allowed the editors to determine such publication by following proper legal and ethical guidelines established by the newspaper's editorial board.

This "all or nothing" policy has troubling First Amendment implications. Victim advocates would applaud such a policy since it empowers victims and protects their privacy. It goes beyond the victims' limited ability to influence coverage, such as turning down an interview request. First Amendment advocates would criticize the newspaper for handing over its decision-making power to news subjects. Surrendering such responsibility undermines the power given to the media by the Supreme Court to identify victims and publish/broadcast other information legally obtained from public sources.

If such power is given to victims of sexual assaults and rapes, then what about victims affected by other crimes, such as burglary or arson? Should the surviving family members of a homicide victim be given such power? Should considerations regarding emotional distress be made for surviving relatives who request that embarrassing private facts be withheld? Or what about the accused, such as public figures or celebrities arrested for drunk driving or prostitution? Should the student newspaper omit the name of a student arrested for drunk driving because of the reaction of his/her parents or the effect on the student's athletic or academic eligibility? These resulting possibilities from such an "all or nothing" policy would seriously undermine the media's power to determine newsworthiness and other crucial factors regarding publication/broadcast.

If the determination was given to law enforcement, the selective release of information, being categorized by what crime affected the victim, would cause serious potential for unconstitutional prior restraint of media publication/broadcast.

Furthermore, the imposition of such special, greater burdens or potential liabilities, departing from the *Florida Star* standard, would pose serious constitutional problems both under the First Amendment and the Equal Protection Clause of the Fourteenth Amendment.

State legislatures and courts have given crime victims statutory and constitutional rights. This limited status, however, does not override the special status given to the news media acting within their First Amendment rights and responsibilities.

Jack Breslin
Iona College

See also Deceptive Newsgathering; Free Press versus Public Safety; Invasion of Privacy; "Out" versus "About": News Media, Politicians' Privacy, and Public Discussion

Further Reading

Arant, Morgan David. "Press Identification of Victims of Sexual Assault: Weighing Privacy and Constitutional Concerns." *Journalism and Mass Communication Quarterly* 68 (Spring/Summer 1991): 238–252.

Benedict, Helen. *Virgin or Vamp: How the Press Covers Sex Crimes.* New York: Oxford University Press, 1992.

Chermak, Steven. *Victims in the News: Crime and the American News Media.* Boulder, CO: Westview Press, 1995.

Coté, William, and Roger Simpson. *Covering Violence: A Guide to Ethical Reporting about Victims and Trauma.* New York: Columbia University Press, 2000.

Davidson, Sandra. "Blood Money: When Media Expose Others to Risk of Bodily Harm." *Hastings Communications and Entertainment Journal* 19, no. 2 (Winter 1997): 225–307.

Johnson, Michelle. "Of Public Interest: How Courts Handle Rape Victims' Privacy Suits." *Communication Law and Policy* 4 (1999): 201–242.

Krajicek, David J. *Scooped! Media Miss Real Story on Crime while Chasing Sleaze, Sex and Celebrities.* New York: Columbia University Press, 1998.

Marcus, Paul, and Tara McMahon. "Limiting Disclosure of Rape Victims' Identities." *Southern California Law Review* 64 (May 1991): 1020.

Smolla, Rod. *Deliberate Intent: A Lawyer Tells the True Story of Murder by the Book.* New York: Three Rivers Press, 1999.

38

Right of Publicity

Imagine the following scenario: One day, the Dalai Lama is visiting Loyola University Chicago (LUC). Samuel Norenberg is one of the few students who obtained a ticket to his public lecture. Samuel is a regular student, a private individual who does not seek publicity. At the event, photographers from the university's marketing department and from the student newspaper are snapping pictures of Samuel attentively listening to the spiritual leader's speech. The following morning, Samuel's photo adorns the front page of the student newspaper as well as the home page of its online version with the caption "Samuel Norenberg listens attentively as the Dalai Lama addresses the university community." (Samuel had been identified by his name badge, which every attendant wore.)

Depending on the kind of person Samuel is, he may feel either pleased or dismayed by this publication. He may not like the fact that his close-up appears in the newspaper without his permission and that his face is the first thing that anyone who picks up a paper or logs on to the website sees. In addition, his picture will also be archived by the newspaper. Searches for his name in Google will link to this photo.

Three months later, as Samuel rides the metro home, he sees another picture of himself at the event, taken by the marketing team this time, on a billboard in the train. His face is featured prominently on an advertisement for his university, with a slogan that reads "Broaden your horizons at LUC."

Depending on the kind of person Samuel is, he may feel either pleased or dismayed by this publication. He may not like the fact that a close-up of him pops up on billboards all over his town's metro system without his consent. On top of this emotional harm associated with having one's photo distributed all over the city, there is also the fact that his image is used in a commercial context. The school's marketing department must have thought that his picture would be successful in attracting prospective students, resulting in higher enrollments and more tuition dollars. It also saved the cost of having to hire professional models for its campaign. In the event that Samuel has ambitions as a model, he may feel exploited that his services have been used without compensation.

What exactly is the nature of the "harm" inflicted on Samuel by the publication of these photos? Is Samuel harmed because his likeness is distributed without his consent or control, therefore violating his right to be let alone? In that case one could argue the newspaper photograph was more harmful as it also included his name, forever associating his name with attending a Dalai Lama event.

Or is the ad inherently more exploitative because of its commercial purpose, reducing his likeness to a mere means to an end, attracting more students? Even though most newspapers are also commercial enterprises, selecting photos with their audience (i.e., their customers) in mind, the main purpose of this photo is illustrating a story, not engaging the audience in a commercial transaction.

The ethical and legal answer to the harm-by-publication question would be that one cannot reasonably expect not to have information about oneself published in connection with a newsworthy event. Allowing people this right would have too much of a chilling effect on the free flow of information. In this case, the picture of Samuel was also not taken at a place where he had a reasonable expectation of privacy; he voluntarily went to a highly publicized event where media were present. Courts very rarely consider the use of one's likeness in a news story to be an invasion of privacy.

The right to privacy is often referred to as the right to be let alone, but this is a limited right that one abdicates by virtue of venturing in the public spaces where there is no expectation of privacy. (European jurisprudence has a different view on this.) In order to have an absolute right to be left alone, one should live as a recluse. But why, then, should one be able to invoke a right to be left alone, to not have one's likeness used, in a commercial context and not in a news context? There are two possible answers to this question.

A first answer could be that the right not to have one's image used without permission is indeed not an absolute right and that it can be overcome by other values. The value to have a free flow of information in our society would trump this right; the value of being able to create advertising would not trump it. A second answer could be that the harm suffered by having one's identity used in the context of commercial speech does not merely result from the exposure suffered, but also from the fact that one's economic interests in one's own image have been misappropriated. This chapter will discuss how courts have struggled to separate these two related interests in cases where someone's likeness is used without permission in a commercial context.

The Right of Publicity as a Right to Privacy?

The Court of Appeals of New York was the first appellate court in the nation asked to grant a defendant remedy for the use of her likeness in a commercial context in 1902. The complaint was filed by the guardian of Abigail M. Roberson and alleged that a flour manufacturer had used a lithograph of the girl's likeness on 25,000 posters advertising the flour. The teenager previously had her portrait taken at a studio, and it is assumed that the photographer sold the negatives to the poster designer, without Roberson's consent.

The posters were on display in warehouses and other public places where friends and acquaintances recognized the image of Roberson. The scoffs and jeers caused her "great distress and suffering both in body and mind." The complaint further argued that "she was made sick and suffered a severe nervous shock, was confined to her bed and compelled to employ a physician." She asked the court to award her $15,000 in damages and an injunction against further use of her image.

The plaintiff acknowledged that the picture was not embarrassing as such, and was in fact a good one. The redress she sought was purely based on the "defendants' impertinence in using her picture without her consent for their own business purposes." In other words, the girl felt humiliated by the fact that her picture was displayed so widely. But did she also suffer extra humiliation because, of all things, her picture was associated with flour? This question is not answered in the complaint.

Distinguishing *Roberson v. Rochester Folding Box Company* from a plethora of other cases where plaintiffs had been granted relief, the court argued—among other things—that the plaintiff had no property right in the subject of litigation, the lithograph of her likeness. Since there was no right to property violated and no libel had been committed, the court stated that this case boiled down to the plaintiff asking compensation for hurt feelings, something the court was not willing to grant. Recognizing a right to privacy, the majority wrote, would result "in litigation bordering upon the absurd," as the right to privacy would also have to

encompass "the publication of a word-picture, a comment upon one's looks, conduct, domestic relations or habits." In other words, the court was worried that pictures such as the one of our hypothetical Samuel Norenberg in the school newspaper could lead to a successful privacy claim.

The majority sympathized with the plaintiff and recognized that the defendant's actions lacked respect for her feelings, but ultimately ruled that the legal system was an unfit instrument to give plaintiffs redress for having one's feelings hurt. Injuries of this nature can be better redressed by the power of sympathy from others instead of through monetary rewards, the court argued. The majority's opinion echoes the rationale of those opposing extensive privacy protections today: It is not clear what right is violated that can serve as the basis for a legal action, and extensive privacy protection based on hurt feelings chills speech.

Consequent Development

Shortly after this decision New York lawmakers passed Sections 50 and 51 of the New York Civil Rights Law preventing anyone from using someone's picture or portrait ("voice" would be added to the list later) for trade purposes without their consent. In 1905, in an opinion critical of the New York court's decision, the Supreme Court of Georgia did recognize a right of privacy in a case bearing similarities to *Roberson*. The defendant, an insurance company, had used Paolo Pavesich's likeness in an ad falsely implying that it insured the plaintiff.

The court heavily focused on the intrusive nature of this action and argued that the invasion was the publishing of "one's picture without his consent by another as an advertisement, for the mere purpose of increasingly the profits and gains of the advertiser." The Georgia Supreme Court based its decision in *Pavesich v. New England Life Insurance Company* partly on a property law analysis, an analysis rejected by its colleagues in New York a few years before.

These early cases were struggling to separate the economic interests and the dignitary (emotional harm) interests that caused the plaintiffs to sue. They relied on the famous and influential 1890 *Harvard Law Review* article by Louis Brandeis and Samuel Warren in which they argued for a general right to privacy, a right to be let alone. Warren and Brandeis were mainly concerned with press intrusions in private lives of high-profile individuals by the emerging gossip press. They relied on property law, mainly intellectual property law, to serve as the basis for recognition of a right to privacy. In other words, they argued for a right to be left alone, which is more or less a dignitary interest, using a property-based argument. The conflating of privacy as a proprietary right and privacy as a dignitary right can be traced all the way back to this seminal article.

A result of viewing the commercial use of one's likeness as a right to be let alone is that it is harder for a celebrity plaintiff to win. If the harm lies in the fact of being exposed, then surely someone who is in the spotlights all the time cannot credibly claim to have his privacy invaded. In *O'Brien v. Pabst Sales Company* (1941) a famous football player was unsuccessful in his lawsuit against a beer company that had used his image on a calendar. The Fifth Circuit Court of Appeals ruled that "the publicity he got was only that which he had been constantly seeking and receiving," effectively barring celebrities from winning a privacy claim stemming from unauthorized commercial use of their image. However, the plaintiff seemed to be particularly upset about being featured promoting beer while he was in fact active in an organization dissuading youngsters from drinking. By reducing the dignitary harm to an interference with the right to be let alone, the court ignored the fact that one can be harmed by being associated with a product one objects to.

Separating the Right to Privacy and the Right of Publicity

In 1960, William Prosser came up with his authoritative categorization of privacy torts in an influential law review article. He identified four privacy-related torts that currently are defined as follows: (1) unreasonable intrusion upon the seclusion of another, (2) misappropriation of name or likeness, (3) unreasonable publicity given to private life, and (4) publicity that unreasonably places another in false light before the public. This categorization has been widely adopted by the courts, even though not all of them have recognized all of the torts.

Around the same time, or slightly before, courts started to recognize a separate but related right, the right of publicity. The right of publicity, like the misappropriation tort, gives plaintiffs redress for unauthorized use of their image or likeness for trade purposes, but it is rooted in property law instead of privacy law. It can be considered more as a protection of the proprietary interest one has in one's personality, whereas the misappropriation tort is more closely associated with what we commonly understand under privacy, a right to be let alone. The distinction between the right of publicity and the misappropriation tort has faded over time to the extent that in many instances they are used interchangeably.

Haelan Laboratories v. Topps Chewing Gum (1953) marked the first time a court recognized a right of publicity as distinct from a right to privacy. The case involved a chewing gum manufacturer that had published baseball cards without consent from the players involved, who already had an agreement with a competing chewing gum manufacturer. Obviously, these players were not harmed by the fact that their image was given publicity in the way that Abigail Roberson was. Unlike Roberson, these players did not crave a life in anonymity. They wanted very much to have their images used on baseball cards; they only did not want their images on the baseball cards issued by the competitor of the chewing gum company they had contracts with.

The case took place in New York, and the court acknowledged that privacy law in New York was codified in Sections 50 and 51 of the New York Civil Rights Law (see above), but Judge Jerome Frank ruled that the right one has in the publicity value of one's photograph is a right that is to be distinguished from the right to privacy. He acknowledged that public exposure could not bruise the players' feelings,

but the unauthorized use deprived them of monetary gain, and he offered them recourse under what he coined as the right of publicity. Shortly after this decision, Melville B. Nimmer called for a recognition of the right of publicity in a famous and influential law review article. Nimmer, an attorney for Paramount Pictures, argued that this was needed to protect the interests of the emerging television and movie industries.

Celebrities and the Right of Publicity

Over the next decades, especially in the 1970s and 1980s, the right of publicity doctrine would pick up steam as it removed itself slowly but steadily from the privacy framework under which it had emerged. Initially, the right of publicity merely protected the likeness and name of a celebrity, but by the late twentieth century the right of publicity covered each feature of a celebrity's persona. A line of cases illustrates this trend.

Bette Midler had a long-standing policy against doing advertisements and endorsements, so when the advertising agency of Young & Rubicam approached Midler's manager to record a song for a commercial, the answer was: "We are not interested." Faced with this refusal, the agency approached one of Midler's backup singers to perform a song that had been covered by Midler a decade earlier ("Do You Wanna Dance?"). The backup singer, who had developed an ability to imitate Midler's voice, did an admirable job, and many viewers thought that the song had been performed by Midler herself.

Midler brought suit, and in reversing and remanding, the Ninth Circuit Court of Appeals (1988) sided with Midler on the basis of a property analysis: "Why did the defendants ask Midler to sing if her voice was not of value to them? Why did they studiously acquire the services of a soundalike and instruct her to imitate Midler if Midler's voice was not of value to them? What they sought was an attribute of Midler's identity. Its value was what the market would have paid for Midler to have sung the commercial in person." The ad agency would end up having to pay Midler $400,000 in damages. The Midler decision allows celebrities with a distinctive, well-known voice to sue those who use their voices without permission for commercial purposes.

Shortly after the Midler decision, singer Tom Waits sued Frito-Lay and its ad agency for deliberately imitating his very distinctive raspy voice in a commercial. The Ninth Circuit Court of Appeals upheld most of the $2.4 million judgment against Frito-Lay, further cementing the validity of the Midler decision in the influential Ninth Circuit and also ruling that damages could be awarded for the humiliation, embarrassment, and mental distress that resulted from this use of one's voice. In other words, the right of publicity was no longer just serving the economic interests one has in one's identity. Waits has won similar lawsuits in Europe as well.

Celebrities have been relatively successful in suing companies on these grounds, and it is safe to say that using look-alikes and soundalikes of celebrities in advertising is a bad idea. Courts have also ruled that other aspects of a celebrity's personality are off-limits for advertising or trade purposes. The Wisconsin Supreme Court, for example, has ruled that football player Elroy "Crazylegs" Hirsch's nickname was part of his identity and that his right of publicity was violated when a shaving gel for women called "Crazylegs" came on the market. Other courts have since followed. In cases like these, plaintiffs will be more likely to prevail if the nickname really identifies a celebrity with consumers and if the name is somewhat distinctive. "Muscles from Brussels," for example, is a more distinctive nickname than "The Beast."

In another famous case, the Sixth Circuit Court of Appeals ruled that catchphrases can also identify celebrities in right of publicity cases. In *Carson v. Here's Johnny Portable Toilets* (1983), late-night television host Johnny Carson successfully sued a company for inserting the phrase that was used to introduce him every night into its company name. The court ruled that the phrase had come to be so closely associated with Carson that it had become part of his identity.

In *Wendt v. Host International* (1997), two actors playing the roles of "Norm" and "Cliff" in the popular television comedy *Cheers* sued Paramount Pictures and a restaurant group over a chain of *Cheers*-themed bars Host wanted to open in airports all over the world. As copyright holder, Paramount had licensed Host to do so, but the actors objected to the fact that the bars would contain two robot-like figurines called "Hank" and "Bob" that resembled Norm and Cliff (this case also illustrates how copyright and right of publicity do not always go hand in hand). By renaming the robots and ensuring that their facial features did not resemble those of the actors (who had refused to grant right of publicity licenses), Host tried to avoid a lawsuit. The actors sued anyway, and after a long court battle the Ninth Circuit Court of Appeals would rule in their favor and let the case go to trial. (The parties would ultimately settle.)

One of the more bizarre suits in this line of cases was brought by *Wheel of Fortune* hostess Vanna White, who sued Samsung Electronics and its ad agency for a humorous ad set in the future, in which a robotic stand-in of Vanna White would turn the cards with vowels and consonants. The Ninth Circuit Court of Appeals ruled in 1992 that the ad violated White's right of publicity, partly because the wig, gown, and jewelry that the robot wore had been selected to resemble White.

For many observers, the *White* decision represented a right of publicity that had spun out of control. While existing law may have been at one point inadequate to protect celebrities against unauthorized uses of their likenesses in a society that placed high value (both economically and culturally) on celebrity, it seemed as if the pendulum had swung too far in the other direction. Some argue that the White case marked the high point of the pendulum's swinging motion and that these types of cases would be harder to win today.

The First Amendment and Limits to the Right of Publicity

The First Amendment, however, presents a restriction on this seemingly unbridled expansion of the right of publicity. Courts have consistently ruled that the right of publicity and common law appropriation cannot be used to restrict the free flow of information. One cannot sue a newspaper for misappropriation because it runs one's photograph or mentions one's name in a story, even though newspapers are for-profit organizations. But what about more hybrid forms such as reality TV shows like *COPS,* ripped-from-the-headlines TV shows, fashion catalogs, documentaries, faux documentaries, and brand journalism?

Judges are traditionally hesitant to determine what constitutes information and prefer to err on the side of free speech in these circumstances. Where entertainment and editorial content overlap, courts tend to still side with defendants when right-of-publicity cases are brought. Even some of the more tawdry reality shows can teach us something about the human condition that renders these programs informative, and entertainment programming is generally also covered by this exception.

However, the entertainment exception has its limits. When Abercrombie & Fitch used an old photograph of former surfer George Downing in its surf-themed catalog to advertise its surf-inspired "Final Heat Tees," the Ninth Circuit Court of Appeals found in *Downing v. Abercrombie & Fitch* (2001) that the news and information exception did not apply. Abercrombie employees had found pictures of Downing and a group of other surfers in a book compilation of photographs by surf photographer LeRoy Grannis. They had obtained the photographs from the copyright holder, but had not asked for permission from the people depicted in them to use the photos in the catalog. The Abercrombie & Fitch catalog also advertised T-shirts like the ones worn by the surfers in the photographs, who sued for misappropriation. The court rejected Abercrombie & Fitch's First Amendment argument that the photos illustrated an article about surfing and constituted information in the public interest. In reversing the district court's summary judgment in favor of Abercrombie, the court ruled that the photographs were merely window-dressing and did not contribute to a matter of public interest

Another, related, defense to right of publicity claims has put a break on the expansion of the right post-*White*. Courts now are more likely to consider whether or not the commercial use of a celebrity is "transformative," whether or not the speaker adds a creative or expressive element that triggers a First Amendment protection. In a 2001 case, the California Supreme Court designed a test to determine under what circumstances the use of celebrities' likenesses is protected speech.

Comedy III Productions v. Gary Saderup centered around a drawing of the Three Stooges by artist Gary Saderup. (At the time of the suit, the Three Stooges had all deceased, but the California statute allows the right of publicity to be passed on after death, another way in which it differs from the common law privacy tort of appropriation, which is not survivable.) Saderup specialized in charcoal drawings of celebrities that he then turned into lithographs or silk-screen images on T-shirts that he would offer for sale. While this merchandise is not commercial speech in the sense that it advertises a product, it still constituted commercial exploitation of the celebrity's likeness covered by the statute.

The court recognized that celebrities have come to take on iconic status in our society and that our societal discourse on values and culture occurs through commenting on the life of celebrities. Oftentimes, when trying to make a point, people creatively appropriate a celebrity's image through artwork, T-shirts, or posters that are offered for sale. For example, if one were to sell a T-shirt with the image of Bill O'Reilly and the message "Fox Lies" on it, should this be protected speech, or should O'Reilly be able to sue for this commercial use of his persona?

The right of publicity, if applied too strictly, threatens to stifle debate, and the court argued for a test balancing the right of publicity with the importance of free and robust debate. The California Supreme Court proposed that courts should consider how much the speaker transformed the original likeness, or whether she added enough to the original so that it becomes a parody or other expression of ideas. In other words, the court asked "whether a product containing a celebrity's likeness is so transformed that it has become primarily the defendant's own expression rather than the celebrity's likeness."

In doing so, the court rejected the rationale of the lower courts that had stated that reproducing a celebrity's image and offering it for sale is never protected by the First Amendment. Ultimately, the court ruled that in the case at hand, Saderup had not met this standard and that his work consisted of "literal, conventional depictions of The Three Stooges so as to exploit their fame." This decision and the test it proposes have been cited favorably by many other courts.

The court's decision in Saderup presented a much-needed infusion of First Amendment consideration in right-of-publicity cases, but the proposed test requires judges more or less to step in the role of art critics. In its decision, the court distinguished the silk screens of Saderup from those of Andy Warhol, who also used images of celebrities such as Elvis Presley and Marilyn Monroe. But, according to the majority, Warhol did so in an attempt to "convey a message that went beyond the commercial exploitation of celebrity images and became a form of ironic social comment on the dehumanization of celebrity itself." Given these subtle distinctions, it should come as no surprise that this test has not created the legal clarity one could have hoped for.

Applying, among other tests, this transformative test, the Court of Appeals for the Sixth District ruled that a painting depicting Tiger Woods titled *The Masters of Augusta* was sufficiently transformative to command First Amendment protection because it consisted of "a collage of images in addition to Woods's image which are combined to describe, in artistic form, a historic event in sports history and to convey a message about the significance of Woods's achievement in that event."

The Right of Publicity in Films and Songs

Films have been considered "a significant medium for the communication of ideas" and have received strong protection from courts against right-of-publicity claims. In a 1979 case, the California Supreme Court rejected requests for damages and injunctive relief by a nephew of Rudolph Valentino for a movie that had been made about the actor's life.

A man suing under the aforementioned New York Civil Rights Law for briefly being portrayed in the movie *Borat* was rebuffed in 2008 by a federal district court judge in New York who stated: "Of course, the movie employs as its chief medium a brand of humor that appeals to the most childish and vulgar in its viewers. As its core, however, *Borat* attempts an ironic commentary of 'modern' American culture, contrasting the backwardness of its protagonist with the social ills afflict[ing] supposedly sophisticated society." Even though the movie made millions at the box office, it fell under the news and information exception.

In May 2013, convicted killer Chris Porco was briefly successful in having an upcoming Lifetime movie about him (and all the promotion surrounding it) enjoined because it used his likeness for advertising purposes or the purposes of trade. However, the ruling was quickly reversed by an appellate court, just in time for the network to promote the movie as "the Lifetime Original Movie Chris Porco doesn't want you to see."

At the time of this writing, sergeant Jeffrey Sarver is suing the makers of the award-winning feature film *The Hurt Locker* because the story is, he claims, clearly based on his life. In 2011, a federal judge in California ruled that the filmmakers were protected under the First Amendment and had transformed the movie into a work of art. In 2014 Sarver is trying to change venue back to New Jersey, but it seems unlikely that he will be able to prevail in the long run. In a similar case, the Sixth Circuit Court of Appeals upheld a summary judgment against "the Original Soul Man" Sam Moore, who claimed that his identity had been misappropriated in the movie *Soul Men*. Applying the transformative use test, the court ruled that the movie added enough expressive elements to the purported use of Moore's identity to trigger First Amendment protection. The implications of a ruling in which moviemakers would be asked to pay damages because they used (elements of) someone's life story in a film would be enormous.

Just like movies, the Supreme Court has labeled songs protective works of art, so in most cases artists can reference people in their songs without fear of being faced with a right-of-publicity lawsuit. One of the seemingly more frivolous right-of-publicity claims in recent times was filed by Lindsay Lohan in 2011, when she sued rapper Pitbull for violating Sections 50 and 51 of the New York Civil Rights Law because her name appeared once in a song ("Give Me Everything") of 104 lines ("so I'm tiptoein', to keep flowin', I got it locked up like Lindsay Lohan"). The district court ruled that using a name in a song, even if the song is made to earn a profit, does not make the use for advertising or promotional purposes, and that even if it were, the isolated nature of the use would sink her claim.

However, more caution should be exercised when using a celebrity's name in a song title or more prominently in a song, especially if the use of the name is not artistically connected to the rest of the song. In that case some courts might conclude that the only reason for using the name was to attract attention to the song by using the person's celebrity. This is how civil rights icon Rosa Parks was allowed by the Sixth Circuit Court of Appeals to pursue a claim against the band Outkast over its song "Rosa Parks." (This decision has been criticized, and some have argued that the fact that Parks was a sympathetic plaintiff played a role. The parties would later settle.)

Ethical Justifications for a Double Standard

As this overview shows, American right-of-publicity law is an amalgam of tort restatements, state laws, and case law resulting in quite some variety between states. The line between the right of publicity on the one hand and the right to privacy on the other hand also has been blurred. In fact, these terms have come to be used interchangeably. Both protect individuals against the unauthorized use of their name or likeness for advertising or trade purposes.

The right of publicity protects individuals, mostly celebrities, against the economic damage of this use and is therefore a property right that in some states can be passed on after death. While theoretically the right of publicity applies to famous and non-famous alike, non-celebrities have a harder time prevailing in right of publicity cases. Some courts require that the plaintiff can show that her personality has an objective value outside of the commercial use at issue in the case, de facto limiting the tort to the famous. In other states courts may assume that a plaintiff's persona has value because it has been used by the defendant for a commercial purpose. But even in those cases, compensatory damages are likely to be limited. Courts have tended to award summary judgments to defendants when plaintiffs were unable to establish that they were well-known.

Non-celebrities, then, are more likely to sue under the privacy misappropriation tort, a legal doctrine that has not been embraced as widely as the right of publicity. Remember, this tort deals more with the dignitary harm associated with the commercial use of one's likeness and has its roots in a right to be left alone. (In some cases, this tort can also cover non-commercial uses when a defendant exploits the plaintiff's identity for her own benefit.)

However, in establishing a dignitary harm, a plaintiff has to show that damage has been done to her mind and dignity, resulting in injury in the form of mental or physical distress. This, of course, is much harder to establish than the mere fact that one's likeness has been used in a commercial context. Establishing in an open court how the alleged misappropriation of likeness or name affected one's mental well-being may be just as traumatizing an experience as the one caused by the misappropriation.

This brings up the ethical question of whether the law as it stands favors the rights of celebrities too much in comparison to those of non-celebrities.

Pro

There is a deeply rooted belief in this society that once you step into the public limelight and reap the benefits from the public exposure that comes with it, you give up benefits and rights that may be freely available to most other people in society. It is much harder—and for good reason—for a private individual to win a libel suit than for a public figure. We believe that public figures should be able to endure the occasional false and defamatory statement, as long as it is not made with actual malice.

So one can argue that there is nothing unequal in having a different regime for celebrities and non-celebrities; this is a distinction that is also made in other areas of law. It was in fact such a distinction that prompted the need for a right of publicity, as celebrities with seemingly valid claims were rebuffed when suing for a violation of their privacy rights because celebrities allegedly had given up this right.

One of the more widely embraced justifications for the right of publicity is rooted in the Lockean theory of labor, which states that people deserve to enjoy the fruits of their labor because they worked for them. Locke saw property acquired through labor as one's "just desert" and a natural right. Commentators and courts alike have used this theory as a foundation for a right of publicity, often in conjunction with an incentive justification, which states that without this just desert for their labor, people will lack motivation to put in the labor to begin with. The court in *Carson v. Here's Johnny Portable Toilets*, for example, stated: "Certainly appellant Carson's achievement has made him a celebrity which means that his identity has a pecuniary value which the right of publicity should vindicate. Vindication of the right will tend to encourage achievement in Carson's chosen field." In other words, in order for more people to want to become the next Johnny Carson, the law ought to protect his right of publicity.

Locke's theory of labor is inscribed into the DNA of this country, as we believe that one should be able to enjoy the fruits of one's labor, as a matter of natural rights. A celebrity works to produce a commodity—himself—that has value on the market, and celebrities therefore should be able to enjoy the fruits of their labor, their lawyers argue. If one takes a picture of a celebrity, puts it on a coffee mug, and sells it for profit, one is free-riding on the labor put into attaining a level of celebrity that could prompt people to fork over $15 for a coffee mug. Additionally, they would argue, one dilutes the "brand" of that celebrity, who may now be perceived as the kind of person who wants to make an extra buck by having her picture printed on all types of tacky merchandise. These perceptions can have significant economic consequences, exactly the reason why celebrities tend to exercise care and caution when doing endorsements.

Celebrities, some argue, have an interest in monitoring the use of their image that regular people simply do not have. In many states, non-celebrities might be able to sue under the privacy tort for the emotional harm of having their name or likeness used, but unless their name or image has economic value independent of the use they should not prevail in a right-of-publicity case, this argument goes. The student in the example used in the introduction, if he is just an ordinary student, has not sustained any real economic damage by the use of his image in the ad.

A criticism of this line of reasoning is that many celebrities have reached celebrity status through sheer luck instead of through hard work, limiting the applicability of the theory of labor. There are a fair number of celebrities out there who only had to put in minimal effort to reach celebrity status and whose career is not the result of hard work and careful planning. For proponents of the right of publicity, this sad truth does not change the fact that however minimal the labor was, the likeness and name have an objective value and should be protected. The value of an object (or in this case a public persona) is determined by the marketplace, not the amount of labor that goes in its production. In the same vein, some people make money by curing cancer, others by winning the lottery or by selling high-risk mortgages. We may have our misgivings about the ways these individuals gather their fortunes, but it does not lessen the property interests they have in the fruits of their labor, the argument goes.

Con

Opponents of the right of publicity as it currently stands tend to question the assumptions inherent in the Lockean theory of labor. They question these assumptions on normative and factual grounds.

They point out that many of today's celebrities are famous for scandalous, immoral, or even criminal behavior. A property right based on the long and arduous road these individuals had to take to reach their celebrity status is unconvincing to them. And even more to the point, critics question whether we—as a society—really should provide an economic incentive for even more fortune seekers to attempt to become celebrities. As explained above, the Lockean labor theory argues that the right of publicity serves as an impetus for people to pursue careers leading to stardom. But too many young people neglect their education in trying to become the next Michael Jordan or Julia Roberts, critics say. It may be understandable that celebrities want to make a profit off their image, but if they want a legal right to do so from society, they should come up with a societal benefit that can serve as the basis for this right, and a celebrity's ability to make money is not a strong-enough policy benefit for some.

Granted, some celebrities have gained their standing in society by being the best in their craft and putting in long hours of work. But even for them, the link between labor and success is tenuous at best, some say. It is doubtful that these people would not have worked to reach the status they have, but for the presence of a right of publicity. After all, the right of publicity does not protect the product of their labor as such; it protects a by-product, their ability to make money from merchandizing and advertising.

Some people also argue that the distinction that is made between the proprietary right and the dignitary harm associated with appropriation of likeness is not absolute. Claims made by celebrities often also include a dignitary harm. Tom Waits did not sue Frito-Lay in order to maintain his marketability in case he wanted to become a spokesperson for Pringles; he sued because he felt hurt that

his art, in which he is emotionally invested, was used without his permission. That is a dignitary harm, acknowledged by the court and allowing him to recover damages. Bette Midler was upset because she did not want to do commercials and felt that her decision not to do so was so brazenly ignored.

The dignitary harm cannot be merely reduced to the harm of having one's image made public, in which case it would indeed not be applicable to celebrities. It is also based on having one's likeness used in a particular context that constitutes a violation of one's autonomy rights. Some people therefore argue that the right of publicity should be seen in terms of autonomy. We all have the ability to define ourselves as human beings through our actions and beliefs, to write the script of our own lives. Commercial appropriation of one's likeness can interfere with this right. Bette Midler and Tom Waits defined themselves as artists who chose not to lend their image to advertising, and this choice should be respected. Staunch opponents of alcohol who are featured in an alcohol commercial are inhibited in defining themselves. Celebrities who lend themselves to every conceivable endorsement might have a weaker case from this perspective.

Non-celebrities may have a better chance at winning if their image were to be used in a commercial context, but still would have to make the case that a commercial use somehow interfered with their autonomy rights. Interpreting the right of publicity in this way would move it away from a property right and bring it back to its privacy roots, without barring the celebrities from winning a case altogether. The autonomy concept also allows for a richer and more nuanced approach to privacy than the reductive "right to be let alone." While it is unclear how this general autonomy right could be applied to specific cases, some think that a thorough rethinking of misappropriation as a violation of one's autonomy rights could mean a new way forward in this area of law that has been influenced disproportionally by the economic interests of the famous.

Looking into the Future: Video Games and Social Media

Some experts have argued that the right-of-publicity law is in serious disarray. It varies from state to state, and the transformative-use defense is applied with widely diverging results, spurring some experts to call for a federal right-of-publicity statute. In addition, different media seemed to be treated differently. Video games, for example, seem to receive a lower level of First Amendment protection than other types of media despite the fact that as recently as 2011 the Supreme Court has stated that they are a medium deserving of such protections.

Recently, two (former) college athletes in two separate cases were allowed by the Ninth Circuit and Third Circuit to pursue their claims against EA Sports for using their personae in its NCAA Football video games. Applying the transformative-use test, the courts found that the avatars used in the games resembled the athletes too closely to be considered transformative. In only considering how the personae were transformed, rather than the transformative nature of the whole work, the courts engaged in a different type of analysis than with other media, such as films. It remains to be seen how the courts will treat this billion-dollar industry in the future.

The principles of right-of-publicity law can be applied straightforwardly to social media, but the potential for misappropriation of identity has ballooned. For example, "Twitterjackers" may be interfering with one's right of publicity when they assume someone's identity on Twitter. However, if they are doing so to parody or critique a celebrity, their actions may be protected by the First Amendment. Social media allow for many ways to appropriate identity and for a blurring of the lines between commercial speech and noncommercial speech. Case law in this arena is still scarce, but bound to grow in the years to come.

The growth of social media, which we mostly use free of charge, has been spurred by their ability to create targeted advertising. An interesting advertising technique for companies that we interact with online is to let our social network contacts know that we like their business. Researchers have long ago found that we tend to follow the opinions of our peer groups in many of our decisions. If a company can create targeted advertising telling people not only about its products, but also whom of their friends it counts among its clients, the ad is likely to be more effective. But does this practice violate the right of publicity of the people who all of a sudden have become endorsers?

A similar practice led to a class-action suit against Facebook of people who claimed that these actions violated their right of publicity. Facebook's Sponsored Stories feature allowed advertisers to repackage users' actions on Facebook and incorporate them in ads that would appear on friends' newsfeeds. The complaint survived a motion to dismiss, and the case would later settle. Facebook later announced it would discontinue its Sponsored Stories feature in 2014. As a result of the settlement, the court did not have to address the validity of Facebook's defense, that its users had given consent to this use of their profile through accepting the users' agreement. Some commentators think this could have been a strong defense.

Conclusion

Commercial appropriation of likeness is somewhat of an ethical no-brainer. Few advertising professionals would argue that it is ethical, or smart business, to include people's likenesses in an advertising campaign without permission. Professional ad agencies have in-house counsel that will insist on written consent of the people involved in campaigns. The legal issue is not as clear cut, mainly because the law has developed on the basis of two different legal doctrines, one based on property law and one based on privacy law. While this distinction has become muddled and to an extent obsolete, its existence is indicative of the relative weakness of privacy as a legal concept in the United States. Privacy understood merely as a right to be let alone does not seem to provide a satisfying framework to deal with the issue of commercial use of likeness. At one point, it excluded celebrities, and it requires a high burden of proof from non-celebrities. As a result, a right of publicity has emerged alongside the misappropriation tort, providing a welcome refuge for celebrities seeking compensation for the commercial use of their likenesses. Courts are still in the process of figuring out the proper balance between this right and free-speech concerns, a balancing exercise that is complicated by an evolving media landscape and a lack of consistency in jurisprudence.

Bastiaan Vanacker
Loyola University Chicago

See also Commercial Speech; The Price of Publicity

Further Reading

Beverley-Smith, Huw, Ansgar Ohly, and Agnès Lucas-Schloetter. *Privacy, Property, and Personality: Civil Law Perspectives on Commercial Appropriation*. Cambridge: Cambridge University Press, 2005.

Black, Gillian. *Publicity Rights and Image: Exploitation and Legal Control*. Oxford: Hart, 2011.

Bunker, Matthew D. "Free Speech Meets the Publicity Tort: Transformative Use Analysis in Right of Publicity Law." *Communication Law & Policy* 13, no. 3 (Summer 2008): 301–320.

Gross, Larry P., John S. Katz, and Jay Ruby. *Image Ethics: The Moral Rights of Subjects in Photographs, Film, and Television*. New York: Oxford University Press, 1988.

Jennings, Jonathan. "Right of Publicity Law Meets Social Media." Paper presented at the American Bar Association 2012 Annual Meeting, Chicago, Illinois,

August 5, 2012. http://www.pattishall.com/pdf/JSJABA%20Right%20of%20Publicity%20Law%20Meets%20Social%20Media.pdf.

Kernan, S. Michael. "Privacy in Social Media: The Right of Publicity." *Hastings Communications & Entertainment Law Journal (COMM/ENT)* 34, no. 3 (Spring 2012): 363–379.

Levine, Jason K. "Can the Right of Publicity Afford Free Speech? A New Right of Publicity Test for First Amendment Cases." *Hastings Communications & Entertainment Law Journal (COMM/ENT)* 27, no. 1 (Fall 2004): 171–232.

McCarthy, J. T. *The Rights of Publicity and Privacy*. St. Paul, MN: Thomson/West, 2006.

Nimmer, Melville B. "The Right of Publicity." *Law and Contemporary Problems* 19 (Spring 1954): 203–223. http://scholarship.law.duke.edu/lcp/vol19/iss2/6.

Prosser, William. "Privacy." *California Law Review* 48, no. 3 (1960): 383–423.

Warren, Samuel D., and Louis D. Brandeis. "The Right to Privacy." *Harvard Law Review* 4, no. 5 (1890): 193–220. http://www.english.illinois.edu/-people-/faculty/debaron/582/582%20readings/right%20to%20privacy.pdf.

SECTION 5

Business Considerations

The Chinese philosophically view copyright ownership differently than do those in the West. As a result, it is difficult to see a realistic hope that a Western concept of copyright can and will take root in the Middle Kingdom. Even in the United States, there is tension between copyright laws and the First Amendment. And, as international copyright laws often differ from those in the United States, it is unclear that the U.S. copyright model is one that can or should be imposed on the world.

It should be no surprise that money talks in sports. Thus, a case might be made that money, not the quality of college sports teams, determines which teams get television coverage and are invited to NCAA end-of-season events.

As legacy media are increasingly having trouble making a profit, media accountability tools also are becoming endangered species, including news councils, ombudspersons, media critics, and journalism reviews. One newspaper, Britain's *Guardian*, however, conducts an "ethical audit." But what are the chances this audit will catch on in other markets and nations?

Speech is an area of concern. As an example of compelled speech, should the government be able to force cigarette companies to include photos of people dying from cancer on product packaging, or do such images involve an emotional element that goes beyond requiring a simple warning label? Too, the law gives less protection to commercial speech than to political speech. But is there an ethical basis for this distinction? And does the narrowing of the gap between commercial and political speech indicate that someday the Court will elevate commercial speech to equal status with political speech?

And finally, how can the business of journalism—of informing the public—most ethically be done without infringing on a person's privacy or ruining his or her reputation? Journalists from different nations answer this question very differently.

Business considerations in *The SAGE Guide to Key Issues in Mass Media Ethics and Law* thus take on a variety of international, legal, and ethics perspectives in Section 5.

39

WOULD CONFUCIUS STEAL THAT BOOK—OR E-BOOK—TODAY?

For a number of decades now, intellectual property has been the subject of often-sticky negotiations between the People's Republic of China (PRC) and the United States of America. Intellectual property, which principally includes copyright, patent, and trademark, has for some time been an evolving concept in China.

Confucius said, "I transmit rather than create; I believe in and love the Ancients." In keeping with the concept of the greater good, creativity is seen as a group activity enhancing and enriching the state. As a result, it would seem natural that intellectual property would be given much less importance in China than would be the case in Western culture and societies. Whether one deals with centuries of dynasties or with events of the late 1980s, China's emphasis has consistently been on political order and stability, as opposed to issues of ownership and private interests.

Accordingly, this article begins by examining the phrase "to steal a book is an elegant offense." It then discusses the omnipresence of digital piracy in Asia, including the rapid penetration of the Internet and mobile devices. Core values of Confucian ethics, such as *yi* (righteousness) and *li* (rites), are employed to analyze the wide acceptance of piracy in this area. China, South Korea, and Singapore are analyzed to discover factors other than Confucian ethics that help shape the core copyright landscape in these Confucianism-influenced cultures. The core copyright industries include "computer software, video games, books, newspapers, periodicals, journals, motion pictures, music, and radio and TV broadcasting," as defined in the *Copyright Industries in the U.S. Economy: The 2013 Report* by the International Intellectual Property Alliance (IIPA). The article also explores the Graduated Response, a possible but controversial alternative approach to this issue. At the end, with a focus on the United States, the authors analyze the drive for international intellectual property protection beyond ethics, legislation, and enforcement.

An Elegant Offense

Within this context, William P. Alford's book *To Steal a Book Is an Elegant Offense: Intellectual Property Law in Chinese Civilization* remains a major work shaping the discussion on this topic, even though it was published some twenty years ago. Alford, a scholar of Chinese law and legal history, says in his book that counterfeiting in the Middle Kingdom is an age-old problem. Such counterfeiting, including everything from computer software to compact discs, has been seen only since the latter part of the twentieth century as being linked to China's larger trade difficulties.

Alford, according to William A. Babcock's *Christian Science Monitor* review of *To Steal a Book Is an Elegant Offense,* says U.S. politicians jumped on this bandwagon, shifting attention from America's domestic economic problems onto foreigners who neither purchased our goods in abundance nor showed compunction about misappropriating the fruits of our technology. And politicians of both parties found it all the more appealing that a sizable number of the key industries raising these concerns were located in such electorally important states as California, Texas, and New York.

In addition, Alford contended in his book that American policy consists largely of the use of extensive pressure to secure formal changes in the PRC's doctrine of intellectual property. This policy, he says, is flawed as it does not take into consideration China's political culture—one that mandates the control of the flow of ideas.

According to Babcock, Alford argues that political culture has impeded the growth of modern intellectual property law in the Chinese world, and without further political liberalization, refinements in intellectual property doctrine itself will be of limited value. "And it follows, according to the author, that a state that has difficulty protecting its citizens' basic civil and political rights is unlikely to be able to protect their property rights. It in turn will have problems protecting the highly sophisticated property interests of foreigners."

Alford concludes by saying the United States "would, in the end, have been far more pragmatic in advancing its intellectual property interests during May 1989 had it not expended considerable political capital on computer software protection, but instead used what leverage it had to more vigorously seek a resolution of the occupation of Tiananmen Square compatible with respect for fundamental human rights, even while recognizing the limits of its ability to shape such events."

Origin in *Kong Yiji*

The statement "to steal a book is an elegant offense" can be dated back to a short novel, *Kong Yiji*, published in 1919 by the revolutionary author Lu Xun. Kong Yiji, inheriting his family name from Confucius, or Kong Fuzi in Mandarin, was an old-fashioned intellectual. When patronizing a local tavern, he dressed in *changshan*, a gown for Chinese males, to distinguish himself from blue-collar customers wearing shirts and trousers. Although dirty and well-worn, the changshan avatar identified Kong as an educated member of the "upper class," or at least that is how he self-identified.

In the ancient meritocratic Chinese society, reading was the only way to a prosperous political career. People were encouraged since their childhood that "the worth of other pursuits is small; the study of books excels them all" (*wan ban jie xia pin, wei you du shu gao;* 万般皆下品，惟有读书高). This is related to the Confucian value of "the student, having completed his learning, should apply himself to be an officer" (*xue er you ze shi;* 学而优则仕), stated when the master mentored his disciple, Zixia, in the *Analects.* Thus, when a bar customer humorously reported he got a scar on his forehead because he stole Squire He's books, Kong Yiji responded, "To steal [*qie,* 窃] a book is not a theft [*tou,* 偷]. For intellectuals, how can you use the word 'theft'?"

The implication of "to steal a book is an elegant offense," therefore, is that if a person uses another's work for self-development—in particular intellectual improvement—it is justifiable.

Some one hundred years have passed since Kong Yiji's defense. Today, digital media are reconstructing the media landscape. The digitization of books, music, movies, and other artistic and innovative works, plus the global diffusion of the Internet, have dramatically changed how these media are delivered to the audience. This article examines digital piracy through the lens of ethics and law enforcement, with the focus on Asia, where digital piracy is widespread.

Digital Piracy in Asia

The intellectual property scenario in Asia is mixed. Japan, South Korea, Singapore, and the Philippines have made great progress toward protecting copyrighted material. While China has made advancements, its future progress will be difficult. In Thailand, Indonesia, Vietnam, and India, instances of copyright infringement are decreasing. But Asia is also a market with robust growth in mobile Internet, and cheaper smartphones and tablets are becoming more available every year. Such an increased digitization brings more piracy concerns.

Digital piracy refers to the illegal copying and/or downloading of copyrighted digital materials such as audio and video documents without permission from and/or compensation to the copyright holder. Music piracy includes illegal downloading and distributing of copyrighted music. Movie piracy includes optical-disc piracy, videocassette piracy, Internet piracy, signal theft, and broadcast piracy of both delayed and real-time public performance. The advent of broadband Internet and mobile technologies makes the dissemination of pirated online information much easier. The Office of the U.S. Trade Representative's 2014 Special 301 Report points out the emergence of pirate servers by which players can access copyrighted games.

Digital piracy is rampant globally. According to the 2011 Global Software Piracy Study conducted by the Software Alliance, an organization composed of innovative companies worldwide advocating for the global software industry, 57 percent of computer users admitted they had committed software piracy. The report also disclosed that Central and Eastern Europe (62 percent), Latin America (61 percent), Asia Pacific (60 percent), and the Middle East and Africa (58 percent) saw more software piracy than did Western Europe (32 percent) and North America (19 percent). Among the top twenty economies, Venezuela (88 percent), Indonesia (86 percent), China (77 percent), and Thailand (72 percent) were the four leading countries in software piracy, compared with Australia (23 percent), Japan (21 percent), and the United States (19 percent). As part of the U.S. government's efforts in protecting intellectual property rights, the 2014 Special 301 Report, the twenty-fifth edition prepared since 1989, identified Brazil, China, India, and Russia as countries with continuing digital piracy challenges. The latter three were on the Priority Watch List along with Algeria, Argentina, Chile, Indonesia, Pakistan, Thailand, and Venezuela.

Despite a growing body of literature that suggests widespread digital piracy in Asia, progress nevertheless is being made. Pirated music files are smaller than software, movies, or games, which makes copying and transferring easier. It is common to find pirated music in China, Hong Kong, Taiwan, Korea, and Singapore, for example. Sarah Mishkin in her *Financial Times* article writes, "Pirated music downloads are the unabashed norm in Asia." Thailand reported rampant theft of cable and satellite signals and illegal video recording in movie theaters. The Indian film industry reportedly suffered losses of approximately $1.1 billion in 2012. The Software Alliance's 2011 report found that software piracy rates were extremely high in Bangladesh (90 percent), Pakistan (86 percent), Sri Lanka (84 percent), and Vietnam (81 percent), even though the accumulated commercial value of unlicensed software in these markets accounted for

10 percent of China's $8.902 billion. However, South Korea and the Philippines have been removed from the Special 301 Report as a result of their continuous legislative and administrative enforcement to protect intellectual property rights on the Internet.

Additionally, Asia is the place where pirated optical discs are made, accounting for 84 percent of the total worldwide, mainly in China, Malaysia, and Taiwan.

An Imported Concept

The Western concept of intellectual property rights has its roots in the European Enlightenment, or Age of Reason. This late-seventeenth-century European cultural movement focused on the betterment of individuals as the way to better society, and it was popular with intellectuals. The thinking behind this movement was embraced by America's Founding Fathers and permeates the U.S. Constitution and its First Amendment. Mankind, accordingly, is considered inherently good and educable, and the most appropriate focus should be on the rights—especially legal rights—of the individual.

The Eastern philosophy, on the other hand, was best articulated by Confucius, and the focus was on the greater good, or the society, instead of on the individual. The significance of one's existence lies in the person's affiliation with family and society. Issues of shame and saving face trump truth. As such, legal rights were not the focus.

Responsibilities rather than rights were for centuries the focus, especially in the minority cultures, or states, now comprising China. Maintenance of tranquility and social order were the goals. And ideas are for sharing, as they benefit all people; ideas are not the purview of individuals. Thus, it is the responsibility, if not the ethical goal, to generously share ideas of others to benefit society.

Fast-forward to the twenty-first century, and each culture has a different view of "ownership": digital "piracy," such as downloading of music and software; "pirated" books and DVDs; trademarks and patents. Such "piracy" in Western culture is—pure and simple—illegal. In China, though, such thinking is seen as simplistic at best, socially irresponsible at worst.

East Asian nations, which are generally more collectivistic than are Western nations, often regard copyright protection as a Western-derived concept, which allows one party to wield monopoly power of knowledge over other parties.

In the late 1800s China was first introduced to the Western concept, and China's then-emperor tried to pass the Regulations on Rewards for the Promotion of Technology in 1898. However, China's court system impeded its implementation. "The lack of enforcement of protection of intellectual property in China was exacerbated by the arrival of Mao Zedong on the political scene, as Chairman Mao strongly denounced individual ownership of any type of property, including intellectual property," Peter Ganea and Jin Haijun noted to Amanda Budde-Sung in the *Journal of Business Ethics*.

It was not until September 7, 1990, that the Copyright Law of the People's Republic of China was adopted at the fifteenth meeting of the Standing Committee of the Seventh National People's Congress.

Not that China is the only nation where individual ownership of property is a foreign concept. Apple co-founder Steve Jobs has been quoted as asking, "Why join the navy if you can be a pirate?" Today, in Chinese slang, "to copy" or "to parody" is referred to as "*shanzhai.*" The literal meaning of shanzhai is "mountain stronghold," or a hideout of bandits and other outlaws. Since Beijing's 2008 Olympics, a new meaning of shanzhai has appeared: the "shanzhai copycat." Now shanzhai has been adopted and used to refer to the places where inexpensive knockoff mobile phones and laptop computers are made, according to William Hennessey. It was chosen by Yu Hua, a well-known Chinese writer, to be one of the ten words to describe China in his 2011 book *China in Ten Words*.

Confucian Concepts of *Yi* (Righteousness) and *Li* (Profit)

In tracing the history of Chinese thought, not all Chinese philosophical schools hold the same opinion on *yi* (righteousness) and *li* (profit). Hsun Tzu, a representative of legalism, maintains that it is the ruler's responsibility to make the society and people rich, though he agrees with the Confucian concept of prioritizing the pursuit of *ren* (benevolence) and yi over li.

However, Confucianism finally became dominant—and became a national standard manipulated by a series of ruling monarchies in feudal China. Confucius contends that it is acceptable for the pursuit of li to be in conflict with that of yi. Otherwise, the former should always be discarded to secure the latter.

618 • BUSINESS CONSIDERATIONS

Confucius's emphasis on yi and his disregard for li can be found in his conversations with his disciples. In the *Analects*, Confucius argues that *junzi* (the superior man) always holds righteousness to be paramount. Thus, junzi increases to *ren* (benevolence), while *xiaoren* (the mean man) deteriorates to profit-seeking. According to Confucius, a virtuous and talented man can only be reckoned as "complete" when he takes righteousness into consideration.

Another *Li* (Rites)

Li (rites, rituals, or propriety) is another key concept of Confucian values. In *Lijii*, or *Book of Rites*, Confucius patterned the correct things to do in a family and in a state. These include the proper manners for cooking, dressing, funerals, marriage, and government proceedings. Sons and daughters should show filial piety to their elders. Wives should be obedient to their husbands. By obeying these rites, one shows deference and loyalty. By making subjects follow such rites, etiquettes, and precedents, the monarch can control social order once conformity is attained. People fulfill their divine duty. As a result, li is the coordinating mechanism controlling the interaction between people of different social strata so they can behave properly and reach social harmony.

As Angela Mia Beam argued, conformity and imitation are complimented in Chinese culture. This helps explain the popularity and acceptance of mass-produced fake and imitation products in China and the popularity of the copycat issues.

Communist Ideology

In China, especially after the Communist Party came to power in the late 1940s, Confucianism was officially replaced by Communist ideology despite its long history. Inspired by Marxism, the Chinese version of Communist ideology further strengthened the collectivistic attributes of the Chinese society. Individual rights were always overshadowed by collective interests. From 1958 to 1983, people worked under a system referred to as "people's commune" in rural China. Peasants shared everything from cooking utensils to land. Resources were assigned by the leadership of the commune. "*Yi Da Er Gong,*" literally "number 1 big and number 2 public," captures the features of communal life, where the commune was big and public ownership was high. Additionally, any private ownership, no matter how small, was considered wicked. When people did not own material belongings, talking about the ownership of spiritual products or intellectual works was out of the question.

The Confucian emphasis on righteousness and dismissiveness of profit, together with the Communist campaign for collective ownership, both contributed to a lack of awareness of intellectual property rights in China.

South Korea

Culturally, South Korea has been influenced by Confucianism. Even today, Confucianism remains a binding power in Korean society. Koreans show great reverence to the senior and superior, obedience of hierarchy, and respect for learning and knowledge—all examples of the legacy of Confucianism to the moral and social system of Korea.

Since the late 1990s, the Korean government has made tremendous investments in broadband infrastructure to promote more efficient government, business, and health care. In the current broadband age, online piracy also has grown. According to a white paper issued by the Global Intellectual Property Center (GIPC), an affiliate of the U.S. Chamber of Commerce, music, printed material, and movie piracy increased by 52 percent, 276 percent, and 312 percent, respectively, from 2007 to 2008.

To counter this trend, the Korean government issued new laws and enhanced law enforcement, in particular, to combat online piracy. This includes the adoption of the Graduated Response measures (which will be discussed in a later section). Public education campaigns were instituted to help change Koreans' perception of intellectual property protection.

Korean pop culture is a great hit in East and Southeast Asia, dubbed the "Korean Wave." K-Pop—South Korean pop music, including dance-pop, hip-hop, etc., such as the "Gangnam Style" that went viral on YouTube—gains 70 percent of its revenue through digital music. South Korea ranked twelfth in the global recorded music market, according to the International Federation of the Phonographic Industry (IFPI). Korean Internet Service Providers (ISPs) have been cooperative in blocking and filtering websites providing unauthorized content. As a result, Korea was removed from the U.S. Special 301 Report in 2009 and praised in 2014 for its outstanding efforts.

As a contrast, China scored 11.62 out of a total of 30 and was particularly low in enforcement and trade secrets, according to the GIPC's 2014 International IP Index. The United States, Britain, and France were the top three countries, scoring 28.52, 27.59, and 27.15, respectively, on this scale.

Singapore: A Piracy Paradise and Intellectual Property Protection Role Model

Much the same as South Korea, Singapore is a Confucian society, especially the Chinese Singaporean community, which is known for its high-speed Internet and high penetration rate of smartphones.

Sycamore, an Asia Pacific brand and research consultancy, conducted research about online piracy behavior and attitudes in Singapore in 2013. It found that youths aged sixteen to twenty-four were the main active group of music, movie, and TV piracy. Singaporeans who said they were current, lapsed, and non-pirates accounted for 49, 12, and 39 percent, respectively. The top two reasons given for pirating behavior were that pirated music, TV programs, and movies are free, and the likelihood of being caught and prosecuted is low. This finding resonates with the survey of American college students, in which about 55 percent of participants said they do not pay for music because they can download it free. Other responses include "habit," "free," "easy," and "no compelling disincentives." Participants also believed that individuals should take the most responsibility for their behavior to refrain from online piracy. Other groups participants believed should bear some responsibility include ISPs and the government, the movie and TV industry, and search engines.

The high online piracy rate in Singapore is detrimental to its own music, film, TV, and entertainment industry. It brings enormous losses to global media creation and production, including Hollywood studios. The low sale of music products meant that the Singaporean music industry hardly survived as of 2012. In the same vein, 36 percent of U.S. participants in a survey said no incentive could convince them to pay for music. As a countermeasure, the Singaporean government was thinking about blocking sites that offer access to pirated content.

On the other hand, Singapore also offers a good example to show how efforts in intellectual property protection can bring economic revenues and attract foreign investment. Overall, Singapore ranked fourth in the GIPC's 2014 International IP Index, after only mature economies such as the United States, France, and Britain.

Possible Solutions

In the modern world, Confucianism no longer appears to provide a workable moral compass to Internet users who tend to access free digital files. Thus, creating new laws and strengthening law enforcement may be alternatives, as illustrated in South Korea and Singapore's success. Only 20 percent of people in mature markets and 15 percent in emerging markets who admitted to frequently committing software piracy were concerned about being caught.

France, Britain, New Zealand, Taiwan, the United States, Iceland, and South Korea have adopted the Graduated Response system to address online infringement, even though this scheme is controversial due to questions about its effectiveness and surveillance. Under this system, ISPs first issue two warnings of possible sanctions after they detect the subscriber at an Internet Protocol address is downloading illegal files. After that, if things still do not change, the user's service is slowed down, suspended, filtered, or terminated. Specific penalties vary from country to country. In Ireland, for example, illegal users may end up with a twelve-month disconnection from broadband Internet. The more severe the infringement is, the more draconian the sanction is. This deterrence has proven to be effective in South Korea. Even after receiving only the first warning, 70 percent of users stopped further illegal activities. France, which ranks high for its successful efforts in intellectual property protection, is the first European country to implement the Graduated Response law known as HADOPI. A subscriber who downloads unauthorized files may face a fine of up to €1,500. With education, warning, and potential sanctions, the law has helped French citizens to buy authorized music. Research found iTunes sales increased by about 25 percent over what they would have been if HADOPI had not been in effect. However, researchers such as Rebecca Giblin, a Monash University law professor, are doubtful whether the efficacy of the Graduated Response is as great as holders of intellectual property rights claimed.

Together with the Graduated Response, some countries are working to block Web services such as the Pirate Bay, the self-claimed world's largest BitTorrent tracker, where anyone can download torrent files, including music, games, software, and videos, for free. The Pirate Bay clarifies its stance to the copyright issue in the "About" section on its site. It says its server only saves torrent files, so there is no copyrighted or illegal material. Now access to the Pirate Bay is blocked by ISPs in some twenty counties. This measure then puts ISP surveillance of users on the agenda.

Search-engine companies also contribute to this joint effort. Baidu, the largest in China, has long been blamed for offering links to unlicensed music in its MP3 search to attract users from foreign competitors. But in 2011, Baidu signed an agreement to distribute free authorized music by Baidu Ting.

As is the case in emerging economies, historically, mature economies experienced a period of piracy as well, such as Europe in the eighteenth century, the United States in the first half of the nineteenth century, and Japan in the twentieth. The necessary investment in development and innovation can only be achieved after a society has amassed sufficient fortunes. Indeed, some researchers say the protection of intellectual property rights is possible only after a society's economy has reached a certain stage. In any case, reducing piracy in low- and middle-income countries remains a big concern.

The U.S. Side of the Story

As would be expected, U.S. companies and organizations are the ones most concerned with anti-piracy. In terms of

computer users' attitudes toward intellectual property, a survey conducted in 2011 by the Business Software Alliance (BSA) found that 29 percent of respondents said that benefits should flow to society, while 71 percent agreed that innovators should be rewarded since this could inspire more innovations, which would, in turn, be good for the progress of society and the growth of business. Therefore, in addition to the respect for creativity and innovation by copyright holders, be they companies or individuals, another drive for anti-piracy campaigns, legislation, and law enforcement is the potential for profit, or the loss of it.

Globally, the commercial value of pirated software rose to $63.4 billion in 2011, according to the BSA software piracy study. For the United States, with the value of legal sales of software reaching $42 billion, the commercial value of the piracy was about $10 billion.

According to the IIPA, the U.S. copyright system contributed 6.48 percent of the U.S. economy, reaching more than $1 trillion in 2012. The total contribution of the whole of copyright industries was $1.7 trillion. Core copyright industries also provided 5.4 million jobs to Americans, accounting for 4.04 percent of the total U.S. workforce. What is more, these are high-paying jobs, 33 percent higher than the average. The growth rate of the copyright industries was more than twice that of the rest of the U.S. economy. Compared with industries making tangible products, such as aerospace ($106 billion), agriculture ($70 billion), food ($64 billion), and pharmaceuticals ($60 billion), copyright industries showed their strength in foreign sales and exports with a market value of $142 trillion in 2012.

Conclusion

The study of China, South Korea, Singapore, and Japan shows that stealing a book is anything but elegant; it indeed is an *in*elegant offense. Nor does Confucianism alone explain how rampant digital piracy has become in Asia. Historically, both Japan and China's progress in intellectual property protection was spurred by trade pressure from the United States. But these Asian nations have all come to realize the importance of intellectual property protection to attract foreign direct investment and enhance the growth of their own national economies.

With the achievement of the U.S. copyright industries, the inspiration of intellectual property endeavors, both in the long and short run, is utilitarian—benefiting society as a whole, including the very intellectuals Confucius considered. Who knows, but were he alive today, he might not advocate stealing of books—or even having them sold at cut rate—but might instead recommend they and their Internet counterparts be sold at full hardcover rates.

Tao Fu
University of International Business
and Economics
William A. Babcock
Southern Illinois University Carbondale

See also Copyright in the United States; International Influence on U.S. Copyright

Further Reading

Alford, William P. *To Steal a Book Is an Elegant Offense: Intellectual Property Law in Chinese Civilization*. Stanford, CA: Stanford University Press, 1995.

Aripin, Nurul Azliah. "7 out of 10 Singaporean Youths Are Active in Online Piracy: Survey." Yahoo! News Singapore, March 18, 2014. https://sg.news.yahoo.com/7-out-of-10-singaporean-youths-are-active-in-online-piracy--survey-124853227.html.

Babcock, William A. "Intellectual Rights Alien Experience to Chinese." *Christian Science Monitor*, October 26, 1995. http://www.csmonitor.com/1995/1026/26b31.html.

Beam, Angela Mia. "Piracy of American Intellectual Property in China." *Journal of International Law and Practice* 4, no. 2 (1995): 335–358.

Budde-Sung, Amanda. "The Invisible Meets the Intangible: Culture's Impact on Intellectual Property Protection." *Journal of Business Ethics* 117 (2013): 345–359. doi 10.1007/s10551-012-1524-y.

Business Software Alliance. "Shadow Market: 2011 BSA Global Software Piracy Study." http://www.bsa.org/~/media/Files/Research%20Papers/GlobalStudy/2011/2011_BSA_Piracy_Study%20Standard.pdf.

Cheng, Chung-ying. *New Dimensions of Confucian and Neo-Confucian Philosophy*. Albany: State University of New York Press, 1991.

"Copyright Law of the People's Republic of China (Revised in 2010)." Ministry of Commerce, People's Republic of China, February 26, 2010. http://english.mofcom.gov.cn/article/policyrelease/announcement/201004/20100406883359.shtml.

Froman, Michael B. G. "2014 Special 301 Report." Washington, DC: Office of the U.S. Trade Representative, April 2014. http://www.ustr.gov/sites/default/files/USTR%202014%20Special%20301%20Report%20to%20Congress%20FINAL.pdf.

Giblin, Rebecca. "Evaluating Graduated Response." *Columbia Journal of Law and the Arts* 37, no. 2 (2014): 147–209.

Global Intellectual Property Center. "Charting the Course—The GIPC International IP Index, 2nd Edition," January 28, 2014. http://dev.theglobalipcenter.com/wp-content/themes/gipc/map-index/assets/pdf/Index_Map_Index_2nd Edition.pdf.

Global Intellectual Property Center. "IP Rights and Broadband Development in South Korea: Lessons Learned for the United States." White Paper Series, n.d. http://www.theglobalipcenter.com/sites/default/files/reports/documents/15652_SK_Broadband.pdf.

Gopal, Ram D., G. Lawrence Sanders, Sudip Bhattacharjee, Manish Agrawal, and Suzanne C. Wagner. "A Behavioral Model of Digital Music Piracy." *Journal of Organizational Computing and Electronic Commerce* 14, no. 2 (2004): 89–105.

Hennessey, William. "Deconstructing Shanzhai-China's Copycat Counterculture: Catch Me If You Can." *Campbell Law Review* 34 (2012): 609–662.

Higgins, George E., and Catherine D. Marcum. *Digital Piracy: An Integrated Theoretical Approach.* Durham, NC: Carolina Academic Press, 2011.

Hille, Kathrin. "Baidu to Launch Free Legal Music Downloads." *Financial Times,* May 4, 2011. http://www.ft.com/cms/s/2/6581f490-7645-11e0-b4f7-00144feabdc0.html#axzz35x7cQNb4.

Husted, Bryan W. "The Impact of National Culture on Software Piracy." *Journal of Business Ethics* 26, no. 3 (2000): 197–211.

IFPI. "Heavy Investment in South Korea," n.d. http://www.ifpi.org/south-korea.php.

International Federation of the Phonographic Industry (IFPI). "Digital Music Report 2012." http://www.ifpi.org/content/library/dmr2012.pdf.

Kong, Xianglin, and James Legge. *The Analects of Confucius.* Chinese-English ed. Beijing: Foreign Languages Press, 2009.

Lin, Yutang. *The Wisdom of Confucius.* Beijing: Foreign Language Teaching and Research Press, 2009.

Mishkin, Sarah. "A Mission to Battle Piracy." *Financial Times*, April 30, 2013. http://www.ft.com/cms/s/0/d6bc4e1c-a852-11e2-8e5d-00144feabdc0.html#axzz33CnhCEqb.

"Not-So-Shocking News of the Day: Thailand Remains on U.S. Piracy Watch List." CNN, May 3, 2011. http://travel.cnn.com/bangkok/life/piracy-watch-list-219339.

"Online Piracy: Rights and Wronged." *Economist*, November 26, 2011. http://www.economist.com/node/21540234.

Shi, Wei. "Cultural Perplexity in Intellectual Property: Is Stealing a Book an Elegant Offense?" *North Carolina Journal of International Law and Commercial Regulation* 32, no. 1 (2006): 1–47.

Siwek, Stephen E. "Copyright Industries in the U.S. Economy: The 2013 Report." http://www.iipa.com/pdf/2013_Copyright_Industries_Full_Report.PDF.

Sycamore. "Online Piracy Behavior and Attitudes in Singapore," March 2014. http://issuu.com/rmrkblty/docs/online_piracy_behaviour_and_attitud.

Upshaw, Danny, and Laurie A. Babin. "Music Downloading: Competing against Online Piracy." *International Journal of Business and Public Administration* 7, no. 1 (2010): 14–26.

Walls, W. D. "Cross-Country Analysis of Movie Piracy." *Applied Economics* 40 (2008): 625–632.

Woolley, Darryl J. "The Cynical Pirate: How Cynicism Effects Music Piracy." *Academy of Information and Management Sciences Journal* 13, no. 1 (2010): 31–43.

Wu, Handong. "Guanyu Zhongguo Zhuzuoquan Fa Guannian de Lishi Sikao (Historical Reflection on Copyright Law Attitude in China)," December 5, 2012. http://www.teachipr.com/j_s/index.php/focus/2012-12-04-21-42-51/146-2012-12-04-22-01-16%3E.

Xianggang Ligong Daxue Zhongguo nongcun dushu xiaozu (Hong Kong Polytechnic University, Rural China Reading Group). "Renmin Gongshe Shijian Yu Gaige De

Zairenshi (A Revisit to the Practice and Reform of the People's Commune)." *Critique and Transformation*, July 23, 2012. http://critiqueandtransformation .wordpress.com/2012/07.

Xiao, Xiaosui. "Rites (Li): The Symbolic Making of Chinese Humanity." *China Media Research* 7, no. 4 (2011): 61–67.

Yoon, Cheolho. "Theory of Planned Behavior and Ethics Theory in Digital Piracy: An Integrated Model." *Journal of Business Ethics* 100, no. 3 (2011): 405–417.

Yu, Peter K. "Intellectual Property and Asian Values." *Marquette Intellectual Property Law Review* 16, no. 2 (2012): 329–399.

Yu, Szde. "Digital Piracy Justification: Asian Students vs. American Students." *International Criminal Justice Review* 23, no. 2 (2013): 185–196.

40

COPYRIGHT IN THE UNITED STATES

Copyright is a legal construct that gives authors and creators control over their expression. The primary function of copyright in the United States is to establish a framework for the economic exploitation of expressive works. As such, copyright provides a legal foundation for the modern cultural, information, and entertainment industries, including print publishing, television, music, radio, film, photography, computer software, theater, architecture, and the fine arts.

Copyright gives the creator limited control over how her original expression is reproduced, distributed, altered, publicly performed, and otherwise used. Individuals or corporations that wish to copy or use the expression need authorization from the copyright holder. Copyright only protects expression, not the facts or ideas that are being expressed. The protection is for a limited time, though that duration has been extended frequently by Congress. There also are important limitations on the copyright holder's control over the expression to ensure that free speech and the advancement of knowledge are not unduly restricted.

Copyright has a relatively short history, having first emerged in the eighteenth century. The law has expanded substantially both in the United States and around the world as technological advancements have generated new ways to create and exploit expressive works. Copyright is regulated globally through multiple international treaties that have taken on increased importance as information products become a more significant portion of international trade. Significant controversies exist regarding the appropriate scope of copyright protection, particularly the use of technological protection mechanisms by copyright holders and restrictions on audience reuse of cultural texts.

Overview

Copyright is a type of intellectual property law, along with patents, trademarks, and trade secrets. Copyright protects expression, not facts, ideas, discoveries, or names. Patents protect inventions and processes, whether a new type of engine, circuit board design, genetically modified plant, pharmaceutical drug, or a new method for manufacturing. Patents are very difficult to obtain and usually expire after twenty years. Trademarks protect the names, logos, and other identifying marks that designate a particular business or product. Trademarks help eliminate consumer confusion regarding the source of a particular product or service and typically remain enforceable for as long as the business exists. A trade secret is proprietary information that a business seeks to keep private. Employees are then obligated to keep the information secret.

Like traditional property law, intellectual property law gives the owner the right to control the use or sale of the property in question. A key difference is that property law governs ownership of tangible objects such as land, buildings, furniture, vehicles, and other physical goods. Intellectual property is intangible and includes ideas, processes, and expression. This makes enforcement of intellectual property rights much more problematic than enforcement of real property rights. One can build a fence or wall to prevent others from trespassing on real property. A fence cannot prevent others from using an idea, process, or expression once the information has been obtained. Another difference between property law and intellectual property law is that ownership of physical property does not expire. A house or other physical object can be owned "forever" and passed down from one generation to the next. Patents and copyrights grant ownership only for a limited time, after which the idea or expression falls into the public domain and can be used freely by anyone.

Copyrighted works can include literary works, musical works, maps, drawings, illustrations, photographs, audiovisual images, computer software, architectural works, choreography, sculpture, sound recordings, and dramatic works. As discussed above, copyright only protects expression, not the ideas, facts, or information being expressed. The thoughts inside someone's head consist of many different facts, emotions, and ideas. That person uses expression to communicate her thoughts to others. Expression can take many forms, such as words, drawings, paintings, sculpture, musical notes, lyrics, photographs, moving images, dance, animation, etc. For example, if an author writes a poem to communicate a love of nature, the author can copyright the particular word choice of the poem since that is her original expression. But the author cannot copyright the *idea* of "love of nature." Anyone else can be inspired to create their own work expressing a love of nature as long as they do not use the first author's expression. Like ideas, facts and discoveries cannot be copyrighted. Suppose a scholar conducts research on the Civil War and discovers a battle that no one else realized took place. Once the discovery is made public, anyone else can write about the battle and incorporate it into their own book, song, painting, or movie without having to get permission from the original scholar. The first scholar cannot copyright the discovery, she can only copyright the expression she used to communicate the discovery.

Originality, Fixation, and Duration of Copyright

To be eligible for copyright protection, expression must be original to the author and fixed in a tangible medium. Original means that the expression did not come from a preexisting source and contains a modicum of creativity. For example, if a songwriter uses a common chord progression that has been used in many songs previously, the songwriter cannot copyright that chord progression since it is not her original expression.

Fixed in a tangible medium means the expression must be made permanent long enough to be perceived for more than a transitory duration. Writing words on paper, saving a file onto a computer hard drive, recording music with a microphone or dance choreography using a video camera, painting on a canvas, or writing musical notation on a sheet of paper all create fixed expression eligible for copyright protection. An improvised jazz solo or extemporaneous speech is not eligible for copyright protection unless the solo or speech is recorded or written down in some fashion. The primary purpose behind the fixation requirement is that copyright protection is supposed to benefit society by making more expression available to the public. If the expression is not fixed in some tangible medium it cannot be retrieved for later use by society.

By international treaty, there are no formal requirements necessary for copyright protection. A work is copyrighted from the moment it is fixed in a tangible medium, regardless of whether the work contains a copyright notice or has been registered with the U.S. Copyright Office. When the first U.S. copyright statute was passed in 1790, copyright lasted for fourteen years with an option to renew the copyright for an additional fourteen years. Congress has repeatedly revisited and extended the duration of copyright. The most recent extension took place in 1998. Copyright in new works now lasts for the life of the author plus an additional seventy years. If there are multiple authors, the seventy years begins when the last author dies. For works created by a corporation, copyright lasts for ninety-five years from first publication, since a corporation might never "die" or cease to exist. Corporations often purchase copyrights from individuals. In those cases, the copyright duration is still tied to the life of the original creators.

Bundle of Rights

The copyright owner is granted a bundle of rights, each of which can be exercised or sold separately. These include the right of reproduction, distribution, public performance, public display, and the creation of derivative works.

Traditionally, the primary focus of copyright has been the reproduction right. No one may reproduce the copyrighted work without the copyright owner's authorization. Reproduction includes making exact copies, such as photocopying or reprinting text, making a copy of a DVD, videotape, or phonorecord, taking a photograph of a painting, or making a copy of a digital file. One does not need to reproduce the entire work before it is considered copyright infringement. Direct copying even of a small portion of the work is sometimes infringing. Nor does the copying have to be exact. Reproduction also includes creating any expression that is substantially similar to the copyrighted work. For example, composing a song that is substantially similar to a copyrighted song or writing a novel that is substantially similar to a copyrighted novel would also violate the owner's copyright even if there are no direct quotes.

The distribution right gives the copyright owner control over how the work is disseminated and made available to the public. For example, placing a file on a website and allowing others to download copies of the file may infringe the distribution right. Similarly, distributing unauthorized copies (such as bootleg records or DVDs) is also a violation of the distribution right. One caveat to the distribution right is the first-sale doctrine. Once a physical copy of a work, such as a book, painting, or DVD, is sold, the copyright owner has no further control over that physical object. The owner of a book or DVD can give away, sell, or destroy the individual copy in her possession, though she cannot make additional copies or publicly perform the work without authorization.

The public performance and public display rights govern uses of a work that do not necessarily involve making a physical copy (which would implicate the reproduction right). Copyright holders have control over public performances or displays of their works, regardless of whether those performances or displays are made for a profit. For example, a theater or acting troupe that intends to publicly perform a play must get authorization from the playwright, even if the performance is nonprofit and no admission fee is charged. A restaurant, bar, or store that plays music (live or recorded) must obtain authorization for all of the copyrighted songs that are played. Radio and television stations, movie theaters, and Internet sites also must get authorization before performing any copyrighted songs, movies, television shows, etc. Even a public recital of a poem

at a bookstore would be considered a public performance of that poem. Note that the public performance right does not extend to private performances, such as playing a song or movie in one's home. The public display right extends the same principle to works without a performance component. For example, a painting or poster visible in the background of a movie or television program is a public display. Placing a copyrighted photograph, drawing, poem, or song lyrics on your website would also constitute a public display (as well as a reproduction).

Perhaps the most complicated right granted to copyright owners is the right to make derivative works. A derivative work is a work based on one or more preexisting works. The author of the derivative work needs permission to use the preexisting works. In addition, the copyright in the derivative work only extends to the original expression that is new to the derivative work. For example, a movie based on a novel or play is a derivative work. If the movie uses the exact same dialogue as the preexisting play, the movie cannot copyright the dialogue. However, the movie can copyright the sound recording of the dialogue being spoken as well as all of the visual images, set decorations, and costumes created for the movie. Sequels, translations, abridgements, and musical arrangements are all common types of derivative works.

Special Case of Sound Recordings

Sound recordings occupy a special place under copyright law. Most sound recordings consist of songs, also known as musical compositions. The underlying song or musical composition is already protected by copyright, which means a sound recording of a song being performed is a derivative work. So every sound recording of a song consists of two separate copyrighted works: (1) the song and (2) the sound recording of the song being performed. In the late 1800s, companies developed player pianos and other mechanical devices that could "perform" a song without a musician present. A perforated paper roll was inserted into the piano and, as it turned, it would cause the piano keys to strike the appropriate notes for the song. Congress, concerned that songwriters would enter into an exclusive arrangement giving one company monopoly control over this industry, amended the copyright law to say that once a "mechanical" copy of a song was publicly released, any other company could release its own mechanical version, as long as the songwriter was paid a statutorily fixed rate for the resulting mechanical reproduction (the piano roll). As recording technology developed in the twentieth century, sound recordings replaced piano rolls but the compulsory mechanical license remained in place. What this means in practical terms is that once a sound recording of a song is released, any other musician or band can record their own "cover" version of the song. No permission from the copyright owner is required as long as no substantial changes are made to the lyrics or melody and the statutory royalties are paid to the copyright owner for each copy of the recording that is distributed. Note that the musician who records the cover version owns the copyright to that sound recording but not the underlying musical composition. This mechanical listening scheme makes it very easy for individuals

to record new versions of existing songs, since they do not need to negotiate permission from the copyright owner of the song. There are hundreds of different sound recordings of many songs, whereas it is rare to see a new version of an existing movie and one almost never sees a new "cover" version of an existing novel. This is because the mechanical license applies only to songs and not other types of expression.

Sound recordings are given a limited public performance right compared to other types of copyrighted works. As discussed previously, any radio station, restaurant, website, arena, or other business that plays music must get permission from the songwriter of any song that is performed, whether the song is performed live or a sound recording of the song is played. But only Internet sites and cable and satellite radio stations must get permission to perform a sound recording. A local bar, restaurant, or other business does not need permission to play a sound recording. If a bar plays CDs or MP3s to provide music for its patrons, the bar must pay a licensing fee for all the songs it plays, but it does not have to pay for any of the sound recordings that it uses. So while songwriters earn performance royalties anytime their songs are performed, musicians only earn performance royalties for their sound recordings in limited circumstances. This anomaly occurred because, in the first part of the twentieth century, the radio industry convinced Congress that radio performances of sound recordings helped promote record sales, so there was no need to give record companies or musicians additional compensation. In the 1990s, as the popularity of Internet radio and illegal file sharing began to reduce record sales, the record industry convinced Congress to create a public performance right for digital sound recordings to help replace the lost revenue. Traditional radio stations lobbied for an exemption, so the public performance right for digital sound recordings only applies to Internet, cable, and satellite radio.

Fair Use and Limits on Copyright

The two most important limitations on copyright are the idea/expression dichotomy and fair use. Each limitation is designed to ensure that copyright contributes to public welfare and does not limit free speech. The idea/expression dichotomy highlights that copyright only protects expression, not the ideas, facts, or discoveries that are being expressed. That anyone can freely use any idea helps ensure the advancement of knowledge and access to information. In the rare situations where protecting expression would also protect the idea being expressed, courts reject copyright protection to ensure the idea remains freely available.

Fair use is a defense to copyright infringement that allows individuals to copy or use portions of a copyrighted work without permission in certain circumstances, such as research, criticism, news reporting, and commentary. Courts examine the purpose of the use, the type of work being copied, how much of the original copyrighted work is used, and the possible impact on the market for the original work to determine whether a use is fair. Quoting from a book in a book review or research paper is likely a fair use. Including a scene from a movie in a film analysis would also be a fair use. The Supreme Court has begun to focus on how transformative a use is when determining fair use. The more the copied expression is transformed (through parody, juxtaposition, or other techniques), the more likely the use will be considered fair. This is because a transformative work is less likely to serve as a substitute for the original work and therefore poses less of a threat to the market for the original work.

Fair use is an expansive concept and has been used to permit a wide variety of uses. For example, home recording of television programs for the purpose of "time-shifting," reproducing photographs in search results for images, creating a parody of a song, and publishing e-mail messages related to security flaws in voting machines have all been considered fair uses. On the other hand, downloading a song for personal use, printing the most important excerpts from a book in a magazine article before the book has been published, and using a painting of a chair as the model for a film set were found to be infringing uses rather than fair uses. So while fair use serves as an important "safety valve" to protect free speech interests, it is highly unpredictable and is decided on a case-by-case basis.

International Copyright Treaties

Though the focus of this chapter is U.S. law, copyright is a key legal aspect of international trade. In recent decades, intellectual property has become one of the largest economic exports for the United States and other developed countries. Copyrighted goods in the form of books, movies, music, art, software, and other products are easily transported across international borders. Broadcasting and the Internet have significantly increased the international flow of copyrighted products and made them more difficult to inspect or control at the border.

Each nation has its own copyright law that is enforced within its borders. Most nations are signatories to one or more international treaties that set out minimum standards of copyright protection for domestic and foreign works. The most important of these treaties is the Berne Convention, first established in 1886 and amended six times since then. Before the Berne Convention, most nations did not grant copyright protection to foreign works or foreign authors unless agreed to by a bilateral treaty.

The Berne Convention is founded on three fundamental principles. First is the principle of national treatment: foreign works should be granted the same protection as domestic works. Second, there should be no formal requirements before obtaining protection; that is, the work should be protected from the moment it is created. Third, an eligible work should be protected even if it is not protected in its country of origin. As an indication of the increasing importance of copyrighted works in international trade, the number of countries that belong to the Berne Convention has grown from 58 in 1970 to 167 in 2013.

In addition to the Berne Convention, the other major copyright treaties include the Agreement on Trade-Related Aspects of Intellectual Property Rights (TRIPS Agreement) and the World Intellectual Property Organization's (WIPO) Copyright Treaty and Performances and Phonograms Treaty. The TRIPS Agreement was negotiated along with the establishment of the World Trade Organization (WTO). Under TRIPS, all WTO member states must adhere to the three basic principles of the Berne Convention even if they are not members of that convention. TRIPS was also significant for adopting WTO enforcement measures, which are seen as having much more force than the enforcement measures included in the Berne Convention. The two WIPO copyright treaties were created in 1996 in response to the proliferation of digital communication technologies. The WIPO Copyright Treaty expands protection for computer programs and databases as well as establishing a "right of communication to the public" that essentially grants the copyright owner the right to control how her work is made available over communications networks, including the Internet. The WIPO Performances and Phonograms Treaty grants musicians, performers, and the copyright owners of sound recordings certain rights related to the reproduction or performance of those sound recordings. More than ninety countries are signatories to each of the WIPO treaties.

Origins of Copyright

Though copyright is entrenched in modern legal systems, it is a law of relatively recent origin. For most of human history, anyone could copy someone else's expression without asking for permission. When the printing press was introduced to western Europe in the fifteenth century, some city-states granted special "printing privileges" to encourage the development of this new technology. Printers were given exclusive rights to print certain books in a given territory. This encouraged printers to invest in developing their fonts and presses, which required substantial capital. Printing privileges also gave government and religious authorities leverage in enforcing censorship against heretical and seditious books. By the eighteenth century, many printers wielded monopoly power within a territory. For example, the Stationers' Company in London was an extremely powerful guild that controlled the publishing industry in England. In 1710, England passed a copyright statute to break the printers' monopoly. For the first time, rights were specifically granted to the author rather than the printer. As more nations passed their own copyright laws, two rationales emerged to shape those laws: economic incentives and moral rights.

Economic Rationale

The economic rationale for copyright law is based on two related concepts, "public goods" and "economies of scale." A public good is an economic term referring to situations where a resource can be consumed without depleting the resource and it is difficult to exclude individuals who do not pay for the use. For example, an unlimited number of individuals can sing or listen to a song without "using it up." Moreover, it is very difficult to exclude nonpayers from listening to the song. Once one individual learns a song, she can teach it to countless others. Few investors would be willing to invest in a product where there is no mechanism for recouping the investment and where it is easy for consumers to use the product or service without paying. Copyright law creates a legal right to exclude nonpayers in hopes of encouraging investment in the production of new expression.

Economies of scale create a similar problem. Economies of scale occur when the average cost per unit to produce a product declines as the number of units produced increases. This often occurs when the fixed cost to produce a product is larger than the marginal cost to produce an additional unit. As production increases, the large fixed cost is spread out over more units. As communication technology has advanced, the cost to reproduce and distribute additional units of content (marginal cost) has declined dramatically. Yet the cost to create the expression in the first place (fixed cost) can still be quite high. For example, some movies cost more than $200 million to create (fixed cost), but a DVD copy of the movie can be made for less than one dollar (marginal cost). Without copyright protection, a competitor could purchase a DVD and then make and sell copies far more cheaply than the producer who had to spend $200 million to make the original film.

The economic purpose of copyright is designed to give the creator an incentive to invest time and money in producing the expression. Copyright creates a market for content and is the legal foundation of modern mass media, including the film, music, television, book publishing, computer software, and video game industries. Ultimately, society benefits because more works are produced. However, economists acknowledge that there is a trade-off in that while more works are created, those works are also more expensive than they would be without copyright, which limits society's access. Theoretically, if additional copies of a work can be created and distributed for free, it would be socially optimal to distribute copies to all individuals. But if copies are given away for free, where will the funding come from to produce the content in the first place?

In recent years, alternatives to the market-based copyright system have been introduced. Open-source software is written by individuals contributing to a project without claiming copyright. Wikipedia is another example of a large project where all of the expression is contributed for free. Nonprofit organizations like Creative Commons have established copyright licenses and websites to encourage creators to share their expression with very few restrictions, creating a regime for individuals to share their content freely.

Moral Rationale

In addition to the economic rationale for copyright, many nations' laws are influenced by the concept of moral rights. From this perspective, an author's expression is an extension of her personality and therefore very personal to her. Moreover, the author invests time and labor in creating the expression. Many argue that the author therefore has a natural right to control how her expression is used. So while the economic rationale for copyright is based on the public policy objective of encouraging creation for the benefit of society, the moral rationale is based on the author's private right to control her expression.

Moral rights include the rights of paternity (attribution) and integrity (the right to prevent mutilation or distortion of the work that would harm the author's reputation). Moral rights are incorporated into the Berne Convention for the Protection of Literary and Artistic Works, but nations can use other "equivalent" rights to comply with the moral rights provisions. For example, the United States does not include moral rights in its copyright statute (except for works of fine art). U.S. copyright law is based solely on the economic rationale. However, other laws, such as trademark and defamation, can at times be used to protect the paternity and integrity of the work.

Digital Millennium Copyright Act

In 1998, Congress passed the Digital Millennium Copyright Act (DMCA) to address Internet Service Provider (ISP) liability issues and strengthen enforcement of technological protection measures, discussed below. Copyright owners had argued that an ISP should be liable for copyright infringement whenever infringing content is stored on the ISP's servers, even if the content was uploaded by a third party. ISPs countered that it would be impossible to police all of the content that users upload and that imposing liability on ISPs would chill free speech by forcing them to limit the ability of users to post their own content. Congress wrote a "notice and takedown" compromise into the DMCA that immunized ISPs from copyright liability as long as ISPs quickly blocked access to infringing content upon notification of infringing activity. The law is considered very controversial since it makes it easy for copyright owners to claim an infringement has occurred without having to prove infringement in court. Once a copyright owner notifies an ISP of an alleged infringement, the ISP must block access to that content expeditiously in order to retain its immunity from liability.

Pro

As discussed earlier, the primary justification for copyright in the United States is utilitarian. Expression (movies, songs, books, video games, computer software, etc.) can be extremely expensive to produce. A writer, painter, sculptor, computer programmer, musician, or cinematographer may require years of specialized training and practice at considerable expense to perfect her craft. Expensive equipment may also be required. In addition, some works, such as motion pictures, can require the collaboration of hundreds of other individuals. While the cost to produce a copyrighted work can run into hundreds of millions of dollars, the resulting work can often be copied and distributed at almost zero cost, especially when taking advantage of digital technology and Internet distribution. If competitors and consumers are allowed to freely copy the work, the price for the work will quickly drop toward zero and the original creator will not be able to recoup her investment in creating the work. This situation will dissuade creators and investors from investing time and money to create new works.

Copyright gives the creator or copyright owner a legal right to exclude others from the market, increasing the likelihood that the creator will be able to recoup her investment. Copyright leads to an increase in the number of works produced, and the assumption is that society benefits from the wider choice of works. Without copyright, fewer works would be produced, especially works that are very expensive to make, such as motion pictures and computer software. As technology makes reproduction and distribution cheaper than before, infringing activity increases and the need for copyright grows stronger.

Critics of copyright often point to the most popular works that make inordinate profits far above the initial cost to create the expression. However, most markets for expression are extremely risky. Most works, whether books, songs, movies, software, etc., never make back the initial investment required for their creation. Thus, the extraordinary profits generated by the most successful works help to cover the losses due to works that do not succeed. For example, a record label may fund the recording of one hundred different albums. The one or two albums that make a huge profit help to fund the ninety-eight albums that lose money. Without copyright to provide those profits, far fewer albums would be recorded and consumers would be left with fewer choices.

Copyright also influences the types of works that are produced. Without copyright, most works would either need to be produced very cheaply or need to recoup their cost very quickly before competitors offer the same work at a lower price. Works that require a large investment or need a long time to recoup their costs would be more difficult to produce without copyright.

Another advantage of copyright is its economic impact. Copyright helps support multibillion-dollar industries such as computer software, video games, movies, music, television, and publishing. According to some estimates, the core copyright industries generate almost $1 trillion of GDP in the United States and close to $150 billion of U.S. exports.

The development of global digital networks has radically lowered the cost to copy and distribute copyrighted content. This has exacerbated the problem of both commercial copyright infringement and private sharing of content. Individuals can easily find and download a limitless supply of content online. Copyright owners argue that these technological changes necessitate stricter copyright laws and the adoption of technological protection measures in order to ensure that creators will still have an incentive to create new works.

Philosophically, other benefits of copyright include individual autonomy and enhanced democracy. Copyright gives a creator some control over how her expression is used. To the extent that expression embodies the personality and beliefs of the author, some commentators feel the author has a moral and ethical right to control her work. From a political-economy standpoint, copyright grants initial ownership over the content to the original creator, which potentially gives the creator more leverage when negotiating with the large corporate entities that market and distribute most works.

Commentators have also noted that copyright helps diversify the selection of works available to the public. Copyright facilitates a private marketplace where creators can choose to produce any content they wish and seek out consumers who may be interested. Without copyright, producers would be more dependent on other sources of funding, such as governments, nonprofit groups, and rich patrons. These groups likely would only fund the creation of expression that supports their specific viewpoints. For example, the government is not likely to fund content that is critical of how the government operates. Religious groups would not fund content that opposes their religious views, and so on. Copyright provides a framework for creators to market their works directly to the public, which leads to less interference regarding what type of expression is produced. In addition, democracy requires a free and independent press that can serve as a "watchdog" on government and private abuse of power. Copyright provides an important funding mechanism for the press and helps ensure independence from government and corporate interests.

Con

Some economists are skeptical of the necessity of copyright and believe its economic benefits are overstated. Copyright has only existed for about three centuries, yet countless expressive works were created before that time. Humans seem to have a strong innate desire to create, which does not require an economic incentive. There are plenty of examples of books, songs, art, movies, even computer software that were created without the economic incentive that copyright provides. Moreover, as the cost to create and distribute content declines, the justification for copyright becomes weaker. If it takes less money to produce the work, there is less need for copyright protection.

The losses due to copyright infringement are overstated. Unlike the theft of physical goods, illegally downloading a song or movie file does not create a replacement cost for the manufacturer. The only economic loss is the loss of revenue due to fewer sales. However, many individuals who download a file would not have purchased the file otherwise. For example, assume one hundred individuals illegally download a song that normally costs one dollar to purchase. The distributor has not incurred any direct cost since no physical items have been removed. The distributor appears to have lost $100 of potential revenue. But if only forty of the individuals would have been willing to pay for the file in the first place, the distributor has actually lost $40 of revenue rather than $100. The other sixty individuals were not willing to pay for the file, so even if copyright infringement were eliminated, the distributor would not generate any revenue from those individuals. So while copyright owners do suffer real losses due to infringement, not every infringing act is a loss and the overall losses due to infringement are greatly exaggerated.

Copyright imposes a social cost that some commentators feel outweighs the social benefit. The social benefit, as discussed earlier, is an increase in the number of works that are produced. However, copyright also imposes a cost on both readers and future authors. Without copyright, the cost of most works would drop toward zero, since that is the cost to create an additional copy. Whatever price the copyright holder charges above zero will exclude some portion of the public that cannot pay. This leads to a social welfare loss, since it would cost society nothing to give those individuals access to the work. Thus, copyright provides an incentive for new works to be created but also artificially raises the price of those works, limiting the number of individuals who get to enjoy them. In addition, future creators typically must consume preexisting works for inspiration and ideas for their own expression. The cost to access the preexisting works increases the total cost to create the new work. For example, an author may need to acquire and read a dozen books while conducting research for her own book. Copyright makes those books more expensive than they would be otherwise. The cost to acquire those books is an expense related to the creation of the new book, ultimately raising the price of the new book as well.

Critics claim that copyright is not necessary even for large-scale works. The success of open-source software such as Linux and collaborative websites such as Wikipedia are two examples where thousands of individuals donate their time and expertise to collaborate on creating content while explicitly rejecting copyright in the resulting work. Creative Commons is a set of licensing standards that many creators are adopting to allow others to freely use their expression. These examples, as well as the countless blogs, forums, YouTube videos, and websites that are created without any attempt at monetization or copyright enforcement demonstrate that copyright is not necessary for creativity to flourish.

Some commentators argue that copyright is inherently exploitative and primarily benefits large corporations rather than individual creators. The copyright industries, including publishing, music, film, and computer software, are dominated by an oligopoly of large corporations that control promotion and distribution. Songwriters, authors, and other creators typically depend on these companies for any chance of commercial success. A new author has no negotiating leverage and must typically sell or assign her copyright to the company in exchange for promotional and distribution opportunities. Recent adjustments to copyright law have assisted these companies in maintaining the power and control they developed in the pre-digital era. Copyright is simply one more example of regulation that favors incumbent corporate interests.

Critics also charge that copyright threatens access to knowledge and information. The widespread adoption of technological measures that "lock" access to copyrighted works restricts the ability of individuals to access and use the information contained in those works. Moreover, these technological locks can prevent legitimate fair uses of the work and continue to block access long after the copyright has expired and the work has entered the public domain.

Another criticism of copyright is its deleterious effect on free speech. The Supreme Court has long recognized that copyright can come into conflict with free speech when individuals are enjoined from using certain expression. Individuals quote from cultural texts for the purpose of comment, criticism, and rhetorical effect. Cultural texts also are signifiers within a culture and can impart a variety of meanings depending on how they are used. For example, using a sentimental patriotic song in a video montage of gruesome war carnage creates a very distinct and thought-provoking juxtaposition. When copyright owners are able to prevent such uses, it potentially limits the marketplace of ideas. Fair use is supposed to allow for this type of copying, but the outcome of any given fair use case is unpredictable and new technological measures can prevent any fair use from taking place.

A similar critique involves empowerment of audiences. Cultural texts such as movies, books, songs, and video games can be interpreted in a variety of ways but often have a "preferred" meaning that the author intends to communicate. Popular texts often support the ideology of the ruling class. When audiences are able to create and communicate resistant and oppositional readings, it acts as a form of empowerment, giving individuals the ability to develop and articulate their own counter-narratives. One popular example of this phenomenon is the fan fiction that developed around the television series *Star Trek*. Many individuals have written and posted their own scripts for alternative episodes of the series, some of which explore homosexual relationships among the characters. Thus, a series that features stereotypical displays of masculinity is subverted in ways that champion gender and sexual orientation diversity. Fan fiction, "mash-ups" that blend multiple songs, and other forms of sampling are all examples of audience empowerment that are threatened by strict enforcement of copyright. These new art forms allow individuals to create new artistic works out of existing works.

Looking to the Future

Copyright law has changed dramatically as new technologies are invented to create, store, and distribute copyrighted expression. Expression contained in a digital file can be copied endlessly and effortlessly, increasing the disparity between the cost to create content and the cost to copy and distribute that content. This extreme form of economies of scale makes it even more difficult for the creator to recoup her costs without some form of legal protection. The proliferation of consumer recording equipment makes it almost impossible for the copyright owner to prevent infringing copies from being made. The Internet makes this problem even greater. Once a copy is made available online, millions of users can copy the content and distribute it globally. One example of this phenomenon was the proliferation of peer-to-peer (P2P) software between 1999 and 2005, when Napster became synonymous with illegal file sharing. Billions of infringing copies of MP3 music files have been made and distributed using P2P software. In a series of legal cases in the United States and elsewhere, a number of P2P software distributors were found liable for contributing to copyright infringement. However, the basic technology of P2P networking remains legal.

Congress continues to propose new laws that would strengthen copyright enforcement and put more pressure on ISPs and other intermediaries to police infringing activity. In 2011, Congress proposed the Stop Online Piracy Act (SOPA), which would have barred advertisers and payment providers from working with websites that host infringing content. The law also would have required search engines to stop providing links to infringing content and ISPs to block access to those websites. While the bill was strongly supported by the copyright industries, First Amendment advocates and a variety of Internet companies protested vociferously that the law would violate the First Amendment, chill free speech, and expose ISPs and other Internet companies to liability. Public pressure, including widespread Internet boycotts, ultimately killed the bill before it could become law.

Another controversy revolves around Google's Library Project, which seeks to scan and index millions of existing works to create a massive, searchable, full-text online library of all published books. While the copyright for many of these books has expired, thousands of others are still protected by copyright. Google has tried to negotiate a settlement with authors' groups to compensate them for reproducing their books, but no final agreement has yet been reached.

Technological Protection Measures

To reduce the economic losses associated with piracy and counterfeit goods, the content industries have lobbied for stricter domestic and international laws that would grant copyright owners and law enforcement agencies more power to investigate infringing activity and increase the penalties for infringement. Moreover, copyright owners have begun to use technological protection measures (TPMs) to prevent users from accessing or copying and distributing content without authorization. The WIPO treaties discussed above mandate that each member country pass legal protection for TPMs to prevent users from circumventing the protection measures. The DMCA, passed by Congress in 1998, prohibits individuals from circumventing any access or copying restrictions that copyright owners insert into their content.

TPMs (commonly referred to as "digital rights management," or DRM, in the United States) are controversial because they utilize encryption technology to prohibit all copying even though the copyright statute allows copying in certain circumstances. For example, copying short passages from a book or movie for a review is a permissible fair use. The reviewer may be legally entitled to copy the passage but physically prevented from doing so by a TPM. In addition, TPMs continue to prohibit access or copying even after the copyright has expired and the expression has fallen into the public domain. The increasing use of TPMs to control access to content has reawakened concerns about the tension between copyright and free speech. But copyright owners argue that the Internet and digital reproduction have made copyright enforcement through traditional legal means much less effective, forcing them to rely on technological measures instead. Copyright owners also

use digital watermarks to trace the origin of infringing works. How TPMs are implemented and regulated is one of the most contentious issues facing regulators.

First-Sale Doctrine

Beginning in the early 2000s, there has been a rapid transition from using physical containers for storing expression to using digital files stored on a hard drive or the Internet via cloud computing. Where individuals used to own physical books, vinyl records, CDs, videotapes, and DVDs, today many individuals purchase digital files stored on an e-book reader, MP3 player, or iTunes account. This has led to an erosion of the first-sale doctrine discussed earlier. An individual is allowed to sell used books, CDs, DVDs, etc. But an individual is not allowed to sell a "used" MP3, e-book, or movie file. As consumers purchase digital files rather than tangible objects, the ability to legally lend, sell, or give away the content is eliminated. Copyright owners now license access to their work rather than selling copies. Some commentators are concerned that this will lead to a "pay per use" society where an individual will need to pay a fee every time she wants to read a passage from a book, listen to a song, or use a software program.

International Harmonization

New technologies such as satellite broadcasting and the Internet also have led to more content crossing national borders. This has increased the trend toward harmonization of domestic laws.

Copyright owners fear that if copying is legal in one jurisdiction, users all over the world will be able to access that content via the Internet. Some commentators argue that each nation should be free to forge its own copyright law in response to its own domestic information policy objectives. Developing nations in particular often argue that they need increased access to content to stimulate their own domestic economies. Economists have noted that weak copyright laws can benefit developing countries that must import intellectual property. This allows for low-cost knowledge transfer. Countries often strengthen their copyright laws once their domestic content industries begin to grow.

Ironically, in the 1800s, the United States had very lax copyright laws that allowed foreign works to be copied freely. Charles Dickens complained that his stories were pirated legally in the United States, depriving him of income. Mark Twain also complained that lack of copyright protection for foreign (British) works made those works cheaper, attracting customers who would have otherwise purchased books by American authors. Once the United States transitioned from a net copyright importer to a copyright exporter, Congress strengthened copyright protection for domestic and foreign works. The United States also began to advocate for tougher international copyright standards. However, not all cultures view copyright in the same way. Scholars have noted that many cultures are more communal and view sharing in a more positive light. These societies often resist the adoption of strong copyright protection. It is clear that the conflict over harmonization, like the tension over

technological protection measures, will increase for the foreseeable future.

Conclusion

Copyright is a legal concept that gives authors and creators control over how their expression—but not their ideas—are used. Expression can be costly to create but very cheap to copy and distribute. Copyright provides an incentive for more works to be created. Economists agree that copyright creates a trade-off; more works are produced, but access to those works is limited to those who can afford to pay. Fair use and other limitations are designed to ensure that copyright law does not impede free speech and access to knowledge.

Proponents note that copyright is the engine of the modern information economy, generating important economic benefits. The copyright industries make a significant contribution to the GDP and the nation's exports. Critics argue that copyright prevents individuals from critiquing and co-opting the cultural texts that dominate the cultural landscape. These critics believe the Internet and new digital technologies can empower individuals to take a more active role in shaping culture, which is a form of political power. They believe that strict copyright enforcement is harmful to democracy.

As society transitions to an information age characterized by digital content and ubiquitous Internet access, the political battles between copyright proponents and opponents will intensify. The focus is shifting from legal control over copying to technological control over access to digital works. At the same time there is increased pressure toward harmonization of copyright with ISPs and other intermediaries at the forefront of enforcement battles.

Matt Jackson
Penn State University

See also Google Books; International Influence on U.S. Copyright; Would Confucius Steal That Book—or E-Book—Today?

Further Reading

Bettig, Ron. *Copyrighting Culture*. Boulder, CO: Westview Press, 1996.

Gillespie, Tarleton. *Wired Shut: Copyright and the Shape of Digital Culture*. Cambridge, MA: MIT Press, 2007.

Goldstein, Paul. *Copyright's Highway: From Gutenberg to the Celestial Jukebox*. Rev. ed. Stanford, CA: Stanford University Press, 2003.

Goldstein, Paul. *International Copyright: Principles, Law, and Practice*. New York: Oxford University Press, 2001.

Gordon, Wendy. "A Property Right in Self-Expression: Equality and Individualism in the Natural Law of Intellectual Property." *Yale Law Journal* 102 (1993): 1533–1609.

Jackson, Matt. "The Digital Millennium Copyright Act of 1998: A Proposed Amendment to Accommodate Free Speech." *Communication Law and Policy* 5 (2000): 61–92.

Jackson, Matt. "Harmony or Discord? The Pressure toward Conformity in International Copyright." *IDEA: The Journal of Law and Technology* 43 (2003): 607–643.

Keller, Bruce P., and Jeffrey P. Cunard. *Copyright Law: A Practitioner's Guide*. New York: Practising Law Institute, 2012.

Landes, William M., and Richard A. Posner. "An Economic Analysis of Copyright Law." *Journal of Legal Studies* 18 (1989): 325–363.

Lessig, Lawrence. *Free Culture: The Nature and Future of Creativity*. New York: Penguin, 2004.

Lessig, Lawrence. *The Future of Ideas: The Fate of the Commons in a Connected World*. New York: Vintage Books, 2001.

Lessig, Lawrence. *Remix: Making Art and Commerce Thrive in the Hybrid Economy*. New York: Penguin, 2008.

Litman, Jessica. *Digital Copyright*. New York: Prometheus, 2001.

Netanel, Neil W. *Copyright's Paradox*. Oxford, UK: Oxford University Press, 2008.

Patterson, L. Roy. *Copyright in Historical Perspective*. Nashville, TN: Vanderbilt University Press, 1968.

Ricketson, Sam, and Jane C. Ginsburg. *International Copyright and Neighbouring Rights*. 2nd ed. New York: Oxford, 2005.

Vaidhyanathan, Siva. *Copyrights and Copywrongs: The Rise of Intellectual Property and How It Threatens Creativity*. New York: New York University Press, 2001.

41

INTERNATIONAL INFLUENCE ON UNITED STATES COPYRIGHT

There is, strictly speaking, no such thing as "international copyright." Since the granting—and the definition—of copyright is determined on a nation-by-nation basis, international copyright law exists only to the extent that individual nations have entered into treaties and other agreements on the issue and have modified their laws in accordance with these agreements.

Thus any examination of similarities and differences between American and international copyright law must examine not only the treaties and copyright agreements that the United States has entered regarding copyright, but also the characteristics and peculiarities of copyright in the United States and other nations.

There are even differences in the underlying understanding of the very nature of copyright. In civil law countries, such as France and its former dependencies, a creator's moral rights to control use of his or her creation—pure copyrights (*droits d'auteurs*)—are considered natural rights that are recognized by the state but not created by it. In these systems, rights created by the government, such as the rights of a publisher (as opposed to an author), are "neighboring rights" (*droits voisins*). But in common law countries, including the United States and Great Britain, ownership rights to a work are created by the government and exist only to the extent that they are granted by law. These two basic ideologies may lead to very different outcomes in otherwise similar situations. For example, under a "natural" system an ownership right exists from the moment of creation, while a policy-based system traditionally requires some formality, such as registration with the government, before copyright protection becomes effective.

As characterized by copyright attorney and writer William F. Patry and others, American copyright policy has undergone three phases. From the origins of the nation and the passage of the first federal copyright law in 1790, America remained isolated in copyright law, refusing to recognize any copyrights beyond its borders. This isolation lasted one hundred years. But as commercial interests became threatened by the growth of international trade in goods, including copyrighted material, the United States and other countries recognized a need for some coordination of their copyright schemes, which led to an era when nations—starting in Europe, but eventually including the United States—took a more international approach toward copyright. This began with European countries negotiating bilateral treaties regarding intellectual property issues, while still retaining their individual copyright regimes, and quickly evolved into a period of multilateralism with the adoption of the Berne Convention in 1886. But while the United States changed its law in 1891 to allow for bilateral copyright agreements with other nations, it waited one hundred years before joining the Berne agreement, finally doing so in 1989. Since then, international standards of copyright have become an integral component of U.S. copyright law, and an important element of international trade agreements.

Nature and Sources of Copyright Protection

Despite the modern incorporation of international norms into American law, U.S. copyright law remains premised on the idea that it is a right granted by the government, by virtue of Article I, Section 8 of the U.S. Constitution, and that its protection applies only in the United States. Professor Paul Goldstein points out that the territoriality of American copyright law is a choice made by Congress, and that the law could have, for example, applied to infringement occurring outside the United States, similar to federal laws regarding patents and bribery.

The nature and length of copyright protection in the United States is generally based on the specific copyright law in effect at the time of a work's creation. This principle applies both to works created in the United States and to those created abroad: a foreign work's eligibility for protection under American copyright law depends on the law that was in effect in the United States at the time of the work's creation, including the terms of any treaties that the United States was party to at that time. Because of the reciprocity provisions of international copyright treaties, foreign countries will usually give equivalent protection to U.S. works, again based on the law in force at the time of creation.

The scope of U.S. domestic copyright law has been expanded to one type of work created abroad, by providing protection under common law principles to unpublished works regardless of the citizenship or residency of the creator. For published works, however, U.S. law directly protects only works produced by American citizens and residents, or first published in the United States. The United States will also provide copyright protection to foreign works under the terms of the copyright treaties and agreements in force at the time that the work was created or published. The major treaties to which the United States is a party are the Mexico City Convention of 1902 (proclaimed effective in the United States in 1908, but mostly superseded); the Buenos Aires Convention of 1910 (effective July 13, 1914, partially superseded); the Universal Copyright Convention (effective September 16, 1955; 1971 revisions effective July 10, 1974; mostly superceded); the Geneva Phonograms Convention (formally, the

Convention for the Protection of Producers of Phonograms Against Unauthorized Duplication of Their Phonograms; effective March 10, 1974); the Brussels Satellite Convention (1974 Convention Relating to the Distribution of Programme-Carrying Signals Transmitted by Satellite; in force March 7, 1985); the Berne Convention (Berne Convention for the Protection of Literary and Artistic Works; last revised 1971; effective in the United States March 1, 1989); the TRIPs Agreement (Trade-Related Aspects of Intellectual Property Rights Agreement; in force April 15, 1994); the WIPO Copyright Treaty (World Intellectual Property Organization Copyright Treaty; effective March 6, 2002); and the WIPO Performances and Phonograms Treaty (effective May 20, 2002). The United States has also proclaimed or ratified additional, bilateral treaties with several dozen individual nations.

Origins of Copyright Law

Copyright law in the United States traces its roots to the licensing schemes for printers that originated in England in the early 1500s, as well as similar systems that emerged at the same time in Venice and France.

In 1566 Parliament created the Stationers' Guild, which was granted the exclusive right to authorize printers to publish books. But some began to question the perpetual rights created under this system, and in 1694 Parliament refused to extend the Stationers' Guild monopoly beyond its expiration in 1695. This left the publishing of books without any regulation for fourteen years, until passage of the Statute of Anne in 1709. This statute gave authors and printers of books existing on April 10, 1710, a twenty-one-year exclusive right to continue to publish their works. Authors and printers of new books received a fourteen-year exclusive grant, renewable for an additional fourteen-year term if the author was still alive. The courts eventually held, in cases such as *Millar v. Taylor* (1769) and *Donaldson v. Beckett* (1774), that an author's rights continued under the common law after the expiration of these terms.

The colonial governments in British North America followed the English system of granting exclusive printing licenses. After independence, the Articles of Confederation did not give the national government any power to legislate in the area. But a lobbying campaign by lexicographer Noah Webster led to a resolution by the Continental Congress asking the states to grant fourteen-year copyrights. Twelve of the thirteen original states—all but Delaware—responded by adopting their own copyright laws by 1786. Six of the states limited protection to U.S. citizens, while four offered protection only to state residents. Only two states—Maryland and South Carolina—offered any copyright protection to non-U.S. residents.

The constitutional framers saw the need for uniformity in copyright protection in the new nation and drafted in the Constitution a provision that "The Congress shall have Power . . . To promote the Progress of Science and useful Arts, by securing for limited Times to Authors and Inventors the exclusive Right to their respective Writings and Discoveries." This provision, which became Article I, Section 8 of the U.S.

Constitution, was adopted without any debate or revision.

The 1790 Copyright Act

Congress did not act on this power until the first federal copyright statute was adopted in 1790. Based on the Statute of Anne, the 1790 Copyright Act included several of the formalities of the English statute, including registration of the work at the local federal courthouse, publication of the registration record (a requirement removed in 1831), and deposit of a copy of the work with the government (initially with clerks of the federal courts, who turned them over to the secretary of state, then in 1846 the Smithsonian Institution and the Library of Congress, then in 1867 the Library of Congress alone). Failure to follow these formalities put a work in the public domain. But, unlike the Statute of Anne, the American law did not include the price controls on printed works that existed under the English law and in five of the colonial statutes.

The 1790 statute provided copyright protection for published works by residents of the United States, regardless of the author's citizenship or the nation in which the work was first published. This meant that foreign citizens who were residents of the United States could receive copyright protection for works published in the United States. But works by non-U.S. residents were protectable only if they were first published in the United States. In addition to limiting copyright on published works to those actually published in America, the United States also imposed high tariffs on imported books.

Unpublished works, however, were protected by common law, regardless of the residency of the author.

The limits on copyright for foreign-published works were justified by citing a need for inexpensive books in the new United States. But other nations took similar approaches at the time. In the United Kingdom the Statute of Anne did not allow copyright protection to nonresidents, although in *D'Almaine v. Boosey* (1835) the Court of Exchequer held that foreigners could assign their copyright to a British publisher, which could then enforce it. Three years later, in 1838, Parliament passed the International Copyright Act, allowing for such protection for authors from nations that agreed to reciprocity with Britain. Other nations based eligibility for protection of a work on the basis of whether the work was published within their nations, without a residency requirement.

Like the Statute of Anne on which it was based, the 1790 U.S. Copyright Act provided for a fourteen-year copyright term, which could be extended for an additional fourteen years if the author was still alive. If the author died during either term, the copyright died with him. Another similarity between the original U.S. copyright statute and the Statute of Anne was that both covered only printed works. As noted above, unpublished works by both American and foreign citizens received their protection in the United States from common law.

Nineteenth-Century Copyright

American publishing blossomed in the nineteenth century, fueled by increasing schooling and literacy and the adaptation of steam technology to run presses. The material was roughly equally American and British, although the British works were cheaper to produce because foreign authors had no rights under American copyright law and there was thus no need to pay royalties for foreign works. As a result, piracy of British copyrighted works was rampant in the United States in the 1800s, and tolerated by the American government. (Britain, meanwhile, took what steps it could to limit this piracy in its territory, including Canada.)

While the United States took no action on the international copyright issue, it did enact significant changes in American copyright law during this period.

The original 1790 Copyright Act required public notice of publication of a copyrighted work, and an 1802 law added the requirement that the notice of copyright be contained within or attached to the work itself. This requirement was strengthened in the first major revision of the copyright law in 1831, when a standard form for the copyright notice was introduced. The 1831 act did, however, remove the requirement that the registration record be published. At the time, such formalities were common among the nations of the world.

The 1831 act also extended the initial copyright term to twenty-eight years, renewable for fourteen additional years if the author or his widow or children were alive. This term was more in line with those of other countries. In 1814 the United Kingdom had extended its initial copyright term to twenty-eight years, and then for life if the author was still living. In France, the term lasted for life of the author plus fifty years, while in Russia it lasted for life of the author plus twenty years. In Germany, Norway, and Sweden, copyright protection never expired.

While the 1831 act brought U.S. copyright terms closer to the length of protection in other nations, this did not indicate any change in America's attitude toward foreign copyrights.

In the 1790 act, the ban on non-U.S. residents obtaining U.S. copyrights was implicit in the law's provision allowing for copyright for U.S. residents. The 1831 act made this prohibition on copyrights for non-U.S. residents explicit. Despite this, an industry practice of "courtesy of trade" arose in which American publishers sometimes paid highly popular British authors to republish their work, even though there was no way those foreign authors could have stopped American publishers from copying their foreign-copyrighted works.

The matter came to the attention of some members of Congress in 1836 with American publishers' opposition to a British publishing house's opening of a New York office. In response, a bill was proposed to grant copyrights to British and French authors as long as the work was published in the United States within a month of publication abroad. But efforts to pass such an international copyright bill faltered, in part because it was primarily pushed by non-Americans, such as by Charles Dickens during an American tour in 1842. Mild lobbying efforts by American publishers were also fruitless, and the issue received little attention until American authors began to press the need for a copyright enforcement system. Then, in 1853, British interests—perhaps, scholar Catherine Seville alleges, through bribery—persuaded U.S. secretary of state Daniel Webster to negotiate a treaty with Great Britain "for the Establishment of International Copyright." The treaty was signed by Webster's successor after his death, but was not ratified by the Senate in the face of intense opposition. Similar efforts for mutual copyright recognition between the United States and Britain were introduced in Congress, without any action, numerous times over the next thirty years. Even though a congressional committee recognized in 1868 that America's treatment of foreign works was an "antiquated and vicious policy," efforts to change the system could not overcome the inertia of the status quo.

During the Civil War, the Confederacy tried to use the failure of the United States to act on the rampant copying of foreign works as a diplomatic tool to gain international support for its cause. In March 1861 the Confederate Congress authorized Confederate States of America ministers soliciting support from European countries to also negotiate copyright treaties with those nations. Although no such agreements were made before the war ended, the Confederacy did enact a copyright statute that, although otherwise virtually identical to the Union act, granted copyright to all copyright holders of other nations who published their works in the Confederacy, as long as their home country extended the same courtesy to Confederate authors.

International Copyright Law Develops without the United States

While the United States was struggling over the question of allowing foreign authors to obtain American copyrights, European nations were beginning to negotiate bilateral international treaties for mutual recognition of copyrights, such as the 1851 treaty between Great Britain and France. In 1852 France went even further, by unilaterally granting foreign authors the same copyright protection they had in their own nation, regardless of whether the author's country reciprocated for French authors. The growth of international copyright treaties led to an international convention on copyright issues, held in Berne, Switzerland, in 1858. While the conference issued a number of reports, it was clear that it would be difficult to harmonize various nations' copyright schemes. Another conference held in Paris in 1878 called for international recognition of authors' rights, based on the French concept of natural law.

The nations continued meeting and at conferences in 1883 and 1885 crafted the Berne Convention for the Protection of Literary and Artistic Works. The United States was not represented at the first of these conferences and sent only an observer to the second. The treaty was signed at a third conference in 1886 by ten mainly European countries (Belgium, France, Germany, Great Britain, Haiti, Italy, Liberia, Spain, Switzerland, and Tunisia) and went into effect on December 5, 1887, after being ratified by all of the signatories except Liberia. The convention created an organization to administer the pact, which was renamed the World Intellectual Property Organization (WIPO) in 1967. With several subsequent revisions, most recently in 1971, and WIPO supplements and clarifications, this treaty—now with

167 members—has become a prime instrument governing international trade in copyrighted materials.

Unlike U.S. copyright law, the convention vested ownership in a work to its creator immediately upon creation. The treaty also provided for moral rights (the rights of authors to control reuse and modification of their work) and prohibited formalities for protection outside the country of origin (while allowing them for domestic protection, since at the time many nations imposed such formalities). The convention also provided for retroactive protection of works still protected by copyright in a nation when it joins the convention.

Works are covered by the convention if they are published by a citizen or domicile of a member nation, or if they are published first or simultaneously in a member state. (Architectural works must be physically located in a member country.) The 1948 and 1971 revisions allow a gap of up to thirty days for "simultaneous" publication. The treaty also requires more than mere publication for protection: a work must also be distributed in sufficient quantities to meet reasonably expected consumer demand for a work to be considered published.

The lack of participation by the United States was a major gap in the treaty's coverage. But America's isolationist attitudes regarding copyright, as well as the Berne Convention's limitations on formalities such as the American manufacturing clause, led the United States to remain outside of the treaty for almost a century. In 1914, a protocol was added to the convention to allow nations to withhold protection from U.S. authors in retaliation for America's failure to prevent copying of works copyrighted in Berne member countries.

U.S. Finally Offers Copyright Protection to Foreigners, but with a Caveat

Within the United States, there was growing concern in the late nineteenth century that America's failure to allow foreigners to obtain copyrights, which allowed rampant copying in the United States of works by foreign authors, in fact stifled the development of a native literature. This began with publishers voluntarily agreeing to pay royalties for some foreign copyrighted works. There was also a long lobbying effort that led the United States to finally recognize foreign copyrights in 1891.

The passage of the International Copyright Act of 1891, also known as the Chace Act, was the result of several years of lobbying and compromise by America's publishers, authors, and typographers. The act, which passed the Senate in the waning hours of the 51st Congress, extended the protections of America's copyright law to foreign authors who otherwise met the statutory requirements (including the formalities of American copyright), but only as long as their home nation provided protection on "substantially the same basis" to U.S. authors, or their home nation had a copyright agreement with the United States.

In either case, the Chace Act required that the material be typeset and printed in the United States. This provision, known as the manufacturing clause, had been included in international copyright bills as early as 1868, although it was opposed by foreign authors and publishers. Once enacted, the clause required that foreign authors, in order to obtain copyright protection in the United States, publish in America simultaneously with publication in their own country. This was an inconvenience for British and other English-language works, but more of a difficulty for foreign-language authors who needed to get their works translated.

Passage of the Chace Act led the United States to enter into reciprocal copyright treaties or agreements with thirteen countries by 1900, including France, Germany, and Great Britain.

Great Britain, concerned about the illicit—but not illegal, under American law—sale in Canada of books by British authors published without permission in the United States, acted quickly to certify that it provided protection on "substantially the same basis" to U.S. authors as it did to British domestic authors, including those in British colonies. This led President Benjamin Harrison to declare in July 1891 that Britain and the United States would offer copyright protection to each other's authors.

Although France and Germany were among the first nations to negotiate agreements after enactment of the Chace Act, their objections to the manufacturing clause led both these nations to threaten to withdraw from their copyright agreements with the United States. The result was a 1905 amendment to the Copyright Act that removed the manufacturing requirement for books published in foreign languages. But the requirement remained for English-language books—including those from Canada and the United Kingdom—and was broadened in the next major revision of the law, in 1909, to require not only typesetting and printing in the United States, but also binding. The 1909 act did give some leeway to translated works, allowing thirty days for a work to be manufactured in the United States after it was published abroad. But the new act also expanded the manufacturing provision to cover illustrations as well as texts. The 1909 act also reinforced the preexisting notice and deposit provisions, although the deposit requirement for foreign works was reduced from two copies to one in 1914.

In 1949, the window for registration and deposit of foreign works was extended from six days to six months, and the period to comply with the manufacturing clause was extended to five years. Subsequent amendments further eroded the manufacturing requirement by allowing printing and binding in Canada and by limiting it to "work consisting preponderantly of nondramatic literary material that is in the English language."

While the manufacturing clause was a significant obstacle for American copyright protection of foreign works, the United States did pass special, short-term copyright provisions for foreign exhibitors at international exhibitions held in the United States. Such provisions were passed for the Louisiana Purchase Exposition held in St. Louis in 1904; the Panama-Pacific Exposition of 1913; the 1933 Chicago World's Fair Centennial Celebration; the 1939 Golden Gate International Exposition; the 1939 New York World's Fair; and the 1940 Pacific Mercado International Exposition, held in Los Angeles.

The exigencies of war also led to relaxation of American copyright formalities. Legislation adopted in 1919 provided for retroactive protection of foreign works published during World War I. During World War II, a 1941 law allowed President Franklin D. Roosevelt to grant extensions for complying with the manufacturing clause during the conflict.

Growing International Focus in the Twentieth Century

As the United States pursued bilateral international agreements under the authority granted by the Chace Act, America also began entering into several of the multilateral copyright agreements that were burgeoning at the time. But it would take almost one hundred years for the United States to join the most inclusive of these agreements, the Berne Convention, because doing so required abandonment of the formalities required under American copyright law.

In 1902 the United States, Costa Rica, Guatemala, Honduras, Nicaragua, and El Salvador negotiated the Mexico City Convention of 1902, which became effective in 1906 but was not ratified by the United States until 1908. The United States did not, however, enact any legislation in accordance with its provisions, which creates some ambiguity regarding the effectiveness of this treaty that was apparently never tested in the courts.

In 1914, President Woodrow Wilson proclaimed U.S. cooperation in the 1910 Buenos Aires Convention on copyright issues with sixteen Latin and South American countries. While the language of this treaty removed the formalities of member states as long as the work contained a notice of reservation of property rights (such as the statement "all rights reserved"), U.S. law was not changed to reflect the treaty, leading the U.S. Copyright Office to reject such a notice as a substitute for the formal notice required under the American Copyright Act. While the Buenos Aires Convention technically remains in effect, it has been superseded by language of subsequent international treaties.

After World War II, the economic implications of the U.S. failure to join the Berne Convention became a major concern. Yet efforts to pass legislation for the United States to join the treaty continued to be fruitless. To deal with this ongoing dilemma, foreign authors would have their works published simultaneously in the United States to be eligible for American protection. And American authors would obtain Berne protection by publishing simultaneously in the United States and a Berne country, such as Canada or Great Britain.

In large part because of the United States' unwillingness to conform its laws with the Berne Convention, in 1952 a new treaty, the Universal Copyright Convention (UCC), was created under the auspices of the United Nations Educational, Scientific and Cultural Organization (UNESCO). It was signed by the United States and thirty-nine other countries, and has been ratified by eighty nations as of 2014. A major reason why the other nations signed this treaty was to get copyright protection for their authors in America, given the United States' unwillingness to join the Berne Convention.

The treaty was ratified by the Senate in 1954, finally bringing the United States into a truly international copyright regime. It became effective in the United States on September 16, 1955, providing protection in the United States to works published outside the United States after that date.

The UCC requires member nations to grant foreign authors the same copyright rights, and on the same terms, as domestic authors. This is known as providing national treatment. It was written to conform as much as possible to existing American law, particularly the notice requirement. Thus, while the UCC bans most formalities as a condition of copyright protection, it does provide that inclusion of a copyright notice—specified by the treaty and virtually identical to the notice required under the U.S. law—is necessary, but otherwise waives any copyright formalities that an individual nation may have.

The changes required in U.S. law for ratification of the treaty, adopted in 1954, were minor. Works from other UCC countries were now eligible for copyright in the United States, were exempt from the deposit requirement and, as long as the copyright notice prescribed by the UCC was affixed, also exempt from the manufacturing requirement. The result of this latter change was that English-language materials first published abroad now could be exempt from the manufacturing requirement, although American works were still subject to it.

A 1971 revision to the UCC allowed developing countries to grant broad rights for translation and reproduction of works for educational use. The United States accepted this language effective 1974, but it did not require any changes in domestic law.

The UCC provides that for members of both the UCC and the Berne Convention, the Berne provisions have priority. Thus, with the subsequent ratification of the Berne Convention by the United States, the UCC now applies in the United States only in regards to countries that are UCC members but are not Berne members. The only such country is Cambodia.

The United States Starts to Bend

Neither the UCC nor the Berne Convention requires member states to provide protection to sound recordings. But as new recording and distribution technologies such as audiotape and videotape became more popular, there was concern in some countries—particularly civil law jurisdictions that acknowledged "pure copyrights" (*droits d'auteurs*)—that authors and performers would lose control over their work. This led to the creation of the 1961 Rome Convention for the Protection of Performers, Producers of Phonograms, and Broadcasting Organizations, which expanded international copyright protection to sound recordings. While ninety-one nations ratified this treaty, the United States, where the performance right encapsulated in the treaty was a foreign concept, never signed or accepted the Rome Convention.

But the United States was more accepting of the 1971 Geneva Phonograms Convention, formally the Convention for the Protection of Producers of Phonograms against Unauthorized Duplication of Their Phonograms. Congress amended the U.S. copyright law to cover sound recordings in 1971 and ratified the Geneva Convention in 1973. Like U.S. law, the convention protects duplication rights, but it does not require member nations to recognize performance rights. The Geneva Convention waives national formalities for sound recordings as long as a recording includes a (P) notice with the date of first publication or information regarding the producer.

The next major revision of the Copyright Act, in 1976, made American law more compatible with some provisions of the Berne Convention by initiating copyright upon creation rather than registration, formally eliminating the registration requirement (while incentivizing it by making it a prerequisite to any infringement suit), and imposing a single copyright term of life of the author plus fifty years. This was the minimum copyright term required by the Berne Convention as revised in 1908, although the treaty allows individual nations to have longer terms. But the 1976 act also retained provisions that were not compliant with the Berne Convention, such as the notice and manufacturing requirements.

The manufacturing provision survived in the 1976 act even though both the House and Senate had passed versions of the bill eliminating that provision: the removal provision did not survive to final passage. In 1982, President Ronald Reagan vetoed a provision extending the manufacturing clause to 1986, but his veto was overridden by Congress. In 1986 the Second Circuit affirmed a district court's dismissal of a First Amendment challenge to the provision,

but a challenge of the provision by the European Economic Community resulted in a finding that the provision violated the international General Agreement on Tariffs and Trade (GATT). The resulting threats of retaliatory action against American tobacco and other products led to failure of an effort in 1985 to again extend the provision. Without the renewal, the manufacturing clause finally expired on July 1, 1986. Nevertheless, the legacy of the provision lives on: the manufacturing requirement still applies to works published between January 1, 1978, and June 30, 1986. And the statutory language of the manufacturing provision was not fully eliminated from the United States Code until 2010.

In 1974 the United States signed the Brussels Satellite Convention, formally the Convention Relating to the Distribution of Programme-Carrying Signals Transmitted by Satellite. But it took ten years for the United States to ratify this agreement, which is aimed at combating international copyright piracy. Member states are obliged to prevent unauthorized satellite distribution—but not reception—of television signals by an unauthorized party. Ratifying the convention did not require any changes in U.S. law.

There were also international copyright agreements during this period to which the United States is not a party. Only one country—Mexico—ratified the Inter-American Convention on the Rights of the Author in Literary, Scientific, and Artistic Works of 1946, which would have created a performance right in member countries. The United States neither signed nor ratified another treaty to create a performance right, the 1961 Rome Convention for the Protection of Performers, Producers of Phonograms, and Broadcasting Organizations. The 1979 Multilateral Convention for the Avoidance of Double Taxation of Copyright Royalties has been accepted by only eleven nations, and thus has not gone into force.

The United States Finally Joins the Berne Convention

The trend of American recognition and accommodation of international copyright reached its apex in the late 1980s, when Congress finally ratified the Berne Convention. While it took several decades for Congress to act, in the end there was general agreement that the failure of the United States to join in the Berne Convention was hurting its international trade efforts, including its efforts to combat international piracy of American works. The Senate formally ratified the treaty and made the necessary changes in U.S. law in 1988, effective March 1, 1989. Finally, the United States had joined the international community on copyright.

American adoption of the Berne Convention required the United States to eliminate its formalities for foreign authors to obtain protection in the United States, and to offer such authors protection equivalent to that offered to domestic authors. Other nations that are parties to the treaty must extend the same courtesies to American authors, although most countries outside the United States had already eliminated their formalities for copyright protection.

So as to not disadvantage U.S. authors, the Berne Implementation Act eliminated the formalities for both domestic and foreign authors. Congress also extended other provisions, such as making the seizure remedy (discussed below) available to domestic as well as foreign authors.

The changes included abolition of the mandatory notice requirement; elimination of registration as a prerequisite for an infringement suit for works from Berne nations other than the United States; replacement of the prior compulsory jukebox license with negotiated rates; elimination of the requirement that a transfer be recorded before initiation of an infringement case; and retroactive protection for foreign works that were still protected by copyright in their home countries but had entered the public domain in the United States due to failure to meet the formalities of prior U.S. copyright law.

Another incompatibility between the Berne Convention and U.S. law identified during the effort to pass the Berne Implementation Act was resolved in 1990, when American law was expanded to allow protection for architectural works.

A question also arose over the Berne Convention's recognition of moral rights. Although the concept was alien to American law, the Visual Artists Rights Act of 1990 took a step in this direction by creating limited moral rights to creators of visual arts works. A 1995 effort to extend these rights to film did not succeed. Later, the United States recognized a limited performance right (see below).

While the Berne Convention bars member countries from imposing formalities as a condition of copyright protection, it does not prohibit member nations from requiring formalities as a condition for certain remedies. Thus American copyright law still requires both domestic and foreign authors to register works in order to obtain statutory damages and attorney's fees. A bill to remove all formalities of copyright for U.S. domestic registrants passed the House twice in 1993, but it was not acted upon by the Senate.

The convention also requires that certain remedies be available for infringement. One of these remedies that the convention requires is the remedy of seizure, which may create a conflict with American law's severe limitations on prior restraints. As professors Mark A. Lemley and Eugene Volokh explain, while courts in copyright cases often invoke the U.S. Supreme Court's stringent, four-part test for prior restraints, as a practical matter they often grant injunctions to prevent alleged infringement on the grounds of imminent irreparable harm.

The late adoption of the Berne Convention by the United States can create some anomalies regarding protection in foreign countries for works published by U.S. authors, because of different effective dates of the Berne Convention and the UCC. David Nimmer, for example, explains that a work by a U.S. author published solely in the United States prior to September 27, 1957, while likely still under copyright in the United States for seventy years after the death of the author, is not eligible for copyright protection in the United Kingdom because the UCC did not go into effect in the United Kingdom until that date.

Copyright as a Subject of Trade Agreements

Five years before joining the Berne Convention, American copyright law became more accommodating of international norms by another route: international trade agreements. A 1984 law providing for duty-free treatment of imports to the United States from Caribbean countries required that these nations respect the copyrights of U.S. authors and was particularly focused on unauthorized rebroadcasts of American video content.

Similar provisions were added to the renewal process in 1984 for the General System of Preferences, which lowers trade barriers for underdeveloped nations, and in the International Trade and Investment Act adopted in the United States that year. The 1988 Omnibus Trade and Competitiveness Act declared protection of American intellectual property to be a priority in negotiating international trade agreements.

The 1994 North American Free Trade Agreement (NAFTA) provides that the member countries—the United States, Canada, and Mexico—may not impose "any formalities or conditions" on authors from the other member nations in order to acquire copyright protection. The agreement also required the United States to provide retroactive coverage to Canadian and Mexican films that had entered the public domain in the United States because of failure to affix copyright notices. This required a change in U.S. law, but the statutory addition went beyond films to also cover works, such as screenplays and musical compositions, that were first fixed as component parts of a film. NAFTA also requires prohibition of rentals of sound recordings and computer software without permission of the creator. The United States had already barred such rentals in 1984, but the provision was due to expire in 1989.

The Uruguay Round of the GATT Agreements, which went into effect on

January 1, 1995, reinforced and built upon the Berne standards through the inclusion—at the insistence of the United States, which was concerned about rampant infringement of American-originated copyrighted works—of the Agreement on Trade-Related Aspects of Intellectual Property Rights (TRIPs). Like the Berne Convention, TRIPs provides that, subject to some exceptions, copyright rights granted by a nation to nationals of another country must also be extended to all foreign copyright owners. But TRIPs goes further by introducing the concept of "most favored nation," which provides that a member nation must treat all foreign authors equally: a nation's domestic copyright law cannot offer privileges to authors of one nation, including domestic authors, that it does not offer to foreign authors from other nations (subject to some exceptions).

Some changes in U.S. law were necessary to comply with TRIPs. One of the most significant was the enactment of a limited performance right, which allowed performers to have a copyright in their live performances in order to prohibit unauthorized recordings. This was the first extension of American copyright law to cover unfixed works, and it represented an erosion of American copyright law's general requirement that a work be "fixed in a tangible medium of expression" in order to be copyrightable.

Thus the Uruguay Round Agreements Act, adopted in 1994, made permanent the interim prohibition on rentals of phonorecords and of computer programs. It also allowed the retroactive coverage that had been granted to Canadian and Mexican films for failure to affix copyright notice to now cover all works from all Berne and WTO nations, but only if the copyright had not expired in the originating country and the copyright holders filed with the Copyright Office during the calendar year 1994. Also, such restored copyrights would last only for the remainder of the originally applicable term. The act also provided protection for users of these works during the period when they were in the public domain, and corrections to the act in 1997 added protections for makers of derivative works.

TRIPs also requires bans on rentals of cinematographic works if such rental has led to widespread copying of such works. Arguing that such piracy of films is not rampant in the United States, America has not adopted such a ban.

But the push for more controls to combat piracy has continued. Thus a 1996 WIPO conference resulted in two new treaties meant to deal with the emergence of digital tools that allow perfect and easy reproduction of copyrighted works: the World Intellectual Property Organization Copyright Treaty and the WIPO Performances and Phonograms Treaty. The former grants copyright owners an exclusive right to communicate their works to the public, while the latter bars circumvention of technology to protect works from unauthorized copying.

The United States adopted both these treaties in April 2002, which required additional changes to U.S. law. These changes were included in the Digital Millennium Copyright Act (DMCA), passed in 1998 and effective in 2002. This statute broadened coverage of prior retroactive copyright provisions and gave American copyright protection to all non-U.S. works not in the public domain in their country of origin that were not protected in the United States because of formality errors. The WIPO Copyright and Performances and Phonograms Treaties Implementation Act of 1998, also effective in 2002, enacted provisions outlawing circumvention of copy-protection schemes and prohibited falsifying, altering, or removing copyright information in order to facilitate infringement.

Since the 1997 WIPO agreements, the U.S. Trade Representative has negotiated free trade agreements with several nations that include intellectual property provisions. In 2011 the United States was one of several nations that signed the Anti-Counterfeiting Trade Agreement, which would create an international enforcement mechanism for copyright infringement on the Internet, as well as for counterfeit goods and medicines. The United States has not ratified the treaty, and the European Parliament has rejected it. There is also some debate on whether the treaty would make substantive changes in U.S. law, and thus require congressional action beyond ratification.

The most recent international copyright treaty, the Treaty to Facilitate Access to Published Works by Visually Impaired Persons and Persons with Print Disabilities, was signed in June 2013 by 186 countries, including the United States. The treaty requires signatories to change their copyright laws to provide exceptions to make books more accessible to the blind and visually impaired by converting them into Braille books, audio recordings, or large-print books without requiring permission of the copyright holder.

Arguments for and against Internationalization of Copyright

Pro

By joining in these international copyright and trade agreements, and conforming its law to match international standards, the United States extends the protections of its copyrights beyond its borders and protects its exports of films, books, television programs, and other forms of intellectual property. According to the U.S. Chamber of Commerce, sales in this category totaled $1 trillion and represented approximately 74 percent of total U.S. exports in 2011.

Con

Critics have questioned the broad scope of these international trade agreements, expressing the fear that a treaty-created international body could hold some tenet of American copyright law or some copyright decision of the U.S. Supreme Court, in violation of one of these agreements. This has already happened over U.S. rules allowing royalty-free use of music by restaurants and stores (see below). With this concern in mind, the Uruguay Round Agreements Act allows the United States to withdraw from the treaty if the WTO "violate[s] U.S. sovereignty three times in five years."

Non-Conforming Copyright Concepts

Despite the general trend toward the internationalization of copyright, individual nations—including the United

States—still maintain some of their own idiosyncratic tenets of copyright law. As scholar Catherine Seville observed, "Local considerations of politics, economics, geography and law result in differences of approach which, once established, are difficult to reconcile."

Scope of Coverage. Both American and foreign law have moved beyond written texts to gradually expand the types of works that can be protected by copyright. But there are some differences. The European Union, for example, provides copyright protection for databases, while U.S. law does not allow copyright for collections of unoriginal data. Another difference involves sound recordings: while they have been eligible for American copyright since 1972, France does not protect sound recordings as part of the core natural rights of copyright in that nation.

Originality. Neither the UCC nor the Berne Convention explicitly require originality for a work to be copyrightable, as U.S. law does. But, as David Nimmer observes, such a requirement is "probably implicit" in both treaties.

Publication. As noted above, the Paris Act of the Berne Convention requires that a work be sufficiently available "to satisfy the reasonable requirements of the public" in order to be considered published for copyright purposes. In other words, it must be made sufficiently available to its potential audience, and a single copy would not constitute publication under this requirement. In the United States, however, one copy is sufficient to constitute publication.

Jointly Owned Copyrights. Countries such as Germany, the Netherlands, and the United Kingdom are stricter in granting a joint copyright than the United States, requiring that multiple authors' contributions be truly inseparable in order for a work to be protected as a joint work. Also, while the United States will allow an individual co-owner of a copyright to grant a nonexclusive license to a work, as long as the proceeds are shared with the other copyright holder(s), many other countries require permission of all co-owners for any licensing arrangement.

Length of Copyright. Most nations provide protection for the life of the author plus fifty years, the minimum required by the Berne Convention. The UCC allows—but does not require—a nation to recognize a shorter term if the author's home country (for an unpublished work) or place of publication (for a published work) recognizes a shorter term. In the United States, the current term of copyright for a single-author work is the lifetime of the author plus seventy years, the same as the United Kingdom.

Moral Rights. Many nations other than the United States recognize moral rights, a creator's right to control use and adaptations of their work. One type of right analogous to moral rights that the United States has granted under its copyright law since 1976 is the right to control public displays of a copy of a copyrighted work. While TRIPs requires adoption of the Berne Convention, which provides for moral rights, TRIPs makes an exception for moral rights. In recent years the United States has recognized some limited forms of moral rights, such as the rights for visual artists enacted in 1990, and the limited performance right in live performances enacted to comply with TRIPs.

Fair Use. The United States has a strong notion of fair use, allowing use for certain purposes of limited amounts of a copyrighted work without compensation. But this principle is not as developed in other nations and does not exist at all in some. The United Kingdom does have a similar "fair dealing" concept. The Berne Convention includes a three-part test for determining when a nation may limit reproduction of a protected work.

Small Business Exemption. The Fairness in Music Licensing Act of 1998 expanded the American copyright law's existing exemption for restaurants and stores up to a certain size to play music without obtaining licenses. The European Communities filed an objection to the expansion with the WTO's Dispute Settlement Body, which ruled against the United States in 2000. After an arbitrator held that the provision cost European copyright holders €1,219,000 a year, the United States paid a $3.3 million award to cover the violation through the end of 2004. Otherwise, the dispute remains unresolved as of 2014.

Cultural Protection Provisions. Several nations have provisions that are aimed at promoting or protecting locally created content that appear to violate international copyright agreements. Countries including Australia and Canada have domestic quotas for media content. The European Union's Television Without Frontiers and Audiovisual Media Services directives, which allow for unfettered movement of television programs within the EU, also require that television channels reserve half their broadcast time for European programs. France, meanwhile, imposes a tax on blank video and audiotapes, with the funds given to authors, video/film creators, and actors to promote works made in the country. The subsidy may go to non-French citizens if there is a copyright treaty between France and the other nation, although the French Culture Ministry has barred the funds for films made by foreigners. This subsidy was a point of contention in the negotiations over the Uruguay Round agreements, until the United States allowed the subsidy to continue for ten years. This would have required the subsidy to end in 2003, yet it persists as of 2014 and no enforcement action has been taken.

International Copyright Reform

Interest groups in several countries have expressed dissatisfaction with the existing copyright regime, both domestically and internationally. In the United States, for example, many documentarians and journalists find the limitations and uncertainty of the fair-use doctrine unnecessarily confusing and constraining. Other issues include restrictions on adapting copyrighted works for those with disabilities. Promoters of Creative Commons, which has fostered the development of a system allowing content creators to grant reproduction and reuse rights on a more granular level than existing copyright law allows, have recently discussed efforts to reform the international copyright system.

Conclusion

The United States has come a long way from its isolationist attitude toward copyright in the eighteenth century, which led to rampant copying of works protected abroad. Now, American law is generally harmonized with the copyright laws of other nations through international copyright treaties and agreements, especially the Berne Convention.

But some differences remain: not just in legal provisions but also in philosophy. As explained above, many common law European countries have a notion of copyright that differs from the American conception.

These different conceptions of copyright, as well as political differences, lead to some of the criticisms that foreigners have of the American copyright system. These criticisms include the record of continuous extensions of the length of copyright protection, with concurrent disregard of the public domain; a legislative process that is too responsive to vested interests and their desires for changes in copyright law; and the American scheme's overreliance on static, permanent creation of a work (fixation), which is arguably an outdated concept in an era of constantly revisable electronic works. Some also argue that the international copyright system based on the Berne Convention discourages experimentation with different concepts of copyright and represents cultural imperialism by major western nations.

The current international copyright regime is a complex collection of national laws and international treaties, which no nation—at least no nation that desires to be part of the community of nations, with global trade and economic relationships—can ignore. The United States took one hundred years to first recognize this, and another hundred to truly become part of the international copyright system. Although some differences remain, American copyright is now firmly entrenched and intertwined with the copyright laws of the international community.

Eric P. Robinson
Louisiana State University

See also Copyright in the United States; Would Confucius Steal That Book—or E-Book—Today?

Further Reading

Bird, Robert C., and Lucille M. Ponte. "Protecting Moral Rights in the United States and the United Kingdom: Challenges and Opportunities under the U.K.'s New Performances Regulations." *Boston University International Law Journal* 24 (2006): 213–282.

Bogsh, Arpad. *Protection of Works of Foreign Origin.* Copyright Office Study No. 32, 86th Congress, 2nd Session, 1960. http://www.copyright.gov/history/studies/study32.pdf.

Dinwoodie, Graeme B. "A New Copyright Order: Why National Courts Should Create Global Norms." *University of Pennsylvania Law Review* 149 (200): 469–622.

Landau, Michael. "Fitting United States Copyright Law into the International Scheme: Foreign and Domestic Challenges to Recent Legislation." *Georgia State Law Review* 23 (2007): 847–892.

Rea, Bryce, Jr. "Some Legal Aspects of the Pan-American Copyright Convention of 1946." *Washington & Lee Law Review* 4 (1946): 10–30. http://scholarlycommons.law.wlu.edu/wlulr/ vol4/iss1/3.

Sandison, Hamish. "The Berne Convention and the Universal Copyright Convention: The American Experience." *Columbia-VLA Journal of Law and the Arts* 11 (1986): 89–97.

Seville, Catherine. *The Internationalisation of Copyright Law: Books, Buccaneers, and the Black Flag in the Nineteenth Century.* Cambridge, UK: Cambridge University Press, 2006.

Stenshoel, Eric. "From Berne to Madrid and Beyond: The Road to International Copyright and Trademark Protection in the United States." *Entertainment, Arts, and Sports Law Journal* 24 (Spring 2013).

United States Copyright Office. *International Copyright Relations of the United States* (Circular 38a). Washington, DC: GPO, 2010. http://www.copyright.gov/circs/circ38a.pdf.

United States House of Representatives. *Copyright Law Revision* (House Report No. 94-1476). Washington, DC: GPO, 1976.

Wolff, Nancy E. "Fair Use: It Stops at the Border." In *International Libel & Privacy Handbook,* edited by Charles E. Glasser Jr., 347–353. New York: Bloomberg Press, 2006.

World Intellectual Property Organization. *International Protection of Copyright and Related Rights* (n.d.). http://www.wipo.int/export/sites/www/copyright/en/activities/pdfinternational_ protection.pdf.

World Trade Organization. *The United States Manufacturing Clause.* Report of the Panel adopted on 15/16 May 1984 (L/5609 - 31S/74). http://www.wto.org/english/tratop_e/dispu_e/83copyrt.pdf.

42

SPORTS COVERAGE

Few words or endeavors elicit such a powerful response as sport. Sport is the epitome of Darwinian ethics. The rules to the games are designed so all players have the same opportunity; everyone should be able to compete on an equal playing field. But from the team captain who picks the squad for the playground game of dodgeball, to the final two players standing in line hoping not to suffer the indignity of being picked last, an inherent unfairness exists. Still, because of the fair set of playing rules, occasionally the group with fewer advantages manages to find a way to defeat a superior foe. Thus, the Darwinian ethics: Within a fair set of rules, the more-talented group will usually win. And because the rules favor no particular group, the possibility of an upset always exists.

College sports operate within the framework of Darwinian ethics. The rules appear to be fair. While the difference should be in talent, this is no longer always the case. The role of television rights contracts slants the playing field toward conferences already having unfair playing advantages in regards to selecting talent.

Media have changed the face of college sports in numerous ways, from changing start times of certain games, to changing traditional game days, and even, in some sports, to changing rules specifically to make the game more television friendly. No change has been more powerful than television rights contracts.

Television rights contracts do more than just bind a team or a conference to a specific network. They serve to give five or six conferences—the Atlantic Coast Conference (ACC), Big Ten Conference, Big 12 Conference, Pacific-12 Conference (Pac-12), and Southeastern Conference (SEC) in football, and these five plus the Big East Conference in basketball—more power than all the other conferences in college sports. Money is always a source of power, and the television rights contracts provide these conferences enough money to create an unfair advantage. New rules set in place in early 2014 give even more power to the conferences with the best television deals. It is more than money. Heavy television exposure leads to a hegemonic belief that teams from the more powerful conferences are superior. It also creates a cycle, promising the best athletes that their future is more secure if they play in a conference that guarantees constant television exposure. Television contracts also lead to a different form of media coverage. Because certain conferences have the advantages that come with expensive rights contracts, media outlets treat these teams differently than they do others. This treatment leads to the perception that teams from the power conferences are inherently better than teams from outside of these conferences. These perceptions lead to an ethical dilemma. No longer is the ability to settle the matter on the playing field the important issue; the issue becomes whether a team is qualified to compete on the same field. And that question is impacted by media attention. Much of that attention is fair; the power conferences traditionally produce the powerhouse teams, from the universities of Oklahoma, Alabama, Notre Dame, and Ohio State University in football to Duke University, the University of Kentucky, and Kansas University in basketball. At the same time, media exposure of teams at the bottom or the middle of these power conferences provides a perception of quality that may not exist.

This chapter looks at the role money plays in building a separate construct for college sports, namely men's college basketball and football, by changing the way the public perceives specific conferences. The chapter begins by examining the difference in the working model of college athletics. It then examines how television rights contracts have changed the dynamic of college sports into a system of the haves and the have-nots. Finally, the chapter examines the Big East Conference, a conference that was a power conference

until college realignment, all over television rights contracts, forced the conference to implode, thus serving as a warning sign for all revenue-producing college sports conferences.

The Entertainment Factor

Universities exist as institutions of higher learning. They have their own special hierarchy and run the business according to an academic model. People assume that athletics are run with the same model, but actually, universities and colleges involved in high-level Division I athletics run their business according to an entertainment model. The entertainment product is responsible for running college sports. Sport administrators at major universities ensure that athletes who attend these universities go to class, make academic progress, stay out of trouble—and, most of all, avoid instances where they become public relations embarrassments to their universities. The entertainment product at universities raises money through marketing, television revenues, licensing of products, ticket revenues, video games, and other forms.

The more prestigious the university, the more important the entertainment product becomes. In his book *Big-Time Sports in American Universities,* Charles T. Clotfelter noted that, of the top one hundred football teams in 1920, sixty were still among the top one hundred today. The same can be said for college basketball. UCLA, North Carolina, Kansas, and Kentucky are almost always among the top teams, and the major conferences have always housed the premier college football and basketball teams (discounting Notre Dame in football, although Notre Dame is joining the Atlantic Coast Conference in all sports, including football, in 2014). The power conferences have always been athletically wealthier than the other conferences, thanks to larger stadiums and higher numbers of alumni interested in their success. Television money amplified the advantages.

The six major conferences work together as an oligopoly within the NCAA cartel and collaborate with major television corporations to dominate the college sports market. An oligopoly is a market structure with a few principal sellers that hold a significant share of the market. An oligopoly occurs when a small group of sellers within an economic construct combines to dominate the market. These sellers understand that whatever action they take will affect the other firms and will elicit a similar response from those firms. An oligopoly works because the sellers need each other, and they can make a larger profit working together instead of in direct competition against each other. Even though these conferences work against each other in terms of building the better product through league expansion and gaining a larger share of television and marketing money, they still work together in controlling the vast profits derived from NCAA television revenues and from college football revenues.

A hegemonic structure of power exists within the dynamic of what Clotfelter defined as "big-time" college conferences and television corporations to maintain control of the demographic target audience. The college sports audience has been conditioned to believe, through years of mediated sports coverage, that the best teams always come from within the six major conferences. Because this has been reinforced by countless sports anchors and in countless sports stories for so long, it becomes common sense and therefore is naturalized as a hegemonic force. This conditioning goes deeper than just the traditional teams at the top of the conference. Teams in the middle (and even near the bottom) of these conferences receive the same hegemonic benefits as teams with history and prestige, because they play in these preferred conferences. These teams are packaged as superior to top-level teams from the other conferences for a reason. Quality teams from other conferences are left out of this paradigm because they become more difficult to sell as quality, according to the set parameters. Teams like Boise State University in football or San Diego State University in football must deal with perceptions that their success is due to weak scheduling and, therefore, these teams do not warrant the attention of teams from major conferences. Still, Boise State raised its national profile by agreeing to play football games midweek to get coverage on ESPN. While that exposure helped, the university still deals with perception issues raised by conference affiliation.

Colleges brand themselves to the public by conference affiliation—the Big Ten on CBS, etc.—while at the same time offering rights to media corporations by representing themselves as something different: as institutions that provide long-term stability. The teams become individualized brands, products designed to draw viewers, or fans, to their teams.

Each individual team brings its own brand equity—which, when combined, strengthens the entire conference. This happens in three ways. First, each individual team or brand acts as a magnet for more fans. Each conference has a number of traditional powers, teams that have excelled over the years, teams that have tremendous fan bases and fans with great loyalty, teams that have tradition behind them, and teams that are high-quality products. Second, fans build an emotional tie with each individual team and that leads to increased identification with the conference. At the end of the season, Big Ten fans root for Big Ten teams in the football bowl games and they root for Big Ten teams in the NCAA Tournament. This becomes value loyalty for the fan. The third way to strengthen the conference occurs when the conference enhances its image through specific actions, such as placing a large number of teams in the NCAA Tournament in basketball or playing in a prestigious bowl game in football.

Media corporations market conferences as high-quality to the fans. Through exposure and news routines, they frame the teams from the six conferences as superior to those from the other twenty-five conferences, including framing the mediocre teams from the top conferences as superior to the top teams from the other twenty-five conferences.

One of the ways media corporations set this frame is through news routine. Media commonly seek out journalists whose values and beliefs mirror those of the audience they try to reach. This also pertains to sports media. ESPN hires analysts who have knowledge mainly of the six conferences. During the 2010–2011 college basketball season, ESPN listed on its website the biographies of a dozen analysts whose specialty was college basketball. Of those, only two—Tom Brennan and Andy Katz—had extensive backgrounds outside of the six major conferences. The others all played or coached a large part of their careers in the six conferences. It is understandable that these sports personalities concentrate on the six major conferences, since that is what they know. An example comes from the February 25, 2011, episode of *College GameDay* on ESPN. During this show, analysts were asked to pick the winners of specific games. One game was the Wichita State–Missouri State matchup in the Missouri Valley Conference. Bob Knight, former University of Indiana and Texas Tech University coach and current ESPN college basketball analyst, when asked to predict the winner, coughed and admitted that he had little to no knowledge of those teams.

Supporting Athletics

All universities have certain ways to earn sports revenues. Those include ticket sales, merchandising, student fees, and television revenues. The largest television revenues come from football bowls, entities that are not negotiated through the NCAA, but instead from television corporations to college conferences and through the Bowl Championship Series (BCS) agreements.

The largest player in this is Disney, which, through ESPN and ABC Sports, controls all six BCS bowls, including the national championship game. ESPN began a new contract in 2014 to televise all six

BCS bowl games and the new college football playoff for about $500 million per year. ESPN also pays these conferences well for basketball. In fact, based on averages that appeared on the Business of College Sports website, conservative estimates show universities that compete in the six major conferences can expect more than $10 million in revenues from television rights deals with ESPN, Fox, and other companies. Some will make more than $25 million per year in television rights revenues. That is before television money from bowl games or the NCAA Tournament is paid to the conferences. Compare this to the deals the Missouri Valley Conference has with ESPN and with Fox. The ESPN deal is worth about $190,000 per year. The difference in media money is important. Conferences that do not have multimillion-dollar contracts from media outlets still have to raise money to pay for athletics at their schools. This often leads to "pay-for-play" games. A pay-for-play game is a game that a smaller university accepts to go to a school from a power conference and play that school for a fee. "We have to play one or two a year," said Dave Kidwell, former sports information director at Eastern Illinois University, of the Ohio Valley Conference. "We make about $700,000 from those games and that supplies a portion of our athletic budget."

Making the athletic budget balance is a chore for the non-power conference schools. But cutting sports or adding a pay-for-play game only goes so far. The largest source of income for schools without large media contracts is the students who go to those schools. Schools from smaller conferences like the Ohio Valley Conference or the Sun Belt Conference depend on student fees. Sometimes as much as 50 to 60 percent of the athletic budget for smaller conferences comes from athletic fees. Television does not just play a monetary role for conferences and individual universities. Exposure is important also. Teams from the six major conferences play in prime television slots on ESPN, CBS, and Fox. A conference such as the Missouri Valley Conference must take a different approach. The Missouri Valley Conference's deal with ESPN is for less than a million dollars, but the conference counts on different media platforms to gain exposure for athletes and alumni across the country. The same is true for teams from the Mountain West Conference or the Mid-American Conference. Those teams have deals with ESPN that pay nowhere near the amount of money that power conferences are paid.

These conferences want the opportunity to play to a national audience. In years past, the Missouri Valley Conference reached approximately 9.5 million homes with its regional television package. Deals that include online streaming of games and weekly games on ESPN networks increase the reach to approximately ninety-one million homes. Commissioners from non-power conferences will take a smaller rights package in exchange for the possibility of raising exposure, even if that exposure is limited in terms of ESPN's marketing of those games.

NCAA College Basketball Revenue Distribution

The NCAA basketball fund is the major means the NCAA has of paying all

Division I schools for television rights, since the NCAA has no say over how the televised football contracts are paid. The NCAA basketball fund accounts for 40 percent of the total revenues the NCAA distributes to its Division I members on a yearly basis. The basketball fund is based on conferences' performance in the NCAA Tournament on a six-year rolling basis. Units are shares of the total amount allotted from the NCAA Tournament rights deal with CBS. One unit is awarded to each conference for each game a team in that conference plays, except for the championship game. If an independent team (one not affiliated with a conference) qualifies, one unit is awarded directly to that university for each game its team plays, except for the championship game.

In 1984, a Supreme Court ruling, *NCAA v. The University of Oklahoma Regents*, ended the NCAA's monopoly on negotiating television rights deals for football, giving each school and conference the opportunity to create its own deals. The result was that conferences started "branding" their teams—and they combined their brands into what eventually became the BCS. The major powers in football did not have to worry about all the other schools; they were able to secure television deals that benefited their particular conferences. Those deals placed most of the football bowl money into the hands of the five BCS conferences. That bowl money became a huge deal. To keep the money centralized, ESPN, which owned the rights to the BCS bowls, promoted schools that were expected to draw the best television ratings. Therefore, ESPN promoted the best teams from the five major football conferences, since these conferences contain the vast majority of national contenders. The BCS ended in 2014 with the advent of a national football playoff, but the power conferences that made up the BCS still retain their power.

College basketball television rights contracts, still controlled by the NCAA and, therefore, all thirty-one NCAA Division I conferences, grew exponentially, from $9.9 million for rights to the NCAA Tournament in 1981 to the current deal of $10.8 billion for television rights. The exposure leads to a perception that all teams from the six major conferences are superior, while the money leads to resources that give teams from those conferences major recruiting advantages. This led to a more pronounced gap between the conferences that had large television resources and those that did not.

The Haves and the Have-Nots

Two types of NCAA Division I college athletics teams exist. The first type are teams from the power conferences—the ACC, Big Ten, Big 12, Pac-12, and SEC—the five major college football playing conferences. These conferences are the recipients of most media attention and generated over $10 billion of television money through football in 2013. The other twenty-five conferences play football at another level or do not receive the same amount of attention as the five major conferences.

The power that comes from football money is used in all other sports. Basketball, the other revenue-generating sport, is the key for the other twenty-five conferences. The amount of NCAA media money college basketball conferences receive and how that money is doled out are important to teams and conferences. The money is needed to meet athletic budgets. The television exposure leads to more money and prestige and, in some instances, increases in overall student enrollment.

In 2010, the University of Texas reported more than $143 million in athletic revenues and nearly $114 million in athletic expenses, and it listed basketball expenses of $8.8 million. The University of Kansas, the top-seeded team that Northern Iowa upset in 2010 to reach the Sweet Sixteen, reported receiving total athletic revenues of $71.8 million, and paying total athletic expenses of $60.2 million and basketball expenses of $10.9 million.

In 2010 in the Big Ten, Michigan State University received more than $80 million in revenues, while it spent $61.6 million in total athletic expenses and $8.3 million in basketball expenses. Ohio State University earned $123.1 million in total revenues, spent $104.9 in total athletic expenses, and spent $4.5 million in basketball expenses.

Using numbers from the same source, the profits for Michigan State (subtracting revenues from expenses) would equal $18.4 million. By comparison, Wichita State University lists its total athletic expenses as $16.7 million. To be more precise, Northern Iowa reported athletic revenues of $14.6 million in 2010, with $14.3 million in expenses. Northern Iowa spent just under $2 million on men's basketball. This disparity does not just exist in the Missouri Valley Conference. Butler, a back-to-back NCAA men's basketball national championship game contender,

also broke even, reporting total athletic revenues in 2010 of $12.3 million, total athletic expenses of $12.3 million, and $2.8 million in basketball expenses. Butler, after making it to the championship game in the NCAA Tournament for two straight years in 2010 and 2011, opted to leave the Horizon Conference in 2012 and move to the Atlantic Ten Conference, partly because the Atlantic Ten Conference gets more television revenue from the NCAA Tournament. A year later, Butler moved to the Big East Conference in hopes of receiving even more television money.

In total, NCAA men's basketball conferences received $10.8 billion over fourteen years for the rights to televise the NCAA men's basketball tournament from CBS and Time Warner's Turner Sports. Thirty-one conferences received disbursements totaling $154,721,003 for the 2008–2009 NCAA rights fees disbursement. Each unit was worth $206,020. The top six conferences received $94,357,147, or 61 percent of that disbursement, an average of $15,726,191 per conference. The other twenty-five conferences split $60,363,856, an average of $2,414,554 per conference. The payouts to the top conferences for the 2008–2009 season were as follows:

- Big East Conference: $19,365,877
- Big 12 Conference: $16,275,578
- Atlantic Coast Conference: $15,863,538
- Southeastern Conference: $15,657,518
- Big Ten Conference: $13,803,338
- Pac-10 Conference (which became the Pac-12 in 2011): $13,391,298

The 2009–2010 season produced total revenues of $168,434,032. The top six conferences received $103,548,057 of this disbursement, or 61 percent of the total revenue. The payouts to the top six conferences were as follows:

- Big East Conference: $23,109,436
- Atlantic Coast Conference: $18,220,902
- Big Ten Conference: $17,109,871
- Big 12 Conference: $15,332,222
- Southeastern Conference: $15,110,016
- Pac-10 Conference: $15,110,016

The money for the top six conferences keeps increasing, and 61 percent of NCAA television revenue heading to the six conferences that already receive more money in regular-season television revenues is quite a lot. In the five years before 2008–2009, the top six conferences received between 61 percent and 62 percent of the total basketball fund disbursement. The other twenty-five conferences shared the other 38 to 39 percent of television revenues.

The only difference was in the disbursement monies per conference, which changed from year to year. The Pac-12 Conference received the lowest payouts of the top six conferences during the five-year span and at that time did not have a television deal with ESPN. The difference between the top six conferences compared to the other twenty-five conferences was extreme. In 2008–2009, six conferences (the Southwestern Athletic Conference, the Summit Conference, the Mid-American Conference, the Mid-Eastern Athletic Conference, the Ivy League, and the Atlantic Sun Conference) received the absolute minimum of $1,236,120. In 2009–2010, they received $1,333,237. In all, sixteen conferences received less than $2 million for the 2009–2010 season.

The top six conferences receive monies from sources other than the NCAA Tournament basketball fund. The conferences are free to make their own deals, usually by combining football and basketball. The Big Ten has television deals with ESPN/ABC, both owned by Disney Corporation, and has its own network, the Big Ten Network, which is partially owned by Fox Sports. The Big Ten makes a little more than $250 million per year in television money. The Southeastern Conference signed a new deal with CBS and ESPN in 2008, makes about $205 million per year in television revenues, and began its own television network in 2014. The Big 12 and Pac-12 conferences make about $78.4 and $57.5 million per year, respectively, in television rights fees as of 2014. The ACC signed a $3.6 billion contract with ESPN in 2010.

The money leads to greater media exposure. The Big Ten deal is guaranteed sixty games to be broadcast on ESPN networks, plus another twenty-six on CBS and at least 105 regular-season Big Ten games on the Big Ten Network. The Big 12 Conference is guaranteed sixty games on ESPN or ESPN2, with ninety-five games guaranteed on all ESPN platforms. The SEC is guaranteed sixty games on ESPN and has games guaranteed to be played on Tuesday, Thursday, and Saturday.

Other conferences have deals with ESPN, but none has the number of games—and none receives the amount of money—that each of the top six conferences do. Most play on ESPN's secondary networks: ESPN2, ESPNU, and others. An example is the Missouri Valley Conference. It earned $4.3 million from the NCAA basketball fund in 2009. In 2011, the conference signed new television deals with ESPN and Fox Sports. The

ESPN deal is worth about $190,000 per year. The schools in the Missouri Valley Conference received about $290,000 (total) from the 2011 NCAA Tournament.

The 2010 projected distribution sheet produced by the NCAA shows the disparity in payouts. The Big Ten received $18.4 million in payouts for the 2010 season, while the Horizon League, at the time the home of Butler, received $4,553,616. The disparity is not just in dollars. There is a difference in exposure, too. What is missing is the exposure provided by getting teams from outside of the six conferences to a national audience.

Conferences want to be covered by ESPN. The exposure reaches larger numbers of people, and the prestige of being covered by ESPN is important to conferences because it helps sell the conference to future recruits and alumni. Conference commissioners have called ESPN exposure the lifeblood of recruiting. ESPN coverage is that important for all conferences. The exposure is so important that conferences outside of the six main conferences will give up money in exchange for exposure. This is in stark contrast to the six major conferences, which get the majority of exposure and are paid for that exposure.

The Mountain West Conference, which placed four teams in the 2009–2010 NCAA Tournament and earned $4.1 million from the NCAA basketball fund in 2008–2009, has deals with CBS College Sports Network and NBC Sports Network and a 2013 deal with ESPN for first-tier games that will pay the conference approximately $18 million per year. The Atlantic Ten Conference, based partially in major media markets on the East Coast, earned $5.5 million from the 2008–2009 NCAA basketball fund and has deals with ESPN, CBS, and NBC that bring the conference approximately $40 million over eight years, or $5 million a year. This conference placed a team in the Final Four in 2011. Along with the success of the conference in recent years, this makes the Atlantic Ten a conference that could rise to the top of the conferences outside of the six major conferences in basketball. The Atlantic Ten's deal with ESPN does not rival that of the major six conferences.

The disparity in coverage and television rights plays a role in building the perception that teams from smaller conferences are not equal to teams from the six conferences. This is one factor that leads to fewer teams being selected into the NCAA Tournament as at-large bids. In 2011, the first year that thirty-seven at-large bids were available, the six major conferences earned all but seven of them. That left seven at-large bids for the other conferences, or one less than in 2010, when eight were picked. The average since 2001 has been 6.8 bids awarded to teams outside of the top six conferences. The low was four in 2009, and the high was twelve in 2004. Eleven schools from outside of the top six conferences were selected in 2012.

These numbers remain stagnant despite the success of the mid-majors in the NCAA Tournament. Since 2006, four teams from conferences outside of the top six have advanced to the Final Four (George Mason in 2006, Butler in 2010 and 2011, Virginia Commonwealth in 2011, and Wichita State in 2013), with Butler coming one shot away from winning it all in 2010. The NCAA payout schedule remains relatively the same, with approximately 60 percent of television rights money going to the six major conferences.

Ratings

The most common reason given for less television coverage of teams from outside of the top six conferences is ratings. In some instances, this is true; most fans want to see the top teams from the top conferences play each other. A deeper examination suggests that this perception may be mediated.

Teams from the other twenty-five conferences traditionally have lower ratings than teams from the top six conferences. An examination of one week of basketball coverage, February 11–17, 2012, from the website Sports Media Watch provides a snapshot that supports that reasoning. On February 11, a Saturday, Alabama and Louisiana State University, two mid-level teams from the Southeastern Conference (a power conference), played at 7:06 p.m. on ESPN2. According to Sports Media Watch, the game drew a 0.3 rating, with 479,000 viewers. This beat the three games between schools from the twenty-five conferences, including a marquee matchup between Missouri Valley Conference leaders Creighton and Wichita State. That game drew a 0.1 rating with 206,000 viewers. Xavier and Temple, a key matchup between two Atlantic Ten teams with a prime 9:06 p.m. start time, drew a 0.01 rating and just 186,000 fans. The games were not marketed as marquee games. The marquee games marketed by ESPN were games between teams from the top six. The University of Kentucky played Vanderbilt

at 9:00 p.m. that night; that contest earned a 1.6 rating and 2,930,000 viewers. Michigan State and Ohio State played on ESPN for a 1.6 rating and drew 2,607,000 viewers, followed by Maryland and Duke with a 1.3 rating and 1,743,000 viewers. The noon start-time game that day took place between Louisville and West Virginia, and that matchup drew a 1.0 rating and 1,310,000 viewers. All of the games with teams from the power conferences were marketed as important games and rivalry games, which they were. These numbers suggest that fans want to see the top teams from the top conferences play.

Television results for the NCAA Tournament were different. The 2011 tournament was the first tournament that showed every game on different channels, and it earned the highest ratings for the NCAA Tournament since 2005. The different channels also allowed researchers a chance to see what games were selected to appear on the main channel (CBS) and what games fans decided to watch.

Two teams from outside of the power six conferences, Brigham Young University and Wofford College, had the highest ratings through the Thursday-Friday games. More than 4.6 million people watched the two teams play. On Saturday, more people tuned in to watch the Atlantic Ten's Richmond play the Ohio Valley Conference's Morehead State than tuned in to watch the University of Kentucky play the University of West Virginia. Through Saturday, three of the five highest-rated games involved teams from conferences outside of the top six.

Similar to the CBS figures, the highest-rated games on cable were played on Sunday. The highest-rated game on cable was the Sunday matchup between

Brigham Young and Florida. The matchup, marketed as the small school against the powerhouse, drew a 3.3 rating, with 5,261,000 viewers. Brigham Young is not a team in the top six conferences. The same story line followed the Butler-Pittsburgh contest that was the fourth highest-rated game on cable through the first weekend, trailing only Arizona-Texas (2.6, 4,408,000) and Kansas-Illinois (2.6, 4,408,000). Nothing in the numbers suggests that teams from conferences outside of the top six draw smaller audiences. In fact, the numbers show similar ratings for teams from both the top six and the other twenty-five conferences. Viewers may be interested in seeing teams they have not seen throughout the course of the year, and they love seeing teams from outside of the power conferences play the big boys.

This offers a different picture than the one offered after eleventh-seeded George Mason University qualified for the Final Four in 2006. Just 14 percent of the nation saw the Sweet Sixteen matchup in which George Mason defeated seventh-seeded Wichita State. After advancing to the Final Four, George Mason's loss to Florida drew 14.5 million fans, down from the 2005 season. The championship game between Florida and UCLA drew just a 17.5 rating, down six points from the 2005 championship game between the University of Illinois and North Carolina. Critics used this to say that fans did not want to see Cinderella teams in the championship game. The reality was that the George Mason Final Four game in the early time slot, while down from the year before, earned a solid rating—one that was not matched until Butler played in the Final Four in both 2010 and 2011. The 2011 Butler-Duke national

title game drew the same rating as the 2005 Illinois-North Carolina game. Still, after the 2012 title game's ratings eclipsed the 2011 ratings, *USA Today* had the following headline: "With No Cinderella in the NCAA Title Game, Ratings Up 5 Percent." The headline reinforced the perception that teams from the six conferences draw better ratings, but the story also said that although ratings were up 5 percent from the 2011 championship game, they were down 3 percent from the 2010 game.

The Big East Conference

The Big East Conference was formed with television marketing in mind. In 1979, a group of East Coast universities decided to form a conference that comprised teams from the top media markets on the East Coast, including New York, New Jersey, Philadelphia, Washington, D.C., and Boston. The major purpose of this conference was to band together to make an appealing brand of college basketball that would be marketable for television. The marketing directors suggested that the conference be named the Big East Conference. And the Big East Conference was created the same year as was ESPN. Since that time, ESPN has been the Big East Conference's primary television rights holder. On June 9, 1982, an article in the *New York Times* reported that the Big East Conference had signed a deal with ESPN and two major networks worth $2 million. Nearly thirty years later, in 2011, the Big East turned down a $130 million annual deal with ESPN, an event that led to the eventual dissolution of the Big East Conference.

The original Big East consisted of Providence, St. Johns, Georgetown, Syracuse, Connecticut, and Boston College. Villanova joined in 1980 and Pittsburgh joined in 1982. The league was originally formed to take advantage of its markets for college basketball. Eventually, the Big East turned to football. In 1991, the Big East used its clout as a power basketball conference to become a power football conference. The Big East added Miami in both basketball and football and Rutgers, Temple, Virginia Tech, and West Virginia as football-only members. West Virginia, Rutgers, and Virginia Tech eventually became basketball and football members, giving the conference influence in the lucrative college football industry.

The money available in college football created a situation in which conferences tried to build larger, more comprehensive media bases and certain markets became important. Conferences need twelve teams to separate into divisions and finish their football season with a highly lucrative conference championship game. As a result, the Atlantic Coast Conference, another conference known primarily for its success in college basketball, announced a desire to expand in 2003. The Atlantic Coast Conference managed to persuade Miami, Virginia Tech, and Boston College to leave the Big East. The Big East countered by adding DePaul, Louisville, Cincinnati, South Florida, and Marquette from Conference USA to enhance its basketball profitability and to raise its profile in markets in the Midwest (Chicago, Louisville, Milwaukee, and Cincinnati) and the Southeast (South Florida). Louisville and

Cincinnati also had football teams, and their football programs profited by joining the Big East. Still, the Big East's football standing was typically the lowest of the six automatic qualifying BCS conferences. In 2010, the Big East announced it was adding Texas Christian University to the conference in an attempt to bolster its football profile. This led to issues within the Big East. Basketball-only schools were becoming unhappy, because the conference was watering down the quality of basketball in hopes of increasing its football profile. Football schools became unhappy with having to share media revenue earned in football, more lucrative than basketball, with the basketball-only schools. In 2011, the Big East Conference turned down the $130 million annual deal with ESPN. Soon after, the major football-playing schools in the Big East started shopping for another conference. Syracuse, Notre Dame, Pittsburgh, and eventually Louisville left the Big East Conference and joined the Atlantic Coast Conference. West Virginia left the Big East Confer-ence and joined the Big 12 Conference. Rutgers left the Big East Conference to join the Big Ten Conference. The remaining basketball schools, mostly Catholic universities, announced they were breaking off from the remaining football schools and formed the new Big East, which consists of Georgetown, Villanova, Providence, St. Johns, DePaul, Marquette, Seton Hall, Butler, and Creighton. The remaining football schools brought in new schools from other conferences and formed the American Athletic Conference. The Big East Conference, again a basketball conference, signed a deal with Fox Sports for

$500 million over twelve years, or $41.6 million per year. The American Athletic Conference signed a deal with ESPN and CBS for approximately $20 million per year. The two conferences' combined deal does not equal the deal that the Big East turned down in 2011.

The implosion of the Big East Conference made a few points clear:

1. Football is more profitable than basketball. Despite being a power basketball conference, weaknesses in football led football schools to leave the Big East Conference for more security and prestige. When the basketball schools broke off and formed their own conference, they were left without football to raise their overall profile and ended up signing a deal that was for considerably less money than the 2011 deal. Also, the conference lost power. As talks continued over the future of the NCAA model and the possibility of paying players, the Big East Conference, as well as the new American Athletic Conference, were left out of the conversation by the remaining power conferences.

2. The marketability of the name of a team matters. Syracuse, Pittsburgh, and Notre Dame make the Atlantic Coast Conference a more palatable football conference as well as adding to the overall profile of Atlantic Coast Conference basketball. The schools the Big East started adding did not increase the overall marketability of the conference. Media outlets play a role in this—a larger role than they want to take credit for. In 2011, as universities changed from one conference to another, Boston College athletic director Gene DeFilippo was quoted in the *Boston Globe* as saying: "We always keep our television partners close to us. You don't get extra money for basketball. It's 85 percent football money.

TV—ESPN—is the one who told us what to do. This was football; it had nothing to do with basketball." Three days later, he recanted his statement in the same newspaper. It did not matter. ESPN's struggles with the Big East over the television rights contract played a role in the departure of the football schools from the Big East to the Atlantic Coast Conference, which signed a $3.6 billion deal with ESPN in 2012. Moving to the Atlantic Coast Conference gave those schools more money ($17.1 million per team per year when all are official members of the Atlantic Coast Conference), and the addition of Syracuse, Pittsburgh, and Notre Dame increased the visibility of Boston College's football profile. DeFilippo's statement established the power that media outlets had in conference realignment.

3. Power in conferences is clearly defined through football. More money exists for fewer entities in football. Currently, sixty-five schools play football at the highest level of NCAA Division I. Most of those universities are housed in the five remaining power conferences. Those conferences have the most money and the most power in determining the future of college athletics.

Conclusion

College athletics are no longer an exercise in Darwinian ethics. Instead, athletics are affected by television rights contracts that place money in the hands of a certain group of conferences. Already stronger than most, the added media emphasis on these conferences creates an unfair advantage, one that affects perception and also selection of specific teams for advancement into major tournaments. College football teams from outside of the five major conferences have little to no chance of playing for a national championship; even with the new playoff format, the top schools from outside will have a difficult time getting invited into the playoffs. Also, top teams from outside of the power conferences have a lower chance of receiving at-large bids to compete in the NCAA men's basketball tournament. Media pundits claim that these teams have not played a schedule strong enough to deserve admission to the tournament, while also promoting teams from conferences that they have a financial interest in promoting. These same media stations have the ability to promote conference realignment, sometimes at the cost of conferences that have not finalized deals with those networks. The power of the media to control who plays in what conference changed the landscape of college athletics, and new rules made by the NCAA that give more power to the five remaining power football conferences only serve to give those conferences more control over their ability to retain the best television deals. Those deals, in turn, provide more exposure and money to the power conferences. In the end, the power conferences become stronger through television contracts and create a playing field that is definitely tilted in their favor.

Scott Lambert
Millikin University

See also Institutional Foundations; The Price of Publicity

Further Reading

Benford, R. D. "The College Sports Reform Movement: Reframing the 'Edutainment' Industry." *Sociological Quarterly* 48, no. 1 (2007): 1–28.

Chittum, Ryan. "ESPN Obscures Its Own Role in the Conference Realignment Mess." *Columbia Journalism Review,* September 22, 2011. http://www.cjr.org/the_audit/espn_obscures_its_own_role_in.php?page=all.

Clotfelter, C. T. *Big-Time Sports in American Universities*. Cambridge, UK: Cambridge University Press, 2011.

Dunnavant, Keith. *The Fifty-Year Seduction: How Television Manipulated College Football, from the Birth of the Modern NCAA to the Creation of the BCS*. New York: Macmillan, 2004.

Hiestand, M. "NCAA Underdogs Might Not Be Ratings Dogs." *USA Today,* March 26, 2006.

Hiestand, M. "With No Cinderella, CBS' NCAA TV Title Game Rating up 5%." *USA Today,* April 3, 2012. http://content.usatoday.com/communities/gameon/post/2012/04/cbs-ncaa-title-game-tv-rating/1.

Jessop, A. "Why Basketball Is Driving Conference Realignment for the Atlantic 10 Conference." *Business of College Sports,* May 30, 2012. http://businessofcollegesports.com/2012/05/30/the-atlantic-10-conference-the-ncaas-new-basketball-powerhouse.

Real, M. *Exploring Media Culture: A Guide*. Thousand Oaks, CA: Sage, 1996.

Real, M. R., and R. A. Mechikoff. "Deep Fan: Mythic Identification, Technology, and Advertising in Spectator Sports." *Sociology of Sport Journal* 9, no. 4 (1992): 323–339.

43

ETHICS TOOLS

With the wave of new communication technologies, everything in the media landscape is rapidly changing, and people are finding new opportunities to interact with the media. In the process, people are commenting on news and events in blogs, on websites, and on social networking sites such as Facebook and Twitter. Scholars have expressed concern about opportunities for Internet users to hide their identities or assume multiple roles online, and there has been a debate about the function of anonymous posting on the Internet. While many of the issues relating to media accountability in the new media age are not unique, the traditional twentieth-century media accountability tools are being used less and less in this century.

Media accountability tools flourished in the decades following the 1947 Hutchins Commission, officially known as the Commission on Freedom of the Press. In particular, this commission promoted the "social responsibility theory," where the media were seen as having a moral obligation to consider and assess society's needs so the press might accomplish the greatest good. Even though people around the world think media are powerful institutions, there has been a long debate on how to ensure a balance in power and thus create a more accountable media system. In the United States, the power of media was guaranteed by the First Amendment to the Constitution of the United States of America in 1791. This amendment provides for freedom of the press and has been used as a precedent for providing freedom for the media in different countries. Nevertheless, scholars have argued that even though the media have constitutional authority to act as watchdogs of society, "we the people" have a responsibility at the same time to act as watchdogs of the press. The major media accountability tools aiding this watchdog process include ethics codes, news/press councils, news ombudspersons, media critics, journalism reviews, and public/civic journalism initiatives.

Today, these six accountability tools are under siege by a press more worried about staying afloat and remaining profitable than focusing on and promoting ethics. A number of factors have come together in a "perfect storm" fashion to undermine the news industry. Newspaper circulation has been shaky at best for decades. In fact, newspaper "household penetration" in the United States was highest around 1910, when the average family subscribed to some three daily newspapers. That figure now is below one-half of a newspaper per household, and falling fast. A number of factors contributed to there being fewer newspapers in fewer homes. In the 1920s radios began to compete with newspapers as sources of news and entertainment in American homes. By the 1950s, television sets were providing even more intoxicating competition to newspapers. At the same time, traffic jams in metropolitan areas made it difficult for afternoon newspapers to be delivered on time, and tens of thousands of newspaper readers canceled their evening papers. And as the baby boomers matured, many members of this generation steadfastly refused to "settle" in a community and begin raising families (at least at an early age, as had traditionally been the pattern), thus making it unnecessary for them to read newspapers chock-full of useful local hints on sewer ordinances, school lunches, and city councils.

And not only has the newspaper industry experienced a sea change this century, but magazines, television, and electronic media have dramatically changed as well. In the wake of these changes, both the media and public have begun to assess various media differently. What follows is a discussion of the six media ethics accountability tools and the challenges these ethics tools are facing today.

Ethics Codes

Of the tools in the media accountability toolbox, ethics codes are one of the most widely used on a global basis. Ethics codes provide some guidelines regarding the roles and responsibilities of journalists. These codes are based on the broader framework of the arguments set forth by philosophers such as Aristotle (the Golden Mean), Immanuel Kant (the Categorical Imperative), and John Stuart Mill (the Principle of Utility). Codes of ethics provide structural outlines to uphold integrity and honesty and thus maintain professional standards. Ethics codes provide road maps for professionals, pertaining to a variety of "dos" and "don'ts." Some codes are more aspirational, some more proscriptive. Through codes of ethics, different professions get an idea about their obligation to the larger society. As they mirror the expectations of society, ethics codes are important to journalism. Professional groups of journalists have been contributing guidelines to members through their codes of ethics. Many media organizations also have specific codes of ethics for their journalists. However, the debate over enforcing and obeying the codes of ethics in journalism has been getting attention by scholars and working journalists. Agreeing upon the pitfalls of codes of ethics in journalism, some media ethicists argue that it is better to have a code of some sort than to not have a code at all. There are many ethics codes, and we will highlight two widely used examples: the SPJ Code of Ethics and the Potter Box Model.

The Society of Professional Journalists (SPJ) is a professional body for journalists in the United States, which started its operation in 1909. SPJ developed a four-part code of ethics: seek truth and report it, minimize harm, be accountable, and act independently. The first part of the code articulates that journalists should ensure truth in their profession. The process of ensuring truth starts with news and information gathering and ends with publishing of news. The second part says that all parties involved in the process of journalism, from subjects and sources to editors and media company owners, should be respected and that harm ought to be minimized. The third part of the code highlights the freedom and independence of journalists. However, the code also mentions that journalists have obligations to serve the people's need to know important news and information about their community and the world. Finally, the fourth part argues for journalism accountability. According to this step, journalists should be responsible to everyone from their sources to their colleagues. This model, specially designed for journalists, is in essence a balancing act—balancing on the one hand truth-telling with minimizing harm, and weighing on the other hand the need for independence against the need to act with accountability.

Harvard University social ethics professor Ralph D. Potter initiated an ethics framework that became known as the Potter Box. Rather than being unique to journalism, Potter argued that his model is appropriate in all ethical situations. The four steps of his model include defining the situation, identifying one's values, identifying guiding principles or philosophies, and choosing loyalties. In the first step, all relevant facts are defined so journalists might better comprehend a situation. The second step involves defining and identifying advantages of different values. For example, if a journalist identifies his or her obligation to uphold the truth as an important value, then this journalist would be hard-pressed to tell a lie

to obtain a news story. In the third step, different philosophies or dimensions of ethical arguments are considered. The fourth step involves considering the loyalties of the decision makers. For example, journalists have often-conflicting loyalties to their audience, owners, editors, colleagues, and society, and they should keep these loyalties in mind when performing their professional duties. Potter argues that the steps of his model could be used in any order and in any situation. Therefore, the Potter Box is a flexible model providing a framework to deal with any ethical issue. It is a circular process, and anyone can start from any step of the model to make any decision.

The Potter Box Model establishes a framework to ensure ethics in all situations and for all professions, including journalism. The model is considered an integrated system. Even though the four steps should be followed to come up with an ethical decision, it is a systematic approach to deal with ethical dilemmas. In summary, the Potter Box Model trusts the conscience of journalists. Moreover, people who are not journalists can also follow the Potter Box Model to aid in their decision-making processes. Today's media companies are part of corporate business organizations and are viewed as profit-making endeavors. The reality is that not only journalists but also corporate executives are major parts of current media organizations. Thus, a general code of ethics such as the Potter Box Model may be more appropriate to handle a variety of issues concerning the ethics of media organizations.

In our increasingly litigious society, however, First Amendment attorneys tend to recommend that media organizations not have ethics codes, with the logic being that a firm cannot be sued for violating something it does not have. As a result, fewer modern-day organizations either have or publicize their ethics codes.

News Councils

News councils have actively monitored the media for nearly a half a century. News or press councils are media ethics organizations that deal with public complaints about the media and media organizations. Based on their investigation of complaints, the news councils meet and make nonbinding recommendations. Although some critics argue news councils are toothless tigers, such councils were never intended to act as sanctions-imposing, extralegal bodies, but rather to provide fodder for discussion of the ethics behind media decisions.

Accordingly, councils provide platforms to bring transparency to the activities of the media. News councils may be seen as ethics clearinghouses for people with complaints about different media organizations. Most news councils around the globe have no legal authority, so compliance with their recommendations is strictly voluntary for media organizations. In the United States, the trend has been toward fewer and less powerful news councils. The National News Council existed from 1974 until 1984 before disbanding. Even though the National News Council first started its operation during the Nixon administration, professional journalists protested the move and said that it would be an obstacle to their work and in direct conflict with the spirit of the First Amendment to the U.S. Constitution.

The twenty-first century has been particularly unkind to U.S. news councils. The Media Council Hawaii, formerly the Honolulu Community Media Council, was established in 1970. Today it appears to be a council in name only. Too, the Minnesota News Council (MNC), founded in 1970 by the Minnesota Newspaper Association, closed shop in 2011. The MNC, like most news councils, fielded complaints by individuals and organizations who claimed they had been harmed by the media. The MNC considered itself to be a "forum of fairness," having and desiring no punitive powers or legal authority. The New England News Council, established in 2006, eventually changed its name to the New England News Forum and decided it would no longer hear public complaints against media outlets, but instead would host discussions about news-coverage issues. The Southern California News Council, despite receiving $75,000 in seed funding by the Knight Foundation in 2006, never got off the ground because of a lack of support from California State University, Long Beach, which was to have been its home base. The last U.S. news council, the Washington State News Council, closed in May 2014.

The Minnesota News Council, the nation's longest-running press council, reported that some 90 percent of the complaints it received were resolved without hearings. The remaining 10 percent of complaints were resolved at council hearings, comprising equal numbers of public and media members. During its forty-one-year existence, the council ruled in favor of the public about half of the time, and for the media about half the time. Gary Gilson, MNC executive director, said it had become increasingly difficult during the 2000s to raise money to support Minnesota's council.

As news council hearings were in no way legal or governmental, no plaintiffs' or defendants' attorneys were involved, and no billable hours were ever generated. It is little wonder that attorneys seldom were big fans of news councils. That said, such media ethics "forums for fairness" are all now extinct in the United States, even though one-time detractor Mike Wallace of CBS eventually changed his tune and called for a national news council. Later in his life, Walter Cronkite also advocated for statewide news councils. Despite such prominent news council proponents, modern-day corporations, institutions, and well-endowed prospective individual donors increasingly were reluctant to financially support media accountability organizations such as news councils. Too, twenty-first-century news councils in the United States found it difficult to accommodate tweets, social media, journalists unaffiliated with traditional mass media—and, in general, a world where journalism and journalists are ever-changing.

The situation overseas is different, however. There are four international press councils: the Alliance of Independent Press Councils of Europe, World Association of Press Councils, Réseau des Instances Africaines d'Autorégulation des Médias (RIAAM), and Eastern Caribbean Press Council. There are also fifty-nine press councils in nations around the world, according to the Media Accountability System Project of the Donald W. Reynolds Journalism Institute.

Media Critics

Media critics, such as Jim Romenesko, are those people who monitor and evaluate the performance of the media. Since these individuals often criticize the role of their colleagues in the media, such critics face many obstacles from their colleagues. As an example, the Media Giraffe Project is a not-for-profit research platform of different media-reform activists who conduct research and monitor the media landscape in the United States. This project started in April 2005 in the Department of Journalism at the University of Massachusetts, Amherst. The word "Giraffe" of the Media Giraffe Project is symbolic and refers to vigilant individuals monitoring the media. In this way, Giraffes work for a strengthened participatory democratic system. The Media Giraffe Project started as a result of the absence of an effective monitoring system to ensure that the media fulfills its role of informing citizens so that they can demand accountability of the U.S. government. The project conducts its activities through research, workshops, symposia, and conferences.

Media critics are key components in the watchdog functions of media, and those critics—including bloggers, political pundits, and others who operate outside of the mainstream media—sometimes are collectively referred to as the Fifth Estate. Such reporters are also seen as an important component of media literacy, as they inform readers and audience members of what the media are doing and saying, which helps people analyze and evaluate the media messages they receive. Some of the major media reporters over the years have run the gamut from the late *New Yorker* press critic A. J. Liebling to modern media critics such as Jack Shafer of Reuters, David Carr of the *New York Times*, Howard Kurtz of the *Washington Post*, and Eric Alterman of the *Nation*. Besides individual critics, there are some organizations that monitor, analyze, and correct misinformation provided by ideological and political groups. For example, Accuracy in Media (AIM) on the right and Fairness and Accuracy in Reporting (FAIR) on the left report on media institutions and publish their findings. The age of new/social media has brought a shift in the scope, function, and role of media criticism. At a time of media retrenchment and cutbacks, many media organizations are reluctant to hire a media reporter or critic when other journalists are needed to cover courts or schools or any number of other local beats.

Journalism Reviews

Journalism reviews are part of media criticism and have played an active role in ensuring accountability in the media by emphasizing self-regulatory issues. The three remaining journalism reviews in the United States—*American Journalism Review, Columbia Journalism Review,* and *Gateway Journalism Review*—evaluate media activities. *CJR* and *GJR* have both print magazines and an online presence. *AJR* publishes online only. These reviews critically analyze media activities and

behavior both in the United States and overseas. Journalism reviews provide platforms for self-regulation and self-criticism for journalists. The reality, though, is that while these reviews have some influence on the quality of the journalism profession, there are few journalism reviews in the world. Scholars generally indicate that the internal and external values of journalists have been influenced by members of the press reading the reviews. However, the reviews have come under some criticism for exhibiting biases in covering public/civic journalism and for not covering self-regulatory issues and international journalism issues.

Attracting advertisers to place ads in either online or print journalism reviews has been particularly difficult during the twenty-first century, when money has been tight and advertisers are reluctant to say anything that might annoy the media. Also, such reviews—especially in print format—have had a difficult time attracting new subscribers, as people are increasingly able to go online for the specific media-related news they seek, rather than relying on review magazines that come out either monthly (*CJR*) or quarterly (*GJR*). Too, younger media-monitors tend to prefer Googling their specific media-related items rather than going to review sites containing both aggregated and original-reporting information.

Ombudspersons

Media ombudspersons, or internal watchdogs, are people who—although they work for the media—mediate disputes between the media and the public. The ombudspersons in news media organizations also provide guidance to address reader or audience complaints about news and comments about the media. The ombudspersons in news media organizations also act as readers' representatives, fielding readers' complaints. Indeed, ombudspersons are known by different names, such as public editors and readers' representatives. By acting as mediators to deal with different complaints of concerned people, ombudspersons try to reach a solution that is mutually agreeable to all parties. So, the main objective of the ombudspersons system is to work for justice and equal rights in an organization. The ombudspersons in media organizations are integral components of the process of ensuring accountability.

The system of ombudspersons first started in the late nineteenth century in Sweden, and other Scandinavian countries followed the Swedish example of designating ombudspersons for government organizations. In the United States, the practice of appointing ombudspersons started in the late 1970s. The first press ombudsman appeared in the United States in July 1967, with the function of listening to the complaints of the readers of the *Louisville Courier-Journal* and the *Louisville Times*, in Kentucky.

In journalism, there has for some time been a debate about how best to ensure accountability in media organizations. Despite the fact that the media ask questions about society, it was an uncommon practice in media organizations to seek answers about the activities of the media. Many scholars argue that it is possible to ensure a more accountable media

organization by having ombudsman. A media organization that creates an ombudsman position for the purposes of enhancing accountability takes a step toward greater social responsibility. The work of some ombudspersons in media organizations has had a positive impact on media accountability. However, there are some criticisms about the effectiveness of ombudspersons, as some media ethicists argue that ombudspersons function as little more than public-relations flacks.

The *New York Times* is one of those media organizations with a public editor. The newspaper first appointed a public editor in 2003, in the wake of the Jayson Blair plagiarism and fabrication scandal, choosing Daniel Okrent. He was succeeded by Byron Calame, former deputy managing editor of the *Wall Street Journal*. Clark Hoyt, former Washington editor at Knight Ridder, was later appointed as the third public editor of the *New York Times*.

Every news organization acknowledges that it makes some mistakes in its day-to-day business. Before asking questions about society, media should ensure that they have a system in place for asking questions about their own job performance. They should also inform the public about this system, because transparency and accountability are key assets of any media organization. Initiating a position of public editor in a media organization will help create an environment of accountable and credible media.

Despite the potential benefits, *USA Today*'s media editor, Rem Rieder, painted a discouraging picture in 2013, noting that just half as many ombudspersons were working in U.S. news organizations as was the case a decade earlier. He also pointed out that more than a dozen media organizations axed the position following the 2008 recession, despite the fact that a handful of new ombudspersons positions were being created in newsrooms in other nations. The Organization of News Ombudsmen's website lists members in twenty-six countries—seventy-five "regular" members, thirty-nine "associated" members, twenty-six "honorary" members, and fifteen "retired" members. According to ONO, news ombudspersons make up the "regular" membership, with "others from the media, press councils, journalism schools, or journalism publications" constituting the "associate" membership.

The acronym "ONO" is apt for an organization of public editors who are likely to utter, "Oh, no!"—at the very least—when they first are made aware of a problem in their publications. But regardless of how they have operated, there are fewer American ombudspersons today, and there is every reason to believe this downward trend will continue. This does not bode well for a press expected by the First Amendment to serve the public responsibly.

Public/Civic Journalism

The theoretical concept of public/civic (P/C) journalism is based on the philosophical argument of "public sphere" provided by German philosopher Jürgen Habermas. The notion of public sphere refers to a platform where people can share their thoughts to build opinion on a particular issue or subject and thus act as watchdogs of society. The term *public sphere* originated from the German word *Öffentlichkeit*, which means an area in social life—a coffeehouse, for example—where people can meet to freely discuss societal problems. In this way, people can raise their voices and express an opinion about any political or social event. According to P/C journalism theory, money and power can prevent productive communication, and thus capitalist mass media can extinguish the public sphere. The development of the Internet will allow commercial media to be a more effective public sphere, with the advent of citizen journalist programs such as CNN's iReport.

Grassroots P/C journalism has grown rapidly since the advent of Internet journalism. P/C journalism empowers members of the public to impact and indeed set the news agenda, thus enhancing, and sometimes threatening, the power of traditional or legacy journalism. Now, any person with a laptop or smartphone and Internet connection can become a public journalist. P/C journalism aims to engage people/audiences in journalism, and the new media have become an integral part of this process. P/C journalism strives to increase citizens' participation in the democratic process by focusing attention on issues that matter to the public. The most important objective of P/C journalism is to provide an opportunity for interactivity with the audience. For example, most mainstream media have been opening up and allowing this kind of interactivity, such as "Have your voice heard" in the BBC and online comments by readers of the *New York Times*.

As a result, "journalists" now write reports and comment on events in different ways, such as blogs, media websites, and social networking sites such as Facebook and Twitter. Of the tools of P/C journalism, blogs have been extensively used, and some scholars argue that blogging is the most efficient method to independently report on any event taking place in society. Web blogs allow people to discuss political issues affecting them. It seems clear that P/C journalism today is in many respects dependent on new media, and the new media are the best means to ensure public and civic engagement in this journalism.

P/C journalism and new media complement each other in several ways. Both P/C journalism and new media have been providing public spaces for discussions, which are operated in a community context. Too, both P/C journalism and new media have improved civic skills, changed public policy, formed new community organizations, and increased volunteerism. P/C journalism and new media both have stimulated discussions on the role and responsibility of journalism in a democratic society.

However, with the perfect storm of P/C journalism and new/social media, defining who a "journalist" is becomes increasingly problematic. Is a thirteen-year-old sitting in her bed and blogging on her laptop a journalist, and if so, are we all now to be considered journalists? Stated another way, in a world where everyone is a journalist, no one is a journalist. In any event, any thought of professionalism—and of professional ethics—is nonexistent, as there are likely to be few if any agreed-upon guidelines. Seen in such an ethics-based light, the P/C journalism–new technology convergence, though an

intriguing intellectual discussion point, is at best worrisome.

Conclusion

These six ethics tools, all of which originated during the mid- to late twentieth century, have often helped enhance and improve media accountability. These guidelines are based on broader philosophical—and, in some cases, universal—perspectives. Now, though, new/social media and new technology are in many cases diminishing the effectiveness of the accountability tools in this media ethics toolbox. At least in the United States, few people or media organizations any longer pay serious attention to media ethics codes, news councils have died out, few established media critics/reporters remain, journalism reviews are an endangered species, ombudspersons are all but irrelevant, and public/civic journalism has been subsumed by new technology.

All accountability tools have the potential of being used in the new-tech twenty-first century. More meaningful new-tech ethics codes could be developed, news council sessions could be Skyped, endowments might fund media critics and journalism reviews, ombudspersons and readers' representatives could work for multiple organizations, and P/C journalism initiatives might become more meaningful if "journalists" were better trained. If these or other new-century mechanisms are employed and found to be successful, there indeed is hope that the media accountability tools still can be useful in continually improving media ethics.

For much of the twentieth century, a couple of small screwdrivers, a lubricant, a rag, and a new ribbon constituted the bulk of the items needed to repair a typewriter. Today, such tools are meaningless when one is faced with a laptop that refuses to boot up. By like token, media ethics accountability tools are quickly becoming rust- and dust-covered. It is now up to twenty-first-century media ethics techies to see how a new toolbox might best be constituted and retrofitted so the public can both participate in and get a fair accounting of the news of the day.

William A. Babcock
Southern Illinois University Carbondale
Delwar Hossain
Southern Illinois University Carbondale

See also Ethical Responsibilities versus Legal Rights; Global Media Ethics: Myth or Reality?; Institutional Foundations

Further Reading

Bertrand, Claude-Jean. *Media Ethics and Accountability Systems*. London: Transaction Publishers, 2000.

Bowman, S., and C. Willis. "The Future Is Here, but Do News Media Companies See It?" *Neiman Reports* (Winter 2005): 5–10.

Carmichael, B. "News Councils Revisited." *American Journalism Review,* October/November 2006.

Christians, C. G., K. B. Rotzoll, M. Fackler, K. B. McKee, and R. H. Woods. *Media Ethics: Cases and Moral Reasoning*. Boston: Pearson, 2005.

Cline, A. R. "Ethics and Ethos: Writing an Effective Newspaper Ombudsman Position." *Journal of Mass Media Ethics* 23 (2008): 79–89.

Commission on Freedom of the Press. *A Free and Responsible Press*. Chicago: University of Chicago Press, 1947.

Evans, H. *Good Times, Bad Times*. New York: Atheneum, 1984.

Fanselow, J. "Community Blogging: The New Wave of Citizen Journalism." *National Civic Review* 94, no. 4 (2009): 24–29.

Farrar, R. "News Councils and Libel Actions." *Journalism Quarterly* 63, no. 3 (1986): 509–516.

Fengler, Susanne. "Holding the News Media Accountable: A Study of Media Reporters and Media Critics in the United States." *Journalism and Mass Communication Quarterly* 80, no. 4 (2003): 818–832.

Gordon, A. D. "Media Codes of Ethics Are Useful and Necessary to the Mass Media and to Society." In *Controversies in Media Ethics*, edited by A. David Gordon and John Michael Kittross. New York: Longman, 1999.

Haas, T. "Alternative Media, Public Journalism, and the Pursuit of Democratization." *Journalism Studies* 5, no. 1 (2004): 115–121.

Haas, T. *The Pursuit of Public Journalism: Theory, Practice, and Criticism*. New York: Routledge, 2007.

Hannigan, J. A. "The Newspaper Ombudsman and Consumer Complaints: An Empirical Assessment." *Law and Society Review* 11, no. 4 (1977): 679–699.

Hickey, Neil. "A Public Editor's Private Story." *Columbia Journalism Review* 44 (May/June 2005): 24.

Hlavach, L., and W. H. Freivogel. "Ethical Implications of Anonymous Comments Posted to Online News Stories." In *Media Accountability: Who Will Watch the Watchdog in the Twitter Age?*, edited by William Babcock, 91–107. New York: Routledge, 2011.

Hossain, M. D., and W. A. Babcock. *Journalism Reviews: Watchdog of the Watchdogs*. Paper presented at the annual conference of the International Communication Association, 2012.

John, B. S., III. "Newspapers Struggle with Civic Engagement: The U.S. Press and the Rejection of Public Journalism as Propagandistic." *Communication Review* 10 (2007): 249–270.

Limor, Y., and I. Himelboim. "Journalism and Moonlighting: An International Comparison of 242 Codes of Ethics." *Journal of Mass Media Ethics* 21, no. 4 (2006): 265–285.

Logan, R. A. "Jefferson's and Madison's Legacy: The Death of the National News Council." *Journal of Mass Media Ethics* 1, no. 1 (Fall–Winter 1985/86): 68.

Maier, Scott R. "Do Trade Publications Affect Ethical Sensitivity in Newsrooms? *Newspaper Research Journal* 21, no. 1 (2000): 41–50.

Media Giraffe Project. *The Media Giraffe Project Mission,* 2013. http://www.mediagiraffe.org/mission1.

Mendes, J. F. *Ombudsman: Self-Criticism in Newspapers.* Organization of News Ombudsmen, November 23, 2009. http://newsombudsmen.org/articles/articles-about-ombudsmen/ombudsman-self-criticism-in-newspapers.

Merrill, J. C. "Commentary." In *Controversies in Media Ethics,* edited by A. David Gordon and John Michael Kittross. New York: Longman, 1999.

Meyers, C. "Creating an Effective Newspaper Ombudsman Position." *Journal of Mass Media Ethics* 15 (2000): 248–256.

Nelsen, D. R., and K. Starck. *The Newspaper Ombudsman as Viewed by the Rest of the Staff.* Paper presented at the annual meeting of the Association for Education in Journalism, 1973.

Nemeth, N. *News Ombudsmen in North America: Assessing an Experiment in Social Responsibility.* Westport, CT: Praeger, 2003.

Nip, J. Y. M. "Exploring the Second Phase of Public Journalism." *Journalism Studies* 7, no. 2 (2006): 212–236.

Northington, K. B. *Media Criticism as Professional Self-Regulation, a Study of U.S. Journalism Reviews.* Unpublished dissertation, presented to the faculty of the Graduate School, Indiana University, 1993.

Organization of News Ombudsmen (ONO). "ONO President Promotes Ombudsmanship in U.K.," 2013. http://newsombudsmen.org/ombudsmen-in-the-news/ono-president-promotes-ombudsmanship-in-u-k.

Schaffer, J. *Civic Journalism: A Decade of Civic Innovation.* Paper presented at the Society of Professional Journalists national convention, 2002. http://www.pewcenter.org/doingcj/speeches/s_spjheadline.html.

Siebert, F., et al. *Four Theories of the Press.* Urbana, IL: Illini Books, 1963.

Society of Professional Journalists (SPJ). "Code of Ethics." http://www.spj.org/ethicscode.asp.

Son, T. "Leaks: How Do Codes of Ethics Address Them?" *Journal of Mass Media Ethics* 17, no. 2 (2002): 155–173.

Steinberg, J. "The *Times* Chooses Veteran of Magazines and Publishing as Its First Public Editor." *New York Times,* October 27, 2003. http://www.nytimes.com/2003/10/27/business/media/27PAPE.html?scp=1&sq=Times%2chooses%20veteran%20of%20magazines%20and%20publishing%20as%20its%20first&t=cse.

Stepp, C. S. "The New Journalist." In *Impact of Mass Media: Current Issues*, edited by Ray Eldon Hiebert. New York: Longman, 1999.

Turkle, S. "Cyberspace and Identity." *Contemporary Sociology* 28, no. 6 (1999): 643–648.

Turkle, S. "Rethinking Identity through Virtual Community." In *Clicking In: Hot Links to a Digital Culture*, edited by L. H. Leeson, 116–122. Seattle, WA: Bay Press, 1996.

Ugland, E. F., and J. Breslin. "Minnesota News Council: Principles, Precedent, and Moral Authority." *Journal of Mass Media Ethics* 15, no. 4 (2000): 232–247.

Walther, J. B. "Selective Self-Presentation in Computer-Mediated Communication:

Hyperpersonal Dimensions of Technology, Language, and Cognition." *Computers in Human Behavior* 23 (2007): 2538–2557.

Ward, S. J. A. *Global Media Ethics: Problems and Perspectives*. Oxford, UK: Wiley-Blackwell, 2013.

Witt, L. "Is Public Journalism Morphing into the Public's Journalism?" *National Civic Review* (Fall 2004): 49–57.

Witt, L. "Participatory Journalism Meets Public Journalism—and a New Era Begins." *Civic Journalism Interest Group News* (Winter 2004): 1–5.

44

COMPELLED SPEECH

Can the government force someone to express something with which that party may not agree? In some cases, yes. This is called "compelled speech" (sometimes "coerced speech"), and the Supreme Court has supported this doctrine in several key opinions. Coupled with the legal question is a significant and thorny ethical component: Should the government have the right to mandate that companies, individuals, or organizations engage in speech acts they would rather not? Conversely, can the government, legally and ethically, force someone not to speak? Moreover, do listeners have any right to hear, or to be prevented from hearing, some points of view?

In many cases, these several notions are combined: for example, forcing a doctor (using government funding) to counsel a woman not to have an abortion when the doctor would rather counsel her to have an abortion, or not counsel her at all, demonstrates the conundrum. The doctor cannot speak about one side of the issue, or would prefer not to speak at all, but must speak about the other side. Under what circumstances should the government be allowed to interfere with a woman and her doctor? More broadly, are there circumstances under which the government should be permitted to interfere with speech? To establish the contours of the conflicting doctrines, it is first important to examine early cases in compelled speech, along with a case that evaluates governmental power to compel private speakers to embrace unwanted ideologies.

Early Compelled Speech Cases

The Supreme Court has handed down a somewhat mixed bag of cases in this area, and the law is not completely settled. The earliest case, *Minersville School District v. Gobitis* (1940), was a challenge to the Minersville, Pennsylvania, public school policy that all students salute the flag and say the Pledge of Allegiance in class or face expulsion. Two children in a Jehovah's Witness family were expelled for refusing to do so. The Court upheld the policy, saying that a free society "is fostered by all those agencies of the mind and spirit which may serve to gather up the traditions of a people, transmit them from generation to generation, and thereby create that continuity of a treasured common life which constitutes a civilization." Moreover, since the Pennsylvania legislature had not provided an exception to the policy on religious grounds, the Court declined to do so.

Public outcry was significant—including by Eleanor Roosevelt, who publicly decried the Court's decision. In 1943, the Court reversed itself, in a case brought by a Jehovah's Witness family who objected to a West Virginia requirement similar to that upheld in Pennsylvania. In *West Virginia State Board of Education v. Barnette*, the Court overturned the West Virginia law. Justice Robert Jackson wrote for a 6–3 majority words that have been repeated many times in First Amendment jurisprudence, "If there is any fixed star in our constitutional constellation, it is that no official, high or petty, can prescribe what shall be orthodox in politics, nationalism, religion, or other matters of opinion or force citizens to confess by word or act their faith therein."

The Court echoed some of the ideas in *Barnette* in a case involving license plates in 1977. The Maynards, a Jehovah's Witness couple, objected to the motto "Live Free or Die" that was standard on New Hampshire license plates at the time, and they obscured the motto on their plates in violation of New Hampshire law. The Court in *Wooley v. Maynard* said that the state could not mandate the display of the motto: "New Hampshire's statute in effect requires that appellees use their private property as a 'mobile billboard' for the State's ideological message—or suffer a penalty, as Maynard already has." Although the state's goal of promoting an ideology can be pursued in different ways, the Court said, the goal cannot

override an individual's moral objections to the ideology.

However, it should be noted that private organizations do not have the same obligations as governmental bodies to refrain from dictating ideology. The Court struck down a Florida right-of-reply law in *Miami Herald Publishing Co. v. Tornillo* in 1974. The state law allowed any candidate for office attacked in a Florida newspaper to have published a reply to the attack in that newspaper. In striking down the law, Chief Justice Warren Burger wrote for a unanimous Court, "The choice of material to go into a newspaper, and the decisions made as to limitations on the size and content of the paper, and treatment of public issues and public official—whether fair or unfair—constitute the exercise of editorial control and judgment. It has yet to be demonstrated how governmental regulation of this crucial process can be exercised consistent with First Amendment guarantees of a free press as they have evolved to this time."

It is worth noting that broadcast organizations *can* be compelled to speak in certain ways—for example, in broadcasting political advertising—but because government regulates the usage of the airwaves via licensing in the public interest, the result is different. Should it be? Should the method of information delivery determine the level of First Amendment protection the information receives? What about the same information delivered on different platforms—should each version of the information, even if it contains the same content, be treated differently?

In a case with a similar question of whether the state can compel a private organization to speak in a particular way,

Hurley v. Irish-American Gay, Lesbian and Bisexual Group of Boston, Inc., the Court in 1995 said that a Massachusetts court order to the South Boston Allied War Veterans Council to include gay, lesbian, and bisexual individuals in the annual Boston St. Patrick's Day parade ran afoul of the First Amendment. Justice David Souter wrote for a unanimous Court, "Disapproval of a private speaker's statement does not legitimize use of the Commonwealth's power to compel the speaker to alter the message by including one more acceptable to others."

Three separate areas of compelled speech will next be examined: compelled commercial speech, compelled speech to receive government funding, and compelled silence (or refraining from engaging in certain expressive activities or content) in government employees.

Compelled Advertising Speech

As discussed in other chapters, the 1980 test developed in *Central Hudson Gas & Electric Corporation v. Public Service Commission of New York* governs most advertising cases today. That four-part test evaluates the legality of the goods or services advertised, the sufficiency of the government's goal in regulating the advertising, the likelihood of the regulation achieving the goal, and the amount of speech regulated (or the quality of the "fit" between the regulation and the goal). In many, if not most, cases, the regulation fails to meet the rather stringent interpretation of the *Central Hudson* test promulgated by the Supreme Court.

Prior to the *Central Hudson* case, in the case of *Abood v. Detroit Board of*

Education (1977), the justices said that forcing charges on nonunion members of a Detroit public school district that would be used to finance expenses for collective bargaining was not a First Amendment violation. However, those dues could not be used to subsidize lobbying or other expenses for ideological causes.

"The fact that the appellants are compelled to make, rather than prohibited from making, contributions for political purposes works no less an infringement of their constitutional rights," wrote Justice Potter Stewart. "For at the heart of the First Amendment is the notion that an individual should be free to believe as he will, and that in a free society one's beliefs should be shaped by his mind and his conscience rather than coerced by the State." Nor could the state compel an individual to agree with a political point of view to keep public employment.

The *Abood* precedent was weakened by a 2014 Supreme Court decision. One question before the Court in *Harris v. Quinn* addressed whether home-care workers, who provide patient services one-on-one, must pay into a public union. The Court answered no, striking down an Illinois law that required all workers to pay for legal services that the state required the union to provide, and in so doing called into question the precedential value of *Abood*. Justice Samuel Alito wrote for the majority, "*Abood* failed to appreciate the difference between the core union speech involuntarily subsidized by dissenting public-sector employees and the core union speech involuntarily funded by their counterparts in the private sector." Calling the in-home healthcare providers "partial public employees," Justice Alito said that to extend the *Abood* principles to them "would invite problems."

Although the Court first extended First Amendment protection to attorney advertising in *Bates v. State Bar of Arizona* in 1977 (discussed in Chapter 46), it has revisited the question of what is permissible in such advertising many times since. Of particular note for compelled speech (or, here, compelled absence of "speech") in the 1985 case of *Zauderer v. Office of Disciplinary Counsel* was an Ohio law that forbade the use of illustrations in ads for legal services. Columbus lawyer Philip Q. Zauderer placed an ad for legal services for women who had been harmed by the Dalkon Shield intra-uterine birth-control device, accompanied by a line drawing of the Dalkon Shield.

There was agreement that the ad did not contain any false or misleading information. The state of Ohio alleged that illustrations were not dignified in legal services advertising but did not provide any evidence or findings to support that allegation. Under *Central Hudson*, the burden on the state was to demonstrate that the ban served a substantial governmental interest and was a good fit for that interest—and the state failed to do so. Justice Byron White wrote, "Thus, acceptance of the State's argument would be tantamount to adoption of the principle that a State may prohibit the use of pictures or illustrations in connection with advertising of any product or service simply on the strength of the general argument that the visual content of advertisements may, under some circumstances, be deceptive or manipulative. But as we stated above, broad prophylactic rules may not be so lightly justified if the protections afforded commercial speech are to retain their force."

Justice White pointed to the efforts of the Federal Trade Commission in regulating broadcast advertising as indicative of the government's ability to regulate images in advertising in a reasoned way. He added, "Because the extension of First Amendment protection to commercial speech is justified principally by the value to consumers of the information such speech provides . . . appellant's constitutionally protected interest in *not* providing any particular factual information in his advertising is minimal."

However, the Court did not use the *Central Hudson* test to overturn a regulation that mandated disclosure of the percentage of charity funds to be paid to the fund-raiser in the 1988 case of *Riley v. National Federation of the Blind of North Carolina*. North Carolina had a statute that mandated fund-raisers to disclose the amount of proceeds paid to the charity to potential donors when soliciting them. Justice William Brennan wrote for a fractured Court that the solicitation of charitable funds is fully protected speech, and the state's attempt to frame the regulation as merely an economic one must fail. The fact that there was a commercial element in the protected speech does not move the speech into the commercial speech category.

Justice Brennan explicitly included compelled silence in the Court's jurisprudence for compelled speech. "Nor is a deferential test to be applied on the theory that the First Amendment interest in compelled speech is different than the interest in compelled silence," he wrote. "The difference is without constitutional significance, for the First Amendment guarantees 'freedom of speech,' a term necessarily comprising the decision of both what to say and what not to say." Rather than tamper with protected speech, he reminded the state of its antifraud laws to protect consumers and charitable donors.

Several recent Supreme Court cases have dealt with regulations on food producers, including several in the area of generic advertising. This type of advertising focuses on general consumption of a product rather than on a particular producer's brand—for example, the famous "Got Milk?" commercials, created by the California Milk Processor Board and licensed to national dairy boards and educational groups like the Milk Processor Education Program.

In *Glickman v. Wileman Brothers & Elliott, Inc.* (1997), a small group of California fruit growers and distributors challenged the Agricultural Marketing Agreement Act of 1937 (AMMA). They objected to the AMMA-mandated marketing orders applied to these California producers that included collective generic advertising for the fruit as part of a larger regulatory scheme—one that promotes a cooperative marketing plan (free from antitrust problems). At issue was a generic ad that read "'California Summer Fruits' are wholesome, delicious, and attractive to discerning shoppers." The California producers challenged the ad and the marketing order mandate as a violation of the First Amendment.

Justice John Paul Stevens, writing for a 5–4 majority, did not agree with the fruit producers and upheld the AMMA marketing order's generic advertising mandate. The fact that the ads may cut into the budgets of the producers did not make

them First Amendment violations. The question, as Justice Stevens put it, was "whether being compelled to fund this advertising raises a First Amendment issue for us to resolve, or rather is simply a question of economic policy for Congress and the Executive to resolve." He found that it was the latter.

Justice Stevens distinguished the Court's holding in *Abood* because in this case, the fruit producers were not being compelled to fund an ideological statement with which they may not agree. He did not apply the *Central Hudson* test (and found the Ninth Circuit in error for having done so) because, as he wrote, "The basic policy decision that underlies the entire statute rests on an assumption that in the volatile markets for agricultural commodities the public will be best served by compelling cooperation among producers in making economic decisions that would be made independently in a free market."

A few years later, in 2001, the Court was faced with a similar generic advertising case, this time for mushrooms. In *United States v. United Foods, Inc.,* the constitutionality of a federal law, the Mushroom Promotion, Research, and Consumer Information Act, was challenged by a group of Tennessee mushroom growers. The justices distinguished this case from *Glickman*, however, because under this law most of the funds were earmarked for generic mushroom marketing. Justice Anthony Kennedy wrote that unlike the California fruit producers, mushroom producers were not forced "to associate as a group which makes cooperative decisions." Thus, because there was not a cooperative agreement for mushroom producers, Justice Kennedy said that the speech was actually compelled: "We have not upheld compelled subsidies for speech in the context of a program where the principal object is speech itself."

Beef producers had their day in court in 2005, challenging a generic advertising scheme required by the federal Beef Promotion and Research Act in *Johanns v. Livestock Marketing Association*. The question before the Court was the same as in *Glickman* and *United Foods*: does forcing the beef producers to fund advertising with which they may not agree violate the First Amendment? The Court said no, but because the speech was considered to be *government* speech, not private speech.

Justice Antonin Scalia pointed out that funding compelled speech in a private setting raises First Amendment concerns, while funding government speech does not. He wrote, somewhat wryly, "'Compelled support of government'— even those programs of government one does not approve—is of course perfectly constitutional, as every taxpayer must attest." The degree of governmental control of the speech in this case was significant; the content was designed and approved by governmental agencies. "Here, the beef advertisements are subject to political safeguards more than adequate to set them apart from private messages," Justice Scalia wrote, indicating that the process of electing government officials provides political control.

In perhaps the most controversial of compelled advertising cases, the Food and Drug Administration (FDA) published a rule that mandated graphic cigarette warning labels under the federal Family Smoking Prevention and Tobacco Control Act. Tobacco companies challenged the labels, which contained a 1–800-QUIT-NOW hotline number and graphic images such as a man smoking through a tracheotomy hole in his neck, a pair of diseased lungs, and a woman kissing a baby wreathed in smoke, and were to have covered a significant portion of the cigarette package. The tobacco companies alleged that in essence, each cigarette package was a mini-billboard for the government's ideological message of smoking cessation. In 2013, a federal appeals court, agreeing with the district court below, found those labels to be in violation of the First Amendment.

A divided three-judge panel of the D.C. Circuit Court of Appeals, in *R. J. Reynolds Tobacco Co. v. Food and Drug Administration* (2012), called the images "inflammatory" and the hotline "provocatively-named." The government, the majority argued, did not portray any factual information in these graphics. Rather, the ads were "unabashed attempts to evoke emotion (and perhaps embarrassment) and browbeat consumers into quitting." The majority then applied *Central Hudson* and found that "FDA failed to present any data . . . showing that enacting their proposed graphic warnings will accomplish the agency's stated objective of reducing smoking rates." (Interestingly, the dissenting judge believed that the *Central Hudson* test was too harsh a standard to be applied and instead would have used a less strict "reasonable relationship" standard under which to evaluate the government's goals and approach.) The FDA did not appeal this decision and instead announced that it would go back to the drawing board and create new labels that were more constitutionally defensible.

All of these cases contain a significant ethical question, as noted earlier: To what extent should government be able to mandate speech (or silence) about legal goods and services? Smoking and drinking are legal for adults in the United States, so what gives the government the right to encourage people to quit smoking or drinking—or to mandate that tobacco or liquor companies do the job for it? What other ethical questions are raised by generic ads and graphic cigarette warnings? Why was alcohol not treated the same way as tobacco?

Government Funding of Speech

As discussed above, different rules apply when government speaks or funds speech. Americans generally have no direct say in the ways in which government speaks for itself and no way to not pay into government funds that support speech acts. As the *Johanns* Court put it, "Citizens may challenge compelled support of private speech, but have no First Amendment right not to fund government speech." Four cases demonstrate the legal landscape in this area.

In 1991, the constitutionality of regulations governing funding of Title X of the Public Health Service Act for family planning services under the Department of Health and Human Services (HHS) were challenged when HHS issued rules that limited the ability of Title X funding recipients to use those funds only in support of preventative family planning

services, not abortion-related activities. Doctors and other Title X grant recipients challenged the rules as a violation of their First and Fifth Amendment rights, but the Court upheld the rules.

Chief Justice William Rehnquist wrote for a 5–4 majority in *Rust v. Sullivan* that the rules were not arbitrary or capricious, but that because the rules were unclear regarding abortion counseling by doctors, the Court would defer to the HHS secretary's interpretation. "We hold that the regulations promulgated by the Secretary do not raise the sort of 'grave and doubtful constitutional questions' . . . that would lead us to assume Congress did not intend to authorize their issuance," he wrote.

The Title X regulations did not unduly interfere with a doctor's relationship with a patient, said the Court. Because the regulation does not provide post-conception medical care, "a doctor's silence with regard to abortion cannot reasonably be thought to mislead a client into thinking that the doctor does not consider abortion an appropriate option for her," the chief justice reasoned.

Interestingly, however, Chief Justice Rehnquist added what many would think to be an astonishing assertion: "Nor is the doctor-patient relationship established by the Title X program sufficiently all-encompassing so as to justify an expectation on the part of the patient of comprehensive medical advice." One would assume that when a patient consults with a doctor, the patient's reasonable expectation would be that the doctor would provide comprehensive medical advice—not simply advice with which the government agreed or financially or otherwise sanctioned. Is this fair, or even moral? To what extent should doctors be financially or morally beholden to anything other than the Hippocratic Oath ("I will prescribe regimens for the good of my patients according to my ability and my judgment and never do harm to anyone")?

In the 1998 case of *National Endowment for the Arts v. Finley*, the question was one of funding for the arts. The National Endowment for the Arts (NEA) had established as broad guidelines for funding of artists "artistic and cultural significance," emphasizing "creativity and cultural diversity" and "professional excellence," and encouraging "public education and appreciation of the arts." In 1990 Congress amended the NEA guidelines to include "artistic excellence and artistic merit taking into consideration general standards of decency and respect for the diverse beliefs and values of the American public." Performance artist Karen Finley, whose art has been deemed controversial due to its raw depictions of sexuality and sexual abuse, was denied NEA funding, and she and other artists brought suit, alleging that the "general standards of decency" guideline was vague and violated the First Amendment.

The Court disagreed. In an 8–1 decision, the justices upheld the NEA guidelines. Relying on *Rust*, Justice Sandra Day O'Connor wrote, "Congress may 'selectively fund a program to encourage certain activities it believes to be in the public interest, without at the same time funding an alternative program which seeks to deal with the problem in another way.'" Moreover, Finley and others could continue to create their art however they wished, as there was no government censorship involved in the NEA's decision not to fund them. As Justice O'Connor put it, "We recognize, as a practical matter, that artists may conform their speech to what they believe to be the decision-making criteria in order to acquire funding. . . . But when the Government is acting as patron rather than as sovereign, the consequences of imprecision are not constitutionally severe."

What about funding going toward humanitarian causes but in violent countries or organizations? The Court faced this question in *Holder v. Humanitarian Law Project* in 2010. The plaintiffs were a group of individuals who supported foreign organizations that engage in both lawful and unlawful activities (for example, the Kurdistan Workers Party). They argued that amendments to the Antiterrorism and Effective Death Penalty Act (AEDPA) making it a crime for individuals to "knowingly" provide "material support or resources" to a group designated as a "foreign terrorist organization" were violations of the First Amendment.

However, the justices did not agree, finding that the provisions were constitutional as applied to the plaintiffs. Chief Justice John Roberts wrote for the majority and said that the terms in question ("training," "expert advice or assistance," "service," and "personnel") were not too vague, unlike terms like "annoying" or "indecent." Moreover, the assistance that the plaintiffs wanted to offer fell within the prohibited statutory definitions. "Plaintiffs do not propose to teach a course on geography, and cannot seek refuge in imaginary cases that straddle the boundary between 'specific skills' and 'general knowledge,'" wrote Chief Justice Roberts. And even if it were not so, as the chief justice pointed out, "Material support meant to 'promot[e] peaceable, lawful conduct' . . . can further terrorism by foreign groups in multiple ways. 'Material support' is a valuable resource by definition."

In a 2013 case involving government funding of speech, *U.S. Agency for International Development v. Alliance for Open Society International,* the question before the Court was whether requiring non-governmental organizations (NGOs) that receive federal funding to adopt explicit policies with which they disagree violates the First Amendment. The answer was yes. The federal United States Leadership Against HIV/AIDS, Tuberculosis, and Malaria Act (Leadership Act) was established in 2003 to fund NGOs to fight HIV/AIDS. To receive this funding, an applicant NGO must adopt a policy that explicitly opposes prostitution. Several NGOs, including the Alliance for Open Society International, challenged this Leadership Act requirement, saying that this restriction on speech, which forced them to promote the government's viewpoint on prostitution, was unconstitutional. The organizations expressed fear that adopting such an explicit antiprostitution position as required for Leadership Act funding not only might alienate some host governments but would make it more difficult in working with prostitutes to combat the spread of HIV/AIDS.

The Court overturned the rule. "A recipient cannot avow the belief dictated by the Policy Requirement when spending Leadership Act funds, and then turn around and assert a contrary belief, or

claim neutrality, when participating in activities on its own time and dime. By requiring recipients to profess a specific belief, the Policy Requirement goes beyond defining the limits of the federally funded program to defining the recipient," wrote Chief Justice John Roberts for a 6–2 majority (Justice Elena Kagan did not participate). Simply put, the chief justice added, "The Policy Requirement compels as a condition of federal funding the affirmation of a belief that by its nature cannot be confined within the scope of the Government program."

Two dissenters, Justice Scalia, joined by Justice Clarence Thomas, felt that the program here was no different than the ones upheld in *Rust* and *Humanitarian Law Project*. Justice Scalia drew a connection with other areas that could receive federal funding: "A federal program to encourage healthy eating habits need not be administered by the American Gourmet Society, which has nothing against healthy food but does not insist upon it." Because the antiprostitution position was central to the government's funding of the Leadership Act, Justice Scalia wrote, "It is entirely reasonable to admit to participation in the program only those who believe in that goal."

What to take away from this discussion? In one case (*U.S. Agency for International Development*), the Court was willing to throw out a law that tied funding to beliefs and speech. But in three cases (*Rust, Finley,* and *Humanitarian Law Project*) the Court was not willing to do so. Where is the difference? To Justices Scalia and Thomas, there should be no difference. When government chooses to fund, it may attach strings to the money. But should it be able to do so? Should participation in a program with an explicit goal be allowed to "only those who believe in that goal," as Justice Scalia wrote? To what extent, then, does government hold a monopoly on American beliefs, or does it at all? Should it? The First Amendment would say no, but the courts have held that there are circumstances under which it might.

As an example, one might reasonably argue that the goal of combating terrorism is not one with which any reasonable person might disagree—but then perhaps it is only a matter of semantics. Is one country's "terrorist" another's "freedom fighter?" Who gets to determine "general standards of decency" for government funding? (Interesting, too, is the fact that Chief Justice Roberts singled out "indecency" as a "vague" word in *Humanitarian Law Project*, but somehow it was acceptably definable in *Finley*. Maybe because *Finley* was "just" an art case, it is less important?) Does a doctor's silence with respect to abortion counseling really mean that he/she has no opinion as to its appropriateness for his/her patient? As with many questions of legal interpretation, such definitions, if not provided by the legislating body, are left to the courts. Is this the right way to do it?

Government Employee Speech

According to the Bureau of Labor Statistics, in January 2014 there were approximately 2.1 million people (excluding postal workers) employed by the federal government, approximately five million employed by state governments,

and approximately fourteen million by county or local governments. To what extent, if any, can governments regulate what their employees say, either on or off the job? The courts have been asked to examine this question many times, and as will be shown, there is no easy answer.

One early Supreme Court case in this area was handed down in 1967, *Keyishian v. Board of Regents*. At issue here was a suit brought by several university professors and a poet challenging New York's Feinberg Law, under which teachers were disqualified from public school employment if they said or wrote "treasonable or seditious" things or advocated or taught "overthrow of the government by force, violence or any unlawful means." The plaintiffs had been asked to sign pledges saying that they were not communists, and they had refused to do so and were fired. The Feinberg Law had been passed during the "Red Scare" of the early 1950s to combat the feared spread of communism through the schools.

Justice Brennan, writing for a 5–4 Court, invalidated the New York law as impermissibly vague. He expressed concern at the vagueness of "treasonable or seditious" acts or words. He outlined a number of scenarios under which the law might be applied. For example, he asked, "Does the teacher who carries a copy of the *Communist Manifesto* on a public street thereby advocate criminal anarchy? . . . And does the prohibition of distribution of matter 'containing' the doctrine [of forceful overthrow of government] bar histories of the evolution of Marxist doctrine or tracing the background of the French, American, or Russian revolutions?" This case is often heralded as one of the strongest defenses of academic freedom because of Justice Brennan's sweeping language: "Our Nation is deeply committed to safeguarding academic freedom, which is of transcendent value to all of us and not merely to the teachers concerned. That freedom is therefore a special concern of the First Amendment, which does not tolerate laws that cast a pall of orthodoxy over the classroom."

The dissenters were less sanguine about the importance of these kinds of freedoms and more afraid of the potential outcomes of teaching or advocating violent overthrow of government. Justice Tom Clark wrote morosely, "I regret to say—and I do so with deference—that the majority has by its broadside swept away one of our most precious rights, namely, the right of self-preservation."

A year later, in 1968, the Court handed down *Pickering v. Board of Education*. Here, teacher Marvin Pickering had written a letter to a local newspaper criticizing his Board of Education and superintendent for how they had managed bond issuance proposals to raise money for school developments, and he was dismissed from his job. The Court agreed that Pickering's First Amendment rights were violated. Justice Thurgood Marshall examined the letter and its intended audience and found that it was not aimed at anyone with whom Pickering would interact in his teaching roles. While the letter did have some errors in it, under the law of libel, Justice Marshall said, it was more important that Pickering have a chance to comment that was the same as any other citizen's right: "In these circumstances, we conclude that the interest of the school administration in limiting teachers' opportunities to contribute to public

debate is not significantly greater than its interest in limiting a similar contribution by any member of the general public." Because the school board did not show that Pickering acted with reckless disregard for the truth, as required in the famous libel case of *New York Times v. Sullivan*, he was unjustly fired.

In 1983, in *Connick v. Myers*, the Court again examined the question of whether speech undertaken by a public employee on matters of potential public concern should be protected by the First Amendment. Sheila Myers was an assistant district attorney in New Orleans who had been required to transfer to another section of the office over her objections. She prepared and distributed a questionnaire for her colleagues about a number of office issues, including "office transfer policy, office morale, the need for a grievance committee, the level of confidence in supervisors, and whether employees felt pressured to work in political campaigns." She was fired for, according to her supervisors, refusing to take the transfer, but also because the distribution of the questionnaire was seen as insubordination.

Justice White saw the issue as "a balance between the interests of the [employee], as a citizen, in commenting upon matters of public concern and the interest of the State, as an employer, in promoting the efficiency of the public services it performs through its employees." In this case, however, the majority believed that most of Myers's questionnaire did not touch upon issues of public concern, but on issues of personal concern, such as office morale and trust in one's supervisors. As Justice White saw it, "the focus of Myers' questions is not to evaluate the performance of the office, but rather to gather ammunition for another round of controversy with her superiors." Thus, her firing was not a First Amendment violation. But, Justice White added, "a State cannot condition public employment on a basis that infringes the employee's constitutionally protected interest in freedom of expression."

The *Pickering* decision was further distinguished in a later case, in 2006. In *Garcetti v. Ceballos*, the Court evaluated the claim of a district attorney who had been passed up for a promotion that this snub was because he had criticized a warrant. Here, the Court made a distinction between speech undertaken as part of one's public employee duties and speech undertaken as a private citizen.

Richard Ceballos was a Los Angeles deputy district attorney serving under Gil Garcetti, the head of the L.A. District Attorney's Office. He was asked to review the issuance of a search warrant; he found that the warrant was problematic and reported the problems in a memo to his supervisors—who went ahead with the prosecution anyway, despite Ceballos's concerns. He was called to testify by the defense in the criminal case and recounted his concerns with the warrant. After this, he claimed he was subject to a number of professional censures.

Justice Kennedy framed the question as whether the memo Ceballos drafted was written as part of his official job duties or as a private citizen and concluded that, of course, it was part of his job duties. "When an employee speaks as a citizen addressing a matter of public concern, the First Amendment requires a delicate balancing of the competing interests surrounding the speech and its consequences,"

he wrote. "When, however, the employee is simply performing his or her job duties, there is no warrant for a similar degree of scrutiny." To allow that level of exacting scrutiny would be to subject all public employees' communication to judicial evaluation. And as such, he stated baldly, "We reject, however, the notion that the First Amendment shields from discipline the expressions employees make pursuant to their professional duties."

Garcetti is the lead case in public employee speech rights today. Is it truly problematic from a First Amendment rights perspective? Critics would argue that individuals who work for private companies and who can be fired on an at-will basis are no better (or worse) off than public employees in this regard. One could reasonably argue that companies should be secure enough in themselves to offer protection to employees who speak out about anything, but that is hardly the case, whether public or private. To what extent should a public employee's speech rights differ from a private company's employee's rights, if at all?

Epilogue: Compelled Speech Today

There are many other areas of compelled speech that cannot be discussed in depth in a chapter. But here are a few tidbits and other cases in which speech has been silenced or compelled.

Campaign Disclosure Laws. While "money is speech" was the big, controversial holding in the 2010 *Citizens United v. Federal Elections Commission* case, there was another "stealth" question that the Court answered in the affirmative by an 8–1 margin: whether laws that mandate that donors and donations be made public are constitutional. Justice Kennedy wrote: "Disclaimer and disclosure requirements may burden the ability to speak, but they 'impose no ceiling on campaign-related activities,' and 'do not prevent anyone from speaking.'"

Is this acceptable? Critics of disclosure laws suggest that first, few voters care enough to go to one of the online sites (like the Sunlight Foundation, www .sunlightfoundation.com) that provides information on which company or individual is supporting what candidate or cause to look up who is funding what, so rules mandating disclosures do not really serve a public interest of providing voters with voting information, and second, those who do care enough are more likely to attempt to exact retribution on those supporting candidates or causes with whom they disagree. In fact, Justice Thomas's dissent focused on exactly such allegations, where proponents of Proposition 8, the California anti-same-sex marriage proposition, said they were fearful for their safety: "Some opponents of Proposition 8 compiled this information and created websites with maps showing the locations of homes or businesses of Proposition 8 supporters. Many supporters (or their customers) suffered property damage, or threats of physical violence or death, as a result."

Clearly, of course, when there are actual threats of violence or death, the law can and does step in to prevent or punish. However, if the "damages" come in the form of boycotts of businesses, is that a sufficient reason to prevent disclosure?

To what extent are critics right—that the loss of privacy in this area is not outweighed by countervailing public goods, such as increased voting information?

Menu Label Laws. Doctors and other medical professionals have noted the rise of obesity in the United States, and many attribute it to the ready availability and affordability of processed and fast food. The FDA requires that producers of processed food and beverages label their goods with nutritional information. The law goes so far as to mandate the display of that information. But many restaurants are under no such requirement. Should they be?

Some cities have passed laws that require nutritional information be made easily available to consumers (New York City and San Francisco). And some restaurants provide that information voluntarily, either online or at the restaurants themselves. For example, if one goes to the McDonald's website, there is a link for nutritional information, so consumers who are interested can see how many calories (550) and fat grams (29) those Big Macs they are planning to order for lunch actually contain. Some McDonald's restaurants provide this information onsite, either posted on walls or on paper mats lining their food trays. Is this voluntary method good enough? Many of the same arguments that are leveled against disclosure in campaign finance can be applied here: many consumers are not going to bother looking at nutritional information, and those who are concerned are not going to be at the average fast-food restaurant. Should governments compel restaurants to speak anyway?

Court-Ordered Apologies. In 2012, the Associated Press reported that a court ruling forced a man to apologize to his estranged wife using the social media site Facebook to avoid a jail sentence. He had posted unflattering comments about her on the site, and he was required to post apologies on a daily basis on Facebook to her and their families and friends. Was this the right resolution to the case?

University philosophy professor Nick Smith has written several thoughtful articles and a book on the meanings of apologies. He discusses the position of philosopher Immanuel Kant on the question of legally forced apologies. Kant put it this way in 1797 in *The Metaphysical Elements of Justice*: "Thus, for example, the imposition of a fine for a verbal injury has no proportionality to the original injury, for someone who has a good deal of money can easily afford to make insults whenever he wishes. On the other hand, the humiliation of the pride of such an offender comes much closer to equaling an injury done to the honor of the person offended; thus the judgment and Law might require the offender, not only to make a public apology to the offended person, but also at the same time to kiss his hand, even though he be socially inferior." So for Kant, the forced apology will result in humiliation and be far more "punishing" than would a fine. In a sense, this would be a form of equity: making the punishment fit the crime more closely rather than simply fining the offender.

Professor Smith does not agree. Rather than serving any public good, he believes that such apologies are less about justice and more about judges: "In practice court-ordered apologies seem driven more by grandstanding retributivist judges attempting to appear tough on crime than from considered ethical, social, and political arguments." Perhaps, but do Kant's arguments about the philosophical good of an apology hold no water at all? Is there a social or moral good to mandating an apology—particularly if the apologist does not feel remorse or is making the apology just to avoid a harsher penalty?

The term *compelled speech* raises the hackles of many Americans. We have been raised as a society to view the First Amendment as not only a bar on government censorship or interference with speech acts but also as a kind of mantra that goes something like, "I can say what I want!" The very notion that government can and does sometimes compel both speech and silence makes some uneasy. It is for this reason that questions surrounding the appropriate legal foundations and uses for compelled speech are so important to consider, from both First Amendment and moral justification perspectives.

Genelle I. Belmas
University of Kansas

See also Commercial Speech; A New First Amendment?

Further Reading

Calvert, Clay. "The First Amendment, Journalism and Credibility: A Trio of Reforms for a Meaningful Free Press More Than Three Decades after *Tornillo*." *First Amendment Law Review* 4 (2005).

Carpenter, Dick, and Jeffrey Milyo. "The Public's Right to Know versus Compelled Speech: What Does Social Science

Research Tell Us about the Benefits and Costs of Campaign Finance Disclosure in Non-candidate Elections?" *Fordham Urban Law Journal* 40 (2012).

Corbin, Caroline Mala. "The First Amendment Right against Compelled Listening." *Boston University Law Review* 89 (2009).

Cross, Ashley M. "The Right to Remain Silent? *Garcetti v. Ceballos* and a Public Employee's Refusal to Speak Falsely." *Missouri Law Review* 77 (2012).

Keighley, Jennifer M. "Can You Handle the Truth? Compelled Speech and the First Amendment." *Journal of Constitutional Law* 15 (2012).

Pomeranz, Jennifer L. "Compelled Speech under the Commercial Speech Doctrine: The Case of Menu Label Laws." *Journal of Health Care Law & Policy* 12 (2009).

Post, Robert. "Transparent and Efficient Markets: Compelled Commercial Speech and Coerced Commercial Association in *United Foods*, *Zauderer*, and *Abood*."

Valparaiso University Law Review 40 (2006).

Roosevelt, Kermit, III. "Not as Bad as You Think: Why *Garcetti v. Ceballos* Makes Sense." *Journal of Constitutional Law* 14 (2012).

Sachartoff, Lawrent. "Listener Interests in Compelled Speech Cases." *California Western Law Review* 44 (2008).

Smith, Nick. "Against Court-Ordered Apologies." *New Criminal Law Review* 16 (2013).

Smith, Nick. "The Penitent and the Penitentiary: Questions Regarding Apologies in Criminal Law." *Criminal Justice Ethics* 27 (2008).

Wentworth-Ping, Alexander P. "Funding Conditions and Free Speech for HIV/AIDS NGOs: He Who Pays the Piper Cannot Always Call the Tune." *Fordham Law Review* 81 (2012).

Zacharias, Fred C. "Flowcharting the First Amendment." *Cornell Law Review* 72 (1987).

45

INSTITUTIONAL FOUNDATIONS

In his novel *The Last City Room*, author Al Martinez subjects newly hired reporter William Colfax to a traumatic introduction to the world of journalism. On his first day, Colfax sees a newsroom veteran expire at his desk, his colleagues slow hand-clapping as the body is carted out; attends an alcohol-drenched wake for the departed reporter; covers a fatal terrorist bombing at the local FBI office; and writes a first-person account of the bombing's aftermath that earns a front-page byline.

Getting a moment to himself, Colfax reflects upon his new employer, the *Herald,* and its staffers: "It was a world in microcosm, a kingdom unto itself that operated with a disturbing sense of isolation even as it reached out to cover the news, bold in its mission yet somehow uncomfortable with its station. Those he had met so far were almost excessively individualistic and yet, in their way, seemed to fit perfectly into the whole unit."

In these few words, Martinez describes two interlocking paradoxes that confound the interplay between news production and media ethics. In one, Colfax puzzled at how *Herald* staffers, "almost excessively" individualists, could put personal interests aside and unite in the common goal of producing news. Putting out a newspaper was a collective enterprise, requiring close coordination among many specialists. But what was the cost of this collaboration, and for our purposes here, its impact on the ethical capacity of the journalists?

The second paradox had to do with the *Herald*'s social role: while an essential part of the community, it was uneasy with its mission. It was a "kingdom unto itself," yet dependent upon public confidence and acceptance for its success. Most news organizations in the United States—newspapers, magazines, or broadcast stations and networks—are private corporations with thousands of employees, centralized management, diverse product lines, demanding financial goals, and stockholders to whom they are beholden. But for the most part, their operating procedures and practices are opaque, isolated in the sense that their internal operations are largely hidden from public view. This matters because of their public mission: they are expected to provide members of society with the information they need to be active, informed citizens. Together, these corporations constitute the only industry that carries a specific constitutional protection from government intrusion, to ensure that this information is independent and credible. As Martinez suggested, not all, like the *Herald,* are comfortable, or successful, in their public mission.

This chapter explores the institutional framework of media organizations, concentrating primarily upon their internal structures, but focusing upon the impact of these structures upon the work of their employees. Specifically, how do their structural characteristics influence the values, ethics, and responsibilities of journalists and of the news organizations themselves?

An Institutional View

News production occurs not in a vacuum, but in a collective context involving actors such as corporate managers, news sources, and audience members. Decisions made by journalists can not only influence the way we comprehend the world, but are themselves products of a complex and contradictory set of relationships that affect the news production process on several levels. Journalists, and the news organizations they work for, also have sets of external relationships with representatives of other social institutions, such as the agencies of government, the political system, the economy, education, and the military, and these external relations also influence the news production process. In social scientific terms, these relationships are studied in terms of their *structures*, or repetitive and consistent patterns of organization. We might consider, for example, how newspapers or television networks are organized, and how their organizational patterns affect the ways journalists work. Structure is usually paired with considerations of *agency*, or autonomy, in considering the extent to which organizational patterns enable or constrain journalists in doing their work. Does the news organization's *structure*, for example, encourage journalists to consider the ethical dimensions of decisions they make in covering the news? More important, how much *agency* do journalists possess in making ethical decisions?

This institutional view of the news media is important, if for no other reason than it reflects the ubiquity of the media presence in contemporary life. This is evident in the way people think and talk about media; while "media" was once defined as a plural noun, referring to a wide array of vehicles of communication, in common usage the word is acquiring a *singular* definition (as in "how did the media react to the president's proposal?"), representing not a diverse collection of newspapers, magazines, radio and televisions stations, but a coordinated, monolithic entity providing news, information, entertainment, and distraction twenty-four hours a day, seven days a week.

It also seems paradoxical that in spite of the fact that people in most countries are spending more and more time and money on media products, the public's trust in media is steadily weakening. The Gallup polling organization, for example, reported in 2012 that 60 percent of U.S. respondents said that they had little or no trust in the media to report news accurately and fairly—the lowest trust figure ever in a presidential election year. (For comparison's sake, in the 1970s over 70 percent consistently expressed high levels of trust in the news media.) "On a broad level, Americans' high level of distrust in the media poses a challenge to democracy and to creating a fully engaged citizenry," the Gallup organization reported. The Pew Research Center in its 2013 *State of the News Media* report noted that because of widespread economic problems in the media industry, news organizations were making significant cuts in staffing levels, thereby reducing the quality of their news products. Nearly one-third of its public respondents said they had dropped a news product in the past year because it no longer provided the news and information they were accustomed to. Another Gallup survey in 2012 found that only 24 percent of the public had a "Very high or High" level of trust in journalists, down from 27 percent in 1992 and 32 percent in 1981—figures that have never been very high, but seem to be getting worse. These trends were also evident in Britain, where a YouGov (an international marketing research firm based in the U.K.) survey in 2012 found for the first time that more respondents distrusted BBC news than trusted it (47 percent to 44), and trust in newspaper journalists ranged from only 38 percent (upmarket or "quality" papers) to 10 percent (tabloids).

Autonomy and Collective Responsibility

These figures describing the public's trust—or distrust—of the news media are based on an institutional understanding of the media and collide with the traditional way of thinking about ethics. Western ethical theory places greater emphasis upon agency than structure, being based upon the notion of the autonomous, self-determining actor. For Immanuel Kant, the essential and necessary condition for being a moral agent, capable of making ethical decisions, was "autonomy of the will." Laws or principles demanded by someone or something external to the rational agent lacked moral force. Moral constraints should be imposed on the individuals only as the result of their own reason, according to Kant. More recently, John Rawls argued that justice must be based upon principles that would be adopted by rational and autonomous agents in a situation in which they were totally free to choose. Other ethicists see autonomy not as a basic condition of moral agents, but as evidence of moral maturity, possessed only by those who are especially self-controlled, independent, or authentic.

However, other philosophers find shortcomings in this view of autonomy. Communitarians, for example, regard it as excessively individualistic, arguing that the truly autonomous individual is only an abstraction, more isolated from community values than people actually are or can be. Others point out that ethics and morality are influenced by cultural values, and a moral person might well be influenced by values based upon such things as loyalty, compassion for others, or commitment to something other than the individual will, such as the general welfare of the community.

A similar zone of contention is evident when notions of collective responsibility are considered. When people form a group, as in joining the staff of a television station, is the group itself or its individual members accountable for the group's actions? Individualists and traditional ethical theory argue that responsibility for the group's action is only an aggregation or summing of the responsibilities of the individuals involved, or "shared responsibility," and to suggest otherwise would be to diminish individual responsibility, relieving people of personal accountability for their actions.

However, other ethicists contend that this view is too limited. Groups and organizations, they argue, resemble individuals in that they generate their own practices and decision-making structures. If a group can act as a unified whole, then the group itself can be held accountable for its actions. People join groups because of their common interests or needs; to the extent that the group meets these needs or serves the common interest, it produces solidarity sufficient to produce collective action by the group, making members accountable for the group's actions. Finally, if group members acquire benefits through their membership that they would not receive as individuals, then they also acquire certain costs, such as being responsible for what the group does on their behalf.

Though Plato wrote extensively about ethics and the city-state, and the Enlightenment fathers of democratic theory such as Thomas Hobbes, John Locke, and Jean-Jacques Rousseau considered the morality of institutions such as government and the family, until recently ethicists paid surprisingly little attention to the institutions that developed in industrialized societies in the nineteenth and twentieth centuries, let alone institutional influence upon ethical choices. However, a number of moral philosophers in recent years have given renewed attention to the ethics of groups or corporate organizations. Building upon the pioneering work of early European sociologists Emile Durkheim and Max Weber, philosophers such as Richard De George, Joel Feinberg, David Copp, Peter French, Virginia Held, and Larry May have offered new consideration as to how we might examine the ethical behavior of formal and informal groups and associations.

May, for example, in *The Morality of Groups*, carefully stated that individuals do not sacrifice their ethical potential when they join a group or are employed by a corporation. As autonomous individuals, they retain a range of ethical choices and accordingly are free to join groups or associations and choose to retain these memberships. And within these organizations, they are accorded some latitude in carrying out their assigned duties. But a group is more than simply the aggregated interests of individual members, May wrote: "The structure of social groups plays such an important role in the acts, intentions, and interests of members of groups, that social groups should be given a moral status different from that of the discrete individual persons who compose them."

These structures, according to May, define how individuals relate to one another within the organization. Of particular importance are the decision-making processes, the supervision provided by corporate managers, and "vicarious agency," the term used by May to describe the capacity of employees to act on their own in representing the interests and objectives of the organization. Acceptance of the decision-making process, management supervision, and the boundaries of vicarious agency, taken together, contributes to a sense of joint action, common interest, or *solidarity* among members of the organization. "Solidarity" is the term used in traditional sociology to, according to May, describe the cohesiveness of a group that exhibits collective intentional behavior:

> Solidarity in the mob and decision-making procedures in the corporation both change individual intentions in the sense that they create a group-based context for one's intentions that is radically different from the context of personal experience outside of the group. This group-based context is comprised of those social relationships among group members which form them into a group. And while it is obviously individuals who participate in these social relationships, the way that these relations or structures change and combine the intentions among these individuals cannot be fully explained by reference to the intentions of individual, isolated people. Like the channel of a river, these social structures shape new intentions out of the previous intentions of individuals, and it is for this reason that it makes sense to talk, in a limited way, about the collective intent of social groups.

The result, according to May, is that structural elements such as corporate beliefs and goals are unquestionably restraints upon the agency of individual employees. But they are more than this. They can lead individuals within the corporation to associate their own aspirations and well-being with that of the

organization itself. He cited organizational research that found that members of highly structured corporations tended to develop different norms that they would hold, or did hold, outside the organizational setting. Therefore, it is plausible that corporations can be held collectively responsible for actions, including harms, caused by their individual members.

Following this line of thought, it is clearly insufficient to think about media ethics as solely the ethical decisions of individual journalists. May's model implies that it is more productive to consider the nature of the corporate environment within which these decisions were made, and how these decisions were made. Finally, the work of May and others suggests that contemporary ethical theory is expansive enough to enable us to consider the ethical performance of media organizations as a whole, and not merely as the acts committed by their employees. Taking this broader approach, how does our knowledge of the organizational environment of news production contribute to our understanding of the ethics of media workers and news corporations?

The Organization of News

The twentieth century witnessed the growth of massive media organizations in industrialized nations that have been called by many names (such as chains, groups, networks, transnational corporations, or conglomerates, to name only a few), but have fundamental similarities. They are hierarchical in nature, characterized by organizational flowcharts, management levels with centralized decision-making authority, and specific job descriptions. They exhibit complex divisions of labor in which employees perform specific tasks as part of a collaborative, collectivized production process. This process is governed by sets of operating rules, regulations, and codes, formulated by managers and intended to govern employees' performance. Like corporate entities manufacturing other types of goods, they represent concentrations of capital used to gain leverage in the marketplace so they might perform their primary function: earn profits for their owners. In the United States, they differ from manufacturers of other products in that they have a specific constitutional protection from government interference because their work is so closely connected to the public interest.

This corporate environment in which news is manufactured has always posed problems for the media ethics field. But given the broad academic and professional interest in media ethics in recent decades, it is surprising how little we know about it. Few systematic studies have been carried out on decision making within media companies, especially decisions involving ethical choices. Most ethics texts and handbooks produced for the journalism classroom are based upon the traditional individual-autonomy model and virtually ignore the environment in which young journalists will eventually work. The supposition of these texts is that the newsroom is nothing more than an aggregation of the individual journalists working there. Ethical blunders such as those committed by Janet Cooke at the *Washington Post* and Jayson Blair at the *New York Times* are nothing more than examples of journalists who were poorly trained or those who ignored the ethical norms of the profession.

But the work of May and his colleagues poses a new set of questions. How much agency, or autonomy, do individual journalists possess within the structure of the corporatized news organization and under what circumstances? At what level are ethical decisions actually made within these organizations? If journalists possess agency, why is there a consistent pattern, or structure, of news stories produced in different media organizations? How is solidarity developed within a news staff, and to what extent do journalists feel a collective responsibility for their work? Most important, how well do media organizations reconcile their private goals with their public mission? And should we consider only the ethics of individual journalists or examine the ethics of the news organizations themselves? This is surely what critical audience members do, when they take issue with something they saw on *60 Minutes* or how the *Chicago Tribune* "played" a particular story. At least partial answers to these questions might be generated by looking at a small selection of research studies that have examined the operations of news organizations, the values inherent in news stories they produce, and the ethics of journalists.

Developing News Policy. Though few systematic studies of the internal operations of news organizations have been carried out, those by Warren Breed, Herbert J. Gans, and Chris Argyris in particular shed light on how organizational structures constrain the agency of news workers.

The formation of newsroom solidarity intrigued Breed, a sociologist who carried out one of the earliest, if not the best, studies of the news production process. Breed, himself a former journalist, studied about 120 journalists on newspapers in the northeastern states. At the heart of his study was "policy," or the consistent content orientation shown, not only in editorials, but also in news selection and news coverage. Every news organization has a policy, but it differs from one organization to another. Though policy is a structural element, journalistic norms and taboos prohibit publishers from directly imposing policy on news workers. Breed's question was: If policy cannot be imposed and journalists often personally disagree with it, why do they follow it and adopt it as their own, even if it does not correspond to the objective reality they comprehend from their newsgathering activities?

News staffers learn policy during their socialization process in their early months with the organization. They read their own newspaper, grasp how editors react to particular news stories, and observe how their reporting is edited to correspond to policy. They learn as well, according to Breed, what sort of situations will grant them agency, or deviation from policy. In some areas, the norms of policy might be ambiguous; in others, the reporter might know more about a given situation than editors or the publisher, and accordingly be given latitude. News stories initiated by reporters are generally given a longer leash than those assigned by editors, who have a preordained sense of how the final product should look. Finally, Breed noted

that experienced reporters, especially those with "star power," could transgress policy because they were trusted by the newsroom management and could be counted upon not to stray too far from policy.

But socialization and deviation aside, Breed was most interested in reasons why journalists willingly conformed to policy. First was a fear of institutional authority and sanctions. Though firings rarely occurred on the newspapers Breed studied, journalists feared demotions, receiving bad assignments, or seeing their colleagues be rewarded with "plum" assignments. More compelling, however, were positive reasons for conforming to policy. Staffers had feelings of obligation and esteem for their superiors who served as models, especially those who had hired them or helped during their socialization. Reporters with aspirations, either to move up in the hierarchy or in the industry generally, thought that bucking policy would be a bar to promotion. Journalists had no conflicting group allegiance; though some of the newspapers were unionized, the union restricted itself to issues connected to conditions of employment and did not interfere with policy. Finally, journalists liked their work: they felt themselves part of an "in-group" or recognized a sense of solidarity with their colleagues. While they were not well-paid, they were close to the pulse of their community, meeting notables and celebrities, getting the "inside dope" ahead of ordinary citizens, and were able to "touch power without being responsible for its use." This made them proud of being news workers and contributed to morale and a sense of well-being.

Breed's final reason for conformity to policy is perhaps the most important for our purposes. Manufacturing news becomes a value in itself to reporters:

> Newsmen define their job as producing a certain quantity of what is called "news" every 24 hours. This is to be produced *even though nothing much has happened.* News is a continuous challenge, and meeting this challenge is the newsman's job. He is rewarded for fulfilling this, his manifest function. A consequence of this focus on news as a central value is the shelving of a strong interest in objectivity at the point of policy conflict. Instead of mobilizing their efforts to establish objectivity over policy as the criterion for performance, their energies are challenged into getting more news. The demands of competition . . . and speed enhance this focus. Newsmen do talk about ethics, objectivity, and the relative worth of various papers, but not when there is news to get. News comes first, and there is always news to get. They are not rewarded for analyzing the social structure, but for getting news. *It would seem that this instrumental orientation diminishes their moral potential* [emphasis added].

This practical orientation had a number of consequences. First, it created harmony between staff and management; as the manufacture of news was a positive value, it nullified potential conflicts and reinforced newsroom solidarity. Second, because solidarity was supported, it ensured that the newspaper would continue to be published, benefiting both ownership and the wider community. Third, as news organizations are capitalist enterprises, policy usually serves to protect property and class interests, thus serving to perpetuate the existing system of power relationships in society. Fourth, this meant news that contradicted newsroom policy might be slanted or buried, thereby denying some important information to the newspaper's readership. Finally, it leaves news workers with difficult choices. Do they attempt to blunt the sharp corners of policy wherever possible, thereby retaining their jobs? Do they attempt to "repress their conflict amorally and anti-intellectually ('What the hell, it's only a job. . . .')"? Do they quit and seek work elsewhere, at news organizations with different policies, or in another occupational field altogether?

While Breed studied policy formation on small- to medium-sized newspapers, Herbert J. Gans applied a similar framework to network news and national newsmagazines. Over a ten-year period, he examined the production processes and their influence on news content at CBS Evening News, NBC Nightly News, *Newsweek,* and *Time.* Ultimately, Gans concluded, the need to meet deadlines in all four organizations overshadowed newsroom power differentials and created story selection processes that led journalists to refer to their organizations as assembly lines, manufacturing news.

Gans characterized these organizations as bureaucracies with top-down power systems. "News organizations are not democratic; in fact, they are described as militaristic by some journalists, and the top editor or producer, and his assistants, have the power to decide what gets into print or on the air . . . subject only to suggestions or vetoes from news and corporate management," Gans wrote. At the top of the hierarchy are corporate executives, responsible for budget and personnel matters, commercial and political interests of the company, and the establishment of policy. More directly connected to story selection and news content are several levels of news editors and managers, and at the base of this pyramid are several levels of writers and reporters. Generally, Gans wrote, editors and managers push an audience orientation in story selection discussions, while reporters and writers are more oriented toward the interests of their sources. Ultimately, compromises are reached, but as editors and managers carry more power in the hierarchy, the decisions tend to favor audience-oriented stories.

Nonetheless, as Breed noted at his newspapers, this is not a coercive process. While news production at the networks and newsmagazines is characterized by assembly lines and bureaucratic structures, the journalists are considered "professionals" and are given "suggestions" rather than direct orders, out of respect for their autonomy and morale. However, according to Gans, "individual autonomy is frequently illusory, especially in a group enterprise. Moreover, the suggestions of powerful superiors are, in fact, thinly veiled orders, requiring polite circumlocutions in which commands are phrased as requests." Reporters and writers play mainly a consulting role in story selection but have more autonomy in story production because they are closer to their sources and what is actually happening outside the newsroom. "Star" writers and reporters are almost completely autonomous, as on Breed's newspapers, and junior writers must earn this autonomy through their performance.

Adherence to policy is maintained largely through employee morale, which Gans described as being shaped by ambience (organizational mood) and good working conditions:

> Nevertheless, morale is primarily determined by the amount of control people have over their work and the ways in which superiors treat their work. Most journalists have a strong commitment to and identification with their product, but they easily become discouraged when their desire to perform well is restrained by what they consider unnecessary bureaucratic obstacles, the unwillingness of superiors to listen to them, and especially undue interference with their autonomy.

Overall, Gans found morale levels to be rarely high, and often low. The organizational hierarchy was both resistant to change and tended to reward employees who were cautious, reluctant to take risks, and supported the status quo.

Chris Argyris produced an organizational analysis of the *New York Times* (thinly disguised as the "*Daily Planet*") during the same period when Gans was examining other national media and found similar levels of low morale. In spite of the fact that the *Daily Planet* was "highly respected," paid high salaries, tried to be objective, and was "admired by the journalism profession to be a leader in maintaining the highest standards of professional competence," Arygyis found the newspaper to be dysfunctional as an organization.

The low morale reported by 87 percent of newsroom employees was a major reason for this dysfunction. Factors leading to low morale were: a growing gap between older employees and newcomers, who tended to be ambitious and eager to achieve early bylines and pay raises; infrequency of pay increases; staffers finding themselves dead-ended in low-status jobs; insensitive actions taken by newsroom supervisors; and staff demotions that resulted in unclear lines of authority.

In spite of these issues, the *Daily Planet*'s system kept operating, producing a consistently high-quality product. Argyris attributed this to the ambience of the newsroom itself. Journalists did not expect a perfect environment and were comfortable with the newsroom's competitive atmosphere. They liked the challenges of reporting and editing. The fact that they were working for one of the top newspapers in the country was confirmation of their importance and career success: They appreciated "the opportunity to feel that one works for an organization that is essential to the nation." The newspaper's policy was broad enough to permit reporters operating under differing conceptions of journalism—as traditionalists, researchers, or activists—to thrive in this environment. Finally, even when given the opportunity to have input into newsroom decisions, reporters and copy editors tended to defer to the authority of their superiors.

While the *Daily Planet* (or *Times*) might be a model for other news organizations to emulate, Argyris thought that its internal dysfunctions had external effects. They made it difficult for the newspaper and its management to examine the organization critically and make improvements in its operations. They damaged its credibility with the public, which tended to isolate it from the very public it intended to serve. And Argyris speculated that dysfunctions in the system might distort news coverage and editorials as well, thereby limiting the newspaper's contribution to the wider society.

Amoral or Immoral?

The practical orientation of news workers within the insulating comfort of the newsroom described by Breed, Gans, and Argyris has been observed by others. Dennis Chase, a media critic and former journalist, wrote in the *Quill*, the journal of the Society of Professional Journalists, that journalists are so focused upon the "hard reality of practice" that they become "aphilosophical," meaning that they ignore questions of fundamental importance. These questions are both theoretical and epistemological, concerned with such issues as: What is news? What is the relationship between news and truth? Is it the job of the news organization to report news or truth?

Without a knowledge-based understanding of journalism, journalists are driven by instinct, subjectivism, or the clichéd concept of the "nose for news," according to Chase:

> The field of journalism is natural prey for this concept. With nothing fixed, with everything continually evolving, the editor is free to unleash his reporters at whatever strikes his or his readership's fancy. There is never an obligation to inquire about the function of a newspaper, or to define a newspaper's chief commodity: news. This last is the most tragic error.

As a result, Chase argued, the field is being torn by an internal disagreement between traditionalist and activist journalists over what words such as "fairness" or "balance" mean, something noted by Argyris at the *Daily Planet* as well. The traditionalists champion a tired "objectivity" that specifies that journalists should tell "both sides of the story," keeping themselves "out of the story." In fact, wrote Chase, this merely substitutes the biases of the journalists for those of their sources and gets the reader no closer to the truth. Activists, on the other hand, practice what they call "personal" or "advocacy" journalism, making no pretense of "telling both sides." To the activists, their personal viewpoints are better informed and less susceptible to self-interest than the material obtained by traditionalists from establishment sources. But to Chase, this provides only the reporter's reaction to the material being reported, rather than a reasoned analysis of the material itself. Both positions, to Chase, have inherent shortcomings because they are suspicious of "true objectivity": patiently accumulated evidence through eyewitness accounts, public and private documents, personal observations, and application of rules of logic. This "true objectivity" would lead to a true science of journalism, according to Chase, which would protect journalists from the whims of their editors and owners.

Chase's argument suggests that if journalists can be considered "aphilosophical," in their lack of interest in knowledge-based questions underlying their work, they might also be considered "amoral," rather than "immoral." The implication here is that journalists do not fail to make good ethical decisions because they are inherently unethical or have not been taught *how* to make ethical decisions. Rather, it is the nature of their work, and the field and organizations in which they perform the process of news production, that rewards them for producing what they call news, rather than thinking about the moral implications of their work.

Further evidence of the influence of the news organizations upon journalists is provided by the national census carried out by researchers at Indiana University over the past thirty years (see *The American Journalist in the 21st Century*). More than 80 percent of journalists reported that newsroom learning had the greatest influence on their ethical understanding. Ranking second was their family upbringing (more than 70 percent), and third was another element of the newsroom: individuals who were employed as senior editors, reporters, or news directors (67 percent). Education was mentioned by 45 percent of respondents and religious training by no more than 30 percent (about two-thirds of more than eleven hundred journalists in the 2002 census said they belonged to some religious group).

Journalists were also asked what most influenced their definitions of newsworthiness, and 77 percent pointed to their journalistic training, closely followed by their supervisors (58 percent) and their newsroom peers and news sources (43 percent each).

As Chase suggested, however, there was not close agreement among journalists as to the appropriate roles and functions of journalists. The Indiana researchers classified journalists' responses into four conceptions of how journalists should operate: as interpreters, adversaries, disseminators, and populist mobilizers. Interpreters constituted the largest group and consisted of journalists who saw their main roles as investigating official claims, analyzing complex problems, and discussing national and international policies. Adversaries were far smaller in number than interpreters and tended to work in print media. They saw themselves as "watchdogs" over government officials and business and hoped their efforts would influence public opinion on these topics. Disseminators were journalists who emphasized the importance of getting information to the public quickly, not publishing unverified facts, reaching the widest possible audience, and providing their audience with entertainment and relaxation, as well as news. Indiana researchers noted that while this group had steeply declined in number over the past twenty years, it represented traditional journalists who were ethically cautious and were likely to think their organizations were doing a good job of informing the public. Populist mobilizers, unlike disseminators, were increasing in number and favored a journalism that encourages audience members to express their own views, motivates them to get involved with issues, helps set the political agenda, and points to possible solutions to public problems. Mobilizers tended to work for small newspapers and magazines and expressed a higher degree of freedom to emphasize what they chose to in their journalistic work.

It is important to emphasize that these are not mutually exclusive categories; as the Indiana researchers pointed out, journalists often embraced more than one of these role conceptions. The overlap between them could be broad or narrow. Over 80 percent of the populist mobilizers,

for example, also rated the interpretive role as very important. But only a quarter of those selecting the adversarial role also thought the disseminator role very important. As the researchers noted: "Journalists have their priorities in terms of role conceptions, but these priorities are not exclusive. Not only do they recognize the existence or necessity of other journalistic roles; they accord those roles substantial importance."

This diversity might be considered one of journalism's strengths. However, this lack of clarity about precisely what journalism is trying to accomplish might, as Chase suggested, be a fundamental weakness.

The Values of News Production

The remaining question is whether structural elements connected to newsroom organization and their conceptions of their roles as reporters and editors influence the news they produce. The evidence suggests that there is an institutional bias in news coverage. Several researchers who have tried to connect the values underlying news content with the way in which the news is reported have found that certain themes are regularly presented, while others are underemphasized or absent from news coverage entirely.

This tendency was evident in the results of an ingenious study carried out by Warren Breed on the role of local newspapers in communities. Using what he called a "reverse content analysis," Breed compared the internal dynamics of eleven cities, as presented in sociological field studies, with the news coverage these events did or did not receive. Breed concluded that newspapers acted to maintain order and social cohesion in the community by ignoring certain events or burying others. The largest category of underplayed events was in the politico-economic area, representing the "undemocratic power of business elites." Generally, favoritism and unequal opportunity for upward mobility—by race, class, or ethnic group—in the delivery of health care, criminal justice, education, and law enforcement, were not covered by the local press. More specifically, the community studies documented about 250 examples in which propertied interests stopped school tax increases, pollution by a locally owned utility was ignored, the chamber of commerce manipulated community affairs, or a prominent family influenced the operation of a local college by making large donations, without these cases being reported in the local press. "Perhaps the most striking fact is that the word 'class' is almost entirely absent from the media," Breed wrote.

This noncoverage extends to other areas, however. Breed found that though almost every newspaper had a weekend section covering church activities, religion as doctrine, faith, or ritual was seldom mentioned. Nor was falling church attendance, competition between churches, troubled church finances, removal of clergy, or religious resistance to curriculum change at local schools. Patriotism, or what Breed referred to as "national ethnocentrism," is protected and promoted by the news media. U.S. complicity and intervention in the affairs of other countries is not questioned; "the media, when depicting history, glorify American deeds and heroes and minimize deviations. Wars are won in the media by

courage and character." Breed also found a tendency toward "local ethnocentrism" and "civic pride"; the progress, growth, and achievements of a city are praised, the failures buried.

In summary, according to Breed, "it appears that 'power' and 'class' as structural strata are protected by media performance. . . . Values of capitalism, the home, religion, health, justice, the nation and the community are also 'sacred cows.'" In this way, the news media, as an institution, "withdraw from unnecessarily baring the shortcomings of other institutions."

H. J. Gans found similar "enduring values" that characterized the news output of national news organizations. Enduring values could be found in many types of news stories over a long period of time and affect what events actually become news. Among those values identified by Gans was *ethnocentrism*, in which other countries are judged by the extent they live up to or imitate American practices. This is most often expressed in war coverage, which tends to personalize the accomplishments of U.S. forces and dehumanize the enemy. *Responsible capitalism* is a news value that expresses an optimistic faith that business people will compete with each other to create economic prosperity for all, but refrain from taking exorbitant profits or gross exploitation of workers or consumers. While monopoly is seen as an evil, there is little criticism of the oligopolistic nature of the economy. *Small-town pastoralism* refers to news values that romanticize rural areas and small towns as they are imagined to have existed in the past, promoting the virtue of smallness against the faults of bigness, as in Big Government,

Big Business, or Big Labor. Bigness is seen as impersonal and inhuman, threatening privacy and tradition. One of the most important news values is *individualism*, protecting the individual against the encroachments of society. Journalists seek out "rugged individualists" who struggle against adversity, act heroically during disasters, or conquer nature or bureaucracy. Other important news values identified by Gans were *altruistic democracy*, *moderatism*, *social order*, and the need for *national leadership* in maintaining order.

Though Gans acknowledged that there was a wide range of news stories produced by these organizations, and that the journalists he interviewed were not interested in ideology, these news values, taken together, resembled an ideology. Their advocacy of altruistic democracy represents a mixture of liberal and conservative values, though he noted that socialist values of Western European nations were ignored or broadly rejected. Their conception of responsible capitalism Gans regarded as right-leaning liberalism, and in their respect for tradition, nostalgia for pastoralism and rugged individualism, defense of social order, and faith in national leadership the news media were "unabashedly conservative."

For over thirty years a team of University of Minnesota researchers studied the longitudinal effects of the press in covering conflict and social change in nineteen Minnesota communities. As an integral part of the community, the newspaper reflects the concerns of the dominant power groupings of the community, they concluded. In conflict situations, the local newspaper only infrequently initiated material that led to the dispute. More often, the local press conferred legitimacy on groups or individuals central to the conflict, or chose to exclude those deemed threatening to the community power structure. Reporters and editors, they wrote, are not independent agents in the process. "Their perspectives on the situation, their range of choices, and their rationales for decisions are constrained by their roles within the community structure and by their linkages with different internal and external substructures."

In this case, it is necessary to understand structures external to the news organization to understand the amount of agency reporters and editors have in making ethical decisions. To the Minnesota researchers, their agency was quite limited:

> The analysis of conflict situations provides abundant evidence that newspapers and other media of communication are not the independent, self-styled social agents that either they or members of the public may imagine them to be. The efficacy of viewing the press, or any other mass medium, as constituting a separate "fourth estate" is doubtful at best. The press is an integral subsystem within the total system, and its strong linkages with other system components impinge upon it as much as it impinges upon them, if not more.

The Ethics of News Organizations

To theologian Reinhold Niebuhr, writing in the 1930s, the problem was deceptively simple. Journalists should expect their personal ethics to be compromised by their employing organizations because *all* institutions, formal and informal, were innately inferior to the moral potential of the individual. As Niebuhr wrote in *Moral Man and Immoral Society*, "In every human group there is less reason to guide and to check impulse, less capacity for self-transcendence, less ability to comprehend the needs of others and therefore more unrestrained egoism than the individuals, who compose the group, reveal in their personal relationships."

This notion of organizational immorality also found expression in the 1940s when the Commission on Freedom of the Press (Hutchins Commission) concluded that press freedom was endangered in the United States because press owners were more concerned with corporate financial health than the informational needs of the wider society. "Members of the Commission were disturbed by finding that many able reporters and editorial writers displayed frustration—the feeling that they were not allowed to do the kind of work which their professional ideals demanded," the commission wrote.

Most recently, the Leveson Inquiry into the phone-hacking scandal of British newspapers also questioned the management morality of news organizations. "The clearest message which comes out of the entirety of this lengthy part of the Report addressing the culture, practices, and ethics of press is that, time and time again, there have been serious and uncorrected failures within part of the national press that have been stretched from the criminal to the indefensibly unethical, from the passing off fiction as fact to paying lip service to accuracy." Among the many proposals for newspaper reform was the establishment of a whistleblowing hotline for journalists who felt pressured by their editors to commit unethical acts.

While there could be merit in this point of view, it seems simplistic to suggest that bureaucratic structures by definition discourage ethical behavior, or that individuals, also by definition, are more ethical than the corporations for which they work. This examination of the institutional framework of the news industry has raised at least three questions of crucial importance.

First, are journalists really moral captives of their organizations? May, French, and their colleagues have been careful to state that joining a formal organization or informal group does not strip individuals of either their moral potential or responsibility. Researchers such as Breed and Gans repeatedly found that journalists were not coerced: they like their work, feel solidarity with their colleagues, and accept their organizations' policies willingly—even when their pay is inadequate or staff morale is low. The news environment appeared to encourage more "amorality" than immorality, suggesting that not only is there a strong element of personal choice underlying journalists' decisions to work in this field, but also that they have latitude in choosing to give greater consideration to the ethical choices they make in the newsroom.

Second, are all news organizations the same in the way in which they address ethical issues? Is "the media" as monolithic as popular usage of the term might suggest? Breed suggested that just as all news organizations have a policy framework, no two newspapers have the same policies. As media organizations differ from one country to another, so can they differ within a country. Research has shown, for example, that the relationship between journalists and their communities can be a function of location and size; in large cities journalists often are members of an educated and income elite relative to the great majority of their readers/viewers, of whom journalists possess little specific knowledge. In smaller communities, they might have greater contact with their neighbors, but they work for organizations that act as forces for harmony and stability, emphasizing "good news" and community-building, rather than independent reporting of local issues.

Conclusion

Equally, the work of May, French, and others suggests that if organizations themselves can act as ethical agents, so can they be differentiated by how they handle ethical issues. This means that media users justifiably might compare newspapers, television networks, or websites and distinguish among them as to how they choose to respond to specific ethics issues. It is only logical that some news organizations might be "more ethical" than others. This also suggests that management of media organizations might be held responsible for ethical transgressions, rather than transferring the blame to lower-level news workers.

And managers of some news organizations might choose to place greater emphasis on ethical and sustainable operations than the management of others.

Finally, the ultimate ethical question for media organizations in democratic societies is: How well do they serve the information needs of the citizens of their community? This examination of the news media's institutional foundations touches upon several problems: the conflict for privately owned media organizations between profit-making and the public service mission, the lack of definition and clarity for news workers as to what news is and how it should be reported, and the tendency for news coverage to be representative of the existing power arrangements of society. Without renewed attention to these problems, it is difficult to see how this final ethical question can be answered. Perhaps Al Martinez, the novelist mentioned at the beginning of this chapter, had these issues in mind when his fictional newspaper, the *Herald,* like so many others newspapers in recent years, closed its doors at the end of his book.

Walter B. Jaehnig
Southern Illinois University Carbondale

See also Ethical Responsibilities versus Legal Rights; Ethics Tools

Further Reading

Argyris, Chris. *Behind the Front Page.* San Francisco, CA: Jossey-Bass, 1974.
Breed, Warren. "Mass Communication and Socio-Cultural Integration." *Social Forces* 37 (1958).
Breed, Warren. "Social Control in the Newsroom." *Social Forces* 33 (1955).
Chase, Dennis. "The Aphilosophy of Journalism." *Quill* (September 1971).
Commission on Freedom of the Press. *A Free and Responsible Press.* Chicago: University of Chicago Press, 1947.
French, Peter. *Collective and Corporate Responsibility.* New York: Columbia University Press, 1984.

Gans, Herbert J. *Deciding What's News.* New York: Vintage Books, 1980.

May, Larry. *The Morality of Groups.* South Bend, IN: University of Notre Dame Press, 1989.

Niebuhr, Reinhold. *Moral Man and Immoral Society.* New York: Simon & Schuster, 1995.

Tichenor, Philip J., George H. Donohue, and Clarice N. Olien. *Community Conflict and the Press.* Beverly Hills, CA: Sage, 1980.

Weaver, David H., Randal A. Beam, Bonnie A. Brownlee, Paul S. Voakes, and G. Cleveland Wilhoit. *The American Journalist in the 21st Century.* Mahwah, NJ: Lawrence Erlbaum Associates, 2007.

46

Commercial Speech

Americans are exposed to dozens of advertisements each day; exposure estimates vary from 250 to 3,000 messages a day. Ads are everywhere: not only on our televisions and radios and in our newspapers, but on our browsers, our smartphones, our grocery carts, and our public bathroom stalls. Advertising is speech, subject to the First Amendment's protection, but it is not afforded the same kind of protection as other kinds of speech because of its commercial nature. Over the past seventy years, the Supreme Court has developed the commercial speech doctrine, which provides a limited level of protection for advertising. But this doctrine has only been around in its current form since the 1980s. Earlier cases offered far more protection to advertising materials. Before turning to the ethical implications of today's advertising and the rules governing it, it is first necessary to trace the path of the commercial speech doctrine and its applications through history.

Early Commercial Speech Cases

The Supreme Court first took an advertising case in 1942, and the outcome was less than satisfying for advertising. In

Valentine v. Chrestensen, the Court said that a handbill containing advertising on one side (for a submarine tour) and political protest speech on the other side (complaints that the submarine owner could not store his submarine at the public New York City wharfs) was still considered to be advertising and thus subject to more stringent regulations than political speech. In holding that the First Amendment did not apply to advertising, the Court said that while the First Amendment properly limits governmental control over speech about public issues, "the Constitution imposes no such restraint on government as respects purely commercial advertising." This distinction remained in place for the next three decades.

It was not until the 1960s and 1970s, in the wake of the civil rights movement, that the Court reconsidered this position. In the famous libel case *New York Times v. Sullivan* (1964), the justices said that the fact that speech touches on advertising does not necessarily render it commercial (in that case, the speech at issue was an advertisement taken out by civil rights activists alleged to have errors in it). Still under the old "no protection" model, the Court in 1973 addressed want ads in newspapers that specified jobs divided by gender ("Jobs—Male Interest" and "Jobs—Female Interest"). A lower court held that this organization of job want ads violated a Pittsburgh ordinance that forbade newspapers from dividing jobs by gender unless there was a bona fide occupational qualification that required a job be performed by one gender or the other (e.g., surrogate mothers or sperm donors). The Supreme Court upheld the ordinance, saying that the ad organization along gender lines was a form of illegal discrimination under the ordinance. "By implication at least, an advertiser whose want ad appears in the 'Jobs—Male Interest' column is likely to discriminate against women in his hiring decisions," suggested the justices in *Pittsburgh Press Company v. Human Relations Commission* (1973).

Two years later, the Court changed course, suggesting that advertising content that was related to issues of public importance had additional protections. In *Bigelow v. Virginia* (1975), the justices considered a law in Virginia that forbade the carrying of advertising in any Virginia publication for abortion services that were legal in other states. A clinic in New York, where abortion services were legal at the time, took out ads in a newspaper advertising those services and was convicted under the law. The state supreme court held that the law was constitutional; the Supreme Court overturned. In this case, the advertising at issue not only offered services for sale that were legal in the state in which they were offered but also touched on an issue of significant national importance—the legality of abortion. "Viewed in its entirety," the Court explained, "the advertisement conveyed information of potential interest and value to a diverse audience—not only to readers possibly in need of the services offered, but also to those with a general curiosity about, or genuine interest in, the subject matter or the law of another State and its development, and to readers seeking reform in Virginia." Moreover, Virginia could not stop its residents from traveling to New York to seek abortion services. Thus the law was an unconstitutional infringement on the advertiser's First Amendment rights. Two justices dissented, maintaining that the Virginia law was a reasonable limitation on speech that served a legitimate public interest.

A year later, in 1976, the Court reached the pinnacle of its protection of commercial speech in *Virginia State Board of Pharmacy v. Virginia Citizens Consumer Council, Inc.* Here, a Virginia state statute said that licensed pharmacists would be considered to have engaged in unprofessional conduct if they advertised the prices of prescription drugs in the media. A group of consumers challenged the law on First Amendment grounds. In overturning the statute, the justices provided the most ringing endorsement of advertising's First Amendment protection to date.

While agreeing that it was an important state interest to regulate pharmacists and pharmacies, the Court did not extend the state's interest to forbidding the publication of truthful information about lawful goods and services for interested parties. Unlike in *Bigelow*, there was no issue of political or social speech or arguments here: as the Court put it, the purely commercial message was simply that "Pharmacist X will sell prescription drug Y at price Z." Is this message outside the protection of the First Amendment? No, said the Court. Noting that the average person's interest in the prices of prescription drugs "may be as keen, if not keener by far, than his interest in the day's most urgent political debate," information imparted through advertising serves an important societal interest. The result of the opinion was to suggest that the state may not prevent truthful information about lawful goods and services from getting to its intended audience, despite what the state may fear about that information's impact.

Justice William Rehnquist's dissent in this case bears mention here. In it, he bluntly stated his fears: "Under the Court's opinion, the way will be open not only for dissemination of price information, but for active promotion of prescription drugs, liquor, cigarettes, and other products the use of which it has previously been thought desirable to discourage." Simply put, said Justice Rehnquist, pharmacists under this new rule are free to encourage patients to seek their doctors' approvals for a whole host of medications that they may or may not need (one example he gave: "Pain getting you down? Insist that your physician prescribe Demerol. You pay a little more than for aspirin, but you get a lot more relief."). One need only tune in for a few hours of prime-time television or flip through a couple popular magazines to find evidence of the justice's fears.

But this freewheeling regulatory regime for advertising did not last long. Only four years later, in 1980, the Supreme Court fashioned the commercial speech test for regulations on advertising that is still used today.

The *Central Hudson* Test

In a case that seemed innocuous enough at first glance, the Court established a four-part test that would be applied to a regulation on advertising. At issue in *Central Hudson Gas & Electric Corporation v. Public Service Commission of New York* (1980)—or what most legal scholars call the *Central Hudson* case— was a New York regulation, passed during the height of the "energy crisis" of the 1970s, that forbade "promotional" advertising that encouraged the use of electricity but allowed "informational" advertising that encouraged shifts of energy consumption. The New York Court of Appeals, the highest court in the state, upheld the regulation, but the Supreme Court reversed.

In reversing the state court and overturning the regulation, the Court put forth a four-part test to be used when a regulation on advertising is challenged. First, it is clear that the government may regulate or ban advertising that is for illegal goods or services or is misleading or unfair in some way. If the advertising is for legal goods or services and is not misleading, then, second, the government must assert a substantial interest to be advanced by the regulation.

The term "substantial" has a distinct legal meaning. In the hierarchy of types of government interests, "substantial" interests are relatively easy to demonstrate—and easier to regulate. "Compelling" and "overriding" interests are higher on the protection scale and harder for the government to regulate; for example, the right to vote, or the fundamental rights contained in the Bill of

Rights, can only be infringed for very specific and critical reasons. "Substantial" interests, on the other hand, are much easier for the government to regulate: enhancing public aesthetics, reducing childhood disease or obesity, and encouraging the cessation of smoking or the curbing of gambling are all examples.

Parts three and four of the *Central Hudson* test examine the regulation itself. Part three is an evaluation of the impact the regulation is likely to have on the government interest. In other words, does the regulation advance the interest that the government has put forth in part two of the test? Finally, part four asks whether the regulation is sufficiently narrowly tailored to achieve its goals. If the regulation would ban too much speech, then the regulation is void. These last two parts are sometimes combined to evaluate the "fit" of the regulation to the government interest. And they are the hardest parts of the test to meet.

Here is a sample application of the *Central Hudson* test: A city council decides that there are too many billboards within city limits, and that the roadways would be more attractive if there were fewer billboards. So the council passes a city ordinance saying that there will be no billboards in the city limits; existing billboards must be removed, and no new ones can be put up. Angry advertisers challenge the ordinance in federal court. The court would apply the *Central Hudson* test. The regulation would easily pass the first two parts of the test, assuming the billboards were for legal services or goods, and the ads themselves were not misleading. And public aesthetics and beauty are substantial government interests. Most regulations do not face

any trouble from parts one and two of the *Central Hudson* test.

Part three, in this hypothetical, is probably not going to pose the city's regulation any problems. The city would have to demonstrate that removing the billboards would improve public aesthetics. That would not be difficult, as most people would rather admire natural scenery than billboards. Part four, however, is another story. Here, the city seeks to eliminate a lot of speech when it bans all the billboards—speech that some consumers, at least, would like to have and that advertisers would like them to have. Part four of *Central Hudson* asks if the regulation is no more extensive than necessary to achieve the government's goal in part two. Here, it is clear even at first glance that the city could put in place other, less drastic restrictions on billboards with a lower impact on speech: limiting the sizes and numbers of billboards, for example, or designating certain areas of the roadways as off-limits to billboard advertising. This more limited response would still achieve the city's substantial goal of more aesthetic beauty on its roadways without damaging too much protected speech. (As noted earlier, sometimes parts three and four of the test are combined to evaluate a regulation's "fit" with the government's interest. An example of that application will be provided below.)

The Supreme Court used this test in 1983 in *Bolger v. Youngs Drug Products Corporation*. Here, the Court applied the *Central Hudson* test to a U.S. Post Office regulation against sending birth control information through the mails. First, there were no allegations in the case that the information Youngs wished to send out was fraudulent or misleading. Second, the

Court acknowledged the importance of "aiding parents' efforts to discuss birth control with their children" as a substantial interest. However, applying parts three and four, the Court found that the statute was problematic because it kept that information away from parents (so it could not be said to advance the government's interest), and, moreover, the statute's effect of "purging all mailboxes of unsolicited material that is entirely suitable for adults" was too broad to survive constitutional consideration and failed the fourth part of the test. Thus, the statute was unconstitutional.

An example of how the third and fourth parts of the *Central Hudson* test are not only the most problematic for government regulation, but how they can be blended into a "fit" requirement, was handed down by the Supreme Court in *Cincinnati v. Discovery Network* (1993). This case involved a challenge to a Cincinnati ordinance that banned newsracks on public property if they contained advertising publications, but not if they contained newspapers or news products. The city asserted a public aesthetic interest, which the Court found worthy. However, the distinction between the allowable publications meant that the regulation did not advance the interest. Justice John Paul Stevens wrote for the Court, "The city had the burden of establishing 'a reasonable "fit" between the legislature's ends and the means chosen to accomplish those ends.'" The city did not meet its burden because, Justice Stevens asserted, "Not only does Cincinnati's categorical ban on commercial newsracks place too much importance on the distinction between commercial and noncommercial speech,

but in this case, the distinction bears no relationship whatsoever to the particular interests that the city has asserted."

The *Central Hudson* test has been used in hundreds of cases since it was handed down in 1980. However, the trend, at least at the Supreme Court level, has been to interpret the test strictly so as to strike down more regulations on commercial speech. And, as will be discussed later, some current justices are unhappy with the *Central Hudson* regime and would like to see it overturned.

Applications of the *Central Hudson* Test to Vice Advertising

"Vice" advertising is that advertising that encourages activities such as drinking, smoking, and gambling—activities that are legal for adults to engage in but that the government may seek to discourage. The Supreme Court has taken a number of these cases, and in most of them, the advertising regulation was overturned after an application of the *Central Hudson* test.

Alcohol Advertising. In the 1995 case of *Rubin v. Coors Brewing Company*, the justices struck down a law that the government claimed would eliminate beer companies from engaging in "strength wars." A section of the Federal Alcohol Administration Act had prohibited beer labels from displaying the beer's alcohol content. The law had been passed to discourage brewers from competing in the marketplace on the basis of the beer's potency.

Writing for a unanimous Court, Justice Clarence Thomas (who, as will be discussed, is one of the chief opponents of the *Central Hudson* commercial speech test) wrote that although the government's goal of reducing "strength wars" was a substantial interest, the regulation failed to advance that interest. Because the ban on alcohol content did not apply to wine and other distilled spirits (in fact, the opposite was true: labels on wines and spirits must include the alcohol content), Justice Thomas scolded, "Rather than suppressing the free flow of factual information in the wine and spirits markets, the Government seeks to control competition on the basis of strength by monitoring distillers' promotions and marketing." Moreover, many states permit the inclusion of strength in advertising, but the government required beer labels to omit that information. Nor had the government provided any solid evidence that the labeling ban had advanced its goal of reducing "strength wars."

A year later, in 1996, a unanimous Court overturned a state law that forbade advertising of liquor prices except at the point of sale. Rhode Island, as well as a number of other states, had a law prohibiting the advertising of liquor prices in places where liquor was not sold. Justice Stevens, writing for the Court in *44 Liquormart, Inc. v. Rhode Island*, agreed that the government's goal of encouraging temperance in alcohol consumption was a substantial one. However, as in the *Coors* case, the government was suppressing too much speech in an effort to achieve that goal.

The complete ban on all liquor pricing information except at the site where the liquor was sold (and even then, signs at the store could not be visible from the street) and even forbidding ads in the media, said Justice Stevens, was simply too broad a ban. The government cannot ban speech to cover up its own hidden goals: "Precisely because bans against truthful, non-misleading commercial speech rarely seek to protect consumers from either deception or overreaching, they usually rest solely on the offensive assumption that the public will respond 'irrationally' to the truth." If the state truly wishes to encourage temperance, there are plenty of ways to do so without affecting freedom of speech; for example, raising taxes on alcohol or engaging in educational campaigns are just a few of the ways.

While Justice Thomas did concur in the case's outcome, he declined to join the reasoning. He would not join the majority's reasoning, he explained, "because I do not believe that such a test should be applied to a restriction of 'commercial' speech, at least when, as here, the asserted interest is one that is to be achieved through keeping would be recipients of the speech in the dark." He went on to attack the *Central Hudson* test in general: "In my view, the *Central Hudson* test asks the courts to weigh incommensurables—the value of knowledge versus the value of ignorance—and to apply contradictory premises—that informed adults are the best judges of their own interests, and that they are not." He asserted that the approach taken in the 1976 *Virginia State Board of Pharmacy* case, where truthful advertising for legal goods and services would be protected, made better sense, and he would return to that approach.

Tobacco Advertising. Perhaps no vice activity has seen as much publicity and litigation as tobacco. Both federal and state governments may regulate tobacco sales and advertising. The Federal Cigarette Labeling and Advertising Act of 1966 forbids broadcast advertising of cigarettes and requires health warnings in ads and on cigarette packages (the ban was extended to smokeless tobacco in 1986, via the Comprehensive Smokeless Tobacco Health Education Act).

In 2000, the Supreme Court forbade the Food and Drug Administration (FDA) to regulate tobacco as a drug in *FDA v. Brown & Williamson Tobacco Corporation*. The question before the Court was whether the FDA could regulate tobacco products as "drugs" or "devices," to which the justices answered no. Justice Sandra Day O'Connor wrote that Congress "has created a distinct regulatory scheme for tobacco products, squarely rejected proposals to give the FDA jurisdiction over tobacco, and repeatedly acted to preclude any agency from exercising significant policymaking authority in the area." This would change with Congressional action in 2010. The Family Smoking Prevention and Tobacco Control Act gave the FDA authority to regulate the manufacture, distribution, and marketing of tobacco. The act put in place new restrictions on tobacco advertising, including the marketing of cigarettes and smokeless tobacco to minors. It also forbade audio ads from containing music or sound effects, and video ads can only be static black text on a white background, with audio limited to spoken words.

The Supreme Court has addressed marketing of tobacco products in several cases in the 2000s and 2010s. In *Lorillard Tobacco Company v. Reilly* (2001), two Massachusetts laws regulating the advertising of tobacco products were challenged. The Massachusetts attorney general had argued that the rules were necessary to reduce the number of minors who smoked. The Court ruled that the state law that regulated outdoor and point-of-sale cigarette advertising was federally preempted—that is, federal law trumps state law in this area—and the state law that regulated ads for smokeless tobacco and cigars violated the First Amendment. "We conclude that the Attorney General has failed to show that the outdoor advertising regulations for smokeless tobacco and cigars are not more extensive than necessary to advance the State's substantial interest in preventing underage tobacco use," Justice O'Connor wrote.

In the 2008 case of *Altria Group v. Good*, the Court said that the Federal Cigarette Labeling and Advertising Act did not preempt state law claims in connection with the advertising of cigarettes as "light" or "lower tar and nicotine." But the FDA's attempt to require tobacco companies to put graphic images of the alleged results of smoking on the actual cigarette package (for example: a man shown smoking with a hole in his throat, or a pair of cancerous lungs compared to healthy lungs) resulted in split lower-court decisions. In 2012, the Sixth Circuit in *Discount Tobacco City & Lottery v. U.S.* upheld the color graphic label requirements of the Family Smoking Prevention and Tobacco Control Act, as well as several other restrictions on tobacco advertising. (The Supreme Court declined to review the case, so the circuit court decision stood.)

But that same year, the D.C. Circuit overturned the graphic labels as not advancing the government's stated interest in reducing the number of smokers (*R. J. Reynolds Tobacco Company v. FDA*). The circuit court said that under *Central Hudson,* the FDA had not provided any evidence "showing that the graphic warnings will 'directly advance' its interest in reducing the number of Americans who smoke." The FDA did not appeal, but it has announced that it will continue to study the problem and make rules that will comply with the federal acts.

Among its other provisions, the Family Smoking Prevention and Tobacco Control Act also bans tobacco product sponsorship of sporting or entertainment events under tobacco brand names and free samples of cigarettes and brand-name non-tobacco promotional items. To date, these provisions have not been challenged.

Gambling Advertising. Another vice area in which governments tend to regulate advertising is in advertising of casinos, lotteries, and other gambling. This area of regulation has seen a bit more success under *Central Hudson* than some other areas. Congress passed several antigambling laws in the 1800s, including the Anti-Lottery Act of 1890, which survived a First Amendment challenge in *Ex parte Rapier* (1892). In this case, the petitioners were arrested and asked for a writ of habeus corpus (an order to appear in court to be released from unlawful imprisonment) after they had mailed newspapers and letters advertising lotteries. The Anti-Lottery Act forbade such mailings ("No letter, postal-card or circular concerning any lottery, so-called gift-concert,

or other similar enterprise offering prizes dependent upon lot or chance . . . shall be carried in the mail or delivered at or through any post office or branch thereof."). Petitioners argued that Congress did not have the right to pass this law, but the Court disagreed: "We cannot regard the right to operate a lottery as a fundamental right infringed by the legislation in question; nor are we able to see that Congress can be held, in its enactment, to have abridged the freedom of the press."

Contemporary cases addressing gambling advertising include a 1986 Puerto Rican case, *Posadas de Puerto Rico Associates v. Tourism Company of Puerto Rico*. The Puerto Rican legislature passed the Games of Chance Act of 1948 that forbade the advertising of legalized casino gambling to Puerto Rican residents, while allowing such advertising to be aimed at tourists. The Puerto Rican Supreme Court upheld the regulation, and the Supreme Court of the United States has jurisdiction to review that holding. In so doing, the Supreme Court showed deference to the findings of the lower court and the legislature.

In applying the *Central Hudson* test, Justice Rehnquist, writing for the Court, found that the legislature's goal of promoting gambling tourism while not harming the local population to be substantial. Moreover, the legislature found that eliminating gambling advertising to the residents of Puerto Rico would advance that goal, and the justices determined this to be a reasonable finding. And, as for the final element of the *Central Hudson* test, Justice Rehnquist noted, "The narrowing constructions of the advertising restrictions announced by the Superior Court ensure that the restrictions will not affect advertising of casino gambling aimed at tourists, but will apply only to such advertising when aimed at the residents of Puerto Rico." Thus the law was sufficiently narrowly tailored to meet the Puerto Rican government's interests.

In the 1993 case of *United States v. Edge Broadcasting Company,* the justices upheld a federal statute (18 U.S.C. § 1304) that forbade lottery advertising from broadcasters licensed in states that do not allow lotteries but allowed such advertising by broadcasters in states that do allow lotteries. A broadcaster licensed in North Carolina (a state that did not allow lotteries) at a location only three miles from Virginia (a state that did allow lotteries) challenged the law. The North Carolina broadcaster claimed that the law did not advance the government's interests with a reasonable "fit" because North Carolina listeners could hear advertisements for Virginia lotteries anyway since broadcast signals do not stop at state lines. But the Court *upheld* the statute because even though the "fit" was not ideal, the justices said that the statute did apply to the overall goal the government sought to address.

Justice Byron White wrote that Congress could have banned all lottery advertising broadcasts, but chose not to: "Instead of favoring either the lottery or the non-lottery State, Congress opted to support the antigambling policy of a State like North Carolina by forbidding stations in such a State from airing lottery advertising. At the same time it sought not to unduly interfere with the policy of a lottery sponsoring State such as Virginia." This balancing under Section 1304, said Justice White, satisfied the government's need to demonstrate a "fit" between the government's balancing of the needs of lottery and non-lottery states with the statute chosen to do so.

In *Greater New Orleans Broadcasting Association, Inc. v. United States* (1999), however, the Court revisited the same federal law it had upheld in the *Edge Broadcasting* case (18 U.S.C. § 1304) and found it inapplicable in another situation. The Court declined to apply the statute to broadcast advertising for private casino gambling by radio or television stations in Louisiana, where this kind of gambling is legal. The Greater New Orleans Broadcasting Association had ignored the federal ban and had been fined.

In a somewhat different application of the "fit" required under *Central Hudson*'s third and fourth parts, Justice Stevens said that Section 1304 disallowed only advertising for private casino gambling but allowed exemptions for advertising other kinds of gambling, such as animal racing and jai alai. Thus, the regulation did not advance the government's stated interest because the regulation included too *little* speech. (Think of it like dieting by just avoiding chocolate-chip cookies and only on Tuesdays. How likely is such a person to lose weight?) Justice Stevens called Section 1304 "so pierced by exemptions and inconsistencies that the Government cannot hope to exonerate it."

Prostitution Advertising. In only one state in the United States—Nevada—is prostitution legal, and only in about half the counties in the state. Clearly state governments may ban advertising for a service illegal in those states, and most do, but in Nevada, where in some counties prostitution is legal, can brothel owners advertise their services? The state of Nevada has fairly severe advertising regulations in place for brothels, and the Ninth Circuit Court of Appeals upheld those laws in 2010 in *Coyote Publishing Inc. v. Miller*.

Under a *Central Hudson* analysis, the court said that not only did the state have an interest in limiting the commodification of sex, the state's restrictions were limited because they were tailored to the counties that permitted prostitution. Simply put, the court said, "Nevada's chosen approach directly and materially advances the state's policy of limiting commodification [of sex] without undermining its competing health and safety goals." The Supreme Court did not review this case.

The Strict Approach. Taken together and as a whole, these cases demonstrate that the Supreme Court tends to apply *Central Hudson* rather strictly, even to "vice" activities, and that many regulations fail to pass constitutional muster because of the third and fourth elements of the test.

It is reasonable to ask whether such a strict reading of *Central Hudson* should or should not be the case, because in all of these lawsuits, the advertisements were for legal goods and services. If governments have the right to ban the activities or products themselves (and in many cases, they do—for example, as many as 10 percent of U.S. counties are "dry," meaning that alcohol cannot be sold in the county in some situations), should they have the lesser right to ban speech about those activities and products? If the government has decided that the vice goods and services should be able to be consumed by adults, to what extent should the government be able to ban truthful speech that provides information about those goods and services? What are the considerations that should go into a government's regulations, or should there be none, even for vice activities?

Political Advertising

Campaign finance reform has a long and storied history, starting primarily with a 1976 Supreme Court case, *Buckley v. Valeo*. In that case, the Court struck down some amendments to the Federal Election Campaign Act as unconstitutional; limitations on independent expenditures for campaigns, on expenditures by candidates from their own resources, and on total campaign expenditures were eliminated. But the justices upheld restrictions on individual contributions to political campaigns and candidates because those limitations enhance the "integrity of our system of representative democracy." This case paved the way for the most controversial First Amendment case of the last decade.

Perhaps no case has garnered as much attention and commentary as the 2010 campaign finance case of *Citizens United v. Federal Elections Commission*. In that hotly debated contest, Citizens United, a conservative nonprofit organization, sought an injunction of the Bipartisan Campaign Reform Act (BCRA, also known as the McCain-Feingold Act). Section 203 of BCRA imposed a number of regulations on campaign donations, including requiring disclosure and disclaimer provisions and forbidding corporations and labor unions from funding "electioneering communications" out of their general funds. An "electioneering communication" was defined as a broadcast, cable, or satellite communication mentioning a candidate within sixty days of a general election or thirty days of a primary election. Citizens United wanted to advertise and show a ninety-minute documentary called *Hillary: The Movie,* which promoted a clear message of Senator Hillary Clinton's suitability for the presidency.

In its opinion, a deeply divided Court overruled some of its precedents in campaign finance law (*Austin v. Michigan Chamber of Commerce* and portions of *McConnell v. Federal Elections Commission*, which had said that corporate identity may be cause for banning political speech). Justice Anthony Kennedy wrote for the 5–4 majority, "If the First Amendment has any force, it prohibits Congress from fining or jailing citizens, or associations of citizens, for simply engaging in political speech." Section 203's limits on expenditures therefore could not stand. The majority relied on a 1978 case, *First National Bank of Boston v. Bellotti*, in which the justices had struck down a prohibition against independent corporate expenditures for ballot initiatives and referenda.

In a bitter ninety-page dissent, with parts read from the bench for emphasis, Justice Stevens blasted the majority opinion's assumption that money does not affect the outcome of campaigns. He wrote, "A democracy cannot function effectively when its constituent members believe laws are being bought and sold." Because the majority had thrown open the floodgates and enabled corporations to fund campaigns without limit, Justice Stevens feared that "the Court's blinkered and aphoristic approach to the First Amendment may well promote corporate power at the cost of the individual and collective self-expression the Amendment was meant to serve."

The Court further chipped away at campaign finance regulations in a 2014 case, *McCutcheon v. Federal Elections Commission.* Here, the question before the justices was whether so-called aggregate limits on an individual person's donations are constitutional. These limitations are based on a two-year election cycle: no more than $48,600 to all candidates combined and no more than $74,600 to political parties and political action committees (PACs). Base limits, which are limits on the amount of money an individual can contribute to a candidate, party, or PAC, were not challenged here. But in *McCutcheon*, the Court struck down the aggregate limits.

Chief Justice John Roberts wrote for the majority that the only kind of corruption that campaign finance laws should try to combat is "quid pro quo" corruption—that is, an exchange of money for an official act, or an "I'll scratch your back, you scratch mine" arrangement. Aggregate limits, then, are not needed to advance this government interest, said Chief Justice Roberts. He explained, "To put it in the simplest terms, the aggregate limits prohibit an individual from fully contributing to the primary and general election campaigns of ten or more candidates, even if all contributions fall within the base limits Congress views as adequate to protect against corruption." Thus, those limits cannot stand.

Justice Stephen Breyer, who also read his dissent from the bench, wrote that the majority "eviscerates our Nation's campaign finance laws, leaving a remnant incapable of dealing with the grave problems of democratic legitimacy that those laws were intended to resolve." His concerns focused in part on his belief that the base limits were not inviolate, and that savvy donors would find ways around them, and that corruption does not only take place in quid pro quo arrangements (an act he baldly called "bribery").

Which side is right here? Does the formula that "money equals speech" work in an era where corporations may spend freely on a candidate, party, or PAC, to the tune of hundreds of thousands of dollars? Do such permissive rules really shut down the political power of the small donor, for whom $1,000 is a significant contribution? What defines "political corruption"? Is it merely quid pro quo corruption, as Chief Justice Roberts suggests, or can it be more, and worse, like Justice Breyer fears? To what extent should government step in to manage how candidates get elected?

Other Advertising

While many regulations focus on vice activities like smoking, drinking, and gambling (and one might argue that politics counts as a vice), there are plenty of other cases in which regulations on advertising are challenged. While this cannot be a comprehensive review, here are a few areas in which significant litigation has taken place.

Lawyer Advertising. It should come as no surprise that attorney advertising has been so heavily litigated in the past several decades. However, attorneys are subject to various legal and ethics rules

by state. The Supreme Court first ruled on lawyer advertising in a 1977 case, *Bates v. State Bar of Arizona.* It is arguably the most important defense of lawyer advertising, even though many cases have come before the Court in the years since. The case provides an excellent opportunity to evaluate the ethical concerns of attorney advertising. At the time, most states forbade attorneys to advertise at all. Two attorneys ran a legal clinic and advertised the prices for some of their services—prices lower than the average.

The Court overturned Arizona's ban, and those of other states, saying that advertising by attorneys could not be wholly banned unless the ads were misleading or fraudulent. However, Justice Harry Blackmun addressed some of the ethical concerns raised by the state bar association: loss of professionalism ("price advertising will bring about commercialization, which will undermine the attorney's sense of dignity and self-worth"); concerns about misleading ads ("advertising of legal services inevitably will be misleading (a) because such services are so individualized with regard to content and quality as to prevent informed comparison on the basis of an advertisement, (b) because the consumer of legal services is unable to determine in advance just what services he needs, and (c) because advertising by attorneys will highlight irrelevant factors and fail to show the relevant factor of skill"); adverse effects on the administration of justice ("advertising is said to have the undesirable effect of stirring up litigation"); adverse effects on the quality of service ("the attorney may advertise a given 'package' of service at a set price, and will be inclined to provide . . . the standard package regardless of whether it fits the client's needs"); and difficulties in enforcement.

Justice Blackmun found none of these issues sufficiently problematic to justify a complete ban on all attorney advertising. But they do raise some ethical concerns. To what extent does the relaxing of regulations on lawyer advertising result in the promulgation of additional litigation, for example, or the commercialization of the law? One need only watch a couple of hours of television to be bombarded with advertisements for new class action claims against pharmaceutical companies, asbestos exposure, and more. Are we as a society more likely to file frivolous lawsuits because of the ubiquity of advertising?

Pharmaceutical Advertising. Long an issue before the justice system, and first addressed in the 1976 *Virginia State Board of Pharmacy* case, drug advertising has been a cause for governmental concern. In 2002, the Supreme Court invalidated a federal law that banned the advertisement of "compounded prescription drugs"—special combinations of drugs prepared for individual patients by pharmacists at a doctor's request. These combinations did not, under this federal law, have to undergo traditional Food and Drug Administration (FDA) testing required of new drugs as long as they were not advertised.

Justice O'Connor, writing for the majority in *Thompson v. Western States Medical Center*, applied the *Central Hudson* test and found that the law failed part four: much more speech was banned than needed to be to achieve the government's goal. Rather than evaluating other means to achieve its goal of streamlining the FDA approval process, the government did not bother. "If the First Amendment means anything," Justice O'Connor wrote, "it means that regulating speech must be a last—not first—resort. Yet here it seems to have been the first strategy the Government thought to try."

As the marketing of drugs continues to proliferate, some companies have taken advantage of a technique called "data mining" to determine doctors' individual prescription rates for purposes of marketing to those doctors. Vermont had a law, the Prescription Confidentiality Law, forbidding pharmacies from sharing information about the drugs prescribed by individual doctors with data-mining companies who would then in turn sell the information to brand-name drug manufacturers to help them target prescribing doctors—and presumably encourage them to prescribe the brand-name drugs. The law was intended to protect doctors from these marketing efforts. The data-mining and drug companies challenged the law on First Amendment grounds.

The Supreme Court heard the case, *Sorrell v. IMS Health Inc.,* in 2011, and overturned the Prescription Confidentiality Law. Justice Kennedy noted that the state had not suggested that the prescribing information was false or misleading. He wrote, "If pharmaceutical marketing affects treatment decisions, it does so because doctors find it persuasive. Absent circumstances far from those presented here, the fear that speech might persuade provides no lawful basis for quieting it."

Off-label drug uses are those uses that are not approved by the FDA but prescribed by physicians because they are shown to help patients. The FDA does not punish doctors for engaging in off-label prescriptions, but what about advertising those off-label uses? In the Second Circuit, at least, such advertising is protected. In 2012, the appellate court said in *U.S. v. Caronia* that a pharmaceutical sales representative's promotion of the drug Xyrem for uses other than those approved by the FDA was acceptable. The Food, Drug and Cosmetic Act does not "criminaliz[e] the simple promotion of a drug's off-label use because such a construction would raise First Amendment concerns." Moreover, penalizing the dissemination of truthful information about a drug could be harmful to the public's making of intelligent medical treatment decisions.

Epilogue: Whither Commercial Speech?

The cases above demonstrate a central ethical concern with advertising regulation: Should the government regulate advertising speech—which does have some First Amendment protection—more heavily because it dislikes the products and services some advertisers tout, or out of fear of what such advertising would produce? And to what extent, if any, should government get involved in the campaign finance world?

There has been an ongoing question of whether advertising speech ought to have more protection than it does—on par with political speech, which has traditionally been given the highest First Amendment protection. The Supreme Court did take on one case, in 2003, called *Nike v. Kasky*, in which it could have addressed a similar question but declined to do so.

In this case, Marc Kasky, a California consumer advocate, alleged that Nike's speech defending its factory conditions in southeast Asia was unfair and deceptive under California's Unfair Competition Law. Before the Court were two questions: "(1) whether a corporation participating in a public debate may 'be subjected to liability for factual inaccuracies on the theory that its statements are "commercial speech" because they might affect consumers' opinions about the business as a good corporate citizen and thereby affect their purchasing decisions'; and (2) even assuming the California Supreme Court properly characterized such statements as commercial speech, whether the 'First Amendment . . . permit[s] subjecting speakers to the legal regime approved by that court in the decision below.'" The California Supreme Court awarded the win to Kasky, saying that Nike's communications were actually commercial speech and thus subject to false advertising law.

After hearing oral arguments, the Court decided not to decide the case (the term is "the writ of *certiorari* is dismissed as improvidently granted"), thus leaving in place the California high court's decision. Several justices, led by Justice Stevens, agreed with the dismissal, saying "For, even if we were to decide the First Amendment issues presented to us today, more First Amendment issues might well remain in this case, making piecemeal review of the Federal First Amendment issues likely." So the overarching question remains unresolved, whether speech from a corporation should be considered commercial, regardless of its content. This, of course, raises questions about the appropriate role of corporations in campaign funding. Clearly, who or what causes or campaigns a corporation chooses to finance speaks volumes about its political stances. How can these issues be reconciled?

Genelle Belmas
University of Kansas

See also Compelled Speech; A New First Amendment?

Further Reading

Boumil, Marcia M., Kaitlyn Dunn, Nancy Ryan, and Katrina Clearwater. "Prescription Data Mining, Medical Privacy and the First Amendment: The U.S. Supreme Court in *Sorrell v. IMS Health Inc.*" *Annals of Health Law* 21 (2012).

Collins, Ronald K. L. "Exceptional Freedom—The Roberts Court, the First Amendment, and the New Absolutism." *Albany Law Review* 76 (2012/2013).

Ehlin, Whitney. "Silencing the Smoking Gun: A Critique of Formalism in Ruling on the Free Speech Implications of the Graphic Label Requirement of Tobacco Products." *Georgetown Journal of Law & Public Policy* 11 (2013).

Greiner, Brienne Taylor. "A Tough Pill to Swallow: Does the First Amendment Prohibit WV from Regulating Pharmaceutical Companies? Advertising Expenses to Lower the Cost of Prescription Drugs?" *West Virginia Law Review* 109 (2006).

Hodge, James G., Jr., Veda Collmer, Daniel G. Orenstein, Chase Millea, and Laura Van Buren. "Reconsidering the Legality of Cigarette Smoking Advertisements on Television." *Journal of Law, Medicine and Ethics* 41 (2013).

Levitt, Justin. "Confronting the Impact of *Citizens United.*" *Yale Law & Policy Review* 29 (2010).

Margulies, Peter. "Advocacy as a Race to the Bottom: Rethinking Limits on Lawyers' Free Speech." *University of Memphis Law Review* 43 (2012).

Moenius, Jill E. "Buying Promises: How *Citizens United*'s Campaign Expenditures Convert Our 'Impartial' Judges and Their Nonpromissory Campaign Statements into an Indebted, Influenced, and Dependent Judiciary." *Kansas Law Review* 59 (2011).

Passalacqua, Matthew. "Something's Brewing within the Commercial Speech Doctrine." *Valparaiso University Law Review* 46 (2012).

Piety, Tamara R. "'A Necessary Cost of Freedom'? The Incoherence of *Sorrell v. IMS.*" *Alabama Law Review* 64 (2012).

Pomeranz, Jennifer L. "No Need to Break New Ground: A Response to the Supreme Court's Threat to Overhaul the Commercial Speech Doctrine." *Loyola of Los Angeles Law Review* 45 (2012).

47

Richard Jewell and the 2013 Boston Marathon

Security guard Richard A. Jewell, who discovered a bomb and notified authorities about it at the 1996 Summer Olympics in Atlanta, should have been noted in the history books as a hero. Instead, because of the subsequent surveillance conducted by the FBI and a "trial by media," his role in the events surrounding the deadly Centennial Olympic Park bombing remains cloaked in a shadow of doubt, even though a man named Eric Robert Rudolph eventually was convicted of the crime, which killed one person and injured 111 others.

In April 2013, another terror scene unfolded in broad daylight in the wealthy commercial district of Boston, when hundreds of runners were on their way to finish the Boston Marathon. A couple of hundred yards away from the finish line, two pressure-cooker bombs exploded, turning a scene of triumph into a landscape of tragedy where three people died and scores more were injured. From the identification of two self-radicalized brothers as suspects in the bombing right up to the terror incident's final episode (covered breathlessly by reporters), in which one of the siblings was apprehended, it took local police fewer than five days to hunt down the two key suspects—one dead, the other in custody.

In this article, two veteran journalists—Irfan Ashraf, whose fifteen-year career has been spent working in the terror-ravaged border areas of Pakistan and teaching journalism at Peshawar University near the Afghanistan border, and John Jarvis, who has worked as a reporter and copy editor for newspapers in Arizona, Indiana, and Texas over the past twenty-six years—discuss what ethical considerations would help journalists do their jobs and inform society in a way that minimizes the infringement on a person's privacy and causes the least damage to a person's reputation. Through a series of questions, each provides a perspective on the two terrorist attacks mentioned above while also discussing the impact of other events on journalists in America and overseas.

Overview

What Did the Media Get Right and Wrong in the Two Terrorist Attacks?

John Jarvis

Ultimately, what the media got right in both cases was the identification of the individuals responsible for the attacks. Unfortunately, the rush to be first with new information as the cases developed left innocent individuals under a cloud of suspicion in both cases—and for Jewell, that cloud never fully dissipated, even after his death in 2007.

In the media, so much of what we do as journalists is akin to reading tea leaves: We spend hours poring over public records, covering press conferences where law-enforcement officials reveal as little information as possible, and filing Freedom of Information Act (FOIA) requests in an effort to piece together a clearer picture of what is going on. When we think we have connected enough dots to make an educated guess about the events surrounding a terrorist attack, we scramble to get that information out to the public, because the pressure to be first in this business is inescapable. That pressure to be first has ratcheted up with the arrival of social media, in which "citizen journalists" can take pictures and videos of breaking news events and upload those images to news sites (or their personal websites) mere moments after the event happens. Would Jewell have had a stronger case to maintain his innocence had cellular telephones capable of recording his discovery of an unexploded bomb been widely available in 1996? Probably so.

German philosopher Immanuel Kant, who perhaps is best known for the concept of the categorical imperative, focused on the actions of an individual instead of the group. Kant espoused acting as if the choices we make as individuals could become universal law—and Jewell did that. He was a security guard who found a bomb, and he alerted authorities to it. But because a newspaper intern saw him under surveillance by law enforcement, the information she relayed to her editors prompted the *Atlanta Journal-Constitution* bigwigs to scrap their hero profile and instead focus on the surveillance he was under. Jewell's life was never the same after that.

In Boston, the city's marathon attracts hundreds of journalists each year. In between the 1996 incident in Atlanta and the one in Boston in 2013, law-enforcement authorities used the lessons they learned from the September 11, 2001, terrorist attacks in New York and Washington, D.C., to try to prepare for another such incident. On November 3, 2012, the Department of Homeland Security conducted a twenty-four-hour emergency-preparedness drill in Boston. The drill, called "Urban Shield," is an example of the caution that permeates life in America after 9/11.

Journalists cannot help but notice that the atmosphere surrounding major public events such as the Boston Marathon has changed. In Boston, the main difference that became apparent almost immediately was the speed at which information (and misinformation) spread about the events. Within moments of the initial blasts, there was live news coverage by professional journalists, as well as personal videos shot on cell phones by people at the scene of the attack.

And just as in the case of the 1996 Summer Olympics bombing in Atlanta, news organizations made mistakes in the rush to be out front with the latest information. On April 18, 2013, three days after the Boston attack took place, a photo of two innocent individuals ran on the cover of the *New York Post,* next to a headline that read, "BAG MEN," and a slightly smaller subhead that read, "Feds Seek These Two Pictured at Boston Marathon." Just like Jewell, these two individuals found themselves under a cloud of suspicion, even though they had nothing to do with the bombing.

I know from personal experience how important it is to get the information out to the public first. Part of my career was spent working on a news copy desk in a Texas city with two competing dailies, and my publication's main mission was to humiliate our competitor across the street by getting the top story of the day first. Then, as now, it was no fun to come in second—but it was even worse to be wrong.

Irfan Ashraf

What have the media learned from both terrorist incidents? I wrestled with this question primarily because I think perfect coverage is impossible. The margin of error will always be there in reporting on sensitive issues. After all, media outlets are not hospitals, where medical surgeons work in a disciplined environment with sterilized tools. Media practitioners deal with unruly variables and rush toward trouble when others are running for their lives. Therefore, making tough decisions is the rule, not the exception.

Given that context, strengths and weaknesses do not play a factor in our estimates of media doing right or wrong. Instead,

these perceptions hinge on the flexibility of the media: How often do media outlets revisit and learn from previous experiences? From Atlanta in 1996 to Boston in 2013, how much the media have learned is significant. This time period shows the impact of technology, but the issue at hand is the ethical faculty of human development.

A few days after the FBI started interrogating Jewell, his mother's contact information was posted on the Internet. The number of unsolicited calls surpassed one thousand a day. Ronald Ostrow, in his investigative report titled "Richard Jewell and the Olympic Bombing," criticized the media circus, writing this about Jewell's mother: "Barbara Jewell attended a news conference called by her son's attorneys and urged President Clinton to intervene and exonerate him. 'My son has no life. . . . He is a prisoner in my home,' she was quoted as saying before breaking down in tears and leaving the podium." Ostrow quoted the ABC poll results that said 69 percent of respondents agreed the media treated Jewell unfairly, 41 percent blamed the media, 32 percent blamed law enforcement, and 25 percent held both responsible for damaging Jewell's reputation.

Looking at the public reaction back then, can we say today's media have learned anything? My colleague John Jarvis may not agree with me, but I see no progress in media understanding of public sentiment. My understanding is very similar to that of *Village Voice* media critic James Ledbetter, who was quoted in Alicia C. Shepard's 1996 article "Going to Extremes." Referring to the Jewell case, Ledbetter said, "There's a way in which you can report that he (Jewell) is a suspect that doesn't constitute the massive character assassination and invasion of privacy that happened to him. There's a world of difference in reporting he's a suspect and camping out at his apartment, writing detailed profiles and having psychologists on the air talking about him."

Therefore, media's dark side lies in its disrespect of privacy, which paints innocent people as devils, outsiders, or deviants. Jewell was publicly psychoanalyzed as possessing "hero syndrome," a condition in which a person first creates a life-threatening situation only to come to the rescue. That label compelled Jewell to fight for his reputation until his death in 2007.

In an interview with Marie Brenner, *Vanity Fair*'s writer-at-large, Jewell said he knew that many people in America would always doubt his innocence. "You don't get back what you were originally," Jewell told Brenner. "The first three days, I was supposedly their hero—the person who saves lives. They don't refer to me that way anymore. Now I am the Olympic Park bombing suspect: '*That's the guy they thought did it.*' "

In a post-9/11 world, Jewell's concerns take on a more serious tone. The unchecked victimization of innocent people has become commonplace in corporate media culture. There are vulnerable communities that cannot put up a fight in the same way a white American citizen such as Jewell can. Therefore, a couple of "swarthy" people around a terrorism site automatically give rise to the definition of the word *terrorist*. Before the identification of the two Chechen brothers in the Boston Marathon bombing, social media cast a shadow of suspicion on an injured Arab student named Abdulrahman Alharbi. Contrasting reports were so confusing that

Alharbi went from "person of interest," to "material witness," to "witness," to "victim." When a terrorist incident happens, the media's witch hunt does not automatically ruin individuals' lives, but almost every vulnerable community lives in fear as long as the crime is unsolved.

Pros and Cons

Did Technological Advances in the Seventeen Years between the 1996 Atlanta Olympics Bombing and the 2013 Boston Marathon Bombing Play Any Role in How These Two Events Were Covered in the American Media?

Irfan Ashraf

When it comes to overall social progress, we have every reason to celebrate technological advances. But we should be cautious not to turn journalism into an impersonal business confined to information gathering and distribution. Too much dependence on information technology has already narrowed the gap between journalism and pizza-delivery services. We also cannot afford to confuse the underlying issues related to the speed of the message and the news media tendency to focus on breaking news. If the former is an outcome of information technology, the latter is a consequence of cutthroat competition. Together, they engender technological determinism—which infringes on public privacy—and a disregard for ethical values in journalism.

American citizens appear to know little about the ethical concerns related to growing technological determinism, which has become a key part of U.S.

foreign-policy objectives. From information gathering on offshore installations in "rogue countries" to surgical strikes against terrorists' hideouts, pilotless drones are a vital component of the high-profile robotic warfare being carried out in Pakistan, Yemen, and Sudan. Hunting down terror suspects has been the justification for using drones, but how do we know that ethically, and also legally, killing people offshore raises the bar on terrorism and data gathering in foreign lands for the airspace violations of other countries?

Understanding the implications of surveillance, and its execution through the violent use of drone technology, is not limited to gathering data or information for any security institution, newspaper, or news channel. For example, the Bureau of Investigative Journalism revealed in a 2013 report that, in Pakistan, between 2,566 and 3,570 people have been killed in 372 drone strikes since 2004. Similarly, the bureau revealed that, in Yemen, anywhere from 240 to 349 people have been killed in 46 to 56 strikes, while in addition to that the unconfirmed number of deaths and strikes are more than 456 and 99, respectively.

Given these facts, can we afford to limit surveillance technology only to its utilitarian purposes? Or should we express confidence in the way authorities are handling the security situation, while media make the case in which surveillance technology dethrones only the bad guys while helping civilians live in peace? Understanding the implications of pilotless drones requires a thorough understanding of the context in which this technology is developed and its present role in overt and covert operations around the world. This is true for any kind

of surveillance technology employed in the civilian sphere. Such observations will help us foresee what lies ahead for journalists—and journalism itself—to benefit from drones' use.

John Jarvis

The answer to this question is an obvious "yes," but going beyond scratching the surface reveals why. Irfan says we in the United States know little about the ethical concerns regarding technology, but that is because Americans have focused our arguments for and against technological eavesdropping on constitutional rights. For some time now, technological advances—telephoto lenses, electronic listening devices, and now unmanned aerial vehicles (UAVs), aka drones—have allowed journalists to monitor and record what in an earlier era would have been considered private conversations. UAVs represent perhaps the most visible—and ominous—means for conducting surveillance in our modern world, but a gnawing sense of vulnerability in public to these electronic eyes and ears is fueling a legislative push to rein in this ever-growing threat to our privacy.

When applying an American view on the problem we are debating, the ethics of John Stuart Mill certainly merit a closer look. To be ethical, Mill said, was to realize that the consequences of a person's actions play a major role in determining whether or not those actions are ethical. In America, the rights of the individual take precedence over the rights of society. As journalists, we must know where the line of privacy can be drawn in the face of this new technology. In the case of drones, state legislatures already are trying to draw that line for everyone. University of Washington law professor Ryan Calo calls drones "privacy catalysts" that could spur the adoption of tougher privacy-protection laws.

Journalists must keep the ethics of their craft in mind when collecting information for their next story. But drones are just the tip of the "Big Brother" iceberg. On August 29, 2013, an opinion column by Ginger McCall for the *New York Times* noted how the Department of Homeland Security has been developing a computer-enhanced tool that officials are calling the "Biometric Optical Surveillance System." (Notice how the acronym of this new system spells BOSS?) This surveillance tool employs video cameras to scan people's faces, either by taking pictures of them in public or by scanning images into the system. The BOSS system will then be able to identify individuals' faces, using cross-references via databases of driver's license photos, police mug shots, or other facial photos that are cataloged by name.

In short, the very nature of journalists reporting on governmental actions is changing—and those changes are being fueled by technological advances hanging like the sword of Damocles over our chosen line of work, threatening to cleave both our profession and our Constitution into pieces.

What Would the Coverage Have Been in the American Media Had These Two Attacks Taken Place Overseas, and Why?

John Jarvis

I do not think the average American would have given the Olympic Park bombing in Atlanta more than a passing glance. "So a security guard found an unexploded bomb and alerted authorities? Ho-hum. Wake me when the bomb goes off; then maybe I'll pay attention. Besides, terror attacks happen in other countries all the time. Why should we care?"

The Boston Marathon bombing probably would have gotten a little higher play and a little more attention had it occurred overseas. It was a sporting event overshadowed by a terrorist attack in which people died. Reading about it in a newspaper, an average American might have even read all the way through the ten-inch wire story (placed on an inside page, no doubt) and thought, "What a shame." Then, when news reports surfaced a few days later about the death of one suspect and the capture of the other—and the fact that they were brothers—that same American might recall reading the original story from a few days ago and think, "The bastards got what they deserved." There would be no consideration for the fate of the victims—and very little thought given to the motives of the terrorists. Although the United States has been called "the world's policeman," unless a crime happens on our turf, Americans do not want to be bothered with details.

I suspect few Americans know that on February 1, 2013, in Ankara, Turkey, a person named Ecevit Sanli set off a bomb near a gate at the U.S. Embassy. Sanli and a Turkish guard were killed in the explosion, which the U.S. government immediately called a terrorist attack by the Revolutionary People's Liberation Party-Front. But because no Americans died, and because the attack happened in a foreign country, average Americans would be hard-pressed to come up with any details about this incident—if they even knew it happened at all.

Terrorists depend on attention to their deadly acts to achieve their political goals, and terrorists of all allegiances know American media outlets will pay more attention to a story if Western targets are involved. However, with a more competitive and decentralized media structure in today's American society, that old axiom "if it bleeds, it leads" no longer holds true in the next day's news cycle. Information about a particularly violent attack, or a brand-new tactic by terrorists, may now be necessary for these same terror groups to earn attention in the nightly news reports in the United States.

Irfan Ashraf

Why should we care? John's understanding of the American media seems simplistic, which makes me wonder if he really means to say that American media do not care about offshore terrorist incidents, especially if such incidents do not relate to common Americans. This conformist view also carries a deceptive tone by making us believe U.S. media get their cues from the American people. If that is so, how do we look at the U.S. media corporate interests in covering offshore news? Does it mean that because the American people do not care about foreign reporting, the U.S. mainstream media blindly accept whatever stories the American Forces Press Service offers?

Given John's line of argument, we should be careful in assessing the U.S. media's coverage of terrorism. For example, John argues that the U.S. media

ignored the U.S. embassy bombing in Ankara mainly because no Americans were killed. I would say that the loss of American lives has little to do with fueling the mainstream U.S. media's overseas coverage. Instead, it is the intertwining of political expediency, militaristic jingoism, and corporate vulturism that influences mainstream U.S. media coverage. Together, such factors put a deceptive spin on humanitarian issues and give them an ideological twist.

Had it not been so, the U.S. antiwar pacifists would have not taken eighteen years to compel the military authorities to remove the ban on media coverage of American war dead as their bodies were returned home. Though the U.S. military has always defended such censorship by arguing that the ban protects the privacy of the soldiers' families, the covert military resolve has always been to control public anger by sanitizing offshore wars. Therefore, saying the American people do not care about overseas terrorist incidents is hard for me to digest. Instead, I think corporate complacency has made the U.S. media blind to civilian interests, which is a big reason selective coverage has benefited U.S. policymakers' offshore militarization projects.

I think the two terrorist incidents in Boston and Atlanta would have invited U.S. media attention even if they had taken place outside America's borders. The apolitical nature of sports activities invites more universal attention, and terrorists have used sporting events as desired sites to grab global attention. Given their violent objectives, terrorists aim at public installations to communicate their message to the target audiences. So far it seems terrorists understand how to manipulate the media more than the journalists know how ethically to report on terror.

How Did American Media Treat Richard Jewell, and Was This Any Different from How the News Media Treated the Boston Marathon Bombing Suspects?

Irfan Ashraf

In journalism, the ends justify the means. Therefore, my disagreement with my colleague John is not conceptual; it also carries ideological underpinnings. My upbringing on communitarian lines in the ethnic Pashtun tribal society in northwestern Pakistan provides a strong base for my ideological and social outlook.

I cannot shrug off worries of family members whose relatives were wrongly implicated as "terror suspects" in the Boston bombing. For authorities to identify the terror suspects, we should not forget that too much dependence on technology did not lead Boston police to mistakenly single out a couple of innocent individuals, as John would have us believe. Rather, a lack of concern for ethical values carried nightmarish repercussions.

Within hours of the Boston bombing, crowdsourcing groups drew upon FBI-released photos of the terror suspects, in which one resembled twenty-two-year-old Pennsylvania native Sunil Tripathi. Tripathi went missing March 16 from his apartment, but new-media sleuths circulated his identity, showing that the FBI suspect wearing a baseball cap closely resembled the missing student. Tripathi's body later was recovered from the water off India

Point Park in Rhode Island. However, before his mysterious death, the social news media website Reddit—which remained instrumental in publishing the Tripathi photo—apologized, declaring that the accusations involving the student constituted "dangerous speculation." Other news outlets started adding their apologies, one after another, until the news of Tripathi's death prompted the replacement of those apologies with remorse.

We do not know what happened to Tripathi, but we do know that his family suffered immensely. Amid the fiery police chase for terror suspects in Boston, newsmen and news vans staked out Tripathi's family home in Pennsylvania. Harassing emails and threatening anonymous calls followed. In a few hours a grainy picture of a terror suspect released on social media compelled the family to seek FBI help. Nothing could explain their worries and concerns more eloquently than the Tripathi family's Facebook message, which said: "These last months have changed our lives forever. . . . Hopefully we are all humbled to see how quickly messages can be distorted, amplified and unleashed. Please be careful, be gentle, and take care of one another."

John Jarvis

I approach this debate with my colleague Irfan from the standpoint of a dyed-in-the-wool American journalist. In both the 1996 Summer Olympics bombing case and the Boston Marathon bombing in 2013, law enforcement sprang into action following a terrorist attack on American soil, intent on identifying suspects as quickly as possible.

Journalists reacted quickly, too. After all, that adrenaline-inducing rush to be first in reporting the details of a breaking news story lies at the very heart of our profession. But in both cases, individual rights were trampled in a headlong rush to be first. In fact, individuals were wrongly identified as potential suspects before the real suspects were apprehended. This "trial by media" turns on its head the due process we cherish in America. Once an individual has been spotlighted by media, that person faces an uphill battle to maintain his or her innocence—and privacy—even though our justice system says that same person is "innocent until proven guilty."

For a Machiavellian take on both cases, one can make the case that "the ends justify the means." In both cases, the rush to identify a suspect as quickly as possible did ultimately end up with the suspects in custody (or dead, as was the case with one of the suspects in the Boston incident). If a couple of innocent individuals were briefly singled out as "persons of interest," the fact that they were not arrested points out that the system ultimately worked—correct?

While someone with a communitarian mind-set might make that argument, I can't. The rights of the individual must come first. In fact, in the United States, certain individual liberties are emphasized in the Constitution. Specifically, the Fourth Amendment protects an American's right against unreasonable searches and seizures, but this only pertains to the limits placed on the federal government. In this new age of surveillance brought on by advances in technology, where can the line be drawn that says a journalist

has gone too far in collecting data on individuals for a story?

When Viewed with the Mind-set of a Communitarian Society, How Does the Lack of Concern for Individuals' Privacy and Reputation Affect Journalism?

John Jarvis

Margaret J. Radin, in a 1982 *Stanford Law Review* article titled "Property and Personhood," wrote that communitarians view the "myth of the self-contained 'man' in a state of nature as politically misleading and dangerous." Radin makes the case that people are immersed in their respective cultures, histories, and languages, all of which constitute creations of society. For Radin, the concept of "person" cannot exist without the overall framework of society.

In communitarian thinking, society benefits from the preservation of individual privacy rights, but there always is an inherent conflict between individual privacy and the needs of the community as a whole.

In their 2011 book *Media Ethics: Issues and Cases,* co-authors Philip Patterson and Lee Wilkins note how totalitarian governments have used government surveillance to squelch individuals' privacy as a way to keep a tight rein on citizens. The authors note that these regimes closely resemble the one detailed in George Orwell's novel *1984,* while making the case that privacy is a crucial component of any democracy. The problem journalists face comes from the conflict between their own consciences and what the law allows. This can lead to ethical overreach that damages the entire profession—and it also fuels the suspicions of the American public that journalists have no ethics or morals when it comes to getting a story first.

Privacy rights protect members of society from governmental excess. The more power a government has, the easier it is to control and manipulate its citizenry.

In Irfan's worldview, the U.S.-led war on terror has heralded an acceptance of curtailing individual freedoms in an effort to thwart more terrorist attacks. I concede to my colleague that the stepped-up U.S. military presence—and in particular the use of Predator and Reaper drones in Afghanistan, Pakistan, and Yemen—has led to increased international insecurity, but there can be no doubt that the 9/11 terrorist attacks changed the way Americans view the rest of the world. Before that day, individual freedoms—those of speech and religion in particular—were seen as paramount not just in this country, but around the world as well. After the attacks happened, more Americans were willing to cede those freedoms to feel more secure. The U.S. government was happy to oblige, ramping up its technological capabilities to thwart terrorist attacks worldwide. This emphasis on security came at a cost: the curtailment of individual freedoms. That, in turn, has affected how we do our job as journalists.

Irfan Ashraf

Surprisingly, the foundational value of *objective* journalism is largely derived from individual rights, yet the lack of concern for individuals' privacy

and reputation is a major issue in mainstream media. One response to this problem is the rising popularity of "civic journalism," "public journalism," "community journalism," and "citizens' journalism," which offer a communitarian approach as a replacement for individualistic libertarianism in mainstream media. There are two reasons the communitarian mind-set is getting increased recognition.

First are the massive electronic surveillance programs of the U.S. and U.K. governments, which carry a chilling effect on societies caused by paralyzing freedom of expression. Spying on the public has raised voices in favor of striking a balance between privacy and security, while at the same time it also has normalized privacy violation in the name of homeland security. In this way, individual privacy is sacrificed to achieve the goal of collective security. Second, despite the fact that mainstream media derive inspiration from individual rights, objective journalism itself has become a threat for individuals' privacy and reputation. We have been analyzing this argument throughout this chapter with the help of the Jewell case and the Boston Marathon terrorist attack. But the issue is far deeper than what it appears in these two cases. On the whole, the critical faculty of mainstream journalism has been lost to the material needs of time. In the absence of critical communication, mainstream media can neither hold the center of power responsible for its disregard for individual rights nor broaden journalists' worldview to look at issues in a larger global perspective. The outcome is evident from rising voices in favor of a communitarian mind-set in journalism, which believes in the bottom-up approach—that is, holding the center of power accountable for making people vulnerable to threats and terror.

Given the context, I want to reframe the argument of my colleague John, who says the 9/11 terror attacks have changed the way Americans view the rest of the world. I expect he would be more critical by not looking at the world from his country's perspective and, instead, helping us know how the 9/11 attacks have changed global views about the United States. In other words, U.S. journalists usually follow a one-sided view by looking at the world from an American perspective. In doing so, these journalists follow a conformist stance; they forget to take into consideration the world perspective, where the U.S. militarization following the 9/11 tragic incidents has played havoc with civilian lives.

Looking to the Future

Knowing What We Know Now, How Would You Suggest Your Media Organization Cover the Boston Marathon Bombing If It Were to Happen Today?

John Jarvis

I would hope that any media organization I work for would see the value of social media to communicate with its subscribers and viewers as quickly as possible. While I do not believe our jobs will be lost to "citizen journalists" anytime soon, I think crowdsourcing information will take on added significance

in our technology-saturated American society.

I also would hope my media organization would not shy away from asking hard questions of government officials in the wake of a terrorist attack, even at the risk of incurring the wrath of those same officials. Make no mistake: The camaraderie that existed between journalists and public-safety officials (police, firefighters, etc.) before the 9/11 terrorist attacks in New York and Washington, D.C., has largely disappeared. It was swept away by a wave of hyperpatriotism that gripped the country in the days and weeks that followed that deadly day.

In an opinion column dated September 9, 2011, and posted on CNN's website, Joel Simon, executive director of the independent and nonprofit Committee to Protect Journalists, wrote that "the global fallout from 9/11 is a stark reminder that while the U.S. failure to uphold democratic standards has obvious implications domestically, the greatest long-term impact is likely to be in the many places where governments are always seeking justifications for unrelenting repression. Ten years on, it's clear that the anti-terror rhetoric and policies developed by the United States after 9/11 have provided effective and enduring cover for the erosion of civil liberties around the world—including press freedom."

More than a quarter-century ago, when I was a freshly minted journalist, the press and law-enforcement officials had a certain understanding of the roles each played at a news event. It generally was understood that journalists could edge their way in a little closer to the action and observe what was going on, as long as they gave those same officials room to do their jobs and did not complicate matters.

American law enforcement changed as a result of the 9/11 terror attacks. Police actions began to take on the feel of military maneuvers, complete with the arrests of journalists who were doing their jobs while standing on public property. In one such example of this new aggressiveness by police directed toward journalists, *Detroit Free Press* photographer Mandi Wright was arrested July 11, 2013, by Detroit police while videotaping the arrest of a suspect on a public street. Wright, who has been working for the *Free Press* since 2000, was handcuffed, then put into an interrogation room *with the suspect whose arrest she had been filming.* After spending nearly seven hours in custody, she was released with no charges filed; her newspaper-issued iPhone was given back to her, but it was missing its memory card. A story written July 16, 2013, by *Free Press* staff writers Jim Schaefer and Gina Damron quoted *Free Press* legal counsel Hershel Fink as saying that courts in the United States have agreed that American citizens and members of the press have the right to take photographs of police officers who are in public areas. Fink cited the video evidence of the incident to emphasize that Wright did nothing illegal and did not interfere with the officers making the arrest. He added that the officer who ordered Wright to stop filming had no right to ask her to do so— and that officer also had no right to confiscate her iPhone.

Given the enhanced aggressiveness of law-enforcement tactics in today's society, we as journalists need media organizations that will stand behind us with legal representation to keep those aggressive law-enforcement tactics in check. That is not to say police and firefighters are the bad guys. But without a willingness to stand up for our rights, journalists will be reduced to stenographers, unwilling—or unable—to ask the hard questions the public wants answered.

Irfan Ashraf

Referring to the complicated nature of challenges confronting the U.S. news media, the late Columbia University professor James Carey once said, "The problem is that you see journalism disappearing inside the larger world of communication. What you yearn to do is to recover journalism from that larger world." Carey was right in his observation that the crisis of the news media is not the lack of resources. Instead, it is the overflow of information choices that has led to a disregard for ethical values. Whatever comes the way of journalists is declared fit to print without it being given a second thought. Why? In the cutthroat competition for news, the quality of information—including verifying the news, balancing a story, and quoting credible sources—does not matter. Instead, the emphasis is on engaging readers by bombarding them with a flurry of information.

This reminds me of the situation in Pakistan, where a local TV channel once asked its senior reporters to do whatever possible to increase viewership. The next day, one of its reporters deliberately aired an erroneous report that said security forces had killed a senior Taliban commander in a helicopter-gunship blitz.

When asked why, the reporter replied, "Today's news says the commander is killed, but tomorrow it will be disclosed that he is still alive." Later, this trend of selling lies flourished so much in the burgeoning media that the official list of twenty-one high-profile militants had on it the names of commanders "killed" more than once already.

John need not fear losing his job to a citizen journalist. Rather, he should worry about the degenerating ethical values of reporting—which otherwise have the potential to rescue journalism from becoming a footnote to media history. After all, the health of journalism will not improve if mainstream media continue to ignore the importance of ethical journalism. Shallow and frequently clichéd approaches to news, incidents of phone tapping, scandals, and growing cases of plagiarism are signs of the degrading quality of mainstream journalism. These not only damage the public interest but also motivate disappointed readers to join the alternative-media camp.

That is why, unlike John, I believe the cardinal sin of journalism is the loss of professional conviction in the long-debated media standards concerning public safety and privacy. To add insult to injury, too much dependence on new-media platforms has also erased the vital attributes of thoroughness and investigation.

My work in Pak-Afghan areas and my interaction with hundreds of Western and local journalists have enabled me to know how often reporters jump to conclusions by searching for simple narratives to make their audiences understand complicated questions. Irresponsible reporting can bring grave consequences for some, while making others into punching bags. Since accountability is generally considered a missing rung on the ladder of professional development in journalism, the absence of fixing responsibility has substantially affected media outlets.

While looking into this background, I would not have covered the Boston Marathon bombing the way the U.S. mainstream media did. True, we cannot reverse the flow of technological development, nor do we need to. But the main question is this: How can we strike a balance between technological development and human faculties? This is purely a managerial issue; we cannot develop a win-win model to drag media out of this complicated scenario. We need to understand that, without adopting business values, media outlets cannot flourish. But without respect for ethical values, quality journalism cannot advance. Journalists need to reflect on the Boston and Atlanta bombings to learn not to fall into terrorists' traps. Instead, they need to critically pitch stories that frame the public's concerns without adding to people's terror.

Conclusion

What Are the Future Challenges and Concerns for Conducting Ethical Journalism in America and around the World?

Irfan Ashraf

The growing need for surveillance has given birth to many related concerns, and one such fear is authoritarianism. In his book titled *The Globalization of Surveillance,* Armand Mattelart writes that "every break with the rule of law has been accompanied by a brutalization of democracy and a regression of the values underpinning it." The loss of democratic values in this way cannot be understood independent of its impact on individual liberties and this issue is discussed in detail in a chapter on drones included in this book. Like the Boston Marathon bombing, isolated incidents have the potential to legitimize technological determinism by monopolizing the rational orbit of security discourse, which is a step toward establishing a culture of insecurity. In other words, any single operation carries seeds of change to enlarge the spectrum of technological determinism to other segments of society. The issue here is not to deny or discourage technological development, but to understand how much preparedness we need for any such change. This exercise is meant to escape the negative social consequences of a technology associated mainly with violence and the intrusion into civilian space.

The business of journalism is not exclusive to any such consideration. Many media organizations are considering drone technology in their newsgathering and distribution efforts, while social media already have justified surveillance in the name of crowdsourcing. Therefore, it is important to analyze how prepared journalists are to accept impending changes, and how they ethically would conduct the business of journalism without infringing on a person's privacy or ruining that person's reputation.

John Jarvis

The ultimate challenge we face as journalists, both here in America and globally, has always been—and continues to

be—to get the story right. There is a river of information coursing through our society at a rate never seen before in history, but that same statement has been true in every era of humankind. Technology has always changed how that river flows, but we have a responsibility to be accurate with what we present to the public. In this age of social media, merely parroting police-scanner traffic during a breaking news event is a recipe for apologies, corrections, and lawsuits. For an ethical consideration of what to do given the state of journalism today, Aristotle's Golden Mean would be a good place to start. After all, his ethical consideration was that virtue could be found in the middle between two extremes. Perhaps we, as reporters and editors, can find a way to balance the need for speed in getting a story to the public first with the realization that being accurate is just as important, if not more so.

But can a happy medium ever be found to conduct the business of journalism and inform society now? The world we once knew no longer exists. What we can strive for now is a way to use the same technological innovations being used by law enforcement and the U.S. government to our advantage. For example, the same UAV technology used to keep tabs on terrorists abroad can also be used for altruistic purposes. These "J-bots," as journalism professor William Allen at the University of Nebraska–Lincoln calls these devices, could help reporters gather information on agricultural methods, natural disasters such as floods, forest fires, hurricanes, and tornadoes, public events such as concerts and parades, and political events such as demonstrations and speeches. In a May 3, 2013, story for *Slate,* Nabiha Syed wrote that "crafting laws to reconcile both privacy and First Amendment interests will be no small feat. For one thing, privacy concerns already seem to dominate the legislative imagination when it comes to drones. What's even more complicated is that the most dystopian vision of our drone future—an all-seeing, all-knowing, all-tracking dragnet—would run afoul of First Amendment freedom of association protections but not newsgathering interests. It's not inconceivable that a drone dragnet would chill all speech—and if seeing more makes us all speak less, we have a problem."

John Jarvis
Southern Illinois University Carbondale
Syed Irfan Ashraf
Southern Illinois University Carbondale

See also The Communitarian Perspective; Drones; Expectation of Privacy

Further Reading

Brenner, Marie. "The Ballad of Richard Jewell." *Vanity Fair,* February 1997. http://www.vanityfair.com/magazine/archive/1997/02/brenner199702.

Kovach, Bill, and Tom Rosenstiel. *The Elements of Journalism: What Newspeople Should Know and the Public Should Expect.* New York: Three Rivers Press, 2007.

Mattelart, Armand. *The Globalization of Surveillance: The Origin of the Securitarian Order.* Translated by Susan Taponier and James A. Cohen. Cambridge, UK: Polity, 2010.

McCall, Ginger. "The Face Scan Arrives." *New York Times,* August 29, 2013. http://www.nytimes.com/2013/08/30/opinion/the-face-scan-arrives.html?_r=0.

Ostrow, Ronald J. "Richard Jewell Case Study." *Critical Issues in Journalism,* June 13, 2000. http://www.columbia.edu/itc/journalism/j6075/edit/readings/jewell.html.

Patterson, Philip, and Lee Wilkins. *Media Ethics: Issues & Cases.* New York: McGraw-Hill, 2011.

Radin, Margaret J. "Property and Personhood." *Stanford Law Review* 34, no. 5 (1982): 957–1015.

Schaefer, Jim, and Gina Damron. "Police Launch Investigations after Arrest of Photographer." *Detroit Free Press,* July 16, 2013. http://www.freep.com/article/20130716/NEWS01/307160018/photographer-free-press-mandi-wright-video-arrested.

Shepard, Alicia C. "Going to Extremes." *American Journalism Review,* October 1996. http://ajrarchive.org/article_printable.asp?id=437.

Simon, Joel. "How 'War on Terror' Unleashed a War on Journalists." *CNN,* September 9, 2011. http://www.cnn.com/2011/OPINION/09/08/simon.press.freedom.911.

Syed, Nabiha. "Privacy Concerns Shouldn't Ground Journalism Drones." *Slate,* May 3, 2013. http://www.slate.com/blogs/future_tense/2013/05/03/drone_regulations_need_to_protect_the_first_amendment_as_well_as_citizens.html

SECTION 6

SOCIAL MEDIA AND THE INTERNET CHANGE THE RULES

Who is a reporter today? Is a fourteen-year-old girl in her pajamas blogging in bed a journalist? Is she all that different from nineteenth-century men with flatbed presses writing, printing, and distributing "newspapers"? Are Bill Kristol, Rush Limbaugh, and Jon Stewart journalists? In a world where everyone may be considered a journalist, can *anyone* really be considered a journalist, and what implication has this on the First Amendment?

How is China, ever mindful of maintaining its great Internet firewall and preserving harmonious news, dealing with and monitoring microblogs? In preserving harmony, is it being ethical?

How is it possible to legally and ethically accommodate readers' comments in the new media era, and do opinionated reader comments belong beneath objective news stories? And although the First Amendment protects people from government censorship, what protects people from censorship by Google or Facebook? What happens when the economic interests of an Internet giant clash with the interests of copyright holders?

Although the U.S. Supreme Court once said students do not shed their free speech rights at the schoolhouse gates, controversial speech now is not about a black armband in a classroom, but rather the nasty parody of a principal on the student's home computer. And while people generally are not liable for passing along nasty rumors by word of mouth, what about publishing them on the Internet—a question that takes on an additional edge with episodes like the MySpace suicide? Banning cyberbullying is ethical, but does it violate the First Amendment?

How is media law adapting to technology, and in particular, how has the First Amendment adapted to the advent of technology unimaginable when it was written? In particular, have legal developments kept pace with ethical developments?

Finally, we live in a world where new media such as Twitter and social media interact with legacy media. Tweets pass along news from traditional media and traditional media pick up news from tweets, and this relationship plays out in situations as disparate as the Arab spring and the Wisconsin labor protests.

Section 6 of *The SAGE Guide to Key Issues in Mass Media Ethics and Law* discusses the ethical and legal implications of social media and the Internet, and how new technology can be a rule—and game—changer.

48

JOURNALISM IN THE
TWENTY-FIRST CENTURY

Each new era of communication has brought with it both a sense of excitement at new possibilities for sharing ideas and an ever-increasing democratization of knowledge. Yet that excitement has also been accompanied by skepticism and even anxiety. With the movement from an oral to a written culture, Socrates and Plato warned that public discussion and the give-and-take of conversation would be threatened by the impersonal nature of the written word. The arrival of the printing press brought a new focus on individualism and disrupted a tradition of community, cooperation, and integration. Along with the electronic age came a fear that we were—in Neil Postman's words—amusing ourselves to death. And the digital age has introduced concerns about information overload, diminishing attention spans, difficulties in sorting truths from falsehoods and, of course, the fate of legacy journalism and the principles that have guided it for a century.

Even though we have seen history repeat itself and discovered that life does, indeed, go on when we move from one communication era to the next, it is difficult not to feel as though the kinds of changes happening in journalism today are particularly important. Rather than asking how the digital age has changed journalism, we find ourselves asking even more fundamental questions: *What is journalism, and who is a journalist?*

The Landscape of Journalism in the Digital Age

To understand what leads to these questions, it is helpful to take a brief tour through the journalism landscape of the past thirty-five years. The digital age is characterized by both the ubiquity of information and ease of access to that information. In fact, the digital age is often called the information age, and those of us living in it have at our disposal information receptacles with seemingly limitless capacities. Although the information age is equated with the development and rise of the Internet, it is important not to overlook the earlier development of cable and satellite TV and radio, a development that brought with it the 24/7 news cycle, news organizations with distinct political points of view, and increased competition among producers of news. In 1980, CNN—the first all-news channel that aired around the clock—was launched, and citizens would no longer have to wait for news. CNN was later joined by other news networks, including HLN, CNBC, Fox News, MSNBC, and recently Al Jazeera America.

The Internet opened to commercial users in 1988, but it was not until the mid-1990s that the first Internet browsers were introduced, and "surfing the Web" entered the lexicon of ordinary people. Very quickly it became clear that we would seek and gather information in fundamentally different ways than we had in the past. In addition to Internet browsers that helped us navigate the World Wide Web, the mid-1990s also saw the arrival of wikis and blogging.

As news organizations were reporting on the potential of the Internet, they simultaneously saw the need to get into the act themselves. In 1995, *USA Today* launched an Internet edition, the first newspaper to do so; CNN followed suit that same year. (Even before the emergence of browsers, the text of the *Chicago Tribune* was made accessible via AOL beginning in 1993.) On January 19, 1996, the *New York Times* Internet edition went online. Social media entered the scene with MySpace (2003), Facebook (2004), YouTube (2005), Twitter, (2006) and Instagram (2010). News organizations have since supplemented their online presence with all of these social media tools.

Today, twenty years after the arrival of the Internet, a number of legacy newspapers, including the *Christian Science Monitor, Detroit News/Free Press, New Orleans Times-Picayune, Portland Oregonian*, and *Seattle Post-Intelligencer,* have cut back on their print editions or abandoned them altogether in favor of online formats. These changes are the result of exiting readers, who have left print in droves, but also of advertisers who have followed readers out the door, taking with them the revenue that made print editions economically viable. Even as *more* people are reading *more* news than ever before, most journalism scholars predict the end of the print newspaper. The rise of the Internet has put similar pressures on other legacy news formats, including news magazines, network and cable TV news, and news radio. While nearly all legacy news organizations now have an online presence—sometimes exclusively—being online is not enough to keep the doors open.

The changing economics of the news industry has brought with it a wave of downsizing that has left many legacy journalists without jobs and the prospects for future "professional" journalists—those who earn a living doing the work—bleak. Frequently, legacy organizations are asking journalists to work alone instead of in teams of reporters, photojournalists, and editors. Or those organizations are moving to a model in which they keep a skeleton crew and then rely heavily on freelancers. All in all, the prospects for journalism as a career—at least in the way it has been conceived for generations—do not look promising.

The reason the adjective *legacy* is used as a descriptor for organizations that have traditionally employed *journalists* and provided *journalism* is that the digital age has brought with it whole new categories of information providers. Not only has the Internet changed the way we seek and gather information, it has also changed the way we create and share it. With the Internet has come unprecedented access to the public sphere. We can opt in to conversations about issues of the day rather than serve as mere observers. This ability to participate via user-generated content and social media tools means that the line between consumer and producer is ever softening.

Often the act of producing content is deliberate and preplanned. A blogger writes an entry and posts it to Tumblr. A Twitter user records the day's events in 140 characters or less and tweets it out. A videographer captures an inspiring performance and posts it to YouTube. At other times, however, citizens become accidental producers. Bystanders film the death of Neda Agha-Soltani, an Iranian woman participating in a Tehran protest, and post it to YouTube. A passenger on a ferry shoots a cell-phone picture of a plane that has just crashed into the Hudson River and shares it via TwitPic. Theatergoers tweet in real time as a man arrives in an Aurora, Colorado, movie theater and guns down twelve people. These and other important acts of citizen journalism reach us directly via social media but are also used by legacy organizations as they tell the stories. In fact, some organizations, including Fox News and CNN, have even set up permanent sections on their websites (uReport and iReport) for citizens to contribute photos and videos of news stories.

The digital age has certainly become one marked by a culture of sharing. Even when we are not creating original content, we are passing along content we have encountered, in effect acting as important distribution channels. Often today, we hear about important news stories first through social media. Some of us stop there, relying purely on information that comes to us; others follow up by seeking additional coverage. Where we get that additional coverage spans a spectrum that includes large legacy news organizations from around the world (CNN, the BBC, the *New York Times*, the *Guardian,* National Public Radio), popular news media websites (the Huffington Post, Salon, Slate), news aggregators (Yahoo! News, Google News), online nonprofits (ProPublica, Texas Tribune, MinnPost), influential blogs (the Dish, Talking Points Memo, Gawker), "fake" news programs (*The Daily Show, The Colbert Report*), and countless other information providers that serve particular audiences.

Some of these providers present news with a detached, balanced stance that has been the hallmark of American journalism since the early twentieth century—an approach commonly referred to as *objectivity*. Others, however, are clearly advocates, and many of the most widely consumed news media today hold no pretense of being objective. What's more, some of these advocates have been recognized by the journalism establishment with awards: Jon Stewart of *The Daily Show* has received two Peabody Awards; Josh Marshall of Talking Points Memo was given a George Polk Award; and David Wood of the Huffington Post won a Pulitzer Prize.

Without a doubt, the journalism landscape of the twenty-first century is remarkably different than the one of the last century. In an age of abundance, almost anything is available at the tips of our fingers. But that abundance has also led to fragmentation. We no longer share the same relatively scarce options for accessing journalism, and we do not necessarily even agree what journalism is. For example, are nightly celebrity news programs journalism, or are they entertainment? Is a story developing in real time and reported with only a few unconfirmed details journalism, or is it a rumor? Is a website that captures a snapshot of viral media—often in a top 10 list—journalism, or is it gossip? And are documents leaked by a government contractor to a blogger who also writes a column for a legacy news organization journalism, or are they treason? In addition, in an age of unprecedented democratization of information, anyone can act as a journalist. But that possibility has led us to question what it means to be a journalist? Is a highly read blogger, a citizen who captures video of an important breaking news event on her cell phone, or a comedian who discusses the important issues of the day on his TV show any less a journalist than someone who covers the city hall for a daily newspaper?

It is certainly true that the Internet and social media are changing the rules, but we have not quite settled on what those new rules are. Before we get there, a number of issues need to be resolved. The remainder of this chapter may not resolve them, but it does attempt to lay them out by further exploring what counts as journalism, and who counts as a journalist.

Two Key Questions

As soon as the power and potential of the Internet began to become evident, journalism scholars and practitioners started to ask questions about the evolving meaning of *journalism* and *journalist*. For example, in 1994, Katherine Fulton wrote an article for *Nieman Reports* headlined "A New Agenda for Journalism." In the article, she asks: "Who is a journalist and what is journalism in a world where data, information and raw video will be plentiful and where everyone with access to a computer and a telephone will own their own press?" Today, we continue to grapple with the questions and sometimes even to debate over which is the *right* question. For some, it is about journalism—the act and the product. For others, the question is about the journalist—the actor and the producer.

Jay Rosen, Yochai Benkler, and Jeff Jarvis prefer to focus on journalism. Who does it is less important. For Rosen, a New York University professor and author of the blog PressThink, journalism is work that should foster citizenship, improve public debate, and enhance democratic life. Anyone who does that work is a journalist. For Benkler, co-director of the Berkman Center for Internet and Society at Harvard, journalism is a "network 'fourth estate'" that includes a number of interrelated roles: witnessing, gathering, selecting, authenticating, explaining, and distributing. Each of these acts can be an act of journalism and can be done by different people who are not necessarily affiliated with a single institution. In a network, Benkler argues, an act of journalism can be performed by anyone. Jarvis, a professor at City University of New York and columnist for the *Guardian*, follows Benkler's line of thinking when he contends, "There are no journalists. There is only the service of journalism," a service "whose goal is an informed public."

These views align well with established beliefs about the role of journalism in a democracy, and they certainly accommodate the twenty-first-century landscape. However, the arguments by Rosen, Benkler, Jarvis, and others who prefer to focus on *journalism* cannot get too far without the issue of *journalist* arising. Put simply, it is difficult to explore the meaning of journalism without simultaneously addressing the meaning of journalist. The day's rhetoric may be that everyone is a journalist, but this claim fairly quickly runs into complications that relate to two overlapping and interdependent domains: law and ethics.

The Legal Domain

Jeff Hermes, director of the Digital Media Law Project at the Berkman Center, calls newsgathering rights in the United States "a structure built on shifting sands." These sands encompass rights, privileges, and protections in the constitutional arena, in statutes and laws, and in informal recognitions.

The Constitutional Arena. The landmark *New York Times v. Sullivan* case established that "debate on public issues should be uninhibited, robust, and wide-open." Therefore, as Erik Ugland and Jennifer Henderson point out in the *Journal of Mass Media Ethics*, the bias in the legal domain, particularly from a constitutional framework, "is toward an expansive definition of journalist" because everyone has a constitutionally protected right to free speech. "A person still needs to be engaged in the underlying behavior that the right protects—in this case gathering and disseminating news," Ugland and Henderson say, "but factors other than behavior, such as characteristics, credentials, or affiliations, should be left out of the equation."

In theory, this approach makes sense; journalists should be able to self-proclaim their status. In practice, however, complexities arise. Regardless of whether someone calls himself a journalist, laws, courts, and institutions with the ability to control access have the power to assign status and grant formal and informal privileges. As David Carr of the *New York Times* notes, "taxonomy is important" because journalists have historically been given special privileges or protections that are not granted to others.

Statutes and Laws. The first of these is shield laws, which protect journalists from being forced to disclose confidential information or news sources. Shield laws are designed to institutionalize limited privileges that reporters have traditionally been given, and in 2013, forty-nine states and the District of Columbia recognized a journalist's privilege through statute or common law. Shield laws give special privileges to journalists, but they are not absolute; a judge can still compel disclosure in cases of extraordinary circumstances or compelling public interest. In addition, these statutes have tended to emphasize occupational status, and they often define journalists as people who are paid by news organizations to do newsgathering.

At this time, no federal shield law exists, but a bill is working its way through Congress. In September 2013, the Free Flow of Information Act (S. 987) passed the Senate Judiciary Committee. One of the difficulties in drafting the bill was in defining *journalist*, and previous efforts to pass a federal shield law stalled because of this. The latest version of the proposed law uses the term *covered journalist*, which includes reporters and editors who work for news organizations and news websites, freelancers, bloggers, and anyone else gathering and disseminating information for the public good. In addition to protecting covered journalists, the bill contains a provision that would allow a judge to extend privileges to anyone if "based on specific facts contained in the record, the judge determines that such protections would be in the interest of justice and necessary to protect lawful and legitimate news-gathering activities under the specific circumstances of the case." David Greene of the Electronic Frontier Foundation, which maintains that a shield law should be linked to the practice of journalism as opposed to the profession, calls the provision "an avenue for non-mainstream and citizen journalists to demonstrate that they are deserving of the shield, even if they otherwise fall outside the law's strict definition of 'covered journalist.'"

Whether a federal shield law would have helped Vanessa Leggett, who was jailed in 2001 for contempt of court after she refused to turn over confidential source material relating to a Texas murder case, is a question up for debate. Leggett, an English and legal writing instructor, had dreams of becoming a true-crime author and had been researching the case for three-and-a-half years when she was incarcerated. Department of Justice lawyers argued that Leggett should not receive a reporter's privilege because none of her works were published. (In fact, she had published two articles in technical manuals.) Regardless of her publication record, Leggett was a freelancer, and her supporters argued that because she did not have a media company to back her up, she was targeted. Leggett would go on to serve 168 days in jail—at the time, the longest anyone had served for refusing to disclose research collected in the course of newsgathering. She was released only when the grand jury ended without handing down any indictments.

The ultimate success of the proposed federal shield law is still up for question, and not every legislator is predicted to embrace the law or its inclusive definition of *journalist*. Earlier in 2013, for example, Senator Dick Durbin of Illinois demonstrated his hesitance about such a broad definition. In a *Chicago Sun-Times* column headlined "It's Time to Say Who's a Real Reporter," Durbin asks, "Is each of Twitter's 141 million users in the United States a journalist? How about the 164 million Facebook users? What about bloggers, people posting on Instagram, or users of online message boards like

Reddit?" His answer: No. "While social media allows tens of millions of people to share information publicly, it does not entitle them to special legal protections."

Some legacy news workers have also spoken up on limiting the definition of journalist for the purposes of a shield law. In their syndicated column, Cokie and Steve Roberts argue that there is a difference between amateurs and professionals: "a difference in training, standards, experience and purpose. And that difference should be recognized by federal law. A shield law that applies to anyone with a laptop or cellphone would be meaningless. . . . The line has to be drawn somewhere."

Questions surrounding the kind of legal protections that journalists receive have become particularly important during a time when major news stories have resulted from documents leaked by Julian Assange's WikiLeaks and by government contractor Edward Snowden. Some claim that Assange and Snowden are journalists; others that they are spies or traitors. Additionally, the people and organizations that reported on the documents are under fire by some critics. In fact, the Obama administration has made hints that it will prosecute leakers using the Espionage Act, and it even branded Fox News reporter James Rosen a co-conspirator in a leak case, although Rosen was never charged. It is becoming increasingly clear that whether the government considers someone a journalist may have serious repercussions.

Informal Recognitions. The third kind of privilege traditionally given to journalists is more informal, and it deals with

rights of access. To be in a position to report on particular issues and events, particularly those that relate to the functioning of the government, journalists need press credentials. Practically speaking, there is only so much space in a press briefing room, in a courtroom, or on Air Force One, and someone needs to determine who gets in. In an introduction to a Nieman Journalism Lab survey about press credentials, Joshua Benton notes,

> Even as the very concept of journalism evolves to accommodate dramatic new ways of gathering and interacting with information of critical public importance, the idea of media credentials remains deeply embedded in the practice of journalism in the United States. Dozens of laws at both the state and federal levels condition the right to engage in newsgathering activity on the receipt of credentials; police departments use press identification to separate journalists from protestors subject to arrest; and political parties limit access to vital aspects of the democratic process to those approved by campaigns.

What the press credentialing process means is that not everyone can act as a journalist because newsgathering rights are not available to everyone. Access to many newsworthy events is still limited, and only those with proper credentials are granted admission. For example, during the 2012 election campaign season, the Mitt Romney presidential campaign sought to exclude BuzzFeed from the campaign's press pool, claiming that the campaign did not have a separate blogger pool. (Interestingly, the Huffington Post was included in the "print" pool.)

At other times, only those with the proper credentials have been allowed to stay. During Occupy Wall Street, several people reporting on the protest were arrested and charged with disorderly conduct because they did not have a press credential issued by the New York Police Department. To get the credential, individuals had to submit an application in person and show six published clips that demonstrated coverage of breaking or spot news. As Erika Fry notes in the *Columbia Journalism Review*, "Simply put, without a press credential issued by the NYPD's Office of the Deputy Commissioner for Public Information (DCPI), you are not a journalist in the eyes of the police."

The Ethical Domain

While the legal questions surrounding who is a journalist are largely practical, the ethical domain covers the theoretical. According to Ugland and Henderson, "Unlike in the law domain where courts and legislatures establish definitions that are imposed upon others, in the professional ethics domain . . . no one has the power to mandate adherence to a particular definition, nor is it necessary to seek any kind of social consensus." Still, if we cannot agree on who counts as a journalist, holding that person to account for ethical standards becomes challenging. To help address the question, at least three interrelated approaches have been proposed: those based on title/status, those based on intent/motivation, and those based on action/product.

Title/Status. Historically, the title *journalist* was conferred upon news workers by organizations that employed them. You were a journalist if you earned a living working for an established news organization. The status was granted, rather than self-proclaimed, and it was easy to recognize a journalist as someone who carried a press pass and a business card that said something like *reporter, photographer,* or *editor*. Of course, that conferral process continues today, but individuals need not wait to be designated a journalist. Everyone can—and many do—call themselves journalists.

Approaching a definition of journalist based on the practice of self-proclamation aligns with the *everyone's a journalist* rhetoric of the day, but it also honors a historical commitment—in the United States and other democracies at least—that journalists should not be defined by any outside entity. (For example, journalists are not licensed to practice.) Under this approach, if someone says she is a journalist, she is a journalist. This also aligns with Jay Rosen's view that the more people who are participating, the better. On the other hand, this approach allows someone to participate in newsgathering and news telling in any number of ways and to call herself a journalist one day but not the next. In addition, one person writing a blog, posting on Facebook, participating on Reddit, or sending tweets may consider himself a journalist; another person doing the very same things may not.

The ethical danger of this approach—not to mention the practical difficulty—is that it tends to leave little room for shared standards. There could be as many definitions of journalist and as many understandings of what the role means as there are people calling themselves journalists. To be ethically justifiable, this all-inclusive approach calls on journalists to be extremely transparent about how they see their role and the ethical commitments that relate to it. In their 2014 book *The New Ethics of Journalism*, Kelly McBride and Tom Rosenstiel formalize this call by including transparency as one of three guiding principles for journalism in the twenty-first century. (Truth and community are the other two.) Transparency replaced the principle of independence, which was featured in an earlier book by Bob Steele. But it is not sufficient to count on journalists following McBride and Rosenstiel's advice to always show their work, offer evidence to back it up, and explain how they gathered it. Citizens, as well, need to commit themselves to learning about the journalists whose work they consume so they can then put that work in a context that makes sense. In other words, the *everyone's a journalist* approach calls for high levels of media literacy among all of us.

The question of shared standards inevitably arises when we try to sort out the difference between a journalist and an activist. Since the age of objectivity began, journalists' professional associations, their colleagues, and their audiences have expected news workers to refrain from having any skin in the game. News reporting (as opposed to commentary or analysis) should be a fair, balanced, and detached enterprise; it should not be activism. In fact, even though some ethicists are leaning toward transparency, the Society of Professional Journalists Code of Ethics continues to list independence as one of four key principles, and the code

guides journalists to "be free of obligation to any interest other than the public's right to know." This includes avoiding real or perceived conflicts of interest and remaining free of associations or activities that could damage integrity or credibility. For most journalists, this has meant refraining from actively and publicly advocating on behalf of an issue or a group, but some have even taken it to the level of choosing not to vote.

However, in the digital age when information comes from so many places, some have argued that the distinction between journalist and activist is a false dichotomy. Jay Rosen, for example, says that comparing activists with journalists may not be the right way of thinking about it. As Rosen explains in a *New York Times* article by David Carr, "We are beginning to realize that journalists come in a variety of shapes and sizes and come with a variety of commitments. It isn't the fact that someone is an activist is irrelevant, it's just that it does not necessarily mean they are the opposite of a journalist."

Still, names do seem to matter. Julian Assange was "openly contemptuous of mainstream journalists," according to George Brock of the *Guardian*. That is, until he faced risk of criminal charges. "At that point, he began describing himself as a journalist." Others prefer to use both titles. When David Carr and Ravi Somaiya wrote an article about WikiLeaks for the *New York Times* and called Alexa O'Brien, who had been covering the trial of Bradley (Chelsea) Manning, an activist, O'Brien requested a correction. O'Brien had been involved in Occupy Wall Street and the U.S. Day of Rage, and she began covering the Manning trial in part to protest the lack of information about the case. In her request for a correction, O'Brien notes, "You are reading my journalistic work, using my journalistic work, capitalizing off my journalistic work, and linking to my journalistic work." For *New York Times* public editor Margaret Sullivan, this is a matter of professional respect. When the media establishment refers to someone as a blogger, "it somehow seems to say, 'You're not quite one of us.'"

For Carr, *activist* and *journalist* are not mutually exclusive. Glenn Greenwald, the blogger and columnist who reported in the *Guardian* on the secrets revealed by Edward Snowden, is clearly an activist. "You need only to read a few sentences of Mr. Greenwald's blog to know exactly where he stands," Carr says. "Mr. Greenwald is an activist who is deeply suspicious of government and the national security apparatus, and he is a zealous defender of privacy and civil rights." He is also, Carr argues, a journalist. Janine Gibson, who oversaw Greenwald's coverage for the *Guardian*, says Greenwald has a point of view, but "he is meticulous and forensic in his approach and is extremely careful about getting it right." Greenwald himself says all real journalists are activists. "Journalism has a value, a purpose—to serve as a check on power."

Intent/Motivation. Greenwald's commitment to serving as a check on power takes us out of the realm of status and into the realm of intent. In an article for the *Journal of Mass Media Ethics*, Sandra Borden and Chad Tew argue that journalists act from "a set of moral commitments that normatively shape [their]

performance of news." These commitments include, among others, reliability, truthfulness, and independence. For Borden and Tew, journalists "demonstrate correspondence between intention and performance." Therefore, people like Jon Stewart and Stephen Colbert cannot be journalists. Even though their performances may look like journalism—even excellent journalism—they are not motivated by the moral commitments of journalists. They are not *intending* to be journalists.

Others who have grappled with the meaning of *journalist* also put motivations at the center of the analysis. For example, Ellyn Angelotti of the Poynter Institute contends that it does not matter whether someone calls himself a journalist. A journalist, she says, "possesses a hunger to pursue the truth and to share it in compelling ways." For Margaret Sullivan, a journalist is "someone who understands, at a cellular level, and doesn't shy away from, the adversarial relationship between the government and the press."

Putting the focus on intention rather than title—either self-proclaimed or assigned—speaks to some of the challenges raised by the latter. If being a journalist means acting from a set of shared moral commitments, then the concern about a lack of standards is mitigated. Of course, these commitments may be in flux. Kelly McBride and Tom Rosenstiel's focus on transparency rather than independence is an example of a suggested shift. But commitments still exist, and anyone who wishes to call herself a journalist—whether she works for a legacy news organization or blogs as a hobby—should be motivated by these commitments.

Although a focus on intention does solve some issues in the *who is a journalist* debate, it is not without its own concerns. Making intention the primary condition for determining who counts as a journalist does not account for all of the "accidental journalists" who have witnessed, recorded, and shared important news stories since the turn of the century. Consider the written accounts, photos, and videos taken by survivors of the 2004 South Asian tsunami. As Steve Outing of the Poynter Institute says, the tsunami story should be considered "the seminal marker for introducing citizen journalism into the hallowed space that is professional journalism." However, those survivors were likely not acting from a set of shared moral commitments when they captured and shared their accounts of the disaster. Therefore, even though the accounts were published and broadcast on traditional media, the word *journalist* would not apply. Likewise, Colleen Owens, a stay-at-home mom who blogged about local IRS offices targeting Tea Party groups (a story that was eventually picked up by the legacy press and made headline news), may not qualify as a journalist. Acting from a set of shared moral commitments requires knowing what those commitments are. Owens saw the story as an important one to tell but described herself as an "amateur" with no journalism experience who was initially acting on behalf of her local Tea Party chapter.

A final challenge to the *intentions* test arises when declared intentions run the risk of being disputed. In both the WikiLeaks and NSA surveillance cases, the status of Julian Assange and Glenn Greenwald as journalists has been challenged. In the case of WikiLeaks, the proposed federal shield law contains a specific exemption for organizations like WikiLeaks. For Greenwald, the challenge came from some within the established journalist community. David Gregory of NBC and Andrew Ross Sorkin of the *New York Times* both publicly suggested that Greenwald could or should be arrested (Sorkin later apologized). For Salon.com writer David Sirota, Gregory's and Sorkin's comments represented the establishment media's "ideological antipathy to journalism"—an antipathy to acting from the very intentions that Angelotti and Sullivan claim are essential for any journalist worth the name.

Action/Product. The third philosophical approach to determining who does and does not count as a journalist focuses around actions and what those actions produce. For many, this gets to the essence of the question (and returns somewhat to whether *what is journalism* is the better question than *who is a journalist*). Using the *actions* test, if someone is producing journalism, he is a journalist. The proof, as they say, is in the pudding. For Matt Welch of *Reason* magazine, journalism may be a calling for many people who share a set of sourcing traditions and political assumptions, but for millions more, journalism is a "legitimate side hobby." Even if they do not share that calling, if they are engaging in the activity of journalism, they are journalists. But does this activity have any requirements? Or is it analogous to the *title* test: If someone calls herself a journalist, she is a journalist.

Often, public interest is used as a barometer. If the work produced serves the public interest, it is journalism, and the person who created it, shared it, or commented on it is a journalist. But do we all have a shared sense of what the public interest is? Clearly not. That is the reason some people judge the stories that came out of WikiLeaks and Edward Snowden's leaks as essential to the public interest; others judge them as treason. Although these two stories are particularly important and contested, others that appear every day add to the debate about what it means to serve the public interest. For instance, on December 23, 2013, the top story in the *Denver Post* was about Broncos linebacker Von Miller being out for the football season due to a torn ACL. On CNN.com, the top story was about a man who wants to let his pregnant wife who is on a ventilator die. On the Huffington Post, the top story was about fifteen Democratic senators who signed on to "sabotage Iran nuclear talks." And on BuzzFeed, the top "Big Story" was about the White House delaying the deadline to sign up for a health insurance plan by one more day. If the public interest test were applied to all of these stories, would we reach consensus?

Perhaps not every journalistic product needs to serve the public interest to count as journalism (and, therefore, for the creator to count as a journalist). Of course, we love to focus on Jay Rosen's ideal of improving civic life and strengthening democracy, but there may be value in other kinds of news products as well. Traditional news values include things like impact, timeliness, prominence, proximity, unusualness, usefulness, conflict,

and human interest. On December 24, 2013, the top Reddit story was one of those that appeals to human interest: a picture and accompanying tweet that said, "The hill behind my house is completely frozen and I'm about to go down it in a laundry basket: Best Christmas Eve Ever." We might be hard pressed to argue that this story serves a compelling public interest, but it does tug at our heartstrings. By telling a story that appeals to the *human interest* value—and by achieving top status on Reddit—rangerbearq, the story's creator, would likely count as a journalist.

Who Gets to Decide?

Examining potential meanings of *journalist* and *journalism* through both legal and ethical lenses helps illustrate the complexity of the news landscape in the digital age, but that examination does not address another important question: *Who should get to decide* what counts as journalism and who gets to be a journalist?

With foundations in the First Amendment and support for a marketplace-of-ideas philosophy, the United States has a history of inclusivity when it comes to these questions. Of course, the professionalization of journalism, which began in the 1900s, led to what Mark Deuze, writing in *Journalism*, calls "a professional identity of journalists with claims to an exclusive role and status in society." But that identity—while powerful—is only symbolic. Journalists have never been subject to the same kinds of requirements (e.g., special training, licensing) as have other professions such as teaching, medicine, and the law. In fact, journalists have actively argued against these kinds of requirements to practice, citing First Amendment concerns. Therefore, although the digital age has only recently made it practical for so many people to create journalism and act as journalists, theoretically, the possibility has existed throughout history.

From an ethical perspective, the need to settle on what counts as journalism and who counts as a journalist appears pressing. However, if we are to heed the advice of ethicists like Clifford Christians, who recommends a return to the general morality rather than a continued focus on professional ethics, then the need diminishes. If, as Christians argues, the goal of all communicators should be to focus on universal principles inscribed in the common good, then it does not much matter whether what we are doing is journalism or whether we call ourselves journalists. Of course, for some journalism ethicists, this might sound like a ticket out of a job. How can we possibly talk about journalism ethics if we cannot agree on the term itself? But perhaps a more inclusive approach is exactly what is needed in an age when everything has the possibility to be journalism and everyone the potential to be a journalist.

This does not, however, settle some of the legal and practical issues. Although organizations like the Society of Professional Journalists (SPJ), the National Press Photographers Association (NPPA), and the Radio Television Digital News Association (RTDNA) support a federal shield law, which, by necessity, defines a journalist, others are less enthusiastic. Columnist and blogger Jack Shafer, writing in Slate, says there is a danger to letting the government define who is a journalist. Doing so is an "excellent foundation upon which to build such a card-issuing ministry of journalism" (aka a licensing bureau). Shafer adds that a federal shield law "imagines that the highest wattage of the First Amendment belongs only to the guild that makes up the media industry. The amendment really belongs to anyone who decides to express themselves." Seth Mandel of *Commentary* magazine agrees, arguing that politicians are not the best qualified to decide who is and is not a journalist. "They are often less informed on the changing digital media landscape than news consumers, and they have an obvious interest in excluding some journalists or news outlets from press protections." For Mandel, like Shafer, narrowing the protections enshrined in the Constitution is a "recipe for trouble."

Perhaps by the time this chapter is published, debate over the federal shield law will be resolved, and the bill will have either passed or failed. A resolution to that legal debate—like the ethical one over what counts as journalism and who counts as a journalist—is not necessary for journalism to continue. Interestingly, it is some of the informal privileges that are the most pressing, particularly those that deal with access. After all, not every person who would like to cover the White House can fit in the press briefing room or on *Air Force One*. There is no question that the power players of the establishment media have an advantage; they have history, they have relationships and, importantly, they have resources. It may be most practical to recognize that not *every* journalist can tell *every* story.

For example, while citizen journalists would certainly bring an interesting perspective to White House coverage, adding them to the press pool would mean replacing others. As of now, journalists in the pool represent a significant number of legacy news organizations but also news websites (Talking Points Memo and the Huffington Post), brand new organizations (Al Jazeera America), and media with different ideologies (*Mother Jones* and Human Events). A group of journalists who cover Congress and the presidency approves White House credentials (although the White House must give security clearance). Journalists seeking credentials must show that they work for an organization whose "principal business is the daily dissemination of original news and opinion of interest to a broad segment of the public" and that is "editorially independent of any institution, foundation or interest group that lobbies the federal government." This, of course, cuts out anyone who is not employed by a news organization. To better recognize the broadening definition of journalist while simultaneously honoring practical limits, the credentialing body—the Standing Committee of Correspondents—should reserve a small number of credentials for journalists who do not meet the employment test but who otherwise demonstrate a commitment to and aptitude for solid political journalism.

Looking to the Future

Taking everything this chapter describes into account, it is easy to understand both the excitement and anxiety the digital age is creating, particularly as it relates to journalism in the twenty-first century. The terms, conditions, expectations, and even the future of journalism are up for debate.

Everyone has a stake in journalism—if we are not producers, educators, and critics, we are certainly consumers—and what we all do now will help settle some of the important questions this chapter has raised. Or, at the very least, what we all do now will help us become more comfortable with the ambiguity. On what, then, should we focus as we move forward?

David Plotz of *Slate* calls this the golden age of journalism (if not the golden age for traditional journalists looking to earn a living doing their work). He has a point. At no time has more information from thorough, thoughtful, and diverse sources been available at our fingertips. This should be celebrated. If we are truly concerned about journalism that will make life—particularly public life—better, we should encourage continuous expansion of the journalism circle.

But there is still something about the words *journalism* and *journalist*. They do and should continue to have meaning. Yes, anyone can proclaim herself a journalist or her work journalism, but that is not enough. People who call themselves journalists (or who are designated as journalists by others) should share a certain kind of commitment, and they should routinely demonstrate that commitment through the work they produce. A solid journalistic product without the intention is not enough, just as intention without the product does not suffice.

With journalism (the act) and journalist (the person) continuing to be important in the twenty-first century, journalism schools, journalism organizations, and citizens alike need to assume shared responsibility for doing good work in both the technical and ethical sense. Many journalism schools are caught between old-world mentality that they are training profes- sional journalists and new-world mentality that everyone can be a journalist. But the schools can be more relevant than ever, and they should have a wider reach, edu- cating all students—not only those who want to pursue a career in journalism— about the value, commitments, and skills of journalism. Canada, Europe, and even some post-Soviet republics offer education in media literacy that focuses on both criti- cal consumption of media as well as media production. This should become a staple of U.S. university education, if not also at the primary and secondary levels.

In addition, the journalism community should welcome new players in journal- ism, including Jeff Bezos of Amazon, who bought the *Washington Post,* and Pierre Omidyar of eBay, who is investing $250 million in a journalism start-up with Glenn Greenwald. Bezos, Omidyar, and others can add their extensive talents and resources to an already rich pool of entre- preneurs working diligently to find new ways of both doing good journalism and remaining financially viable. Good jour- nalism does not come without a cost, and hobbyists alone cannot meet our needs. We need to find ways of compensating people for their work.

At the end of 2013, as part of a Nieman Journalism Lab project, a number of observers offered outlooks for journalism in the next year. Those outlooks are over- whelmingly positive, and several speak of a shift in attitude away from what Jan Schaffer, executive director of J-Lab, calls "the handwringing over losses in legacy journalism." With a focus on moving for- ward, Dan Gillmor of Arizona State University predicts that "journalists will increasingly recognize the value of col- laboration and cooperation—and of shed- ding their 'not invented here' attitudes." Concurrently, Gillmor says, "Information providers of all kinds, including bloggers, Facebook managers and others who care about their communities, will share what they know, and will leverage traditional methods of organizing to get the public to focus on things that matter." If the future truly holds this in store, perhaps our excitement about journalism in the twenty- first century should trump our anxiety, and we should actively work to help foster a continually reimagined journalism that does a better job of accomplishing what it has always been about: helping people focus on, care about, understand, and act on the things that matter.

Wendy N. Wyatt
University of St. Thomas

See also Access to Information; Ethical Responsibilities versus Legal Rights; Reporter's Privilege/Poster's Privilege; Twitter and Traditional Media

Further Reading

Angelotti, Ellyn. "A Broader Definition of Journalist." *New York Times,* December 12, 2011. http://www.nytimes.com/ roomfordebate/2011/12/11/are-all- bloggers-journalists/we-need-a-broader- definition-of-journalist.

Benton, Joshua. "Reporters, Bloggers, News Photogs, Citizen Journalists: Please Take This Survey about Press Credentials." Nieman Journalism Lab, September 24, 2013. http://www.niemanlab.org/2013/09/ reporters-bloggers-news-photogs-citizen- journalists-please-take-this-survey-about- press-credentials.

Borden, Sandra L., and Chad Tew. "The Role of the Journalist and the Performance of Journalism: Ethical Lessons from 'Fake News' (Seriously)." *Journal of Mass Media Ethics* 22, no. 4 (2007): 300–314.

Brock, George. "Does David Miranda Count as a Journalist? That's Not the Point." *Guardian,* August 29, 2013. http://www.theguardian.com/profile/george-brock.

Carr, David. "Journalism, Even When It's Tilted." *New York Times,* July 1, 2013.

Deuze, Mark. "What Is Journalism? Professional Identity and Ideology of Journalists Reconsidered." *Journalism* 6, no. 4 (2005): 442–464.

Durbin, Dick. "It's Time to Say Who's a Real Reporter." *Chicago Sun-Times,* June 26, 2013. http://www.suntimes.com/news/otherviews/20978789-452/sen-dick-durbin-its-time-to-say-whos-a-real-reporter.html.

Friend, Cecilia, and Jane B. Singer. *Online Journalism Ethics: Traditions and Transitions.* Armonk, NY: M. E. Sharpe, 2007.

Fry, Erika. "Who's a Journalist?" *Columbia Journalism Review*, October 7, 2011. http://www.cjr.org/behind_the_news/whos_a_journalist_1.php?page=all.

Fulton, Katherine. "A New Agenda for Journalism." *Nieman Reports* 48, no. 1 (1994): 15.

Gillmor, Dan. "Building on the Snowden Effect." Nieman Journalism Lab, December 20, 2013. http://www.niemanlab.org/2013/12/building-on-the-snowden-effect/.

Greene, David. "Senate Revises Media Shield Law for the Better, but It's Still Imperfect." Electronic Frontier Foundation, September 20, 2013. https://www.eff.org/deeplinks/2013/09/senate-revises-media-shield-law-better-its-still-imperfect.

Hanson, Jarice. "Authors, Authority, Ownership, and Ethics in Digital Media and News." In *The Handbook of Global Communication and Media Ethics*, Vol. II, edited by Robert S. Fortner and P. Mark Fackler, 803–822. Malden, MA: Wiley-Blackwell, 2011.

Jarvis, Jeff. "BuzzMachine." http://buzzmachine.com

Jarvis, Jeff. "Who Is a Journalist? Manning Trial Poses Question of Vital Public Interest." *Guardian*, July 11, 2013. http://www.theguardian.com/global/2013/jul/11/who-is-journalist-bradley-manning-trial.

Lee-Wright, Peter, Angela Phillips, and Tamara Witschge. *Changing Journalism*. Milton Park, Abingdon, UK: Routledge, 2012.

Mandel, Seth. "Should the Government Decide Who Is a 'Legitimate Journalist'?" *Commentary*, July 1, 2013. http://www.commentarymagazine.com/topic/shield-law.

McBride, Kelly, and Tom Rosentiel, eds. *The New Ethics of Journalism: Principles for the 21st Century*. Thousand Oaks, CA: Sage, 2014.

Meyers, Christopher, ed. *Journalism Ethics: A Philosophical Approach*. New York: Oxford University Press, 2010.

Peters, Chris, and Marcel Broersma. *Rethinking Journalism: Trust and Participation in a Transformed News Landscape*. New York: Routledge, 2013.

"Pew Research Journalism Project." http://www.journalism.org.

Postman, Neil. *Amusing Ourselves to Death: Public Discourse in the Age of Show Business*. New York: Penguin Books, 2006.

Roberts, Cokie, and Steve Roberts. "Who Is a Journalist, and Why Does It Matter?" *Mercury News,* September 26, 2013. http://www.pottsmerc.com/opinion/20130926/cokie-steve-roberts-who-is-a-journalist-and-why-does-it-matter.

Rosen, Jay. "PressThink." www.pressthink.org.

Schaffer, Jan. "Lost in the Gloom, an Entrepreneurial Bloom." Nieman Journalism Lab, December 16, 2013. http://www.niemanlab.org/2013/12/lost-in-the-gloom-a-boom-in-entrepreurship/.

Shafer, Jack. "We Don't Need No Stinkin' Shield Law, Part I." *Slate,* April 16, 2008. http://www.slate.com/articles/news_and_politics/press_box/2008/04/we_dont_need_no_stinkin_shield_law_part_1.html.

Singer, Jane B. "Journalism Ethics in a Digital Network." In *The Handbook of Global*

Communication and Media Ethics, Vol. II, edited by Robert S. Fortner and P. Mark Fackler, 845–863. Malden, MA: Wiley-Blackwell, 2011.

Sirota, David. "Meet the "Journalists Against Journalism Club." Salon.com, July 2, 2013. http://www.salon.com/2013/07/02/meet_the_journalists_against_journalism_club.

Sullivan, Margaret. "Who's a Journalist? A Question with Many Facets and One Sure Answer." *New York Times,* June 29, 2013.

http://publiceditor.blogs.nytimes.com/2013/06/29/whos-a-journalist-a-question-with-many-facets-and-one-sure-answer.

Ugland, Erik, and Jennifer Henderson. "Who Is a Journalist and Why Does It Matter? Disentangling the Legal and Ethical Arguments." *Journal of Mass Media Ethics* 22, no. 4 (2007): 241–261.

Wyatt, Wendy, ed. "Special Topic: Who Is a Journalist?" *Journal of Mass Media Ethics* 22, no.4: (2007): 239–347.

49

CHINA WORRIED?

Except for the first several years after it was founded, China has adopted "good news only" as a journalism policy. The Ministry of Propaganda of the Communist Party of China (CPC) aims at promoting the achievements of this country under the leadership of the Party. Article I of the Professional Code of Ethics for Chinese Journalists released in 2009 specified that journalists shall serve the people wholeheartedly. They shall be loyal to the Party, the motherland, and the people. Media reports shall be the integration of the ideas of the Party and the thoughts of the people. Positive reports shall be dominant, combined with reports serving the enhanced watchdog function. An earlier code of ethics for broadcasting editors and journalists issued by the then-State Administration of Radio, Film and Television (SARFT) also underlined ardently carrying out the good-news policy and creating a positive and healthy media environment. More recently, when negative news related to disasters was disclosed, as in the case of the 2008 Wenchuan Earthquake, the stress was put on how those victims could not have been evacuated or rescued without wise

decisions and quick action by the Party. As Doug Young summarized, the role of Chinese media is to tell the Party's stories to Chinese people and the world. Or, to use a catchphrase popularized in 2012 and 2013, it is to *shifang zheng nengliang*, meaning to radiate positive energy, a physics term now used to refer to propagating news that makes people more confident, optimistic, and vibrant.

This chapter will examine the key characteristics of weibo, or microblogs; weibo's roles in the "good-news-only" Chinese society; and the technology, laws, and regulations employed by the Chinese government to try to put weibo under control. These sections are followed by the ethical consideration of such practices.

Everybody "Knits Her Scarf"

The half-truth stories propagated in the Chinese media were effective when China was closed to the world until the late 1970s. However, after China started to open up, especially after the advent of new information and communication technologies, the way information is disseminated has changed. Social media, represented by weibo, have posed a challenge to the good-news-only or "harmonious" model.

Weibo is the Chinese translation of microblogs, a Twitter-like service. Chinese weibo users refer to their tweeting as "knitting the scarf" because the sound "weibo" is the homophone of both "microblogs" and "scarf" in Mandarin. Twitter was blocked in China after violent riots happened in July 2009 in Xinjiang with nearly two thousand casualties. Sina Weibo was the first microblog service provided by Chinese operator Sina.com in August 2009. The number of registered users of Sina Weibo had reached five hundred million as of the end of 2012. Several other big Web companies, such as NetEase.com, Tencent.com, and Sohu.com, all launched weibo service in 2010, each claiming more than one hundred million registered users. By the end of November 2013, the total number of weibo accounts had reached 1.3 billion. Sina Weibo is the dominant player and Tencent Weibo a challenger.

Although both take the form of micro-blogging, weibo is not exactly the same as Twitter. Twitter allows 140 words while weibo allows 140 Chinese characters, which is believed to express three to five times more information than the same number of English words. Weibo users can follow other microbloggers, repost others' tweets to their home pages, and broadcast tweets of their own. Sina Weibo, for example, enables users to upload videos, pictures, music, and emotion icons. It also encourages interactivity and participation of tweeters, such as tweeting consecutively for certain days, by awarding virtual medals. Sina Weibo also enables its users to make comments on others' posts without having to retweet that post, another difference from Twitter.

The demographic profile of Chinese weibo users shows that male microbloggers slightly outnumber females, and two-thirds of users are under thirty. Nearly 80 percent had monthly income of less than 3,000 yuan in 2010 (about US$441 based on the then-exchange rate). These microbloggers use weibo mainly to seek information and express opinions. Topics such as public welfare, political affairs, and entertainment gain most of the attention.

Roles of Weibo

Considering the general unanimity, voluntary or involuntary, of the mainstream Chinese media in their news stories, weibo is a conduit for many Chinese to hear a different voice. It is conducive to the propagation of opinions and formation of the public sphere. Weibo may set the agenda for traditional media. Some incidents are first disclosed via weibo tweets, then gradually attract the mainstream media's attention and coverage. A case in point is the bullet-train collision in Wenzhou in July 2011. No state-run newspaper had reported it until a Sina Weibo user first tweeted it. PM2.5, a tiny particle smaller than 2.5 micrometers that may cause serious respiratory diseases, first became a buzzword on weibo. Its weibo popularity, combined with other factors, finally urged the Chinese government to include it in the air-quality index and monitor it beginning in 2012, four years earlier than the original schedule.

Weibo not only has efficacy in public security and environmental activism, but it promotes social change in other ways. In the case of the 2011 Wukan land-dispute incident, local villagers and national elites used weibo to ignite national debate on democracy and political reform in China. This incident shows weibo's role in mass incidents and social protests. Weibo has become a weapon for Chinese citizens to defend their rights. Migrant workers tweet to get the media and the public's attention so as to receive their due wages their employers are unwilling to pay.

Weibo also plays a role in anti-corruption, which is in accord with the goals of the new Chinese leadership. Luo Changping, an outspoken investigative journalist, exposed on his weibo account that Liu Tienan, the then-deputy minister of China's National Development and Reform Commission, had taken bribes. This charge led to Liu's being removed from the position and placed under investigation. What was interesting is Luo did not run the story in the print version of *Caijing*, a magazine where he worked as deputy editor, but on his personal weibo account.

Luo's courage inspired his colleagues. A few other reporters took the same measure. Wang Wenzhi, who works for the *Economic Information Daily*, is another whistleblower. In an open letter he posted at his weibo account, Wang accused Song Lin, head of China Resources, a *Fortune* Global 500 state-owned enterprise, of intentionally overpaying for a coal-industry acquisition, which resulted in the loss of state property.

With the penetration of Sina Weibo and Tencent Weibo, there have been many VIP-like microbloggers who are verified by the service provider with a capitalized letter *V*. They are dubbed "da V," or Big Vs. Big Vs usually have at least one hundred thousand followers. There are about nineteen thousand such Big Vs at Sina Weibo and Tencent Weibo. Among them, about thirty-three hundred accounts have more than one million followers. There are two hundred Big Vs who have more than ten million followers. With millions of followers, each of their tweets might incur the so-called butterfly effect, a small change that triggers big repercussions. Pan Shiyi, who was invited by Sina.com to be one of the first twenty accounts of Sina Weibo, told the *Economist* that he was well aware of the greatness and quickness of his tweets, which may go well beyond his original intention.

Putting Weibo under Control

Given the potential of weibo to reach a large audience within a short period of time, China has taken stern measures to try to put this influential media form under control. The government's stated concerns include, but are not limited to, national security, social stability, ethnic unity, libel, rumors, fraud, and pornography. Its control measures include monitoring weibo posts with software and human labors, as well as promulgating relevant rules and regulations.

Armed with Technology

In the United States, the Internet is recognized by the Supreme Court as less subject to regulation than other forms of communication. Even profane speech, hate speech, and anonymous astringent comments are protected by freedom of speech. Section 230 (c)(1) of the Communications Decency Act of 1996 says that "an online computer service must not be treated as a speaker or publisher when the content comes from someone else."

However, Internet Service Providers (ISPs) and Internet Content Providers (ICPs) whose servers or operations are located in China have to censor users' messages and even disable clients' accounts if they want to renew their operating license. Microblog service providers in China must guarantee they implement censorship techniques to put information flows under scrutiny. Sina Weibo came under verbal attack for its removal of tweets concerning the *Southern Weekly* incident, in which employees of an investigative newspaper protested against censorship of their New Year's Day editorial on constitutionalism. Supportive weibo posts were quickly removed after Sina had received directives from higher administration. If Sina Weibo did not follow censorship instructions and delete such tweets, one manager explained, it would go game-over just like treading on an ant. Sina Weibo reportedly employs about one thousand censors to monitor microblogs.

The speed at which tweets are deleted is stunning. Again, taking Sina Weibo as an example, 30 percent of the deletion of original tweets happened within five to thirty minutes after they were posted. Ninety percent of such removals happened within twenty-four hours.

The rate of deletion varies from area to area. Microblogs sent in western China, such as Tibet, Qinghai, and Ningxia, where ethnic riots are a big concern, tend to be deleted more quickly than those originating in eastern provinces and municipalities.

The weibo censoring system is both proactive and retroactive.

Proactive measures refer to filtering in all forms or even using camouflaged posts to prevent certain tweets from being sent out. Weibo users will receive a message declaring either that the tweet has violated relevant rules and regulations so it cannot be processed, or that a delay has been caused by server data synchronization. The user has to wait for one or two minutes. This would be the time for the tweet to be manually checked for sensitive content. A camouflaged post is one that makes the user believe that the tweet has been released but, in fact, no other users can see it. Keyword alerts usually give censors the hint about what to censor. In 2011, blocked search terms included Ai Weiwei, an artist and activist who was arrested and then released but is still prohibited from traveling abroad; Jasmine Revolution, the Tunisian revolution that developed into the Arab Spring and inspired pro-democracy protests in China; Jon Huntsman, then–U.S. ambassador to China who attended a protest in downtown Beijing; and Zengcheng, where migrants held a demonstration that escalated into a mass incident. According to a study monitoring microblog removal at Sina Weibo from January 1 to June 30, 2012, top keywords censored were mostly related to Bo Xilai, former top leader of Chongqing Municipality who was removed in March 2012 and sentenced to life imprisonment in September 2013; Wang Lijun, former police chief of Chongqing, who traveled to the U.S. consulate in Chengdu seeking political asylum in February 2012; Chen Guangcheng, a blind activist who had been under house arrest, was sentenced, and later came to the United States in May 2012 after diplomatic efforts; Gary Locke, then–U.S. ambassador to China; refuting rumors; seeking confirmation; and content deletion. Later that year, censored words included Beijing rainstorm, a flash flood that killed seventy-nine people; Diaoyu Islands, China's disputed territory; and group sex.

Retroactive mechanisms remove tweets that have already been broadcast, monitor certain users, and even close the account of sensitive users. Sina Weibo screens some words so that the search results will not be shown. Microbloggers who often make sensitive posts are subject to more censorship attention than those who do so by chance. When a sensitive post is removed, all corresponding reposts will disappear, too. The list of sensitive words that cannot be searched is updated frequently. When a banned term is searched, a message will pop up saying, "According to relevant regulations and policies, the result of your search term is not shown."

As a countermeasure, Chinese microbloggers turn to coded language—homophones, puns, or neologisms—to circumvent the filtering. For example, "草(艹)," pronounced *cao*, a homophone of the Chinese equivalent of "fuck," is used to avoid being censored for vulgarity. The river crab, pronounced as *hexie*, is a better-known homophone of "harmony." Microbloggers satirically say they are harmonized after their tweets have been deleted. "六三" was coined

for "六四." "六" means six while "三" symbolizes one (一) on top of three (三), which equals four or "四." It refers to the student movement that happened on June 4, 1989, at Tiananmen. But the filtering system is so advanced and powerful that even such devices may not be searchable at weibo. Examples include "令jh" for "令计划" or Ling Jihua, a top-ranking official of the Communist Party whose son reportedly died in a traffic accident when driving a Ferrari with two female passengers, leading to the father's demotion; "粥涌康/州永康/洲永糠" for "周永康," a former Politburo member who supervised China's security forces and law-enforcement institutions and reportedly is under investigation for the corruption in China's state-owned oil enterprises; and 8qb4 for 8964, referring to June 4, 1989, since dates are shown in the order of year-month-day in Chinese.

Promulgating Rules and Regulations

Since weibo was introduced to Chinese Internet users, relevant rules and regulations have been in effect. Among them, the real-name registration, Sina Weibo Community Pact, and recent "7 bottom lines and 500 reposts" rules deserve more attention.

Real-Name Registration

To strengthen Internet regulations, major Chinese cities such as Beijing, Shenzhen, and Guangzhou, where Sina Weibo, Sohu Weibo, and Tencent Weibo users are registered, ordered a real-name registration for microbloggers in December 2011.

Take Beijing as an example. On December 16, 2011, the Beijing Municipal

Government issued a regulation concerning the development and supervision of micro-blogs. The sixteen-item regulation took effect on the same day. The regulation is often oversimplified as the real-name registration rule because Article 9 requires that any organization or individual that registers a microblog account to produce, reproduce, publish, or disseminate information shall use real identity information.

However, a close scrutiny of the regulation will show its amazingly wide scope.

The regulation specifies that microblog operators shall apply for a telecommunications operator's license and be subject to examination, verification, and approval. It requires Internet companies that provide microblog services to be responsible for disseminating core socialist values and advancing socialist culture to serve the goal of constructing a harmonious socialist society. Microblog operators have to abide by the regulation, otherwise they cannot run their business, as stated earlier in this article. It is left to the Internet company to decide whether they want to be a compliant player or a challenger to the authorities. If they want to earn revenues, they need to behave in accordance with the interest of the government, which is often propagandized as being the same as national interest. The implication of a harmonious society is consensus and uniformity. Discordant voices are susceptible to being stifled. The regulation provides the legal framework for microblog operators to supervise and to be supervised.

The regulation also stipulates, based on the number of registered users and microblogs, that Internet companies that run a microblog service shall set up a corresponding department and assign technicians with professional knowledge and expertise to guarantee information security. These Internet companies have a liability to report to the police once users violate laws and regulations to disseminate harmful information. The vagueness of words such as "information security" and "harmful" accommodates extensive interpretations. It could be the security of personal information belonging to each microblogger or information pertinent to national security. Information with the tint of harmfulness has great variety, as well. It could be unhealthy, defamatory, libelous, obscene, and even lethal.

Article 10 specifically provides what types of information are banned on weibo. Any organization or individual shall not post, repost, or spread information that may violate the basic principles of the Constitution of China; jeopardize national security, leak state secrets, subvert the government, or undermine national unity; harm the honor of China or its interests; incite hatred and discrimination or undermine the solidarity among different ethnicities; violate state religion policy, preach heresy and feudal superstitions; spread rumors, disturb social order, destroy social stability; spread vulgarity, pornography, gambling, violence, terrorism, or instigate crimes; humiliate or defame others and infringe upon others' legitimate rights; instigate illegal assembly, protest, demonstration, and undermine social order; organize activities in the name of illegal civil organizations; or contain content that violates laws and administrative regulations. Article 10 is so sweeping that an administrative punishment or even lawsuit could be inflicted upon microbloggers due to just a slip. As the old Chinese saying goes, if you want to punish someone, you can always find excuses.

The rule requires microbloggers to use their real name and national identification number before they post comments at the weibo site. This applies to new users. For those who had already registered before the regulation became effective, they would have to do it within the next three months, before March 16, 2012. Registration is done at the backstage. Tweeters can still use screen names. They have to register before posting their comments. If they only browse, it is not necessary to register.

But these efforts have failed to compel all users to register.

Some researchers believe that one of the reasons is that weibo is more content-driven than social-driven. Weibo users come to this platform for content, or what people say, rather than who says it. Anonymity does not bother tweeters. They are more interested in the tweet itself. Anonymity also makes microbloggers feel free from persecution when they express opinions that may be against the government. Research supports that the real-name registration may have a chilling effect to microbloggers who are stationed in mainland China, do not have a verified identity, are open to comments by other microbloggers, but have a small online social network.

Real-name registration may impair revenues to microblog operators. Sina admitted in its Form 20-F filing with the U.S. Securities and Exchange Commission that it had not been able to verify the identities of all users. Sina's explanation was that users' behavior, the nature of

microblogging service, and the lack of clarity in implementation procedures all made the mission difficult. In this annual report, Sina expressed concerns over the competitiveness of microblogging service in China and the intensive censorship and even potential shutdown of this service by the Chinese government. Sina said potential users were hesitant to register when it was hoping to monetize weibo. When potential users migrated to other weibo sites, Sina would lose its advertising clients. The registration regulation may also cause service providers to incur big economic expenditures to check the identity of such a huge number of users and keep the data safe.

Sina's case shows that the implementation, though abortive, of the microblog management regulations not only affected freedom of speech of Chinese tweeters but posed potential impairment to China's thriving Internet business entities.

On the whole, the predicament of microblog operators makes them have to yield to the government in some situations. On March 31, 2012, both Sina and Tencent had to shut off the comment function before it was resumed three days later. Users could post their own tweets but they could not comment on posts by others. In a message to their users, the two microblog titans said that lots of harmful and illegal information existed in the comments and shutting down the commenting service would facilitate a centralized cleanup. In this campaign, six people were detained and sixteen small websites were closed. The State Internet Information Office (SIIO) official said these sites had spread the rumor of a military coup. It happened when Bo Xilai was removed from office and placed under investigation.

China is not the only country that has adopted real-name registration. South Koreans were required to use their real names when expressing their opinions on online forums. In 2012, the regulation was ruled unconstitutional. The law was implemented out of concerns about anonymous criticism of politicians and celebrities. Koreans' public resentment toward the real-name rule focused on its infringement on privacy. Technically, it was difficult to verify the real identity of users. The hacking of the databases of the verification system exacerbated the situation, with thirty-five million users' information being stolen.

Sina Weibo Community Pact and Relevant Regulations

On May 28, 2012, Sina Weibo launched its Community Pact, together with the Sina Weibo Community Management Regulations (Trial) and the Sina Weibo Community Committee System (Trial), to further regulate weibo users' conduct and build the legal framework for possible punishment.

Sina declared that the aim of the pact was to establish a harmonious, law-abiding, and healthy network environment, safeguard the order of the Sina Weibo community, and better guarantee the lawful rights and interests of users. Article 13 of the pact resonates with Article 10 in the real-name registration regulation. The target is untrue information that may undermine social order and jeopardize national security. Article 21 is eye-catching because it stipulates that any user whose real name has been verified by Sina can use the reporting function to help

discover conduct that violates the regulations. Article 23 stands out as it specifies the punishment. If a weibo user violates the pact, the posts shall be subject to deletion and barred from reprinting, comment, or marking. The user shall be prohibited from posting and being followed. That weibo account may be closed.

The Seven Bottom Lines and the 500-Repost Rule

On August 10, 2013, Lu Wei, minister of China's SIIO, talked with more than a dozen Big Vs at the Forum on Social Responsibilities of Internet Celebrities. The SIIO was set up in May 2011 to tighten the government's control of the Internet. Lu emphasized that Big Vs should abide by the "seven bottom lines." These include the legal bottom line, the socialist system bottom line, the national interest bottom line, the legitimate interest of citizens bottom line, the public order bottom line, the moral bottom line, and the authenticity of information bottom line. It is said that the seven bottom lines are also red lines, which means nobody should go beyond them. These bottom lines are not only the responsibility of Big Vs, but of the whole society. Anhui Province launched a chant on advocating the seven bottom lines and building a civilized Internet. Then a directive was issued instructing major websites to publicize and popularize this song. The last few lines say, "Social harmony is what we share. The baseline of the law is what we shall not breach. National revival and the Chinese dream start with me. It is my great glory and honor."

This is a big move to deter vocal and popular microbloggers. Sina penalized

103,673 weibo accounts that were claimed to have violated the bottom lines from mid-August to mid-November of 2013. Some Big Vs have also been targeted by law enforcement, including Charles Xue, who was arrested on charges of soliciting prostitution. Xue, a Chinese American investor in Internet and telecom companies and active online commentator, known as Xue Banzi at Sina Weibo, had close to twelve million followers. When Xue was detained, China Central Television (CCTV), China's state television broadcaster and the largest TV network, ran a story that featured Xue confessing his adultery. Wang Qinglei, a journalist who worked ten years for CCTV, was fired after he questioned the practice of his former employer for running this story before a court trial.

The *People's Daily* ran an editorial warning that Big Vs might become big rumor mongers.

On September 9, 2013, the National Supreme People's Court and the Supreme People's Procurator jointly published a rule stipulating that if a posting has been viewed more than five thousand times or retweeted five hundred times, the person who posted it may be subject to a libel penalty of up to three years in jail. It is taken as a continuing struggle to intensify Internet control.

Ethical Considerations

China's good-news-only journalism tradition, the inherent characteristics of weibo and its users, as well as the technology and regulations employed to censor weibo all focus on the concerns that weibo, this hard-to-control medium, may be manipulated to challenge the legitimacy of the ruling party and call for mass protests or political change.

Before the advent of new media such as weibo, it was easier to put the press and broadcasting media under control to serve an authoritarian regime, no matter which country it was. The public had to receive what the ruling party wanted them to know—the achievements of the government and activities of leaders, all positive publicity. When people died of famine in the 1960s in China, the media were still feeding citizens the news of good harvests and high agricultural output. Even news of an earthquake with a death toll of approximately 240,000 in Tangshan in 1976 was blocked at first and reached domestic and international audiences later.

The Decision on Certain Important Questions Concerning the Building of a Socialist Harmonious Society, adopted by the CPC Central Committee and released in 2006, borrowed the Confucian concept of harmony and steered China toward the construction of a harmonious society. Article V, about constructing harmonious culture and consolidating the ideological and moral foundations of a harmonious society, pinpoints that new media should be the venue for enhancing societal harmony by intensifying the supervision of the Internet and guiding public opinions. The harmonious society motif is in reaction to the great social discrepancy and tumult triggered by the full-fledged economic development but slow-paced political reform.

Sifting and removing weibo posts that do not sound "harmonious" aims at preventing the formation of large-scale unrest that may result in political upheaval. The quantity of mass incidents has been increasing, from eighty-seven hundred in 1993 to tens of thousands in the early 2010s. The size of mass incidents, the degree of violence, and the level of organization all make this an issue of great magnitude. Such group events, as they are referred to sometimes, usually originate with income discrepancies, ethnic conflicts, or forced land transactions that result from China's social milieu—quick socioeconomic transformation and slow responses of the local government to the change. The large-scale mass incidents may easily grow out of control, especially with the Internet, and weibo in particular, facilitating information propagation. Censoring, or "harmonizing" as users would say, weibo tweets can cut off the blasting fuse so as to maintain political stability.

Weibo is a mediated public space that is characterized by persistence, searchability, replicability, and invisible audiences. The electronic footprint one leaves on weibo is permanent, searchable, and can be copied and pasted. This may have led to the abhorrence some users felt once the real-name registration came into effect. The technical property also empowers the regime to crack down on any sensitive posts and their initiators in an easier way. The invisibility of the audience, especially those with power at hand, such as the authorities, poses a lurking danger to weibo users. The state mechanism against weibo users functions like a panopticon. The real identity of each tweeter is clear to the authorities, like the prisoner who can be monitored in the cell by unseen guards. Under such surveillance, some tweeters would be very self-disciplined. They would become observant

rather than articulate. If the panopticon-like surveillance is vertical and top-down, then the Sina Weibo Community Pact adds a touch of peer surveillance. At social networking sites (SNSs), users voluntarily disclose in the profile aspects of their identity, such as their location and sexual orientation, to the surveillance of others, a process referred to as "participatory surveillance" by Anders Albrechtslund. Article 21 of the pact makes the participation go to the extreme of reporting the misconduct of peer users to the authorities. The seamless vertical and horizontal surveillance makes freedom of speech more difficult to attain.

The dynamism of weibo, as with other SNSs, depends on three cornerstones: profiles, friends lists, and comments. If, out of the fear of being punished for five hundred reposts or five thousand views, microbloggers retreat to no comments and no retweets, then the networking would lose its sense. The concept of rhizome developed by Deleuze and Guattari captures the interconnectedness on the Internet. By following and commenting, users disseminate information in all directions and nonstop. However, filtering and removing techniques, plus the moral and legal constraints imposed by the real-name registration regulation and the five-hundred-repost rule, snip the network of free information flow.

Even worse, China's long feudal and Confucian legacy has resulted in a highly hierarchical and patriarchal society. The regime has overwhelming power over the masses. Individuals tend to put national interest well above their own rights due to China's collectivist tradition. The justifications provided for the real-name registration regulation, Sina Community Pact, and five-hundred-repost rule constrain microbloggers from expressing different opinions since they may not want to do anything that is labeled as undermining or disgracing the motherland. These factors have already encouraged some microbloggers to self-censor what to tweet. Furthermore, Chinese history has seen the change of dynasties and social upheaval, which has taught the Chinese a lesson: to be ambiguous on principles and stay away from potential mire for self-protection. Even though the absolute number of registered microbloggers is huge, most of the tweets are contributed by a small number of people. Less than 5 percent of the participants in a study created more than 80 percent of the original posts. Another study found that even though verified Sina Weibo users accounted for 0.1 percent of the total, they contributed 46.5 percent of the "hot" weibos. Put another way, most Chinese microbloggers are observing or retweeting the posts from a handful of other users instead of making their own voices heard.

On the other hand, verified Sina Weibo users have 9,455 followers on the average, while unverified microbloggers have 57.5. About 75 percent of microbloggers have less than twenty followers. Weibo posts by verified users and those with pictures are more likely to be reposted, a study shows. The five-hundred-repost rule can be broken so easily, since there are active weibo users. And it obviously targets this small group rather than the majority of people who tweet. They are the online opinion leaders who have the power to wage an opinion war.

Shi Shusi, *Worker's Daily* magazine's editorial director, posted his observations about the changes that had happened recently on his weibo account on December 5, 2013, after the five-hundred-repost rule became effective. Shi commented that there had been fewer Big Vs but more official accounts of government institutions. He noted that some "morons" joined the Fifty-Cent Party, a term used to ridicule those who are hired to post pro-government weibo. Shi claimed that public intellectuals who still kept their weibo accounts either remained reticent or made "egg drop soup for the soul." Yet he acknowledged that users chose to stay at weibo because there were no other places where they could go.

Shi's observation is satirical but telling. The recently issued rules and regulations are exerting their chilling effect. A most recent but not unexpected blocked search term at Sina Weibo is *meiti guanzhi*, or supervising the media.

Undoubtedly, there are users taking advantage of weibo for vicious purposes. They post profane, defamatory, and irresponsible tweets. They use weibo to spread rumors. Neither zombie followers who are paid to follow the user nor purchased tweets or comments are surprising to those who have been into weibo for a long time. That said, none of these offenses could justify the cyclopean work of censoring weibo.

Tweets, retweets, and comments to tweets provide a free participatory discussion. Although some opinions might be wrong, comments help people get close to truth. Let alone the fact that some information spread via weibo is not wrong at all. It is "harmonized" simply because it is a harsh but true voice that the government does not want to hear or want more people to hear. Considering China's transformation, and the low authenticity of the Party-supervised media, weibo has to assume the role of bringing Chinese closer to veracity in some cases. As John Stuart Mill argued, "The only way in which a human being can make some approach to knowing the whole of a subject, is by hearing what can be said about it by persons of every variety of opinion, and studying all modes in which it can be looked at by every character of mind."

Weibo is the channel for China's new middle class, after becoming economically well-off, to pursue more political rights, gain a higher quality of life, and cast their concerns about society. Chinese weibo users tend to follow strangers, such as stars, celebrities, and experts in certain fields. Many Big Vs fall into this category. They are social and political elites and, more importantly, online opinion leaders. Most of them have already gained status, fame, and authority in their own field. It would not be exaggerating to say these Big Vs are guiding, influencing, and even educating their followers. They have brought their insight and expertise into the discussion of contentious issues. Kai-Fu Lee, former Google China chief, has more than fifty-one million followers at Sina Weibo. Most of them are tech-savvy male students in their twenties. Lee tweets the latest developments in global high technology and calls for more freedom of expression. He tweets his humor, wisdom, outspokenness, and experience. He nurtures the younger generation with his prolific tweets. His weibo accounts at Sina Weibo and Tencent Weibo were closed for three days in February 2013, after he questioned the management of a search engine, Jike, run by the *People's Daily*, the Party's mouthpiece.

In this sense, those weibo opinion leaders are contributing to social change in China. Employing state-of-the-art communication technologies and promulgating rules and regulations to compel microbloggers to self-censor, even to reticence, is morally wrong. It constrains people from expressing what they deem is right and true.

Maybe one of Kai-Fu Lee's weibo posts could best summarize the attitude toward weibo: "Reposting weibos is a power, and responsibility. We spread messages, not rumors; observe, not follow blindly; be critical, without violating truth; straightforward, not foul-mouthed. You and I are not just visitors, but active participants. Let weibos be clear and warm, starting with ourselves."

Despite the thorough censorship, weibo users are still talking about censored issues using veiled references. Research shows that weibo works as a conduit for the Chinese to develop a better understanding of politics, since it is one of the few media platforms where anti-government voices may be heard.

The wise way is not to stifle such voices but to let them go, as the legend about how Yu the Great controls the waters says.

Tao Fu
University of International Business and Economics

See also Ethical Censorship; Global First Amendment; Twitter and Traditional Media

Further Reading

Albrechtslund, A. "Online Social Networking as Participatory Surveillance." *First Monday* 13, no. 3-3 (2008). http://firstmonday.org/article/view/2142/1949.

Ansfield, J. "How Crash Cover-up Altered China's Succession." *New York Times,* December 4, 2012. http://www.nytimes.com/2012/12/05/world/asia/how-crash-cover-up-altered-chinas-succession.html.

Ansfield, J., and C. Buckley. "China Focusing Graft Inquiry on Ex-official." *New York Times,* December 15, 2013. http://www.nytimes.com/2013/12/16/world/asia/china-presses-corruption-inquiry-of-powerful-former-security-official.html?_r=0.

Bamman, D., B. O'Connor, and N. A. Smith. "Censorship and Deletion Practices in Chinese Social Media." *First Monday* 17, no. 3-5 (2012). http://firstmonday.org/ojs/index.php/fm/article/view/3943/3169.

"Beijing Orders New Controls on 'Weibo' Microblogs." BBC, December 16, 2011. http://www.bbc.co.uk/news/world-asia-china-16212578.

"Beijingshi chutai weibo guanli guiding: Fabu shiyi lei neirong weifa (Beijing Released Regulations to Supervise Weibo: Posting 11 Categories of Tweets Will Be Ruled Unlawful)." *Beijing Evening News,* December 16, 2011. http://news.xinhuanet.com/politics/2011-12/16/c_122436394.htm.

"Big Vs and Bottom Lines." *Economist,* August 31, 2013. http://www.economist.com/news/china/21584385-authorities-move-against-some-chinas-most-vocal-microbloggers-big-vs-and-bottom-lines.

Bishop, B. "Translation of Beijing's New Weibo Regulations." *DigiCha,* December 16, 2011. http://digicha.com/index.php/2011/12/translation-of-beijings-new-weibo-regulations.

boyd, d. "Social Network Sites: Public, Private, or What?" *Knowledge Tree* 13 (May 2007).

Branigan, T. "China's Leadership Faces Fresh Scandal over Fatal Ferrari Crash." *Guardian,* September 3, 2012. http://www.theguardian.com/world/2012/sep/03/china-scandal-fatal-ferrari-crash.

Caragliano, D. "Why China's 'Real Name' Internet Policy Doesn't Work." *Atlantic,* March 26, 2013. http://www.theatlantic.com/china/archive/2013/03/why-chinas-real-name-internet-policy-doesnt-work/274373.

Chan, M., X. Wu, Y. Hao, R. Xi, and T. Jin. "Microblogging, Online Expression, and Political Efficacy among Young Chinese Citizens: The Moderating Role of Information and Entertainment Needs in the Use of Weibo." *Cyberpsychology, Behavior, and Social Networking* 15, no. 7 (2012): 345–349.

Chao, L. "Sina, Tencent Shut Down Commenting on Microblogs." *Wall Street Journal,* March 31, 2012. http://online.wsj.com/news/articles/SB10001424052702303816504577314400064661814.

Chen, S. J. "China's Weibo Guru, Kai-fu Lee." *Forbes,* January 20, 2012. http://www.forbes.com/sites/china/2012/01/20/chinas-weibo-guru-kai-fu-lee.

Chen, Z., P. Liu, X. Wang, and Y. Gu. "Follow Whom? Chinese Users Have Different Choice." *ArXiv,* December 1, 2012. http://arxiv.org/abs/1212.0167?.

Chin, J., and P. Mozur. "Gloom Falls over Chinese Web as Lee Kai-Fu Reveals Cancer Diagnosis." *Wall Street Journal,* September 6, 2013. http://blogs.wsj.com/chinarealtime/2013/09/06/gloom-falls-over-chinese-web-as-lee-kai-fu-reveals-cancer-diagnosis.

"Decisions by the CPC Central Committee on Several Important Questions Concerning the Building of a Socialist Harmonious Society." *Xinhua,* October 18, 2006. http://cpc.people.com.cn/GB/64093/64094/4932424.html.

Deleuze, G., and F. Guarrati. *A Thousand Plateaus: Capitalism and Schizophrenia.* Translated by B. Massumi. Minneapolis: University of Minnesota Press, 1987.

Demick, B. "Former China's Security Chief Zhou Yongkang Reportedly Probed for Graft." *Los Angeles Times,* December 16, 2013. http://www.latimes.com/world/worldnow/la-fg-wn-china-corruption-zhou-yongkang-20131216,0,5889055.story#axzz2o2nJHsGf.

Foucault, M. *Discipline and Punish: The Birth of the Prison*. Translated by A. Sheridan. New York: Vintage Books, 1995.

Freivogel, W. H. "Does the Communications Decency Act Foster Indecency?" *Communication Law and Policy* 16 (2011): 17–48. doi:10.1080/10811680.2011.536496.

Fu, K., C. Chan, and M. Chau. "Assessing Censorship on Microblogs in China: Discriminatory Keyword Analysis and the Real-Name Registration Policy." *IEEE Internet Computing* 17, no. 3 (2013): 42–50. doi:10.1109/MIC.2013.28.

Fu, K., and M. Chau. "Reality Check for the Chinese Microblog Space: A Random Sampling Approach." *PLoS ONE* 8, no. 3 (2013). doi: 10.1371/journal.pone.0058356.

Guan, W., et al. "Analyzing User Behavior of the Micro-Blogging Website Sina Weibo during Hot Social Events." *ArXiv,* October 24, 2013. http://arxiv.org/abs/1304.3898?.

Hachten, W. A. "Development and Theory of the Media." In *New Media for a New China,* edited by J. F. Scotton and W. A. Hachten, 28–42. Malden, MA: Wiley-Blackwell, 2011.

Hewitt, D. "Weibo Brings Change to China." BBC, July 31, 2012. http://www.bbc.co.uk/news/magazine-18887804.

Hille, K. "Real Name Rule to Add to Sina Weibo's Woes." *Financial Times,* February 28, 2012. http://www.ft.com/cms/s/0/e995b7aa-6201-11e1-807f-00144feabdc0.html#axzz2nw58I5vX.

Internet Regulation and Data Privacy in China. Pillsbury Law, 2013. http://www.pillsburylaw.com/siteFiles/Publications/Internet_RegulationChina_032613.pdf.

Jiang, S. "Chinese Netizens Outraged over Response to Fatal Bullet Train Crash." CNN, July 26, 2011. http://www.cnn.com/2011/WORLD/asiapcf/07/25/china.train.accident.outrage/index.html.

Jiang, S. "Why Has Chinese Media Coverage of Beijing's Smog Been So Unflinching?" *Tea Leaf Nation,* January 15, 2013. http://www.tealeafnation.com/2013/01/why-has-chinese-media-coverage-of-beijings-smog-been-so-unflinching.

Johnson, I. "Coup Rumors Spur China to Hem in Social Networking Sites." *New York Times,* March 31, 2012. http://www.nytimes.com/2012/04/01/world/asia/china-shuts-down-web-sites-after-coup-rumors.html?_r=0.

Lam, O. "China: Sina Weibo Manager Discloses Online Censorship Practices." *Global Voices Advocacy,* January 7, 2013. http://advocacy.globalvoicesonline.org/2013/01/07/china-sina-weibo-manager-discloses-internal-censorship-practices.

Larson, C. "How China Censors Weibo." *Businessweek,* March 12, 2013.

Lee, J. "First Amendment Essay: Regulating Blogging and Microblogging in China." *Oregon Law Review* 91, no. 2 (2013): 609.

Li, Y., et al. "What Are Chinese Talking about in Hot Weibos?" *ArXiv,* May 10, 2013. http://arxiv.org/abs/1304.4682v2.

Liu, W. "China Draws Seven 'Red Lines' in the Sand for Internet Conduct." *Context China,* September 2013. http://contextchina.com/2013/09/china-draws-seven-red-lines-in-the-sand-for-internet-conduct.

Lu, J., and Y. Qiu. "Microblogging and Social Change in China." *Asian Perspectives* 37 (2013): 305–311.

Lu, W. "Liberty and Order in Cyber Space." *China Daily,* September 9, 2013. http://usa.chinadaily.com.cn/china/2013-09-09/content_16955871.htm.

Meriwether, A. "A User Contract for Chinese Microbloggers." Herdict Blog, June 7, 2012. http://blogs.law.harvard.edu/herdict/2012/06/07/a-user-contract-for-chinese-microbloggers.

Miles, P. C., and L. Zhang. "China Turns to Tweeting: Exploring the Problematic Use of Tweeting in China." *International Journal of Business and Social Science* 3, no. 2 (2012): 91–94.

Mill, J. S. *On Liberty*. New York: Gateway, 1955.

"Minitrue: Song of the Civilized Internet." *China Digital Times,* December 19, 2013. http://chinadigitaltimes.net/2013/12/minitrue-song-civilized-internet.

"The Power of Microblogs: Zombie Followers and Fake Retweets." *Economist,* March 12,

2012. http://www.economist.com/node/21550333.

Public Opinion Research Laboratory of Shanghai Jiaotong University. "Annual Report on Chinese Microblog in 2011." In *The Report on Chinese Social Opinion and Crisis Management 2012,* edited by G. Xie, R. Liu, and P. Wang, 364–394. Beijing: Social Sciences Academic Press, 2012.

Ramstad, E. "South Korea Court Knocks Down Online Real-Name Rule." *Wall Street Journal,* August 24, 2012. http://online.wsj.com/news/articles/SB100008723963904440829045776067941676 15620.

SARFT. *Zhongguo guangbo dianshi bianji jizhe zhiye daode zhunze* (Professional Code of Ethics for Chinese Broadcasting Editors and Journalists), February 7, 2005. http://www.sarft.gov.cn/articles/2005/02/07/20070920151122290888.html.

"Shi Shusi: The State of Weibo." *China Digital Times,* December 18, 2013. http://chinadigitaltimes.net/2013/12/shi-shusi-state-weibo.

"*Shifang zheng nengliang* (Radiating Positive Energy)." *China Daily,* February 22, 2013. http://www.chinadaily.com.cn/opinion/2013-02/22/content_16246125.htm.

Tanner, M. "China Rethinks Unrest." *Washington Quarterly* 27, no. 3 (2004): 137–156. doi:10.1162/016366004323090304.

Tong, J., and L. Zuo. "Weibo Communication and Government Legitimacy in China: A Computer-Assisted Analysis of Weibo Messages on Two 'Mass Incidents.'" *Information, Communication and Society* 17, no. 1 (2014): 66–85. doi:10.1080/1369118X.2013.839730.

Tong, Y., and S. Lei. "Large-Scale Mass Incidents and Government Responses in China." *International Journal of China Studies* 1, no. 2 (2010): 487–508.

Wan, A. "Former Google China Head Lee Kai-Fu Sows Seeds of Change." *South China Morning Post,* August 8, 2013. http://www.scmp.com/news/china/article/1295061/lee-kai-fu-nurtures-start-ups-and-hopes-better-china.

"*Wangyi xuanbu weibo yonghu chao 2.6 yi, tengxun 4.69 yi, xinlang 3.68 yi* (Netease Declares 260 Million Registered Users with Tencent at 469 Million and Sina 368 Million)." Techweb, October 19, 2012. http://www.techweb.com.cn/internet/2012-10-19/1247107.shtml.

"Weibo to Start Real Name Registration." *Global Times,* December 17, 2011. http://www.globaltimes.cn/NEWS/tabid/99/ID/688778/Weibo-to-start-real-name-registration.aspx.

Wu, L. "Mass Incidents of Ethnic Minorities in China: A Political Sociology Perspective." *Modern China Studies* 16, no. 4 (2009): 34–48.

Young, D. *The Party Line: How the Media Dictates Public Opinion in Modern China.* Singapore: John Wiley & Sons, 2013.

Zeng, F. "Discussion on Media Report on Group Events." *Asian Culture and History* 4, no. 1 (2012): 54–64.

Zhang, L., and I. Pentina. "Motivations and Usage Patterns of Weibo." *Cyberpsychology, Behavior & Social Networking* 15, no. 6 (2012): 312–317. doi:10.1089/cyber.2011.0615.

"*Zhongguo xinwen gongzuozhe zhiye daode zhunze xiudingban quanwen* (Professional Code of Ethics for Chinese Journalists)." *China News,* November 27, 2009. http://www.chinanews.com/gn/news/2009/11-27/1988722.shtml.

Zhu, T., D. Phipps, A. Pridgen, J. R. Crandall, and D. S. Wallach. "Tracking and Quantifying Censorship on a Chinese Microblogging Site." *ArXiv,* November 26, 2012. http://arxiv.org/abs/1211.6166?.

50

READER COMMENTS

This article explores legal and ethical issues that arise from reader comments on others' work in digital media, such as blogs or professionally produced news articles. It extends the legal and ethical analysis to other contexts that arise in interactive media when a service or individual that provides digital content allows users to make contributions: for example, posts of status updates on Facebook, images on Instagram, videos on YouTube, or comments on any of these. The two main legal issues explored are liability for contributions that are defamatory or include copyright-protected content. Ethical issues include when a host should allow comments, and the extent to which hosts should moderate contributions to advance goals like quality and balance. Practices and technical mechanisms that hosts use to achieve these goals are also explored.

Legal Liability

Legal questions about contributions arise in multiple contexts. Some services, like online versions of newspapers, provide professionally edited content but also allow readers' comments. For content like blogs, questions include whether a blog-hosting service is responsible for content its users post, as well as whether the owner of a particular blog is responsible for comments that visitors post to the blog. For social media, analogous questions are whether a service provider like Facebook or Twitter is responsible for users' content and whether a particular Facebook user is responsible for comments on her posts. Finally, for Internet Service Providers that deliver all of these kinds of content to their users, there are questions about the circumstances in which they are legally responsible for it.

Though the details of these matters quickly become technical, they involve fundamental questions of freedom of expression: Under what conditions is the host of a conversation liable for content that others contribute? The next sections address how, in many jurisdictions, legislatures and courts have taken measures to limit liability for users' contributions.

This summary emphasizes Anglo-American law. The United States has been a leader in developing both the technology and the law in this area, in some instances on the basis of common law with origins in the United Kingdom. Moreover, the United States is home to many online services that benefit from these limits on liability, including Facebook, Twitter, Yelp, and YouTube.

Defamatory Contributions

In the United States, many of the legal issues that user contributions present were resolved in the early years of the Internet's proliferation by Congress's passage of the Communications Decency Act (CDA). The CDA, part of the Telecommunications Act of 1996, was originally introduced in the U.S. Senate, and it focused on regulation of decency online— i.e., sexual content. The U.S. House of Representatives amended the law to include Section 230, which has a broader scope. Section 230 says that "No provider or user of an interactive computer service shall be treated as the publisher or speaker of any information provided by another information content provider." The provisions of the CDA that prohibited indecency, and inspired the act's name, were ruled unconstitutional by the U.S. Supreme Court on grounds that they were vague and overbroad, i.e., they regulate more expression than is constitutionally permissible. But CDA Section 230 was unaffected by that ruling, and thus provides immunity against liability for comments uploaded by others, including defamation liability. Though many Section 230 cases involve defamation, immunity has also been upheld in state contract and criminal cases, as well as a variety of federal claims. The Electronic Frontier Foundation, the U.S.-based civil liberties organization, calls Section 230 "the most important law protecting Internet speech."

In defamation law—the law that allows a party to obtain a legal remedy for published content that tends to harm reputation— legal liability for off-line material may depend on whether one is deemed an author of the material, a publisher of it, or a distributor. An author creates material. A publisher has knowledge of the material and the opportunity to exercise editorial control over it. Classic examples are a publisher or editor of a newspaper or a book. If one is a mere distributor of material, one may not be fully liable for defamatory content. Classic examples of distributors are a librarian, bookstore, or newsstand. Such distributors are generally not legally liable for content unless they have actual knowledge that it is defamatory, e.g., a bookseller is made aware that a book is libelous. Thus, in the early days of the Internet's proliferation, before Section 230, a legal question became whether service providers are publishers or distributors of information.

If an online service is not deemed a publisher of defamatory content, it may still be deemed a distributor. Does this mean that if an online service has actual knowledge that material is defamatory, it is liable? Section 230 was introduced in response to the decision in *Stratton Oakmont v. Prodigy* (1995) that because an Internet Service Provider took measures to edit content, it was deemed a publisher of the content rather than a distributor and could be held fully liable for defamation. The decision thus created a disincentive for a service provider to exercise editorial control: If a content provider chose to exercise editorial control, it could then face liability.

However, a leading case on the issue of liability of distributors, decided on the basis of Section 230, found that distributors are a subset of publishers, and that distributors have immunity even when they have knowledge of unlawful expression. In *Zeran v. America Online* (1997), Ken Zeran sued America Online (AOL), the Internet Service Provider, for posts to an AOL bulletin board by anonymous users that were potentially defamatory because they alleged that Zeran was selling T-shirts with slogans celebrating the 1995 bombing of the Oklahoma City federal building. Zeran contacted AOL, requesting removal of the messages. AOL complied, though Zeran and AOL disputed the date on which AOL complied. More messages were posted, and AOL again removed them. Zeran sued AOL for defamation, arguing that AOL was negligent in allowing the material to be posted. The Fourth Circuit Court of Appeals ruled that AOL was not liable, and that the scope of Section 230 was broad, barring causes of action for torts under federal law against service providers for content originating with third parties. Thus, whether a service is deemed a publisher or distributor, and whether it has received notice of defamatory content (and thus, may have actual knowledge of it), is not relevant.

The court in *Zeran* explained that Congress chose to create legal immunity even when the service provider has notice of the defamatory content. If a law were to allow liability when the service provider has notice, the law creates an incentive for the service provider to remove content upon notification that it is defamatory, whether or not it is actually defamatory,

rather than risking further legal proceedings for failing to remove it. The court in *Zeran v. America Online* explained that the intention of Congress, which the text of the statute as well as the *Congressional Record* reflect, was to create broad immunity, regardless of notice, because it is more protective of online expression. Congress noted that it would be impossible to successfully screen millions of user contributions for legally actionable content, but it sought to remove disincentives for service providers to exercise at least minimal control over content, such as by screening for and blocking content containing offensive words.

Experts appear to be interpreting the CDA broadly to include blogs and social media, though cases are few. An individual blog owner who is the author of a post, or the contributor of a comment to another blog, can both be deemed the "information content providers" of those posts and suffer liability for them. A blog owner can also be deemed an "interactive computer service" because others can comment on her blog, but cannot be held liable for comments that others make. The blog-hosting service, and the Internet Service Provider that transmits the blog (among other content), can also be deemed "interactive computer services" that cannot be liable for the contents of the blog owner or the commenters on her blog. Selecting and editing comments have been deemed protected under Section 230, though the Electronic Frontier Foundation suggests that perhaps a blogger can lose immunity by changing the meaning of another's comments or contributions, thus crossing the line into being an author. Section 230 appears to apply in analogous ways to social media like Facebook, insulating the owner of a Facebook page from liability for others' comments, as well as insulating Facebook itself, and Internet Service Providers, from liability for Facebook content. Authors of Facebook posts, on their own or others' pages, are legally responsible for their content.

CDA Section 230 immunity has its limits. There are contexts in which it is not applicable, though that does not of course mean that one has no defenses in those contexts. Section 230 does not create exemptions from liability under federal criminal law. The CDA specifically provides no immunity for violation of intellectual property law, which is addressed more specifically by statutes including the Digital Millennium Copyright Act, a U.S. federal law addressed in the next section. Regarding state law, the CDA, a federal statute, says, "No cause of action may be brought and no liability may be imposed under any State or local law that is inconsistent with this section." Thus, state law that is inconsistent with Section 230, in the sense that it creates greater liability than under federal law, is preempted. But in *Perfect 10, Inc. v. CCBill* (2007), a federal circuit court ruled that CDA Section 230's reference to copyright law applied only to federal copyright law; Section 230 could provide immunity from liability under state law for intellectual property violations. State intellectual property law can involve causes of action that are not part of federal copyright law, as was true in that case, which involved the state of California's law of right of publicity—the right to control the commercial use of one's name and image.

Critics have suggested that Section 230 creates extra protection for online defamation beyond what is available off-line, but the law's defenders claim that Section 230 is only meant to ensure that liability for defamatory content is allocated to those actually responsible for creating it. One consequence is that one may have no legal remedy if one is libeled online but cannot identify the publisher, or the publisher is judgment proof, i.e., financially insolvent.

Many nations, including Canada and Japan, lack limitations on third parties' liability analogous to Section 230. In the United Kingdom, the Defamation Act of 1996 provides that one is not a publisher for purposes of defamation law if one is merely the operator or provider of equipment and services for transmitting messages. However, the exceptions to this general rule are important in some cases. In a landmark 2001 ruling in the United Kingdom, *Godfrey v. Demon Internet Service,* physics lecturer Laurence Godfrey asked a major U.K. Internet Service Provider, Demon Internet, to remove a post from a discussion group on Usenet, an early Internet technology. Godfrey alleged that the post, which appeared to be from him, was forged and defamatory of him. Demon did not remove the message, which remained on the server for ten days before it was automatically deleted, like all old messages. Godfrey, who was unable to identify who posted the message, sued Demon Internet for not removing the message when he complained. The court ruled that an ISP's transmission of the message could be a publication for purposes of defamation law. Under additional provisions of the Defamation Act of 1996, it is a defense to defamation that one "did not know, and had no reason to believe, that what he did caused or contributed to the publication of a defamatory statement" and took "reasonable care in relation to its publication." The court ruled that once Godfrey alerted Demon to the posting, Demon could no longer claim that it took reasonable care and did not contribute to the publication. Demon then settled out of court, paying Godfrey £15,000 plus legal costs of over £200,000.

Copyright-Infringing Contributions

In intellectual property law, similar questions arise as in defamation law: when does one enjoy immunity, referred to as a legal "safe harbor," for material that others post? Section 230 of the Communications Decency Act does not affect federal intellectual property law. It specifically says, "Nothing in this section shall be construed to limit or expand any law pertaining to intellectual property." It is the Online Copyright Infringement Liability Limitation Act (OCILLA), passed as part of the Digital Millennium Copyright Act (DMCA), that addresses limitations on the liability of service providers for copyright infringement in some circumstances.

The DMCA safe harbor applies if one does not know of copyright infringement. When one has "actual knowledge" of illegal activity, one may face liability. The law includes "notice and takedown" provisions under which one can escape liability if one is given notice of illegal content (i.e., notified about it by the copyright holder) and acts expeditiously to remove it or disable access to it.

DMCA also obliges services to terminate users for repeated or blatant copyright infringement, to designate an agent to receive notifications of infringement, and to inform users of such policies. A user whose material was removed can file a "counter-notice" demanding that the service provider restore the material or face liability for taking it down.

The safe harbor provisions have been interpreted broadly to apply not only to Internet Service Providers that provide service to users' homes, businesses, and mobile devices, but also providers of all sorts of online content, including e-mail, news, music, and movies. DMCA safe harbor has been interpreted to apply to search engines, which now receive millions of requests annually to remove content, although they may not have been liable merely for linking to infringing content. Experts have interpreted the safe harbor to apply not only to blog-hosting and social media services but also to their individual users, though cases are few.

The question arose in the *Viacom v. YouTube* (2013) litigation of whether general knowledge of widespread infringement or actual knowledge of specific infringement is required to trigger this obligation to act expeditiously. The court ruled that it was specific instances of infringement that triggered this obligation. YouTube went beyond the requirements of the DMCA and installed an automated system known as "ContentID" in 2008 that checks for content that matches uploaded material against tens of millions of samples that copyright owners have registered. Once a match is detected, the policies of the content owner are followed: it is either blocked, or if the copyright owner's policy is to "monetize" the content, the content is allowed and the copyright owner shares revenue from advertising that runs next to the content. Thus, even if material like a recording of the performance of a song at a concert is technically infringing, the original copyright owner can choose to make money off the advertising that runs on YouTube. Though the DMCA does not require such proactive policing for infringing content, in its litigation Viacom did not seek damages for any allegedly infringing activity after it was installed.

Because one can be held liable if one has been notified of infringing content but does nothing, immunity under the DMCA is arguably not as broad as that offered by Section 230 for defamation. Though the burden on the service provider to respond to takedown requests can be substantial, the DMCA places the onus of pursuing copyright infringement primarily on the copyright owner, rather than the service provider.

The European Union (EU) has adopted some broadly similar exemptions of service providers from copyright liability and from obligations to police users' activity on their services. The EU Parliament's Electronic Commerce Directive of 2000 lays out provisions for member states to follow. It exempts service providers from liability if the service does not have actual knowledge of "illegal activity or information." If a service provider becomes aware of infringing activity, it must "expeditiously" remove or disable access to the material. The European Court of Justice ruled, in response to a case from Belgium, that national courts cannot order ISPs to monitor customers' communication to police illegal file sharing. Among

justifications the court cited were customers' rights to privacy and free speech.

One difference from the U.S. copyright law is that the EU rules fail to lay out notice and takedown provisions, but encourage member states to do so. Because most member states have failed to do so, questions remain about how a service provider should be notified, how quickly it must take down infringing material, and whether there is a right to argue that the material is not illegal. Critics charge that these questions leave a lack of "legal certainty," which is the ability of those governed by the law to guide their conduct in accordance with the law.

Ethics: Building in Accountability

The Society of Professional Journalists, based in the United States, includes an obligation in its 1996 ethics code to be accountable to readers, which includes the sub-obligation to "clarify and explain news coverage and invite dialogue with the public over journalistic conduct." Such dialogue can of course occur through reader comments. Accountability is an obligation that is recognized to some extent by creators of media such as blogs as well, whether or not they view themselves, or others view them, as engaging in journalism. In any medium in which third-party comments and other contributions appear—such as audience comments on professionally produced work, comments on a blog entry, or comments on social media such as a Facebook page—comments can enhance accountability to users. Comments that expose the harms a content creator causes, or the creator's errors or biases, can advance the goal of holding the creator ethically accountable.

Reader comments are part of a long tradition in journalism of inviting reader feedback, with origins in publishing letters to the editor. There is social-scientific evidence from experiments suggesting that readers make inferences based on comments about public support for their own and others' positions, about the news articles they accompany, and even about the underlying issues. If comments influence readers' views, some may wish to treat them more carefully, though it is of course difficult to draw ethical lines about what is inappropriate influence on users' views.

Digital media often give creators the power to moderate third-party comments, so questions arise about the extent to moderate, if at all. In any normative ethical theory in which deception is potentially unethical, appearing to be viewpoint neutral while actually engaging in viewpoint discrimination is an ethical issue. Moderators of comments may be tempted to select comments in a biased way without revealing their bias. They may be tempted to remove critical comments, or comments they disagree with, or not approve them for posting in the first place.

How should editors and content creators operationalize obligations of accountability regarding user comments? The discourse ethics of Jürgen Habermas (1990) and of Theodore L. Glasser and James S. Ettema (2008) identify decisions as ethically justified when they can be justified through free and open dialogue with stakeholders. Mark Cenite and Yu Zhang (2010) draw upon discourse ethics to propose obligations for news content providers to follow regarding user comments, which can be part of a dialogue between readers and viewers with journalists. Cenite and Zhang suggest that news content providers set general policies on when to allow and moderate comments, in order to guard against making biased decisions about whether to include comments in individual cases; allow relevant, non-abusive user complaints about their work; and respond to such feedback, in order to promote journalistic accountability.

Allowing a varied selection of comments can go far to advance the ethical goal of journalistic accountability while also enhancing the reader experience. Content providers vary in the policies they use to advance these goals. Some allow a free-for-all, in which comments are unmoderated. Some allow anonymous and pseudonymous comments to facilitate the broadest range of uninhibited views. Others, such as the *Wall Street Journal*, require commenters to use actual full names, in an attempt to encourage commentators' accountability and more civil discourse. In many sources, moderation of comments is undertaken, including deletion of content based on quality, relevance, offensiveness, legality, or to ensure a balance of views. Some content hosts adopt point systems, where readers or individual comments may be featured more prominently if they are rated highly by others. Some allow commenters with high ratings to bypass such moderation.

Looking to the Future

In the pages of a printed newspaper, the publisher might be held liable for libel and copyright infringement even if material was contributed by a reader in a letter to the editor. In interactive digital media, where user contributions are rapid and high volume, legal liability has been limited in the United States and elsewhere to reduce the burden to screen content and thus to promote growth of these media. Authoritative rulings are few on the extent to which legal immunity applies to social media. Ethical issues of how much to moderate content that others post take on a new urgency in those news media and blogs that attempt some editorial control over contributions. Some interactive media are adopting technical measures to assist in moderation, whereas others have abandoned moderation entirely.

Mark Cenite
Nanyang Technological University

See also Journalism: Communications Decency and Indecency; Online Reporting; Reporter's Privilege/Poster's Privilege

Further Reading

Cenite, Mark, and Yu Zhang. "Recommendations for Hosting Audience Comments Based on Discourse Ethics." *Journal of Mass Media Ethics* 25, no. 4 (2010): 293–309.

Electronic Frontier Foundation. "Section 230 of the Communications Decency Act," n.d. https://www.eff.org/issues/cda230.

Glasser, Theodore L., and James S. Ettema. "Ethics and Eloquence in Journalism: An Approach to Press Accountability." *Journalism Studies* 9, no. 4 (2008): 512–534.

Habermas, Jürgen. *Moral Consciousness and Communicative Action*. Cambridge, MA: MIT Press, 1990.

Society of Professional Journalists. "Code of Ethics [SPJ Code]," 1996. http://www.spj.org/ethicscode.asp.

51

FROM PACKET SWITCHING TO PORN AND POLITICS

Protection and Censorship in Online Search

There was a time when questioning Google's search algorithm was the height of any assumed wrongdoing by an online search provider. Wondering if it was ethical to provide search results by popularity rankings might seem trivial now in light of the many other issues facing search users, search providers, and Internet Service Providers in general. While often considered the "Wild West" of many things, the Internet and its users have faced and will continue to face many dilemmas. Court rulings dealing with Net Neutrality, the FCC, and big business in early 2014 put a new spin on what we might begin seeing as consumers online as search giants like Google move outside the search box and into ever-expanding markets, including everything from technology gadgets and applications to education and lifestyle products. At the time of this publication the debate over whether the Internet or access to it should be a public utility was reaching a boil but simmering down quickly on the side of the commercial marketplace.

As we look at the issue of censorship and online search, we should remember that while the network that eventually became the Internet was created with purpose through the work of many interested scientists and researchers in the 1960s, the World Wide Web that we know today is very much the result of organic growth fed by the public, the private, the governmental, and the commercial sectors of our world. It is the product of a kind of growth that has been mostly unhindered by rules or previously imposed structures. This fact presents a very interesting study in how injustice is defined and dealt with. It is also worth noting that the terms Internet and World Wide Web essentially describe two different things but will be used interchangeably throughout this chapter.

This will be a brief look at the beginnings of the Internet and how its foundational structure set the path for the growth and change we have seen over time. With that perspective in mind we will look at the potential pitfalls of giant search engines and the control they wield over how and what we consume online. In addition, advances in tangible technologies like smartphones will be discussed in regard to their relationship to these search giants.

History

When looking at the legal and ethical health of an organism like the World Wide Web, an understanding of its history offers valuable perspective on current issues. When four host computers were connected together to form ARPANET at the end of 1969, the "budding Internet" was off the ground, according to the Internet Society's *Brief History of the Internet*. ARPANET was the seedling of what was to become what we now understand as the living and breathing Internet. The successful ARPANET experiment was followed in 1972 by the development of the first basic electronic-mail application. As with most Web-related applications, the initial development was quickly expanded and enhanced by other developers within just a few months to include even more operations and uses. E-mail was the largest network application for over a decade and remains a foundational and vital part of our working and personal digital lives.

As ARPANET evolved it was the first of many efforts to connect network nodes on the "information superhighway." It is important to note that this developing Internet was built on the concept of open-architecture networking. According to the Internet Society, in an open-architecture network "the individual networks may be separately designed and developed and each may have its own unique interface which it may offer to users and/or other providers, including other Internet providers." The open-architecture concept meant very specific elements could be created for the environment and user, and while there were no official constraints on type or geography, pragmatic considerations were important. This very open approach was the foundation for the resource we know today and set the tone for its future growth.

That rapid and amazing growth took the young Internet, just a simple collection of separate computer networks linked together, and helped it evolve into the World Wide Web, a global system for identifying, organizing, linking, and locating information on those networks. Most of the early motivations for development in this arena were primarily for resource sharing. E-mail applications that used the Internet architecture changed how people collaborated and can be considered a first step toward more intense forms of collaboration, such as social media. Even the devices we carry every day in our pockets, packed with collaboration applications and opportunities for information sharing, can be seen as the offspring of these early applications and developments.

Technology has always played a key element in our evolving social structures and norms. Whether one has more impact over the other can be left for debate by the technological determinists and their opponents, but the relationship between the two remains important. The Internet Society poignantly concludes its brief history of the Internet by alluding to "the next social structure" and how it will guide the Internet in the future. It predicts the form of that new structure will be harder and harder to find, and it cites the cause of that challenge as being the ever-growing number of concerned stakeholders in the Internet. These stakeholders include commercial, public, and private interests that can often be at odds. Any stumbling along the way, it says, "will not be because we lack for technology, vision, or motivation. It will be because we cannot set a direction and march collectively into the future." While the Internet Society's brief history is somewhat dated, this closing sentiment still rings true and the future of the Internet remains up for debate as stakeholders continue to argue over best practices, next steps, and ownership.

The Ethics of Search

To put it in numbers, the Pew Research Center tracked American adult Internet use from 1995 to 2014 and saw a rise from 14 percent to 87 percent. While this is only a study of American use, it still presents a picture of just how many people navigate the World Wide Web. Online search engines are the most used method for that navigation. With that in mind, another Pew project in 2005 found that one of the early issues with search online was the implementation of paid search results. The study found, however, that

users felt displaying certain results at the top of a search return list was acceptable so long as it was clear it was a paid result, or the practices were fully disclosed. While paid search results are not as much of an issue in today's search landscape, there are other issues. Within the current population of search users there seems to be a fairly widely held assumption that a user receives authentic or organic (unaltered) results when searching online; keywords typed into a box return information, factual entries devoid of partiality. This may be true of some lesser-known search engines that draw from the results of many other search providers; however, the most popular engines, such as Google or Bing, operate on algorithms complicated with popularity rankings and commercial interests and held in secret under lock and key. A 2007 study on user trust in search engines used eye-tracking technology (partially funded by Google) and found that users would benefit from receiving more information on a search results page explaining how the results were cultivated.

If we want an analogy for the ethics of search, we can look to libraries. A librarian who only wants to perpetuate information and texts that support certain ideas, and guides patrons to those texts only, would be seen as unethical. Large engines can operate in much the same way by tailoring algorithms, allowing discriminatory autocompleted search terms, and limiting or not limiting search results. Google's mantra of "do no evil" has come under fire for such actions and more. They have often fallen into the "damned if you do, damned if you don't" trap with their products. From Google

Street View to ad-tailoring based on user searches to some of the company's other applications, such as Google Now, some would say Google just knows too much about us. Others would say Google just does good business. Data mining is not the company's only potential sin, but nor should Google be locked in the stocks just yet. Google has been seen as both villain and champion of copyright, another major issue of the digital world. As a champion, for instance, it has made image searches based on usage rights much easier, providing transparency to search users, as well as issuing over fifty million takedown notices for copyright infringement in 2012 (upon legal request), according to Mashable. Very much the middleman in many battles, Google has also upheld the tenets of free speech in other countries when governments would limit searches very strictly for their citizens. Google is first and foremost a commercial product, a for-profit business online; however, because of the services it provides, it has unceremoniously been yoked with the tasks (to name just a few) of upholding the tenets of free speech and protecting intellectual property, copyright, and the innocence of our children, all while providing seamless search functions and cool, new, and useful Web applications for business and education. Not a small task, to say the least. All while doing "no evil."

Why Google?

So why do we care what Google does? Google is really not the whole Internet though it may seem that way at times. It is most definitely a main entry point for the bulk of Internet users. The focus on Google is justified in that it remains leaps and bounds above other search engines in terms of users. In 2013, comScore data placed Google with a 65.2 percent share of search traffic. The second-place engine (China's Baidu) came in with just an 8.2 percent share. Online advertising company Chitika released a study that shows in the United States alone the population of all fifty states uses Google at least 50 percent of the time. Another study, conducted by the Pew Research Center in early 2012, cites respondents at 83 percent who use Google as their engine of choice. One *New York Times* article from 2008 still accurately portrays (based on the previously mentioned study results) Google as having more control over the shape of online expression than anyone else in the world. In this sense, Google is one huge juggernaut of speech protection, censorship, and bottom-line satisfaction decision making. It is potentially one of the most complicated systems of speech, communication, and information access in existence.

The Politics of Search Engines takes an in-depth look at the issues surrounding some of the more technical aspects of search online, but also highlights why these issues are political in nature and why they deserve inspection. The authors write that the issues are important because "what people (the seekers) are able to find on the Web determines what the Web consists of for them. And we all—individuals and institutions alike—have a great deal at stake in what the Web consists of." If we take a satirical view of what the Web consists of presently we might say the

Web is simply a collection of cat videos, humorous memes, and pornography. Since satire is also a pretty strong form of social criticism, what does that say about us as a society of search-engine users whose search entries ultimately create the Web? Our own participation online with search and other content creation plays an increasingly important role in how we in turn may be protected from various forms of injustice online.

The Censorship of Search

If we go back to the idea that Google is like some kind of ultimate librarian, keeper of the keys to unfathomable amounts of information, we can look at the discussion of censorship in categories. Search results removal, autocompletion of search terms, and autocorrection are just three of the forms of censorship (be it "soft" censorship or otherwise) Google has been known to participate in. These are also considered to be functions used and provided in order to create a more user-friendly or helpful environment online. As with many ethical debates we can ask whether good intention is enough to create an act worthy of being deemed "ethical" in the end. Is it acceptable for Google to remove a search result that leads to materials that violate copyright or is considered low quality while leaving results intact that lead to offensive, but otherwise legal materials? The Internet was once considered a very important tool for eliminating information gatekeepers in the big media landscape; it would now seem the evolution of the World Wide Web has essentially

created one ultimate gatekeeper. The big difference with this arrangement is the role Internet users have in controlling content, enacting change, and demanding corrections. Accessibility is a powerful tool, and every Internet user has potentially the same ability to right the wrongs of online censorship or misinformation.

In the cases of outright search results removal, the search giant can be like a massive eraser creating a revisionist history. Most of us feel that once something is put online (like that embarrassing vacation photo) it can never really be deleted, but what about items smudged out by Google, the archivist of archives? While not gone forever, it is decidedly more difficult to find something without assistance from a search engine. Are you more likely to use a link on page 2 of your search results or on page 72? Just like a librarian cultivates the collection for their patrons, Google cultivates the collection of Internet data for its users through various mechanisms.

In terms of actual censorship, examples are muddy, depending on your perspective. In 2006, Google dealt with issues in Turkey when a video posted on YouTube (a Google entity) sparked controversy and led the Turkish government to ban YouTube access in the country. While Google ostensibly resolved the issue by blocking certain content to Turkish IP addresses, YouTube users in the meantime voluntarily removed the offending video that sparked the debacle. This is one of many examples of the self-correcting nature of the Internet, a characteristic that will ultimately be the resource's most valuable protection against the majority of intrusions, be they on privacy, freedom of speech, or otherwise. While Google worked to solve the problem while maintaining its own Web traffic (it is a business after all), it can be said the search giant essentially censored materials to one population while preserving access to the same materials by the majority of YouTube users. The result was a "greater good" approach in a situation where others may have taken an all-or-nothing approach.

The Turkish example is a good one because it is fairly common in terms of video content, and often the material deemed offensive is removed by Internet users before any other action is taken. Users seem to be the first to cry foul; be it an erroneous tweet, Facebook post, or search result, they create a collective wisdom that acts as judge, jury, and executioner online more quickly than any corporate office or legal entity ever could. It is undeniable, however, the power Google has over what we see online, as mentioned previously. A *TechNewsWorld* opinion piece during the height of the 2012 U.S. presidential election highlights the potential impact search results can have on politics. While Google had seemingly cleaned up certain aspects of its algorithm in years previous to prevent third-party reputation managers from having too much influence over search results (referred to as Google bombing), Google itself still has control over the end product. The piece makes a bold claim that manipulation of search results during election season could heavily impact election results. Taking into account the fact that someone who is already in office will likely have more search results turn up in general, *TechNewsWorld*'s unofficial test

showed some disturbing results. It was fairly easy to see how the results might lead a journalist, for example, researching a political story toward many more negative pieces of information for a particular candidate. Whether or not Google itself was guilty of manipulating search results to favor one candidate over another during the 2012 election (which is the claim made by the author), the ease with which this kind of manipulation of search results can be accomplished should disturb us all. Simply comparing search results from one engine to another typically will reveal differences in how the results are returned, especially for hot topics. In addition, location services now offered by most search engines can further skew results. Someone in South Africa will receive much different returns on the term "Egypt" than will someone in the United States, even on the same engine.

The Huffington Post picked up where the *TechNewsWorld* piece left off and conducted a pilot study regarding search results. The study looked at what the potential impact of online search bias might be on public opinion. One example of this bias was described as something as simple as changing the order of the links returned when searching for stories about events or issues. In brief, the results of the study (which included six hundred subjects in the population sample) indicated that public opinion indeed can be altered by manipulating the order of results. Based on the study findings, the researchers allude to the ability to manipulate results as "entirely too easy" (though they do not offer further details on this), and further they opine "that search engine companies are at best delinquent and at worst complicit in allowing manipulation of order to be so easily achieved, and that the concentration of search represents a significant threat to our First Amendment rights to a free press." The study claimed that manipulation of results happens all the time through processes like Search Engine Optimization (SEO), whereby companies and individuals can develop their Web assets in such a way as to influence the order of appearance in keyword search returns. Study authors Eric Clemons and Steve Barnett indicate that "search engine vendors not only do not prevent manipulation, they help users perform manipulations" and suggest that a possible explanation for this is because it enables vendors to deflect problems with search results with responses like "it's not our fault you don't engage in SEO" when a company, website, or other content does not show up on the results list where they assume they should be. Another claim made in the report is drawn from comparing search vendors like Google to journalists or other media outlets. Clemons and Barnett highlight that vendors seem to be held to a lower standard and that lack of transparency makes manipulations easier to hide and harder to eliminate.

If we go back to the idea that Google might be able to influence an entire election, Clemons, in another Huffington Post article in 2012, indicates they can. Clemons points to previous testimony to the Senate Judiciary Subcommittee on Antitrust, Competition Policy, and Consumer Rights that documents a history of manipulation to organic search (meaning the search is understood to be free from manipulation and results presented are not of the paid variety). The authors target fairness in Google's practices and express concern in regard to the impact on public opinion. They write, "The key question here is whether this bias can have an impact on public opinion in a way that interferes with the public's ability to learn about candidates, and that interferes with candidates' ability to present themselves to voters." They go on to leverage their research, which indicates Google can "indeed abridge the public's ability to become and remain fully informed, by limiting the public's ability to hear what Google does not want heard," and further assert the power to manipulate public opinion is far greater in Google's hands than in those of any newspaper.

This opens another dark alley where a discussion as to whether search engine results qualify as protected speech is to be had. When legal issues online first arose in the early days of the World Wide Web, Internet Service Providers like America Online (AOL) served as intermediaries who could not really be held accountable for questionable materials (offensive, illegal, or otherwise) that appeared on their portals or passed through their channels online. Labeling Google as a publisher would change that categorization, and has already done so. A 2012 *New York Times* article exploring whether search results are protected speech focuses on a white paper commissioned by Google that builds the argument for Google-as-publisher. The paper, written by Eugene Volokh, professor at the University of California, Los Angeles, indicates Google operates more like a news editor, that "when Google assembles search results, it is communicating with its readers, and making selections about what to communicate." He likens this to a news editor deciding what to communicate to readers, where to place stories, and making judgment calls on the importance of items. Volokh even indicates this affords Google benefits from two sides. As an intermediary, it would be protected from accusations of copyright infringement if material in search results violates those laws, while as a publisher, it is protected by other existing laws (as in potential antitrust cases). Steven Shaw at ZDnet.com, in response to the Volokh paper, succinctly points out that "since actual people at Google manipulate the results—exactly how and how much Google won't say—the content is editorial in nature and is therefore as protected by the First Amendment as the front page of the *Wall Street Journal*." Shaw also very bluntly admits to Google being his choice engine and challenges legislators to try and make Google "more fair and less gigantic." In another example of how self-correction is important online, Shaw puts faith in Web users as a more effective disciplinarian online than government. He says if Google ever slips up or stops being the best, "the users will take care of the situation by the end of the week."

Another area of concern regarding search censoring and manipulation is Google's autocomplete function. When searching, the function creates a list of possible suggestions as you begin to type in your search terms. This essentially suggests terms that might complete the search you have begun to type. Sometimes this is immensely helpful, but often it is immensely offensive. A *Search Engine Watch* article from 2013 reviewed a UN

Women campaign to end misogynistic autocomplete suggestions regarding women on Google. When typing "women should" in Google's search bar, autocomplete suggestions included "stay at home, be slaves, be in the kitchen, not speak in church" and so on. The campaign was visually powerful and brought the important issue to light; however, it also managed to make the problem worse as people who saw the campaign went to Google and tried to replicate the autocomplete terms to see if it was true. This only served to solidify those autocomplete results as popular because of how the function is programmed. According to Google's help files: "Autocomplete predictions are algorithmically determined based on a number of factors, like popularity of search terms, without any human intervention. Just like the Web, the search terms shown may include silly or strange or surprising terms and phrases."

In addition to explaining how the terms are provided, Google also attempts to address discord with autocomplete in its help files, stating: "We try to reflect the diversity of content on the Web, some good, some objectionable. We also have a small set of removal policies for things like pornography, violence, hate speech, and terms that are frequently used to find content that violates copyrights." The company did use that "small set" of policies in 2011 to do away with autocomplete terms that were more likely to lead people to sites where pirated materials could be found. Jessica Lee in the *Search Engine Watch* article alludes to how protection from such ills may be found, saying, "Perhaps marketers have the greatest opportunity to make a change with their knowledge of how algorithms work. Maybe it's time we help take control of those results by putting content out there that is thought provoking and balanced for popular search queries." Again, as with other examples, this highlights how powerful the collective intellect and efforts of Internet users as a society can be. At the time of this writing in 2014 I was still able to produce the results "stay at home, not work, and be seen not heard" when searching the term "women should" in Google. Alternatively, when typing in the term "men should," no autocomplete results were provided. Digging deeper into Google and the relationship between the company and its applications and the users of those applications, you can quickly see how Google performs much like a mirror in terms of culture and society.

The third category focuses on auto-correction. This function is a much-loved and similarly hated function that operates as a foundation in many programs we use every day. Entire websites have been dedicated to the often hilarious, yet embarrassing communication situations created when we battle auto-correct, particularly on smartphone applications. At the end of 2013, with the release of the latest Android (Google-owned) operating system, Google banned 1,400 words from the 165,000-word dictionary included with the operating system, according to *Wired*. Effectively known as a "kill list," these words are loaded into the system and, when used, will either be redlined as being mis-spelled or, if the word is actually mis-spelled, no correction will be offered. In many text message or other chat applications, the words will be automatically corrected to the term Google's operating system deems most appropriate. According to the article and from personal experience, Google is not comfortable with or does not deem it appropriate for its customers to use anatomically correct terminology, discuss women's undergarments, use sexual (safe or otherwise) terms, and many other bizarre categories of words. *Wired* points out that while terms like "morphine" and "Demerol" are forbidden, "marijuana," "methamphetamine," and even "bong" pass muster. The article also highlights that "Islam-related words 'Sunni' and 'Iftar' are censored, but many others related to Muslim faith and other religions are kosher." Some of the determinations are almost laughable. "Butt" and "geek" are offered no assistance in autocorrect, and comedian George Carlin's seven dirty words, of course, are effectively "banned," according to the *Wired* article. The selection of words is noticeable and questionable. "Lactation," for instance, along with "thud" and "LSAT," "uterus" and "STI" are all effectively excluded. "Penis" is immediately corrected to "pen is." The function can of course be turned off, however we cannot ignore the fact that with the Pew Research Center reporting 56 percent of all American adults as smartphone users in 2013, and 28 percent of those being Android platform users (3 percent more than Apple's iPhone), Google reigns (if only slightly) in the mobile arena as well as in the search engine arena. More troubling than the situation itself is that most users may only see it as a minor annoyance rather than an infringement on their rights to speak freely as society becomes more accustomed to the "assistance" they receive from their smart devices. The *Daily Beast* asked the Electronic Frontier Foundation (EFF) about these kill lists. Jillian York, EFF's director of international freedom of expression, noted that the situation is not outright censorship but "it is annoying, and it's denying choice to customers." These comments were in reference to Apple's even larger (fourteen thousand) list of vocabulary no-no's.

In addition to autocorrect functions, the Google Hangouts chat system has an interesting way of handling those times when you just need to vent. When using the speech-to-text function, the system will kindly add asterisks in place of the letters in your favorite four-letter words.

Protection through Collective Intelligence

Many examples of data manipulation, censorship, or heavy-handed "guiding" in online search and retrieval include instances of correction through a very democratic process of heeding the cry of the populace. As with many organic elements of nature, the World Wide Web displays a knack for self-correction. When information considered incorrect is promoted online, the cry of "foul" is never far behind. The world is watching online, and the mechanism for correction appears to be quicker and stronger than any legal structure for enacting discipline or justice in the World Wide Web. One could argue the Internet changes too fast

to create an all-encompassing structure of law and justice. Legislation is simply too slow for the digital world. An alternative seems to be the concept of collective intelligence and how users and devices, data banks and people are finding a balance online. In perhaps an interesting twist of irony, Google executive chairman Eric Schmidt discussed this concept in 2011, at the MIT Sloan School of Management. When confronted with questions of whether increased human-computer interaction was a good thing, he pointed to how the situation may lead to positive changes in society. In his talk titled "The Future of the Global Mind," he stressed how technology really is about data collection, rather than just hardware and software. His belief is this data will be used (as collective intelligence) to help us make better decisions. In this sense, collective intelligence may be our biggest ally in guarding against infringements on speech, copyright, and other rights online.

A telling statistic in regard to the relationship between online search users and the search engine itself came from Schmidt's talk. In an *MIT News* article, reporter Zach Church highlighted what Schmidt said about increased knowledge sharing and how it is comparable to the invention of electricity: "At 2,000 tweets per second and 48 hours of YouTube uploads per minute, the world, [Schmidt] argued, is getting smarter. And the thirst for new information is overwhelming: On a daily basis, 16 percent of Google searches are new search terms." This brings to the surface not only the speed of knowledge sharing (which has most likely increased since the 2011 talk) but also how we contribute to the content of what is shared. New searches in Google build on the existing data bank of possible results returned in a search query. The relationship is very symbiotic and dynamic. This symbiosis makes it even more important to keep our role in the World Wide Web ever-present. We create, we publish, we request, and we correct. In a sense, it is more accurately called the "World Wide WE."

Conclusion

This topic also brings to light a concern more general and broad, yet just as important as specific instances of censorship and intellectual property rights violations. It is the notion that our basic free will is somewhat hindered when using these giant, complicated, and complex search engines online. We are guided to information through a process of which we are not wholly aware. We are not privy to potential bias; we essentially lose our autonomy and invest our trust in an engine to lead us to what we hope and perhaps assume is a list of choices that represents the entirety of possible selections online. Seems like a tall order, but an important one nonetheless when considering the power that is potentially leveraged by something so widely used and accessed as a search engine. Clemons, in his attack on Google's influence on public opinion, emphasizes Google's power as a gatekeeper and paints a picture that portrays Google as more dangerous than blatant acts of censorship like book burning because "most of us do not know that it

is occurring. . . . No one should trust them or any other company with this much power."

With that in mind, it seems even more important as we forge ahead in a world of data mining, collective intelligence, and even heavier dependence on Internet-capable gadgets, that we weave into our learning systems a strong foundation of information literacy. If society at large is to be the most effective protection within a structure of collective intelligence, we must arm ourselves with skills that will enable us to differentiate between valid and invalid, trustworthy and untrustworthy sources and results. Building Internet-using societies that can swiftly and effectively differentiate between biased and unbiased information is not necessarily a feasible goal, but being able to identify an existing bias and analyze it within a larger body of information would be a potentially more important and powerful way to create stronger protection for everyone online.

We, the users, influence all aspects of the Internet. Whether it is through content creation, programming, development, marketing, feedback, logging in, or choosing to log off, we are all part of the organism. As such, we have a responsibility to police this vast universe of knowledge. Like any other resource, it deserves and necessitates protection. So, if we ask "who will protect us from Google," we may not need to look any further than ourselves.

Stacy Elizabeth Stevenson
Kent State University

See also Access to Information; Ethical Censorship; Google Books

Further Reading

Baker, Paul, and Amanda Potts. "'Why Do White People Have Thin Lips?' Google and the Perpetuation of Stereotypes via Auto-complete Search Forms." *Critical Discourse Studies* 10, no. 2 (2013): 187–204.

Christian, Jon. "From 'Preggers' to 'Pizzle': Android's Bizarre List of Banned Words." *Wired,* December 2, 2013. http://www.wired.com/2013/12/banned-android-words

Church, Zach. "Google's Schmidt: 'Global Mind' Offers New Opportunities." *MIT News,* November 15, 2011. http://newsoffice.mit.edu/2011/schmidt-event-1115.

Clemons, Eric K., and Josh Wilson. "Can Google Influence an Election?" *Huff Post Tech: The Blog,* October 9, 2012. http://www.huffingtonpost.com/eric-k-clemons/google-election-2012_b_1952725.html.

Clemons, Eric K., and Steve Barnett. "Quick: Is Someone Trying to Steal Your Agora?" *Huff Post Tech: The Blog,* December 22, 2010. http://www.huffingtonpost.com/eric-k-clemons/quick-is-someone-trying-t_b_800536.html.

Cohen, Noam. "Professor Makes the Case That Google Is a Publisher." *New York Times,* May 20, 2012. http://www.nytimes.com/2012/05/21/business/media/eugene-volokh-ucla-professor-makes-a-case-for-google-as-publisher.html?pagewanted=all&_r=0.

"Collective Intelligence: A Conversation with Thomas W. Malone." *Edge,* November 21, 2012. http://edge.org/conversation/collective-intelligence.

Efrati, Amir. "Rivals Say Google Plays Favorites." *Wall Street Journal,* December 12, 2010. http://online.wsj.com/news/articles/SB10001424052748704058704576015630188568972?mg=reno64-wsj&url=http%3A%2F%2Fonline.wsj.com%2Farticle%2FSB10001424052748704058704576015630188568972.html.

Enderle, Rob. "The United States of Google." *TechNewsWorld,* October 1, 2012. http://www.technewsworld.com/story/The-United-States-of-Google-76273.html.

Google, Inc. "Autocomplete." n.d. https://support.google.com/websearch/answer/106230.

Google, Inc. "Our History in Depth." September 2013. http://www.google.com/about/company/history.

Google, Inc. "Ten Things We Know to Be True." n.d. http://www.google.com/about/company/philosophy.

Internet Society. "Brief History of the Internet." http://www.internetsociety.org/internet/what-internet/history-internet/brief-history-internet.

Introna, L. D., and H. Nissenbaum. "Shaping the Web: Why the Politics of Search Engines Matters." *Information Society,* July 29, 2006: 169–185.

Lee, Jessica. "Google's Misogynistic Autocomplete Suggestions: Who's Responsible?" *Search Engine Watch,* October 22, 2013. http://searchenginewatch.com/article/2302295/Googles-Misogynistic-Autocomplete-Suggestions-Whos-Responsible.

Pan, Bing, et al. "In Google We Trust: Users' Decisions on Rank, Position, and Relevance." *Journal of Computer-Mediated Communication* 12, no. 3 (2007): 801–823.

Pew Research Center. "The Web at 25." February 2014. http://www.pewinternet.org/files/2014/02/PIP_25th-anniversary-of-the-Web_0227141.pdf.

Purcell, Kristen, Joanna Brenner, and Lee Rainie. "Search Engine Use 2012." *Pew Internet & American Life Project,* March 9, 2012.

Rosen, Jeffrey. "Google's Gatekeepers." *New York Times Magazine,* November 28, 2008. http://www.nytimes.com/2008/11/30/magazine/30google-t.html?pagewanted=all&_r=0.

Shaw, Steven. "Google's Search Engine Results Are Free Speech and I Don't Care." *ZDNet,* May 29, 2012. http://www.zdnet.com/blog/btl/googles-search-engine-results-are-free-speech-and-i-dont-care/78265.

Smith, Aaron. "Smartphone Ownership—2013 Update." *Pew Research Internet Project,*

June 5, 2013. http://www.pewinternet.org/2013/06/05/smartphone-ownership-2013.

Sullivan, Danny. "Google Still World's Most Popular Search Engine by Far, but Share of Unique Searchers Dips Slightly." *Search Engine Land,* February 11, 2013. http://searchengineland.com/google-worlds-most-popular-search-engine-148089.

52

WHERE ARE THE SCHOOLHOUSE GATES?

In 1969, at the tail end of the great expansion of rights during the Warren Court, the justices boldly proclaimed that public school students did not "shed their constitutional rights to freedom of speech or expression at the schoolhouse gate." *Tinker v. Des Moines School District* was the first explicit recognition of First Amendment free speech protections for public school students. As it turned out, that decision was the high-water mark for student expression. Although the precedent still stands, it has been narrowed repeatedly through the years. And no one knows for sure what the free speech rights are for students and student journalists outside the schoolhouse gates when they blog nasty comments about teachers, principals, and other students from their home computers.

Today, student journalists and those in other school-sponsored expressive activities shed most of their First Amendment rights at the gate. Even as the Supreme Court has recognized expanded free speech rights for corporations, makers of violent video games, and fundamentalist picketers at veterans' funerals, it has continued to limit the free speech rights of students in the public schools. First Amendment experts say that this area of the First Amendment marks the Court's most significant limitation on speech over the past half century.

What is uncertain is whether school administrators can reach beyond the school gates into the homes of their students to censor speech from home computers or mobile devices outside of school that causes a disruption back inside the schoolhouse gates. Different courts have split on this new media issue and the U.S. Supreme Court has dodged the split.

Tinker

Early in the Vietnam War, seven young schoolchildren in Des Moines, Iowa, decided to wear black armbands to school to protest the Vietnam War. This was long before antiwar protests had begun to grip the nation's college campuses. Four of the children lived in the home of the Reverend Leonard Tinker, a local Methodist minister who had been assigned to the American Friends Service Committee. The Tinker children were Paul, who was eight and in second grade; Hope, eleven and in fifth grade; Mary Beth, thirteen and at Warren G. Harding Middle School; and John, sixteen and at Theodore Roosevelt High School. The Tinkers recalled that their parents had been involved in civil rights and antiwar demonstrations as long as they could remember. John said in a court statement that the idea was to support a Christmas season call to remember the dead in Vietnam and hope for peace. The local school board heard about the planned protest and passed a preemptive ban. When children got to school, administrators ordered them to remove the armbands. Counselors told one of the students he would never get into college because colleges would not accept protesters. Others accused the children and family of being communists. At one point red paint was slashed on the Tinker home.

When the children refused to remove the armbands, the schools sent them home. After Christmas vacation, the students returned without the armbands but several wore black clothing for the rest of the school year to remind the school of their protest. They also went to court.

Justice Abe Fortas, in one of his last opinions for the Court, wrote as if it was self-evident that students had First Amendment rights at schools. "It can hardly be argued," he wrote, "that either students or teachers shed their constitutional rights to freedom of speech or expression at the schoolhouse gate."

Fortas based that conclusion on two important liberty decisions from the first half of the twentieth century. He cited the 1923 *Meyer v. Nebraska* decision in which the Court ruled that states could not ban the teaching of foreign languages in the public schools. (At the time, a majority of states banned the teaching of German because of World War I.) He also cited the 1925 *Pierce v. Society of Sisters* decision in which the Court ruled that states could not bar parents from sending their children to parochial school. In addition, Fortas pointed to the famous 1943 decision in *West Virginia v. Barnette* in which the Court eloquently upheld the right of children to refuse to salute the flag based on religious scruples of Jehovah's Witnesses against worshiping graven images.

Fortas held that school officials had to show "more than a mere desire to avoid the discomfort and unpleasantness that always accompany an unpopular viewpoint." If a public school wanted to censor speech, it would have to show that the "forbidden conduct would 'materially and substantially interfere with the requirements of appropriate discipline in the operation of the school.'"

There was no realistic fear of public disruption in the *Tinker* case, Fortas wrote. He said,

in our system, undifferentiated fear or apprehension of disturbance is not enough to overcome the right to freedom of expression. Any departure from absolute regimentation may cause trouble. Any variation from the majority's opinion may inspire fear. Any word spoken, in class, in the lunchroom, or on the campus, that deviates from the views of another person may start an argument or cause a disturbance. But our Constitution says we must take this risk . . . and our history says that it is this sort of hazardous freedom—this kind of openness—that is the basis of our national strength and of the independence and vigor of Americans who grow up and live in this relatively permissive, often disputatious, society.

But the proposition that students are clothed with First Amendment rights in school was not self-evident to some of the other justices. Nor was the notion that a permissive society was one that made American strong. By the time the Court announced the decision in 1969, it reflected the divide in society over the Vietnam War, civil rights, and the notion that the younger generation of protesters had grown up in a permissive atmosphere.

Even Justice Hugo Black—the First Amendment absolutist also about to leave the Court—argued that the First Amendment had nothing to do with student speech at schools. He strongly criticized—and reading between the lines ridiculed—the Court's decision to protect the right of students to express their political views "from kindergarten through high school."

Wrote Black, "While I have always believed that, under the First and Fourteenth Amendments, neither the State nor the Federal Government has any authority to regulate or censor the content of speech, I have never believed that any person has a right to give speeches or engage in demonstrations where he pleases and when he pleases."

Black conceded that the armband students did not disrupt the classwork, but he wrote that "the armbands did exactly what the elected school officials and principals foresaw they would, that is, took the students' minds off their classwork and diverted them to thoughts about the highly emotional subject of the Vietnam War." He noted that the record showed that the armbands "caused comments, warnings by other students, the poking of fun at them, and a warning by an older football player that other nonprotesting students had better let them alone. There is also evidence that a teacher of mathematics had his lesson period practically 'wrecked,' chiefly by disputes with Mary Beth Tinker, who wore her armband for her 'demonstration.'"

Black concluded with a warning that reflected society's backlash against young protesters. "If the time has come when pupils of state-supported schools, kindergartens, grammar schools, or high schools, can defy and flout orders of school officials to keep their minds on their own schoolwork, it is the beginning of a new revolutionary era of permissiveness in this country fostered by the judiciary. The next logical step, it appears to me, would be to hold unconstitutional laws that bar pupils under 21 or 18 from voting, or from being elected members of the boards of education."

Indecency in the College Press

The tame expression of the little Tinker children was a far cry from that in the underground newspaper that Barbara Papish distributed at the University of Missouri and that led to her being expelled from the journalism school. The Court's opinion in *Papish v. Board of Curators* in 1973 described the offensive content of the magazine this way: "First, on the front cover the publishers had reproduced a political cartoon previously printed in another newspaper depicting policemen raping the Statue of Liberty and the Goddess of Justice. The caption under the cartoon read: ' . . . With Liberty and Justice for All.' Secondly, the issue contained an article titled 'M—-f—-Acquitted,' which discussed the trial and acquittal on an assault charge of a New York City youth who was a member of an organization known as 'Up Against the Wall, M—-f—-.'"

Papish was expelled for having failed to follow accepted standards of student conduct that included a prohibition on indecent conduct or speech. The Supreme Court acknowledged "a state university's undoubted prerogative to enforce reasonable rules governing student conduct," but pointed to *Tinker* for the proposition that "state colleges and universities are not enclaves immune from the sweep of the First Amendment." It added that "the mere dissemination of ideas—no matter how offensive to good taste—on a state university campus may not be shut off in the name alone of 'conventions of decency.'" The Court pointed to its recent 1971 decision of *Cohen v. California* in which it had found that the First Amendment protected a person who wore a "F—- the draft" jacket through a courthouse.

But the lay of the land in the Supreme Court had changed substantially by the late 1980s when two important student speech cases came before the Supreme Court. When *Papish* was decided, William H. Rehnquist was an often-lonely dissenter. By the time of *Bethel School District v. Fraser* in 1986 and *Hazelwood v. Kuhlmeier* in 1988, the more conservative Burger Court was giving way to the Rehnquist Court.

Matthew N. Fraser was a student at Bethel High School in Pierce County, Washington. He delivered a nominating speech at a school assembly in which he referred to his candidate in what Chief Justice Warren E. Burger referred to as "an elaborate, graphic, and explicit sexual metaphor." Justice William Brennan was less Puritanical in his concurrence, quoting Fraser's speech:

> I know a man who is firm—he's firm in his pants, he's firm in his shirt, his character is firm—but most . . . of all, his belief in you, the students of Bethel, is firm.
>
> Jeff Kuhlman is a man who takes his point and pounds it in. If necessary, he'll take an issue and nail it to the wall. He doesn't attack things in spurts—he drives hard, pushing and pushing until finally—he succeeds.
>
> Jeff is a man who will go to the very end—even the climax, for each and every one of you.
>
> So vote for Jeff for A.S.B. vice-president—he'll never come between you and the best our high school can be.

According to the Court record, "some students hooted and yelled; some by gestures graphically simulated the sexual activities pointedly alluded to in respondent's speech. Other students appeared to be bewildered and embarrassed by the speech. One teacher reported that on the day following the speech, she found it necessary to forgo a portion of the scheduled class lesson in order to discuss the speech with the class."

An appeals court had ruled in favor of Fraser, but Burger said the appeals court had not appreciated the "marked distinction" between the "sexual content of respondent's speech in this case" as opposed to the careful expression of a political view in *Tinker*. He added that the Court had stressed in *Tinker* that Mary Beth Tinker's speech did "not concern speech or action that intrudes upon the work of the schools or the rights of other students."

The chief justice also pointed out that students' rights inside the school are not as strong as their rights outside the school. A student clearly would not be protected wearing the "F—- the draft" jacket of Cohen inside of the schoolhouse gates, he wrote.

Even Justice Brennan, the Court's strongest First Amendment advocate, agreed that the public schools could intervene to teach Fraser a more persuasive way of expressing himself.

The decision in *Bethel* stood for the proposition expressed by the Court that "the constitutional rights of students in public school are not automatically coextensive with the rights of adults in other settings."

Hazelwood

Almost two decades after *Tinker*, the U.S. Supreme Court announced a devastating blow to student speech and the student press when it validated the authority of the principal of Hazelwood East High School to remove controversial stories about teen pregnancy and divorce from the school newspaper without even talking to the students.

The Court did not overrule *Tinker*, but that was the practical impact on all school-sponsored expressive activities. The Court's decision in *Hazelwood v. Kuhlmeier* was one of the most far-reaching

decisions restricting free speech in the past half century.

The Hazelwood East case began at the end of the school year in 1983, when the Journalism II class, which produced the *Spectrum,* compiled two full pages of stories under the headline: "Pressure Describes It All for Today's Teen-Agers. Pregnancy Affects Many Teens Each Year."

From a journalistic viewpoint, the student work was excellent. It was the kind of work that wins high-school journalism prizes. The stories showed reportorial enterprise as well as independence of judgment.

Principal Robert Reynolds objected to two of the six articles. One was an account of three Hazelwood East students who had become pregnant. The article made references to birth control and sexual activity and reflected the positive attitude of the girls toward their pregnancies. The principal thought the article's references to sexual activity and birth control were inappropriate for younger students at the school. The names of the pregnant girls had been changed, but Reynolds was concerned that they could be identified from other information in the articles.

The other article he objected to was an account of a student whose parents were divorced. The student complained that her father "wasn't spending enough time with my mom, my sister and I" prior to the divorce, "was always out of town on business or out late playing cards with the guys," and "always argued about everything" with her mother. The *Spectrum* planned to delete the name of the student in the divorce article, but the real name was on the proof read by Reynolds.

Reynolds thought it unfair that the father did not have a chance to respond.

The principal decided time was too short to make the necessary changes and ordered the two pages removed from the *Spectrum,* excising four unobjectionable articles along with the two controversial ones. He did not consult the students about his decision because he did not think there was time before publication.

Three students on the staff, led by Cathy Kuhlmeier, challenged Reynolds's action. With the help of the American Civil Liberties Union of Eastern Missouri, the students won in the federal appeals court in St. Louis. But the lawyers handling the case botched the argument in the U.S. Supreme Court, according to the recollections of former ACLU leaders.

Fred Epstein, past president of the ACLU in St. Louis, said: "As I recall, *Hazelwood* was argued by a couple of incompetent lawyers who would accept no advice from the ACLU or other lawyers who had Supreme Court experience. Worst of all, the two ACLU lawyers handling the case would not even let friendly lawyers conduct a mock court to prep the two lawyers handling the case."

White's Opinion

Justice Byron White, who wrote a number of decisions hostile to the press, wrote the 5–3 majority opinion in which he said high school newspapers were part of the school curriculum, not public forums for the exercise of free speech.

White disagreed with the Eighth U.S. Circuit Court of Appeals' decision that the school newspaper was a public forum for student views. Instead, he said the school had clearly treated it as a part of the curriculum and not a public forum. If the school paper were a public forum, student journalists would have broader free speech rights.

White, pointing to the *Bethel* case, noted that just because students do not shed their rights at the schoolhouse gates does not mean that their rights inside those gates are "coextensive" with their rights outside the gates.

The student speech issue in *Hazelwood* was entirely different from the issue in *Tinker,* White maintained. *Tinker* was about "educators' ability to silence a student's personal expression that happens to occur on the school premises," he wrote. But *Hazelwood* concerned "educators' authority over school-sponsored publications, theatrical productions, and other expressive activities that students, parents, and members of the public might reasonably perceive to bear the imprimatur of the school. These activities may fairly be characterized as part of the school curriculum, whether or not they occur in a traditional classroom setting, so long as they are supervised by faculty members and designed to impart particular knowledge or skills to student participants and audiences."

White concluded that the Court would not use the standard it had applied in *Tinker.* "The standard articulated in *Tinker* for determining when a school may punish student expression need not also be the standard for determining when a school may refuse to lend its name and resources to the dissemination of student expression," he wrote. "Instead, we hold that educators do not offend the First Amendment by exercising editorial control over the style and content of student speech in school-sponsored expressive activities so long as their actions are reasonably related to legitimate pedagogical concerns."

Alan Howard, a First Amendment expert at Saint Louis University Law School, explained White's distinction in an interview for the *St. Louis Beacon*:

> The court recognized a distinction between kids *at* school and kids *in* school. So the court found that students (even those too young to vote) are still citizens, and when at school in their capacity as citizens can express their views on matters of public concern—in *Tinker*'s case, express opposition to a war. So when walking in the halls from one class to another class, or playing outside at recess, or eating lunch in the cafeteria, the school can't punish kids talking to other kids about political issues—even if school officials don't like what the students are saying or just don't want kids expressing views on controversial topics.
>
> *Hazelwood* was not a case where the school officials were seeking to suppress student/citizenship speech that occurred at school. Rather, it was a case where school officials were engaged in "teaching" kids in their capacity as students—in this setting, the school was playing the role of educator, not sovereign, and the kids were playing the role of student, not citizen—and, in this context, the court concluded that schools should have more leeway to regulate student speech.
>
> The high school had a journalism class, a component of which was putting out a newspaper—but the purpose of the newspaper was not primarily to serve as an outlet for students as citizens to comment on matters of public concern, but was to provide a means by which the school would teach good journalism practices.

Reynolds thought the story about divorce was poor journalism because it criticized the father without having contacted him. Most journalists would agree that this is poor journalistic practice. But many journalism educators consider the *Hazelwood* stories to be examples of extraordinarily good high school journalism.

Brennan's Dissent

Justice Brennan wrote a stinging dissent, saying "The mere fact of school sponsorship does not . . . license . . . thought control in the high school."

First, Brennan disagreed with White's conclusion that the newspaper was not a public forum. He pointed to the newspaper's and school board's policies about the *Spectrum*. Those policies announced that the paper "was not just a class exercise in which students learned to prepare papers and hone writing skills, it was a . . . forum established to give students an opportunity to express their views while gaining an appreciation of their rights and responsibilities under the First Amendment to the United States Constitution."

The student journalists published a statement at the beginning of each year stating that "Only speech that 'materially and substantially interferes with the requirements of appropriate discipline' can be found unacceptable and therefore prohibited." The school board itself vowed that school-sponsored publications "will not restrict free expression or diverse viewpoints within the rules of responsible journalism."

Even if he were to agree that the journalists' controversial articles could be excised, Brennan wrote that he would "emphatically object to the brutal manner" in which Reynolds exercised his authority. "The principal used a paper shredder," Brennan wrote. "He objected to some material in two articles, but excised six entire articles. He did not so much as inquire into obvious alternatives, such as precise deletions or additions (one of which had already been made), rearranging the layout, or delaying publication. Such unthinking contempt for individual rights is intolerable from any state official. It is particularly insidious from one to whom the public entrusts the task of inculcating in its youth an appreciation for the cherished democratic liberties that our Constitution guarantees." Brennan concluded,

The Court opens its analysis in this case by purporting to reaffirm *Tinker*'s time-tested proposition that public school students "do not shed their constitutional rights to freedom of speech or expression at the schoolhouse gate." That is an ironic introduction to an opinion that denudes high school students of much of the First Amendment protection that *Tinker* itself prescribed. Instead of "teach[ing] children to respect the diversity of ideas that is fundamental to the American system," and "that our Constitution is a living reality, not parchment preserved under glass," the Court today teach[es] youth to discount important principles of our government as mere platitudes. The young men and women of Hazelwood East expected a civics lesson, but not the one the Court teaches them today.

Significant Setback for Free Expression

Gregory P. Magarian, a professor at Washington University law school, says *Hazelwood* "remains a very important speech-restrictive decision" and "represents perhaps the most important instance of the Court's steady retreat from protecting students' free speech rights."

The *Hazelwood* decision was the most important of several decisions cutting back on student speech rights. The Supreme Court's weaker protection of free student expression is consistent with weak support on the Court for the press in general, Magarian says.

"The idea of press rights, as a specific, separate category of free speech rights, has all but died on the vine," he wrote in an e-mail. "That has more than anything else to do with changes in media economics and technology. But even before the Internet, the Court had largely embraced an attitude toward press rights that was indifferent at best. *Hazelwood* is part of that."

Also part of that cold shoulder toward the press are decisions where the Court refused to extend constitutional protection for journalists to protect confidential sources and held newspapers responsible for abiding by reporters' promises of confidentiality to sources.

"It is striking that the limitations on student rights and press freedom have come over a time when the Court has expanded other First Amendment rights," Magarian wrote. But, he added, "First Amendment speech rights haven't simply expanded over the past twenty-five years. Instead, First Amendment speech rights have changed shape. The Court has put much more energy into expanding the free speech rights of politically or economically powerful speakers while largely disdaining First Amendment concerns of politically and economically disempowered speakers.

On the other side of the ledger, we can see the Court's expansion of commercial speech rights—and, especially, its conversion of campaign finance regulation into a First Amendment preserve."

In an interview with the Freedom Forum a decade ago, Kuhlmeier recalled a girl coming up to her at a symposium on the case and calling her a "freedom fighter" while asking for her autograph.

"I never thought of myself as a freedom fighter," she said. "But I guess I did at least try to make a difference. Students don't have enough First Amendment freedoms. There are a lot of very intelligent kids out there, and we should listen to them more. Maybe, if we did, the world would be a better place."

Now Cathy Kuhlmeier Frey—and a risk manager for Bass Pro Shops—she continues to see things differently from Reynolds. The two appeared in 2013 at a forum on student speech marking the twenty-fifth anniversary of the decision.

Education Week described a tense exchange. "I was so angry because we had worked so hard" on those articles, Frey said, as she and Reynolds argued over the details of the controversy. "I stood up for what I believed in. That has molded me into someone who is not afraid to speak up."

Bong Hits

From *Tinker* through *Kuhlmeier,* the issue was how much First Amendment protection a student retained after passing through the schoolhouse door and walking into the classroom. The "Bong Hits 4 Jesus" case, *Morse v. Frederick,* began to probe how far school authorities can reach off campus to limit student speech affecting the school.

Joseph Frederick says he wanted to get on TV when the Olympic torch parade passed his Juneau, Alaska, high school. When students were dismissed from class to attend a rally as the torch passed, Frederick went home and picked up a banner that read, "Bong Hits 4 Jesus." He and his snowball-throwing friends unfurled the fourteen-foot banner and held it in a way that the media and other students across the street could see it. His principal Deborah Morse saw him, took him into her office, and suspended him for what she saw as a pro-drug message.

Frederick argued that his speech was not on school premises and that it was not school speech because it was not made in a school program such as a newspaper. And he maintained he was not promoting drugs.

But, in a narrow decision, the Supreme Court supported the principal. Chief Justice John Roberts pointed to *Fraser*'s sexually charged nomination speech in school for the proposition that "the constitutional rights of students in public school are not automatically coextensive with the rights of adults in other settings." And he pointed to *Hazelwood* for the proposition that the rights of students "must be 'applied in light of the special characteristics of the school environment.'"

Had Fraser given his speech outside of the school in a public meeting, his speech would have been protected, the chief justice wrote. Similarly, if Frederick's speech had been outside of the school and not at a school event, it would have been protected, he suggested.

The chief justice rejected Frederick's argument that his was not school speech. He pointed out that the assembly occurred during school hours, that it was sanctioned by the principal as a class trip, and that teachers were interspersed among the students enforcing school rules. He also pointed out that the high school band and cheerleaders performed, that Frederick was standing in the midst of the students, and that his banner was directed toward the school.

The chief justice acknowledged that the words could be viewed as political, nonsensical, and possibly humorous to some. He noted that Frederick had said the words "were just nonsense meant to attract television cameras." But he added that the principal had reasonably interpreted it as a pro-drug message that violated school policy.

The chief justice acknowledged that the main holding of the *Hazelwood* case did not apply to *Bong Hits* because no one could reasonably conclude that the school was approving the message on the banner. But he noted that in *Hazelwood* the Court had based its decision in part upon a non-free speech case—*TLO v. New Jersey*—in which the Court had approved a search of a school locker for drugs based on reasonable suspicion rather than probable cause. The Court had said in its 1985 *TLO* decision that the lesser Fourth Amendment protection for searches in school was justified by the war on drugs. *TLO* had cited *Tinker* for the proposition that "the special characteristics of the school environment" justified some easing of constitutional rights, particularly when it came to the campaign against drugs.

The narrowness of the Court's opinion in *Bong Hits* was underscored by Justice Samuel Alito's concurrence, which was joined by Justice Anthony M. Kennedy. Both justices were necessary to Roberts's majority. Justice Alito wrote that he was joining the opinion "on the understanding that (a) it goes no further than to hold that a public school may restrict speech that a reasonable observer would interpret as advocating illegal drug use and (b) it provides no support for any restriction of speech that can plausibly be interpreted as commenting on any political or social issue, including speech on issues such as 'the wisdom of the war on drugs or of legalizing marijuana for medicinal use.'"

One justice refused to recognize any First Amendment rights by students—Justice Clarence Thomas. He wrote that he would overturn *Tinker,* which was an unwarranted intrusion on the authority of school administrators.

Thomas cited the history of educators controlling the expression of students under the doctrine of *in loco parentis.* He added: "In short, in the earliest public schools, teachers taught, and students listened. Teachers commanded, and students obeyed. Teachers did not rely solely on the power of ideas to persuade; they relied on discipline to maintain order."

In conclusion, Thomas wrote,

In light of the history of American public education, it cannot seriously be suggested that the First Amendment 'freedom of speech' encompasses a student's right to speak in public schools. Early public schools gave total control to teachers, who expected obedience and respect from students. And courts routinely deferred to schools' authority to make rules and to discipline students for violating those rules. Several points are clear: (1) under *in loco parentis*, speech rules and other school rules were treated identically; (2) the *in loco parentis* doctrine imposed almost no limits on the types of rules that a school could set while students were in school; and (3) schools and teachers had tremendous discretion in imposing punishments for violations of those rules.

Speech in the Student's Bedroom

Most of the free speech disputes in the public schools today involve student tweets, Facebook posts, Internet blogs, and other social media written from home or from a friend's house but directed at a teacher or principal. Often these comments are in the form of crude parodies that have more similarities to Fraser's speech than to Tinker's sedate armband.

To date, the Supreme Court has dodged conflicting opinions from the lower courts.

One student who lost in the Second U.S. Circuit Court of Appeals was Avery Doninger, the former class secretary of Lewis S. Mills High School in Burlington, Vermont, who got angry when principal Karissa Niehoff canceled the Jamfest, an annual school musical event.

Doninger tried to whip up opposition to the principal's actions by calling on allies to contact the school board. She also wrote an online message on LiveJournal. com calling Niehoff and other school officials "douchebags." In response, the principal refused to allow Doninger to run for reelection for student office. When she won in a write-in campaign, the school awarded the office to a second-place finisher. Students responded by wearing "TEAM AVERY" T-shirts, which the principal ordered them to take off.

The appeals court upheld the principal's actions on the basis that there is no clear law on whether a school can punish a student for speech created off-campus and directed at the school, with the potential that the speech could disrupt the school.

Ken Paulson, president of the First Amendment Center, criticized the school and the court for punishing good citizenship. "One irony to the case is that Doninger's punishment was justified on the grounds that she was not engaging in 'good citizenship.' She was a member of the student council, was upset about the school's failure to schedule an arts activity for students, spoke out about what she believed to be misconduct by government employees, and tried to run for public office. Outside the four walls of a public school, that activity would be the very definition of a good and engaged citizen."

The decision in Doninger's case conflicted with the Third Circuit Court of Appeals decision involving Justin Layshock, a seventeen-year-old senior at Hickory High School in Pennsylvania who created a fake MySpace profile about his principal on his grandmother's computer. The parody contained offensive answers to some of the stock questions posted by MySpace. Here are a few of the questions and the answers Layshock entered for the principal.

In the past month have you smoked: big blunt

In the past month have you gone Skinny Dipping: big lake, not big dick

Ever been beaten up: big fag

Under interests, Layshock wrote, "Transgender, Appreciators of Alcoholic Beverages."

On a number of occasions, Layshock showed fellow students the profile in school. On one occasion a teacher had to disperse a group that had gathered around the computer.

Eventually, after he and his parents were called to school, Layshock apologized to the principal. The school board went ahead with discipline, suspending Layshock for ten days, assigning him to a segregated school setting for half the school day, and barring him from graduation. The Hermitage School District said the profile violated school rules on "Disrespect; Harassment of a school administrator via computer/Internet remarks that have demeaning implications; Gross misbehavior; Obscene, vulgar and profane language; Computer policy violations."

The parents sued and won. The court ruled that the school could not punish the student for speech created off campus that did not interfere with the school environment.

Academic Criticism

One of the more trenchant academic criticisms of the limitations on school expression came from University of Colorado scholars Robert Trager and Joseph A. Russomanno at the Association for Education in Journalism and Mass Communication 1993 convention. They said:

> When free expression is limited in order to instill majoritarian societal values in their schools, this turns the First Amendment on its head. Rather . . . students' expressive rights should be at the core of the societal values that public schools teach—and that schools should allow students to practice.

> The First Amendment is instrumental in providing the foundation for dissent,

self-fulfillment, human dignity and liberty—all vital in the realization of both the polity and the individual.

Every organization, including the school, has a culture, serving to inform its membership about how to interpret and respond to social life. . . . Schools are societal surrogates for students. The school is one of the few—perhaps the only—institutions with which the pre-adult has contact outside the home.

By providing structure and standards, the school can bestow a sense of significance to its students, letting them "know they belong to a functioning and complete society." Alternatively, a system that distinguishes between what is permitted within the school and outside its door symbolically conveys to students—citizens who are in their politically formative years—that viewpoints can be constrained based not merely on their content, but also on their location.

A school environment devoid of free expression is not likely to produce an adult ready to support the sentiment attributed to Voltaire: "I disapprove of what you say, but I will defend to the death your right to say it."

Pro

Student free speech is essential to the civic education of the public school student. The nation's democracy is centered around contentious discussion of public issues with dissenters to the norm protected in their expression. To wall off the public school from this robust discussion is to exclude an essential—possibly the essential—ingredient of democratic decision-making from the public schools. An independent student press—one that is a forum for student opinion and a check on abuses by school administrators—is as essential to the life of a public school as it is to the life of a civil society.

The *Hazelwood* decision limiting the speech of public school journalists and others in school expressive activities was one of the most devastating blows to the First Amendment over the past half century. It is incoherent for the Court to expand the rights of corporations to make unlimited political contributions, while it limits the rights of students and student journalists.

Con

Tinker, while extremely broad in its sweep, was limited from the start by the Court's reference to "special characteristics" of the school setting and to speech that did not cause a disruption in the classroom. The court decisions that have followed—limiting a vulgar election speech, limiting the rights of students in school expressive activities, and limiting student speech involving drugs—are consistent with the special characteristics of the school setting. Just as educators can require students to use proper grammar and punctuation, they also can require them to follow good journalistic practice in student publications. One could even go so far as to argue that *Tinker* never was justified under the Court's precedents or the original meaning of the First Amendment. Both Justice Black in the beginning and Justice Thomas today point out that public school administrators have always had the role and duty of inculcating values and discipline in students.

Looking to the Future

The vast majority of today's conflicts involving student speech grow out of student posts to social media on their home computers. A big legal question mark lingers over whether this kind of speech is protected. One would expect the Court to conclude, as the Third Circuit did in the Layshock case, that student expression created on a home computer that does not materially disrupt the school setting would be protected. But the Court could well decide that expression from home is not protected where it creates a disturbance in the hallways at school. The Court would also be more likely to limit that home-produced speech if it advocated drug use or other activities that threatened the health and welfare of students.

Conclusion

The revolution in the protection of student speech that was heralded by *Tinker* was short-lived. What had at first seemed like the inauguration of a new era of protection for student speech has quickly devolved into a series of decisions limiting student speech. Many legal scholars argue that the debilitating impact of *Hazelwood* is more important than the empowering impact of *Tinker.* Looked at across the range of First Amendment law, and especially across the range of First Amendment law pertaining to the media, the *Hazelwood* decision is one of the most destructive of the past half century to free expression.

William H. Freivogel
Southern Illinois University Carbondale

See also Cyberbullying and Student Expression; Generational Expectations; A New First Amendment?; New Technology: Free Speech Messiah or First Amendment Traitor?

Further Reading

Bonner, Alice. *Death by Cheeseburger: High School Journalism in the 1990s and Beyond.* Washington, DC: Freedom Forum, 1994. http://www.first amendmentcenter.org/madison/wp-content/uploads/2011/03/dbc_web.pdf.

Eveslage, Tom. "25 Years of Stifled Student Press Freedom Deserves Attention." *Gateway Journalism Review,* April 2013.

Freivogel, William H. "*Hazelwood* Reverberates 25 Years Later." *Gateway Journalism Review,* April 2013.

Freivogel, William H. "History Lesson: Milestone *Hazelwood* Case Curbed Free Speech of Students." *St. Louis Beacon,* January 14, 2013. https://www.stlbeacon.org/#!/content/28846/hazelwood_supreme_court.

Paulson, Ken. "2nd Circuit Sides with Connecticut School in Dispute over Off-campus Speech." First Amendment Center, April 26, 2011.

Trager, Robert, and Joseph A. Russomanno. "Free Speech for Public School Students: A 'Basic Educational Mission.'" Paper presented at the Association for Education in Journalism and Mass Communication annual convention, 1993.

53

CYBERBULLYING AND STUDENT EXPRESSION

When twelve-year-old Rebecca Sedwick jumped to her death from a tower near her Florida home in September 2013, many asked what could have been done to prevent this tragedy. Her mother wondered if she had done enough. Learning that Rebecca was being taunted and ridiculed by classmates, her mother contacted school officials, sought counseling for her daughter, closed her Facebook account, and tried to monitor Rebecca's social media use.

School officials took steps to limit Rebecca's face-to-face interaction with the bullying students while in school but did little to address these students' online assaults, many from outside the school. Lawmakers had passed cyberbullying legislation, but it focused on responding to offenders more than preventing the offense.

Reacting like many twelve-year-olds would if their social media use were curtailed, Rebecca found other online applications, created a new user name, and—perhaps fearful of losing social-network privileges again—did not tell her mother about a new wave of hateful, hurtful messages. So a dozen or so middle-school students continued to tease and taunt Rebecca to the day she died.

Bullying that once was a one-on-one playground scuffle today includes a communication maze called cyberbullying and has become a growing epidemic with a nation scrambling for answers. Unfortunately, proposed remedies have posed problems, and solutions remain elusive.

* * * * *

Is cyberbullying best addressed as a legal matter or an education issue? Is resolution solely in the hands of lawmakers and judges, or better left to teachers and administrators, parents, and the students involved? Finally, is there a way to protect everyone's best interests—victims, students told they have free-speech rights, and school officials who have a duty to protect and properly educate their students?

Introducing the Problem

Bullying and cyberbullying are different. Sort of. Bullying is not new. Most of us can recall from childhood what face-to-face taunting and terrorizing were like. Cyberbullying still has those traumatic qualities, but the delivery system has changed. Instead of a school confrontation with the threat of immediate abuse, a cyber attack can come anonymously, from a distance, with words as the weapon, and before a broader audience. The result is no less harmful. In fact, the bruises or humiliation you might get from a bully's physical encounter may pale in comparison to the psychological effects of hurtful words permanently engraved in cyberspace.

Bullying—a repeated physical, abusive, face-to-face confrontation—usually is more conduct than expression. It is an offensive power play with threatened (and often actual) physical harm to a vulnerable victim. It is not surprising that school officials will exert their authority when such hateful and hurtful conduct occurs on school grounds. Parents and other citizens logically expect educators to protect students in school and ensure a safe and productive learning environment.

Despite how bullying and cyberbullying may differ in delivery and consequences, the message from society and the courts is clear: adults—from parents to school officials to law enforcement—are to protect children from physical and mental abuse. Still unclear, especially when the assault involves school-age youth and is more verbal than physical, is where protection of expression ends and punishment for conduct begins. A student can be punished for verbally assaulting a classmate face-to-face, but can a student be punished for posting off campus a targeted cyber assault if not interacting face-to-face or encouraging physical harm? Where does an educator or a judge draw the line between protected and unprotected speech? Unfortunately, the courts and lawmakers have not given school officials clear, consistent, educationally sound answers to these questions.

Bullying has become a more complex concern. Physical contact is not the bully's only recourse today. An attack can occur from a distance, by not just one but a multitude of bullies. When the assault is ongoing and online, and persists indefinitely, it becomes cyberbullying.

With the growth of new technology and its social media progeny, communication and confrontation easily and more frequently occur in cyberspace. And technology has introduced another complication. It has blurred school boundaries. School officials have slowly been extending their authority outside of school, prompted by state laws and parental pressure to respond to damaging student messages that originate off campus, but are disseminated by classmates through social media.

This new technology has spawned many yet-unanswered constitutional questions. School officials, student victims, and those disciplined for involvement are looking for answers, as are concerned students who wish to discuss a cyberbullying issue online. In this chapter, the respective interests of law and education will be examined.

- Where is the line between protected student expression and unprotected speech by a cyberbully?

- Where is the line between justified punishment for unprotected speech and questionable punishment for antagonistic, insensitive speech unlikely to inspire physical or emotional harm?
- When, if ever, are school officials legally justified to investigate and regulate social media posts that are generated off campus but show intent to harm students?
- Are options available to educators who prefer to protect the bullied through teaching strategies, guidelines, and better-informed students and staff?

The Issues

An estimated thirteen million American children are teased, taunted, or physically assaulted by their peers every year. One in six American children in 2012 reported being bullied verbally, physically, or online at least twice a month. Every day, 160,000 American children miss school because of physical or psychological attacks. The FBI's Internet Crime Complaint Center reported that in 2013 there were more cyberbullying complaints than ever. And as evidence of its severity, cyberbullying is in violation of the law in forty-nine states.

Dan Olweus, creator of the Olweus Bullying Prevention Program, says a bullied person is "exposed, repeatedly and over time, to negative actions on the part of one or more other persons, and he or she has difficulty defending himself or herself." Student bullies use their popularity, their physical strength, or access to embarrassing information to control or harm a vulnerable classmate. That "imbalance of power," real or perceived, empowers the bully physically, socially, or emotionally, according to the National Bullying Prevention Center.

At its simplest level, cyberbullying is bullying through electronic technology. That includes e-mail, text messaging, chat-room exchanges, and social-network posts. The same "imbalance of power" relationship exists between the cyberbully and the victim. What makes it different from in-person bullying are elements that add intensity, influence, audience, and permanence to the hurtful message.

Anonymity emboldens the now-more-aggressive cyberbully and intensifies the stress and vulnerability of the exposed victim. Cyberbullying from an unknown source can instantly be delivered 24/7, not just to the bullied but to others the bully wants to join in the attack. So many more students "observe" cyberbullying than would see a physical confrontation at school. These solicited participants are more likely to take part in an online assault than they would be to join a fight that broke out in the school. And once that cyberbullying message is sent, it takes on a life of its own and is almost impossible to retrieve or delete. All of this can make cyberbullying more emotionally and psychologically harmful than a face-to-face physical confrontation with a bully.

The numbers from separate studies show the growing threat of cyberbullying. In 2009, 6 percent of students in grades 6–12 reported being cyberbullied. In 2011, 16 percent of students in grades 9–12 reported being cyberbullied during the past year. Statistics the federal government and the Cyberbullying Research Center released in May 2013 indicate that 37 percent of teens reported being bullied while at school, but 52 percent reported being cyberbullied. Of those bullied face-to-face, 85 percent said the bullying occurred inside the school. One in three teens experienced cyber threats online; one in four were repeatedly bullied via cell phone or the Internet.

Victims of bullying (and cyberbullying) usually are reluctant to report the assault. Students fear retaliation if they report their peers' bullying and believe their parents will cut off phone, computer, and social-media access if those are instruments of bullying. It underscores the importance of vigilant educators when more than half (52 percent) of teens do not tell their parents when cyberbullying occurs.

A 2011 study found that while 33 percent of teenagers reported having been cyber-bully victims, only 7 percent of parents were worried about cyberbullying. However, 68 percent of young people said cyberbullying is a serious problem and 81 percent said that bullying online is easier to get away with than bullying in person. And 80 percent think it is easier to hide online bullying from parents than in-person bullying.

Balancing Conduct and Speech

Cyberbullying clearly is a speech/conduct conundrum. Traditional in-person bullying most often involves physical contact or unprotected fighting words likely to incite violence. Cyberbullying, though, does not easily fit this "bullying conduct" model. Cyberbullies use written words or visual images to communicate hateful or hurtful messages, but not personal confrontation or immediate physical assault of a victim. With more threads

of expression, and authoritative legal acknowledgment that young people do enjoy First Amendment freedom of expression, the challenge is to fairly balance the obligation to protect students' physical well-being *and* protect their free-speech rights.

School officials face a balancing act of their own when informed that a student has been bullied or cyberbullied. They are expected to investigate, though not necessarily required to punish. Within legal parameters, many administrators prefer to resolve the bullying problem through education instead of heavy-handed restrictions and punishment. Upon learning of a bullying incident, an administrator's first response would be to determine whether and how the incident is connected to the school. If a bullying incident occurred outside school property, there may be little an administrator can do to discipline the bully. With cyberbullying, unless school officials can determine the nexus between an online assault and harm in school, affecting the bullied student's education or the rights of other students, legal barriers limit the authority of administrators to punish or restrict even the cyberbully's speech.

This is one reason school officials will resist the wishes of a bullied student's parents to simply retaliate and discipline the bully, whether the attack occurs online or in person. Besides weighing the legal consequences of their response, administrators often focus first on whether they can resolve the problem in a way that supports the victim and serves other students in the school.

This chapter's focus is on legal tension in public schools—protecting students from hateful and harmful online speech without violating the First Amendment rights of students engaged in protected online expression. School officials, students, parents, lawmakers, and judges must weigh the many interests involved and determine boundaries.

The Legal Dilemma

So what is protected speech immune from punishment or restraint and what is unprotected verbal assault subject to restrictions? There seems to be little consensus on the legal front.

This was an easier conflict to address when bullying was always face-to-face, with a personal attack on school grounds. This was unacceptable *conduct*, with an easily identifiable bully and victim. And the legal system always made it easier for government (or here, public school personnel) to regulate and punish action than restrict speech.

Conduct is usually controlled through written laws and policies. Regulations about driving, drinking, dress, public behavior, and the like protect citizens from harming themselves—and one another. Rules can be more restrictive for minors. Both social responsibility and the law limit the actions of our impressionable young citizens. Regulations dealing with what they can and cannot do, and when and where, are well within the purview of adults—parents, educators, store owners, and others.

When government has a valid interest (e.g., preserving order and protecting students), officials can clearly define acceptable behavior and regulate where, when, and how students who violate these behavioral rules can be punished. What

the bully said, before or during confrontation with a victim, was seldom of concern, since the speech was part of the bullying behavior being punished.

But cyberbullying has a different context, one impossible to address solely as conduct. While school officials can regulate the where, when, and how of behavior on school grounds, they cannot punish students engaged in a fight at the local shopping mall. So what happens when hateful expression that spouts from the mouth of a bully in school becomes a cyberbully's posted tirade from an off-campus computer or mobile device? It is easy to understand why school officials can quiet a shouting match in the hallways or a verbal attack in the classroom, but what can they do to the student who, from off campus, e-mails or texts a message that urges classmates to ridicule or name-call a targeted student? Cyberbullying has a *speech* component that can bring more harm to the victim than words alone uttered by a playground bully. And when the bully's message is shared not just with those personally viewing a student confrontation, but with an unknown number of electronically connected classmates, this could affect the school day for many students.

Bothersome cause-effect concerns have to be addressed. When does teasing become bullying? When is there sufficient evidence, or likely imminence, of harm to the bullied victim? When is an online statement *not* cyberbullying but instead protected opinion or comment?

To take a step back in time, state legislation and school policies on bullying emanated from state laws dealing with harassment. Both of these harmful acts were face-to-face, personal assaults of a physical nature, identified by law or policy as unlawful behavior. When cyberbullying emerged as a comparable threat in the late 1990s, it was logical to also treat this corollary to bullying as unlawful conduct. It was only when the harmful personal assaults were delivered through cyberspace, not in-your-face, that free-speech questions arose. One might prevent harm from a bully by avoiding him in school, by ducking when he tries to hit you, or by fighting back. But how do you avoid a cyber attack, control how and when you are hit, or hope to fight back against what may be many attackers?

Administrators, teachers, students, school-board members, parents, lawmakers—everyone wants answers. It seems logical to start with existing and acceptable regulations on bullying. Certainly the school's interests—student safety and disruption-free education—remain the same. But terms must be defined. "Harm" from cyberbullying is more than physical; defining and restricting harassment and intimidation amplify the harm beyond physical assault to psychological damage. But harm must come from more than an unpopular idea or an insult. When determining whether a post is a hyperbolic threat or prelude to a physical assault, the challenge is to distinguish between protected and unprotected speech.

Cloudy Court Guidance

During the past four decades, two separate civil rights issues have evolved on parallel tracks—one from lawmakers, the other from judges—providing mixed advice to schools dealing with cyberbullying. Prevention of measurable harm to students goes back to federal laws offering civil rights protection from harassment on the basis of gender, race, or disability. Student rights of free-expression emanate primarily from the 1969 U.S. Supreme Court ruling in *Tinker v. Des Moines Independent Community School District*, protecting individual speech that does not disrupt the learning process or intrude upon the rights of other students.

The *Tinker* thread through the courts validated students' constitutional right of free expression—what they could say in school, free of restriction, and what public-school officials could stop or punish based on the Supreme Court's ruling. The harassment thread from legislation focused on what government has a right to regulate—the conduct of citizens (who, as *Tinker* acknowledged, include students). With more latitude to regulate behavior than speech, legislators passed laws identifying inappropriate, hurtful conduct, and instituted policies and practices to guide public officials responsible for protecting students from such harm. The U.S. Constitution permitted defensible time, place, and manner regulations and justified punishment for unlawful conduct.

When the courts were asked to resolve conflicts between students and school officials in these matters, it was for different reasons. Expecting the school to control conduct, parents went to court believing, in a harassment or unfair-treatment case (and later with bullying), that the administration had *not* taken appropriate steps to protect a student. One lesson school officials learned early was that failure to act, and to protect students from harm, would be negligent in the eyes of a judge.

But when parents (representing their sons or daughters) went to court with a constitutional rights question, it usually was because of what school officials did, not what they failed to do. Students argued that they were harmed because their ideas were suppressed in ways inconsistent with Supreme Court standards. Lower courts repeatedly, in case after case during the 1970s and early 1980s, agreed that overzealous school officials had exceeded their authority by stopping merely unpopular or disagreeable speech, not content that was disruptive or harmful to students.

During these years, bullying took its long-standing position of physical conduct, not to be confused in any way with student expression as a constitutional freedom involving protected ideas and beliefs. School officials knew that they were obligated to act and protect students from physical harm, but that they should not interfere with students' expression unless they could show they followed specific guidelines for content-neutral restrictions and had valid justifications for such limits.

That was the message when, in *Tinker*, the Supreme Court overturned lower court rulings that had affirmed longstanding deference to the *in loco parentis* role of school officials. The High Court did not reject this precept, but added the caveat that students retained the free-speech rights of all citizens. Not all student expression in school was protected. Just as government is obliged to justify limits placed on adults exercising this freedom, the Court said, so must public-school officials offer evidence that they have valid reasons for restricting student expression. School officials were told they can restrict student speech in two ways. Unprotected, *Tinker* said, is speech that "might reasonably (lead) school

authorities to forecast substantial disruption of or material interference with school activities" or that collides "with the rights of other students to be secure and to be let alone." Neither of these was present when Mary Beth Tinker, her brother John, and their friend Christopher Eckhardt were suspended from school for merely wearing black armbands to school to protest the Vietnam War.

This landmark case marked a dramatic shift in the schools. Administrators could no longer rely on their authoritative role to control what their students said. It was now assumed that students could express their personal beliefs while at school unless such expression was demonstrably disruptive or invasive of other students' rights.

Administrators, concerned that student speech would undermine authority and disrupt the schools, reluctantly and modestly set new policies to regulate student speech. Almost all regulations challenged in court were found to be unconstitutionally vague and overbroad. Courts ruled that schools too often imprecisely defined "substantial disruption" and/or insufficiently supported administrators' assertions that sanctioned student speech contributed to expected, if not actual, disruption. Little attention was given in court to the legal argument that *Tinker* also said that speech was unprotected if it infringed on the rights of other students. Cyberbullying may have changed that.

Supreme Court's Path toward Cyberbullying Case

For seventeen years after *Tinker*, the burden of proof in free-speech cases remained on school officials, not students. But then the U.S. Supreme Court began retreating from the rigid requirements facing school officials. Never totally abandoning the students-have-speech-rights message of *Tinker*, the High Court in several rulings during the next two decades made it easier for administrators to justify restrictions on student expression.

After the 1969 *Tinker* ruling, courts repeatedly cautioned school officials not to overreact when students express themselves in school. The High Court lightened the burden on administrators in 1986. In *Bethel School District v. Fraser*, the Court said that the school appropriately punished a student who at a school assembly used a less-than-subtle sexual metaphor in a two-minute campaign speech for a student council candidate. The speech led to no "substantial disruption," but the Court said that beyond the constraints of *Tinker*, school officials have the authority to punish speech that is lewd, vulgar, or indecent. *Tinker* standards remain, the Court said, but Chief Justice Warren Burger added, "The undoubted freedom to advocate unpopular and controversial views in schools and classrooms must be balanced against the society's countervailing interest in teaching students the boundaries of socially appropriate behavior."

Two years later, the High Court upheld censorship of a student newspaper, ruling in *Hazelwood School District v. Kuhlmeier* that school officials deserve breathing room in speech cases. The Eighth Circuit Court of Appeals ruled for the students, saying that the newspaper did not substantially disrupt the school or interfere with the rights of students. The Supreme Court did not refute this, but chose to neither apply nor overturn *Tinker*. Instead, the Court expanded on its message in *Bethel* and said that administrators also have a valid interest in regulating expression that is inconsistent with the school's "basic educational mission," messages that the public could incorrectly perceive as reflecting the school's beliefs. Although *Hazelwood* dealt with a school-sponsored venue, the Court's reasoning has been applied since then in some off-campus cyberbullying cases where someone considered a school's failure to act to be educational malpractice.

The court will consider an important point before deciding whether administrators can regulate what is said: Are ideas expressed in a school venue within the school's purview (thus seen by the public to have the administration's OK) or do they come independently from a student beyond the school's reach? This question was asked again in 2007 when an Alaska high school student unfurled a banner that said "Bong Hits 4 Jesus." In *Morse v. Frederick*, the Supreme Court once more ruled in favor of the school. Joseph Frederick said he was outside school grounds when he displayed his silly, meaningless banner as the Olympic Torch bearer came by on the street across from his school. Though Frederick argued that there was no public disturbance from his personal message expressed on a public street, the principal suspended him from school.

In a close decision, the Court upheld the suspension. *Tinker* again was acknowledged, but not applied, as the majority in *Morse* ruled that this was a school-related event, since students were excused to attend and teachers were there to supervise. And using a theme from both _Bethel_ and _Hazelwood_, the Court said that Frederick clearly was saying _something_ about drug use, so school officials understandably would not want the public to believe the school tolerated drug use.

Before the dust had settled in the _Morse_ case, administrators knew that they had more to worry about than a student carrying an objectionable banner near the school. With the rapid growth of communication technology came the emergence of online bullying. Judges in the lower courts soon realized the apprehension of school officials fearful that the mobile devices readily available to students could make it harder for the schools to protect students from harm.

Beginning with _Bethel_, the legal burden shifted from the school administrator back to the student, as it was in the pre-_Tinker_ years. The _Tinker_ legacy also was eroding in school. For thirty years after _Tinker_, when students' non-disruptive speech was stifled in school, they could create and distribute a written "underground" protest outside of school, beyond an administrator's legal reach. School officials seldom interfered with off-campus speech (or conduct). But as technology emerged and computers, smartphones, and social-networking sites became common carriers for student speech, school boundaries became blurred.

Administrators, emboldened by new legal latitude to ensure safety and smooth school operations, began using the "substantial disruption" standard beyond the boundaries set by the _Tinker_ Court that established that criterion. Courts have been divided on whether _Tinker_ can be applied off campus in this way, but they seem receptive to an educator's argument that where the speech originated is less important than the likelihood that its negative impact will be felt by students within the school.

For decades, student free-speech litigation has focused on the "substantial disruption" standard. But with the recent growth of cyberbullying, the second tenet of _Tinker_ has emerged. Also unprotected, the Court said then, is student expression that intrudes on the rights of others. This is seldom argued when student speech concerns school policies or education issues— often the focus of student press coverage. But cyberbullying usually targets an individual. In school, that is seldom a teacher. Because power is often an incentive and almost always a factor in bullying (or cyberbullying), students are far more vulnerable. It is not surprising that school officials, obligated to protect their students and offer them a safe school environment conducive to learning, argue in court that a cyberbullying attack, using social media and crossing school boundaries, intrudes on the rights of a bullied student.

Proponents of student expression are concerned that _Tinker_ today is being used in ways that do not protect but instead threaten free speech. They argue that extending the regulatory authority of school officials to social media content generated off campus will intimidate or punish students commenting on school-related issues. Not defending cyberbullying, civil libertarians fear that dealing with this volatile issue in terms of speech rather than conduct could result in unjustified restrictions on free expression. Interpreting and applying Supreme Court rulings, judges are to balance respective rights of students and school officials. In cyberbullying cases, concern for all students means considering the rights of *all* students—not just the victims, but also other students who may want to discuss the issue.

As of 2014 the U.S. Supreme Court has not yet ruled on cyberbullying, or any case concerning student online communication, but is likely to hear such a case. With cyberbullying laws in virtually every state, and district and appellate courts at odds on how to reconcile and apply the High Court's rulings in *Tinker, Bethel, Hazelwood,* and *Morse*, school officials are searching for solutions in the face of demanding parents who want assurances that their schools are safe and their children protected.

Guidelines clearly are needed to protect or prevent harm to bullied victims—not just those bullied in school, but students targeted anonymously in posted threats or personal, hurtful half-truths. School officials reason that cyberbullying, akin to harassment, is worthy of off-campus monitoring when victims can feel the effects of such attacks while in school. But if administrators intervene because of what the cyberbully says, prior court rulings on student expression must be considered.

Because the U.S. Supreme Court has not dealt with off-campus student speech, schools (and lower courts) usually have applied *Tinker v. Des Moines*. Though it determined the rights of student speakers and obligations of administrators inside the school, *Tinker* gave school officials two justifications for restricting student speech—threat of substantial disruption and intrusion on the rights of others.

Believing that preserving the educational process and ensuring the safety of students trumped an individual's right to speak, school officials argued that *Tinker* permitted punishment for off-campus speech when they could demonstrate one of the Court's free-speech exceptions.

Almost every time the school was challenged in court for punishing off-campus speech, administrators argued that the expression was substantially disruptive. Judges made school officials demonstrate that they could "reasonably foresee" substantial disruption inside the school and tie it to specific off-campus speech. Before the dramatic increase in cyberbullying, and the violent school shootings in Columbine and Newtown, the courts pressed school officials hard for evidence of the link between off-campus speech and school disruption. For the past decade, however, judges have given administrators more latitude, easing the burden-of-proof requirements. If an online message connected the sender in any way to school gun violence, courts were likely to justify intervention on the basis of either substantial disruption or intrusion on the rights of students in that school.

Frank LoMonte, executive director of the Student Press Law Center, acknowledges that it is harder these days to defend the free-speech rights of young citizens. LoMonte believes that *Tinker* should be applied only to student expression within the school, where speech can be narrowly defined and its effects measured. Off-campus speech takes too many forms, he says, and comes from too many different sources and circumstances. *Tinker* offers too little protection to such an array of speech outside of school, LoMonte argues, adding that most well-intentioned, anti-bullying legislation uses vague and overbroad language that is either difficult to fairly enforce or doomed to defeat as unconstitutional if challenged in court.

Blurred Boundaries for Student Speech

All U.S. Supreme Court student-speech cases have dealt with expression in school-related venues. So why have lower courts subsequently, in cyberbullying cases, allowed schools to use the free-expression exceptions of *Tinker*—substantial disruption and intrusion on the rights of others—when regulating speech outside of school?

Laws in at least eleven states authorize school officials to discipline students for off-campus behavior that substantially disrupts the school's learning environment. Federal circuit courts are split on this legal interpretation of Supreme Court precedents regarding the school's authority beyond school boundaries, but within judicial circuits allowing off-campus scrutiny and sanctions, state legislatures have given their schools off-campus authority.

The saturation of social media and the ease with which connected students communicate across school boundaries have pressured schools to use that power. As lawmakers move closer to equating cyberbullying with unprotected conduct, and require schools to have compatible school policies on bullying, it is easy to understand why administrators believe they are expected to intercede whenever and wherever a communicated message could qualify as "bullying."

The Supreme Court has never reversed its *Tinker* declaration that students have free-speech rights. School authorities therefore should be careful not to quickly label as "bullying" messages that qualify as harsh, critical, but protected free expression. Administrators can be tempted to intervene. They have seen federal courts for almost two decades retreat from the students-as-citizens free-speech posture of the 1970s and early 1980s. Today, judges seem more concerned that, at a time when school gun violence has frequently and tragically taken student lives and communication and technology have made it harder to insulate students from harm, school officials need more latitude to fulfill their responsibility to ensure a safe school environment. If this means sacrificing some of a student's speech freedom, so be it. That is the message many school officials are hearing—from the courts, lawmakers, and parents.

* * * * * *

Defenders of free expression worry that limits will be placed on students who are *not* bullies but who communicate online extensively—often frankly, sometimes critically. Examples would be students who take an unpopular position on a religious or political issue, who criticize a teacher for what they believe is an unfair grade, who express disgust when an administrator enforces a school policy, or who offer an unflattering opinion of the school's Homecoming queen.

If school officials believe that a student's post constitutes cyberbullying, is unprotected speech, and is a punishable offense, what recourse does the student have? The line between protected and unprotected speech fades when cyberbullying is at issue. The mandate to protect student victims from the harmful effects of bullying has blurred school boundaries to the point where restricting off-campus speech can easily seem justified. What regulatory limits remain?

There is little doubt that school officials can and should intercede when *on-campus* conduct (bullying) or speech (harassment) poses an imminent threat to a student or the educational system. It is when the taunting and cyberbullying originate *off-campus* that the school must reasonably foresee that the speech contributes to substantial disruption or the invasion of student rights in school.

School officials since *Tinker* have consistently used the "substantial disruption" prong of *Tinker* to justify punishment of off-campus speech. The main reason is simple: Most content objectionable to school officials has dealt with criticism of school policies, practices, or personnel. That made it hard for administrators to argue that such speech was unprotected because criticism of the school would "interfere with the rights of students." It was more judicious, and perhaps easier, to argue that attacks on school decision makers and their actions substantially disrupt the workings of the school.

Cyberbullying changed this. Posted content, while still addressed to other students, called for harmful, if not disruptive, action against a student. Ostensibly, this meant that school officials could use both of the *Tinker* exceptions to protected speech—content that was disruptive *and* infringed on the rights of students victimized online. Courts have given school officials more discretion in one other circumstance: When there is evidence that an electronic message a student posts off campus threatens serious physical violence, as per Columbine or Newtown, or the student is engaged in illegal activity. The greater the threat of physical harm that could result from an online post, the less likely courts are to require evidence that violent action truly could result.

An example is the Ninth Circuit Court's ruling in *Wynar v. Douglas County School District* in late 2013. When Nevada high-school sophomore Landon Wynar told friends on MySpace about rifles and other weapons he owned, and identified classmates he intended to shoot and dates matching the Columbine and Virginia Tech shootings, school officials were notified. Wynar fought his expulsion from school, claiming that he had been joking and that his Instant Messages were protected by the First Amendment. The court disagreed, citing *Tinker*.

Nationally, circuit courts of appeals are split on whether *Tinker* should be applied when off-campus student speech is involved. But this split has occurred among schools arguing *Tinker*'s "substantial disruption" prong. The Third and Fifth Circuit courts require school officials to use *Tinker*'s cause-and-effect "substantial disruption" standard to justify the regulation of off-campus speech. The Fourth and Eighth Circuit courts have supported school officials' findings of substantial disruption.

In *Wynar*, the Ninth Circuit said that because of the severity of this threat, both prongs of *Tinker*—disruption and student rights infringement—could support the school's position. The Court said that "when faced with an identifiable threat of school violence, schools may take disciplinary action in response to off-campus speech." The appellate court also acknowledged *Tinker*'s seldom-used second free-speech exception, noting that violent threats clearly "invade the rights of others," in this case, students' right to be safe in school. The *Wynar* ruling left open the question of whether cyberbullying qualified, in a milder, less violent way, as an intrusion on the rights of students.

* * * * * *

Just as the U.S. Supreme Court ruled in the "Bong Hits 4 Jesus" case, and lower courts in social media and cyberbullying cases, how the free-speech standards of *Tinker* apply is less a matter of where speech occurred. More important to the courts is what was said and what are the likely consequences of the ideas expressed.

It may seem peripheral to the concern for victims of cyberbullying, but to be sure the bully's speech is targeted, and not just anyone's speech about bullying, another Supreme Court case and legal concept deserve mention. When a hurtful message calls for harm to someone, whether that speech is protected or unprotected can depend on what was said, to whom, and with what result.

When the problem is cyberbullying, should the student be punished who encourages others to bully—in violation of law or policy—or should it only be the students who act because of the speech? What constitutes punishable advocacy distinct from distasteful or offensive expression? This requires a review of how—outside the context of cyberbullying—courts distinguish between protected and unprotected

advocacy of illegal action. Supreme Court guidance comes from a landmark case dealing not with the specific issue of bullying, but a broader concept. Can someone legally deliver a message that encourages listeners to break the law? How close must the advocate's speech be to the illegal action of those who hear the message?

In 1969, the Supreme Court ruled unconstitutional an Ohio statute used to convict a Ku Klux Klan speaker who told his followers to rid the country of Jews and Blacks. In *Brandenburg v. Ohio*, the Court said that advocacy of an illegal, but improbable, act was protected speech unless it posed an imminent danger by inciting receptive listeners likely to immediately engage in the illegal act. Subsequently, the questions asked of government or law-enforcement officials wishing to stop or punish proponents of illegal acts were "Is the illegal act likely to occur as an immediate response to the speech?" and "Were those who heard the call for illegal action likely to do what they were told?"

Questions of imminence and incitement have guided advocacy litigation, but a third factor has been given more credence. In *Rice v. Paladin Enterprises*, the Fourth Circuit Court of Appeals ruled in 1997 that the publisher of a how-to manual on ways to kill people could be sued by the families of victims whose killer followed in detail the book's directions. The appellate court ruled that the book was not protected advocacy of an abstract idea, and the publisher had to know that readers would use the manual to commit crimes. The Supreme Court allowed the court's ruling to stand.

Courts since have said that the speaker's intent to harm someone deserves more attention in advocacy cases than whether the harm is imminent. If there is a cause-effect link between the speech and the illegal act, whether the action takes place immediately is less important than whether the speaker wants and expects listeners to engage in the illegal act.

These advocacy criteria could be applied when school officials consider punishing a student who criticizes school policy or rants against a teacher he believes gave an unfair grade to the student.

What about the accused cyberbully? If the focus is on what is said, and whether the individual's off-campus speech disrupts school activities or infringes on a student's right to a safe learning environment, the legal precepts of advocacy might help balance protected free expression and unprotected provocation of illegal behavior (which cyberbullying *is* in forty-nine states). Was the cyberbully proposing immediate harm to a student? Were those who received the bully's proposal likely to follow the bully's lead? Did the bully who posted the threat intend to harm or have others harm the victim?

SPLC executive director Frank LoMonte wants to see *Brandenburg*, rather than *Tinker*, applied to off-campus speech, but few courts have done so. The Ninth Circuit Court in *Wynar* said that when off-campus expression goes beyond mocking students or cursing school policies to detailing gun violence toward students, *Tinker* should apply, with broad discretion going to school officials.

* * * * * *

School officials face another challenge when deciding whether to intercede after a parent reports that her daughter is being bullied online. What are the options if there is no early evidence of an emotional toll on the targeted student? If the off-campus taunting and name-calling have not resulted in any observable effect in school, when and how can an administrator respond? Officials know that they are to ensure students a safe and sound learning environment, and that when dealing with an individual student's speech, they will have to link student expression and substantial disruption. If the online attack originates from a school computer or from a bully's use of a social network in school, administrators are clearly justified to promptly act. They realize that their failure to act could imply to the public that the school condones such behavior, and they know that school officials who do not act promptly when bullying occurs can find themselves in court—and losing.

Tinker remains a legal reminder to school officials that students should be encouraged to think, speak, and learn active citizenship. *Bethel, Hazelwood* and *Morse*—all upholding administrators' decisions to curtail or punish speech—tell school officials they are obligated to protect all students, not just those who speak out. So many administrators search for a way to protect everyone's interests.

Seeking Answers

With a growing number of state laws and school policies on cyberbullying, there has been a comparable increase in the number of students whose speech is stifled by such regulations. Young citizens and education leaders are searching for guidelines, if not answers. Students want the latest technology to communicate today, and school officials strive to stay one step ahead of these trial-and-error learners. Where *are* the trail markers?

This examination of cyberbullying and its troublesome communication/conduct components has revealed the challenges facing educators and students. We have seen how the courts have not clearly or consistently told student speakers and school administrators where the boundaries are between protected and unprotected speech. Can state and/or federal legislation help?

Cyberbullying has the attention of lawmakers, who have amended laws on harassment and bullying or enacted new legislation addressing "the willful and repeated use of cell phones, computers and other electronic communication devices to harass and threaten others." Colorado in 2005 was the first state to do so, with Idaho and South Carolina following in 2006. By 2009 twenty-one states had cyberbullying laws, and the total increased to thirty-six states by the end of 2010, according to the National Conference of State Legislatures. By 2013 every state but Montana had a cyberbullying law. All required schools to have policies on how to deal with cyberbullying, and forty-four states gave school officials the authority to discipline violators.

If school officials found consolation in having laws or local policies to help navigate the shifting terrain of cyberbullying, they learned that there is truth to the maxim "the devil is in the details." New laws and policies frustrated—for different

reasons—administrators, parents, and free-speech proponents. Laws varied among the forty-nine legislative bodies that fashioned them, and differences were amplified because each school district adopted its own policies.

Precise definitions and clear parameters are required if a school's rules and regulations are to withstand a constitutional challenge in court. That goes for state and federal laws, as well. Rules and regulations will be judged unconstitutional if written in vague or overbroad language. Saying that "disruptive speech can be punished" is vague (because one does not know how the enforcer will define "disruptive" or "be punished") and is overbroad (because the vagueness allows the enforcer too much discretion, likely leading to punishment not just of unprotected speech but also of speech that is protected). Students and school officials both must clearly understand what is permitted as protected free expression and what speech has no constitutional protection.

The American Bar Association, in *School Bullying: How Long Is the Arm of the Law?*, noted how this posed problems for school officials. Knowing they were to protect their students, schools struggled to understand the new laws and policies, plagued by vague, overbroad, and imprecise wording, inadequate due process for accused bullies, even failure to offer evenhanded protection to some targeted students. If any problem kept a school from complying, and a bullied child suffered as a result, school officials in growing numbers found themselves facing irate parents in a courtroom. And those defending free speech, such as

Frank LoMonte of the Student Press Law Center, argued that well-intentioned regulations often punished not only harassment and serious threats, but also offensive or annoying speech protected by the First Amendment.

Protecting Every Student's Interests

When courts have not clearly answered the legal question of "Can we or can't we?" school officials may feel more comfortable responding from an educator's perspective, answering the question "What should we do?" It can be safer to focus on the educational environment and what is best for the students involved in a cyberbullying incident. If a simplified solution narrows options to punishment or suppression based primarily on what a student has posted online, what started as a fair way to protect the victim can easily become a legal debate over free speech.

There are challenges when legal mandates and sound education are decision-making, should-we-or-shouldn't-we considerations. Ethicists remind us that many more actions and expressions are legally permissible than are ethically sound. With student expression, courts have set limits on both what students can say, and when and how they can say it. But school officials have court-mandated limits too, regarding what student speech can be stopped or punished, and when and how schools can regulate student speech. Students and administrators can remain within the boundaries of lawful speech and regulation and still act and express themselves as responsible citizens and educators.

So there is no easy way to resolve the speech/conduct issues of cyberbullying. Brandishing the legal arguments of each side—student free-speech rights and administrative authority to protect the rights of *all* students and ensure student safety and a productive school environment—bullying students and protective school officials are easily tempted to exceed their legal boundaries, using instead the farther-reaching arguments in defense of what they choose to do.

Judges have been sympathetic to the school's protective efforts, but the cost of litigation, the questionable effectiveness of simply punishing bullies, and the risk of violating free-speech rights have convinced many administrators to focus instead on students' understanding of cyberbullying and the values of civil behavior. Guidelines have come from scholars researching this problem, professional education associations, and federal agencies.

Taking Preventive Steps

Prevention and intervention are both part of the educators' response. Some schools have created a "digital citizenship" thread through their K-12 curriculum that, among other things, encourages all students to actively participate in efforts to curb and counter cyberbullying. A school district may create an anti-bullying task force to educate students and the adult community about what bullying is, how and why it is harmful and inappropriate, and what schools can do to protect victims. Students and parents are central to early intervention.

The Robert F. Kennedy Center for Justice and Human Rights launched

Project SEATBELT (Safe Environments Achieved Through Bullying Prevention, Engagement, Leadership and Teaching Respect) in late 2013 to underscore this effort to protect victims by reducing bullying instead of punishing bullies. An educational response to cyberbullying teaches students to value civility, follow guidelines for ethical behavior, and rather than stifle or discourage communication among students, encourage a respectful exchange of ideas.

In her 2012 book *Bullied*, Carrie Goldman has a chapter on restorative justice. She says this response to bullying is "not about rules and punishment, but about values and relationship. . . . [It is] not about a violation of rules; it is about a violation of people." Having a specific policy that defines and prohibits cyberbullying can be part of the solution, she says, but "protocols also must be in place for intervening when incidents occur."

Schools required by law or policy to have procedures in place for dealing with cyberbullying must clearly define boundaries for protected and unprotected student *behavior*. Educators often are unsure of their authority beyond school boundaries, especially in terms of student expression. Most believe they cannot stop or punish cyberbullies attacking from outside of school. Courts have required even more specificity when school policy defines what *speech* is subject to punishment. Few policies explain the rationale behind specific regulations. Instead, school policy, like state law, becomes a mandate for student behavior and an instrument for punishment, not an incentive for better teaching and learning.

Educators believe that vague or sweeping laws and school policies may console the public, but they do little to help the victims of cyberbullying. An appropriate response must protect the victim and educate the bully and other students affected, school officials say, adding that their response as educators should be to see that the problem is resolved and will not recur. Acting in concert with law or policy can punish offenders and protect the interests of school officials if the issue goes to court, but a broad, multi-faceted assault on cyberbullying can be of more help to bullies and bullied students.

As early as 2008, the U.S. Department of Justice issued a Model Acceptable Use Policy for Information Technology Resources in the Schools. Its first two of eight rules told students to engage in "kind and respectful" communication and "report threatening or upsetting materials to a teacher." Students were told not to "transmit, copy, or create material that violates the school's code of conduct, such as messages . . . meant to bully or harass." The U.S. Department of Education today encourages schools to have a long-term plan that includes preventive steps, such as creating an anti-bullying curriculum, placing an accent on responsible citizenship, teaching digital literacy, and involving parents in anti-cyberbullying initiatives.

As more schools consider electronic devices essential to the curriculum and distribute tablets to all students, school officials know they have to remind both students and parents of their added responsibility. Students have to learn to follow their conscience when communicating in this wired world, one educator said.

Acknowledging that bullying and cyberbullying are similar assaults, defined as "willful and repeated infliction of harm," some schools have adopted a companion Code of Conduct that defines and accents appropriate student behavior. Just as clearly stated school policies help administrators meet their legal and professional obligations, so can a Conduct Code guide students' actions while they learn the importance of civility and respect for one another.

But school officials face more legal hurdles if they decide that a comparable Speech Code can help them curtail or punish cyberbullying. As noted earlier, authorities can regulate a person's conduct (i.e., time, place, and manner) for valid reasons, but if they want to stop or restrict someone's speech, limits cannot be subjectively based on liking or disagreeing with what a person says. There are only narrow, specific legal justifications for suppressing someone's expression.

Charles Haynes is director of the Religious Freedom Education Project and co-producer of *Harassment, Bullying and Free Expression: Guidelines for Free and Safe Public Schools*, published in 2012. Seventeen groups representing the interests of religion, education, and civil liberties proposed ways to balance "the need for school safety vs. the need for free expression." In a news release about the guidelines, Haynes said, "When we take freedom seriously, we create a safer environment. When we overreact and try to shut down speech, . . . we make people angry, we polarize people. And students don't respond well to being told they can't express what they believe."

In search of common ground for student expression and student protection, educators and free-speech advocates are finding that the road toward Cyberbully Control remains under construction. Ambiguous or unclear road signs have made it hard for decision makers to deal with cyberbullying. The legal and learning landscape calls for concessions. More discussion of the problem is preferable to heavy-handed suppression of student speech. But unbridled expression that is hateful and hurtful, if not disruptive, is no solace to a bullied victim.

* * * * *

No clear template has emerged for addressing cyberbullying incidents such as that of Rebecca Sedwick, the twelve-year-old who, unable to cope with the posted tirades of her classmates, jumped to her death from a tower near her Florida home. County prosecutors tracked the cyberbully taunts to a dozen other students posting on Facebook.

Two girls—one twelve years old, the other fourteen—were charged as felons for criminal acts related to Rebecca's death. But two months after Rebecca's death, prosecutors dropped the charges. According to the *New York Times*, those close to the case said there was too little evidence that the postings from these girls were criminal acts. Experts said that so many factors are a part of cyberbullying cases that one of many potential contributing factors in a suicide is unlikely to justify criminal charges.

If blame/fault cannot easily be tied to one action (or one's comments), it is unlikely that simply stopping or punishing the speaker, even a bully, is a productive alternative. Regulation of speech is justifiable. But the where-when-why-and-how circumstances are important. Not just what is said, but the context and consequences as well must be weighed if speech protection is to be preserved.

Thomas Eveslage
Temple University
Scott T. Eveslage
Lower Merion (PA) School District

See also Free Press versus Public Safety; Generational Expectations; New Technology: Free Speech Messiah or First Amendment Traitor?; Where Are the Schoolhouse Gates?

Further Reading

Alvarez, L. "Suicide of Girl after Bullying Raises Worries on Web Site." *New York Times*, September 14, 2013. http://www.nytimes.com/2013/09/14/us/suicide-of-girl-after-bullying-raises-worries-on-web-sites.html?pagewanted=all.

American Jewish Committee and Religious Freedom Education Project/First Amendment Center. "Harassment, Bullying and Free Expression: Guidelines for Free and Safe Public Schools," May 22, 2012.

Calvoz, R. R., B. W. Davis, and M. A. Gooden. "Cyber Bullying and Free Speech: Striking an Age-Appropriate Balance." *Cleveland State Law Review* 61, no. 2: 357–389 (2013).

"Cyber / Bullying Statistics." Cyberbullying Research Center, May 7, 2013. http://www.statisticbrain.com/cyber-bullying-statistics.

Davis, M. R. "Schools Tackle Legal Twists and Turns of Cyberbullying." *Education Week*, February 4, 2011. http://www.edweek.org/dd/articles/2011/02/09/02cyberbullying.h04.html.

Goldman, C. *Bullied: What Every Parent, Teacher and Kid Needs to Know about Ending the Cycle of Fear.* New York: HarperCollins, 2012.

Hilden, J. "Why North Carolina's New Law Making It a Crime for Students to Bully Teachers Online Is Deeply Troubling from a First Amendment Standpoint." *Justia Verdict*, December 10, 2012. http://verdict.justia.com/2012/12/10/why-north-carolinas-new-law-making-it-a-crime-for-students-to-bully-teachers-online-is-deeply-troubling-from-a-first-amendment-standpoint.

Hinduja, S., and J. W. Patchin. "State Cyberbullying Laws: A Brief Review of State Cyberbullying Laws and Policies." Cyberbullying Research Center, July 2013. http://www.cyberbullying.us/state-cyberbullying-laws-a-brief-review-of-state-cyberbullying-laws-and-policies.

Ivester, M. l0l . . . OMG!: What Every Student Needs to Know about Online Reputation Management, Digital Citizenship and Cyberbullying. CreateSpace Independent Publishing Platform, 2011.

Keenan, C. "State of Cyberbullying." *SPLC Report*, Winter 2010–11. https://www.splc.org/news/report_detail.asp?id=1582&edition=54.

LoMonte, F. "'Cyberbullying' and First Amendment." *Quill & Scroll*, Spring 2011.

LoMonte, F. "Effective Statewide Policy to Combat Cyberbullying in Delaware Schools." Testimony of the Student Press Law Center in Delaware cyberbully legislation hearings, April 27, 2012. http://www.splc.org/pdf/del_testimony42712.pdf.

LoMonte, F. "Zero Tolerance for Online Bullying Can Hamper Free Speech." American Bar Association: Children's Rights Litigation, September 28, 2012.

Magid, L. "When Schools Can Discipline Off-Campus Behavior." *Threshold*, Summer 2009. http://www.safekids.com/2010/02/25/when-school-can-discipline-off-campus-behavior.

Noguchi, S. "Teaching Crude Teens Good Digital Citizenship." *San Jose Mercury News*, August 31, 2011.

Olweus, D. *Bullying at School: What We Know and What We Can Do.* Hoboken, NJ: Wiley-Blackwell, 2013.

Patchin, J. W., J. A. Schafer, and S. Hinduja. "Cyberbullying and Sexting: Law Enforcement Perceptions." *FBI Law Enforcement Bulletin*, June 4, 2013. http://www.fbi.gov/stats-services/publications/law-enforcement-bulletin/2013/june/cyberbullying-and-sexting.

"RFK Center Launches Project SEATBELT, an Anti-Bullying Project." Robert F. Kennedy Center for Justice and Human Rights, June 5, 2013. http://rfkcenter.org/rfk-project-seatbelt-bullying-prevention-program-launched-5.

54

GOOGLE BOOKS

Google Books embodies what might be characterized as a cyber-utopian vision: to be a permanent, openly accessible repository of the world's knowledge. Google describes the purpose of Google Books as making the content of books discoverable through searching. Google scans books, converts them to machine-readable text using optical character recognition technology, and stores them in a searchable database. Google likens Google Books to a digital card catalog: it includes bibliographic information like a traditional library's card catalog. But unlike a card catalog, which only provides keywords for topics, Google Books also allows searching of the full text of all its books simultaneously and the display of excerpts of text of most of these books. Google Books, in its current form, does not make a scanned book available in its entirety unless the book has no copyright protection. Google provides links so users can buy the books online from major retailers or borrow them from libraries. Since Google Books began in 2004, over twenty million titles have been digitized. Its partner libraries and many observers have praised the underlying vision. Some publishers and authors have objected that copying and display of works violate copyright, and some have sued Google.

Google Books involves two programs, the Partner Program and the Library Project. The Partner Program, formerly named Google Print, is more like a bookstore in that it aims to promote books so they can be discovered and sold. In this program, partners, who are the copyright holders of books, cooperate with Google, which scans a book (if an electronic copy is not already available), then stores and displays the book's contents. Google also gives the partner a digital copy of the book. Partners decide how much of a book will be displayed, from 20 percent to 100 percent, and they may even allow free downloads. The Partner Program ran ads next to displayed books until 2013. Partners can also choose to make their books available through Google Play, Google's e-book store.

Google Books' largest program, the Google Library Project, refers to Google's efforts to scan the contents of some of the world's major research libraries. The Library Project began in 2004 and its partner libraries originally included major universities such as Harvard, Michigan, Stanford, and Oxford, and the New York Public Library, but now include more partners, most of them university libraries. Google spearhead this effort to digitize books, with the help of partner libraries, and provided proprietary technology for scanning the books.

Copyright Issues Involving the Google Library Project

Many of the works that Google digitizes for the Library Project are in the "public domain," the term used in copyright law for when no copyright protection is available. Google makes available many public domain works in their entirety to view online or to download. Many works are in the public domain because they had no copyright to begin with, such as the works of William Shakespeare (1564–1616), which were published around a century before the first copyright law took effect England in 1710. Thus, early editions of the works of Shakespeare are available for free download from Google Books. (However, some later editions, which may have additions such as modern spellings of words and text annotations, are still under copyright protection of their own, and thus their availability may be limited.) Other works are in the public domain because their copyright terms have expired, so reproducing and displaying them present no legal obstacles. Examples include the works of Charles Dickens, including his 1843 novella, *A Christmas Carol*. (Under the United Kingdom's copyright law at the time, copyright expired after a term of the author's

life plus seven years, or a term of forty-two years, whichever was longer; Dickens died in 1870, twenty-seven years after publication of *A Christmas Carol*, so copyright expired forty-two years after its publication.) Works lacking copyright protection also include one-of-a-kind items such as historical documents found in the collections of participating libraries. Libraries receive digital copies of the books Google scans.

The legal questions that the Library Project raises involve two classes of works: those that are definitely still copyright protected, and those that may still have copyright protection. Partner libraries in the Library Project decide whether only works definitely lacking copyright protection are scanned, or whether in-copyright works (i.e., still under copyright protection) are scanned as well. The tendency since copyright's beginnings has been to extend copyright terms. In the United States and in many other countries, copyright terms last for the life of the author plus seventy years, or ninety-five years for works of corporate authorship. For in-copyright books for which the copyright holder is identifiable, the default view that the Library Project makes available, in addition to bibliographic information, is limited to snippets, i.e., a few sentences surrounding the search term (typically about one-eighth of a page). Copyright holders can also choose to make more of their books available—e.g., entire pages—by granting a license to Google. For example, they can allow browsing but limit the total amount of the book available, e.g., by not allowing access to one out of every ten pages. Copyright holders can also choose to opt out of making available even snippets—so that no preview is available, only bibliographic information. Some dictionaries have chosen this option. Copyright holders can also request that a book not be scanned, or even choose to make a book entirely unavailable in searches. Out-of-print books— i.e., books that are no longer being printed and shipped by their publisher—constitute the majority of Library Project titles. The Library Project makes these books searchable, and therefore discoverable, by a wider audience. Google provides links to major online book retailers where users can buy a book that appears in a search and links to libraries where users can borrow them.

A second set of legal issues that the Library Project raises involves "orphan works," which were produced sufficiently recently that they may still have copyright protection, but the copyright owners cannot be identified or located. Because only a minority of books remain in print during long copyright terms, many works fall in this category. For the millions of such works that Google has scanned, its current policy is that, if the copyright holder does not come forward and claim a book it scans, a digital copy of the book will be searchable and snippets will be made available in Google Books. This "opt out" approach—so named because access to books is allowed unless copyright holders come forward and opt out—facilitates wider distribution of orphan works while imposing only a minimal burden on copyright holders who wish to remove their works. How much access Google was to allow for works in this category, and on what

terms, proved to be key issues in early litigation about the Library Project.

Litigation over the Library Project

Google did not seek the permission of copyright holders when it began scanning books for the Library Project. In 2005, the Authors Guild, the largest organization of American authors, which advocates for their interests, sued Google for copyright infringement, as did publishers who are members of the Association of American Publishers (AAP), specifically McGraw-Hill, John Wiley and Sons, Simon and Schuster, and Pearson.

A Settlement Is Rejected

In 2008, Google and both groups, the authors and publishers, reached a settlement in which Google agreed to pay $125 million in exchange for the rights to sell access to the works it had digitized. Under the proposed settlement, research libraries and other institutions could purchase subscriptions to Google Books. In March 2011, Judge Denny Chin of the Southern Federal District Court of New York rejected the settlement, saying that it was not "fair, adequate, and reasonable" and would "simply go too far." Among his reasons was that the settlement agreement would make forward-looking business arrangements for Google that, under U.S. law, are not properly within the scope of the settlement of a current dispute. A central issue became how the settlement dealt with orphan works.

Google had scanned millions of in-copyright, out-of-print works, many of them orphan works, without permission.

Unless a copyright owner came forward and opted out of inclusion in the Google database, the proposed settlement would have allowed Google to sell access to the full text of these works, without the threat of legal action for copyright infringement from copyright owners. The settlement would have allowed Google to sell access to these works to libraries that subscribe to its database of scanned books, and Google could sell copies of works to individuals for viewing in the cloud. Copyright owners of some out-of-print works would likely come forward and opt out, but many of the works are surely orphan works that no one would claim. Potential competitors to Google had not scanned such works. Judge Chin wrote that because Google's database included these orphan works, Google would have an advantage over potential competitors who lacked similarly comprehensive collections. Through the settlement, Google would essentially have an exclusive license (i.e., permission) to market access to millions of orphan works, without the threat of liability for copyright infringement. But if a competitor were to scan orphan works, the competitor, who was not involved in the settlement, would not have similar legal immunity from infringement claims. Thus, the settlement would "reward" Google "for engaging in wholesale copying of copyrighted works without permission," Judge Chin wrote.

In his decision rejecting the proposed settlement, Judge Chin quoted critics who stated that Google "took a shortcut by copying anything and everything regardless of copyright status" and acted "in calculated disregard of authors' rights. Its business plan was: 'So, sue me.'"

Although Google's contracts with libraries do not grant rights exclusively to Google to digitize their books—i.e., libraries are free to digitize books with other partners—Judge Chin was also concerned that no other organizations would be able to build a library to compete with Google's, giving it a "de facto monopoly" over such works. These were among the potential violations of antitrust law, the set of laws designed to preserve economic market competition, that the settlement agreement raised. Foreign copyright holders also raised concerns under international law that were among other factors Judge Chin considered in rejecting the settlement.

Rejection of the settlement meant that the full texts of orphan works remained searchable and available to users in snippet view, but Google could not sell access to the full text for viewing or download, as the settlement had proposed.

Publishers Settle

Google and the AAP plaintiffs reached a separate settlement in 2012 that was not subject to court approval. It did not resolve any legal issues, and the AAP appears to have yielded to Google but gained little. The terms of the settlement were not fully disclosed, but it was reported that it provided that publishers can choose to opt out of making an in-copyright book available to Google. If publishers fail to opt out, Google makes 20 percent of the book available for browsing and may make it available for sale on Google Play, its online store. Publishers can also make their own arrangements with Google under the settlement. For orphan works, this settlement preserved the status quo after the rejection of the previously proposed settlement in 2011. Orphan works remain searchable unless the copyright owner comes forward and objects.

The Authors Guild Seeks Class Certification

The Authors Guild continued its copyright infringement litigation as a class action lawsuit, an option available in U.S. law in which multiple plaintiffs can pursue their claims together as a "class," rather than filing individual suits. The court must "certify" the class, meaning that it must find that there are common factual and legal issues among the class members and that they suffered the same kinds of harm. For class certification, the case arrived for a second time in the court of Judge Denny Chin, and he granted certification of the class of "all persons residing in the United States who hold a United States copyright interest in one or more Books reproduced by Google as part of its Library Project."

Google appealed the grant of the class certification, arguing that the Authors Guild was not representative of the entire proposed class, because many members of the proposed class benefit from the Library Project and hundreds of class members had made written objections to the Authors Guild's position or opted out of the class. Google also argued that it has a fair use defense—a defense to copyright infringement—that could moot the litigation, i.e., make it irrelevant.

In July 2013, a three-judge panel of the Second Circuit Court of Appeals vacated the class certification, saying it was granted prematurely, before the lower court determined the merits of Google's fair use defense. The panel did not rule on the issue of whether the plaintiffs were representative of the proposed class, but noted that Google's arguments against certification "may carry some force." The panel remanded (i.e., assigned) the case to a lower court for determination of the merits of the fair use defense; the case went back to Judge Chin for a third decision.

In November 2013, Judge Chin dismissed the remanded case, ruling that Google Books has a valid fair use defense for its use of copyrighted works. He ruled that the Authors Guild had made out a case for copyright infringement because Google had, without a "license" (i.e., permission), engaged in unauthorized reproduction of the plaintiffs' works (i.e., by making digital copies); engaged in unauthorized distribution (i.e., by making copies available for download to its Library Project partners); and engaged in unauthorized display of the works (i.e., displaying plaintiffs' works to the public), all in violation of the copyright holders' exclusive rights. However, Google's actions were fair use, for the reasons explained next.

Google Books as Fair Use

The decision in the case represents a significant development of the fair use doctrine. Years before the decision, media law scholar Siva Vaidhyanathan observed that with Google Books, Google "hopes to rest a huge, ambitious, potentially revolutionary project on the most rickety, least understood, most provincial, most contested perch among the few remaining public interest provisions of American copyright: fair use." With Judge Chin's ruling, Google has prevailed in this effort.

This section briefly describes the fair use defense and how it was applied in this case. A quintessential example of the fair use that has long been recognized is use of quotations from a book in a book review, but fair use has been recognized in many other contexts, online and off-line. In the American courts, fair use requires balancing of four factors, as described next.

The Purpose of the Use. Use of parts of the original work for news reporting, reporting of current events, or educational purposes all count toward fair use. So do transformative uses, i.e., use of a work for a different purpose than the original. Examples of transformative uses include using parts of a work in a criticism or review of the original work, or a parody of the original. If the purpose of the use is primarily commercial, that counts against fair use, though fair use has been found even in some cases in which the defendant benefits commercially.

In the Google Books case, the purpose of the use is "highly transformative," Judge Chin ruled, because the book's text was being used to find books. Scholars also use Google Books to conduct searches on millions of books simultaneously and to trace the frequency with which words are used and track trends in their usage, and this is another transformative use, Judge Chin said. Such uses of text as data for research mean that "words in books are being used in a way they have not been used before," he wrote. Judge Chin

acknowledged that Google Books is "largely a commercial enterprise" that relies on advertising revenue. It benefits commercially when users come to Google to search Google Books, and this traffic is used to justify the price it charges for advertising. But Judge Chin considered that because Google Books does not sell scans of books or snippets, it does not engage in the "direct commercialization" of in-copyright works. Further, Google Books also serves educational purposes. So, on balance, he concluded that the first factor in the fair use test favored Google.

The Nature of the Original Work That Is Borrowed From. Some works are closer to the core of copyright-protected expression than others, according to American fair use case law, and at this core is creative expression, such as a poem or novel. Facts are not subject to copyright protection, and nonfiction works such as news articles, which consist of copyright-protected expression but are based largely on underlying facts, are considered further from the core of copyright-protected material. When considering the nature of the work, a finding that a work is close to the core of copyright-protected expression makes it less likely that the fair use defense will succeed. Another consideration in analysis of the nature of the work is whether the original work is published; if it is not, this counts against fair use. The parties in the Google Books case did not dispute that most of the works that Google scanned are nonfiction and they are published, so he found this factor favored Google's fair use defense.

Amount and Substantiality of the Original That Is Used. Courts consider both the amount of what is borrowed and how substantial, or important, it is to the original work. Thus, for example, copying a small number of words from a long mystery novel is more likely to be considered fair use than copying a long passage. But if, for example, that short passage reveals "whodunit"—who committed the crime that the novel is about—that short passage of text is substantial, and its substantiality counts against fair use. Google Books scans entire works, Judge Chin noted, but displays only snippets of in-copyright works, unless the copyright holder granted permission for Google to display more. He did not dwell on analysis of this fair use factor in the case, but found this factor weighed "slightly against" fair use. His conclusion on this factor was criticized by those who argued that the crucial consideration was the amount displayed to users.

Potential Market Effect of the Use on the Original Work. The court considers the effect of the use of the material on the market for the original work. The key question is whether the use supersedes or substitutes for the original work; replacing the original work counts strongly against the fair use defense. So, for example, a book review is generally not a replacement for a book, and a parody is generally not a replacement for the work it targets, so the potential market effect of these uses does not count against fair use. However, an unauthorized copy of a music file can be a replacement for the original. This fourth factor in the fair use test is sometimes referred to as the most important. Judge Chin observed that the security measures Google has in place to limit the

display of a text ensure that the results of a Google Books search cannot replace the original work. Moreover, he found that the only reasonable conclusion was that Google Books enhances book sales by facilitating the discovery of relevant books through searches and providing links for users to purchase the books. Thus, this factor favors Google's fair use defense, he found.

Balancing the four factors in the fair use defense, Judge Chin ruled that Google had a strong fair use defense. In addition to his step-by-step analysis of the fair use defense, Judge Chin also considered whether Google Books serves the public interest and advances the purpose of copyright—"to promote the progress of science and the useful arts"—stated in the U.S. Constitution. Judge Chin concluded that "Indeed, all society benefits" from Google Books: It helps users find books, and instead of hurting authors' and publishers' rights, it allows them to benefit. It allows scholars to search many books simultaneously. It preserves books in digitized form, and gives "new life" to out-of-print and old books. It allows users who are disabled or part of "remote or underserved populations" to access works, he found.

Continuing Litigation over Google Books

Shortly after Judge Chin rejected the Authors Guild's copyright infringement claims, the Authors Guild filed a notice that it was appealing the decision to the Second Circuit Court of Appeals. The Second Circuit was also deciding another appeal of a lower court's ruling in a 2012 case, *Authors Guild v. HathiTrust*. Hathi-Trust, consisting of partner libraries who were participants in the Google Library Project, kept digital copies of works scanned through the Library Project in a digital repository. The lower court ruled that HathiTrust had a valid fair use defense against the Authors Guild's claims of copyright infringement. The judge emphasized that an important transformative use of the scans was that the platform allowed access and searching for those who are "print disabled," that is, unable to effectively read print because of a visual, learning, or physical disability.

Policy Debate

The copyright concerns in the litigation discussed raise policy considerations that underlie the fair use test: whether it serves copyright's goals to allow usage of work, without permission, to create something new—in this case, a database—that arguably serves the public interest. There are additional policy considerations about whether a private corporation is the best entity to create a digital library, as well as privacy concerns.

A Private Corporation and the Public Good

Is it optimal for a private corporation to build and control a repository of the world's knowledge? This is the main policy question debated about Google Books. Internet scholar Evgeny Morozov is among critics who have suggested that policymakers should make decisions about whether a digital library should be publicly funded. Public libraries are a public good that governments have traditionally provided through public funding. Many off-line libraries are nonprofit entities, and they are free to conduct themselves in ways that they may not if they were constrained by profit considerations, e.g., by acquiring and preserving books that are not popular. Google's corporate obligations may influence the execution of the Library Project in negative ways, critics assert. In the past, when a member of the Partner Program gave permission, Google used contextual advertising, i.e., targeted advertising that runs next to their books displayed online, to generate revenue that was shared with the Partner Program member. If Google were to reintroduce the use of advertising, its choices of which books to scan and make available may be influenced by the popular appeal of the works.

Google, a private corporation, acted on the bold vision to build a comprehensive digital library and was willing to undertake the negotiations, logistical coordination, and expense to build it rapidly. No rivals have moved so quickly. The Library of Congress, which is the publicly funded library serving the Congress of the United States, and is often considered the United States' national library, announced plans to build a national digital library in the 1990s. The plans have not fully materialized, though the Library of Congress has made millions of files in the public domain available at the American Memory site. Another site, the Internet Archive, is a nonprofit organization supported by donations and some revenue-generating activities. It archives Web pages, and it has a book collection numbering in the millions of titles, but its collection is dwarfed by that of Google Books. One small digital archive is Project Gutenberg, which posted its first document in 1971 and includes about 45,000 scans, mostly of public domain works. It has been hosted at universities, and as of 2014 is hosted at the University of North Carolina at Chapel Hill.

A newer digital archive that is in part publicly funded is Harvard's Digital Public Library of America (DPLA), operated by a nonprofit organization that seeks to digitize America's biggest research libraries and make them available to all Americans, and eventually internationally. Harvard pulled out of the Google Library Project in 2008 because of concerns about legal risks of copyright infringement. In 2013 it launched the DPLA, which is funded by the National Endowment for the Humanities and private foundations. So far, the DPLA has been collecting works in the public domain only, but hoping the law changes so that it can make in-copyright, out-of-print works available.

Google Books presents a case study of the consequences of privatization of what was traditionally a public institution, the library. Google had the will and the resources to execute the project when others were still formulating their visions or attempting to raise money. But commercial considerations that likely underlie Google's bold actions may shape the future of the project and the terms on which it can be accessed.

Privacy Concerns

Privacy concerns about Google Books have received surprisingly little scrutiny, given that its off-line counterparts,

off-line libraries, have strong traditions of protecting readers' and borrowers' privacy. Privacy groups, including the Electronic Privacy Information Center, have raised objections that Google Books may pose a threat to anonymous reading, but privacy concerns were not a major focus in the litigation over Google Books.

When a reader browses in an off-line library, no one keeps track. One can read anonymously. Google states that in order to enforce limits on the pages made available in Google Books, it tracks non-personally identifiable information like IP address, books, and pages read. Google says that it uses cookies, i.e., files placed on one's computer that it can access, to keep track of this information, so that it can be collected regardless of whether one is logged into a Google account. The collection, use, and disclosure of this information is subject to Google's privacy policies. In addition to concerns about how Google and its partners use data on books accessed, Google is among the giant companies that reveals requested data to the authorities in many countries that request it.

Looking to the Future

Legal scholar Lawrence Lessig called Google Books "the most important contribution to the spread of knowledge since [former American president Thomas] Jefferson dreamed of national libraries." How might Google Books change in the future? In decades and perhaps centuries to come, as more and more books are added, and copyright expires for existing titles, it will likely become an even more valuable resource. How much of each of the books in its collection will be available? Unless copyright law changes, access to in-copyright books may remain limited. In the early days of Google Books, there appeared to be confusion over the scope of what Google would make available to its users. It is important to note that even though Google was indiscriminate about whether the works it scanned were in copyright or not, from its early days, Google has made available only parts of in-copyright books, not the whole text of these works. The value of making even this limited amount of each book available should not be underestimated, some have argued, observing that Google Books makes a large and growing number of books, old and new, discoverable through searching.

If Google is able to negotiate arrangements globally, the offerings of Google Books are likely to become more diverse. Google's early partner libraries are based in the United States (and Oxford). Though it is important to note that these major research libraries have many items that are not in English, critics raised concerns that the large number of English works scanned might contribute to the global dominance of the English language. After its launch, Google added some partners based in countries where English is not the primary language.

For better or worse, Google Books may signal the demise or transformation of the university library. Access to a university library's collection is typically available to those in a university community (and in some cases, guests) who are in geographical proximity, are able to physically access the library during its hours of operation, and are able to read printed text. By removing some of these constraints, Google Books opens the possibility of much wider access to research libraries. Some libraries may be replaced one day by online access—by subscription or not—to Google Books. Convenience of online access, across multiple platforms including mobile devices, may have a powerful influence on the actual utilization of library resources, including both old works that might otherwise be forgotten and contemporary works available through the service.

If Google Books were able to negotiate deals with rights holders, it might develop a service with even greater reach and impact. A new model for music distribution has emerged in recent years. Listeners can now access much of the world's music through free music-streaming services that are advertiser-supported, or they can pay a flat-rate subscription and listen without advertising. Perhaps one day Google, or another service, could negotiate arrangements with owners of in-copyright books to provide full-text access to more works, either for free with the support of advertising, or on a flat-rate subscription basis. Such a service could provide unprecedented access to the world's knowledge.

Mark Cenite
Nanyang Technological University

See also Copyright in the United States; From Packet Switching to Porn and Politics: Protection and Censorship in Online Search; International Influence on U.S. Copyright

Further Reading

Darnton, Robert. "Google and the Future of Books." *New York Review of Books,* February 12, 2009. http://www.nybooks.com/articles/archives/2009/feb/12/google-the-future-of-books.

Electronic Privacy Information Center. "Google Books Settlement and Privacy." http://epic.org/privacy/googlebooks.

Lessig, Lawrence. "Google Sued." Lessig.org, September 22, 2005. http://www.lessig.org/2005/09/google-sued.

Samuelson, Pamela. "Mass Digitization as Fair Use." *Communications of the ACM* 57, no. 3 (2014).

Vaidhyanathan, Siva. "Copyright, Creativity, Catalogs: The Googlization of Everything and the Future of Copyright." *University of California Davis Law Review* 40 (2007).

55

NEW TECHNOLOGY

Free Speech Messiah or First Amendment Traitor?

Alexandra Wallace sat in front of a computer and delivered a diatribe about Asians that would be preserved online infinitely. The University of California, Los Angeles student mocked Asian accents, complained about how Asian students talk on the phone in the library, and made several other racist comments about Asian people. She uploaded the video to YouTube and became an instantaneous, infamous celebrity.

The video was viewed by millions, shared on other social-networking sites, and discussed in the media. Wallace removed the video and apologized for publishing it in the UCLA student newspaper, but by then it was too late. Other people had already copied the video and continued to share it online. Parodies of the video also flooded the Web. News stories reported that the university was considering disciplinary charges against Wallace. Following death threats and other harassment, she left the university.

Wallace was practicing her First Amendment right to free speech when she uploaded that video to the Web. She was never charged with doing anything legally wrong. Yet, Wallace committed her own digitized social suicide when she decided to express her free speech via social networking. She made a mistake that she could never take back. That is the power of social networking. It is a technology that is difficult to regulate and riddled with ethical challenges.

The First Amendment empowers the masses to gather peacefully, challenge their government, spew a homophobic diatribe, launch an anti-Christian tirade, or prattle on about the superiority of one race over another. Some may see the First Amendment as the heart of democracy, but the promise of free speech and freedom of the press can come with a price. If one is going to promise free speech to one person, he also must grant that freedom to another person. In the end, we do not always like the speech that we hear. Can we ever draw a line between what speech should be free and what speech should not?

Technology has muddied the First Amendment waters even further. Recent advances have given people with little technological skill the ability to share their thoughts to a wide audience. The technology has provided Internet Service Providers with exceptional power over what information is shared and what is not. Might those companies have agendas that come into conflict with individual freedom of speech? Geolocation devices and mobile phones have given the government the ability to track and watch the activities of individuals. Could those technological advances conflict with an individual's First Amendment rights to gather and associate with whomever he or she chooses? How can one balance copyright protection in the digital age against creative free speech? This chapter will delve into how the legal system has attempted to deal with these technological challenges to the First Amendment.

Technological Threats to the Right to Assemble

Federal authorities placed a wiretapping device on a California pay phone in the mid-1960s. They were suspicious that Charles Katz was gambling. Through their eavesdropping device, they overheard Katz placing bets with bookies. Katz was charged with multiple counts of illegal transmission of wagering information. Katz fought back, arguing that authorities should have obtained a warrant before they placed a wiretap on the phone. The Supreme Court ruled in Katz's favor. In *Katz v. United States*, the court argued that the wiretap violated the Fourth Amendment. That case paved the way for the development of the Omnibus Crime Control and Safe Streets Act of 1968. The new act specified when wiretaps could be applied to telephone communications. As time progressed, new technologies emerged.

The Electronic Communications Privacy Act of 1986 was passed to expand that legislation. It extended federal protection to computers and cellular devices. The act specified when law enforcement needed a warrant to access information rather than a much-easier-to-receive subpoena. The act emphasized protecting communication as it was happening. E-mail that was undeleted for 180 days was considered abandoned, so it was considered fair game for a subpoena rather than a warrant. That act has continued to serve as the primary federal legislation governing mobile devices and computers.

A plethora of concerns have emerged as time has progressed. New technologies and new uses of technologies have developed, but the law has not changed to address those developments. For example, the law allows warrantless searches of e-mail messages that are stored on a third-party server such as Yahoo! or Gmail. When the legislation was initially written, individuals were not saving emails for an unspecified period of time in the cloud. There are concerns that the lapses in those laws could interfere with an individual's First Amendment rights to free speech and to free association with people who have unpopular views.

Current law also does not address non-communication-based issues related to new technology, such as the government's ability to obtain location data from cell towers. As one travels with his or her mobile phone, the device is registered on a cell tower. As the device moves out of the range of one tower, it registers on the next tower and so forth. Law enforcement can request a telecommunications company to divulge all of the mobile phone data from a specific tower during a particular time period. This allows officers to know which mobile phones are in a particular area at a specific point in time.

Reports from the *New York Times* and the American Civil Liberties Union suggest that there is a lot of variation in how law enforcement chooses to collect mobile phone data from users. It is not unusual for officers to request mobile phone data from a telecom company when there is an emergency, such as a kidnapping. Some departments require a warrant in non-emergency cases, but other departments have far more flexibility, allowing data to be collected without a warrant. The situation gets sticky when one considers just how much information the officers are obtaining. For example, officers might request the data for all phones that have registered on a particular cell tower during a particular time period. While this data might yield the information that officers need, it also will reveal information on countless individuals who are not involved in a particular investigation. This could raise Fourth Amendment privacy concerns, but it also could raise First Amendment concerns regarding the right to freely associate, as officers discover who is gathered in a particular place at a particular time.

It is difficult to determine how frequently the police are using mobile phone data without a warrant. Legislators have proposed new regulations that would update the Electronic Communications Privacy Act. Thus far, new federal legislation has not been approved. As a result, states have resorted to developing their own varying laws.

One important mobile phone issue was recently resolved when the U.S. Supreme Court ruled unanimously that police officers generally cannot search the cell phone of a person arrested unless they first obtain a search warrant. This decision expands the privacy rights of mobile phone users, whether they use flip phones or smartphones. The Court commented that carrying around a smartphone was like taking along a library of books.

Copyright versus Free Speech

A college student downloaded a *Time* magazine cover featuring an image of President Barack Obama. Using some software on his computer, he altered the image so that Obama looked like the notorious Joker from the Batman film *The Dark Knight*. He uploaded the image to his Flickr account. As time passed, the image spread across the Web. A few months later, Flickr removed the image and all of the comments associated with it from the student's Flickr site. The image was removed due to copyright concerns under the Digital Millennium Copyright Act (DMCA). The removal of the image inspired conspiracy theories. People across the Web questioned who had made a copyright claim. Flickr protected the name of the person who made the claim for privacy purposes.

Before the DMCA was passed, an individual complaining about a copyright violation had to win a copyright suit to ensure that material was removed from the Internet. The individual could ask the Internet Service Provider (ISP) to remove the content, but the law did not motivate the ISP to grant the request. That changed after the Digital Millennium Copyright Act was passed in 1998. The law allows an ISP to be sued over material that has been posted by individuals who use that site. In other words, a company such as Flickr could be sued because of content that was posted by one of the individuals who used the popular photo-sharing website. The law also allows the ISP to avoid liability if the company removes the material that has violated the copyright. In other words, the safest thing for a company such as Flickr to do is to remove content the moment someone claims a copyright infringement. Some argue that this law has placed a great deal of Internet content power in the hands of private companies.

Many people worry that freedom of speech has been sacrificed in an effort for Internet Service Providers to avoid those lawsuits. Supporters of DMCA, however, argue that the digital age has made it easier than ever for individuals to violate copyrights. They argue that it is more important than it was in the past to have laws that protect the original content producers. Unfortunately, cases have demonstrated DMCA abuse across the Internet. For example, a group of students at Swarthmore College obtained

access to a series of e-mail messages and memos from Diebold Election Systems, a major producer of voting machines. The content suggested that Diebold employees had seen weaknesses in their own software that made it vulnerable to hackers. The students chose to publish the material online at Swarthmore in 2003. Shortly after the publication, Diebold contacted the university and complained of a copyright infringement via DMCA. The university removed the content and the students' voices were quashed. The students did not have a chance to take their case before a judge. DMCA makes the court process unnecessary.

Technically, DMCA allows for the material to be republished if individuals demonstrate that a copyright has not been violated. How often is a middle-class individual or college student, for that matter, going to be willing to fight back against a corporation that has claimed a copyright violation?

Additional copyright laws have been proposed. The Stop Online Piracy Act (SOPA) and the Protect IP Act (PIPA) were hotly debated in 2012. The acts were proposed as an attempt to stop piracy by restricting user access to sites that were known to feature pirated content. Essentially, the act would close off part of the Internet to users. Many people viewed this as governmental interference into free speech. Major online companies such as Google and Facebook opposed the bill because they argued that it would force them to police users of their sites. Creators of the popular website Wikipedia protested the act by taking their site offline for 24 hours. The acts were never approved, but officials with the Department of Commerce's Internet Policy Task Force have proposed restoring a portion of SOPA. They have recommended making it a felony to stream copyrighted work without authorization. That proposal also has been greeted by severe criticism.

The Government Is Watching

While new technology has put a great deal of power into the hands of consumers, it also has placed enormous control in the hands of the government. The government has a responsibility for making sure that individuals or corporations do not abuse technology. The government also has a responsibility for making sure that citizens are safe. Technology gives officials a whole new way to ensure that protection. The question is, how far should the government go to protect citizens? At what point does the government breach constitutional rights in its pursuit of national security? The attack on the World Trade Center in New York City provided a test of the government's power over technology.

Terror and confusion swept across the United States after the Twin Towers came crashing down on September 11, 2001. Many people remember seeing armed military officers standing inside the airport, or recall the anthrax fears that made them wary of opening the mail, but there was something else happening behind closed doors. President George W. Bush's administration enacted a vast, secret wiretapping program. The initial program allowed the National Security Agency to eavesdrop on conversations when an individual was believed to be associated with al Qaeda or other terrorist groups. No warrant was required. News reports have indicated that the NSA logged the phone calls of millions of people within the United States.

The program marked a major change in NSA power. Previously, the NSA was charged primarily with surveillance abroad rather than within the country. Also, the government was only allowed to eavesdrop on phone calls or e-mails within the United States after receiving a court order from the Foreign Intelligence Surveillance Court, which meets in sessions that are closed to the public. Traditionally, probable cause also was important to justify the use of a wiretap. The secret surveillance program changed all of that. Officials have said that the secret NSA program successfully prevented terrorist attacks. The degree to which terrorism has been curbed is unclear.

The wiretapping program received severe criticism, with many people arguing that it violated other American laws. In time, President Bush put the warrantless surveillance program on the books by approving the 2008 Foreign Intelligence Surveillance Amendments Act. In addition to making the surveillance program official, this new law gave retroactive legal protection to telecommunication companies that had assisted the government with the surveillance. The FISA Amendments Act was challenged when a federal appeals court heard a case that consolidated thirty-three different lawsuits that were filed against telecom companies such as Verizon and AT&T. The court ruled that the law was constitutional. The Supreme Court declined to hear an appeal of the case.

President Barack Obama signed an extension to the FISA program in 2012, which will keep the wiretapping act on the books until 2017. The law was challenged in the *Clapper v. Amnesty International* case, but the Supreme Court ruled that the groups involved in the suit failed to demonstrate that they had been targeted by warrantless surveillance and, therefore, could not pursue the case. The Court did not determine whether the wiretapping law was constitutional.

Much of what is known about the NSA's surveillance program was revealed after whistleblower and former NSA contractor Edward J. Snowden leaked classified documents to the media. The documents revealed that one of the many powers enacted by the NSA's surveillance program has been the agency's practice of collecting mass quantities of phone records. These phone records reveal what number was dialed and when the call was made. The courts have offered differing opinions as to the constitutionality of this data collection. Within a few days of each other, one judge ruled that the metadata-collection program was likely unconstitutional, whereas another judge ruled that it was legal. Additional documents have indicated that the NSA has recorded e-mail metadata from individuals, such as the sender and recipient of messages.

The government clearly has not come to an agreement as to how far the NSA's power should stretch. The Obama administration has defended NSA surveillance programs, but a plethora of lawsuits and a variety of court opinions have demonstrated the public's concerns about the NSA spying programs. While the content of calls and e-mail messages may not be recorded, the data can reveal who people have contacted.

Net Neutrality: The Battle for Content and Innovation

One of the most significant legal issues regarding First Amendment rights and the Internet revolves around a single question: can the Federal Communications Commission regulate the Internet? In essence, the content that is provided to individuals by a broadband Internet Service Provider could be determined on the basis of that single question.

The Telecommunications Act of 1996 made a distinction between two different types of services: telecommunication and information. Under the act, common-carriage regulations applied to telecommunication services. Common-carriage regulations require that telecommunication companies allow communication without discrimination. Those regulations did not apply to information services. In the *FCC v. Brand X Internet Services* case of 2005, the Supreme Court ruled that broadband Internet Service Providers were not telecommunication service providers. This decision has meant that broadband ISPs are not required to follow the common-carrier regulations that telecommunication providers such as telephone companies must follow. Rather, ISPs have a sort of editorial control. If a cable provider does not want to allow a competing ISP to use its cable lines, it has the right to deny that ISP access. As another interpretation, if a cable provider does not want the public to see content from a competitor, the cable provider has the right to withhold that content.

The FCC's Open Internet Order, commonly known as net neutrality, takes a different approach to those issues. Net neutrality went into effect in 2011. The order assumes that the FCC has the ability to regulate the Internet. The FCC does not claim that it can control content, but rather that it can regulate those companies that are providing content through the Internet. Among other things, net neutrality rules stipulate that ISPs cannot block legal content from their customers. The idea is that broadband providers do not have the right to determine what content an individual can access from the Internet. The rules state that the ISP must provide all legal content to the user. The ISP cannot discriminate as to which content is provided and which is withheld.

Verizon filed a lawsuit against the FCC shortly after the net neutrality rules went into place. At the time this chapter was written, a federal appeals court ruled that the FCC did not have the right to institute the rules. Those who are opposed to the net neutrality rules claim that the regulations will interfere with progress. They argue that there are situations when ISPs need to be able to block content that could slow down their services. Companies such as Verizon also feel that they should have the right to charge fees to content providers who want their content to be distributed through their broadband cables. ISPs may not own the Internet, but they do own the cables that are being used to deliver that content. They feel they

have the right to determine how their broadband cables are being used. In other words, the broadband company should be able to charge an online content streaming site such as Netflix a fee before an audience member can stream a movie. Both content and lots of money ride on the resolution to this case.

We All Have Digital Cameras in Our Pockets

There are countless ways that individuals can acquire inexpensive digital cameras. Those cameras might be the size of a typical camera, or they can be more discreet and tucked away inside of a mobile phone. With little training an individual can quickly upload videos or photos to social media sites such as YouTube, Vine, or Vimeo. The simplicity of that technology has put a great deal of power in the hands of eager individuals. It also has created a complex legal environment, which pits First Amendment rights against a host of other laws.

Digital video has had a profound effect on our society. The film *Innocence of Muslims,* which portrayed the prophet Muhammad as, among other things, a womanizer, is believed to have ignited violence in Egypt and Libya. The film made more headlines when actress Cindy Lee Garcia argued that her own copyright was violated when the film was published on YouTube. The actress said that she was misled as to the film's content when she participated in the filming and that her voice was dubbed. Garcia filed lawsuits against YouTube as well as the filmmaker.

The film's creator, Nakoula Basseley Nakoula, was convicted of bank fraud in 2010. When the film was published, he was on probation. Shortly after the violence in the Middle East erupted, Nakoula was arrested and charged with probation violations including using aliases and lying to the police. His Internet use also had been restricted in accordance with his probation. Eventually, Nakoula pled guilty to four probation violations and was sentenced to one year in prison. As part of his plea arrangement, Nakoula was not sentenced for any probation violations that were directly connected to his work on the film. Nonetheless, the Nakoula case has raised a number of concerns for people who worry that he was prosecuted in an attempt to stifle his First Amendment right to publish the controversial film. Undoubtedly, First Amendment advocates will be on the lookout for similar cases in the future.

Animal rights activists also have turned to digital video as a means for spreading their message. On several occasions individuals have secretly recorded videos of animal cruelty, which have been posted online for public viewing. The animal activist may have shot video at a farm while posing as an employee. The videos have shocked and offended the public. They also have caused problems for the agricultural groups that work with animals, who frequently argue that the videos are not representative of all the activities that take place at a particular farm. Prompted by agribusiness complaints, state governments have responded by proposing what is commonly called ag-gag legislation. These laws make it illegal for people to shoot photographs and videos on farms. Some legislation makes it illegal for activists to apply for jobs at farms while lying about their affiliations to animal rights groups. States such as Iowa and Utah approved ag-gag laws during 2011 and 2012. States such as Nebraska, Tennessee, and California unsuccessfully attempted to approve other ag-gag laws during 2013. The content of the legislation varied from one state to the next. In California, the law would have made it illegal for anyone to shoot photographs of animal cruelty without reporting it to authorities within forty-eight hours. An Indiana law would have made it illegal to shoot farm video without the business owner's consent. It is highly likely that more ag-gag legislation will be proposed in the future. Some people argue that these laws violate First Amendment rights by stifling the voices of activists. In this case, there is a concern that animal cruelty will continue or even grow as individuals are afraid they will be prosecuted for collecting video or photographic evidence of a crime. Meanwhile, farm owners argue that the whistleblowers are unfairly damaging the reputation of the farm industry. It is difficult to predict how states across the nation will eventually resolve this issue.

The government has not yet found its footing in regards to free speech and digital video. The legal system simply has not been able to keep up with the rapid adoption of digital cameras or the public's thirst to share amateur videos. A multitude of people have accused the police of forcing them to stop recording video of police activity on public streets. Some have accused officers of charging individuals with an infraction such as disorderly conduct merely to stop them from shooting video of officers. The ACLU sued the Baltimore Police Department in 2010 after the police allegedly deleted the videos an individual had on his mobile phone. The U.S. Department of Justice sent a widely circulated letter to the police department in 2012, which specified that individuals have the First Amendment right to shoot video of police activity. So, while there may continue to be some variation in how police officers respond to the public's use of video cameras during police action, it would seem that the federal government supports the individual's right to use cameras—even when law enforcement is involved.

That being said, digital video censorship does not always come from the government. The American Civil Liberties Union of Arizona criticized YouTube for removing the video *Border Patrol in the Bushes* in 2011. The amateur video showed authorities arresting an individual. The faces of officers and an officer's nametag could be seen in the video. YouTube removed the video after it received privacy complaints from the border patrol. As a private institution, YouTube has the right to remove videos, but this case raises yet another question as to the important role that private institutions may now play in regards to free speech. As corporations increasingly have more control over the Internet, they have the ability to both promote and restrict free speech.

GPS: Friend or Foe?

It was a mechanic who first discovered a strange device hidden beneath Yasir Afifi's car. The San Jose college student would later learn that the device was a Global Positioning System (GPS) tracker that was secretly attached to the car by the FBI. The authorities had not received a warrant before they placed the device on Afifi's car. A Muslim advocacy group filed a lawsuit in 2011 against the FBI on behalf of Afifi. The Council on American Islamic Relations' lawsuit alleges that the FBI violated the college student's Fourth and First Amendment rights.

GPS devices have become a common aspect of our society. We install the devices in our cars and use them within our mobile phones. They act as a system of live maps. GPS can serve another function as well. GPS can allow someone else to know where you are and where you have been. This aspect of the technology has made GPS a useful tool for law enforcement. Officers can secretly install a GPS device onto someone's car and use it to track the individual's movements. One issue that the legal system is struggling to determine is whether the police must obtain a warrant before they attach a GPS device to an individual's vehicle. Some scholars have questioned whether the warrantless use of GPS devices by law enforcement tramples on the Fourth Amendment's protection against unreasonable search and seizure. The technology, however, also raises a question about First Amendment rights. Similar to the warrantless searches of telephone records conducted by the NSA, could law enforcement's use of GPS interfere with an individual's right to freely associate with other people? The First Amendment guarantees individuals the right to gather with people regardless of what ideologies those people may have.

Thus far, the Supreme Court has suggested that the warrantless use of GPS is a violation of constitutional rights. In 2012, the Court ruled in *United States v. Jones* that officers should not have used a GPS device without a warrant in a drug-trafficking case. The use of such devices constitutes a search, according to the Supreme Court. The government had argued that it did not need a warrant for the GPS by citing a previous case, *United States. v. Knotts*. In that 1983 case, officers placed a beeper inside of an item that was purchased by one of the defendants. After the item was placed in the defendants' automobile, officers used a radio receiver to monitor the signals produced by the beeper. In that case, the Supreme Court ruled that it was legal for officers to use the beeper to follow a car. The 2012 ruling, however, determined that a GPS is a different kind of device from a beeper because GPS devices can enable law enforcement to monitor an individual's movements constantly over a long period of time. The *United States v. Jones* ruling may affect a wide variety of other GPS cases, such as Afifi's lawsuit against the FBI. The Court also said that secretly installing a GPS device amounted to trespass, but the justices did not rule on whether law-enforcement officers have the right to use GPS devices that already are installed on an individual's vehicle or inside of someone's mobile phone. Similarly, the Third Circuit U.S. Court of Appeals ruled in 2013 that law-enforcement officers had overstepped the law when they attached a warrantless GPS device to a vehicle owned by a suspect in a burglary case. Officers used the GPS to track the vehicle to a drugstore that was recently robbed. After checking the GPS data, they searched the automobile and found the items that had been taken from the store. The suspects were arrested and charged with the burglary. The officers had spoken with the U.S. attorney's office before they attached the device to the automobile, but they had failed to obtain a warrant. The court ruled that the officers had violated the Fourth Amendment.

There certainly are other issues related to GPS. The New York Court of Appeals heard a case in which a state labor department employee was fired for misconduct, including lying on his travel records. Investigators collected evidence about his travel—both work-related and personal—continuously for more than a month after they attached a GPS device to his automobile. Investigators did not seek a warrant before the device was attached to Michael Cunningham's car. Cunningham wanted the department to reconsider his dismissal without the use of the GPS records. He argued that the state had discriminated against him. The court ruled in 2013 in favor of Cunningham, saying that the state should have sought answers without tracking the employee's movements outside of business hours.

The Facebook Conundrum

Benjamin Franklin and George Washington never could have imagined a world where one measures a person's "friends" by his or her contact list on Facebook. The social-networking site has created a platform where individuals may express their opinions about everything from bologna sandwiches to political races. The courts generally have perceived comments made on Facebook as being protected by the First Amendment. That being said, the legal system is still struggling with applying the First Amendment in regards to specific types of posts. One challenge has been the handling of posts that suggest some sort of a threat.

When rapper Antavio Johnson had a beef with the police in Florida, he wrote the song "Kill Me a Cop." The song was published on the social media site MySpace. In the song, Johnson named two Florida police officers and made a reference to another officer and a police dog that had died. In 2009, Johnson was sentenced to two years' imprisonment on two counts of corruption by threat of a public servant. Johnson pleaded no contest to the charges, but many people questioned whether his First Amendment rights were violated when the charges were filed. He certainly is not the only rapper who has ever issued threats in a song. Nonetheless, he did name specific individuals in his song, and Florida law makes it a crime to threaten individuals who are public servants. On the other hand, a high school student in Florida received probation in 2012 after she made assassination threats against President Barack Obama on Facebook. At the very least, these two cases demonstrate that the courts have taken an inconsistent approach to threats that are posted online.

Social media activity involves more than merely posting comments, however. With the click of a button, Facebook users also have the ability to "like" a particular news story, organization, photo, etc. Other Facebook friends and, in some cases, the

public can see the items that an individual has "liked." The courts have had to decide whether those Facebook "likes" are protected by the First Amendment.

Six former employees of the Hampton County Sheriff's Office argued that they lost their jobs because they had demonstrated their support for the sheriff's political rival. One way that they showed that support was by using the "like" button on the Facebook page of the sheriff's opponent during the election. The Fourth Circuit Court of Appeals ruled in 2013 that clicking the "like" button is similar to sharing a traditional political poster. In other words, the "like" button is a type of political speech, which is protected by the First Amendment. The ruling shows that the court recognizes that new technology presents a variety of ways for individuals to engage in speech, assembly, etc. Social media provides us with constantly evolving means to engage in activities that are protected by the First Amendment. One does not necessarily need to publish a line of text in order to actively speak. As the Internet continues to evolve, it is imperative that the courts continue to recognize the multiple ways that it offers opportunities for free speech. Just as one might hold a picket sign or post a bumper sticker on his or her car, there are many ways that social networking offers the opportunity for individuals to express themselves.

Facebook has presented other challenges to the First Amendment as officials have struggled to find ways to protect the public without interfering with the right to free speech. For example, the state of Indiana approved a statute that prevented registered sex offenders from using social-networking services such as

Facebook as well as instant-messaging services. The Seventh Circuit U.S. Court of Appeals ruled in 2013 that the Indiana law violated the First Amendment. The court argued that Indiana's statute was too broad. The ruling suggested that a law restricting sex offenders' activities online could potentially be acceptable, but that law would need to be very specific. A broad law that prevents all usage of social media inevitably restrains speech. A more narrow law would be designed to prevent particular activities online rather than restricting all speech.

Pro: The First Amendment Must Adapt to New Technology

There are two clear sides to the relationship between the First Amendment and technology. On one side, one can argue that the government has acted correctly in its use of technology. This section will examine that argument.

The government has acted wisely in allowing the NSA to wiretap and gather data that could be useful in preventing terrorist attacks. The NSA does not intend to infringe upon First Amendment rights. Its mission is one of security. While we must protect the First Amendment, this does not mean that we should prohibit law enforcement from being able to take advantage of new technology in order to protect the people. Presidents Bush and Obama have merely granted the NSA the ability to wield that technology. Similarly, additional laws should be developed to grant local law enforcement the ability to take advantage of existing technology. Officers should not be penalized for attaching a GPS device to the automobile of a suspected criminal. This technology is widely available to anyone. Why should law enforcement not have the opportunity to use it?

Likewise, the Digital Millennium Copyright Act is necessary. The First Amendment must be protected, but copyrights must also be guarded. Technology has moved so quickly that it is difficult for every potential copyright case to go through a court system. The DMCA gives copyright holders a way to protect themselves, while also ensuring that Internet Service Providers are also protected from lawsuits. The law protects the First Amendment by giving people the opportunity to have material restored once they prove that a copyright was not violated.

The FCC has overstepped its boundaries by approving net neutrality rules. While these rules may be designed to prevent discrimination online, they intrude upon the rights of the Internet Service Providers. These companies should have the right to use their technology as they choose. Net neutrality legislation would prevent ISPs from being able to operate as efficiently as they would like. These rules also may stand in the way of technological progress as they force the ISP to allow access to websites that create technical problems for the ISP and may slow down Internet access.

States should continue to have the opportunity to propose ag-gag laws. These laws are not designed to interfere with the First Amendment. Rather, these laws exist to protect farmers and other business owners from unscrupulous tactics by activists. These laws can be particularly effective when they encourage someone who has shot video of animal abuse to submit that video to law enforcement. It is not necessary for these videos to be shared with the world in order for law enforcement to put a stop to animal abuse. By uploading the videos for public viewing, individuals are acting as vigilantes. It is appropriate, however, for those who witness a crime to share that information with law enforcement.

The courts have acted intelligently by penalizing individuals who have published threats on social media. The people who publish those comments might not have intended for them to be taken seriously, but we cannot allow threats to go unpunished. People should learn to use social media and other technology responsibly. A threat online should be treated exactly the same as a threat that appears in a letter or another form of media.

Con: New Technology Threatens First Amendment Rights

On the other side of the ongoing tug-of-war between the First Amendment and new technology, one can argue that the First Amendment should take precedence and be protected against emerging threats from technological development. This section will examine that argument.

Regulations are imperative to ensuring that the First Amendment is protected. Existing laws must be updated to accommodate advances in technology. The antiquated Electronic Communications Privacy Act of 1986 must be revised. The updated law should take into account locational data, which law-enforcement officers can request from telecom companies.

The law should specify if and when it is appropriate for law enforcement to request records of all of the mobile phones that have registered on a particular cell tower at a given time. Restrictions should ensure that those records are not haphazardly available without a warrant. People must not fear associating with others even if those people have unpopular opinions. That being said, the regulations should allow flexibility that ensures that law enforcement can get access to the information it needs in an emergency. There are situations where technological access can mean the difference between life and death. Law enforcement needs to have access to that information in those cases.

The Digital Millennium Copyright Act is an affront to the First Amendment. It places too much power in the hands of corporations and businesses. The Internet and new technology should be viewed as the ultimate avenue for the First Amendment. By removing copyright cases from the court system, individuals have their speech stifled. The DMCA forces individuals to prove their First Amendment right to publish rather than forcing the person who owns the copyright to demonstrate that that copyright was actually violated. The act should be revised so that the First Amendment is properly protected.

The government has gone too far with approving the FISA Amendments Act. The powers given to the NSA are staggering. They represent a clear infringement upon First Amendment rights. The government has no right to collect massive quantities of data from people who have committed no crime. Likewise, the government should not do anything that threatens our right to assemble with other people—even if those people have unpopular views. The NSA should not have access to that information. Similarly, the courts made a wise decision in *United States v. Jones*. Law enforcement must be curbed from using technology in ways that interfere with the First Amendment. Officers should not be able to place a GPS device on a given individual's automobile. Just because the technology is available does not mean that law enforcement or anybody else has a right to abuse it.

The courts have made outstanding progress in recognizing that the First Amendment should extend beyond comments that are published in social media. Often, clicking the "like" button on Facebook is only one way that an individual can share his or her opinion online.

Regulations: A Mixed Bag

The Internet has become society's most significant means for attaining information. It is not merely an entertainment device. It is the way that we go about understanding the world around us, as well as ourselves. Whether we like what we see and hear online or not, the Internet has become a powerful tool for expressing opinions and ideas. Social media sites such as Facebook and Twitter give us the ability to communicate with a broad audience. The simplicity and availability of cameras extends that ability even further, allowing us to capture moments in time or express ourselves creatively. New technology, which gives us the ability to connect with people who share our opinions, is directly connected to First Amendment rights. As a result, regulations regarding new technology should be managed at the federal level.

While some efforts have been made to update regulations to account for emerging technology, the United States still has a long way to go to ensure that citizens' First Amendment rights are maintained in the digital age. One of the key issues for the future is determining what the government's role should be in managing new technology. Leaving individual states to make their own rules about new technology is dangerous, as it leaves room for divergent regulations. Those states that have addressed such issues may have outstanding regulations, but what about those other states that have not developed their own regulations yet? Do people in those states not deserve the same First Amendment rights as people in the states that have those regulations?

There is promise for the future with courts recognizing that First Amendment rights online extend beyond the specific words that an individual uses and legislators discussing enhancements to the existing Electronic Communications Privacy Act. Yet, there is still work that needs to be done. The Electronic Communications Privacy Act and other federal laws must be revised to take into account new technology.

Jenn Burleson Mackay
Virginia Tech

See also Data Privacy; Invasion of Privacy; A New First Amendment?; Shark Tweets: The Implausible Expectation of Privacy as a Basic Human Right

Further Reading

Barclay, Eliza. "2013 Was the Year Bills to Criminalize Animal Cruelty Videos Failed." NPR, December 27, 2013. http://www.npr.org/blogs/thesalt/2013/12/19/255549796/2013-was-the-year-every-new-ag-gag-bill-failed.

Kravets, David. "10 Years Later, Misunderstood DMCA Is the Law That Saved the Web." *Wired*, October 27, 2008. http://www.wired.com/threatlevel/2008/10/ten-years-later.

Lessig, Lawrence. *Code 2.0.* New York: Basic Books, 2006.

Lessig, Lawrence. *Free Culture: How Big Media Uses Technology and the Law to Lock Down Culture and Control Creativity.* New York: Penguin Press, 2004.

Nunziato, Dawn C. *Virtual Freedom: Net Neutrality and Free Speech in the Internet Age.* Stanford, CA: Stanford University Press, 2009.

Phillbeck, Justin, Alina Buccella, and Jordan Crews. "*Bland v. Roberts*: Facebook Likes Are Protected by the First Amendment." *Wake Forest Law Review*, September 22, 2013. http://wakeforestlawreview.com/bland-v-roberts-facebook-likes-are-protected-by-the-first-amendment.

Policinski, Gene. "The Chilling Power of GPS Surveillance." First Amendment Center, November 11, 2011. http://www.firstamendmentcenter.org/the-chilling-power-of-gps-surveillance.

Samoriski, Jan H., John L. Huffman, and Denise M. Trauth. "Electronic Mail, Privacy, and the Electronic Communications Privacy Act of 1986: Technology in Search of Law." *Journal of Broadcasting & Electronic Media* 40 (1996): 60–76.

Solove, Daniel J. *The Future of Reputation: Gossip, Rumor, and Privacy on the Internet.* New Haven, CT: Yale University Press, 2007.

56

TWITTER AND TRADITIONAL MEDIA

In less than a decade of existence, Twitter has become a dominant part of the modern journalist's toolbox, providing a distribution channel, access to sources, and a mode of feedback from the public. This has notably occurred as more and more newsrooms face cutbacks, and the journalism labor market becomes more transitory and freelance-driven.

For individual journalists, Twitter provides a platform through which they can promote their work, build name recognition, and develop a network of sources. It also allows journalists to communicate with each other, both to discuss the material content of their work and to engage in story analysis. For news organizations, Twitter provides the same promotional opportunities, and it also gives them a way to provide a constant stream of updates to their followers, guaranteeing nearly instant audience awareness for any new piece they put online.

Twitter is part of an interdependent ecosystem of social media, playing a role in connecting its users that is derived from its specific technological characteristics,

and which is different from most of the functions performed by other social media systems. Many scholarly and popular accounts elide all social media into one broad category, overlooking important and essential differences. Indeed, these differences are so wide-reaching that scholars have not yet arrived at a consensus definition of "social media" at all. Nevertheless, research and discussion of "social media use," "social media content," and "social media effects" abound, often connecting Facebook and Twitter. Before exploring concerns about Twitter, it is worth examining how Twitter stands apart in terms of both its functionality and its user base.

Twitter in the Context of Other Social Media

Most notably, as of 2013, Twitter is used by only 18 percent of American adults who use the Internet, compared with 71 percent for Facebook; Twitter's reach is comparable to that of LinkedIn, Pinterest, and

Instagram. Twitter users are much younger than the general population, are disproportionately African American, and are more likely to live in urban or suburban than rural areas. They also have different psychological traits than do Facebook users, notably being less sociable and extroverted. It is not surprising, therefore, that Twitter itself is a poor tool with which to gauge public opinion. The broad sentiment found through Twitter's semiautomatically curated "trending topics" tends to be much more politically liberal than the general population, likely owing to the skewed demographics of its users.

However, Twitter's functionality, and that of many social network platforms, presents an additional wrinkle to any examination of it as a pathway for the distribution and reception of news information. Because Twitter is based on users constructing social networks within it, no two users receive the same content from it—all users receive tweets from the other users that they follow, as well as "promoted" tweets (that is, advertisements) targeted to their characteristics. As message senders, no two users have the same audience. Instead, users' tweets are only seen by those other users who follow them. The practice of retweeting—sending another user's tweet out to your own network of followers, sometimes with additional text attached—helps to cross-pollinate those egocentric networks and expose users to each other in organic ways that help build new networks of shared interests, values, and beliefs.

Twitter's unique characteristics are also key to understanding how information is presented and received within it. Unlike its closest cousin, Facebook, Twitter transmits only text, which is limited to 140-character chunks. Other media can only be sent through URLs included in text, which Twitter has built side systems to roughly accommodate (such as its picture-hosting service). As a result of this limitation, tweets must be brief, often using abbreviations and sentence structures similar to newspapers' headlines. In order to provide some context and system-level organization, early Twitter users began appending the pound symbol (#) to keywords to create searchable "hashtags," though this functionality was not specifically supported by the system. Similarly, conversation in Twitter is created by appending the at symbol (@) to usernames to target a message to that user. These two user-driven innovations are responsible for much of the organization of Twitter content that is available above and beyond simply following users and observing their tweets.

By default, all tweets are publicly viewable, both to followers and to the general public, who may find a tweet through a keyword search or a link from another site. One's account can be made "protected," so that only those in a reciprocal following relationship can see it, and users can send "direct messages" privately to their followers. Nonetheless, the vast majority of tweets are part of the broad public flow of information contained within Twitter.

It is worth noting that the common content of Twitter, while sometimes derided as frivolous, bears many key similarities to that found in eighteenth- and nineteenth-century personal diaries. These diaries were key outlets for reflection and accounting in their time, and have often provided historians with important information about their authors. Twitter, though perhaps greater in scope and volume, would seem to have the same potential for contemporaneous journalists today. This is particularly important because it provides the opportunity for journalists to find and report on new kinds of information that would previously not have been available to them or that they may not have even thought to seek out.

Twitter in the Process of Journalism

Because it is an open system into which any 140-character chunk of text can be placed, Twitter can play a variety of roles in the processes of newsgathering, assessment, production, distribution, and reception. Indeed, because of its social sharing capability, Twitter (like other social media) can add to the traditional news processes by allowing news consumers to repackage and redistribute news content within their social networks and to more readily influence the production of news by traditional sources.

For journalists working in the traditional model of journalism, Twitter can provide easy access to information and to sources of information. This is especially true during an ongoing or breaking news event, when traditional access to information or sources—that is, via telephone or face to face—is not possible, though the faster speed and lower cost of Twitter make it an attractive way to connect with sources in any event. This contact may come in the form of general inquiries for

information about new or ongoing stories, providing a way for the public to get involved with stories that matter to them, or the equivalent of cold-calling sources, by sending individuals tweets asking them for an interview or for specific information. It may also involve tweets themselves being directly quoted in news. Using the wisdom of the crowd in this way creates the potential for journalists' blind spots to be filled in—that is, for them to hear and address viewpoints they might not otherwise know about.

Different kinds of stories appear to lend themselves more or less to the use of tweets as direct sources of information. In sports journalism, particularly on television and online, athletes' tweets are increasingly being used as story content, suggesting a weaker gatekeeping role for these news organizations and a greater ability for athletes to engage in public relations through electronic news media. While the attitudes and beliefs held by sports reporters, and especially print reporters, tend to be that Twitter has not changed the work that they do, analysis of the actual use of Twitter by sports journalists suggests otherwise. Specifically, while journalists think they use Twitter primarily for its speed and direct access to the public—that is, for things like breaking news or promoting new pieces added to their organizations' websites—they actually engage primarily in commentary and opinion. For example, in the case of the Penn State child sexual abuse scandal that broke in 2011, reporters covering the story engaged in broad speculation about the direct and ancillary outcomes of the case; criticism of the university, football program, and other media outlets;

reframing of the story in order to balance dominant narratives; and empathy with the victims. Additionally, Twitter allowed these reporters to engage in conversation about the story directly with members of the public, in some cases to find story information, but also to engage in argumentation and name-calling.

Although these findings suggest serious concerns about the professional conduct of sports reporters who use Twitter, particularly regarding verification and objectivity, sports journalism has long been an area where standards have been different in practice than they are in other types of journalism, especially on television. However, Twitter also provides fodder for breaking and ongoing stories in more traditional "hard" news areas.

Twitter in Election Coverage

Over the last several years, elections have provided perhaps the best context to observe this behavior in action, because they have predictable timelines and narrative patterns, but also involve a competitive race for new information. The starting point for Twitter playing a significant role in election coverage—perhaps a necessary condition—is for politicians themselves to be active in the system. In many recent elections around the world, most candidates have not been active on Twitter, but sizable minorities have, and they have been able to produce tweets that brought them additional coverage through direct quotation and by prompting follow-up reporting by journalists in traditional media.

This relationship between tweets and coverage has the potential to significantly bias election coverage in favor of those candidates able to devote the most staff time to savvy social media communication, targeted either at the press or at the public (which the press would also pick up). Incumbent or otherwise established candidates would be privileged by this press behavior, as well as those that were particularly well funded. The effects are likely to increase going forward, as journalists find themselves with less time and fewer resources with which to gather news; that is, tweets will become relatively more valuable to the newsgathering process and relatively less worth following up on.

The use of tweets as a news source also allows politicians a route around the traditional method of press gatekeeping—interviews, press conferences, and other forms of source questioning. This allows candidates to refuse to interact with some or all news agencies, address their publics via Twitter, but still get the benefit of exposure to the broad populace via quotation in the press. This might also be seen as a new kind of agenda setting or information subsidy, in which the source wrests away some of the press's power or exists in a symbiotic, cross-promotional relationship with it. Contrary to the idea of sports reporters using Twitter to reframe a story through their own tweets, this behavior finds journalists ceding power to sources and to the Twitter-using public.

Indeed, trends that emerged from the Twitter public were actually more prevalent in coverage of the 2010 British elections than were politicians' tweets, and that coverage also included tweets from nonpolitical elites (celebrities, for example) for entertainment purposes. Moreover, tweets were not only used for quotes or to illustrate stories that were already being reported; tweets and source interactions via Twitter also led to new coverage being initiated, creating new potential exposure for the candidates in question.

Of course, the primary draw for politicians to Twitter is not that they may be quoted in the press, but that they have unfettered access to members of the public. When viewed from the point of view of the public, then, Twitter itself may be seen as a news source, aggregating breaking news, links to new stories, citizen journalism, commentary, and original source information from politicians and other news figures. Users might follow news about a story through a curated set of sources—specific reporters, pundits, politicians, etc.—but might also follow tweets with a particular hashtag. This phenomenon could be seen during the 2010 Australian elections, when #ausvotes became an important source of information for those looking to stay current with the campaign. Of course, such a hashtag includes not only (perhaps not even mostly) news and campaign information; it is also chock-full of public discussion and conversation, and likely even some unrelated tweets whose authors hope a popular hashtag will make them more visible. As such, the nature of #ausvotes as a campaign news source was shaped by traditional news coverage and official campaign events, but also by the existing interests of its users, through which that traditional campaign information was filtered. Based on this shared negotiation of importance within the campaign dialogue, as determined by extent of

discussion, the hashtag user network can be conceptualized as an "ad hoc issue public"; however, this may be too restrictive an approach for the broad and ostensibly nonpartisan discussion that happens around an election. Instead, we might think of this as an emergent news public, providing official information, traditional news reporting, and argumentation across a broad issue agenda. When considering the benefits and risks of the public using this kind of outlet as a primary news source, it is also important to address how broad a given hashtag's coverage remains.

Twitter as a News Source

When thinking about the idea of people using Twitter as a news source—whether by following a hashtag or a particular set of other users—it is important to keep in mind that there is no one person or organization coordinating the information that is made available. Some will come directly from traditional news sources, some will be traditional news content posted by other users with their own commentary, and still more will be from alternative or firsthand sources. The balance of traditionally reported information and rumor in this context is completely dependent on what sources a user chooses to use and how those sources behave while the story is unfolding. Research has not reliably identified the extent to which Twitter users use it for news, but those who do are likely to also seek information from other social media sources, such as Facebook or YouTube, in which traditional news content is less prominent.

A helpful illustration of concerns about how Twitter works for news consumers exists in another area in which it has come to be seen as an invaluable source of news and information: protest movements. The Wisconsin labor protests of 2011 prompted significant discussion in Twitter and other social media. At the outset of the underlying political debate, one local newspaper created a hashtag, #wiunion, that it used for related stories and media, and which it also encouraged readers to use for their tweets, photos, videos, and so on, across social media platforms. This value-neutral hashtag, meant to aggregate news and information about the protests without supporting one side or the other, quickly became the center of a predominantly pro-protest information network. While about half of the original tweets tagged with #wiunion during the early protests were straight news or links to news, greater than 40 percent contained sentiments supporting the protests, sometimes combined with links to blogs or visual media about the protest movement. This kind of social media movement structure was adopted by labor activists in neighboring states (e.g., #miunion in Michigan) without going through an early stage as a site of news aggregation, and #wiunion continued to be used for pro-labor organizing and information dissemination after the protests ended.

An obvious concern, then, is that a user turning to Twitter for an up-to-the-second cross section of news and opinion on a particular hot topic has no effective way of understanding the extent to which voices on one side or another might be dominating discussion. Complicating matters further, retweets in the #wiunion stream were not evenly distributed. Tweets of opposition to the protests were retweeted significantly more frequently than supporting tweets, part of a broad pattern of differences between retweeted and non-retweeted messages, suggesting that the perception one gets of the issue by following the hashtag may not even reflect the collective view of all #wiunion users, let alone the general public, or the competing claims found in traditional reporting. Notably, even some of the most active #wiunion users had concerns about the accuracy and provenance of the information that was made available via the hashtag.

Thus, as the story progressed, it was still easy for #wiunion followers to find news as it is traditionally conceived and from the same kinds of news organizations one would follow on television or in print. However, it also became nearly impossible to follow the story via Twitter without also being exposed to a considerable amount of opinion and activist communication. Because Twitter does not do its own categorization, and instead relies on identifying patterns and trends within tweets, taking one story and separating it into "news" and "opinion" is quite impractical and counter to the way Twitter is typically used for news consumption.

Twitter as a Site of "Affective" News

Wisconsin's protests took place in the context of local and national democratic systems and a robust civil society. They were organized by unions, joined by supportive organizations and individuals, and featured no violence and few arrests. As such, ample information about the protests could be found in both traditional media and more in-depth online media, making reliance on Twitter one option of many for individual news consumers. This is much less true when it comes to the protests following the 2009 Iranian elections or the various uprisings that comprise the Arab Spring, events that occurred away from the auspices of open press systems and that held the interest of observers around the world. During those events, Twitter and other social media were used for intra-movement organizational purposes, but also provided much greater information to journalists and the global public than would have otherwise been available in real time.

In the sudden and breaking event of the Tahrir Square protests that began January 25, 2011, speed and drama were on display as key values of the news distributed via the #egypt hashtag. These contribute to "instantaneity," perhaps Twitter's greatest appeal as a news medium. The difficulties for mainstream media in covering the protests directly, as opposed to at a distance, created a vacuum that firsthand reports via Twitter were able to fill. This notion of speed, immediacy, proximity, and experiencing the news as it happens is a common feature of research about Twitter in the January 25 uprising.

Research also strongly emphasizes the collective and organic nature of how breaking stories develop on Twitter, with regard to both the specific pieces of information that are made available and the broader set of values that emerge from users' aggregated behavior. The coverage found in Twitter's #egypt stream mixed new, collectively negotiated news values with those of traditional media. Emergent keywords kept the trends relevant to the story, though this is not a given in Twitter's architecture. Tweets mostly focused on the dramatic, large-scale protests in Cairo, but also provided information about smaller events around the country, and connected the events in Egypt to the then-recent protests in Libya. In other words, the crowdsourced newsroom of Twitter provided, sorted, and contextualized relevant information about the story, in a similar way to what one would expect from the traditional media.

However, Twitter also introduced new news values to the mix. Where traditional media generally relies on official elites as sources, Twitter made elites of official and nonofficial sources alike, including individuals reporting live from the protest without any prior elite status. That is, individuals' access to information in the moment was more important than their position in a hierarchy of official information. Tweets in #egypt also overwhelmingly expressed solidarity with the protesters, a clear break from traditional news values, but one that was actually used by some traditional journalists active in the Twitter discussion. These new news values combine to make up a form of "affective news," blending information and opinion so deeply that in #egypt it was impossible to sever the two, either amongst the whole stream or even in many individual tweets. The personal connection to the story and the ultrafast nature of its updates may have had the effect of suggesting that the story was actually moving and changing faster than it really was—many triumphalist tweets of late January 2011 have different connotations now, as Egypt's political situation remains unsettled.

Part of the impulse for this kind of tweeting may also have been as a way to interact with traditional media and its values, particularly among those users who were not strongly engaged in the social media conversation. While protest movements often aim to create spectacles that will attract the attention of traditional media, ultimately amplifying their message, the Egyptian protests created a "media spectacular," in which the media system itself became a site of protest, a news source, and an object of news coverage. Indeed, an early spike in citizen media activity preceded both a decline in citizen content creation on YouTube and a significant, persistent leap in traditional media coverage of the protests appearing on YouTube. This suggests that the protest movement understood the traditional media to have a valuable reach to the global public, and that the traditional media still exercise a significant amount of influence, even in a social media space. This phenomenon can be seen in Twitter as well, where traditional media actors are often central figures in a news discussion network by virtue of the large audiences and recognition they can pull over from their traditional venues. It is worth noting that the reverse phenomenon—social media content filtering into traditional media coverage of the protests—appears not to have been very prevalent. While international newspapers cited social media sources more than did nearby newspapers, none cited them often.

This power imbalance can be seen in retweeting relationships amongst journalists, bloggers, activists, and others taking part in Twitter's Egypt coverage. The most frequent kinds of retweets in the Egypt information flow were activists, bloggers, and other users retweeting journalists; journalists themselves were also much more likely to retweet other journalists than any other kind of user. Thus, the journalism that emerged took the form of a conversation, directed by journalists, but with the cooperation of activists and bloggers. Notably, this activity was driven by individual journalists, rather than by news organizations, suggesting that perceptions of those individuals played an important role in determining the credibility and utility of what they had to say. Individual journalists in social media were also able to step away from the protest paradigm that was maintained in traditional media coverage, and gave greater voice to nonelite than elite sources, suggesting that this kind of information may allow journalists a way out of problematic traditional reporting routines, while also privileging personal brands and credibility over a more straightforward evaluation of the information contained in a report.

This way of thinking about Twitter as a news source holds up when examining other breaking news events as well. Coverage of the United Kingdom's 2011 riots in Twitter feeds from reporters with the *Guardian* and the *New York Times* gained significant notice as the story was unfolding, sending their own eyewitness accounts, quoting and retweeting other eyewitnesses, retweeting other news reports, and linking back to live blogs about the riots. When a man began firing shots on the campus of the University of Texas in September 2010, Twitter users in nearby buildings were the first to report on the events, providing live warnings and updates about the shooter's location for several minutes before local traditional media had begun to cover the story, also via social media.

Twitter as Ambient Journalism

All of these characteristics of the Twitter coverage of breaking news events support the idea that Twitter and similar systems have created an environment of "ambient journalism," a flow of information that, according to Alfred Hermida, is "broad, asynchronous, lightweight, and always-on." This model is at odds with traditional journalistic norms in a number of ways. An ambient news flow cannot be understood to be complete in the way that a traditional news piece typically is, even if all the same information can be found in both sources, because the ambient news environment is designed around occasional sampling, while the traditional news piece is meant to be consumed at once. Instead, one's network (and the algorithms used by Twitter to determine exactly what a user sees and when) acts as a kind of aggregate-level, crowdsourced editor, providing and promoting pieces of information as they become available and relevant. Journalists today can influence this flow only indirectly, adding pieces to it that the network will move from person to person. Moving forward, the role of journalists may have more to do with the development of tools and routines that

help shape the aggregation process, rather than simply contribute to it. The characteristics of overall discussion on Twitter suggest that this is not simply a niche issue within broader forms of Twitter use. Over 85 percent of Twitter's trending topics are related to headline news, about half overlap with concurrent cable TV news coverage, and Twitter tends to lead other media when it comes to breaking news, but follow for longer-term stories.

This ambient model, in which "social awareness streams" provide constant piecemeal updates, is notably open and lacking in order. It privileges an iterative process of collective understanding in which the broadly participating public comes to some consensus about a piece of information or a story as an aggregation of those pieces. Although research suggests that the Twitter public is well-suited to quash rumors and incorrect information, this is a model that is entirely the reverse of the traditional model of institutional journalism.

Indeed, the logic of traditional journalism is borne from a filter-then-publish model, in which the filtering process happens inside the professional enclave of the newsroom. Having gathered information via reporters, news organizations use the expertise and experience of those reporters, editors, producers, and other journalism professionals to determine what reality is, and publish that for the audience to consume. This amounts to what Stephen J. A. Ward and Herman Wasserman call a "closed" ethical foundation. That is, the process of turning disparate pieces of information into news happens away from public view, using guidelines meant for those few who have been accepted as practitioners, and without input from those outside the internally accepted boundaries.

Notably, this is not a new concern, but is very similar to the different approach espoused by the citizen journalism movement, which tends to use a more open, publish-then-filter model. Though this has become more common in the Internet era, this type of citizen journalism has a significant pre-digital history, and its open ethos informs the collectively oriented news communities that exist in Twitter and other social media today. Although many of these individuals do not think of themselves as journalists, or their behavior as journalism, they report and sort pieces of information in what can be thought of as a massively open news production process that provides the whole public with access to truth-finding mechanisms as well as to what they produce.

Pro

Those who see Twitter as beneficial to journalism point to a number of ways in which it either enhances existing approaches or upends them. For news organizations, Twitter provides quick and direct access to interested members of the public, helping organizations to build and maintain their online audience, and allowing the public to learn about potentially important information as quickly as possible. For journalists, it creates greater potential for individual recognition and credibility, which can be especially important as the news industry transitions away from long-term staff positions and toward more freelance work. These impacts help support the viability of the news business and encourage trained journalists to continue their participation in the broader Twitter conversation, which they are less likely to do in other social media.

For proponents of Twitter, this ties into more general perceived benefits of the platform. Because it is not just a discussion among untrained, everyday citizens, but rather features significant participation by traditional journalists, the news and information that is collectively filtered by the Twitter community has professional guidance of both its source material and the process by which it sifts and winnows that material. Traditional journalists remain by far the most significant sources of news within the Twitter ecosystem, through their own direct contributions of information and links, and through being linked by other people. Thus, while journalists retain their primacy as information sources at a reduced level, they take on new responsibilities in cooperating with the public to contextualize, explain, and provide narrative structure to the bits and pieces of information made available in disparate, individual tweets. Because it is based on Twitter's massively open system—as opposed to the more closed Facebook, or the more one-way YouTube—this process is made accessible to the entire news-consuming public, rather than only those few who actively participate.

Supporters of Twitter also see significant benefits for those participators and for the general public. Because of the much broader availability of information and information sources online, Twitter provides an outlet for an extremely wide range of viewpoints, and thus a more complete understanding of important civic and political debates. For the same reasons, it also provides journalists access to those viewpoints, meaning that it may have the effect of expanding the range of voices that are heard through traditional media sources and routing around journalists' blind spots. Those who provide the additional viewpoints can benefit from the feeling that their concerns and interests are being heard and that they are contributing to informing the public on an issue they care about. This is one potential advantage of Twitter over previous citizen journalism platforms. Members of the public who want to become involved in citizen journalism may see themselves as unable, because they perceive journalism as something that is necessarily based in institutions (for example, newspapers). Twitter allows these individuals to participate in a collective form of journalism, and to come and go from it as they please, even though they may not understand their actions to be journalistic.

Con

Those who see Twitter as problematic for journalism interpret this new model differently, focusing on concerns about credibility, accuracy, and completeness. This is part of a broader critique of the publish-then-filter approach. Specifically, those who advocate for filtering and news production to happen within the confines of the newsroom see a public process as potentially misinforming the audience,

who may see or participate in only part of the process that turns disparate information into a cohesive story. A primary part of this concern is that the information added by the public to an ongoing Twitter conservation about the news could come from anywhere—a person who tweets a piece of information may be an eyewitness, an expert, or someone with other firsthand knowledge, or they could be passing along a rumor, contributing their own speculation, or simply making things up as a form of information vandalism. Though the process of discussion might reveal the truth about that piece of information, it may not happen until many people have seen it, forwarded it, or taken it as correct. Journalists may feel compelled to report on and debunk such false information, even though that can have the effect of spreading belief in it just by giving it more exposure.

The speed with which Twitter moves complicates this potential problem. Although traditional media sometimes print or broadcast inaccurate information, their somewhat longer process of developing a story allows more problems to be caught before they are released. The rush to be first on Twitter provides journalists an incentive for tweeting and retweeting information that may not have been fully vetted and provides news consumers an incentive for following and taking in every new and immediate piece of information. This speed also causes significant turnover in any given Twitter feed, meaning that someone who only casually follows a breaking story may see only part of it. For these users, not only have they missed any potential benefits of observing the public process of figuring out what the story is, they have also been presented with an essentially incomplete version of the story, lacking whatever information passed through the stream when they were not actively watching.

There are additional concerns about Twitter encouraging triviality amongst not only members of the public, but journalists as well. This echoes concerns about the sound-bite nature of television news—that depth is sacrificed for speed, and that the tendencies of the medium lead to news being presented as entertainment. This argument against Twitter points to the conversational and jocular nature of some Twitter interactions among journalists and between journalists and members of the public, as well as the inclination for journalists to engage in speculation and opinion-mongering in these contexts. Because Twitter is a somewhat informal environment, but also a competitive promotional platform, some have also expressed concern that it could encourage the reporting of trivial stories, or framing of stories in especially sensational ways—a tendency toward so-called "click-bait." Each of these issues separately, and all of them working in concert, could also have the effect of diminishing the credibility of journalists and news organizations that provide or share incorrect information, promote stories in a way that trivializes their news value, or interact unprofessionally with other people in the Twitter environment.

Looking to the Future

Twitter is neither the first nor the last Internet platform to challenge journalism's traditional standards for ethics and professionalism. The World Wide Web itself provided many of the capabilities that characterize Twitter when it comes to news; it was what allowed Matt Drudge to break the Monica Lewinsky scandal in 1998 when reporters from *Newsweek* were sitting on the story. Later, blogs lowered the technological barriers to entry and created new networks of partisan news and opinion flow that traditional media often interfaced with, cable television in particular. News consumption, production, and evaluation at blogs is driven not only by bloggers but also by their readers and commenters, a community of individuals similar to the networks that arise in Twitter.

Thus, preparing for the future of the news media requires thinking less about Twitter as a specific communication platform operated by a specific company and thinking more about the features and characteristics of Twitter as a medium and how people use those features. Twitter already shares space with other social media and will share space with new ones in the future; all of them have common affordances to which journalists, news organizations, and the news-consuming public must give consideration.

Journalists' role in the future of open, networked, digital media may be the most straightforward. There is nothing inherent to Twitter or any of its contemporaries that requires journalists to engage in opinionating, rumormongering, rushed publishing of unverified information, or any of the platform's other potential pitfalls. They can self-police and monitor one another's behavior, as they already do somewhat, with existing standards to guide them. Perhaps the biggest hurdle to this kind of ethical protection is the lure of clicks as a way to grow the bottom line. For both freelance and staff journalists, the need to deliver an audience will continue to exist and to put pressure on the professional concerns of their work.

News organizations face a different challenge. Open, networked media by their nature usurp part of the role that news organizations have traditionally played in society. They no longer have a monopoly on setting the news agenda or on determining what is true or important about a news story. Instead, news organizations may focus on providing structure, context, and centers of expertise to the participatory news processes that happen online. This transition also allows news organizations an opportunity to engage more in community journalism, emphasizing reciprocal connections with the audience, which allow for a deep and guided understanding of the issues that are important to the news-consuming public.

Those news consumers have their own set of opportunities as a result of Twitter and its related technologies. The future likely holds a greater level of "news participation"—that is, reporting first-hand information, sharing news, commenting on news, and engaging in the collective process of determining truth, relevance, and importance. Digital technologies allow individuals to engage in one-off instances of citizen journalism without any particular commitment to an organization or to additional work. The flip side of this openness for participation is that the amount of available information will likely continue to grow, meaning that news consumers seeking credible information about issues in the news will have to do more work to follow the collective truth-seeking process that sifts through it all.

Conclusion

Twitter and the digital media that share its basic features give good reason to rethink some of the assumptions that traditional journalism is built on. In particular, they open the journalistic process to a much wider range of sources and viewpoints and give the public a way to get involved in the news that gives them a personal stake in it. However, they also expose the process to potential sources of misinformation and approaches to news-gathering that may violate basic standards of journalistic ethics, from both professional and citizen journalists alike. They also present different and potentially clashing new incentives for individual journalists and the organizations they work for.

These technologies are not going away. Though Twitter itself may become more or less popular, its underlying open network structure is an inherent part of the online world and will continue to affect news and information flows in one form or another. Journalists, news organizations, and news consumers all would be wise to understand their actions on Twitter in the context of their considered goals, and not only the system's short-term incentives.

Aaron S. Veenstra
Southern Illinois University Carbondale

See also Journalism in the Twenty-first Century; Reader Comments

Further Reading

Broersma, Marcel, and Todd Graham. "Social Media as Beat: Tweets as a News Source During the 2010 British and Dutch Elections." *Journalism Practice* 6 (2012): 403–19. doi: 10.1080/17512786.2012.663626.

Bruns, Axel, and Jean Burgess. "#Ausvotes: How Twitter Covered the 2010 Australian Federal Election." *Communication, Politics & Culture* 44 (2011): 37–56.

Hermida, Alfred. "Twittering the News: The Emergence of Ambient Journalism." *Journalism Practice* 4 (2010): 297–308. doi:10.1080/17512781003640703.

Holton, Avery E. "Case of the #UTShooter: The Public Working with, for, and around the News Media." *Journal of Applied Journalism & Media Studies* 1 (2012): 125–142. doi:10.1386/ajms.1.2.125_1.

Kwak, Haewoon, Changhyun Lee, Hosung Park, and Sue Moon. "What Is Twitter, a Social Network or a News Media?" Paper presented at WWW 2010, Raleigh, North Carolina, April 26–30, 2010.

Lasorsa, Dominic L., Seth C. Lewis, and Avery E. Holton. "Normalizing Twitter: Journalism Practice in an Emerging Communication Space." *Journalism Studies* 13 (2012): 19–36. doi:10.1080/1461670X.2011.571825.

Lewis, Seth C. "The Tension between Professional Control and Open Participation: Journalism and Its Boundaries." *Information, Communication & Society* 15 (2012): 836–866. doi:10.1080/1369118X.2012.674150.

Nanabhay, Mohamed, and Roxane Farmanfarmaian. "From Spectacle to Spectacular: How Physical Space, Social Media and Mainstream Broadcast Amplified the Public Sphere in Egypt's 'Revolution'." *Journal of North African Studies* 16 (2011): 573–603. doi:10.1080/13629387.2011.639562.

Papacharissi, Zizi, and Maria de Fatima Oliveira. "Affective News and Networked Publics: The Rhythms of News Storytelling on #Egypt." *Journal of Communication* 62 (2012): 266–282. doi:10.1111/j.1460-2466.2012.01630.x.

Sanderson, Jimmy, and Marion E. Hambrick. "Covering the Scandal in 140 Characters: A Case Study of Twitter's Role in Coverage of the Penn State Saga." *International Journal of Sport Communication* 5 (2012): 384–402.

Singer, Jane B. "Journalism Ethics amid Structural Change." *Daedalus* 139 (2010): 89–99. doi:10.1162/daed.2010.139.2.89.

Veenstra, Aaron S., Narayanan Iyer, Chang Sup Park, and Fawaz Alajmi. "Twitter as 'a Journalistic Substitute'? Examining #wiunion Tweeters' Behavior and Self-Perception." *Journalism: Theory, Practice, and Criticism* (forthcoming). doi:10.1177/1464884914521580.

Ward, Stephen J. A., and Herman Wasserman. "Towards an Open Ethics: Implications of New Media Platforms for Global Ethics Discourse." *Journal of Mass Media Ethics* 25 (2010): 275–292. doi:10.1080/08900523.2010.512825.

Zelizer, Barbie. "When Facts, Truth, and Reality Are God-Terms: On Journalism's Uneasy Place in Cultural Studies." *Communication and Critical/Cultural Studies* 1 (2004): 100–119. doi:10.1080/1479142042000018095.

Zubiaga, Arkaitz, and Heng Ji. "Tweet, but Verify: Epistemic Study of Information Verification on Twitter." *Social Network Analysis and Mining* 4 (2014): 163. doi:10.1007/s13278-014-0163-y.

INDEX

Bolded numbers denote volume numbers.

Hutchins Commission. *See* Commission on Freedom of the Press (Hutchins Commission)

Hutchins, Robert, **1:**52

Hyde, Sandra, **2:**585

Hyde v. City of Columbia, Missouri, et al. (Missouri, 1982), **2:**585–586, 591

Hyperbole, **2:**508, 510, 512, 516–517

Idaho Dairymen's Association, **2:**559

Impressible content, **2:**542–543

IMS Health, **1:**355

In loco parentis, **2:**822–823, 833

In re January 11, 2013 Subpoena (New Jersey, 2013), **1:**176

In re Oliver (1948), **1:**240

Incitement, crime victims' claims of, **2:**587–589

Independence, as journalistic principle, **1:**11, 204, 205, 264, **2:**765

Independent Counsel Act (1978), **1:**335

Independent Media Center, **1:**433

Indiana Daily Student (newspaper), **2:**592

Individualism. *See* Libertarian/individual focus

Information literacy, **2:**809

Information Technology, Files, and Freedom Act (France, 1978), **1:**427

Innocence of Muslims (film), **2:**865–866

Inside Edition (television show), **1:**295

Instagram, **2:**758

Institutions, ethics of, **2:**705–720

Intellectual privacy, **1:**352

Intellectual property. *See also* Copyright; Trademark

China, **2:**613–618

digital piracy, **2:**615–621

Singapore, **2:**619–620

South Korea, **2:**618–619

tangible property vs., **2:**626

United States, **2:**621

Inter-American Convention on the Rights of the Author in Literary, Scientific, and Artistic Works, **2:**653

International Copyright Act (1891), **2:**649–650

International exhibitions, copyright provisions for, **2:**650

International Trade and Investment Act (1984), **2:**655

Internet. *See also* New media

censorship, **1:**425, 431

China, **1:**21–22, **2:**539–540

civility, **1:**55

credibility, **1:**4

historical background, **2:**800–801

impact of, **2:**758

news sites, **2:**758

persistence of information, **1:**190

Internet Content Providers, **2:**542, 778

Internet Movie Database, **1:**360

Internet Policy Task Force, U.S. Commerce Department, **2:**863

Internet Service Providers (ISPs)

access to users' online activities, **1:**361

China, **2:**542, 778

content control, **2:**864–865

equal treatment of content, **1:**69

liabilities and protections, **1:**3, 8–9, 186–187, **2:**439–454, 633–634, 791–796, 862, 870

privacy concerns, **1:**179

Intrusion, **1:**178, 312, 334, 350–351, 388–392, **2:**522, 576–577, 582–584

Investigative Reporters and Editors (IRE), **1:**199

Investigative reporting, **1:**193–209. *See also* Undercover reporting

changing nature of, **1:**193–195, 205–206

deceptive practices in, **1:**161–162, 165–173, 203–206, **2:**555

decline of, **1:**200

ebbs and flows of, **1:**207–209

ethics, **1:**203–207

future of, **1:**172–173, 200, 208–209

historical background, **1:**196–197

new-media environment, **1:**205–206

nonprofit organizations' role in, **1:**198, 201–203

purpose and impact of, **1:**195–200

watchdog role, **1:**200–202

Iravani, Heide, **2:**444

Isaacks, Bruce, **2:**500–501

Isaacman, Alan, **2:**495–497

IsAnyoneUp.com, **1:**325

ISPs. *See* Internet Service Providers (ISPs)

Jackson, Robert, **2:**690

Jacobs, Katrien, **2:**545

Jaffee v. Redmond (1996), **1:**280

Jarvis, Jeff, **2:**761

Jaspers, Karl, **1:**32

Louisville Courier-Journal (newspaper), **1:**270, **2:**683
Louisville Times (newspaper), **2:**683
Louw, D. J., **1:**34
Love, Courtney, **1:**408
Lu Wei, **2:**782
Lu Xun, *Kong Yiji*, **2:**614
Luce, Henry, **1:**52
Luo Changping, **2:**777
Luther, Martin, **1:**62
Luttig, Michael, **2:**588–589
Lynch, Jennifer, **2:**465
Lyon, Matthew, **1:**6

MacIntyre, Alasdair, **1:**31
Mack, Erin, **1:**306
MacKinnon, Catharine, **1:**69
Macon Telegraph Publishing Company v. Tatum (Georgia, 1993), **2:**580
Mad-cow disease, **2:**565
Madison, James
 access to information, **1:**148, 159
 freedom of speech, **1:**117
 freedom of the press, **1:**5, 73
 Ninth Amendment, **1:**310
 U.S. Constitution, **1:**106, 117
Magarian, Gregory P., **2:**820–821
Magee, Robert G., **2:**449–450
Magna Carta, **1:**112
Magnusson v. New York Times Co. (Oklahoma, 2004), **2:**518
Mandel, Seth, **2:**769
Manning, Chelsea (Bradley), **1:**182, 258–259, 267, 321, 419–420, 428–430, **2:**765–766
Mano, D. Keith, **1:**409–410
Manola, Marion, **1:**306
Mansbridge, Peter, **1:**88
Manziel, Johnny, **1:**369, 374–375, 376
Mao Zedong, **2:**617
Marbury v. Madison (1803), **2:**476
Marceau, Justin, **2:**559
Marcotte, Amanda, **1:**295
Marketplace of ideas
 critiques of, **1:**23–26, 69–70, 71
 freedom of the press and, **1:**48–53, 56, 58
 Holmes's *Abrams* opinion and, **1:**66
 Milton as precursor of, **1:**63
 new media and, **2:**454
 theory of, **1:**68–70

Marshall, Josh, **2:**759
Marshall, Thurgood, **1:**76, 335, **2:**497, 699
Marshall, William, **1:**72
Martin, Eric, **1:**4
Martin, Trayvon, **1:**217
Martin v. City of Struthers (1943), **1:**150
Martinez, Al, *The Last City Room*, **2:**705–706, 720
Mattel Inc. v. MCA Records Inc., **2:**492
Mattelart, Armand, **1:**426, 427, **2:**751–752
May, Larry, **2:**708–710, 719–720
Mayersohn, Andrew, **1:**98
MCA Records, **2:**492
McBride, Kelly, **1:**172, 195, 205, 207, **2:**765, 766
McBurney v. Young (2013), **1:**181
McCain, John, **1:**147, 356
McCall, Ginger, **2:**744
McCarthy, Carolyn, **2:**576
McClure's (magazine), **1:**208
McConnell, Jackie, **2:**557
McConnell v. Federal Elections Commission, **2:**733
McCullen v. Coakley (2014), **1:**335
McCutcheon v. Federal Elections Commission (2014), **1:**100, 104, **2:**733
McDermott, James, **1:**261, 314
McDonald's, **1:**387, **2:**701
McGraw-Hill, **2:**849
McIntyre v. Ohio Elections Commission (1995), **2:**451
McKevitt, Michael, **1:**278
McKevitt v. Pallasch (2003), **1:**278–279
McLaughlin, John, **2:**547
McLean, Deckle, **2:**527
McNealy, Scott, **1:**384
McRoberts, Flynn, **1:**278
McVeigh, Timothy, **1:**250
Media. *See also* Freedom of the press; Journalism; New media; News media; Ownership of media; Social media
 business model of, **1:**85–86
 checks on government, **1:**253, 265
 college sports, **1:**369–381, **2:**663–676
 credibility of, **1:**14, 81–91, **2:**706–707
 crime victim coverage, **2:**573–592
 cutbacks and understaffing, **1:**83
 defined, **2:**706
 globalization of, **1:**128–129

⑤SAGE video

We are delighted to announce the launch of a streaming video program at SAGE!

SAGE Video online collections are developed in partnership with leading academics, societies and practitioners, including many of SAGE's own authors and academic partners, to deliver cutting-edge pedagogical collections mapped to curricular needs.

Available alongside our book and reference collections on the *SAGE Knowledge* platform, content is delivered with critical online functionality designed to support scholarly use.

SAGE Video combines originally commissioned and produced material with licensed videos to provide a complete resource for students, faculty, and researchers.

NEW IN 2015!

- Counseling and Psychotherapy
- Education

- Media and Communication

sagepub.com/video
#sagevideo